THE COMPREHENSIVE GUIDE

WINES OF CALIFORNIA

MIKE DESIMONE & JEFF JENSSEN

FOREWORD BY MICHAEL MONDAVI
PREFACE BY KEVIN ZRALY

STERLING EPICURE
New York

New York

An Imprint of Sterling Publishing
387 Park Avenue South
New York, NY 10016

STERLING EPICURE is a trademark of Sterling Publishing Co., Inc. The distinctive Sterling logo is a registered trademark of Sterling Publishing Co., Inc.

Additional information courtesy The Wine Institute and the US Department of Agriculture.

Interior designed by Christine Heun
Maps by Philip Buchanan

A complete list of picture credits appears on page 568.

ISBN 978-1-4549-0448-9

Library of Congress Cataloging-in-Publication Data

DeSimone, Mike.
Wines of California : the comprehensive guide / Mike DeSimone & Jeff Jenssen.
pages cm
Includes index.
ISBN 978-1-4549-0448-9
1. Wine and wine making--California. I. Jenssen, Jeff. II. Title.
TP557.D45 2014
663'.209794--dc 3

2014008145

Distributed in Canada by Sterling Publishing
c/o Canadian Manda Group, 165 Dufferin Street
Toronto, Ontario, Canada M6K 3H6
Distributed in the United Kingdom by GMC Distribution Services
Castle Place, 166 High Street, Lewes, East Sussex, England BN7 1XU
Distributed in Australia by Capricorn Link (Australia) Pty. Ltd.
P.O. Box 704, Windsor, NSW 2756, Australia

For information about custom editions, special sales, and premium and corporate purchases, please contact Sterling Special Sales at 800-805-5489 or specialsales@sterlingpublishing.com.

Manufactured in the United States of America

2 4 6 8 10 9 7 5 3 1

www.sterlingpublishing.com

Wines of California is dedicated to ALL the families of winemakers and grape growers in California, past, present, and future, and to our many friends in the wonderful world of wine.

Cheers to you all!

CONTENTS

FOREWORD

I'VE HAD THE PLEASURE OF KNOWING JEFF AND MIKE FOR MANY YEARS AND HAVE constantly been impressed with their love of food, wine, travel, culture, history, and storytelling, so when they asked if I would consider writing a foreword for *Wines of California: The Comprehensive Guide*, I jumped at the chance.

While countless books have crossed my desk over the decades, it was the depth of study they were prepared to undertake—not only on wine and wineries in California (everyone's favorite cornerstone), but also the history of food, culture, community, and the arts—that impressed me the most. I feel that this information has been missing in recent times for books of this kind.

Born and raised in the Napa Valley and in the wine industry, I felt that I was quite knowledgeable on the history of California wines, but through their words, Mike and Jeff made the early pioneers come alive and taught me much of the wonderful detail I had either forgotten or never learned.

The flow of the book is ingenious, starting with the history of California music, the geography, the geology, the way the mission fathers developed the wine industry—all of it is a wonderful history lesson in itself. The extensive research on the California pioneers, from Father Junípero Serra, to Charles Krug, Karl Wente, and so many others, is a joy to read and an integral part of the history that has shaped California's vibrant wine industry today.

This work is also a testament to the amazing American spirit and creativity. The impact of phylloxera in the early 1900s, then World War I, and Prohibition in 1919 did not break the spirit of the California wine pioneers. They were, and remain, a true inspiration.

Also, the history of many of the innovations that we take for granted today is beautifully documented. From the development of improved sanitation to the reduced oxidation of wines to the adaptation of cold stabilization, the book clearly explains so many techniques that now are widely used. In fact, during the late '50s and early '60s during my formative years at Charles Krug Winery, I vividly remember the flavor differences in the wines being made before and after the implementation of cold fermentation. It was wonderful to be reminded of those times of innovation, change, and the quest to constantly improve on what had gone before.

Mike and Jeff also have succeeded in making the many wine regions of California accessible. The personalities and styles of the wine regions are captured in the detailed descriptions of the wineries. I think you will appreciate the clarity they bring to the importance of place in the wines produced.

For the last 25 years, I have used English author Hugh Johnson's *World Guide to Wines* as my reference book on wines, families, and producers, and I think Mike and Jeff have accomplished this for California. With the rapid changes and development over the last 10 years, *Wines of California* provides accurate and timely information on the people, the families, and the regions of California.

Although Jeff and Mike's original objective may have been to create a book brimming with history, colorful stories, and educational nuances, this work also serves as a great reference book for everyone who wants to learn about California wines and visit the many regions that are covered in this comprehensive guide.

Part Two, "In Their Own Words," showcases many of the pioneers and great winemakers of California and their personal insights—the unedited conversation is an absolutely wonderful foray into the many visionaries, personalities, and people who comprise our diverse and dynamic industry.

I know you will look forward to reading and enjoying this book as well as keeping it nearby for reference. Please enjoy.

Michael Mondavi

PREFACE

Mike DeSimone and Jeff Jenssen truly are movers and shakers in the world of wine. I know I can breathe easy any time I invite them to step in as guest speakers at the Windows on the World Wine School or for my master classes. I often say that if we compare wine educators and writers to doctors, I am a general practitioner, but when I need expertise in a particular area, I refer to a specialist. This is where folks like Mike and Jeff come in: they put in the long hours crafting *Wines of California* (just as they did on their prior title, *Wines of the Southern Hemisphere*), homing in on the state that is now the fourth largest producer of wine in the entire world. I have long felt that the time for a new book on California has come, and these two gentlemen have finally done it.

In 1970, there were only around 240 wineries in the state of California, and today there are more than 3,700. Beyond the exponential growth in the number of wineries itself, the entire culture of winemaking has changed and continues to change. Winemaking in California is a constantly moving target; it was in its infancy when I first visited wine regions there in the early 1970s, and today it remains in its formative years and has not yet begun to peak.

The two words *fun* and *exciting* don't often come to mind when considering wine writing or wine tastings, yet those are exactly the words I and many of my peers and friends use when talking about Mike and Jeff. Each half of this duo has been blessed with the abilities to both speak and write well. They are engaging and enjoyable speakers as well as prolific writers. By combining history, culture, personality, and intimate knowledge of their subject with the necessary facts and figures, they have turned what in other hands could be a dry book of statistics and listings into a compelling read.

The ability to take what we normally do in a wine tasting or master class and put that into words on paper is extremely difficult, and yet it appears that Mike and Jeff are able to do this effortlessly. I cannot imagine the number of hours they spent traveling to and from California, tasting wines, compiling all the information, and then putting it all together in such a comprehensive yet easy-to-read volume. It is quite obvious that they have done the requisite legwork. Not only have they incorporated the timeline of wine in the state, they also have focused on the particularities of the varied wine regions and brought to life the personalities of dozens of major players. In other words, they have successfully brought the story of the entire culture of wine in California to life.

The authors have a great respect for the past and for the "founding fathers" of California wine. They also have chosen to include stories of the second and third generations of many great California wine families through the series of interviews titled "In Their Own Words." Many of their subjects are old friends of mine, and it makes me happy to see the story of California wine, especially that of the late twentieth and early twenty-first centuries, told through their eyes. Mike and Jeff have generously opened the pages of their book to winemakers and winery owners, allowing each to give his or her unique outlook on winemaking in California. Collectively, these interviews add another dimension to the story of California wine.

The first time I visited California in 1972 you could count the number of wine-country restaurants on one hand. Then, simultaneously, the United States grew to become the number one consumer of wine in the world, with much of that wine coming from California, and the popularity of the farm-to-table movement took off. The result has been a renewed interest in food and an enormous number of restaurant choices in all the wine regions of California. Naturally, many of these establishments offer locally grown specialties paired with wines from the immediate area. The inclusion of recipes from winery kitchens and wine country restaurants in this tome gives great insight into what is going on in the California food movement today, and also serves as a travel guide to the best meals when you visit these regions yourself. This keeps the culture of wine in perspective—wine is meant to be enjoyed, not drunk in a vacuum.

The way we view wine has changed in the past 40 years. California wine used to just be described as white or red, and then we moved on to calling those same wines (however incorrectly) Chablis or Burgundy. People then started to request wine from a few specific wineries, and then they began seeking out bottles first from Napa and then Sonoma. As wine drinkers became more sophisticated, they looked for particular vineyard names on labels, and then they got savvy in terms of AVAs. Although many writers have glossed over the regions of California beyond Napa and Sonoma, Mike and Jeff have been both inclusive and forward thinking by delving into the other less popularized regions of California and discussing them in depth.

These two seasoned wine professionals have brought us an up-to-date, modern look at what is happening in one of the most exciting wine regions in the world, and they have done it with style. As much as I have enjoyed reading *Wines of California*, I look forward to the next edition, as a testament to the innovation and tenacity of the grape growers and winemakers of California.

Kevin Zraly

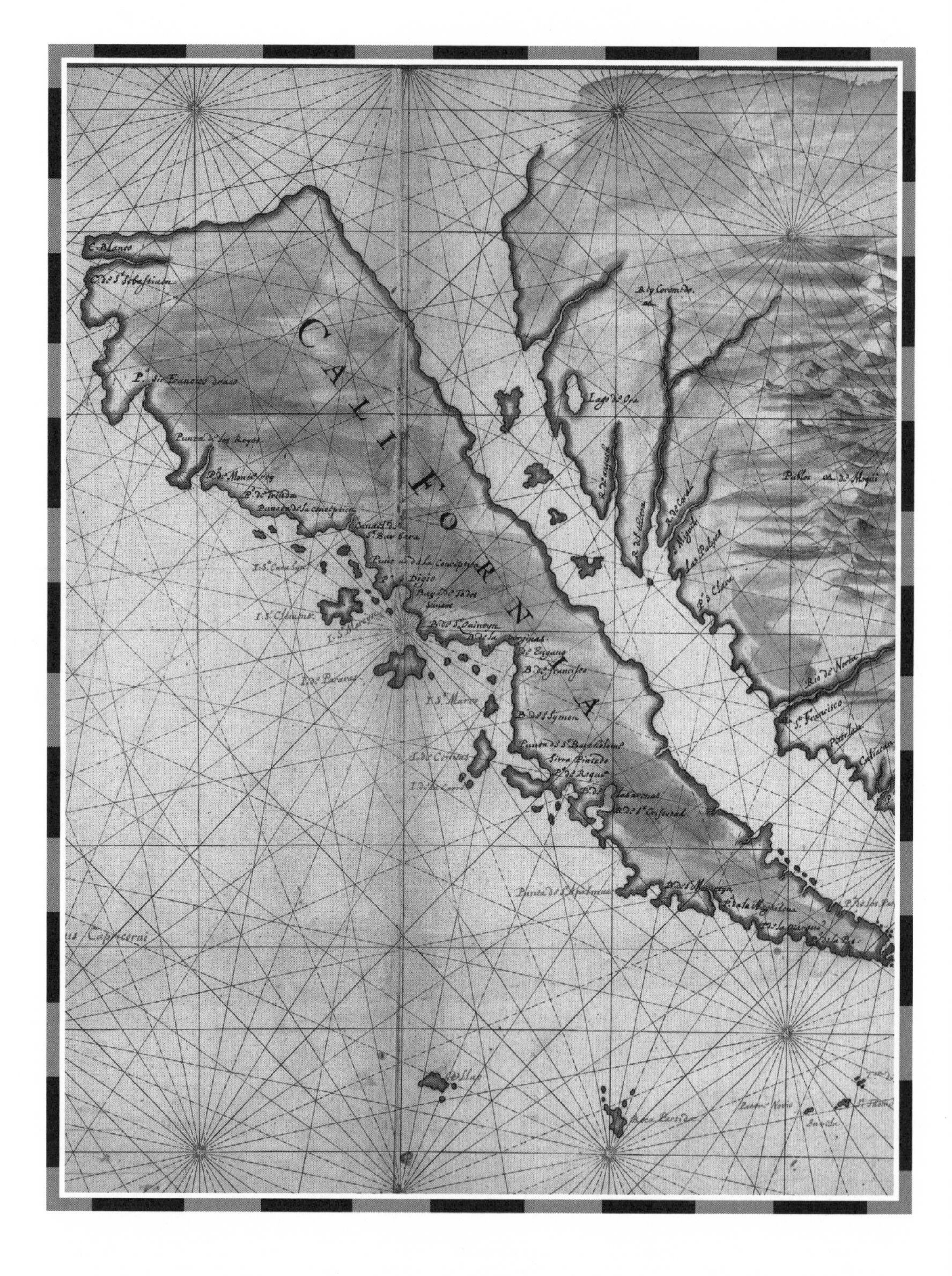
CALIFORNIA

INTRODUCTION

CALIFORNIA LOOMS LARGE IN THE PSYCHE, not only its own but that of residents of the other 49 states and indeed the whole world. It has been mythologized in every recent generation through the lexicon of popular music, starting with "California Here I Come," originally written for the Broadway stage in 1921 and then popularized by Al Jolson in 1924. The eminently memorable tune launched a multitude of television and movie characters as well as countless real people on their journey to a better life or at least an unforgettable vacation in the Golden State. Audible impressions of California pepper the playlists of oldies, easy listening, and classic rock stations alike, including the Beach Boys' "California Girls," the Mamas and the Papas' "California Dreamin'," the Eagles' "Hotel California," Albert Hammond's "It Never Rains in Southern California," Led Zeppelin's "Going to California," and the Red Hot Chili Peppers' "Californication." Younger music lovers may be inclined to load their iPods with Katy Perry's "California Gurls," Rihanna's "California King Bed," or Train's "California 37," but whether your favorite California song was first bought on vinyl or over the Internet, we know that one of these iconic tunes is buzzing through your head right now, bringing thoughts of sandy beaches, convertibles, and beautiful people with sun-kissed features and a perpetual glow.

California has been legendary since the mid-sixteenth century, when the first Spanish explorers arrived. The name "California" came from a 1510 Spanish novel, *Las Sergas de Esplandián,* in which it was used to describe an island ruled by beautiful Amazon warriors. It is believed that the book's author, Garci Rodríguez de Montalvo, based the place name on the Spanish word *califa*, which in turn was based on the Arabic word for ruler or leader. Even before its boundaries or interior was known, California inspired the imagination of the people who set out to explore and conquer it. California first appeared on a map in 1562, at a time when it was thought to be a paradisiacal island. If we take into account the rugged terrain that makes up its borders, including the Sierra Nevada, the Mojave Desert, the Colorado River, and the rough-hewn shores of the Pacific Ocean, it might just as well have been one in the days before mechanical transportation.

Those of us who arrive in the nation's most populous state by air after choosing our dinner location and booking a car via an in-flight app can only marvel at the idea of Spanish explorers traveling by ship and then on horseback to an unknown land, reading by candlelight a novel whose fantastic locale gave a name to the place on the map that remains to this day the stuff of tales and dreams.

The very features that make California so perfect for those wishing to live the dream, including bright, sunny days that are ideal for driving around with the car top down and refreshing, humidity-free evenings that seem designed for a hint of fur on the red carpet, also make it unequaled for the cultivation of the fruit of the vine. The state's ample sunshine provides daytime conditions that are exemplary for the ripening of grapes, and its 800 miles of coastline provide fog and breezes that are essential to maintain the cool environment that promotes the retention of acidity, a necessary component in a balanced glass of wine. Inland valleys receive similar cooling action from nearby rivers and lakes.

Spanish missionaries planted the first grapes, but California as a grape-growing state is a melting pot as diverse as the United States itself, with viticulturists from all over the world bringing their hometown varieties to plant in the state's varied soils, from Covelo in the north to the Ramona Valley in the south. Although many wine drinkers think of California primarily as the home of high-alcohol Cabernet Sauvignon and buttery Chardonnay (or worse, the home of "blush" wine or White Zin), the number of different varietals vinified there—from Albariño to Zinfandel—and the wide array of styles would astound all but the most immersed student of the state's wine industry.

As of this writing, there are 116 federally approved American Viticultural Areas, or AVAs, in the state, and petitions have been filed with the Federal Alcohol and Tobacco Tax and Trade Bureau for an additional 18 AVAs, including 11 subappellations in Paso Robles alone. The state is divided into four major regions: North Coast AVA, Central Coast AVA, South Coast AVA, and the Central Valley, which is not an AVA. All these are further subdivided into multiple AVAs.

California is the number one producer of wine in the United States, responsible for 90 percent of all the wine made in the country. The state boasts 3,800 bonded wineries, an increase of 2,100 in the last decade, and 4,600 grape growers. Its 163,695 square miles contain 546,000 acres of wine grapes, and in 2012 just over four million tons of grapes destined to become wine were harvested. Over 207 million cases of California wine were sold in the US market that year, representing a total retail value of $22 billion, with an additional $1.43 billion of US wine, 90 percent from California, exported to a growing roster of nations around the world. Perhaps the most startling fact about the California wine industry is that it is the world's number four producer of wine in total volume, behind France, Italy, and Spain.

California's first vineyard was planted by a Jesuit missionary at Mission San Bruno, near modern-day San Francisco, in 1683, though it is believed that the grapes were never harvested and no wine was made there. A more successful vineyard was established in 1779 by Father Junípero Serra, known today as "the Father of California Wine." Father Serra was a Jesuit who planted vines at Mission San Diego de Alcala in 1779 in what was known as the *Provincia de Las Californias* in the Viceroyalty of New Spain. He built a rudimentary winery on the site one year later. Before his death in 1784 he was responsible for the founding of eight other missions, most of which had their own vineyards. The first—and for many years the only—grape grown here was the Mission grape, known in Chile as *Pais* and in Argentina as *Criolla Chica*.

The cultivation of European grape varieties, or *Vitis vinifera,* came to North America about two hundred years later than it did to South America, although the route of introduction was the same: among the entourages of the Spanish conquistadors were Catholic priests who planted vines and made wine for Mass and the table. It is interesting to note the similarity of latitude of the first vineyards to flourish in the opposing hemispheres. Mendoza, Argentina, and Santiago, Chile, sit at latitudes of 32.89 South and 33.45 South, respectively, while San Diego, California, the site of Father Serra's first mission and vineyard, is at a nearly corresponding point in the Northern Hemisphere at a latitude of 32.71 North.

It is more than just analogous latitude and a shared origin that connect the grape-growing regions of California to those of Chile and Argentina. The one major influence on all three that moved wine production forward from a by-product of the sacrament of Communion to a highly quaffable beverage was the introduction of French grape varieties and the pioneering efforts of French and other European viticulturists and enologists.

The first non-Mission vines were planted near Los Angeles in 1833 by Jean-Louis Vignes, a businessman whose occupations included winemaker, distiller, and cooper. Vignes was not pleased with the quality of wine he was able to make using available stock, and so he sent to his native France (he was born near Bordeaux) for Cabernet Franc and Sauvignon Blanc cuttings. He is thought to be the first Californian to have aged his wines, using barrels he made himself out of wood garnered from his property in the

San Bernardino Mountains. Within about ten years he was shipping wine by sea north to Santa Barbara, Monterey, and San Francisco, and by 1850 he was producing upward of 150,000 bottles annually. Although people from many other nations, notably Italy and Germany, have made their mark on the California wine industry as a whole, the influence of the French continues today through the efforts of winemakers, winemaking consultants, and winery owners such as Jean-Charles Boisset, Michel Rolland, Stephane Derenoncourt, Philippe Melka, Christian Moueix, and Pierre Seillan.

Just as a Spanish priest is known as the Father of California Wine, a Hungarian "Count," Agoston Haraszthy, the founder of Buena Vista Winery (owned today by Jean-Charles Boisset), is sometimes called "the Father of California Viticulture." Over the course of several years he imported cuttings from over 150 of Europe's great vineyards to California. After growing grapes close to San Francisco, in 1856 he settled on a small vineyard near Sonoma. He transplanted some of the French varieties he originally had planted nearer to the city and brought on Prussian immigrant Charles Krug—the same Charles Krug who in 1861 founded his eponymous winery in Napa Valley, owned today by Peter Mondavi and his family—as his winemaker. Krug previously had worked for John Patchett, who planted a Napa vineyard in 1854 and opened what has been called the first winery there in 1858.

By 1857 Haraszthy had begun construction on a stone winery complete with the latest in winemaking equipment and underground cellars. He ultimately owned more than 5,000 acres of land that included many vineyards, and he built a large stone mansion in the Buena Vista vineyards for himself and his family. In addition to his pioneering efforts planting grapes on the steep hillsides of Sonoma, Haraszthy's greatest contribution to California wine is the 19-page document he authored in 1858, his *Report on Grapes and Wine of California*, which is still identified as the first written study of vineyard practices and winemaking in California or indeed the whole of the United States.

The scene for European immigration to California had been set a few years earlier with the California Gold Rush. Gold was first discovered at Sutter's Mill in Coloma in January 1848. Word spread quickly, and within the next couple of years over 300,000 people from across the country and around the world headed to California. The site where gold was first discovered is in modern-day El Dorado (Spanish for "the Golden") County in the Sierra Foothills AVA. The first known grapes in the Sierra Foothills were planted during the Gold Rush, but the more lasting effect of this geological phenomenon has been the increase

in population in California, particularly San Francisco and the surrounding area. The age of California dreamin' had truly just begun.

San Francisco increased in size from a town of about 200 residents to over 36,000 between 1846 and 1852. California became a state in 1850 as part of a legislative package that also involved the territories of Texas, New Mexico, and Utah. Steamships had just begun plying the seas, bringing populations from China and South America, and by 1869 railroads stretched from east to west across the United States, making the passage much more secure than one by horse and wagon. As cities and towns across the new state grew, European immigrants, whether they were fresh off the boat or previously had settled elsewhere in the United States, set out for California to purchase inexpensive land, establish farms, and provide produce, meat, and dairy products to the ever-increasing population.

Talk to any fifth- or sixth-generation grape grower today and it is highly likely that he or she is a descendant of Italians or Germans who started out raising melons or peaches or dairy cows before some enterprising relative planted row upon row of grapes to provide raw material for the burgeoning wine industry. Karl Wente, a German immigrant who was taught winemaking by none other than Charles Krug, started his own winery in 1883 and was among the grape-growing avant-garde in Livermore Valley with his purchase of 48 acres. Jacob Beringer, another Charles Krug protégé, bought land in Napa Valley with his brother Frederick in 1875 and founded their winery—said to be the oldest continually operated winery in Napa Valley—one year later. The histories of every winemaking region and many individual wineries in the state are crisscrossed with the names of farmers and winemakers whose heirs and progeny continue their legacy today either in the latter-day rendition of the family business (if it is still family-owned) or elsewhere in the industry.

Shortly after California became a state and at about the same time that cross-country railroad tracks were completed, phylloxera was ravaging the vineyards of Europe, causing grape farmers from France, Italy, Spain, and Croatia to abandon their vineyards and seek their fortunes across the seas. Many of those emigrants with an agricultural bent headed to South America,

Australia, New Zealand, and North America to ply their trade, further spreading European vineyard and winemaking practices throughout the New World. With its wide open stretches of farmland, newfound statehood, growing population, and nearly mythic status the world over, California was the North American destination of choice for anyone who could afford passage, even if he or she went bankrupt in the process of getting there. By the beginning of the twentieth century California had a somewhat mature winemaking industry. California wines had begun to win awards in international and European wine competitions, including Captain Gustave Niebaum's Inglenook Wine, said to be the first Bordeaux-style wine in the United States, which took a gold medal at the Paris World's Fair in 1889. That same year, Livermore Valley's Cresta Blanca won two gold medals at the Paris Exposition, including best of show, thanks to a pioneering grower named Charles Wetmore.

A thriving export business had begun as well, with California wine being shipped to Australia, England, Germany, and the countries of Latin America.

Just as the vine-destroying insect known as phylloxera decimated the vineyards of Europe in the late nineteenth century, the temperance movement came close to destroying winemaking in the United States, Australia, and New Zealand in the early to middle twentieth century. The 18th Amendment of the US Constitution, also known as the National Prohibition Act and the Volstead Act (after the chairman of the House Judiciary Committee, Andrew Volstead), took effect on January 17, 1920. This nationwide ban on the production, sale, or transportation of alcoholic beverages remained in effect until December 5, 1933, when it was formally repealed by the ratification of the 21st Amendment. (The 18th Amendment is the only amendment to the US Constitution that has ever been repealed.)

Wine remained legal for sacramental and religious purposes, and wine and other spirits remained legal for medicinal purposes, available by doctor's prescription from a pharmacy. Because of these loopholes in the law, a handful of wineries remained operational during the 13 years that Prohibition reigned, and several Sonoma and Napa wineries lay claim to the title "Oldest Continually Operating Winery in the USA." Another provision of the law allowed for the head of each household to "make 200 gallons of non-intoxicating cider and fruit juice each year," and much of the ongoing grape production in California was shipped by rail across the country to home winemakers who may or may not have consumed all of their allotted 200 gallons under their own roofs.

Italian immigrants Cesare Mondavi and his wife, Rosa, had already shown their entrepreneurial prowess by opening a grocery store, saloon, and boardinghouse in their new home of Minnesota. It was there that they began making wine with grapes sourced from California. The Mondavis saw the promise in California even during Prohibition, causing them to bring their young family, including sons Robert and Peter, to Lodi, California, where they began buying grapes and shipping them around the country to others interested in making wine in their own domiciles.

Before Prohibition there were over 2,500 wineries across the United States, and by 1933 fewer than 100 remained. California accounted for more than 700 wineries as of 1920, and it took until well into the 1980s before the same number were open again. From 1933 into the 1960s fortified wines gained a stronghold in the domestic wine market. Made with the addition of brandy or grain alcohol, which retains a high sugar level (giving them a sweet taste) and an alcohol level of 20 percent as opposed to around 11 to 14 percent for other wines and 40 percent or higher for spirits, fortified wines were taxed at the same levels as wine. This made them less expensive than hard liquor and thus offered more bang for the buck to those who were drinking for purposes other than to enhance the experience of dining.

Two of the characters who figure strongly in California's post-Prohibition resurgence are Beaulieu Vineyards' André Tchelistcheff and Brother Timothy, a member of the Christian Brothers order who was a science teacher turned winemaker. Beaulieu's founder, George de Latour, met Tchelistcheff at the French National Agronomy Institute in 1938 and invited him to come to Napa to become his chief winemaker. Tchelistcheff focused his attention on high-quality California Cabernet Sauvignon and was among the first winemakers to utilize the practice of aging wine in small French oak barrels in California. He also made important advances in the understanding and implementation of now-common techniques such as vineyard frost protection, malolactic fermentation, and cold fermentation (which was first introduced to California by Peter Mondavi Sr.) He was also instrumental in the development of vineyard sites in Carneros and other California regions. He stayed on at Beaulieu until his retirement in 1973, after which he consulted for a number of high-profile wineries in Napa and Sonoma and throughout the Pacific Northwest. Many prominent winemakers who have been in the business since the 1960s and 1970s name Tchelistcheff among their most important mentors or influences in the wine business.

His contemporary Brother Timothy first worked as a wine chemist at the Christian Brothers' Mont La Salle Winery in 1935. After Prohibition, the order determined that it should produce wine commercially rather than just for the Mass, and Brother Timothy moved into winemaking, becoming the face of the popular brand throughout the country. Brother Timothy's role at Christian Brothers continued until his retirement in 1989, when the winery was sold to a large corporation. Prior to that Christian Brothers was one of the top brands of wine and brandy in the United States.

By the late 1960s, a generation after World War II veterans returned home with a taste for French and Italian wine and at the time Julia Child was introducing French cuisine to American readers and television audiences, dry wines finally became more popular than sweet fortified wines, prompting a revolution in California's vineyards. The California State University system's viticulture and enology program began in 1880, but the program stalled during the years of Prohibition. In 1955, the University of California, Davis, acquired 40 acres of vineyard land in Oakville, Napa Valley, for purposes of research and education. Three years later, the Department of Viticulture and Enology's current home, Wickson Hall, was built. Many of today's luminary winemakers and vineyard managers and their recent predecessors are graduates of UC Davis, which had a large hand in training those who revitalized California's wine industry from the 1960s onward.

Ernest and Julio Gallo founded their winery in 1933, almost immediately after the repeal of Prohibition, using money borrowed from Ernest's mother-in-law, Theresa Franzia, and winemaking pamphlets from UC Davis that they had found in a basement in a public library in Modesto. By 1960 Gallo was the largest wine brand in the country, a position it has firmly held since the middle of that decade. In addition to the entry-level labels that fueled its explosive growth into and throughout the 1960s, the Gallo family today produces many mid- to high-level brands, including the Gallo Signature Series, Frei Brothers, William Hill Estate, Louis M. Martini, and MacMurray Ranch.

Robert Mondavi left his father's Charles Krug winery in 1965 to establish the first large, purpose-built winery in Napa Valley since the start of Prohibition. Robert Mondavi was among the first in California to begin labeling wines with varietal names, such as Cabernet Sauvignon and Chardonnay, as opposed to the names of famed European wine regions, such as Burgundy for red wines and Chablis for white, regardless of the grape varieties used in production. This was the beginning of a new gold rush in Napa, with a growth spurt in the number of new wineries and a meteoric rise in the quality of the wine produced there. In 1965 there were only 232 wineries in the state, a number that has grown 15-fold in the nearly 50 years since then.

From the 1960s and into the 1970s the popularity of wine from California was growing in the United States, but the image of California wine in the global market ranged from nonexistent to persistently negative. French wine still reigned supreme in the minds and glasses of the establishment until the wine competition that has since become known as "the Judgment of Paris" took place on May 24, 1976. Also called the Paris Wine Tasting of 1976, it was organized by Steven Spurrier, who at the time was a wine merchant living in Paris. (He has since become a renowned wine educator, journalist, and author.)

Spurrier set up a blind tasting pitting top California Chardonnay against the best Burgundian whites, and highly rated California Cabernet Sauvignon against the finest reds from Bordeaux. Spurrier was a strong proponent of French wine, and it is said that he expected the French wines to win. The eleven judges were asked to taste each wine and rate it on a scale of 20 points, ranking the wines in order from high to low. The rankings of Spurrier and his American colleague at l'Académie du Vin, Patricia Gallagher, were not included in the average scores, leaving the final judging to the nine French winemakers, sommeliers, winery owners, and restaurateurs in attendance.

Although the results were first ignored and then spurned by the French press, it is fortunate that *Time* magazine's George M. Taber was present and able to share the results with the rest of the world. The number one white wine was Chateau Montelena Chardonnay 1973 from Calistoga in Napa Valley. The winemaker at the time was Mike Grgich, who had yet to establish his own winery, and among the French wines beaten were Joseph Drouhin Beaune Clos des Mouches 1973, Ramonet-Prudhon Batard-Montrachet 1973, and Domaine Leflaive Puligny-Montrachet Les Pucelles 1972. Other California whites that made a strong showing were Chalone Vineyard Chardonnay 1974, Spring Mountain Vineyard 1973, and Freemark Abbey Vineyard 1972. The winning red wine was Stag's Leap Wine Cellars Cabernet Sauvignon

1973, which took top honors over esteemed wines such as Château Mouton-Rothschild, Château Montrose, and Château Haut-Brion. Ridge Vineyards Monte Bello Cabernet Sauvignon 1971 came in second place among the California reds and fifth place in reds overall.

The Judgment of Paris was a definitive triumph not just for the individual wines included but for the entire California wine industry. As word spread—slowly, as this was long before the advent of the Internet or social media—the wines of California began to be taken more seriously by American wine lovers and wine drinkers around the world. California wine regions are now visited by 20.4 million tourists annually, who spend $2.1 billion each year. Take a tour through Napa, Sonoma, Paso Robles, or Santa Barbara today and you are as likely to see a mix of tourists from as far away as Japan, Australia, and France as you are to see day-trippers from nearby cities.

Of the more than $1.4 billion in US wine shipped around the world in 2012, 90 percent of it was grown and produced in California. The largest foreign market as a whole consists of the 27 countries that make up the European Union, especially the United Kingdom, France, Spain, and Italy. The largest individual country California wine is exported into is Canada, followed by the United Kingdom, Hong Kong, Japan, China, Vietnam, Mexico, and South Korea. In 2012 the United States became the largest wine-consuming nation in the world by total volume, and 58 percent of the wine drunk within its borders was from California. Not even taking into account California's 116 AVAs or 3,800 wineries, the vast array of wine from California is staggering, with a multitude of varieties, styles, and price points. From the famed "Two Buck Chuck," Bronco Wine Company's private label Charles Shaw wines for Trader Joe's (which now retails for $2.49 in its home state and up to $3.79 elsewhere in the nation) to cult-status icon wines available to only the lucky few for upward of $500 upon release, the Golden State has something for everyone who likes wine.

Off-dry Moscato is the fastest-growing category in the United States among wine drinkers, Pinot Noir from the extreme Sonoma Coast is the favorite of a small but enthusiastic group of wine connoisseurs across the country and around the world, and allocation-only Napa Valley Cabernet Sauvignon is still being stockpiled by captains of industry in Silicon Valley and beyond. As might be expected, Chardonnay is California's most widely planted wine grape as well as the most popular varietal in the United States. Next in line is Cabernet Sauvignon (again, no surprise), which is the state's most widely planted red grape. Other important varieties are, in order of total acreage, Zinfandel, Merlot, Pinot Noir, Syrah, Sauvignon Blanc, Pinot Grigio, and Riesling.

One category of wine that is strictly a New World (or American) designation is "Meritage," which refers to a blend using at least two of the acceptable Bordeaux varietals: Cabernet Sauvignon, Merlot, Cabernet Franc, Petit Verdot, Malbec, and Carménère, with no more than 90 percent of one of those varietals included in the blend. White Meritage blends must include two or more of the following grapes: Sauvignon Blanc, Sémillon, and Muscadelle de Bordelais, again with no more than 90 percent of a single varietal in the final blend. The name "Meritage" (pronounced to rhyme with "heritage") is licensed from the Meritage Alliance, founded in Napa Valley in 1988 using the name the Meritage Association. Since its establishment, the organization has grown from a handful of members to over 250 wineries.

The wine-labeling laws in the state of California are generally consistent with US wine labeling laws but in a few instances hold wine producers to a higher standard. For example, US wine that is labeled with a vintage year must contain 85 percent wine from grapes harvested that year, which is also true for wines that bear the "California" designation. However, if a more specific AVA is listed on the label, such as Napa or Oakville, the bottle must contain at least 95 percent wine from the stated year. California law stipulates that 100 percent of the grapes in wine labeled "California" come from within the state's borders, whereas wine from a specific AVA may contain only 85 percent wine from that appellation. Wines that are labeled with single-varietal names, such as Pinot Noir or Sauvignon Blanc, must contain at least 75 percent of the stated variety. If a single-vineyard designation is noted on the label, at least 95 percent of the grapes had to have been grown in that vineyard.

Wine labels must include the bottler and location. If a label reads "produced and bottled by" this indicates that at least 75 percent of the wine was fermented by the company that bottled the wine. If it simply reads "bottled by," the wine has been bottled at that winery, but it may have been grown, crushed, fermented, and aged by another entity. Alcohol content is mandatory on wine labels, with a margin of error of plus or minus 1.5 percent. For wines with over 14 percent alcohol, the margin of error or tolerance is not used. For sweet wines, which may have an alcohol content between 14 and 21 percent, the margin of error is 1 percent.

THE GRAPES

An estimated 546,000 acres of wine grapes were growing in California in 2012. The US Department of Agriculture tracks the total acreage, by county, of 69 of the most populous grape varieties. In addition to widely planted varieties such as Chardonnay, Cabernet

Sauvignon, Zinfandel, Merlot, Pinot Noir, Syrah, Sauvignon Blanc, and Pinot Grigio, each of which totals well into five digits in terms of acreage, double-digit totals are tracked as well, in amounts as low as 55 acres. This is the range in which we find grapes beloved by winemakers and wine geeks alike that do not have large market share or traction when originating from California, such as Aglianico, Carménère, Counoise, and Pinotage. Although bottlings are small, many fine examples are found at winery tasting rooms and are hand-sold by sommeliers at fine restaurants throughout the state. At the opposite end of the continuum are Rubired and Ruby Cabernet, which grow on 12,220 and 6,074 acres, respectively, but hardly merit discussion because one would be hard pressed to find a high-quality wine made from either.

In addition to the individual 69 grape varieties that are tracked, another 10,000-plus acres fall under the headings of "Other White Wine" (4,011 acres) and "Other Red Wine" (6,220 acres). It will be interesting to note which grape varieties, if any, are cultivated in sufficient quantity to make a break from "Other" into their own categories in the coming years.

Scanning statistical data is hardly anyone's idea of a good time, but thanks to the Department of Agriculture's breakdown by county and totals over the past decade, the ability to spot rising stars in the wine world moves beyond merely anecdotal by both increase in quantity and the counties in which they proliferate. For example (and the sake of the alphabet), let's start with Albariño. Although the total acreage in the state amounts to a mere 180 acres, it becomes obvious that although the total output is minuscule, the fact that in 2004 there were only 28 total acres in the state and that the highest current concentration—55 acres—is found in San Luis Obispo County, home to Paso Robles, itself a rising star of a region, tells us that this is a grape to be reckoned with, however small the scale.

WHITE GRAPES

ALBARIÑO

Small in quantity but big on flavor, Albariño is a transplant from Spain's Rias Baixas region. (It is said to have been brought to Spain by French monks in the twelfth century.) Some winemakers bottle it under its Portuguese name, Alvarinho. It covers 180 acres in total throughout the state, particularly in the counties of San Luis Obispo, Monterey, Napa, and Yolo, where it has found a home in the Clarksburg AVA. The grape loves hot, sunny days bracketed by foggy mornings and cool nights, and its citrus, tropical fruit, and stone fruit flavors and aromatic floral notes shine through the brightest with a minimum of oak or no oak at all.

CHARDONNAY

Despite cries in recent years of "ABC!" (Anything but Chardonnay!), consumers can't get enough of this French transplant. Much of the backlash against the grape had more to do with the high-alcohol, overoaked style that made its way to wine shops around the country than with any of the natural qualities of the grape itself. The number one choice among American wine drinkers as well as the most prolific variety in the state, blanketing 95,074 acres, Chardonnay is produced across the entire range of wine styles and price points from "cheap and cheery" to expensive, rare, and ageworthy. Chardonnay's flavors of lemon and Granny Smith apple work equally well in crisp, steel-fermented bottlings, a buttery, well-oaked style, and sparkling wine. Colder temperatures coax the mineral notes of Chardonnay to the forefront, whereas vines growing on warm valley floors yield grapes with more prominent tropical fruit flavors. It is grown throughout the state, most notably in Monterey (16,882 acres), Sonoma (15,255 acres), San Joaquin (14,410 acres), and Napa (7,165 acres) counties. Besides still wine production, Chardonnay is an important component in Champagne-style sparkling wine.

CHENIN BLANC

This native of the Loire Valley that is known to most wine drinkers as the most popular variety from South Africa also thrives in California's rich soils. A total of 6,090 acres is found across the state, with the highest concentrations in Fresno and Madera counties. Smaller but still notable acreage thrives in Yolo, San Luis Obispo, and Santa Barbara counties, with a high concentration of standout bottlings coming from the Santa Ynez Valley. The conical bunches of green grapes ripen late in the season, so they are among the last to be picked each year. Flavors of pear and apple are complemented by rich minerality and racy acidity.

FRENCH COLOMBARD

Also known simply as Colombard, this workhorse grape lent acidity and citrus fruit flavors to inexpensive bottles and even jugs labeled "Chablis" before consumer demand for single-varietal whites such as Chardonnay and Sauvignon Blanc took off in the 1980s. It was once the most extensively grown grape in California, where it thrived on more than 90,000 acres as recently as the late 1980s. Still grown on an astounding 22,487 acres but mostly unheralded in entry-level blends, it is starting to be seen in single-varietal bottlings by innovative producers such as Jean-Charles Boisset of Buena Vista Winery. Expect flavors of peach, apricot, and citrus rind with light floral touches. It is also used in the production of brandy in California, as it is in its home country of France, where much of it is distilled into Cognac and Armagnac.

GEWÜRZTRAMINER

This northern Italian native mainly known to wine drinkers through the wines of Germany and Alsace is noted for its bright acidity and floral notes, most distinctively that of rose petal. This aromatic white covers 1,752 acres of California soil, with predominance in Monterey, Mendocino, Santa Barbara, and Sonoma. It thrives in cool-weather regions, and the finest versions feature little to no oak.

GRENACHE BLANC

There is not a lot of Grenache Blanc in California—267 acres in total—but its proliferation in Santa Barbara and San Luis Obispo, counties both known for their Rhône blends, offers a clue to its primary use. It is closely related to red Grenache (or *Garnacha*), which originated in Spain and spread to southern France. Primarily blended with Roussanne but increasingly vinified on its own by daring winemakers, Grenache Blanc is noted for its citrus flavors and herbal notes.

MARSANNE

A small-production grape with a big reputation, this is another Rhône valley variety that has found a home on the sunny slopes of California. Although it is grown on only 114 acres and is found mainly in blends, it is an increasingly important player in Santa Barbara, San Louis Obispo/Paso Robles, Monterey, and Sonoma. Marsanne's rich flavors of peach, jasmine, and a dusting of Christmas spice are enhanced by its zesty acidity. Single-varietal bottlings are hard to come by, but if you find some in your travels, make sure to bring at least one home.

MUSCAT (MUSCAT OF ALEXANDRIA, MUSCAT BLANC, MUSCAT HAMBURG, ORANGE MUSCAT)

Although for winemaking purposes Muscat is classified as a white grape, its color can range from pale green to pink to reddish brown or almost black on the vine. It is believed that all

Vitis vinifera grapes descended from Muscat of Alexandria, which originated in North Africa. It was used by the ancient Egyptians to make wine and is known for its large, oval, pale amber berries. It is the most prominent of the Muscat varieties in California, where it blankets 4,180 acres. Next in line is Muscat Blanc, whose official name is Muscat à Petit Grains, a description that refers to its small berries. It covers 2,293 acres. The third most promulgated Muscat variety in the state is Muscat Hamburg, which for statistical purposes is considered a red grape because of its dark color. Also called Black Muscat, it is grown on 661 acres. The acreage of Orange Muscat, named for its aroma rather than its color, totals 329. It is often used on its own or blended with others in small amounts as a dessert wine. In general, Muscat grapes are blended together and made into off-dry or sweet wines. Wine made from Muscat is noted for its aromas and flavors of orange, peach, apricot, honey, and flowers. With the growing popularity of sweet wines and particularly still and sparkling Moscato, it will be interesting to see the increase in acreage and production in the coming years. The most recent total of these four is 7,463 acres throughout the state.

PINOT GRIGIO/PINOT GRIS

It's practically two grapes in one, going by both its Italian and its Alsatian name, depending on winemaker preference and style. An aromatic white whose color on the vine varies from bluish-gray to light brownish-pink, it takes its name from the pinecone-like clusters its grapes form and the French word for gray, *gris*. The primary flavors are apple, lemon, and pear with light floral notes and crisp minerality. Wines labeled "Pinot Grigio" trend toward a lighter, fruitier style, and those bearing the name Pinot Gris are often fuller and riper with more pronounced spice notes. It is one of the most populous grapes in the state, found on 12,866 acres of California farmland. About one-third of that (4,148 acres) is growing in San Luis Obispo, and conspicuous concentrations are found in Monterey, Yolo, Sacramento, and Fresno counties. While there is not a particularly large amount of Pinot Gris in Sonoma (475 acres) in comparison to other areas, we have noticed quite a few higher-end Pinot Gris bottlings being produced there.

RIESLING

Officially called White Riesling by the Department of Agriculture, this German native is now at home on 4,452 acres in California, with almost half of that in Monterey and the balance distributed throughout the state. It may be made in dry, off-dry, and sweet styles, but Riesling's high acidity is a nice foil for its powerful fruit and floral flavors. Its bulblike green-yellow berries, sometimes tinged with purple, do best in cold-weather areas, where its acidity is retained by significant diurnal temperature variation. Riesling was once one of California's most popular white grapes, grown there originally by German immigrants such as Charles Krug and Jacob and Frederick Beringer. Though its popularity waned with the rising demand for Chardonnay and Pinot Grigio, California Riesling is experiencing a bit of a comeback as consumer tastes shift toward the aromatic white category. In 2004 there were only 2,121 acres of it in the state, a number that has more than doubled in the intervening years.

ROUSSANNE

Fully ripened Roussanne grapes, native to the Rhône Valley, are deep brown with an orange red–tinged color. This color, known as *roux* in French, is the root of the variety's name. Its total of 324 acres is barely a blip on the radar compared with more prevalent grapes, but Roussanne's clear-cut flavors of pear and honeysuckle and luscious floral aroma make its presence known in white blends and the rare single-varietal bottling in a number of places, especially San Luis Obispo, Santa Barbara, Napa, Sonoma, and Monterey. Roussanne is most frequently blended with Marsanne and Viognier, and it is noted for the combination of floral and herbal notes and fine-edged acidity it brings to the mix.

SAUVIGNON BLANC

Now cultivated the world over, Sauvignon Blanc most likely originated in France, where it is most at home in Bordeaux and the Loire Valley. Its name is derived from the French words for "wild" (*sauvage*) and "white" (*blanc*). The second most widely planted white grape in California and the seventh in total acreage, it is grown on 15,407 acres. Its flavors can vary from crisp and clean with strong tropical fruit and citrus flavors to more structured and elegant, especially when grown in a colder climate or tamed with the judicious use of oak. Stronger notes of asparagus, freshly cut grass, and green bell pepper are often present as well, adding to its *sauvage* reputation. It is also known here as Fumé Blanc, a name credited to Robert Mondavi in the late 1960s. The largest concentration of Sauvignon Blanc vines can be found in Napa (2,736 acres) and Sonoma (2,553 acres), and both San Joaquin and Lake counties boast upward of 1,800 acres each. Monterey, Mendocino, San Luis Obispo, and Santa Barbara are also host to significant acreage of Sauvignon Blanc, whose rising popularity may be tied to consumer trends toward fresh white wines paired with spicy Mexican, Central American, and Pacific Rim cuisine.

VIOGNIER

Grown on 3,001 acres of California ground, Viognier is distinguished by its highly aromatic, perfumed nose and flavors of apricot, peach, honey, and soft spice. It has moved far beyond its perceived home in France's Rhône Valley to become a favorite among winemakers and consumers alike—plantings have increased from 2,120 acres since 2004. Often vinified on its own, it is also blended with Marsanne and Roussanne, its hometown companions. Almost a third of California's Viognier is grown in San Joaquin County, the home of Lodi, and large contingents are found in Santa Barbara, Sonoma, San Luis Obispo, and Yolo counties. Viognier's graceful flavors and intense acidity are a good match for seafood and richly spiced dishes.

RED GRAPES

ALICANTE BOUSCHET

This hearty red-fleshed grape was heavily planted throughout California during Prohibition because, once harvested, it survived the long cross-country trip by rail to be used by home winemakers back east. Easy to maintain and offering high yields, it was also very widely planted across France, Spain, and Portugal in the years after the nineteenth-century phylloxera epidemic. It is a cross between Petit Bouschet and Grenache created in 1866 by Henry Bouschet, who successfully fulfilled his quest to create a durable grape with deep red color. Currently cultivated on 1,091 acres, it is mostly grown in inland counties. This is a far cry from the upward of 40,000 acres that existed here in the 1930s. Quite a bit of it is used for blending, often with Zinfandel, but single-varietal versions are made by Ridge Vineyards and Francis Ford Coppola Winery.

BARBERA

Far from its home in Italy's Piedmont, Barbera was first vinified in California at the end of the nineteenth century. It was a mainstay of the Italian Swiss Colony winery's red blends at that time, and although it fell out of favor in the years following Prohibition, plantings remain fairly high at a total of 6,328 acres. Its forceful flavors of blackberry, cherry, and blueberry and accents of spice and vanilla (picked up during barrel aging) are the backbone of many a bottle of "red table wine" and a smattering of single-varietal versions as well. Widely utilized by the first wave of Italian immigrants in California, Barbera is being rediscovered by a new generation of winemakers who are making high-quality interpretations as a nod to the state's winemaking history and in many cases to their own heritage as well. More than two-thirds of the state's crop is grown in El Dorado County, and another 15 percent is grown in Madera County.

CABERNET FRANC

One of the parents of Cabernet Sauvignon, Cabernet Franc is most at home in Bordeaux-style blends, which may be referred to by the name Meritage in California. Most noted for its assertive peppery character, Cabernet Franc also has flavors of cherry, cassis, violet, and earth. It is cultivated on 3,429 acres across the state, with over one-third of it grown in Napa (1,219 acres). This is no surprise given the number of high-profile—and high-priced—reds produced there, many labeled Cabernet Sauvignon but vinified with the addition of other grapes. There are also significant amounts in Sonoma (598 acres) and Santa Barbara (364 acres). We have seen a lot of single-varietal Cabernet Franc coming out of Sonoma, much of it available only at tasting rooms or direct from the winery.

CABERNET SAUVIGNON

This French offspring of Cabernet Franc and Sauvignon Blanc is one of the most widely cultivated grapes in the world. It is the second most widely grown grape in California and the most populous red grape, found on 80,630 acres. Almost a quarter of all the Cabernet Sauvignon in the state is grown in Napa, where it thrives on 19,516 acres. It is also widely planted in San Joaquin (11,595 acres), Sonoma (11,480 acres), and San Luis Obispo (10,114 acres) counties, and it is found to some degree in every county in the state. "Cali Cab" is a category unto itself in this country and now in many parts of the world, although like Chardonnay it is offered across the spectrum of prices and styles, from entry level and easy to find to hyperscarce and stratospherically priced. One of the reasons Cabernet Sauvignon receives high scores from critics, which only drives up prices more, is that its rich tannic structure makes it built to age, so collectors can amass these wines now and pull them out later for special occasions or simply to impress. Cabernet Sauvignon's general profile of black cherry, cassis, plum, violet, and pencil lead is enhanced by oak aging to include flavors of vanilla, caramel, butterscotch, and spice. Despite California Cabernet Sauvignon's reputation as high-alcohol, overoaked fruit bombs, there are a startling number of well-produced California Cabs across the entire spectrum of price that exhibit remarkable restraint and balance.

CARIGNANE

A large, dark, round grape that grows in tight clusters, Carignane, also known as Carignan, is a native of Spain (where it is called *Mazuelo* and *Cariñena*) that rose to prominence as the most widely planted variety in the Rhône Valley. It now grows on 2,558 acres in California, where it often is blended anonymously into red table wine. As a single variety it offers bright flavors of red cherry and nutmeg, and in blends it adds strong acidity, healthy tannins, and dark red color. Almost half of it is grown in Madera County (1,119 acres), but there is also a healthy showing in San Joaquin (460 acres), Mendocino (357 acres), and Sonoma (179 acres).

GRENACHE

Often said to be the most widely grown red grape on the planet, Grenache—known as *Garnacha* in its native Spain—works equally well on its own or as a blending grape. It flourishes in hot, dry climates, and its thin-skinned, medium purple berries are low in tannin, producing wines that are perfect for drinking when they are young. Flavors include raspberry, strawberry, honeysuckle, and light spice. Grenache grows on 6,020 acres in California, with over half of that divided between Fresno (2,032 acres) and Madera (1,579 acres) counties. It was long used throughout the state to make inexpensive, easy-drinking (for some) red and rosé wines, but its cultivation and vinification have been championed by the Rhône Rangers, a group dedicated to the promotion of Rhône-style wines in California and throughout the United States. Respectable acreage is noted in both San Luis Obispo (316 acres) and Santa Barbara (238 acres), which boasted only 172 acres each as recently as 2004. This makes sense to anyone who is aware of these two areas as hotbeds of Rhône-style winemaking. Grenache is often blended with Syrah and Mourvèdre in what are increasingly referred to as GSM blends.

MALBEC

Originally from France, where it is mainly blended with other grapes, especially in Bordeaux, Malbec made a name for itself in a big way in Argentina. (It is now being marketed as a single variety in the Cahors region of France, rightfully billed as the "original home of Malbec," where it has been grown and produced for hundreds of years.) Malbec is remarkably dark in color both on the vine and in the glass, and its flavors of black cherry, plum, chocolate, violet, and licorice are equally at home on their own or as part of the ensemble. It is grown on 2,689 acres, although around a third of that (944) is currently nonbearing, meaning the vines are not yet old enough to produce wineworthy grapes. Napa is home to 392 of those total acres, and Sonoma boasts 365, one for each day of the year. Most surprising is that of San Joaquin County's 665 acres, well more than half (391) are nonbearing vines. Given the growth in the state as a whole—the total has doubled since 2004, when there were only 1,255 acres of Malbec here—this is another variety to keep your eye on.

MERLOT

Despite disparaging comments made about the variety in the movie *Sideways*, California Merlot reigns strong, planted on 45,689 acres here. Like its blending partner and rival Cabernet Sauvignon, Merlot grows in every county in the state. Its smooth tannins and bright flavors of black cherry and blueberry, often backed by a touch of mint or eucalyptus, lighten the tannins in Cabernet-based blends and add freshness in the glass. Because of its softer tannic structure, Merlot does not require as much aging as other varieties and can be brought to market earlier. Merlot takes its name from the French word for blackbird (*merle*) due to its deep bluish-purple color. That color carries over into the glass, where Merlot may range from intense black cherry to inky purple. Stylistically, Merlot can run from young, fruity, and fresh to deep and rich, depending on growing conditions, winemaker technique, and length of aging. The county with the most Merlot is San Joaquin (7,818 acres), but there is plenty to go around: there are 5,975 acres of Merlot in Napa, 5,778 acres in Sonoma, 5,424 in Monterey, and 4,143 in San Luis Obispo.

MISSION

Mission is the grape that started it all, long before California was even a state. The grape that was first brought over by Spanish missionaries who were part of the original wave of immigration into California was initially the only variety and then the most highly propagated one until the arrival of French, German, and Italian grapes. There are still 643 acres of Mission here, mainly in the center of the state. The same grape that was first grown in South America, it is known as *Pais* in Chile and *Criolla Chica* in Argentina. Although the first wines made from Mission were rudimentary and would be considered barely drinkable by today's standards, a style of fortified wine known as Angelica uses Mission as its primary variety and is still produced in an elegant fashion by a very small number of producers.

MOURVÈDRE

Officially called Mataro (one of its Spanish names) for statistical purposes in California, Mourvèdre is an essential component in the GSM (Grenache–Syrah–Mourvèdre) blends, to which it adds a necessary dose of ageworthy tannins. It currently blankets 954 acres throughout the state, with a strong showing in San Luis Obispo County (217 acres, double 2004's 113 acres) and Santa Barbara (83 acres).

There are also large pockets of Mourvèdre in Contra Costa County (192 acres) on the northern Central Coast, near San Francisco and Oakland, and in Madera County (206 acres), where it was traditionally used in fortified dessert wines. Mourvèdre is noted for its flavors of mixed berries, spice, and anise. It can also have some strong elements of earth or even green notes that can be tamed by the hand of a talented winemaker.

PETIT VERDOT

Petit Verdot is most commonly used in small quantities in Bordeaux-style blends, although it is also crafted into single-varietal bottlings that are available at many California winery tasting rooms. It adds color, tannins, and a marked violet flavor and aroma when blended with other grapes. The name translates from French as "small green," a reference to the fact that the berries may not ripen properly if weather conditions are less than perfect at the beginning of the growing season. When fully ripened, Petit Verdot grapes are small and nearly black in color. It is grown on 2,228 acres in California, a significant increase from the 1,613 acres that existed in 2004. The largest proliferation is in Napa, with 753 acres, up from 485 acres in 2004. There are also high concentrations in Santa Barbara (384 acres), San Luis Obispo (319 acres), and Sonoma (233 acres).

PETITE SIRAH

Known in France and Australia as Durif, its original name, Petite Sirah was first brought to California in the late nineteenth century. It has been used in sweet fortified wines and also to add color and tannins to entry-level red blends, but this offspring of Peloursin and Syrah is striking out on its own in high-quality dry wines made throughout the state. The "petite" in its name is a reference to the size of the grapes on the vine, but Petite Sirah is big on flavor, with strong notes of plum and blueberry and hints of spice and mint. A high level of tannins contributes to its excellent aging potential. It grows on 8,637 acres across all of California, an increase of over 30 percent since 2004, when it covered only 6,363 acres. There are 2,001 acres in San Joaquin County, and relatively large plantings are also found in San Luis Obispo (1,435 acres), Napa (845 acres), and Sonoma (597 acres). A large part of the upsurge in both acreage and popularity no doubt is due to the efforts of PS I Love You, an advocacy group for Petite Sirah growers and producers.

PINOT NOIR

It takes its name from the pinecone-like clusters of grapes and the French word for "black" (*noir*), but in the glass Pinot Noir tends to be more cherry to medium garnet in color. The famed red grape of Burgundy is now at home all over the world, and the best versions are coming from cool climates. The extreme west Sonoma Coast is an area that is producing a large amount of high-quality, small-batch Pinot Noir. The variety offers flavors of cherry, chocolate, coffee, light spice, and orange zest. Aging in the barrel and bottle will add flavors of vanilla and Mediterranean herbs. It is cultivated on 39,610 acres of California vineyard land, a serious expansion of the 25,181 acres it covered in 2004. Sonoma is responsible for 12,062 acres of Pinot Noir, Monterey is home to 8,764 acres, and Santa Barbara boasts 4,499 acres. While some of the increase in attention to Pinot Noir is attributable to the movie *Sideways*, its popularity also is due to the general trend toward lighter, higher-acid, food-friendly wines. In addition to still wines, Pinot Noir is used in Champagne-style sparkling wines, particularly from the Anderson Valley and Carneros.

SANGIOVESE

The famous grape of Tuscany gets its name from the Latin *sanguis Jovis*, or "blood of Jove." It has been grown in California since about 1880, brought over from their home country by Italian immigrants. It is planted in amounts large and small in every region in the state, covering 1,894 acres, with 383 of those in Sonoma and 264 in Napa. It is usually seen as a single variety but sometimes is blended with Cabernet Sauvignon, Merlot, or Cabernet Franc, "Super Tuscan"–style. Young Sangiovese will taste of black plum, tart cherry, strawberry, and orange peel; age will bring on desirable secondary flavors of earth, tar, or truffles. It is also made into lovely rosé.

SYRAH

Syrah's numbers are as strong in California as its rich, fruity flavor. This is the same grape that is called Shiraz in Australia, and the origin of its name is a mystery. It may be named for a city in Persia, which is where the variety may have originated, and it may have first been called either Shiraz or Syrah. Either way, this Rhône Valley transplant blankets 18,798 acres of California hillsides and valleys, and it is found both on its own and in GSM or other red blends. In the New World, Syrah is known as a big, powerful wine, with flavors of plum, black cherry, cassis, anise, black pepper, and leather. It is also made in a more elegant style, with an emphasis on the savory notes of Mediterranean herbs and earth. The county with the highest concentration of Syrah is San Luis Obispo, with 2,553 acres; other quadruple-digit counties include San Joaquin (2,007 acres), Sonoma (1,895 acres), Madera (1,808 acres), Monterey (1,786 acres), and Santa Barbara (1,339 acres.) California Syrah is also made into luscious rosé with the refreshing qualities of white wine and the rich mouthfeel of a red.

TEMPRANILLO

A native of Spain, Tempranillo is an up-and-coming winemaker favorite in California. In 2004, it graced only 649 acres in the state, a total that has grown to 925 acres. Although in the past it was used to make inexpensive table wine here, today it is being produced as a single variety in both fresh and more heavily oaked styles. Its name comes from the Spanish word for "early," *temprano*, referring to the fact that this variety ripens early in the season. It has a deep garnet color and flavors of cassis, cherry, plum, mocha, and cigar box. There are 178 acres of Tempranillo growing in Fresno County and 164 acres in San Luis Obispo County.

ZINFANDEL

No one knows exactly how the first Zinfandel vines got to the state or even where the name comes from, but Zinfandel is a pure California success story. The third most prolific grape in California, Zinfandel blankets 49,136 acres here and is grown from stem to stern throughout the state. Far and away the largest plantings are in San Joaquin County, which features 18,999 acres of Zinfandel among its many acres of grapevines. Sonoma trails in distant second with 5,358 acres; other four-digit growers include Madera County (2,928 acres), Fresno County (2,747 acres), San Luis Obispo County (2,725 acres), Amador County (2,019 acres), Mendocino County (1,945 acres), Sacramento County (1,512 acres), and Napa County (1,492 acres). Although a lot of Zinfandel is made into inexpensive pale rosé or blush wine misleadingly labeled "White Zinfandel," a true Zinfandel is inky purple in color, offering rich flavors of raspberry, blackberry, licorice, and black pepper. Cooler-climate versions can be a bit more restrained, with hints of herbal notes or green pepper. Because of its high sugar content, it is easy to make high-alcohol Zinfandel, but there is now a trend toward a more elegant, lower-alcohol style. Zinfandel is closely related to the Italian grape Primitivo and the Croatian grape Plavac Mali and has been said to be genetically identical to the Croatian grape Crljenak Kastelanski. Many old-vine Zinfandel vineyards include plantings of other varieties such as Carignan, Petite Sirah, and Alicante Bouschet, sometimes called "mixed blacks," that were accidentally included in field blends in the past and are now intentionally blended in. One of the forces that has played a strong part in Zinfandel's transition toward a fine-wine variety is ZAP, or Zinfandel Advocates and Producers, a group dedicated to the study and celebration of this flavorful grape.

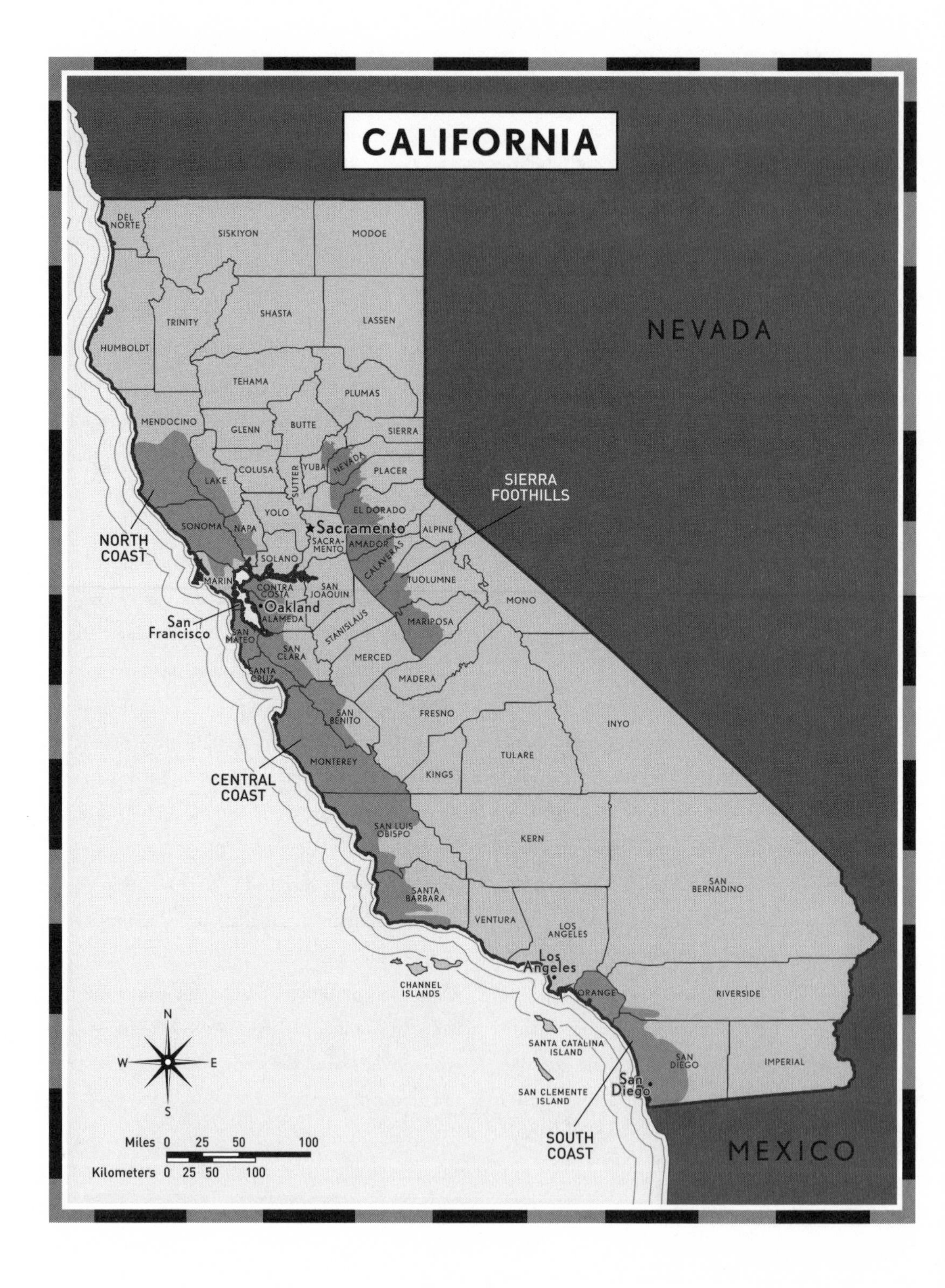
CALIFORNIA
NEVADA
MEXICO
DEL NORTE
SISKIYOU
MODOE
TRINITY
SHASTA
LASSEN
HUMBOLDT
TEHAMA
PLUMAS
MENDOCINO
GLENN
BUTTE
SIERRA
COLUSA
SUTTER
YUBA
NEVADA
PLACER
LAKE
YOLO
EL DORADO
SONOMA
NAPA
Sacramento
ALPINE
SACRA-MENTO
AMADOR
SOLANO
CALAVERAS
MARIN
CONTRA COSTA
SAN JOAQUIN
TUOLUMNE
MONO
Oakland
ALAMEDA
STANISLAUS
MARIPOSA
San Francisco
SAN MATEO
SAN CLARA
MERCED
SANTA CRUZ
MADERA
SAN BENITO
FRESNO
INYO
MONTEREY
TULARE
KINGS
SAN LUIS OBISPO
KERN
SANTA BARBARA
VENTURA
LOS ANGELES
SAN BERNADINO
Los Angeles
ORANGE
RIVERSIDE
SAN DIEGO
IMPERIAL
San Diego
CHANNEL ISLANDS
SANTA CATALINA ISLAND
SAN CLEMENTE ISLAND
NORTH COAST
SIERRA FOOTHILLS
CENTRAL COAST
SOUTH COAST
N
W
E
S
Miles 0 25 50 100
Kilometers 0 25 50 100

PART 1

THE WINE REGIONS OF CALIFORNIA

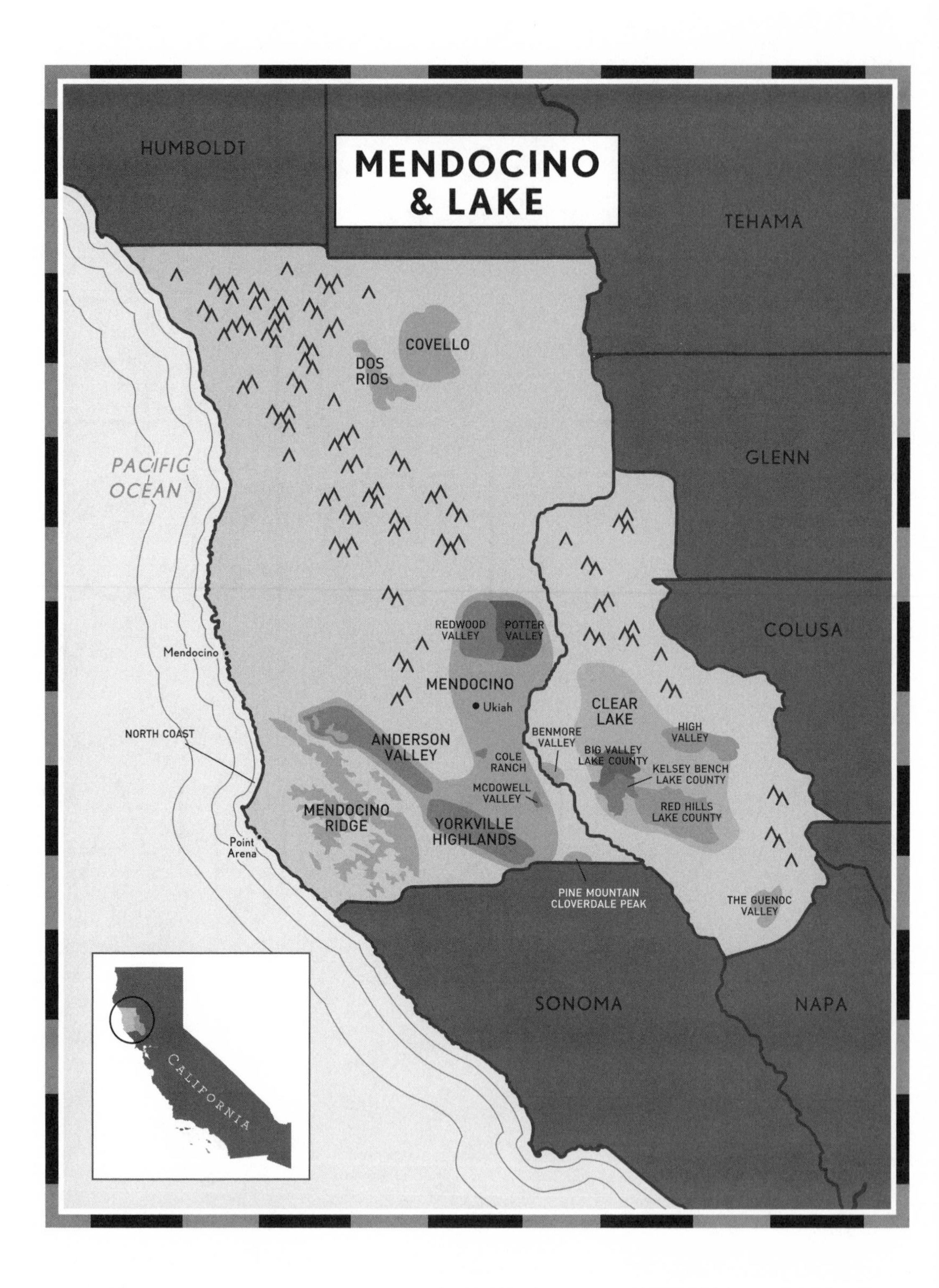
MENDOCINO & LAKE
HUMBOLDT
TEHAMA
GLENN
COLUSA
SONOMA
NAPA
PACIFIC OCEAN
COVELLO
DOS RIOS
REDWOOD VALLEY
POTTER VALLEY
MENDOCINO
Ukiah
Mendocino
NORTH COAST
ANDERSON VALLEY
COLE RANCH
MCDOWELL VALLEY
MENDOCINO RIDGE
YORKVILLE HIGHLANDS
Point Arena
BENMORE VALLEY
CLEAR LAKE
HIGH VALLEY
BIG VALLEY LAKE COUNTY
KELSEY BENCH LAKE COUNTY
RED HILLS LAKE COUNTY
PINE MOUNTAIN CLOVERDALE PEAK
THE GUENOC VALLEY
CALIFORNIA

CHAPTER 1

MENDOCINO COUNTY AND LAKE COUNTY

NORTHERN CALIFORNIA IS A NATURE LOVER'S paradise where statuesque redwoods shade ferns, orchids, and moss along the weather-beaten Pacific coast, and farther inland, hikers, mountain bikers, and sailors enjoy the pristine surroundings of one of the most ancient lakes in North America. To the west, Mendocino County, which is 60 percent redwood forest, is home to the world's tallest living tree, which stands at a towering 370 feet. Lake County, to the east, boasts the largest lake in the state, Clear Lake, which is 19 miles long by 8 miles wide and is believed to be one of the oldest lakes on the continent.

The northernmost wine-growing regions in the large North Coast AVA, Mendocino County and Lake County sit side by side, each just north of its higher-profile neighbors, Sonoma and Napa. Established in October 1983, the North Coast AVA has a total area of 3,008,000 acres (4,700 square miles) and contains within these four regions the highest concentration of wineries in the state. Both Mendocino and Lake counties trace their winemaking histories to the days of the California Gold Rush, and both have been used extensively for the past 40-odd years as grape-growing centers for large corporate wineries' entry-level bottlings. Both are entering into a golden age of winemaking as young winemakers, many the descendants of area wine industry pioneers, are branching out on their own and making high-quality, small-batch wines. Although they have many things in common—including latitude—Mendocino and Lake are worlds apart in terms of geography, climate, soils, and top grape varieties.

MENDOCINO

Mendocino County borders Sonoma County to the south; Lake, Glenn, and Tehama counties to the east; Humboldt and Trinity counties to the north; and the Pacific Ocean to the west. The natural border between Mendocino and Lake counties is the Mayacamas Mountain Range. The largest AVA in the county is simply called Mendocino, and this and its largest sub-AVA, Anderson Valley, form an angled V, with Mendocino in the east and Anderson Valley in the west. Even farther west than Anderson

Valley is the Mendocino Ridge AVA, noted for high-elevation plantings.

The large north-to-south portion of the Mendocino AVA is traversed by the 110-mile-long Russian River, which runs parallel to Highway 101 and flows southward into Sonoma. The top portion of Anderson Valley is cut through by the 28-mile-long Navarro River, which starts in the Coastal Mountain Range and flows northwest, first through the Yorkville Highlands sub-AVA in the southwest corner of Mendocino and then through a portion of the Mendocino Ridge AVA before continuing through the Anderson Valley and coursing into the Pacific about 10 miles south of the coastal city of Mendocino.

The Mendocino AVA encompasses 275,200 acres, of which 16,700 are planted with grapes. One of its most notable features is that 28 percent of its vineyards are certified organic or biodynamic. Green and sustainable vineyard practices are widespread and seem to be put to use by almost all the boutique and midsize wineries in the region. As you read through the winery listings, you will notice a significant number of wineries using solar power in part, with one winery relying completely on the sun for all of its energy needs. Fish Friendly Farming is growing in popularity, with more and more vineyard owners and wineries enrolling in the certification program each year. The first organic winery in the United States, Frey Brothers, was founded here in 1980; Frey was also the first producer of certified biodynamic wine. The largest certified organic grower in the state, Fetzer Vineyards, is located here, as is the nation's largest producer of wines from organically grown grapes, Bonterra. One-third of California's total organic wine grape acreage is found in Mendocino County, which also has the highest percentage of certified organic vineyards in the state and the entire country.

The majority of wineries here are family-owned, and many of today's winemakers can trace their roots back to the founding families of the 1850s. The intergenerational stewardship of the land combined with an influx of back-to-nature types in the 1970s have been two separate forces leading to a regional commitment to protect the earth and to farm using natural practices. There are 343 growers and over 90 wineries in Mendocino County. Chardonnay is the number one variety here, growing on 4,660 acres, followed by 2,430 acres of Cabernet Sauvignon, and 2,251 acres of Pinot Noir. Zinfandel is not far behind with 2,010 acres, and there are 1,727 acres of Merlot. In addition to 735 acres of Syrah, there are many vineyards growing Petite Sirah, Carignane, and Barbera, some of which date back to the early part of the twentieth century. Other white varieties that are grown here are

Sauvignon Blanc, Gewürztraminer, Viognier, and Chenin Blanc. White grapes tend to do well in the alluvial soils along the Russian and Navarro rivers, while reds thrive in the higher-elevation benchlands.

There are two small AVAs within Mendocino County that are north of the Mendocino AVA: Dos Rios and Covelo. Dos Rios, established in November 2005, has a total area of 15,500 acres. Spanish for "two rivers," it is situated between the Eel River and one of its forks, and there is only one winery operating within its boundaries. It is noted for its rocky soils and steep slopes. Covelo, to the northeast, is the newer and larger of the two, having been established in March 2006. It contains a total area of 38,000 acres. Covelo has mainly flat terrain, and the high mountain peaks surrounding it protect the region from the effects of the Pacific Ocean.

The Anderson Valley AVA, 16 miles long and 5 miles wide, was established in September 1983. It is home to what many consider some of the finest Pinot Noir vineyards in the area. Because of its proximity to the Pacific Ocean—between 10 and 15 miles—it enjoys cool temperatures in the morning and evening and ocean-generated fog that helps create the ideal growing conditions for not just this variety but also other cold-weather lovers such as Gewürztraminer and Riesling. Day-to-night temperature swings during the growing season can be as great as 40 to 50 degrees Fahrenheit. Anderson Valley Pinot Noir is so sought after that it is used in a number of appellation-specific bottlings by a Who's Who of high-profile producers in Napa, Sonoma, and elsewhere in California.

The Yorkville Highlands AVA, situated north of Sonoma County's Alexander Valley and just southeast of Anderson Valley, received official status in June 1998. Composed of 40,000 acres on either side of Highway 128, it has the highest concentration of red grapes in the county at 83 percent. Among the more than twenty varieties grown here, Cabernet Sauvignon is the most abundant, followed by Syrah, Pinot Noir, Merlot, and Chardonnay. About 450 acres are planted, divided among twenty-five family-owned vineyards. Most vineyards are planted between 1,000 and 2,200 feet of altitude, a position that benefits from cool afternoon breezes blowing in from the nearby Pacific Ocean. Cool late-day temperatures are essential to prevent overripening that may lead to "cooked" flavors in finished wine, and much colder nighttime temperatures help preserve acid balance in the grapes.

Among the more than 200 viticultural areas in the United States, the Mendocino Ridge AVA is the only existing AVA that is noncontiguous. Only vineyards planted at elevations of

1,200 feet or higher are considered part of the AVA; lower elevations fall into the Anderson Valley or Mendocino County appellation. Whereas lower altitudes are covered with fog in the early part of the day and the late afternoon, the high peaks of Mendocino Ridge poke through the fog, offering continuous sunshine to its vineyards during daylight hours. Established in December 1997 and covering 87,466 acres, Mendocino Ridge is home to just 75 acres of vineyards. Italian pioneers with a love of Zinfandel and no fear of heights planted the first Zinfandel vineyards here at the end of the nineteenth century, and Mendocino Ridge is still noted for this variety.

The Redwood Valley AVA in the northwest of the Mendocino AVA achieved recognition in February 1997. It is cooler than the broad valley floor of the larger Mendocino AVA and is home to Cabernet Sauvignon, Zinfandel, Barbera, and Petite Sirah. Italian immigrants planted some of the first vines in the red soils of Redwood Valley, which is named for the altitudinous trees that dominate the landscape. Directly to the east of Redwood Valley is the Potter Valley AVA, which sits at elevations more than 200 feet higher than its neighbors. Valley temperatures can soar during the day, but it is downright cold once the sun goes down. Pinot Noir, Chardonnay, Riesling, and Sauvignon Blanc do very well in Potter Valley, which has a total area of 27,500 acres and was established in November 1983.

The McDowell Valley AVA—a tiny region composed of just 540 acres—is in the southeast of Mendocino, just east of the Russian River. Situated mainly on benchland with altitudes up to 1,000 feet, McDowell Valley, which was recognized as an AVA in February 1987, is home to Zinfandel, red Rhône varieties such as Grenache and Syrah, and small amounts of white Rhône varieties.

Across the Russian River and to the northwest is the even smaller Cole Ranch AVA, established in May 1983, which covers an area of only 150 acres. The smallest AVA in the United States is home to 60 acres of Cabernet Sauvignon, Merlot, and Riesling growing at elevations between 1,400 and 1,600 feet above sea level.

Mendocino's newest viticultural area, the Pine Mountain-Cloverdale Peak AVA, became official in November 2011. Its 4,750 acres are home to 230 planted vineyard acres, mainly red varieties. It crosses county borders, with a portion of the appellation in Sonoma County. The AVA, above the town of Cloverdale, begins at an altitude of 1,600 feet and runs as high as 3,000 feet at the peak of Pine Mountain. Grapes have been grown here since the Gold Rush era, mostly on plots smaller than 30 acres.

There are also two AVA petitions pending before the Alcohol and Tobacco Tax and Trade

Bureau (TTB): Ukiah Valley and Sanel Valley. The Russian River is the dominant feature of the Ukiah Valley, dividing it roughly in two in a straight line from north to south. The folksy town of Ukiah is the county seat of Mendocino. Sanel Valley, just north of Sonoma County, is a six- by two-mile swath of alluvial plain on either side of the Russian River. It is home to Sauvignon Blanc, Chardonnay, Merlot, and Cabernet Sauvignon.

The vineyards of Mendocino County are just a couple of hours north of San Francisco, and wine tourism is booming as Californians discover the pleasures of the far north coast. Once drivers get past Cloverdale, they have a big decision to make. They can bear left up Highway 128 to savor the delights of the Anderson Valley from Yorkville to Boonville and beyond or keep straight on Highway 101 along the Russian River to enjoy the small-town ambience of Hopland and Ukiah and the wonderful wines of "Mendo." Either way, they will not be disappointed.

LAKE COUNTY

It is amazing to think that the fertile soils surrounding one of the oldest lakes in all of North America—which is also the largest lake wholly within California's borders—has just recently become known for the high quality of its wines. After the Gold Rush turned into the gold bust, many immigrants who chose to seek their fortune in fields rather than mines turned to the untouched shores of Clear Lake. Vineyards flourished in the volcanic or shale soils of hillsides and the alluvial soils of terraces and valleys from the mid-nineteenth century until the advent of Prohibition. Farmers turned their land over to walnuts and fruit trees for a good part of the twentieth century, but once wine industry pioneer Jess Jackson bought a farm here in the 1970s and began growing grapes, a new rush was on, bringing a significant number of grape growers to the region, most of whom sold their grapes to large wineries for use in entry-level California appellation bottlings. Although about 90 percent of the grapes grown in Lake County are still sold to wineries in other areas, there is a lot of buzz about the wines of Lake County and the new generation of innovators drawn to this special place at the foot of the glorious Mount Konocti.

Taking into account the Clear Lake AVAs four sub-AVAs, there are seven AVAs within Lake County. The largest, Clear Lake, surrounds the lake of the same name, which takes up half of the AVA's geographic area. There are two "older" sub-AVAs within Clear Lake: High Valley to the northeast of the midpoint of the lake and Red Hills Lake County on the southern shores of the lake. The Clear Lake AVA covers an area of 168,960 acres and was established in June 1984. Its first two sub-AVAs were granted official recognition 20 years later: Red Hills Lake County in September 2004 and High Valley in August 2005. High Valley AVA vineyards range in elevation from 1,600 to 3,000 feet above sea level, and Red Hills Lake County's vineyards, at the base of the 4,300-foot extinct volcano Mount Konocti, run from 1,400 feet up to 3,000 feet as well. The Kelsey Bench-Lake County AVA encompasses a total area of 9,100 acres, with 900 of them planted to grapevines, mainly red varieties. There are twenty-seven vineyards and one winery. The Big Valley-Lake County AVA is 11,000 acres in size, with 1,800 acres planted to vines. Six wineries and 43 vineyards make their home here.

There are a total of 8,600 acres of grapes growing in the county, with the bulk of them in the Clear Lake AVA and its sub-AVAs, and 170 grape growers farm there.

Although many inland areas in California suffer from extreme daytime heat, the Clear Lake AVA enjoys the lacustrine effect of the large body of water in its midst. The dominant grape variety is Cabernet Sauvignon, planted on 3,300 acres, followed by Sauvignon Blanc, on 1,790 acres. Other Bordeaux varieties are also planted here, as are Chardonnay, Petite Sirah, Syrah, Tempranillo, and Zinfandel. The vast majority of vineyards are planted within shouting distance of Clear Lake. There are more than thirty wineries in Lake County, mostly small and family-owned, and every major English-language wine magazine has lauded the attributes of Lake County Cabernet Sauvignon in recent years.

The small Benmore Valley AVA, established in November 1991, is 1,440 acres in size. There are no wineries within its borders yet. It is west of the Clear Lake AVA, on the border with Mendocino County. The Guenoc Valley AVA, just north of the county's border with Napa County, was recognized as an official viticultural area in December 1981. The AVA sits within the borders of nineteenth-century British actress Lillie Langtry's estate and is believed to be the first established single-proprietor AVA in the nation.

While Lake County's tourism options could best be described as rustic through the early years of this century, with the influx of upscale wineries there is an increasing range of lodging and dining options. In addition to mountain biking, rock climbing, white water rafting, hiking, sailing, and fishing, locals and tourists alike now add wine tasting to their list of must-do activities in Lake County.

THE WINERIES

BLACK KITE CELLARS

22686 Greenwood Ridge Road, Philo, CA 95466,
(415) 923-0277
www.blackkitecellars.com

Tom Birdsall and Rebecca Green Birdsall were cycling in Burgundy when the idea of owning a winery first struck them. As luck would have it, Rebecca's parents, Donald and Maureen Green, had purchased 40 acres of land in 1995 that now include Kite's Rest Vineyard. In 2004 the family hired Paul Ardzrooni to manage the vineyards and Jeff Gaffner to direct the winemaking. Black Kite Cellars' wines consistently garner high scores from many respected wine publications, including *Wine Enthusiast* and *Wine Spectator*. Black Kite Kite's Rest Vineyard Anderson Valley Pinot Noir 2010 has aromas of bright red cherry, red currants, Christmas baking spices, and a touch of talc in the complex bouquet. It is fruity yet elegant and restrained in the mouth with a delightful finish. Black Kite Stony Terrace Block Anderson Valley Pinot Noir 2010 is fruit-filled and bright on the nose and exuberant on the palate. It has soft flavors of red fruits with a touch of spice. The finish is long and elegant. Drink it now or cellar it for a few years; you'll be pleased either way.

BONTERRA VINEYARDS

2231 McNab Ranch Road,
Ukiah, CA 95482,
(707) 462-7814
www.bonterra.com

The concept for Bonterra Vineyards originated in 1990, and the wines were first released in 1992 under the name "Fetzer Organic." In 1994 the name "Bonterra" began appearing on the label, and today they are the leading producer of organically grown wines in California. Bob Blue is the head winemaker and has been with Fetzer since 1988, and Dave Koball has been the vineyard director since 1995. Dave oversees 970 acres of Mendocino County certified organic land, 284 of which are certified as biodynamic, and produces 4,400 tons of grapes per year. Together Bob and Dave oversee a staff of 110 employees, making this one of the largest organically minded wine producers in the state. Bonterra Organic Vineyards Mendocino County Chardonnay 2011 is straw yellow, with aromas of caramelized pineapple, lemon blossom, and lemon curd. In the mouth the first impression is buttery with notes of beeswax and hazelnuts, but the finish is crisp, clean, and fruity with a nicely restrained minerality. Bonterra Organic Vineyards Mendocino County Merlot 2010 is cherry red, with notes of dark plums and black cherries in the bouquet. The palate shows big dark fruits with a nice oak frame. The finish is long and is characterized by soft tannins.

BRASSFIELD ESTATE

10915 High Valley Road,
Clearlake Oaks, CA 95423,
(707) 998-1895
www.brassfieldestate.com

Jerry Brassfield acquired 1,600 acres of land in 1973 and over the years purchased additional property so that today Brassfield Estate consists of 2,500 acres in the High Valley AVA of Lake County. The estate's vineyards include Monte Sereno, Volcano Ridge, Ridge Top, and High Serenity. David Ramey is the consulting winemaker, with Jason Moulton as the associate winemaker. Brassfield Estate Serenity 2011 is a blend of 56 percent Pinot

Grigio, 31 percent Sauvignon Blanc, and 13 percent Gewürztraminer. It has aromas of white citrus blossoms, honeycomb, and white stone fruits. In the mouth flavors of white peach and tropical fruits dance on your tongue before the long, crisp finish. Brassfield Estate Eruption 2011 is composed of 39 percent Syrah, 27 percent Mourvèdre, 10 percent Malbec, 8 percent Petite Sirah, 8 percent Tempranillo, 4 percent Zinfandel, and 4 percent Grenache. It is garnet-ruby in the glass, with aromas of black cherry, cocoa powder, and Indian spice in the complex bouquet. In the mouth the fruit flavors come forward with a bit of spice in the smooth tannic finish.

BREGGO CELLARS

11001 County Road 151, Boonville, CA 95415,
(707) 895-9589
www.breggo.com

Napa Valley winery owner Cliff Lede partnered with the team at Breggo Cellars in the Anderson Valley, and together with winemaker Ryan Hodgins and president Jack Bittner the group is making delicious wine in Mendocino County. Breggo Cellars Savoy Vineyard Anderson Valley Chardonnay 2010 is medium straw, pale yellow colored, with aromas of white peach and lemon blossom, and a whiff of petrol. In the mouth flavors of white peach and green apple are accentuated by a creamy mouthfeel and a bright lemon finish. Breggo Anderson Valley Riesling 2011 is medium straw, with notes of citrus, citrus blossom, and orange zest in the bouquet. Bright pineapple, lemon-lime, and grapefruit flavors come alive on your palate, with a crisp, clean finish.

CEAGO VINEGARDEN

5115 E. Highway 20, Nice, CA 95464,
(707) 274-1462
www.ceago.com

Jim Fetzer, former president of Fetzer Vineyards, has created a beautiful biodynamic winery estate and farm on the shores of Clear Lake. From a Pomo Indian word, *Ceago* (pronounced "shee-ye-ho") literally means "grass-seed valley," but Jim takes it to mean that we must respect the land in a nurturing fashion. Visitors to Ceago Vinegarden are always impressed with the natural beauty of the estate and enjoy taking a long walk on Ceago's lakefront pier. If you're lucky enough to reserve one of the two rooms available for an overnight stay, you may never want to leave. Ceago Vinegarden Estate Grown Reserve Lake County Chardonnay 2010 is straw yellow, with notes of Christmas spices, toasted almonds, and tropical fruits in the bouquet. On the palate it is rich with a buttery mouthfeel and creamy finish. Ceago Vinegarden Del Lago Syrah 2010 has aromas of red raspberry, black cherry, and cinnamon. It is fruity in the mouth with a nice amount of spice on the finish.

DALLIANCE WINES

13151 East Highway 20, Clearlake Oaks, CA 95423,
(707) 998-9656
www.dalliancewines.com

The owners of Dalliance enjoy a little playful witty repartee and double entendre when it comes to the name of their winery. From the French for *un affaire romantique*, the word "dalliance" refers to playful frolicking or amorous play on the side. What better wine to enjoy on a Sunday afternoon picnic in the park with that someone special? Dalliance

Lake County White Wine 2011 is a blend of 60 percent Viognier, 20 percent Riesling, 18 percent Sauvignon Blanc, and 2 percent Chardonnay. It is straw yellow in color, with aromas of citrus blossom, honeydew melon, and white stone fruits. It has flavors of pineapple, guava, and peach, with a pleasant mouthfeel and a crisp clean finish. Dalliance Lake County Red Wine 2010 is a blend of 46 percent Zinfandel, 18 percent Barbera, 17 percent Syrah, 14 percent Tempranillo, and 5 percent Grenache. Deep ruby garnet in the glass, it has aromas of red cherry, Christmas baking spices, and cassis. It is soft upon entry into the mouth with good balance and a smooth tannic finish.

DREW FAMILY CELLARS

P.O. Box 313, Elk, CA 95432,
(707) 877-1771
www.drewwines.com

After several years managing vineyards in Sonoma and working as an assistant winemaker for a number of different wineries, Jason Drew and his wife, Molly, packed their belongings and moved to Australia to study at the University of Adelaide. Eighteen months later they returned home with Jason's degree in enology and their newborn son, Owen. Jason began working at Corison Winery and then moved to Babcock Vineyards, but the culmination of the Drews' dream of owning a vineyard occurred in 2004, when they purchased a 26-acre apple orchard in the Mendocino Ridge AVA. Drew Morning Dew Vineyard Anderson Valley Pinot Noir 2010 has aromas of black cherry, red raspberry, and fennel bulb. It is fruit-forward in the mouth with a delightful sweet tannic finish.

ELKE VINEYARDS

12351 Highway 128, Boonville, CA 95415,
(707) 246-7045
www.elkevineyards.com

mary elke

Boonville Barter
2011 Pinot Noir Anderson Valley

Mary Elke began making wine from grapes grown on her land in 1997. Before that time her fruit was used in wines made by others, including Au Bon Climat, Far Niente, Mumm, and Roederer, to name only a few. Her winemaker, Matt Evans, actually lives in New Zealand but returns each year to make Elke's wine. Mary Elke Pinot Gris 2011 is pale straw in color, with aromas of ripe melon, Bartlett pear, and citrus blossom. In the mouth there are flavors of fruit and toasted almonds. It is clean and crisp and perfect for a hot summer afternoon. Mary Elke Boonville Barter Pinot Noir 2011 is cherry red in color, with notes of dried cherry and ripe black cherry in the pleasant bouquet. It is fruit-forward on the palate with a persistent finish of fruit and cocoa powder.

FETZER

12901 Old River Road, Hopland, CA 95449,
(707) 744-1250
www.fetzer.com

Barney and Kathleen Fetzer purchased 720 acres of land in 1958 and together with their sons, Jim and John, produced 2,500 cases of their first commercial red wine in 1968. Over the years the Fetzers acquired additional large parcels of land, and in 1978 Fetzer was one of the first California wineries to produce white wine made from Chardonnay. The company was sold to the Brown-Forman Corporation in 1992, and production reached 2.2 million cases that year. Today, Fetzer is owned by Concha y Toro and winemaking is under the direction of Dennis Martin, Charlie Gilmore, and Michael Chupp. Fetzer makes a wide array of wines from thirteen varieties. Fetzer

Sundial Chardonnay 2011 has delightful aromas of tropical fruit and pleasant acidity on the palate. This is a perfect wine to take to a picnic or a family gathering on the beach. As Fetzer likes to say, "We'll never disappoint you with our Chardonnay: it's like saying hello to an old friend."

FOURSIGHT WINES

14475 Highway 128,
Boonville, CA 95415,
(707) 895-2889
www.foursightwines.com

Homer Albert "Twink" Charles, his wife, Margaret, and their son Homer "Norman" settled in Anderson Valley in 1943 to join the lumber trade. They built a small sawmill and eventually purchased their current property in 1950, but it wasn't until 2001 that subsequent generations planted Charles Vineyard and until 2006 that the family started Foursight Wines. Foursight Charles Vineyard Sauvignon Blanc 2011 is pale straw in color. Bright citrus, apple, and pear notes are accented by a touch of freshly picked wheat grass. It is vibrant in the mouth with bright fruit flavors and a crisp, clean finish. Foursight Charles Vineyard Clone 05 Pinot Noir 2010 (only five barrels made) has a rich dark cherry color and perfumed aromas of red cherry and dried black cherry with just a touch of anise to excite your nose. A mix of red fruits and dark berry flavors mingle on your palate and carry you through the sweet tannic finish.

FREY VINEYARDS

14000 Tomki Road,
Redwood Valley, CA 95470,
(707) 485-5177
www.freywine.com

New York City–born Paul and Beba Frey met and married while in medical school and settled down to raise a family in Northern California in the early 1960s. Twelve children later the family decided to plant Cabernet Sauvignon and Riesling and sell grapes to nearby wineries. In 1980 the family bonded the winery and became the first organic winery in the United States, and in 1996 they became the first producer of Demeter-certified biodynamic wines in North America. Frey Vineyards is in the Redwood Valley AVA in Mendocino County, and all of its wines are made with no added sulfites. Frey Organic Mendocino County Petite Sirah 2010 is garnet purple in color, imparting aromas of purple flowers, ripe cherry, and a touch of vanilla from oak aging. Nice rich flavors of strawberry preserves and ripe cherry abound before the sweet tannic finish. Frey Organic Mendocino County Sangiovese 2010 is garnet in color, with concise aromas of freshly picked cranberry and red raspberry. It gently coats your mouth with ripe fruit flavors and then leads you to a smooth tannic finish with just the right amount of spice.

GOLDENEYE WINERY

9200 Highway 128, Philo, CA 95466,
(707) 895-3202
www.goldeneyewinery.com

Looking for a place to plant Pinot Noir, Dan and Margaret Duckhorn found the perfect *terroir* in the Anderson Valley in 1996. The next year they harvested the first grapes that they used to make Goldeneye's inaugural 375 cases of wine. Zach Rasmuson became the winemaker and general manager in 2003 and over the last decade has earned the winery a well-regarded reputation in the world of California Pinot Noirs. Goldeneye is one of a few California wineries to have earned the coveted LEED Gold Certification for its environmental practices. Goldeneye Anderson Valley Estate Grown Gewürztraminer Confluence Vineyard 2010 is straw yellow in color. Notes of Anjou pear, kumquat, and citrus rind delight the nose while crisp clean flavors excite the tongue. It has nice acidity and a touch of sweetness on the finish. Goldeneye Anderson Valley Pinot Noir 2010 is cherry red. Seductive aromas of mixed berry preserves, ripe red fruits, and cracked black pepper rise through your nose while flavors of cherry and red raspberry spread across your mouth. There is nice spice in the finish, with a touch of creamy mocha cappuccino at the very, very end.

GREENWOOD RIDGE VINEYARDS

5501 Highway 128, Philo, CA 95466,
(707) 895-2002
www.greenwoodridge.com

The Greenwood Ridge tasting room is a sight to see. It was designed by owner-winemaker Allan Green's father, the architect Aaron Green, an associate of Frank Lloyd Wright. Only one fallen redwood tree—with a diameter of 13 feet—was used to provide all the lumber to build the octagonal structure. The tasting room runs on solar power from panels attached to the roof, and the excess energy is diverted back to the electric company. Winemaker Allan Green limits the production of his highly rated wines to 2,500 cases per year, and his efforts have garnered international attention from a variety of wine publications. Greenwood Ridge Vineyards Sauvignon Blanc is composed of 76 percent Sauvignon Blanc and 24 percent Sémillon. It has aromas of honeydew melon and Red Delicious apple. There are nice touches of herbal characteristics and minerality on the palate. It has a clean, balanced acidic finish with lingering notes of Meyer lemon. Greenwood Ridge Pinot Noir 2010 is cherry red. Indian spice, red fruit, and saddle leather hit high in the nose, with sexy black cherry fruit flavors in the mouth. It has a great, smooth tannic finish. This wine is wonderful with food or without—you decide.

GREGORY GRAHAM WINES

13633 Point Lakeview Road, Lower Lake, CA 95457,
(707) 995-3500
www.ggwines.com

Gregory Graham established his own label in 1992 while working at Rombauer Vineyard in Napa Valley, but it wasn't until 2004 that he began to produce wine from grapes grown on his own vines. He and his wife, Marianne, now live among those vines. Their winery was completed in 2006, and since 2011 it has been operating under solar power. Their current production is 4,500 cases of wine made from varieties that include Sauvignon Blanc, Riesling, Viognier, Chardonnay, Grenache, Pinot Noir, Syrah, Zinfandel, and Cabernet Sauvignon. Gregory Graham Wines Cinder Cone Reserve 2008 is the first blend from the estate. It is a blend of Syrah, Cabernet Sauvignon, and Grenache from Graham's Crimson Hill Vineyard and a touch of Malbec sourced from nearby Red Hills Ranch. Ruby purplish in the glass, it has aromas of purple flowers, violets, cracked black pepper, and blueberry pie. It is dense and fruit-forward on the palate with a savory finish. Gregory Graham Roumiguiere Vineyard Riesling 2009 is made with just a touch of residual sugar. It has aromas of Granny Smith apple, honeycomb, and white flowers. With bright fruit flavors in the mouth and a delightful amount of sweetness, this makes the perfect wine to pair with hot and spicy Asian cuisine.

HANDLEY CELLARS

3151 Highway 128, Philo, CA 95466,
(707) 895-3876
www.handleycellars.com

Milla Handley graduated from the University of California, Davis, in 1975 and worked at Chateau St. Jean before moving to the Anderson Valley in 1978. After working at Edmeades Winery she began making her own Chardonnay in her basement. Today her estate vineyard consists of 12 acres of Pinot Noir, 5 acres of Gewürztraminer, and 13 acres of Chardonnay. The vineyard was certified CCOF (California Certified Organic Farmers) organic in 2005, and her team consists of vineyard manager José Jimenez, co-winemaker Kristen Barnhisel, and consultant Bill Oldham. Handley Cellars Anderson Valley Gewürztraminer 2012 has aromas of white flowers and tropical fruits. There are nice flavors of ripe melon and lemon meringue pie on the palate with a touch of spice in the finish. Handley Cellars Estate Anderson Valley Chardonnay 2011 is straw colored. Notes of white stone fruits and crisp minerality hit the nose just right. Granny Smith apples, Christmas baking spices, and toasted hazelnuts flood the palate before the clean finish.

HAWK AND HORSE VINEYARDS

13048 Highway 29, Lower Lake, CA 95457,
(707) 942-4600
www.hawkandhorsevineyards.com

David Boies purchased the historic 900-acre El Roble Grande horse ranch in 1982 and planted vines in 2001. The first vintage, in 2004, received high praise in international competitions. Hawk and Horse remains tied to its past, and visitors to the property can see American Saddlebred and American Quarter horses as well as Scottish Highlander cattle grazing the land. The ranch and winery are Demeter Biodynamic and CCOF Organic Certified. Vineyard management is under the direction of Mitch Hawkins, and winemaking is performed by Richard Peterson and Tracy Hawkins. Hawk and Horse Vineyards Cabernet Sauvignon 2009 is dark garnet in color, with aromas of ripe black raspberry, blueberry pie, and cigar box in the complex bouquet. In the mouth it is velvety with flavors of black plum, dark chocolate, and freshly ground black pepper. The tannins are well integrated, and the finish is persistent.

JERIKO ESTATE

12141 Hewlitt and Sturtevant Road,
Hopland, CA 95449,
(707) 744-1140
www.jerikoestate.com

San Francisco Judge J.H. Sturtevant built the original mansion in 1898, and 100 years later Jeriko Estate was acquired by Daniel Fetzer. Daniel immediately began replanting vineyards using techniques learned as a young man because of his Fetzer family ties, and he added an estate winery and wine bar in 1999. Jeriko Estate is certified organic by Stellar Certification Services and biodynamic by Demeter. Jeriko Estate Reserve Syrah 2009 is inky purple. It has loads of big ripe fruit and a touch of white pepper in the nose, with sweet fruit and balanced tannins in the finish. Jeriko Estate Dijon Clone Pinot Noir 2011 is ruby garnet in color. Cherry cola, freshly ground black pepper, Indian spices, and ripe red fruits transfer from nose to palate effortlessly. It has a classic Burgundian finish.

LANGTRY ESTATE

21000 Butts Canyon Road,
Middletown, CA 95461,
(707) 995-7521
www.langtryestate.com

Grapes were first planted here in 1854, but it wasn't until famed British stage actress Lillie Langtry bought the property in 1888 that Guenoc Valley wines received any attention. In Victorian times Lillie was known as "the most beautiful woman in the world" and was courted by Edward, Prince of Wales. She purchased her 8,000-acre property with Fred Gebhard, a friend who was also counted among her many suitors. Today the Langtry Estate is one of the largest contiguous private land holdings in California, with 21,349 acres, and its corresponding Guenoc Valley AVA is considered by many to be the first single-proprietor American Viticultural Area. Langtry Estate Guenoc Lake County Sauvignon Blanc 2011 has aromas of mango, white stone fruits, and grapefruit rind. It is crisp and fruity in the mouth with a clean finish. Langtry Estate Guenoc Lake County Petite Sirah 2011 is purple in color with aromas of violets, lavender, and freshly picked blueberries and red raspberries. It has a nice amount of heft on the palate with fruit flavors accented by a touch of spice. The finish is long, smooth, and fruit-driven.

MASÚT VINEYARD AND WINERY

1301 Reeves Canyon Road,
Redwood Valley, CA 95470,
(707) 485-5466
www.masut.com

Brothers Ben and Jake Fetzer were raised on the Fetzer Home Ranch and learned the winemaking business from the ground up. By the time they reached the eighth grade they were making blends of Sangiovese and Cabernet Sauvignon. As third-generation winemakers and grape growers they farm their 1,500-acre Masút Ranch together and make wines that have begun to capture the attention of wine critics and consumers alike. This is a winery to keep your eye on. Masút Vineyard and Winery Estate Pinot Noir 2010 is dark ruby in color. Bright red cherry, cinnamon, and clove aromas are enticing as ripe fruit flavors, balanced acidity, and velvety tannins fill your mouth.

MCFADDEN VINEYARD

13275 Highway 101, Hopland, CA 95449,
(707) 744-8463
www.mcfaddenvineyard.com

Guinness McFadden fell in love with Potter Valley, planted 23 acres of vineyards in 1970, and over time has planted 140 more. Over the years he has sold grapes to Beringer, Fetzer, Piper Sonoma, Chateau Montelena, and Robert Mondavi, but he decided to make his own Pinot Gris in 2003. In 2004 he added Riesling; in 2005, Sauvignon Blanc, Zinfandel, and Pinot Noir; and in 2006, Chardonnay. McFadden Vineyard is certified organic by California Certified Organic Farmers and is well known in the area for its farm stand that sells beautiful bay leaf wreaths and garlic braids. Guinness also is credited for his commitment to energy sustainability because of his hydroelectric power plant and solar panels. McFadden Old Vine Zinfandel 2010 is garnet in color. Dried cherry, red raspberry preserve, and freshly ground white pepper combine to make an intensely pleasant first impression. The fruit carries on to the palate with a long, luscious finish. McFadden Sauvignon Blanc 2012 has great notes of lime rind, orange blossom, and Ruby Red grapefruit juice. It is crisp and clean in the mouth with a balanced acidic finish.

PARDUCCI

501 Parducci Road, Ukiah, CA 95482,
(707) 463-5357
www.parducci.com

The Parducci family moved from Tuscany to Mendocino and established their eponymous winery in 1932. It is considered by many to be Mendocino County's oldest winery and has been producing wine continuously for over 80 years. Bob Swain has been the head winemaker for more than 15 years and crafts wine in the Small Lot Blend and True Grit Reserve collections. Parducci Small Lot Blend Sauvignon Blanc 2011 is pale yellow, with aromas of pineapple, guava, and lemon zest. In the mouth it has flavors of ripe melon, Ruby Red grapefruit, and lime with a crisp, clean finish. Parducci Small Lot Blend Pinot Noir is cherry red, with aromas of freshly picked strawberries, ripe red cherries, and dried black cherries with top notes of cigar box and Indian spices. It is fruity on the palate with rich berry flavors shining through before the persistent finish.

PAUL DOLAN VINEYARDS

501 Parducci Road,
Ukiah, CA 95482,
(888) 362-9463
www.pauldolanwine.com

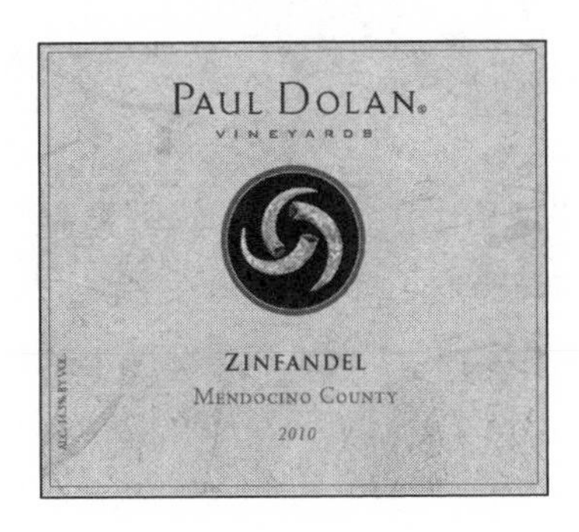

Inspired by Paul Dolan's role as a leading proponent of biodynamic and organic grape farming, these wines exclusively utilize grapes grown in accordance with organic and biodynamic principles. Paul Dolan Vineyard Mendocino County Chardonnay 2010 is straw yellow, with aromas of Gala apple, citrus blossom, and vanilla caramel. It is full-bodied in the mouth with balanced acidity and a persistent finish. Paul Dolan Vineyard Mendocino County Zinfandel 2010 is garnet in color, with aromas of blackberry preserves, fresh black raspberry, and freshly ground white pepper. It is fruit-forward in the mouth with a touch of spice in the finish.

ROEDERER ESTATE

4501 Highway 128, Philo, CA 95466,
(707) 895-2288
www.roedererestate.com

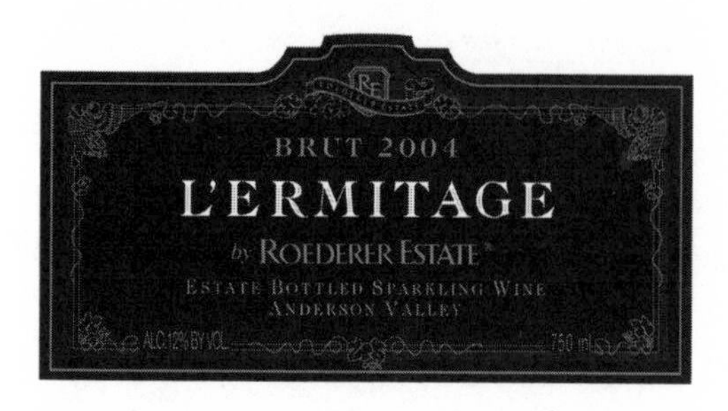

Fifth-generation Champagne-born winemaker Jean-Claude Rouzaud selected this 580-acre Anderson Valley parcel in 1982 to continue his family's sparkling wine legacy in California. He has since handed over command to his son Frederic, and the estate continues to make delicious bubbly using the traditional Champagne method. Only grapes grown on the estate are used in the cuvée, and the family is very careful to use only 70 percent of the first press and none of the *deuxieme taille,* or second press, to craft its high-quality California sparkling wines. Roederer Estate Brut NV is composed of 60 percent Chardonnay and 40 percent Pinot Noir. It is straw colored, with enticing aromas of green apple, ripe pear, and toasted hazelnut that transfer seamlessly onto the palate. It is refreshing in taste with a nice amount of bubbles. Roederer Estate L'Ermitage 2004 is one of the estate's Tete de Cuvée wines that are made only in exceptional years. It is wonderfully bubbly with a delightful mousse and aromas of Granny Smith apples and toasted brioche. It is persistent on the palate and continues to invite you in for another sip.

SCHARFFENBERGER CELLARS

8501 Highway 128, Philo, CA 95466,
(707) 895-2957
www.scharffenbergercellars.com

John Scharffenberger founded his eponymous Anderson Valley winery in 1981. The name was later changed to Pacific Echo because of the winery's proximity to the Pacific Ocean, but since Maisons Marques and Domaines took over the winery in 2004, the name has been restored to the original. Tex Sawyer has been the winemaker since 1989 and is known for his highly rated Méthode Champenoise sparkling wines. Scharffenberger Cellars Brut Excellence Non Vintage is crafted from one-third Pinot Noir and two-thirds Chardonnay. It is straw colored with an abundance of tiny bubbles and has aromas of freshly baked brioche, green apple, and ripe pear. In the mouth flavors of fruit mixed with toasted hazelnuts combine nicely before the pleasant finish.

SHANNON RIDGE

13888 Point Lakeview Rd., Lower Lake, CA 95457, (707) 994-9656
www.shannonridge.com

Clay and Margarita Shannon were raised in Sonoma and Napa, respectively, and met while working at a winery in the Napa Valley. They began their business by growing grapes for other wineries, but a visit to Clear Lake got them started on the road to making wine under their own label. Their first vineyard was Terre Vermeille, on which they planted Sauvignon Blanc, Barbera, Cabernet Sauvignon, and Zinfandel vines. They have solidified their commitment to Lake County by adding additional vineyards and building a home that overlooks their vineyards. Shannon Ridge High Elevation Chardonnay 2011 is straw yellow, with aromas of honeycomb, white peach, and crème caramel. In the mouth it is creamy with bright fruit flavors and a clean finish. Shannon Ridge Lake County High Elevation Sauvignon Blanc 2011 has crisp clean aromas of tropical fruit that flow seamlessly onto the palate. The finish has a nice level of acidity that makes this a perfect wine to pair with briny shellfish.

SIX SIGMA RANCH

13372 Spruce Grove Road, Lower Lake, CA 95457, (707) 994-4068
www.sixsigmaranch.com

The land that Six Sigma Ranch sits upon was first settled in the mid-1800s by twenty families who each owned a 160-acre parcel. In 1926 Norval Brookins was able to amass a very large ranch by buying many of those families' holdings, and in 1963 he sold to Bob and Beverly Kleeman, who ran a dude ranch here for a few years. It later became a cattle ranch, and in 2000 the present owners, Danish-born Kaj and Else Ahlmann, acquired the property and began making wine. In 2009 they hired winemaker Matt Hughes, whose provenance includes stints at Kendall-Jackson, Verité, and Wildhurst Vineyards. Six Sigma Asbill Valley Sauvignon Blanc 2012 is light straw in color, with aromas of white grapefruit, white stone fruit, and tropical fruits. It is crisp and light in the mouth with a pleasantly balanced acidic finish and bracing minerality. Six Sigma Christian's Vineyard Pinot Noir 2010 is cherry red, with aromas of black cherry, powdered cocoa, and cranberry juice. It is full in the mouth with ripe fruit flavors and a touch of spice in the finish.

STEELE WINES

4350 Thomas Drive at Highway 29,
Kelseyville, CA 95451,
(707) 279-9475
www.steelewines.com

In 1968 Jed Steele started out as a Napa Valley cellar rat before entering UC Davis for a master's degree in enology. After that he worked at Kendall-Jackson for nine years and moved on in the same year that production hit the million-cases-per-year mark. In 1991 he started his eponymous Steele Wines, and to this day he enjoys making small-lot bottlings, many with fewer than 1,000 cases produced. Steele Wines Writer's Block Counoise 2011 is garnet in color, with aromas of toasted hazelnut, toasted oat, red fruit, and black plum. It is full bodied in the mouth, with dominant fruit flavors that lead to a balanced tannic finish. Steele Wines Viognier 2011 is straw colored, with aromas of white stone fruits and dried apricots. It is light and fruity in the mouth with a crisp, lemon zesty clean finish.

ZINA HYDE CUNNINGHAM

14077 Highway 123, Boonville, CA 95415,
(707) 895-9462
www.zinawinery.com

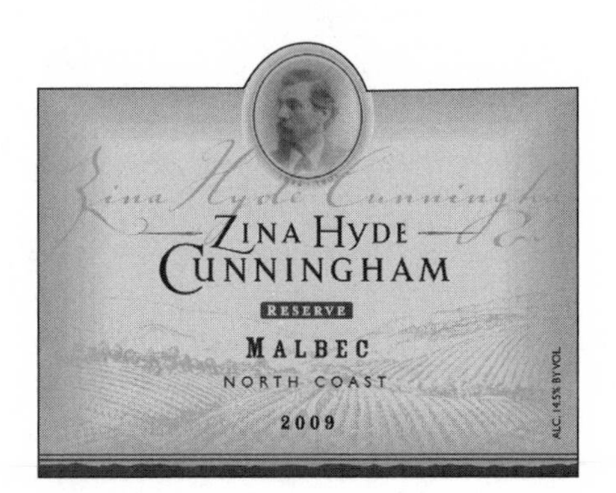

Zina Hyde Cunningham left Maine and traveled across the country in 1849 to strike it rich in the Gold Rush. He didn't become fabulously wealthy, but he did find enough gold to purchase a small property in San Francisco, where he became a blacksmith. Tired of city life, he purchased a 160-acre ranch in Windsor in 1859 and became a winemaker. By 1865 he began planting vines in Ukiah in Mendocino County. Today, Zina's great-grandson Bill carries on the family tradition in Boonville. Zina Hyde Cunningham Russian River Valley Sauvignon Blanc 2012 is straw colored, with light aromas of pineapple, tropical fruit salad, and freshly cut grass. It is soft in the mouth with delightful fruit flavors and a pleasant, lightly acidic finish. Zina Hyde Cunningham North Coast Malbec Reserve 2009 has aromas of Grandma's blueberry pie, black raspberry, and a touch of smoked meat. It is silky in the mouth with nice persistence.

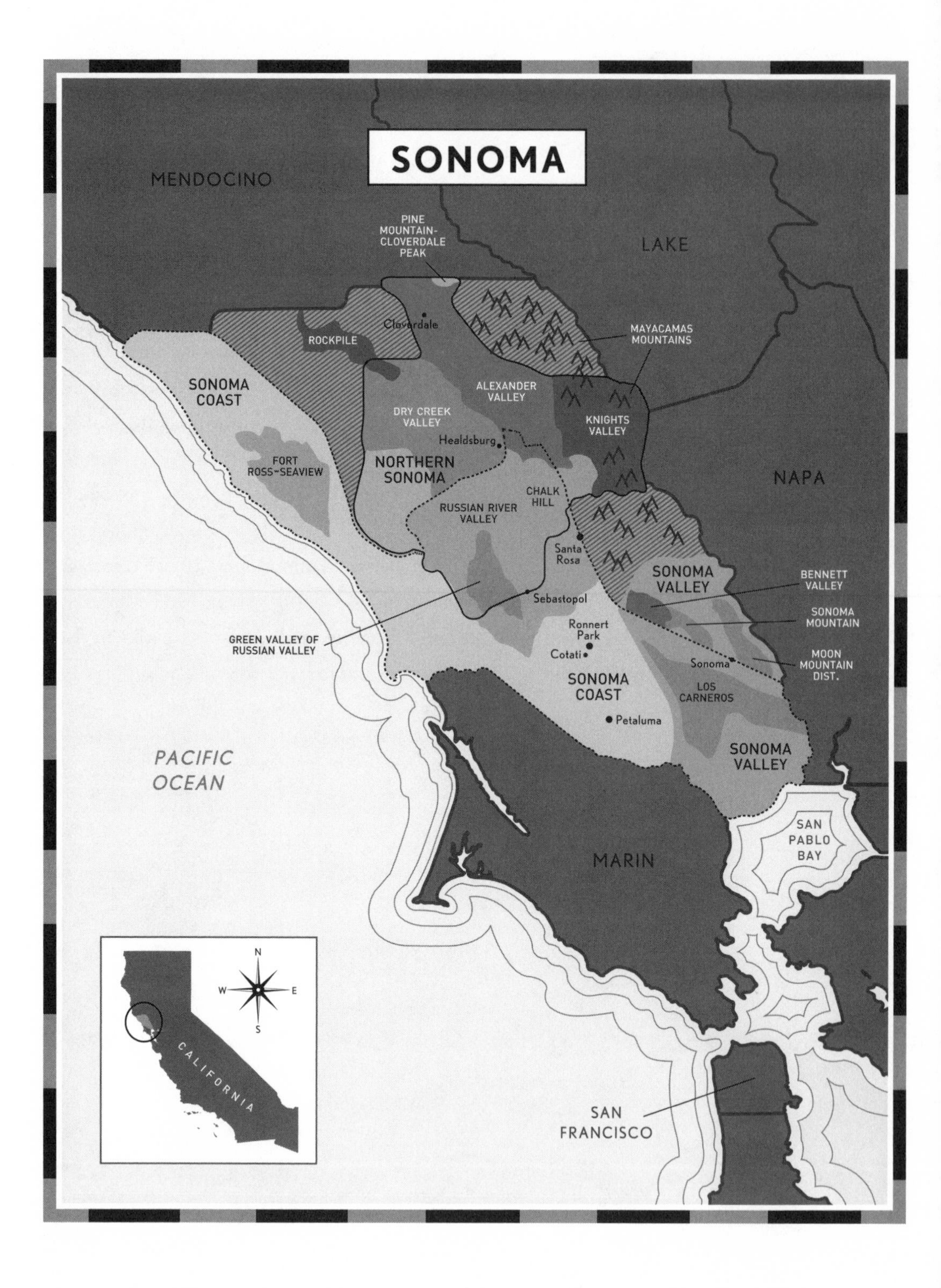

SONOMA
MENDOCINO
LAKE
NAPA
MARIN
PACIFIC OCEAN
SAN PABLO BAY
SAN FRANCISCO
PINE MOUNTAIN-CLOVERDALE PEAK
Cloverdale
ROCKPILE
MAYACAMAS MOUNTAINS
SONOMA COAST
ALEXANDER VALLEY
DRY CREEK VALLEY
KNIGHTS VALLEY
Healdsburg
FORT ROSS-SEAVIEW
NORTHERN SONOMA
CHALK HILL
RUSSIAN RIVER VALLEY
Santa Rosa
SONOMA VALLEY
BENNETT VALLEY
Sebastopol
SONOMA MOUNTAIN
GREEN VALLEY OF RUSSIAN VALLEY
Ronnert Park
Cotati
MOON MOUNTAIN DIST.
Sonoma
SONOMA COAST
LOS CARNEROS
Petaluma
SONOMA VALLEY
N
W
E
S
CALIFORNIA

CHAPTER 2

SONOMA COUNTY

SONOMA IS TRULY A NATURAL PARADISE, and some portions of it seem so isolated that we cannot begin to imagine how remote this area must have been when the first European settlers arrived in the early nineteenth century. Driving along its almost 60 miles of twisting Pacific coastline or along unpaved roads through seemingly endless redwood forests, it is hard to believe that Sonoma County is home to more than 370 wineries and 60,000 acres of grapevines. The laid-back vibe and hands-on touch of winemakers, farmers, and chefs have made this a nearly perfect environment for enjoying the pleasures of the field and vine. Whether you enjoy driving along winding back roads for long stretches or like to park the car and flit from tasting room to restaurant to gallery in a homey Mission- or Gold Rush–era downtown, Sonoma—which incidentally is larger than Rhode Island—has something to offer you.

To the west of Napa County, positioned between Mendocino County to the north and Marin County to the south, Sonoma is due north of San Francisco and is easily reachable by car. Sonoma County contains sixteen AVAs with wildly varying topographies and soils, and its wineries range in size from tiny boutique operations to enormous corporate entities. If you name a grape variety, someone in Sonoma is growing and vinifying it, although specific subregions are becoming known as the home for particular varieties, blends, and winemaking styles. Sonoma County often seems to live in the shadow of its neighbor to the east, but considering the high quality of Sonoma fruit and the role the development of Sonoma has played in the simultaneous evolution of Napa, it may turn out that Sonoma is really the wind beneath Napa's wings. To cite one example along a lengthy historical time line, it is said that George Yount, after whom the Napa town of Yountville is named and who is regarded as one of the first to plant vines in Napa Valley, actually planted cuttings acquired from Sonoma County vineyards. Another example: a portion of the grapes that Mike Grgich used in the 1973 Chateau Montelena Chardonnay, which stunned the world by coming in first among white wines in the 1976 Judgment of Paris tasting, were sourced from Sonoma vineyards, including the Bacigalupi Vineyard in the Russian River AVA.

The Sonoma Valley was settled 12,000 years ago by a number of native peoples, including the Miwok, Wintun, Wappo, Miyakmah, Pomo, Koskiwok, and Patwin tribes. Drawn here by the same abundant resources that anchored later settlers to the area, these people gave Sonoma its name, which is based on their word for "many moons." The early inhabitants also gave name to the Mayacamas Mountains, the portion of the Coastal Ranges that divides Sonoma from Napa; the name most likely derives from a village called Maiya'kma or from the Miyakmah people themselves. If one watches the mountains intently at night—or just looks east while driving through the Sonoma Valley—the moon really does appear to rise and set over a series of undulating peaks multiple times in the course of an evening.

Since 1542 Sonoma has been under the flag of several different nations, including Spain, Russia, Britain, the Mexican empire, the Republic of Mexico, and the short-lived Republic of California, finally becoming part of the United States when California gained statehood in 1850. Russian trappers planted grapes in Sonoma at Fort Ross on the Sonoma Coast in 1812, the first in the area. In 1823 Spanish missionaries who had been slowly working their way up the California coast planted grapevines at Mission San Francisco Solano de Sonoma under the direction of Father Jose Altmira. This was the northernmost and the last of the twenty-one Franciscan missions in California and the only one to be established under the flag of Mexico, which was newly independent from Spain. Ten years after the mission was built the Franciscan missions became secularized by the Mexican government, and it was turned into a fortified town led by General Mariano Guadalupe Vallejo. This mission-cum-fortress became the center of what is now the city of Sonoma, which was the capital of the California Republic for 26 days in the summer of 1846. In addition to wine bars, tasting rooms, and restaurants, visitors to Sonoma can tour well-preserved adobe structures near the main plaza that include the mission, the army barracks, and Vallejo's home.

A Hungarian "count" named Agoston Haraszthy, who sometimes is called "the Father of California Viticulture," is credited with bringing the largest collection of European grape varieties to California and to Sonoma County. The founder of Buena Vista Winery (which today is owned by Jean-Charles Boisset), Haraszthy imported cuttings from more than 150 great European vineyards to California. He originally replanted his vines near San Francisco, and in 1856 he chose a small vineyard near Sonoma to which he transplanted many of his vines. He then hired a German immigrant named Charles Krug—who went on to found his own winery across the Mayacamas Mountains in St. Helena—and built a stone winery replete with state-of-the-art (for the time) winemaking equipment and underground cellars.

Franciscan missionaries are credited with first planting grapes and making wine in California, but they used only Mission grapes and their technique was rudimentary at best, whereas Haraszthy is considered to be the person who brought a wide array of grapes to northern California and to have used modern European processes in his winemaking. His vineyard holdings eventually grew to 5,000 acres containing many vineyards and his large family home. Besides his visionary efforts planting grapes in Sonoma, Haraszthy is noted for the important nineteen-page document that he wrote in 1858, *Report on Grapes and Wine of California,* which is recognized today as the first written study of winemaking and vineyard practices in California and the entire United States.

Toward the end of the nineteenth century, immigrants from Italy, Germany, and other European countries were planting grapes and making wine in Sonoma, and some of those original wineries exist to this day. The Gold Rush of 1849 brought many people from other nations to California, and when the gold petered out, many bought land and turned their hands to farming. Still more winemakers abandoned fields in their home countries when phylloxera struck the vineyards of Europe shortly thereafter, bringing their skills to the New World. This was the period of time that in grape growing and winemaking spread to South America, South Africa, and Oceania, as well as to California.

German immigrant Jacob Gundlach bought 400 acres in Sonoma in 1858 and built a winery three years later along with partners. Another immigrant from Germany, Charles Bundschu, joined the business in 1868, and today Gundlach Bundschu is considered the oldest family-owned winery in the state of California. Simi Winery, now owned by Constellation Brands, was established in Healdsburg in 1876 by the Italian brothers Pietro and Giuseppe Simi, who had come to California during the Gold Rush. The Martinelli Winery owes its existence to the teenage Giuseppe Martinelli and Luisa Vellutini, who eloped in 1887, abandoning Tuscany for the Russian River Valley, where they began growing grapes and making wine. The Sebastiani family's Mission Vineyard was part of the original San Francisco Solano de Sonoma Mission's vineyard. Founded by Samuele Sebastiani in 1904, Sebastiani Winery is now part of the Foley Family Wines portfolio.

By 1920 Sonoma County was home to more than 250 wineries and had grapes growing on 22,000 acres, supplanting Los Angeles as the number one grape-growing region in the state. The effects of Prohibition, the Great Depression, and two world wars hurt the entire California wine industry, Sonoma included. A handful of wineries were able to remain open through Prohibition as a result of loopholes in the law that allowed wine consumption for sacramental or medicinal purposes, but many vineyards were sold and their land was converted to fruit orchards.

By the 1960s Americans were becoming exposed to different types of international cuisine, especially French and Italian, and were increasing their consumption of wine. At the same time, they moved away from drinking sweet fortified wines toward a drier style of food-friendly wines. In the early 1970s a new wave of vineyard and winery owners began moving into Sonoma. By the middle of that decade plantings returned to pre-1920 levels, with 24,000 acres of vineyards recorded.

By the 1980s Sonoma County was transitioning from being a center of dairy, grain, and fruit, with wine grapes taking center stage. At the end of that decade wine grapes became Sonoma County's number one agricultural crop, and as northern California became the "birthplace" of the farm-to-table movement (which somehow had gotten lost in the postwar packaged food boom of the 1960s), the stage was set for Sonoma to become known as the home of high-quality wine.

One can still marvel at the fact that as inflation raged throughout the country and real estate prices broke new barriers every year, individuals, couples, and families with a dream, a desire to make wine, and not all that much money headed to Sonoma in the 1970s and 1980s and bought large tracts of land on which to grow grapes. Enormous farms and ranches were snapped up for the price of a four-bedroom house in an East Coast suburb, and many of Sonoma's best wineries were founded during this period.

Among Sonoma County's 60,000 acres of grapevines, Chardonnay rules the roost, growing on 15,255 acres. Used in both still and sparkling wines, it is grown throughout the region but seems to have a particular affinity for the Russian River Valley and what is unofficially known as the "real Sonoma Coast" or the "extreme Sonoma Coast." It also does very well in the Los Carneros AVA, which straddles both Sonoma and Napa counties. The next most prolific white variety in Sonoma is Sauvignon Blanc, trailing behind on 2,553 acres. It is most prominent in the Russian River Valley, Dry Creek Valley, and Sonoma Coast. Almost every other white variety you can name is grown in

Sonoma, and we have tasted many fine examples of Pinot Gris, Riesling, and Viognier.

It appears that the balance of power has finally tipped in Sonoma, with a larger amount of Pinot Noir than Cabernet Sauvignon. The most widely planted red grape in the county is Pinot Noir, which is found on 12,062 acres. It does especially well in Los Carneros (where, like Chardonnay, it is used in both still and sparkling wine), the Russian River Valley, and one of the newest AVAs in Sonoma, Fort Ross-Seaview on the Sonoma Coast, which was officially recognized in late 2011. Coming in a close second is Cabernet Sauvignon, on 11,480 acres. Although from a reputation standpoint Napa seems to have Cabernet Sauvignon embedded in its DNA, we have opened many bottles of top-quality Sonoma Cabernet Sauvignon that are equal to their counterparts from over the mountains, often at a fraction of the cost. Merlot, vinified on its own or used in Meritage blends, is grown on 5,778 acres, especially prospering in Bennett Valley and Sonoma Valley.

Another widely grown red variety is Zinfandel, which blankets 5,358 acres of Sonoma vineyards. Some of the oldest Zinfandel vines in the state are found in Sonoma, especially in the Sonoma Valley, Dry Creek Valley, and Rockpile AVAs. Syrah is found on just over 1,895 acres throughout the county, including the Sonoma Coast, Russian River Valley, and Alexander Valley AVAs. A host of other red grapes are grown within the borders of this large county, including Petite Sirah, Sangiovese, Petit Verdot, Malbec, and even Pinotage.

As of January 1, 2014, all wine produced with grapes from a Sonoma County AVA must include the words "Sonoma County" on the label. For example, a wine made with grapes from the Russian River Valley AVA, in addition to being labeled "Russian River Valley" will also have to be labeled "Sonoma County." The purposes of this conjunctive labeling legislation are to both strengthen the image of Sonoma County as a world-class wine region and increase consumer awareness of the sub-AVAs of Sonoma County so that people know where these viticultural areas are located.

Sonoma County offers many different environments for grape growing. Days are generally cool, with an average daily temperature of 70 to 72 degrees Fahrenheit, and even in high summer the temperature rarely rises above 85 degrees except in inland areas farther north, such as the Alexander Valley. Large bodies of water contribute cooling effects on the county as a whole: the Pacific Ocean, which runs along the county's western coast, and San Pablo Bay, to the south of Los Carneros and the southernmost tips of the Sonoma Coast and Sonoma Valley

AVAs, offer late-morning fog and cooling breezes. The Russian River, which enters the Alexander Valley from the north, at the border with Mendocino, and then veers west, meandering through the Russian River Valley, Green Valley, and Sonoma Coast AVAs before coursing into the Pacific, offers a water source and also provides a natural break in the hills to pull Pacific fog inland and north.

ALEXANDER VALLEY AVA

The northernmost AVA in Sonoma County, Alexander Valley stretches from the southern border of Mendocino to the northern edge of the Chalk Hill AVA. This AVA was established in June 1988 and covers a total area of 32,536 acres, with its southern half bordering Dry Creek Valley to the west and Knights Valley to the east. The eastern edge of the Alexander Valley AVA runs into the foothills of the Mayacamas Mountains. Named for Cyrus Alexander, a homesteader and farmer who planted grapes there in the 1840s, the valley was known more for prunes and other orchard fruit than for wine grapes until quite recently. Twenty-two miles long by two to seven miles wide, it is home to over two hundred grape growers and more than forty wineries.

The nearby Pacific Ocean provides cooling maritime breezes and fog, which rolls in at night and flows up the Russian River, the dominant feature of the valley floor. Altitudes vary from 200 to 2,000 feet above sea level. Soil types in the river valley are alluvial with gravel and silt characteristics, and at higher elevations we find volcanic ash soils. Grapes are grown on over 15,000 acres here, and although Pacific breezes and fog help cool the fruit during the day, this inland region is known for a fully ripened, warmer-weather style of wine, as opposed to the AVAs closer to the coast. The number one variety in the Alexander Valley is Cabernet Sauvignon, which is grown on more than 6,000 acres. Merlot also thrives here, as does Zinfandel, including a significant quantity of old-vine vineyards. The number one white variety is Chardonnay, which is planted on over 2,000 acres.

BENNETT VALLEY AVA

Gaining official AVA recognition in December 2003, Bennett Valley's 8,140 acres are home to a little more than 650 acres of grapevines. It overlaps the Sonoma Valley and Sonoma Coast appellations, lying north of the town of Sonoma and the Sonoma Mountain AVA and just south of the city of Santa Rosa. Cradled by three mountain peaks, Bennett Valley varies in elevation from 250 to over 1,800 feet. Its well-drained volcanic rock soils are blessed with cool coastal breezes and morning fog. Almost forty small family vineyards, most less than 20 acres, share space among gentle slopes, and there are only four wineries within the AVA, with only one open to the public. Merlot, Syrah, and Sauvignon Blanc appear to be Bennett Valley's standout varieties.

CHALK HILL AVA

Occupying the northeast corner of the larger Russian River Valley AVA and sitting just south of Alexander Valley and Knights Valley, Chalk Hill covers an area of 22,400 acres, of which more than 1,400 are planted with grapevines. The five wineries here are all on the western slopes of the Mayacamas Mountains. Named for its volcanic ash chalk-colored soils, Chalk Hill was first granted AVA status in 1983 and then amended in 1988. Chardonnay and Sauvignon Blanc thrive here, as does Cabernet Sauvignon. Because of the high elevation, Chalk Hill's vineyards avoid the fog that rolls up along the Russian River, and so this AVA is generally warmer than the larger Russian River Valley AVA.

DRY CREEK VALLEY AVA

Dry Creek Valley was among the first American Viticultural Areas in the country, established in October 1983, and its history of grape growing reaches back over 140 years. Italian and other European immigrants gravitated toward its rich farmland shortly after the Gold Rush ended, and by the 1880s there were almost 900 acres of vineyards and nine wineries here. The most widely grown variety at the time was Zinfandel, which remains Dry Creek Valley's shining star to this day. Although Prohibition was not kind to Dry Creek Valley and many vineyards were converted to fruit orchards and fields of grain at that time, vineyard plantings have increased steadily since the 1970s, and today there are 9,300 acres of vines and more than seventy wineries here.

Just north of the Russian River Valley AVA and to the west of Alexander Valley within the larger Northern Sonoma appellation, Dry Creek Valley is 16 miles long by 2 miles wide. The gorgeous town of Healdsburg, home to a panoply of tasting rooms and wine-themed restaurants, sits at the southeast corner of the appellation, at its convergence with the Alexander Valley and Russian River Valley AVAs. Soils on the valley floor are primarily well-drained alluvial gravel and sandy loam, while benchland and hillside soils are gravelly clay loam, often tinged with noteworthy streaks of red earth.

The most prolific grape varieties here are Cabernet Sauvignon, Zinfandel, Merlot, Chardonnay, and Sauvignon Blanc. Quite a few vineyards in Dry Creek Valley are studded with ancient gnarled Zinfandel vines that are over 100 years old.

FORT ROSS-SEAVIEW AVA

One of the newest AVAs in Sonoma County, Fort Ross-Seaview is wholly surrounded by the larger Sonoma Coast AVA. It was granted official status in December 2011, with a total area of 27,500 acres. Out of those acres, just over 500 are planted. A high-altitude region affected by both elevation and nearness to the Pacific Ocean, Fort Ross-Seaview features vineyards at heights of 800 to 1,800 feet above sea level, many of which sit above the fog line and are afforded long daylight hours of warm sunshine. In a short amount of time it has gained a reputation among wine lovers for its Pinot Noir and Chardonnay, and we have tasted fine examples of Zinfandel, Syrah, Petite Sirah, and Pinotage cultivated in its well-drained gravelly loams. White Rhône varieties are planted in small amounts as well and are already showing promise.

Fort Ross was the first site in Sonoma County to be planted with grapes in the early part of the nineteenth century. This Russian stronghold was home to cuttings said to have been brought to the area from Peru and to have been cultivated by Russian fur trappers. It is within the area that many call the "true Sonoma Coast" because the Sonoma Coast AVA is very large, with some southern portions completely inland, between Marin and Napa valleys. The Fort Ross Vineyard and Winery is said to be the closest vineyard to the Pacific Ocean in the whole state and offers staggering views of the rugged coast below. Many esteemed Pinot Noir producers own vineyards within the Fort Ross-Seaview AVA or source fruit for appellation or vineyard-designate bottlings.

GREEN VALLEY OF RUSSIAN RIVER VALLEY AVA

Located in a rough triangle between Occidental, Sebastopol, and Forestville and extending a bit north of the latter, the Green Valley of Russian River Valley sits within the southwest portion of the larger Russian River Valley AVA. At the time it was established, in December 1983, it was known as the Sonoma County Green Valley AVA. The name change took place in April 2007 so that the AVA would be more closely associated with the well-known Russian River Valley appellation, which has definitely achieved a level of cachet with both professional and amateur wine lovers.

Closer to the Pacific than many other portions of the Russian River Valley, Green Valley is said to be one of the coolest regions in Sonoma County, in particular because of the breezes and fog that approach via the Petaluma Gap. Its total area is 19,000 acres, out of which 3,600 are planted to grapevines. It is noted for its Goldridge soil, a type of fine sandy loam that is yellow in color. Just ten wineries make Green Valley of Russian River Valley their home, but a stellar roster of wineries both large and small either own vineyards or purchase grapes from those who do from among the hundred prized vineyards in the AVA. As would be expected, Pinot Noir and Chardonnay are the main grapes here and are vinified in both still and sparkling styles. Top-notch Syrah and Gewürztraminer are produced here as well.

KNIGHTS VALLEY AVA

Knights Valley shares its eastern border with the southwest edge of Lake County and the northernmost reaches of Napa, near Calistoga, and it nestles into the Mayacamas Mountains and Mount St. Helena. To the west it is bordered by the Alexander Valley and Chalk Hill AVAs. Protected from the cooling effects of the Pacific Ocean, it is said to be the warmest appellation within Sonoma County. It was among the original AVAs in the county, having been established in November 1983. Two thousand acres of grapes grow among a total area of 36,240 acres. Bordeaux varieties thrive here, especially Cabernet Sauvignon, Merlot, and Cabernet Franc, as does Sauvignon Blanc. Due to the warm climate, the latter is produced in a ripe style, with rich nuances of tropical fruit.

LOS CARNEROS AVA

Los Carneros (also referred to as just *Carneros*) is Spanish for "the rams," a reference to this wine region's former role as pastureland for grazing sheep. Crossing county borders, it is shared by both Sonoma County and Napa County. Wineries in the western portion may also include Sonoma County and Sonoma Valley on their labels, while on the other side of the county line they may be identified as coming from the Napa Valley AVA as well as Carneros. The total surface area is 32,000 acres, among which 8,000 are cultivated with grapes. Twenty-two wineries make their home here, and from the early 1980s onward (the AVA was established in 1983) it has been the American vineyard and winery base of a prominent catalog of European sparkling wine producers, including Moët & Chandon (Chandon), Champagne Taittinger (Domaine Carneros), Freixenet (Gloria Ferrer), Champagne G.H. Mumm (Mumm Napa), and Codorniu (Artesa, previously Codorniu Napa).

Because of its proximity to San Pablo Bay and its east-west orientation (both the Napa and Sonoma valleys run north to south), Los Carneros is generally a cold-weather region, although its former title of "coldest" has been rightfully claimed by AVAs farther north and west. Both Pinot Noir and Chardonnay have been grown here for many years, although a late 1980s phylloxera outbreak necessitated a major replanting effort. Both of these varieties are made into still and sparkling wine, and they have recently been joined by sizable plantings of Merlot and Syrah.

MOON MOUNTAIN AVA

The newest AVA in Sonoma County and the most recent to be added in the state as of this writing, Moon Mountain falls within the confines of the larger Sonoma Valley AVA. The total area of this AVA is 17,633 acres, with 1,500 acres planted to grapevines. Most vineyards here are on mountainsides rather than the valley floor, with vineyard altitudes ranging from 400 to 2,200 feet above sea level. There are eleven wineries and more than forty vineyards in the AVA, including the historic Monte Rosso vineyard, now owned by E & J Gallo, which was planted in the late nineteenth century.

NORTHERN SONOMA AVA

The very large Northern Sonoma AVA (first established in 1985 and then amended in 1986 and 1990) covers 348,000 acres. Appropriately named, it covers much of the northern portion of Sonoma County, including all or most portions of the Alexander Valley, Chalk Hill, Dry Creek Valley, Green Valley of Russian River Valley, Knights Valley, Rockpile, and Russian River Valley AVAs, portions of which also fall into the Sonoma Coast AVA. Although wine produced from a mélange of grapes grown within the borders of the Northern Sonoma AVA may be labeled as such, for most purposes it is more meaningful for wines to bear the designation of one of the more recognizable AVAs inside its boundaries, such as Russian River Valley or Alexander Valley.

PINE MOUNTAIN-CLOVERDALE PEAK

The small Pine Mountain-Cloverdale Peak AVA became official in November 2011. Its 4,750 acres are home to 230 planted vineyard acres, mainly red Bordeaux varieties with small amounts of Sauvignon Blanc. Tucked into the northwest corner of the Alexander Valley AVA, it crosses county borders, with a portion of the appellation in Mendocino County. The AVA, above the town of Cloverdale, begins at altitudes of 1,600 feet and runs as high as 3,000 feet at the peak of Pine Mountain. Grapes have been grown here since the Gold Rush era, mostly on plots smaller than 30 acres. There are no wineries built here.

ROCKPILE AVA

Named for the dominant feature of the local landscape, Rockpile owes its name to the Rockpile Ranch, which was founded here in 1858 by sheep farmer Tennessee Carter Bishop, who became the local sheriff in that same era.

Its name goes back even further than that—the indigenous Pomo people called it *kabe-chana,* or "place with many rocks." Just north of the man-made Lake Sonoma, Rockpile sits in the center of Sonoma County's northern border with Mendocino. At 15,400 acres in size, Rockpile, established in 2002, can claim only 150 acres planted to grapevines. Sheriff Bishop was said to have planted vines on his ranch in 1872, and in 1884 the Swedish immigrant S. P. Hallengren planted vines as well. Today, Hallengren's descendants, the Mauritson family, continue to farm grapes in this high-elevation, rock-strewn region. Elevations run between 900 and 1,900 feet, and vineyards planted above the fog line benefit from long hours of sunlight, making this prime territory for red grapes such as Cabernet Sauvignon, Zinfandel, and Petite Sirah.

RUSSIAN RIVER VALLEY AVA

The Russian River Valley has one of the longest-standing traditions of grape growing of any AVA in the region, with a history going back to the 1870s. By the end of that decade more than 7,000 acres of vines were planted in the Russian River Valley, and 500,000 gallons of wine were produced annually. Although vineyard acreage declined through the long years of Prohibition, the modern era of Russian River Valley winemaking began in the 1960s, when Bob Sisson, a University of California farm advisor, counseled viticulturists to plant Chardonnay and Pinot Noir. First established in November 1983, the Russian River Valley AVA had an original footprint of 96,000 acres, which was expanded to 126,600 in October 2005 and then to its present size of 169,029 acres in November 2011. The most recent expansion added land in the south and east of the AVA, including an area sometimes called the Sebastopol Hills. The entire Russian River Valley AVA is overlapped by the larger Sonoma Coast AVA to the south and east and by the Northern Sonoma AVA in its northern portion. While the original, northern portion of the Russian River Valley is prime real estate for Pinot Noir and Chardonnay, the flatter area added in late 2011 is also the home of vines bearing Zinfandel, Cabernet Sauvignon, and other red Bordeaux varieties.

As might be expected, the Russian River flows through the valley in a southwesterly direction, drawing Pacific fog inward each day, providing a cooling action for the region's grapes, which cover 15,000 acres. The Russian River was so named by Russian fur trappers who built Fort Ross a bit farther to the north-west and planted the first grapes there. The Russians pulled up stakes in 1841, but Gold Rush–era settlers, many from Italy, gravitated here over the next 15 years and began planting fruit trees, grain, and other crops. Although Gravenstein apples were king through the first two-thirds of the twentieth century, wine grapes are the Russian River Valley's current claim to fame. Westside Road, home to a string of high-profile wineries whose releases earn high points vintage after vintage, is affectionately called the Russian River Gold Coast and the Russian River's Rodeo Drive. While the emphasis throughout the AVA is on Pinot Noir and Chardonnay, a fair amount of Zinfandel, Syrah, Petite Sirah, and Sauvignon Blanc is grown here too.

SONOMA COAST AVA

Established in July 1987, the large Sonoma Coast AVA—the largest in the county—covers 480,000 acres, or 750 square miles. It partially overlaps with the Northern Sonoma AVA and contains segments of the Russian River Valley, Green Valley, Los Carneros, and Chalk Hill AVAs within its borders. It also has a wholly enclosed sub-AVA, Fort Ross-Seaview, in the northwest. This falls within the area that people refer to as the "true Sonoma Coast" or "extreme Sonoma Coast" to differentiate it from the southern half of the AVA, which is east of Marin County. The eastern edge of this lower portion abuts Sonoma Valley to the east and San Pablo Bay to the south. The city of Petaluma is in the center of this lower area of the AVA, which is cooled by breezes entering the land via the Petaluma Gap.

Not counting wineries within the sub-AVAs, the Sonoma Coast AVA has seven wineries within its boundaries and 2,000 planted vineyard acres. It is known for its cool climate caused by the nearness of the Pacific Ocean and the moderating effects of fog and breezes, but some elevated coastal areas are too high for fog to reach, allowing warm sunshine to penetrate vineyards for the full length of the day. A group called West Sonoma Coast Vintners banded together in 2011. It is comprised of winemakers who produce bottlings from the northwest region of the AVA, with a focus on Pinot Noir. Syrah is making a name for itself here as well.

SONOMA MOUNTAIN AVA

A small AVA within the greater Sonoma Valley AVA, Sonoma Mountain is just south of the Bennett Valley viticultural area. The town of Glen Ellen is within its boundaries, and it is a high-elevation region known for rich Cabernet Sauvignon, Zinfandel, Chardonnay, Sauvignon Blanc, Sémillon, and Pinot Noir. Many vineyards are at altitudes too high for fog to reach, and a multitude of crannies and fissures within steep mountain slopes provide for a variety of microclimates; this is why such a diversity of grape varieties thrive on its 800 planted acres. Established in February 1985, Sonoma Mountain's total expanse is just 5,000 acres.

SONOMA VALLEY AVA

Known locally as the Valley of the Moon, Sonoma Valley has been planted with grapes since Franciscan missionaries arrived in 1823, which were expanded by General Vallejo 11 years later. This is also where Agoston Haraszthy founded Buena Vista Winery in 1857. It is bordered to the east by the Mayacamas Mountains, which separate Sonoma and Napa counties, and to the west by the Sonoma Mountains. The Bennett Valley, Moon Valley, and Sonoma Mountain AVAs fall within its outline, as does a portion of Los Carneros. The southern portion of the Sonoma Valley AVA overlaps with the southeastern area of the Sonoma Coast AVA. As a result of its fortunate location between mountain ranges, cooling breezes from the Santa Rosa Plain move north to south through the valley, which also benefits from cooling influences from San Pablo Bay that move in the opposite direction. The Sonoma Mountains shelter the valley from daytime fog and more direct Pacific Ocean breezes.

Granted formal AVA status in 1981 (and amended in 1985 and 1987), the Sonoma Valley AVA is home to 15,000 acres planted to grape vines. A wide array of varieties is cultivated here, from Alicante Bouschet to Zinfandel. The latter exists in a number of vineyards dating back to the 1880s and 1890s, featuring untrellised gnarled vines supported by surprisingly thick bases. Many vines bearing the former variety are eligible for the old-vine designation as well, including some growing alongside Touriga Nacional, Petite Sirah, and other "mixed blacks," almost always in close proximity to same-age Zinfandel vines. Cabernet Sauvignon thrives here as well, in particular in the northern reaches of the AVA. Chardonnay, Pinot Noir, and Merlot are also notable varieties of the region. There are 114 wineries and 76 tasting rooms within the Sonoma Valley AVA, many ringing the eight-acre Mission-era Sonoma Plaza.

THE WINERIES

ACORN/ALEGRÍA VINEYARDS

12040 Old Redwood Highway,
Healdsburg, CA 95448,
(707) 433-6440
www.acornwinery.com

Bill and Betsy Nachbaur purchased the Alegría Vineyard in Russian River Valley in 1990 and have farmed it ever since, first selling their grapes to other wineries and then producing their own wines starting in 1996. Their production is small—just 3,000 cases per year—so the name Acorn is a nod to their diminutive size and the oak aging their wines receive. Acorn specializes in field blends, cofermenting multiple varieties that grow side by side in its 120-year-old vineyard. The wines are made by Bill Nachbaur and Clay Mauritson. The Acorn Hill and Medley are proprietary vineyard blends, and the "single-varietal" bottlings such as Syrah, Sangiovese, Cabernet Franc, and Zinfandel also include small amounts of other varieties. Acorn Alegría Vineyards Russian River Valley Zinfandel 2010 is 80 percent Zinfandel blended with 11 percent Petite Syrah and 7 percent Alicante Bouschet; the remaining 2 percent consists of thirteen different grapes. It has a bouquet of mixed-berry tart with a hint of chocolate-covered espresso beans. In the mouth the rich fruit flavors are wrapped up in luscious tannins as notes of baking spices and black pepper zip across your tongue.

ADOBE ROAD WINERY

1995 South McDowell Boulevard,
Petaluma, CA 94954,
(707) 939-7967
www.adoberoadwines.com

Pro race-car driver Kevin Buckler and his wife, Debra, opened Adobe Road Winery with a passion to create quality wines in sync with the local *terroir* and the natural rhythms of the seasons. As a nice juxtaposition to racing around a track at 180 miles an hour, Kevin can often be found spending

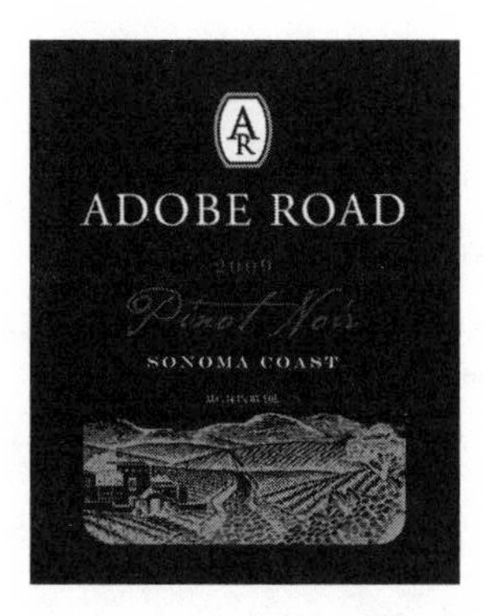

quiet, almost contemplative time in the vineyards for hours at a time. Kevin and Debra opened a new boutique wine facility in 2008, and their wines have garnered accolades from their numerous fans. Their tasting room is on the historic Sonoma Plaza, and visitors can often find winemaker Michael Scorsone in the house to answer any questions. Feel free to visit at the Petaluma location to see Kevin's racing trophies on display. Adobe Road Winery Russian River Valley Bacigalupi Vineyard Chardonnay 2009 is straw yellow in the glass, with aromas of canned peaches, white flowers, and English toffee. In the mouth this is a big and full wine with a very creamy texture. Adobe Road Winery Sonoma Coast Pinot Noir 2009 is cherry red, with notes of black cherry, dried lavender, and red plum in the nose. On the palate flavors of dried blueberry and cherry preserves are presented nicely before the long floral-laced finish.

ADRIAN FOG

2064 Gravenstein Highway North,
Sebastopol, CA 95472,
(707) 431-1174
www.adrianfog.com

Winemaker Stewart Dormand and his wife, Jane, started Adrian Fog in the late 1990s. From the outset they have received high marks all around for their small-lot Pinot Noir from vineyard sites in Mendocino, Sonoma Coast, and Russian River. Cool-climate grapes are selected with an eye toward the influence of fog patterns, vine age, sun orientation, and clonal selection. For their most recent vintage, the largest bottling was 330 cases and the smallest was 23. Adrian Fog Savoy Vineyard Anderson Valley Pinot Noir 2007 is deep garnet in the glass, with aromas of blackberry, cranberry, and a trace of anise. Mixed fruit-of-the-wood flavors with touches of anisette and forest floor endure on the palate through the long finish, boosted by gorgeous acidity.

ANABA

60 Bonneau Road, Sonoma, CA 95476,
(707) 996-4188
www.anabawines.com

Anaba takes its name from a type of wind that blows warm air up steep slopes, and it is more than a coincidence that owner John Sweazey was the first in Northern California to install a wind turbine on his property to provide power to the winery's tasting room and offices. Winemaker and director of vineyard operations Jennifer Marion works with Burgundy and Rhône varieties, producing stellar Chardonnay, Pinot Noir, and blends and single-varietal wines using Grenache, Syrah, Mourvèdre, Roussanne, Marsanne, and Viognier. Anaba Gap's Crown Vineyard Chardonnay 2010 mingles bright flavors of pineapple and mango with a creamy texture and notes of buttered toast. Anaba Las Madres Syrah 2009 bursts in the mouth with flavors of blackberry, black pepper, and fennel bulb. Silky tannins and zippy acidity create a sense of harmony on the palate.

ANAKOTA

4611 Thomas Road,
Healdsburg, CA 95448,
(707) 433-9000
www.anakota.com

A joint venture between Pierre and Monique Seillan and the Jackson family, Anakota shares winery space with the highly acclaimed Verité. Only two wines are made under the Anakota label, both of them single-vineyard Cabernet Sauvignon from estate-owned Knights Valley vineyards on the slopes of Mount St. Helena on the eastern edge of Sonoma. If you are lucky enough to score one of each from the same vintage, enjoy them side by side and ponder the subtle effects of *terroir* on wine. Anakota Helena Montana Vineyard Knights Valley Cabernet Sauvignon 2008 is deep black cherry to the eye. Fragrances of blueberry and cassis lead on the nose, backed by notes of mocha and cigar box. In the mouth flavors of black cherry and espresso bean mingle with touches of butterscotch and spice. Silky tannins endure through the rewarding finish. Anakota Helena Dakota Vineyard Knights Valley Cabernet Sauvignon 2008 is deep ruby red in the glass, with rich aromas of blackberry, black currants, mocha, and graphite. Dark berry flavors are intertwined with strong notes of baking spices, forest floor, vanilla, and bacon, with a lift of menthol in the long, pleasing finish.

ARISTA

7015 Westside Road, Healdsburg, CA 95448,
(707) 473-0606
www.aristawinery.com

Founded in 2002 by Al and Janis McWilliams and their sons Mark and Ben, Arista has quickly joined its neighbors on Westside Road, including Rochioli and Williams Selyem, on a short list of the best wineries in Russian River. Winemaker Matt Courtney joined the team in November 2012 after an eight-year stint under Helen Turley at Marcassin. In addition to their Two Birds and Harper's Rest vineyards on the 36-acre Westside Road property, in April 2012 the McWilliams family purchased the Martinelli Road Vineyard in order to add Chardonnay and old-vine Zinfandel to their lineup of exceptional Pinot Noirs. Vineyard management is under the direction of Ulises Valdez. Simple tastings are available, but visitors to Arista are encouraged to wander among the serene Japanese gardens or book a private feast and wine pairing in the glass-walled "dojo." Entry-level Pinot Noir from Sonoma Coast, Russian River Valley, and Mendocino County are joined by a selection of single-vineyard versions whose subtle differences make for a primer on *terroir*-driven variations within a single vintage. Arista Toboni Vineyard Russian River Valley Pinot Noir 2010 opens on the nose with equal amounts of ripe cherry and forest mushrooms. In the mouth cherry leads to black plum, and earthy flavors are enhanced by Mediterranean herb notes and a sprinkle of baking spice, all wrapped within a creamy mouthfeel. Arista Bacigalupi Vineyard Russian River Valley Pinot Noir 2010 gives up a bouquet of fresh blackberry and raspberry mingled with overturned earth notes. Fresh fruit opens on the palate, joined by oregano and a hint of rosemary, with a satiny texture and a bright finish. Arista Two Birds Estate Vineyard Russian River Valley Pinot Noir 2010 is deep cherry red in color and offers aromas of fruits of the wood with a suggestion of Andes mints. Flavor abounds, with black currant, fresh raspberry, and forest floor encased in an elegant tannic structure.

ARROWOOD VINEYARDS & WINERY

14347 Highway 12, Glen Ellen, CA 95442,
(707) 935-2600
www.arrowoodvineyards.com

Richard and Alis Arrowood founded Arrowood in 1986, releasing their first vintage in 1988. Arrowood had previously worked at Chateau St. Jean, where he made some of the first single-vineyard wines in California. Arrowood is now part of the Jackson Family Wines portfolio, and current winemaker Heidi von der Mehden worked with Richard Arrowood for three years before taking over full winemaking duties in 2010. The spotlight is on Chardonnay and Cabernet Sauvignon, but Syrah, Malbec, Merlot, and Viognier are produced too. Grapes are sourced from choice vineyard sites in the Sonoma, Russian River, Dry Creek, Alexander, and Knights valleys. Arrowood Sonoma County Chardonnay 2010 is medium straw in the glass, with a nose of vanilla custard, white peach, and honeysuckle. In the mouth flavors of peach and Gala apple merge with notes of vanilla and spice, leading to a crisp finish. Arrowood Reserve Spéciale Sonoma Valley Cabernet Sauvignon 2007 is deep garnet to the eye. Aromas of mixed wild berries, spice, and baking bread yield to flavors of black currant, black cherry, blackberry, violet, and forest floor. Well-structured tannins are present from the first sip through the persistent finish.

AUTEUR

PO Box 1554, Sonoma, CA 95476,
(707) 938-9211
www.auteurwines.com

Winemaker-owner Kenneth Juhasz crafts fine cool-climate Pinot Noir and Chardonnay using fruit sourced from Sonoma Coast, Carneros, Mendocino Ridge, and Oregon's Willamette Valley. Before settling in Sonoma with his wife and business partner, Laura, Juhasz honed his craft in Central Otago and the Willamette Valley. Winery club members and lucky residents of a handful of states in which Auteur is distributed have access to Juhasz's wine. Seated tastings of five wines with Kenneth or Laura at their Sonoma winery cottage can be arranged. Auteur Durrell Vineyard Chardonnay 2010 releases flavors of clementine, peach jam, and white flowers, with a mouth-filling texture and a not unexpected splash of citrus on the finish. Auteur

Sonoma Stage Pinot Noir 2009 opens with notes of cherry and black plum that continue on the palate, joined by a medley of dark fruits, a touch of coffee, and a dusting of Mediterranean herbs.

BEDROCK WINE CO.

554 Michael Drive, Sonoma, CA 95476,
(707) 364-8763
www.bedrockwineco.com

Morgan Twain-Peterson started Bedrock Wine Co. in 2007. The son of Ravenswood's Joel Peterson, he started out making wine at his father's side and then progressed to his very own 550-square-foot chicken coop. Six years later he enticed his good friend New Yorker Chris Cottrell to join him in the wine business. They have since transferred to larger digs, but their winemaking maintains a hands-on approach. Their wines are highly rated by *Wine Advocate* and *Wine Spectator*. Bedrock Wine Co. Heirloom Bedrock Vineyard 2010 is a blend of 60 percent Zinfandel, 25 percent Carignane, and 15 percent mixed field blend. It has aromas of anise, black plums, and dried cherries. In the mouth the sweet fruit flavors are accented by nuances of dried Mediterranean herbs, pencil lead, and a whiff of peppermint. The tannins are well balanced, and the finish is long and luscious. Bedrock Wine Co. Heirloom Compagni Portis 2012 is a field blend of aromatic and nonaromatic white grape varieties. It is straw colored and has aromas of stone fruits, freesia, and tropical fruits. It is generous in the mouth with delightful flavors that tickle the tongue. The finish invites you in for another sip.

BELLA VINEYARDS AND WINERY

9711 West Dry Creek Road,
Healdsburg, CA 95448,
(707) 473-9171
www.bellawinery.com

Scott and Lynn Adams and their winemakers Michael Dashe, Joe Healy, and Dave Majerus make small batches of Zinfandel, Syrah, and Petite Sirah from their three vineyards. The vines in their Big River Ranch in Alexander Valley are over 100 years old, and their Dry Creek Valley Lily Hill Estate nurtures Zinfandel vines that are over 85 years old. Tastings that include visits to the vineyards and large wine caves are available by appointment. Bella Maple Vineyards Dry Creek Valley Zinfandel 2010 bears lush flavors of wild raspberry, cassis, espresso, and anise wrapped in tannins that are at once chewy and totally smooth. Bella Big River Ranch Zinfandel 2010, composed of 94 percent Zinfandel and 6 percent Petite Syrah, is a full-bodied elegant wine featuring juicy red and black fruit tastes with a dusting of fresh ground pepper and Christmas baking spices.

BENZIGER

1883 London Ranch Road, Glen Ellen, CA 95442,
(888) 490-2739
www.benziger.com

All of Benziger's vineyards are certified biodynamic, organic, or sustainable, and the health of the vines shows through on thrice-daily tram tours and in your wineglass. General manager, winegrower, and Tribute winemaker Mike Benziger found the land he and his family currently farm in the late 1970s. Shortly thereafter Mike, his wife, his parents, and his six siblings relocated from New York to Sonoma Mountain to begin life anew as a winemaking family. In the 1990s, after noticing that the earth and vines didn't look as healthy and vibrant as they had previously, the Benziger family transitioned to using natural farming methods. The rolling hills of their Glen Ellen estate are home to not just grapevines but sheep, cattle, and a host of bugs and birds that help keep the vineyards in balance. Their equally well-balanced lineup of wines includes Cabernet Sauvignon, Merlot, Syrah, Sauvignon Blanc, and Chardonnay. Benziger Signaterra San Remo Vineyard Pinot Noir 2010 from the Russian River Valley opens with aromas and tastes of gingerbread spices, which open to reveal bright cherry pie flavors whose subtle undertones of peat are revived by a bright splash on the back of the palate. Benziger Tribute 2009 is an estate-grown Bordeaux-style blend made mostly of Cabernet Sauvignon. Delicious

brambleberry notes enriched by splashes of tart cherry, pencil lead, and pine needles set the stage for structured tannins and a zesty finish.

BEVAN CELLARS

3468 Silverado Trail,
St. Helena, CA 95504,
(707) 542-0123
www.bevancellars.com

KICK RANCH
SAUVIGNON BLANC
Bevan
SONOMA COUNTY
2011
Cellars

Russell Bevan and Victoria De Crescenzo caught the bug while they were living in Minneapolis and traveling to California wine country on vacation. They began searching for property and eventually bought a dream home on eight acres of land in Bennett Valley. Their friend Kal Showket gave them one ton of Cabernet Sauvignon grapes so that they could try their hand at winemaking the same year, and as they say, the hook was set. Bevan Cellars wines are highly rated by *Wine Spectator* and *Wine Advocate*. Bevan Cellars Showket Vineyard Bab's Cuvée Cabernet Sauvignon 2009 is deep garnet in color, with aromas of ripe black plum, black raspberry, and a touch of blueberry. On the palate the mouthfeel is amazingly full yet light with pronounced dark fruit flavors and just a hint of dark chocolate. The tannic structure is elegant and focused. Bevan Cellars Kick Ranch Sauvignon Blanc Robin's Cuvée 2011 is pale straw-colored with aromas of tropical fruits and white peach. It is light yet crisp in the mouth with great depth and pronounced minerality.

BLUE ROCK VINEYARD

Cloverdale, CA 95424,
(415) 435-1946
www.bluerockvineyard.com

Originally settled by Italian immigrants who came over to work at the Italian Swiss Colony Winery in the 1880s, Blue Rock began life anew when Cheryl and Kenny

Kahn purchased the 100 acres of vineyards and olive trees, restored the original buildings, and replanted the vineyards to the five Bordeaux varieties and a small amount of Syrah. Today, a total of 1,800 cases per year are made from Alexander Valley estate-grown fruit, consisting mainly of Cabernet Sauvignon and blends. Although wine club members have first crack at new releases, small amounts of winemakers Kenny Kahn and Nick Goldschmidt's output find their way onto the wine lists of fine restaurants in about fifteen states. Blue Rock Baby Blue 2010, the estate's entry-level blend made from the younger vines on the estate, is composed of 52 percent Cabernet Sauvignon, 25 percent Merlot, 13 percent Cabernet Franc, and 10 percent Syrah. The nose is heavy on blackberries and cassis with a light touch of Grandma's spice rack, joined in the mouth by nuanced flavors of violet and earth. The rich mouthfeel belies Baby Blue's easy-to-stomach price. Blue Rock Best Barrels Cabernet Sauvignon 2009, a blend of 85 percent Cabernet Sauvignon and 15 percent Petit Verdot, is a powerhouse of mixed-berry pie flavors with a heady dose of espresso bean and toasted vanilla bean, wrapped nicely in a splashy tannic bow.

BUENA VISTA

18000 Old Winery Road, Sonoma CA, 95476,
(800) 926-1266
www.buenavistawinery.com

It is more than fitting that the historic Buena Vista Winery, founded in 1857 by the self-proclaimed count Agoston Haraszthy de Mokesa, should find itself in the portfolio of the Boisset family under the guidance of wine-world royalty Jean-Charles Boisset. Said to be California's first winery to produce fine wine, Buena Vista has been through several incarnations in its rich history, including long periods with no wine production. The Boissets' 2011 acquisition has already resulted in a renovation project that was completed in 2012; visitors are treated to a tour of the lovingly restored winery and cellars. A wide array of dry, sparkling, and sweet wines are produced under six tiers, with a focus on Carneros Chardonnay, Pinot Noir, Merlot, Zinfandel, and Syrah. Buena

Vista Carneros Merlot 2010 is an autumn fruit pie on the nose, with vibrant flavors of black cherry, fresh ground pepper, and mace. Soft tannins and balanced acidity make for a nice mouthfeel and a satisfying finish. Buena Vista Vinicultural Society Sonoma Pinot Noir 2010 tastes of blackberries and cherries blessed with touches of forest floor and caramel, with a bold mouthfeel tapering to a velvety finish.

THE CALLING

205 Concourse Boulevard,
Santa Rosa, CA 95403,
(877) 289-9463
www.thecallingwine.com

The Calling is a collaboration between Emmy Award–winning sports commentator Jim Nantz and Peter Deutsch, CEO of W.J. Deutsch & Sons. It began innocently enough in a Greenwich, Connecticut, restaurant when Peter approached Jim to compliment him on *Always by My Side*, a book about Jim's relationship with his father, who was coping with Alzheimer's disease. The two immediately hit it off, and a friendship and business partnership was formed. For both men, The Calling is about pursuing one's passions and motivating others. Jim is also extremely excited to bring more attention to the Nantz National Alzheimer Center through sales of The Calling wines. Winemaking is under the direction of Marco DiGiulio, and fruit is sourced from a variety of vineyards, including Dutton Ranch. The Calling Russian River Valley Dutton Ranch Jewell Vineyard Chardonnay 2010 is straw colored, with delightful aromas of vanilla, white peach, and white flowers. It is generous in the mouth with a nice heft on the palate. The finish is long and full with a pleasant final note of lemon curd and crème brûlée. The Calling Russian River Valley Dutton Ranch Pinot Noir 2012 is garnet colored, with aromas of freshly picked cherries, forest floor, and a touch of brown baking spice. In the mouth delicious fruit flavors are followed by a touch of spice and pleasant acidity. The finish is long and luxurious.

CARLISLE

PO Box 556,
Santa Rosa, CA 95402,
(707) 566-7700
www.carlislewinery.com

Carlisle founder Mike Officer fell hard for wine while in college, and within a few years after graduation he and his wife, Kendall Carlisle Officer, were making five-gallon batches of Zinfandel in their kitchen sink. That soon turned into a barrel-a-year habit, and after moving to Santa Rosa in the mid-1990s they were up to 300 cases of "garage" Zinfandel per annum. Carlisle Vineyards & Winery was officially launched in 1998, focusing on old-vine Zinfandel and red Rhône blends and single varieties. Jay Maddox joined Mike and Kendall in 2001, bringing along his joint degrees in enology and viticulture from UC Davis. Carlisle sources fruit from some of the oldest and finest vineyards in Sonoma County, including their own Zinfandel vineyard, which was planted in 1928. Carlisle Papa's Block Russian River Valley Syrah 2011 is deep purple to the eye. Fragrances of wild brambleberries and dried Mediterranean herbs lead to palate-expanding flavors of blackberry, wild raspberry, and a pinch of savory herbs and baking spices, straight through the zesty finish. Carlisle Carlisle Vineyard Russian River Valley Zinfandel 2011, dark ruby in the glass, has a heady aroma of black cherry and freshly picked fig. Rich berry and plum flavors backed by a nice dose of Sichuan pepper and Chinese five spice roll across the tongue, bracketed by full tannins and fresh acidity.

CAROL SHELTON WINES

3354-B Coffey Lane,
Santa Rosa, CA 95403,
(707) 575-3441
www.carolshelton.com

Having worked with such wine-world legends as Andre Tchelistcheff and Robert Mondavi over the course of an esteemed and honored career, Carol Shelton and her husband, Mitch Mackenzie, established their own brand in 2000. Working with Zinfandel from a variety of California *terroirs*, Carol lets her original major at UC Davis—poetry—shine through in the clever names she gives her wines, such as Wild Thing Zin, Sweet Caroline, and Karma Zin. Currently producing about 5,000 cases annually, Carol has added other varieties, including Cabernet Sauvignon, Pinot Noir, and those from the Rhône, and she is working on increasing production capacity to satisfy the countrywide demand for her first-rate wines. Carol Shelton Wild Thing Mendocino County Old Vine Zinfandel 2009, made from 78 percent old-vine Zinfandel, 12 percent Carignan, 7 percent Petite Sirah, and 3 percent Cabernet Sauvignon, bursts upon the nose and palate with fresh fruit notes of blackberry combined with an opulent dose of vanilla custard. The creamy mouthfeel and smooth finish invite you back for another sip. Carol Shelton 'Xander Zin 2009, a blend of 90 percent Zinfandel, 5 percent Carignan, and 5 percent Petite Sirah, is a bit like a layered fruit dessert, although it is not by any means a sweet wine. Flavors of raspberry and cherry seem to predominate, then vanilla and chocolate take over, and then a pleasant wave of spice hits, all nicely enveloped in a casing of polished tannins. Carol Shelton Coquille Blanc 2010, a blend of 40 percent Grenache Blanc, 30 percent Roussanne, 15 percent Marsanne, and 15 percent Viognier, is a welcome diversion from the enticing lineup of Zinfandels. Fragrances of ripe peach, almond blossom, and jasmine give way to rich flavors of white peach, pear, and toasted nuts with a captivating floral lift.

CHALK HILL ESTATE

10300 Chalk Hill Road,
Healdsburg, CA 95448,
(707) 657-4837
www.chalkhill.com

Founder Fred Furth was flying his plane over the Russian River in 1972 and spotted the land that eventually was to become his vineyard. Currently, Chalk Hill Estate is owned by Bill Foley and winemaking is handled by Lisa Bishop Forbes, who prefers a noninvasive, sustainable, light touch in her craft. Chalk Hill Estate Sauvignon Musque 2011 has delightful tropical aromas, including freshly cut pineapple and orange peel. There are notes of dried sweet herbs and flavors of mango, grapefruit, and white stone fruits. The finish is crisp and clean with a lingering florality at the roof of your mouth. Chalk Hill Estate Pinot Noir 2011 is cherry red and has aromas of red cherry, red raspberry, and a touch of cedar. It is generous in the mouth, with flavors of red fruits and Chinese black tea. The tannins are well balanced, and the finish is long with a final touch of spice.

CHARLES HEINTZ VINEYARDS

PO Box 238,
Occidental, CA 95465,
(877) 874-3852
www.heintzvineyards.com

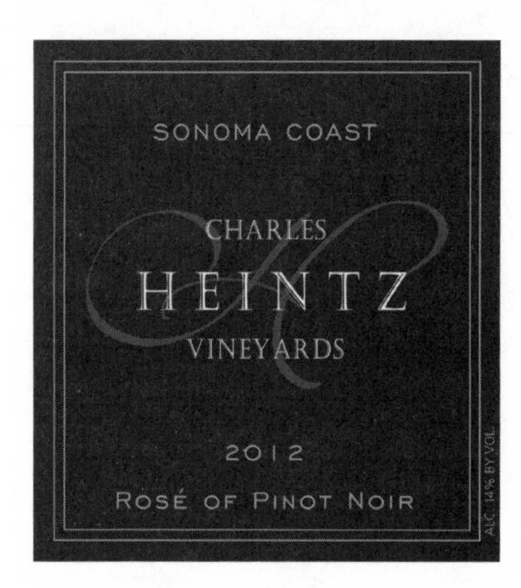

Family-owned since 1912, Heintz Ranch is known for producing quality cool-weather grapes, especially Pinot Noir, Chardonnay, and Syrah. Its wines are truly artisanally handmade, and production between both labels—Heintz and Dutch Bill Creek—comes in at less than 1,000 cases total. Heintz Sonoma Coast Syrah 2009 is inky purple with delightful aromas of crystallized violets, red fruits, and black plums. It is fruit-forward in the mouth with restrained elegance in the finish. Heintz Rosé of Pinot Noir 2012 is salmon pink and makes you think of summer days tubing down the Russian River with a floating cooler filled with delicious wine. It has ethereal aromas of strawberries and cream and white flowers that transfer seamlessly onto your palate sip after sip.

CHASSEUR

2064 Gravenstein Highway North,
Sebastopol, CA 95472,
(707) 829-1941
www.chasseurwines.com

French for "hunter," Chasseur was launched in 1994 by winemaker Bill Hunter. After stints at Rombauer and Bonny Doon, Bill wanted to make Pinot Noir and Chardonnay that best expressed his own philosophy, and he later added small amounts of Syrah to the mix. Chardonnay is sourced from vineyards in the southern reaches of the Sonoma Coast appellation and from the Russian River Valley, whereas the Pinot Noir comes only from vineyards in and around the Russian River Valley. In 2009, Andrew Berge joined Bill in an assistant winemaker capacity. The well-deserved accolades earned by Chasseur may seem out of proportion to its 2,700-case annual output, but they are surely doing things right. Hunter Wine Cellars Chasseur Graton's Choice Chardonnay 2010 is a mouth-pleasing mash-up of stone fruits and citrus, with a dusting of spice and grated lemon rind.

Hunter Wine Cellars Chasseur Russian River Valley Pinot Noir 2010 gives up whiffs of bright fruit and orange essence on the nose, while the more subdued palate offers flavors of black cherry, cassis, baking spices, and chocolate, with a pleasing balance of tannins and graceful acidity.

CHATEAU ST. JEAN

8555 Sonoma Highway, Kenwood, CA 95452,
(707) 833-4134
www.chateaustjean.com

Walking through the main entrance and gardens, you can forget that you're in California for a moment and think you've been transported to a Mediterranean villa. But don't be fooled: Chateau St. Jean embodies the spirit of Sonoma hospitality. The tasting room staff always makes you feel like you're family, but for a special experience call ahead and ask to visit the reserve room. You'll be glad that you did—and make sure to add extra time in your schedule to take in the scenery. Winemaker Margo Van Staaveren is responsible for overseeing the production of Chateau St. Jean's thirty or so wines. Chateau St. Jean Sonoma County Chardonnay 2010 is straw colored, with aromas of pineapple upside down cake, crisp apple slices, and toasted almonds. It is creamy in the mouth with refreshing acidity in the finish. Chateau St. Jean Sonoma County Pinot Noir 2010 has aromas of red raspberry, Christmas baking spices, and red plums. It has a touch of spice on the palate along with generous fruit flavors. Well-balanced tannins lead the way to a long, luscious finish.

CLINE CELLARS

24737 Arnold Drive, Sonoma, CA 95476,
(707) 940-4000
www.clinecellars.com

After receiving a degree in agriculture management from UC Davis, Fred Cline founded Cline Cellars in Oakley, California, where his mother's father, Valeriano Jacuzzi, had taught him to love the land and to make wine. Fred and his wife, Nancy, moved from Oakley to the Carneros appellation of Sonoma County in 1992 and planted Syrah, Marsanne, Roussanne, and Viognier. Today Cline Cellars is known for its acclaimed red and white Rhône varieties and for Zinfandel that is still grown in Oakley. Cline's vineyards are naturally and sustainably farmed. A circa-1850s farmhouse serves as the tasting room, set amid grounds featuring spring-fed ponds and thousands of rosebushes, and the California Mission Museum is a testament to the Spanish Catholics who first brought wine grapes to California. Wine is produced and bottled in six tiers: Oakley, California, Sonoma, Cool Climate, Ancient Vines, and Single Vineyard. Cline Cool Climate Sonoma Coast Syrah 2010 is inky blue violet and tastes of blueberry pie and freshly ground black pepper, made even more delicious by the velvety mouthfeel and zingy finish. Cline Contra Costa County Bridgehead Zinfandel 2010 is a powerhouse that knows when to show restraint. It fills the nose with equal parts just-picked berries and baking spices and then caresses the mouth with these flavors joined by smooth white chocolate and a hint of toast.

CLOS DU BOIS

19410 Geyserville Avenue,
Geyserville, CA 95441,
(800) 222-3189
www.closdubois.com

Founder Frank Woods introduced Clos du Bois's first Chardonnay and Pinot Noir wines in 1974 after traveling extensively throughout France. The company has certainly grown since the early days, and today director of winemaking Gary Sitton works with long-term growers in Sonoma County and coastal California and oversees approximately 800 acres of vineyards to make an extensive portfolio of white and red bottlings. Clos du Bois North Coast Sauvignon Blanc 2012 has aromas of white flowers, lemongrass, and grapefruit zest. It is crisp and fruity in the mouth with a nice touch of minerality in the finish. Clos du Bois North Coast Zinfandel 2010 is composed of 76 percent Zinfandel, 9 percent Tempranillo,

8 percent Petite Sirah, and 7 percent Syrah. It is dark garnet, with aromas of anise, black plum, and Christmas baking spices. It is big and bold in the mouth with flavors of fresh fruit and dark berry conserves. There's a nice amount of spice in the finish.

COBB WINES

18100 Fitzpatrick Lane,
Occidental, CA 95465,
(707) 799-1073
www.cobbwines.com

David and Ross Cobb made the first vintage of their Coastlands Vineyard Pinot Noir in 2001, but the path that led to this venture had long been under way. Originally a marine biologist, David first crafted homemade wine in the late 1970s while living and working in Saudi Arabia, where it was not possible to buy beer or wine. David and his wife, Diane, first planted their vineyard in 1989, working with many different Pinot Noir clones, and sold their grapes to other wineries until their son Ross came aboard in 2001. Ross had gained wide experience with winemaking and particularly Pinot Noir while working at such noted wineries as Ferrari-Carano, Bonny Doon, Williams Selyem, and Flowers. Together David and Ross focus on small-lot, single-vineyard Pinot Noir from the Sonoma Coast appellation. Cobb Jack Hill Vineyard Sonoma Coast Pinot Noir 2009 offers aromas of black cherry and perfectly ripe black plums. Abundant dark fruit is most evident on the palate, with dollops of spice and chocolate, amid a full mouthfeel and a bright finish. Cobb Coastlands Vineyard Sonoma Coast Pinot Noir 2009 is deep cherry to the eye, with fragrances of mixed-berry marmalade, citrus, and spice. The elegant and richly nuanced palate moves through fruit into mint tea, Moroccan spice, and cedar before giving way to a smooth yet vivid finish.

COPAIN WINES

7800 Eastside Road,
Healdsburg, CA 95448,
(707) 836-8822
www.copainwines.com

After a two-year apprenticeship under Rhône Valley icon Michel Chapoutier, Wells Guthrie began making wines that are classic California in style with an eye to the craftsmanship of France. Working with Syrah, Pinot Noir, and Chardonnay mostly from nearby Mendocino County, Guthrie's Copain produces three tiers of wine, *Tous Ensemble*, *Les Voisins*, and Single Vineyard. The majority of Copain goes to fortunate club members, but many bottles are sold at its Russian River Valley winery and tasting room and online. Copain Les Voisins Syrah 2010 offers a bright nose of blueberries and wildflowers whose exuberance belies the restrained wine in the glass. Flavors of blueberry, blackberry, and lavender are encased in velvety tannins with a touch of river rocks.

DAVIS BYNUM WINERY

8075 Westside Rd, Healdsburg, CA 95448,
(866) 442-7547
www.davisbynum.com

In 1973, former newspaper reporter Davis Bynum built the first winery on Westside Road in Healdsburg and then, using grapes from neighbor Joe Rochioli's now-acclaimed vineyard, made what is claimed to be the first single-vineyard Russian River Valley Pinot Noir. Today, under the ownership of the Klein family and Rodney Strong Wine Estates, Davis Bynum is known for artisanal Russian River Valley Chardonnay and Pinot Noir. Winemaker Greg Morthole has been with the winery since 2005, advancing to head winemaker in 2010. Davis Bynum River West Chardonnay 2011 has aromas and flavors of Granny Smith apple and Bartlett pear, with a nice dose of butterscotch and a touch of lemon zest. Davis Bynum Jane's Vineyard Pinot Noir is a classic cherry vanilla parfait joined on the nose by floral aromatics. Delicious fruit continues in the mouth with a velvety texture and a satisfying finish.

DEHLINGER

4101 Vine Hill Road, Sebastopol, CA 95472,
(707) 823-2378
www.dehlingerwinery.com

Enologist Tom Dehlinger studied at UC Davis and then planted 14 acres of vines in 1975. Today, in addition to himself, his wife, Carole; daughters Carmen and Eva; and vineyard manager Martin Hedlund, Tom and a small staff create 7,000 cases of estate-bottled Chardonnay, Cabernet Sauvignon, Pinot Noir, and Syrah from what has grown to 45 acres. The small-scale ethos is apparent in the high-quality wines crafted by this dedicated team. About three-quarters of their wine is set aside for wine club members, with the balance available at the winery (by appointment) and on restaurant wine lists. Dehlinger Winery Estate Russian River Valley Chardonnay 2009 has a rich nose of orange marmalade on buttered toast that endures on the palate, aided by a creamy mouthfeel and zippy acidity. Dehlinger Goldridge Russian River Valley Syrah 2009 proffers flavors of blackberry and raspberry infused with cocoa, espresso, aniseed, and freshly ground pepper.

DELOACH VINEYARDS

1791 Olivet Road, Santa Rosa, CA 95401,
(707) 755-3309
www.deloachvineyards.com

Cecil De Loach, a San Francisco fireman who fell in love with winemaking, planted his first grapes in 1973. The Boisset family of Burgundy, France, took the reins at DeLoach in 2003 after scion Jean-Charles Boisset became enamored with the Russian River Valley, likening Sonoma County to Burgundy in terms of climate and *terroir*. After the 2004 vintage, the new owners ripped out the existing vineyards and replanted them using biodynamic techniques; 2010 saw the first wines produced from newly planted stock. Winemaker Brian Maloney, assisted by Katie Cochrane, works with Chardonnay, Pinot Noir, and Zinfandel grown under the hand of winegrower Eric Pooler for the Estate Wine, Vineyard Designate, and OFS tiers. DeLoach Estate Chardonnay 2010, from the first harvest of the newly planted Russian River Valley Estate Vineyard, is a delight to the nose and mouth. Flavors of caramelized pear tart with hints of Mediterranean herbs and jasmine are encased in a rich mouthfeel with a rewarding burst of brightness. DeLoach Estate Collection Pinot Noir 2010 is a testament to the Boissets' Burgundian heritage. Black cherry and raspberry lead the charge, with a full complement of autumn spices on hand to lend finesse.

C. DONATIELLO

320 Center St.,
Healdsburg, CA 95448,
(707) 431-4442
www.cdonatiello.com

Chris Donatiello made his name on the sales and marketing side of the wine and spirits industry and then headed to the Russian River Valley to focus on his eponymous winery, producing small-lot, single-vineyard Pinot Noir and Chardonnay. Donatiello and winemaker Webster Marquez forge wines (available via online order and at their downtown Healdsburg tasting room) that are a testament to *terroir* and the art of viniculture. C. Donatiello Peters Vineyard Chardonnay 2009 puts forward aromas of Granny Smith apple and toast with butter and orange marmalade and then washes over the taste buds with flavors of apple, citrus, Christmas spice, and a touch of wet stones. C. Donatiello Russian River Valley Floodgate Old Vines Pinot Noir 2009 offers notes of cassis, mocha, and forest floor on the nose that are accompanied in the mouth by flavors of fresh summer berries and a smidgen of earthy spice, leading to a rewarding finish.

DRY CREEK VINEYARD

3770 Lambert Bridge Road, Healdsburg, CA 95448,
(707) 433-1000
www.drycreekvineyard.com

Kim Stare Wallace and her husband, Don Wallace, continue the legacy begun by Kim's father, David Stare, in 1972. A pioneer in many ways, David was an early advocate of sustainable farming in the wine industry. A proponent of Dry Creek Valley's AVA status, in 1983 David was the first to label a wine from this appellation. Against all advice, he also insisted on planting Sauvignon Blanc and introduced the first Sonoma County Sauvignon Blanc. In most parts of the world, 40 years is just a blip on the time line, but in that amount of time Dry Creek Vineyard has earned many accolades and been "first" in several endeavors. Wines are made in two series, Signature and Single Vineyard, and a small amount of dessert wines is made. Dry

Creek Vineyard Dry Creek Valley Sauvignon Blanc 2012, a blend of 90 percent Sauvignon Blanc and 10 percent Sauvignon Musqué, has a clean nose of bright tropical fruits. On the tongue it is a mélange of citrus, notably grapefruit and lemon-lime sorbet, with the tiniest hint of florality, all of which add up to a wine that is as elegant as it is refreshing. Dry Creek Vineyard Heritage Zinfandel 2010 offers a strong nose of blackberry, mocha, and nutmeg. These notes continue onto the palate, where blackberry and chocolate are joined by North African spices and velvety tannins.

DUTTON ESTATE WINERY

8757 Green Valley Road,
Sebastopol, CA 95472,
(707) 829-9463
www.sebastopolvineyards.com

Joe and Tracy Dutton were both born into farming families, and they carry on their traditions today. Joe continues to manage Dutton Ranch, founded by his parents, whose 1,300 acres are graced by 1,150 acres of Pinot Noir, Syrah, Zinfandel, Chardonnay, Sauvignon Blanc, and Pinot Gris, plus 150 acres of apples. Their vineyards are situated in the Green Valley of the Russian River Valley and Sonoma Coast appellations, and in addition to being used in their own wines, Dutton Ranch grapes are sold to about sixty other producers. Joe and Tracy purchased a Chardonnay vineyard in 1995 close to Dutton Ranch and to Kozlowski Farms, Tracy's family's farm. Their initial release of 1,000 cases of Pinot Noir and Chardonnay was bottled under the Sebastopol Vineyards label. Dutton Estate Russian River Valley Kyndall's Reserve Chardonnay is almost sweet on the nose, with touches of vanilla, spice, and citrus, leading to flavors of orange crème brûlée and a hint of clove, with a lush mouthfeel. Dutton Estate Russian River Valley Karmen Isabella Pinot Noir 2010 presents aromas of cherry, blackberry, and Turkish delight. On the palate, rich berry fruit and honeysuckle give way to light tannins and a zesty finish.

DUTTON-GOLDFIELD

3100 Gravenstein Highway North,
Sebastopol, CA 95472,
(707) 823-3887
www.duttongoldfield.com

A collaboration between two friends and colleagues Steve Dutton and Dan Goldfield, Dutton-Goldfield was formed in 1998 with a focus on Pinot Noir and Chardonnay. Steve is the fifth generation of his family to live in this area, and he began farming grapes with his father at age five. Dan started on a path toward research chemistry, but after graduating from UC Davis with a master's in enology he developed a devotion to Pinot Noir while making wine at La Crema and then Hartford Court. Most of their fruit comes from Dutton Ranch vineyards in the Green River of the Russian River Valley AVA, and their portfolio also includes small amounts of Syrah, Zinfandel, and Pinot Blanc.

Dutton-Goldfield Dutton Ranch Russian River Valley Chardonnay 2011 is pale yellow to the eye, with a nose of citrus, lemon zest, and custard. It is full on the palate, with flavors of tangerine, lemon, and butterscotch, with a satisfying finish featuring equal amounts of acidity and minerality. Dutton-Goldfield Dutton Ranch Russian River Valley Pinot Noir 2011 offers aromas of black cherry with notes of incense and spice. Cherry continues on the tongue, mingling with vanilla and nice spice notes. The smooth, mellow finish is backed throughout by sweet tannins.

ENKIDU

8910 Sonoma Hwy,
Kenwood, CA 95452,
(707) 833-6100
www.enkiduwines.com

Owner and winemaker Phillip Staehle conceived his winery based on the principles embodied by Enkidu, the best friend of Gilgamesh in *The Epic of Gilgamesh*, who was the protector of animals and the land. Using naturally farmed grapes and traditional winemaking techniques, Staehle works with Chardonnay, Syrah, Petite Sirah, Zinfandel, Cabernet Sauvignon, and Pinot Noir to create wines that are balanced and complex but most of all are appealing to the senses. Enkidu Tin Cross Vineyard Pine Mountain-Cloverdale Peak Chardonnay 2011 is a lean, mineral-driven expression of the varietal, with flavors of lemon sorbet and flint that coat the mouth lusciously before a final burst of clean acidity. Enkidu Kick Ranch Sonoma County Syrah 2009 offers aromas of cassis and cherry, bacon, and black olive. Rich on the palate, cherry jam and fresh cherry fight it out with dashes of Mediterranean herb and baking spice.

ENROUTE

PO Box 2358,
Sebastopol CA 95473,
(707) 944-2312
www.enroutewinery.com

Focused solely on Russian River Valley Pinot Noir, EnRoute's first vintage, 2007, came to market in 2009. The winery was started by Beth, Erik, and Jeremy Nickel, Dirk Hampson, and Larry Maguire, who also own Far Niente, Dolce, and Nickel & Nickel; its sole bottling at this time is Les Pommiers Pinot Noir, named for the apple orchards that gradually have been replaced by grapevines in the Russian River Valley. Their 21.5-acre Graton Vineyard in Russian River's Green Valley AVA is a former apple orchard now planted to a variety of Pinot Noir clones. The slightly larger Amber Ridge Vineyard is also home to Pinot Noir vines. Winemaker Andrew Delos works under the able hand of director of winemaking Dirk Hampson.

EnRoute Les Pommiers Russian River Valley Pinot Noir 2010 offers aromas of tart cherry and black plum with a whiff of violet and earth. In the mouth flavors become apparent gradually, opening with a punch of raspberry and black cherry, backed by graceful notes of peat and gravel wrapped in solid tannins. Although you will want to drink every bottle you buy, do yourself a favor and lay a few down.

FERRARI-CARANO VINEYARDS AND WINERY

8761 Dry Creek Road,
Healdsburg, CA 95448,
(707) 433-6700
www.ferrari-carano.com

Don and Rhonda Carano founded Ferrari-Carano Vineyards and Winery in 1981 after visiting Sonoma County on a wine-buying trip for their Eldorado Hotel and Casino in Reno, Nevada. Ferrari-Carano has been making fine wine since 1985, and visitors to the property always marvel at how the gardens and main buildings remind them of an Italian villa. If you're looking for a romantic getaway, go ahead and splurge and spend a night or two at Ferrari-Carano Vintners Inn in Santa Rosa, set on 92 acres of beautiful vineyards in the Russian River Valley; it's also home to the John Ash & Co. restaurant. Winemaker Aaron Piotter is responsible for red wine production while Sarah Quider makes the whites. Vineyard management is overseen by Steve Domenichelli. Ferrari-Carano's Fumé Blanc 2010 has notes of tropical fruit, citrus blossom, and stone fruit in the complex bouquet. In the mouth there are fresh fruit flavors and bright acidity in the finish, making this a perfect wine as an aperitif or with briny seafood. Ferrari-Carano Merlot 2011 has aromas of cigar box, red raspberry preserves, and Christmas baking spices. It is full-bodied in the mouth with lots of fruit, and it leaves a lingering impression of dark chocolate that persists for a long time.

FLOWERS VINEYARD & WINERY

28500 Seaview Road,
Cazadero, CA 95421,
(707) 847-3661
https://flowerswinery.com

Walt and Joan Flowers owned a nursery in Pennsylvania before transferring their lives and passion cross-country. In 1989, they bought 321 acres on the northern Sonoma Coast and planted Pinot Noir and Chardonnay. Today they have developed a partnership with the Agustin Huneeus family, and their highly sought-after wines earn well-deserved accolades from industry insiders and wine civilians alike. Using grapes grown in their own Camp Meeting Ridge Vineyard and Sea View Ridge Vineyard or sourced from other vineyards in the Sonoma Coast AVA, head winemaker Jason Jardine's bottlings are available via Flowers's wine club and at fine restaurants and wine shops throughout the country. Flowers Sea View Ridge Pinot Noir 2010 opens with a volley of freshly picked berries, backed by lush flavors of grilled wild mushrooms and pancetta on lightly buttered toast; this wine is a delight to the palate.

FOPPIANO VINEYARDS

12707 Old Redwood Highway,
Healdsburg, CA 95448,
(707) 433-7272
www.foppiano.com

Started by Giovanni Foppiano in 1896, Foppiano Vineyards is one of the oldest family-run wineries in Sonoma. Today, fourth- and fifth-generation family members work side by side to create Petite Sirah, Chardonnay, Pinot Noir, and Syrah from their sustainably farmed Russian River Valley vineyards. Louis J. Foppiano, one of the founders of the Russian River Valley AVA, passed away in 2012 at the age of 101. Foppiano is known worldwide for its award-winning Petite Sirah; in 2002, Louis M. Foppiano, son of Louis J., became the first charter member of PS I Love You, an advocacy group for Petite Sirah. Vineyards are now under the direction of Louis J.'s grandson Paul Foppiano, and winemaking is performed by Natalie West. Foppiano Vineyards Estate Bottled Petite Sirah Russian River Valley 2009 emits fragrances of fruits of the wood, mocha, and a hint of fennel seed. In the mouth blueberry pie, cherry conserves, and a smear of Nutella are presented in an elegant wrapping of tannins and are finished with a bright, fruity splash.

FORT ROSS VINEYARD & WINERY

15725 Meyers Grade Road,
Jenner, CA 95450,
(707) 847-3460
www.fortrossvineyard.com

Lester and Linda Schwartz first met as students at South Africa's University of Cape Town in the 1960s. Before moving to California in the mid-1970s, Lester worked as an attorney and Linda, who is a musician and composer, worked as a music teacher and arts administrator. They continued in those professions after their relocation and purchased a large swath of land in the coastal mountains above the old Fort Ross settlement. After building their home, they began ordering rootstock in 1991, which prompted Linda to study viticulture. Their early vineyard experiments proved that the area was perfect for Pinot Noir and Chardonnay, to which they added a small amount of Pinotage in homage to their native South Africa. Their first vintage was 2000, and in 2009 Jeff Pisoni, who also makes wine from his family vineyards in the Santa Lucia Highlands, came aboard as winemaker. Fort Ross Vineyard Symposium Sonoma Coast Pinot Noir 2009, composed of 97 percent Pinot Noir and 3 percent Pinotage, is dark red in the glass. Fragrances of black cherry, green tea, and white pepper open on the palate to flavors of blackberry, black plum, brioche, and baking spices with pleasant farm stand notes. Fort Ross Vineyard Sonoma Coast Pinot Noir 2009, deep ruby to the eye, offers a luscious nose of wild berries and dried herbs. Gorgeous mouthfeel, zesty acidity, and a firm tannic structure provide an elegant setting for flavors of mixed brambleberries, sage, thyme, and chocolate.

FRANCIS FORD COPPOLA WINERY

300 Via Archimedes, Geyserville, CA 95441,
(707) 857-1400
www.franciscoppolawinery.com

Academy Award–winning director, producer, and screenwriter Francis Ford Coppola's eponymous Alexander Valley winery, the former Chateau Souverain, reopened in July 2010

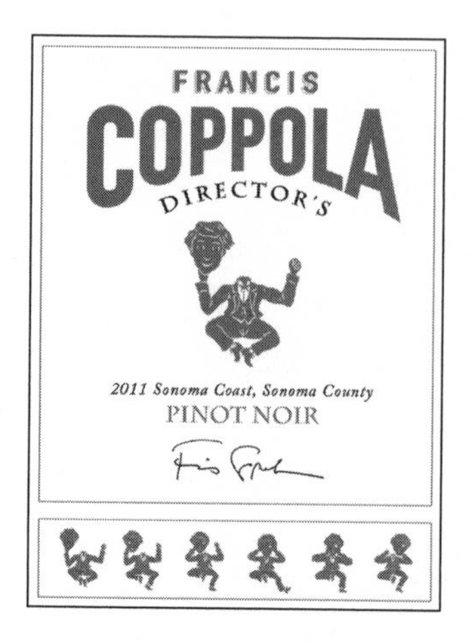

after extensive renovations. Coppola teamed with another Academy Award winner, Dean Tavoularis, whose production design skills were put to good use in creating a family-friendly "wine wonderland" featuring two wine-tasting bars, two restaurants, a park area, a swimming pool, a movie gallery, and a performing arts pavilion. The grounds were designed with Copenhagen's Tivoli Gardens in mind, and this unique wine country destination quickly became a Sonoma favorite. Many different types of tours and tastings are available for a variety of interest levels, time commitments, and price points, and the entry-level Rosso & Bianco wines are offered at no charge. Wines are made in a dizzying array of tiers, including Su Yuen, Votre Santé, Sofia, Rosso & Bianco, Diamond Collection, Director's, Director's Cut, Eleanor, Archimedes, and FC Reserve. Francis Ford Coppola Director's Cut Russian River Valley Chardonnay 2011 is medium straw in the glass, with aromas of tropical fruits and spice. On the palate ripe peach and Asian pear join the tropical fruit flavors, with a touch of crème brûlée on the finish. Francis Ford Coppola Director's Sonoma Coast Pinot Noir 2011 offers a fresh fruity nose of cherries and citrus. Flavors of mixed red and dark berries and baking spices mingle on the tongue through the sleek finish.

FREEMAN VINEYARD & WINERY

1300 Montgomery Road,
Sebastopol, CA 95472
(707) 823-6937
www.freemanwinery.com

Ken and Akiko Freeman spent several years searching California for a vineyard site from which to make cool-climate Chardonnay and Pinot Noir comparable to the wines they love from Burgundy. They founded

Freeman in 2001, collaborating with winemaker Ed Kurtzman, who now works in a consultant capacity with his protégé, Akiko. In addition to estate-grown grapes, Freeman sources from other well-known vineyards in the Russian River Valley such as Keefer and Heintz ranches; total production is 5,000 cases per year. Freeman Vineyard and Winery Ryo-fu Chardonnay 2010 fills the nose with scents of ripe stone fruits and Bartlett pear and then washes the tongue with flavors of lightly toasted pineapple and mango sorbet with a hint of creaminess. Freeman Vineyard and Winery Akiko's Cuvée Pinot Noir 2010 feels bigger than a Pinot Noir on the nose, with strong fragrances of raspberry and blackberry joined by notes of freshly ground pepper, graphite, and clove. Berry flavors are the first thing to hit the taste buds, backed by touches of freshly baked bread and a hint of mushroom. Rich mouthfeel and a final dash of orange zest invite you to taste again.

FREI BROTHERS RESERVE

3887 Dry Creek Road, Healdsburg CA 95448,
(866) 346-3963
www.freibrothers.com

Swiss immigrant Andrew Frei bought part of what is now Dry Creek Valley's Frei Ranch in 1890 and then built a winery that was producing 20,000 cases of wine per year by 1895. Frei's sons, Walter and Louis, took over the winery in 1903. In the 1930s Julio Gallo began buying grapes from Frei Ranch. The Gallo family bought Frei Ranch and the winery in the 1970s after the remaining members of the Frei family retired. Viticulturist Jim Collins manages the estate vineyards and helps source grapes from within Sonoma's finest growing regions. Chardonnay, Sauvignon Blanc, and Pinot Noir come from Russian River Valley; Cabernet Sauvignon is from Alexander Valley; and Merlot and Zinfandel originate in Dry Creek Valley. The California Sustainable Winegrowing Alliance has given Frei Brothers Reserve the California Sustainable Winegrowing Certification Frei Brothers Reserve Russian River Valley Chardonnay offers aromas of Granny Smith apple with a dash of citrus. Granny Smith apple continues in the mouth, with vanilla custard notes and a very light touch of spice. Frei Brothers Reserve Dry Creek Valley Merlot 2010 has a nose of wild brambleberries with a suggestion of vanilla latté. Flavors of raspberry and blackberry are joined by strawberry jam, mocha, and white chocolate. Soft tannins and invigorating acidity make for a satisfying sip.

FROSTWATCH VINEYARD & WINERY

5560 Bennett Valley Road,
Santa Rosa, CA 95404,
(707) 570-0592
www.frostwatch.com

Owners Brett Raven and Diane Kleineke make small-batch wines from grapes that are almost all grown in their Bennett Valley Frostwatch Vineyard. Their 15-acre vineyard was originally planted with Chardonnay, Merlot, and a small amount of Zinfandel, but for the last several years they have undertaken a replanting effort to replace Merlot with mainly white varieties. Fortunately, they have kept about two acres of Merlot, but they have added in Sauvignon Blanc, Sémillon, and a bit of Pinot Noir. An attorney by trade, Brett studied winemaking at University of California, Davis, and had the opportunity to hone his skills at Alderbrook Winery, Matanzas Creek Winery, and Ramey Wine Cellars before turning his attention to Frostwatch full time. Wines are made at the vinify facility in Santa Rosa, which also features a tasting room called Vinoteca. Frostwatch Bennett Valley Kismet 2011 is a blend of 88 percent Sauvignon Blanc and 12 percent Sémillon, all grown in the Frostwatch Vineyard. Understated aromas of tropical fruit, freesia, and freshly chopped herbs lead to flavors of grapefruit and pineapple with a pleasant lift of spice. Keen acidity and a touch of creaminess add up to a nicely balanced wine. Frostwatch Bennett Valley Pinot Noir 2010 has a nose of cherry and spice with a whiff of juniper. On the palate cherry predominates, but the rich mouthfeel makes one think of cherry preserves or a splash of cassis. Elegant spice notes carry through to the bright finish.

GARY FARRELL VINEYARDS & WINERY

10701 Westside Road,
Healdsburg, CA 95448,
(707) 473-2900
www.garyfarrellwines.com

Gary Farrell honed his craft with Robert Stemmler, Davis Bynum, Tom Dehlinger, and Joe Rochioli before starting out on his own and launching Gary Farrell Winery in 1982. Sourcing Pinot Noir and Chardonnay from the finest vineyard sites in the Russian River Valley and Zinfandel from there and Dry Creek Valley, Gary Farrell produces wines of exceptional quality. Farrell sold the winery in 2004 but was the winemaker until 2006. In 2011 the winery was again sold, to Sonoma-based Vincraft Group. Current winemaker Theresa Heredia joined the team after stints at Saintsbury, Joseph Phelps, and Freestone, where she perfected her skill with Chardonnay and Pinot Noir. Gary Farrell Russian River Valley Russian River Selection Chardonnay 2010 has a nose that combines the best of tropical fruits and autumn fruit pies. Flavors of pineapple, Fuji apple, honeysuckle, and vanilla pudding with cinnamon play across the tongue in textured waves, leading to a final splash of brightness. Gary Farrell Russian River Valley Russian River Selection Pinot Noir 2010 bears fragrances of cherry and cassis with notes of crème brûlée. The art of winemaking is apparent on the palate, where cherry and cassis merge with flavors of bread pudding and a sprinkle of orange zest, all kept alive by soft tannins and sprightly acidity.

GLORIA FERRER CAVES & VINEYARDS

23555 Arnold Drive,
Sonoma, CA 95476,
(707) 933-1917
www.gloriaferrer.com

Barcelona, Spain, natives José and Gloria Ferrer arrived in Sonoma County in the 1980s, when there was no other sparkling wine producer in Carneros. Inspired by the rolling hills and Mediterranean climate, the Ferrers realized that this land would be ideal for planting Chardonnay and Pinot Noir. The Ferrer family has a rich background in sparkling wine production. Their Catalonian homestead, La Freixeneda, dates back to the twelfth century, and they are well known for the Spanish sparkler Freixenet. Gloria Ferrer Caves & Vineyards opened its doors in 1986 and has continued to win accolades for over 25 years. Their original 160-acre Carneros ranch has expanded to 335 acres, and in addition to sparkling wine, executive winemaker Bob Iantosca and head of production Mike

Crumly now make still wines. Gloria Ferrer Blanc de Noirs NV offers scents of red berries with a whiff of custard. On the palate flavors of black cherry, lemon zest, and caramel predominate through the bright finish. Gloria Ferrer Carneros Cuvée 2001, which was first released in 2013, is blended from 53 percent Pinot Noir and 47 percent Chardonnay. On the nose cut green apples and sliced pear are intertwined with soft notes of baking bread. In the mouth apple and pear are joined by citrus, and a rich mouthfeel and zesty acidity lead to a lasting finish.

GUNDLACH BUNDSCHU WINERY

2000 Denmark Street,
Sonoma, CA 95476,
(707) 938-5277
www.gunbun.com

In 1858, German immigrant Jacob Gundlach purchased 400 acres in Sonoma and named it Rhinefarm in honor of his homeland. Three years later he brought in some partners and built a winery. Another immigrant from Germany, Charles Bundschu, joined the business in 1868, and today Gundlach Bundschu is considered by many to be the oldest family-owned winery in the state of California. Although the original property was divided over the years, in 1997 the Bundschu family purchased a portion of the old Dressel parcel and restored Rhinefarm to a single contiguous estate vineyard. Gundlach-Bundschu Estate Vineyard Sonoma Coast Gewürztraminer 2012 is pale straw in color, with aromas of tropical fruits, citrus blossoms, and lychee. It is round in the mouth, with refreshing fruit flavors, crisp acidity, and a touch of austere minerality in the finish. Gundlach Bundschu Estate Vineyard Sonoma Valley Cabernet Franc 2010 is inky garnet, with aromas of espresso, blueberry pie, and tobacco leaf. It is fruit-forward in the mouth, with nice heft on the palate and a silky tannic finish.

GUSTAFSON FAMILY VINEYARDS

9100 Stewarts Point Skaggs
Springs Road,
Geyserville, CA 95441,
(707) 433-2371
www.gfvineyard.com

With 20 acres of Zinfandel, Petite Sirah, Syrah, Cabernet Franc, Cabernet Sauvignon, Riesling, and Sauvignon Blanc situated among almost 250 acres of forest and meadow above Lake Sonoma, Dan Gustafson and his family appear to be sitting on top of the world. Dan, a landscape architect from

Minnesota; his wife, Phyllis; and their children have worked within the natural beauty of this former sheep ranch to create winery grounds that are a favorite picnic spot for locals and visitors alike. Dan discovered the land and got into the world of wine in 2002 and then expanded the property to its current size in 2006. Gustafson Estate Sauvignon Blanc 2011 displays a complexity often missing from this varietal, which is first apparent from the delicate aromatic notes of jasmine, honeysuckle, and orange rind. In the mouth citrus and floral flavors are joined by a touch of toasted vanilla bean, followed by a zingy finish. Don't be fooled by the fruit-forward nose on Gustafson Estate Petite Sirah 2010. Black cherry and blackberry are joined on the palate by flavors of baking spice, with an underlying earthy foundation; grippy tannins promise a satisfying finish that does not go unfulfilled.

HALLECK VINEYARD

3785 Burnside Road, Sebastopol CA 95472,
(707) 829-8170
www.halleckvineyard.com

In 2002 Ross and Jennifer Halleck entered their 2001 Pinot Noir in the competition at the Pinot Noir Summit and walked away with the designation number one Pinot Noir in the United States, setting the stage for successive vintages of highly rated Pinot Noir. After starting a highly successful branding agency in 1980, Ross moved to Sonoma County in 1991 to plant a Pinot Noir vineyard in the Sonoma Coast region. They planted in 1993, and their first harvest was in 1999. Jennifer had sourced the Dijon clones for their vineyards, and while she and Ross developed their business and raised three sons, she also worked at outside jobs in the wine industry in cellar, tasting room, and sales positions. Although Ross and Jennifer are no longer married to each other, they continue as business partners, alongside winemaker Rick Davis. Halleck Three Sons Cuvée Russian River Valley Pinot Noir 2008 opens with aromas of black cherry and vanilla. Flavors of cherry and blackberry are heightened by notes of baking spices, freshly ground pepper, and cedar, all leading to a smooth and enjoyable finish that just keeps on keeping on. Halleck Hallberg Vineyard Russian River Valley Pinot Noir 2008 is deep garnet in the glass. Scents of cassis, cherry compote, and gingerbread spice mingle with hints of flint. Strong tannins and rich minerality underlie flavors of sweet and slightly tart cherry, cigar box, and star anise.

HANNA

9280 Highway 128, Healdsburg, CA 95448,
(707) 431-4310
www.hannawinery.com

Christine Hanna's father, Dr. Elias Hanna, a San Francisco cardiac surgeon, bought 12 acres of farmland in the Russian River Valley in the 1970s and began making homemade Chardonnay and Cabernet Sauvignon. In the mid-1980s he hired a winemaker and bought more property. Today Christine runs a winery that includes 250 acres of vineyards planted on a total of 600 acres. Their vineyards are in the Russian River appellation, where they grow Pinot Noir and Chardonnay; Alexander Valley, where Cabernet Sauvignon, Merlot, and Malbec are planted; and on top of the Mayacamas Mountains, the range that divides Sonoma from Napa. It is here, on the Bismark Mountain Ranch, that the Hanna family grows Merlot, Cabernet Sauvignon, Cabernet Franc, Petit Verdot, Malbec, Syrah, Petite Sirah, and Zinfandel. Jeff Hinchliffe has been in charge of winemaking for over 15 years, and Hanna now has two tasting rooms: one in Alexander Valley and one in Russian River. Hanna Alexander Valley Cabernet Sauvignon 2009 offers scents of black cherry conserves, cassis, fennel seed, and espresso bean. On the tongue flavors of black cherry, raspberry, mocha, vanilla bean, and a sprinkling of freshly ground pepper are wrapped in smooth, pleasing tannins. Hanna Bismark Mountain Vineyard Zinfandel 2007 is deep garnet to the eye, with aromas of cassis, black cherry, and baking spices. In the mouth flavors of mixed-berry pie, butterscotch, and a pinch of spice are encased in velvety tannins.

HARTFORD FAMILY WINERY

8075 Martinelli Road,
Forestville, CA 95436,
(800) 588-0234
www.hartfordwines.com

Since their first vintage of 1996 was released, Don Hartford and Jennifer Jackson-Hartford's wines have received accolades and acclaim from many wine publications. Winemaker Jeff Stewart works with Chardonnay, Pinot Noir, and old-vine Zinfandel from some of the finest vineyard sites in Russian River Valley, the Green Valley subappellation, and the Sonoma Coast. Hartford Four Hearts Vineyard Russian River Valley Chardonnay 2010 is an elegant expression of fruit and mineral flavors. Bright citrus, floral notes, and minerality play across the tongue in a delightful show of harmony, leading to a nice wave of butterscotch on the finish. Hartford Highwire Vineyard Zinfandel 2010 gives off aromas of raspberry and black cherry with violet and lavender undertones. In the mouth rich berry fruit mingles with violet and anise through the luscious finish.

HIDDEN RIDGE

110 Camino Oruga, Napa, CA 94558,
(707) 481-7021
www.hiddenridgevineyard.com

Entrepreneurial couple Casidy Ward and Lynn Hofacket originally bought the Hidden Ridge Vineyard site to build and then flip a home but ultimately decided that the steep slopes and elevation (700 to 900 feet) were better suited for grapes than for people. Originally selling their grapes to other winemakers, Hofacket and Ward made their first small-scale vintage of Cabernet Sauvignon in 2001, eventually growing to today's still small by any standards 3,600 cases per year, crafted by winemakers Tim Milos and Marco DiGiulio. Vineyard slopes are as steep as 55 degrees, and the 60 acres of vines are on the Sonoma side of Spring Mountain, in the Mayacamas range. Hidden Ridge 55% Slope Cabernet Sauvignon 2008 offers aromas of black cherry, cassis, and light baking spices. In the mouth a mix of fresh berries and fruit compote is joined by mocha and Chinese five spice, all wrapped in a luscious tannic structure.

HIRSCH VINEYARDS

45075 Bohan Dillon Road,
Cazadero, CA 95421,
(707) 847-3600
www.hirschvineyards.com

Self-described "owner and chief bug" David Hirsch bought his first vineyard plot on the Sonoma Coast in 1978 and planted it with Riesling and Pinot Noir in 1980. He planted 44 more acres between 1990 and 1996 and an additional 25 in the early years of the twenty-first century. Vineyard manager Everardo Robledo has been with Hirsch for many years and is an expert in cultivating grapes in this rugged landscape whose face has been shaped by the San Andreas Fault. Winemaker Ross Cobb's first vintage here was 2010, but he worked with Hirsch fruit in his previous positions at Flowers and Williams Selyem. The entire team is dedicated to David Hirsch's vision of creating site-specific wines that speak of the *terroir* of the extreme Sonoma Coast. Hirsch Vineyards San Andreas Fault Sonoma Coast Pinot Noir 2010 offers fragrances of black cherry, blackberry, Earl Grey tea, and honeysuckle. On the tongue rich red fruit mingles with floral and earthy notes. Smooth tannins and bright acidity perform a pas de deux filled with ease and grace.

HOOK & LADDER WINERY

2134 Olivet Road,
Santa Rosa, CA 95401,
(707) 526-2255
www.hookandladderwinery.com

San Francisco firefighter Cecil De Loach and his wife, Christine, purchased 24 acres of Russian River Valley old-vine Zinfandel in 1970 and sold grapes to other wineries before founding the successful DeLoach Vineyards. After selling DeLoach in 2003, they started Hook & Ladder, a smaller-scale family-run winery that focuses on estate-grown Russian River Valley fruit. Jason, Michael, and Joshua De Loach are heavily involved in the family business, respectively working as winemaker, president, and head of sales. Their vineyards spread over 375 acres in the Russian River Valley, producing Chardonnay, Sauvignon Blanc, Gewürztraminer, Zinfandel, Merlot, Cabernet Sauvignon, and Pinot Noir. Hook & Ladder Russian River Valley Chardonnay 2011 gives off aromas of Granny Smith apple, jasmine, and orange zest. In the mouth you will note flavors of crisp apple and lemon zest with a smattering of buttered toast. Hook & Ladder Russian River Valley Zinfandel 2010 offers fragrances of raspberry, cassis, and a touch of cigar box. In the mouth raspberry is joined by blackberry, a splash of tart cherry, and a ribbon of caramel, heading into a lusty, well-deserved finish.

HOP KILN WINERY

6050 Westside Road,
Healdsburg, CA 95448,
(707) 433-6491
www.hkgwines.com

Named for the large historic Walters Ranch Kiln that was used for drying hops, Hop Kiln offered its first release in 1976. Later, in 2006, the winery produced the first vintage of its premium brand, HKG. The original kiln building now is the estate's tasting room, which serves as a reminder of the importance of the California North Coast as a hop-growing region before grapes and wine changed the agricultural landscape. Winemaker Chuck Mansfield, the son of an El Dorado grape grower, became head winemaker in 2007, immediately earning high marks from the major wine publications. Vineyard manager David Smith, who came aboard in 2008, is a fifth-generation California farmer. HKG Estate wines are wholly sourced from the winery's 250-acre Russian River Valley estate. Releases include Pinot Noir, Chardonnay, Pinot Grigio, Rosé of Pinot Noir, and Sparkling Rosé of Pinot Noir. HKG Russian River Valley Chardonnay 2011 offers aromas of Bartlett pear and caramelized pineapple with a touch of brambles. On the tongue, flavors of tropical fruits, apricot, and chopped green herbs endure to the bright finish. HKG Russian River Valley Pinot Noir 2010 is garnet to the eye, with a fresh nose of cherry, orange zest, and dried herbs. Black and tart cherry mingle on the tongue, joined by notes of chocolate, dried Mediterranean herbs, and river rocks.

IMAGERY ESTATE WINERY

14335 Highway 12,
Glen Ellen, CA 95442,
(707) 935-4515
www.imagerywinery.com

After working with his family at their Sonoma winery, Joe Benziger wanted to create his own label, showcasing small-production, single-vineyard wines. While in the planning stages for his new project, Joe met Bob Nugent, a local artist who designed Joe's first label. Twenty years on Joe is still handcrafting wines, and Bob curates the Imagery art collection and brings on artists to create their original labels. Imagery's vineyards are Demeter-certified biodynamic. Their gallery tasting room features artwork from a variety of international artists who have worked on their unique labels. Joe loves to work with unexpected varieties, including Barbera, Lagrein, Tempranillo, and Sangiovese. Imagery Estate Winery Sonoma County Barbera 2009 has a nose of ripe fruit and mocha. In the mouth black cherry, blackberry, and blueberry mix and mingle with chocolate-covered espresso bean straight through the mouth-pleasing finish. Imagery Estate Winery Sonoma County Tusca Brava 2010, a blend of 48 percent Sangiovese, 30 percent Merlot, 19 percent Cabernet Sauvignon, and 3 percent Malbec, is deep berry red in the glass. A bright nose of fruits of the wood signals the fruit and berry flavors that will first appear on the palate but barely hints at the spice, vanilla, and cigar box notes that join them on the tongue, wrapped up in rich tannins.

IRON HORSE VINEYARDS

9786 Ross Station Road,
Sebastopol, CA 95472,
(707) 887-1507
www.ironhorsevineyards.com

Barry and Audrey Sterling first happened upon 300 acres of rolling hills while driving along Ross Station Road in 1976 and bought this beautiful property two weeks later. They took the name Iron Horse from a train that stopped at Ross Station in the early part of the twentieth century, and the weathervane that became their logo was discovered on the grounds while they were building the winery. The original 100 acres of vines had been planted by Forrest Tancer, who became the Sterlings' partner in the winery and retired in 2005. Audrey and Barry's daughter Joy is Sterling's CEO, and her brother Laurence is director of operations. Iron Horse is known for its exquisite sparkling wines and still Pinot Noir and Chardonnay. The first vintage of Pinot Noir was released in 1979, one year before the first Iron Horse sparkling made its way into the world. Iron Horse Thomas Road Pinot Noir 2010 offers aromas of black cherry and cassis with a dash of alluring earthiness. On the palate intricate flavors of cherry jam, black plum, and vanilla custard wash across the tongue in pleasing waves. Iron Horse Classic Vintage Brut 2008, disgorged in November 2012, is blended from 72 percent Pinot Noir and 28 percent Chardonnay. Scents of pink grapefruit, toasted almond, and crème brûlée waft toward the nose, and the palate is rewarded with opulent flavors of clementine, lemongrass, and almond tart.

J. RICKARDS WINERY

24505 Chianti Road, Cloverdale, CA 95425,
(707) 758-3441
www.jrwinery.com

Jim Rickards bought a 60-acre ranch in Alexander Valley in 1976, revitalized an old Zinfandel vineyard originally planted by the Brignole family in 1908, and then branched out into Cabernet Sauvignon. He proved his critics wrong when he found water on the ranch after being told there was none, adding two wells and two ponds for irrigation. Despite being informed that his land was suitable only as a rock quarry, Jim became a successful grape farmer while still working full-time as a registered nurse at Santa Rosa Memorial Hospital and still sells grapes to other highly lauded wineries in the area. In 1991 he and his wife, Eliza, added Petite Sirah, Malbec, and Shiraz, and in 2005 they founded J. Rickards Winery, specializing in small-lot wines that highlight the varied soils and microclimates of their 45 acres of vineyards. Jim brought Blaine Brazil in as assistant winemaker in 2011, and together they produce estate-grown old-vine Zinfandel, Malbec, Petite Sirah, Sauvignon Blanc, Blanc de Blancs, a Cabernet blend, and two dessert wines. J. Rickards Winery Alexander Valley Five Sisters Blend Cabernet Sauvignon 2010 is composed of 85 percent Cabernet Sauvignon, 8 percent Malbec, 3 percent each Petit Verdot and

Merlot, and 1 percent Cabernet Franc. It is dark ruby in the glass and gives fragrances of cherry, black currants, espresso bean, and Turkish delight. It is full in the mouth, and flavors of dark fruits commingle with black cherry, dark chocolate, baking spices, and a light florality right through the long, rewarding finish. J. Rickards Winery Brignole Vineyard Alexander Valley Old Vine Zinfandel 2010 is deep red violet to the eye. Aromas of dark fruits of the wood and Christmas spices lead to rich flavors of raspberry, black plum, chocolate-covered coffee bean, and clove wrapped in a sheath of mouth-pleasing tannins.

J VINEYARDS & WINERY

11447 Old Redwood Highway,
Healdsburg, CA 95448,
(888) 594-6326
www.jwine.com

Judy Jordan credits her father, Tom Jordan, for introducing her to the wine business, helping to start her career, and inspiring her sense of entrepreneurship. She is also grateful to her mother, Sally Jordan, for instilling her sense of elegance, style, and etiquette into Judy from an early age. Judy set out on her own in 1986, leaving the family business behind, and purchased the old Piper Sonoma property, which she christened J Vineyards & Winery. Although she started out producing highly rated sparkling wines, Judy saw the potential in cool-climate varieties such as Pinot Noir, Chardonnay, and Pinot Gris for still wine production and ventured into that realm as well. Judy holds a degree in earth sciences and geology from Stanford, and her belief that we are stewards of the land has led to the implementation of sustainable practices in the vineyard and winery. Winemaking is under the direction of Melissa Stackhouse, and the vineyards are under the care of John Erbe. J Vineyards Cuvée 20 Russian River Valley Brut NV, a blend of 50 percent Chardonnay, 49 percent Pinot Noir, and 1 percent Petit Meunier, is pale straw in the glass with persistent bubbles. A nose of white peach and crushed almonds broadens on the tongue, revealing flavors of crisp green apples and pears, orange zest, and a hint of brioche. J Vineyards Estate Grown Russian River Valley Pinot Noir 2011 is rich garnet in color, offering fragrances of ripe and tart cherry with hints of herbes de Provence. Flavors of cherry cola, smoke, and Mediterranean herbs intertwine on the palate, leading to a soft but satisfying finish.

JACUZZI FAMILY VINEYARDS

24724 Arnold Drive, Sonoma, CA 95476,
(707) 931-7575
www.jacuzziwines.com

Fred Cline is the maternal grandson of Valeriano Jacuzzi, whose last name is a household word thanks to the water pump, spa, and hot tub business founded by his family. After successfully starting up Cline Cellars in 1982 and then moving it to the Carneros region of Sonoma in 1992, Fred and his wife, Nancy, established Jacuzzi Family Vineyards across the road from Cline Cellars. Their first Jacuzzi Family Vineyards wine was produced in 1994, and their 18,000-square-foot winery opened in 2007. Winemaking is under the direction of Charlie Tsegeletos, who brought over 20 years of experience with him when he came aboard in 2002. Vineyards in Sonoma-Carneros and the Sonoma Coast are naturally and sustainably farmed. In a tribute to the Jacuzzi family's Italian heritage, Italian grape varieties predominate, including Arneis, Tocai Friulano, Aglianico, Primitivo, and Sangiovese. However, this being California, Chardonnay, Cabernet Sauvignon, and Merlot are vinified as well. Jacuzzi Family Vineyards Sonoma Coast Chardonnay 2010 has a nose of just-picked green apple. In the mouth there are flavors of fresh apple, Seckel pear, and lemon blossom with just a touch of lightly buttered toast. Jacuzzi Family Vineyards Sonoma Coast Sangiovese 2010 is deep garnet in the glass and gives aromas of cherry, blackberry, and a pinch of spice. Flavors of cherry and blackberry come through on the palate, bolstered by a hint of black pepper. Soft tannins and balanced acidity make for a very nice wine.

JOHN TYLER WINES

4353 Westside Road, Healdsburg, CA 95448,
(707) 473-0115
www.johntylerwines.com

The John in John Tyler is John Bacigalupi, and Tyler is he and his wife Pam's nephew, Tyler Heck. Pam's parents—and Tyler's grandparents—Paul and Anna Marie Heck were co-owners of Korbel Champagne Cellars, and John's family planted one of the Russian River's most well-known vineyards. Bacigalupi Chardonnay was included in Mike Grgich's 1973 Chateau Montelena, the wine that turned the world on its head in the 1976 Judgment of Paris. Today John runs the vineyards, Tyler makes the wine, and John and Pam's twin daughters, Katey and Nicole, head up the family's marketing efforts. Their Westside Road tasting room is a great place to try their Pinot Noir and Zinfandel. John Tyler Bacigalupi Vineyard Russian River Valley Zinfandel 2008 is deep red violet to the eye. Fragrances of fruits of the wood mingling with clove and nutmeg lead to flavors of blackberry and black cherry. Spice gives way to subtle notes of forest floor, all enveloped in rich tannins. John Tyler Bacigalupi Vineyard Russian River Valley Pinot Noir 2009 offers aromas of fresh cherry and wild strawberries with a touch of Mediterranean herbs. In the mouth a balance of medium-weight tannins and fresh acidity lays the groundwork for flavors of dark cherry mingling with oregano, sage, and a pinch of citrus zest.

JORDAN VINEYARD & WINERY

1474 Alexander Valley Road, Healdsburg, CA 95448,
(800) 654-1213
www.jordanwinery.com

Tom and Sally Jordan, a young couple with a passion for French food and wine, moved to California from Denver and started Jordan Winery & Vineyard in the 1970s. They had previously flirted with the idea of owning a winery while traveling through France, but their first glass of Napa Cabernet made them realize they didn't have to cross the ocean to fulfill their dream. Their original purchase was 250 acres in Alexander Valley, and two years later they began construction on a winery and bought 1,300 more acres. In 1976, winemaker Rob Davis—who still holds the winemaking reins—came aboard under the direction of consulting winemaker André Tchelistcheff. The Jordans' son John, born in 1972, the same day his parents signed the deed on their first piece of land in Alexander Valley, became CEO in 2005. Only two wines are made here: Chardonnay and Cabernet Sauvignon. Jordan Russian River Valley Chardonnay 2011 offers a fresh nose of apple, ripe peach, and freesia. Flavors of Granny Smith apple and white peach and a light florality are present in the mouth. Creamy mouthfeel and vanilla spice notes carry through to the bright finish. Jordan Winery Alexander Valley Cabernet Sauvignon 2008, composed of 77 percent Cabernet Sauvignon, 18 percent Merlot, and 5 percent Petit Verdot, is deep violet in color. Fragrances of cherry, black plum, violet, and spice broaden on the palate in a mouth-pleasing configuration of soft tannins and bold acidity.

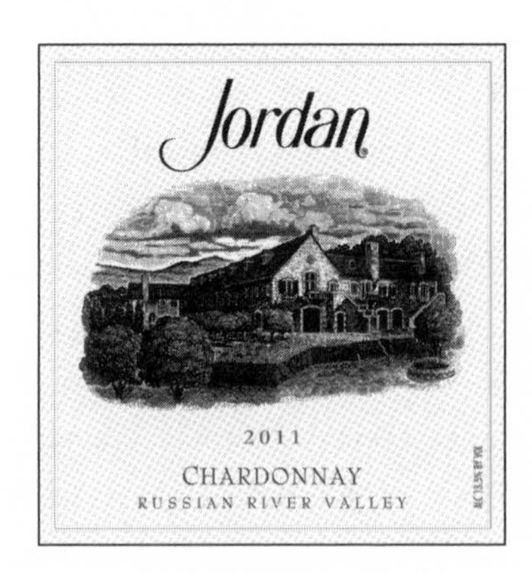

JOSEPH SWAN VINEYARDS

2916 Laguna Road,
Forestville, CA 95436,
(707) 573-3747
www.swanwinery.com

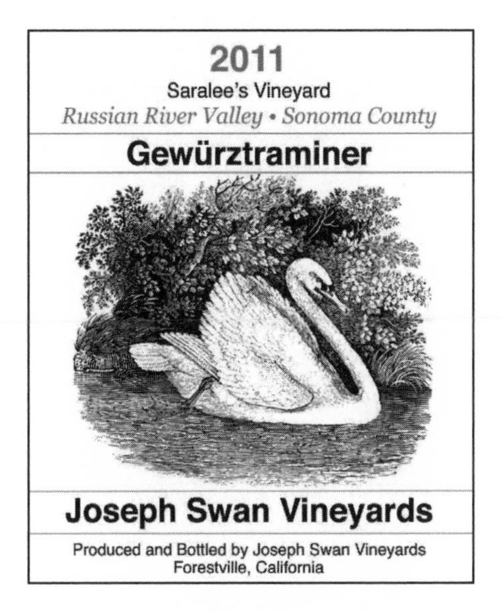

Joe Swan, the son of teetotaler parents from North Dakota, purchased a small farm near Forestville in 1967 that included 13 acres of Zinfandel vines. Taking advice from his friend and mentor André Tchelistcheff, Swan began planting Chardonnay and Pinot Noir. He made his first few vintages in the cellar of the 100-year-old farmhouse that had come with the property and built a simple winery in 1974. Current owner and winemaker Rod Berglund became a winemaker in 1979 and married Joe's daughter Lynn, in 1986. His first vintage at Swan was 1987, shortly before Joe's untimely passing. Joseph Swan Vineyards is well known for Chardonnay, Pinot Gris, Gewürztraminer, white Rhône varieties, Pinot Noir, Zinfandel, and Syrah. Joseph Swan Vineyards Saralee's Vineyard Russian River Valley Gewürztraminer 2011 is light straw in the glass, with aromas of apricot, honeysuckle, orange blossom, and a whiff of spice. On the tongue ripe summer peach and citrus blossoms mix it up with baking spices, wet stone notes, and balanced acidity. Joseph Swan Vineyards Trenton Estate Vineyard Russian River Valley Pinot Noir 2009 is deep red violet to the eye. Fragrances of black cherry, Portobello mushroom, and a touch of crème brûlée waft toward the nose, and on the palate black cherry, raspberry, mocha, and a hint of orange zest caress the tongue amid satiny tannins.

KAMEN ESTATE WINES

111B East Napa Street,
Sonoma, CA 95476,
(707) 938-7292
www.kamenwines.com

Robert Mark Kamen sold his first screenplay in 1980, and while celebrating by hiking through the rugged Sonoma Coast, he happened upon a tract of land with awe-inspiring views of San Francisco Bay. Within a week he acquired the 280-acre property, with a plan to grow Cabernet Sauvignon. He continued a successful screenwriting career while Phil Coturri, an organic viticulture pioneer, oversaw the vineyards. All the grapes were sold to other wineries until 1996, when a fire destroyed half the vines as well as Kamen's home. After a replanting effort, Kamen began making estate-grown wine; the first vintage was 1999. In addition to Cabernet Sauvignon, Syrah and Sauvignon Blanc are vinified under the direction of winemaker Mark Herold. Kamen Sonoma Valley Cabernet Sauvignon 2009 is deep red violet to the eye. A complex nose of mixed wild berries, Mediterranean herbs, and espresso bean is just a suggestion of what the palate reveals, including layers of sweet and tart cherry, blueberry, blackberry, toasted almond, baking spices, and lavender. Fruit, floral, and spice notes play across the taste buds straight into the voluptuous finish.

KANZLER VINEYARDS

PO Box 1977,
Sebastopol, CA 95473,
(707) 824-1726
www.kanzler.com

Kanzler Vineyards is truly a family business in every sense of the word. Steve and Lynda Kanzler purchased their vineyard land in 1993; Steve is in charge of the vineyard and winery, and Lynda is CFO. Daughter Melissa Kanzler Grant heads up marketing, while her husband, James Grant, takes care of legal matters. Winemaking tasks fall to Steve and Lynda's son Alex, who was raised on the vineyard estate and gained experience working with Pinot Noir with some of their high-profile neighbors as well as in New Zealand and Oregon. Kanzler Vineyards Sonoma Coast Reserve Pinot Noir 2010 is deep garnet to the eye, with lush fruit fragrances of black cherry and fruits of the wood joined by mocha and butterscotch. In the mouth cherry and raspberry open to flavors of cassis and blueberry. Espresso and vanilla flavors continue through the lasting finish.

KELLER ESTATE WINERY

5875 Lakeville Highway,
Petaluma, CA 94954,
(707) 765-2117
www.kellerestate.com

While driving the back roads of Sonoma over 30 years ago, Arturo and Deborah Keller fell in love not just with the idea of owning a vineyard but with a 650-acre ranch in the Petaluma Gap. They planted their first Chardonnay vineyard in 1989, all the while maintaining a sense of balance and harmony with the natural ecosystem. Their first grape crop was sold to Rombauer, and within 10 years Pinot Noir plantings were added to their holdings. In 2000 a beautiful architect-designed, gravity-fed winery was constructed on the site, where winemaker Alberto Rodriguez works alongside Ana Keller to produce estate-grown Pinot Gris, Chardonnay, Pinot Noir, and Syrah. Keller Estate La Cruz Vineyard Pinot Gris 2011 alights on the nose with succulent aromas of white peach, toasted pineapple, and light spice. In the mouth peach and pineapple are joined by flavors of apricot and star anise. Keller Estate La Cruz Vineyard Pinot Noir 2010 is garnet in the glass, with fragrances of black cherry, aniseed, and citrus blossoms. On the tongue cherry and red raspberry flavors are revealed, merged with notes of milk chocolate, orange zest, and soft spice.

KENDALL-JACKSON WINE ESTATES

5007 Fulton Road, Fulton, CA 95439,
(707) 571-8100
www.kj.com

Jess Jackson was a police officer and attorney before buying a Lakeport, California, fruit and nut orchard in 1974, which he converted to a vineyard. In 1982 he produced the first vintage of Kendall-Jackson Vintner's Reserve Chardonnay, which has grown to become one of the most popular wines in the United States. Over 30 years later Kendall-Jackson is one of the best-known American wineries, making wine in five tiers: Avant, Vintner's Reserve, Grand Reserve, Highlands Estate, and Stature. Sauvignon Blanc, Chardonnay, Pinot Noir, Cabernet Sauvignon, Merlot, Syrah, and Zinfandel are the mainstays of its production. Kendall-Jackson owns 15,000 acres of California vineyards, and Jackson Family Wines owns over thirty wine brands in total. Jess Jackson passed away in April 2011, and his legacy continues via his wife, Barbara Banke, and five children. Visitor experiences at the Fulton Road Wine Center include tastings of small-batch wines available only at the winery, tours, and custom wine-and-food-pairing experiences. In addition to the Fulton Road Wine Center, Kendall-Jackson has a tasting room-cum-small plates experience in downtown Healdsburg called Partake by K-J. Kendall-Jackson Grand Reserve Chardonnay 2010, made with estate-grown fruit from Santa Barbara and Monterey counties, offers tropical fruits and white peach on the nose. The palate combines ripe peach and citrus blossoms with soft notes of custard. A creamy mouthfeel and zesty acidity add up to a well-balanced wine. Kendall-Jackson Grand Reserve Sonoma County Merlot 2009, a blend of 93.6 percent Merlot, 3.3 percent Malbec, and 3.1 percent Cabernet Sauvignon, is deep red violet in the glass, with a bright nose of cherry and violet. On the tongue flavors of black cherry, cigar box, mocha, and a light floral lift cavort within smooth tannins. Kendall-Jackson Stature 2007 is a blend of 73 percent Cabernet Sauvignon, 18 percent Merlot, 8 percent Malbec, and 3 percent Petit Verdot, all estate-grown in Napa Valley. This is the zenith of winemaking at Kendall-Jackson, from the deep garnet color in the glass, through the aromas of raspberry, blueberry, and Mediterranean herbs, and into the rich flavors of fruits of the wood, cherry conserves, hillside herbs, and luscious crème brûlée, presented in a lush but never overpowering tannic structure.

KENWOOD VINEYARDS

9592 Sonoma Highway,
Kenwood, CA 95452,
(707) 833-5891
www.kenwoodvineyards.com

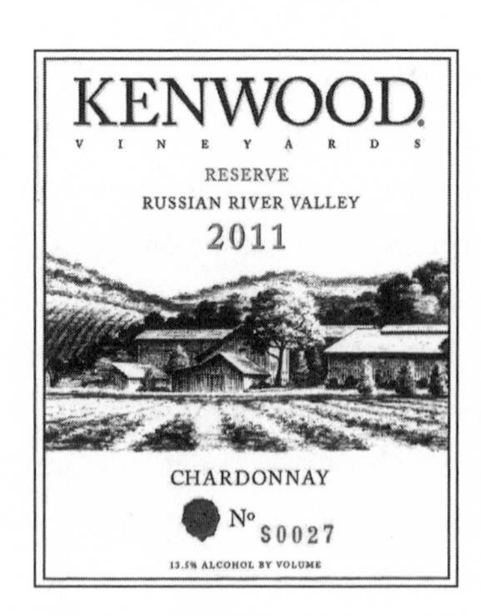

The old Pagani Brothers winery, founded in 1906, was brought back to life when winemaker Mike Lee, along with investors and family members, bought and refurbished it in 1970. Winemaking still takes place in the original buildings, which have been extensively renovated. Kenwood, currently owned by Gary Heck, president of F. Korbel & Brothers, produces 500,000 cases of wine in six different tiers at prices ranging from under $10 to upward of $70. In addition to Chardonnay, Pinot Gris, Sauvignon Blanc, Cabernet Sauvignon, Merlot, Syrah, and Zinfandel from its 22-acre estate, Kenwood sources grapes from throughout Sonoma County, producing appellation-based and single-vineyard wines. Kenwood Jack London Vineyard Sonoma Mountain Cabernet Sauvignon 2010, composed of 97 percent Cabernet Sauvignon and 3 percent Merlot, is deep garnet to the eye, with aromas of blackberry, mission fig, and eucalyptus. Dark fruit and soothing herb notes continue on the palate, entwined with flavors of tobacco and crème brûlée. Kenwood Vineyards Reserve Russian River Valley Chardonnay 2011 offers fragrances of Granny Smith apple and ripe stone fruits. On the tongue flavors of citrus fruit and white peach mingle with notes of vanilla bean and buttered toast, nicely supported by a smooth mouthfeel and a bright finish.

KETCHAM ESTATE

1083 Vine Street, Suite 218,
Healdsburg CA 95448,
(707) 395-0700
www.ketchamestate.com

After taking early retirement from his computer company and setting up a business importing vintage Italian cars, Mark Ketcham fulfilled a lifelong dream in 2000 by buying a 17-acre Pinot Noir and Chardonnay vineyard in the Russian River Valley. Chardonnay was replanted to Pinot Noir, and the vineyards are now under the direction of Roberto Ordaz. Mark and his wife, Allison, built their home in the middle of the vines, some of which are more than 25 years old. Ketcham Estate Ketcham Vineyard Pinot Noir 2010 yields aromas of black cherry, red raspberry, and licorice root. Flavors of black cherry, Dr Pepper, Mediterranean herbs, and fresh peat swirl across the palate through the rich, lasting finish.

KISTLER VINEYARDS

4707 Vine Hill Road,
Sebastopol, CA 95472,
(707) 823-5603
www.kistlervineyards.com

When the Kistler family established their winery in 1978, the annual production was 3,500 cases of wine. Today under the direction of winemaker and vineyard manager Steve Kistler, lab technician and business manager Mark Bixler, and assistant winemaker Jason Kesner, the winery produces 25,000 cases of highly regarded Chardonnay and Pinot Noir. The wines are decidedly Burgundian in style and score highly in all the major wine publications. Kistler Vineyard Chardonnay 2009 is medium straw color, with aromas of freshly cut white stone fruits, dried yellow peach, and jasmine blossom. It fills the mouth with delightful fruit flavors and light florality. There's a nice level of minerality in the finish. This is a truly delicious French-style Chardonnay. Kistler Vineyard Pinot Noir 2009 has a brilliant cherry-red glow with amazing aromas of red plum, red raspberry, red cherry, anise, and Christmas baking spices. It is generous in the palate, with remarkably balanced soft tannins and a light touch of salinity in the finish.

KOKOMO WINERY

4791 Dry Creek Road,
Healdsburg, CA 95448,
(707) 433-0200
www.kokomowines.com

Erik Miller "traded in the soybeans and cornfields" of his hometown, Kokomo, Indiana, for the rugged beauty of Sonoma. After graduating from Purdue University, he headed west, enrolled at UC Davis to study enology, and started working as a cellar hand at Amphora Winery. He made his first Kokomo vintage in 2004, a Dry Creek Valley Cabernet Sauvignon, and a year later was joined by his best friend and college roommate, Josh Bartels. In 2008 Erik and Josh brought in a winery partner, fourth-generation farmer Randy Peters. Kokomo Peters Vineyard Russian River Valley Chardonnay 2011 gives off scents of Granny Smith apple, tropical fruits, and jasmine. Its creamy mouthfeel is boosted by crystalline acidity, and flavors of apple, buttered brioche, and toffee persist through the crisp finish. Kokomo Dry Creek Valley Zinfandel is deep red violet, with aromas of black cherry, blackberry, and hillside herbs leading to a palate dominated by rich fruit with haunting undertones of rosemary, sage, and white pepper.

KOSTA BROWNE

PO Box 1555,
Sebastopol, CA 95473,
(707) 823-7430
www.kostabrowne.com

It is hard to believe that two waiters who pooled their tip money with the dream of making wine could one day become the founding partners of a highly acclaimed winery, but that is exactly what happened to Dan Kosta and Michael Browne. The dream began in the summer of 1997, and after eight months the pair had saved enough to buy a half ton of grapes and some winemaking equipment. In 2001 they joined forces with Chris Costello and his family, and the three of them remain the guiding hands behind Kosta Browne, which was acquired by the Vincraft Group in 2009. Michael Browne is the executive winemaker, assisted by a team that includes Ryan O'Donnell, Nico Cueva, and Jeremiah Timm. Single-vineyard Pinot Noir and regional versions from the Santa Lucia Highlands, Russian River, and Sonoma Coast are available to wine club members and at select restaurants nationwide. Kosta Browne Russian River Valley Pinot Noir 2011 has a nose of mixed berries, herbes de Provence, and Turkish delight. The taste buds first become aware of black cherry and blackberry layered with mocha and cranberry, all of which linger through the smooth finish. Kosta Browne Sonoma Coast Pinot Noir 2011 is garnet to the eye, with a bouquet of blueberry, cassis, and mocha. Raspberry and blueberry open on the tongue, followed by a burst of mixed fruit with a touch of dried savory herbs, which hang in a delightful balance of grippy tannins and pleasing acidity.

KUNDE FAMILY ESTATE

9825 Sonoma Highway,
Kenwood, CA 95452,
(707) 833-5501
www.kunde.com

Louis Kunde left Germany for California, and in 1904 he bought the Wildwood Ranch, the foundation of what is now the 1,850-acre Kunde Estate in Sonoma Valley. Fourth- and fifth-generation family members continue to farm the land, growing and vinifying

Sauvignon Blanc, Viognier, Chardonnay, Merlot, Syrah, Barbera, Cabernet Sauvignon, and Zinfandel. A variety of visitor experiences are offered, from walk-in samplings to customized mountaintop tastings and vineyard hikes. Winemaker Zach Long's goal is to let the *terroir* shine through in each bottle of Kunde. Kunde Family Estate Sonoma Valley Chardonnay 2011 offers scents of fruit salad in a glass, starting with green apple, Bartlett pear, and clementine. Soft touches of gingerbread spice work their magic within the fruit flavors of this full-bodied wine, right up to the zippy finish. Kunde Family Estate Sonoma Valley Cabernet Sauvignon 2009 is deep garnet in color, with a nose of black cherry, blackberry, and mocha. Black cherry and pure cocoa carry over onto the palate, where a strong tannic structure and a smooth finish make this a wine you will mourn when your glass is empty.

KUTCH WINES

21660 8th Street East, Building A, Suite C,
Sonoma, CA 95476,
(917) 270-8180
www.kutchwines.com

Heeding Horace Greeley's call to "go west, young man," Jamie Kutch traded in his Wall Street trading desk in 2005 and headed to Sonoma County to make wine. Armed with no practical experience but filled with passion and a dream, Kutch worked a harvest at Kosta Browne and began visiting prime vineyard sites on the Sonoma Coast and Anderson Valley to procure the best possible grapes for his handcrafted—and foot-treaded—Pinot Noir. Kutch and his wife, Kristen Green, jokingly refer to their tanks, barrels, and fermenters as "our condo," but if success can be measured in quality and accolades, Jamie's move was a wise one. Kutch Wines are available via wine clubs and on some of the area's finest wine lists. Kutch McDougall Ranch Sonoma Coast Pinot Noir 2011 is deep black cherry in the glass, with a richly perfumed nose of raspberry, violet, and lavender. Lush texture and soft tannins make a gorgeous backdrop for elegant blackberry layered with pine needle and light floral notes. Kutch Falstaff Sonoma Coast Pinot Noir 2010 is deep red to the eye. Aromas of blackberry and citrus zest give way to opulent flavors of blackberry, grapefruit pith, and a touch of forest floor. While you may want to savor a glass of this on its own, the food-friendly nature of the Falstaff cannot be overstated.

LA CREMA

235 Healdsburg Avenue,
Healdsburg, CA 95448,
(800) 314-1762
www.lacrema.com

La Crema was founded in 1979 and became part of Jackson Family Wine Estates in 1993. The focus is on cool-climate Chardonnay and Pinot Noir from the Sonoma Coast, Russian River Valley, Anderson Valley, Carneros, and Monterey. Winemaking is directed by Elizabeth Grant-Douglas, who uses Burgundian technique with California flair. Grant-Douglas started here in 2001 and took the top position in 2010. She is assisted by Eric Johannsen and Craig McAllister. Vineyards are sustainably farmed, and wines are produced in four tiers: Monterey, Sonoma Coast, Appellation Series, and the top-level Nine Barrel. La Crema Monterey Chardonnay 2011 is medium straw in color and offers a complex nose of toasted pineapple, Cavaillon melon, and orange blossom. In the mouth juicy peach pie flavors meld with vanilla bean and a hint of river rocks, leading to a bright and delicious finish. La Crema Russian River Valley Pinot Noir 2011, from the Appellation Series, is deep garnet to the eye. Fragrances of black cherry, sassafras, and anise are released upon pouring, and on the palate raspberry, black cherry, chocolate-covered espresso bean, and aniseed present themselves slathered in velvety tannins.

LANCASTER ESTATE

15001 Chalk Hill Road,
Healdsburg, CA 95448,
(707) 433-8178
www.lancaster-estate.com

Lancaster Estate was founded in 1995 with a commitment to producing high-quality estate-grown wines, mainly Cabernet Sauvignon, from grapes grown on the estate's 52 acres in Alexander Valley. Consulting winemaker David Ramey works with winemakers David Drake and Jesse Katz. Drake is also in charge of the vineyards, and Katz joined Lancaster in 2010 after a couple of years at Screaming Eagle. Foley Family Wines has owned the property since 2012. Lancaster Estate Alexander Valley Cabernet Sauvignon 2009 is composed of 85 percent Cabernet Sauvignon, 7 percent Malbec, 6 percent Merlot, and 1 percent each Cabernet Franc and Petit Verdot. It is deep violet to the eye, with a nose of cherry, black currants, and Chinese five-spice powder. Luscious flavors of black plum, blackberry, crème brûlée, and dark chocolate remain on the palate straight through the sublime finish. Lancaster Estate Alexander Valley Samantha's Sauvignon Blanc 2011 has a nose of honeydew melon, lemon, and jasmine. Pink grapefruit, lychee, lemongrass, and floral notes play on the tongue, swathed in a bold mouthfeel and an invigorating minerality.

LANDMARK VINEYARDS

101 Adobe Canyon Road,
Kenwood, CA 95452,
(707) 833-0053
www.landmarkwine.com

Founded in Windsor in 1974, Landmark moved to the base of Sugarloaf Mountain in Sonoma Valley in 1989. Winemaker Greg Stach's workshop is a state-of-the-art winery set amid beautifully landscaped grounds. Stach succeeded Eric Stern, whom he worked alongside for seven years before Stern retired in 2010. Stern previously had toiled alongside consulting winemaker Helen Turley, who was brought in in 1993. Landmark sources grapes for its Chardonnay, Pinot Noir, Syrah, and Grenache from diverse sites throughout the Sonoma Coast, Sonoma Valley, Russian

River Valley, Carneros, Bennett Valley, and Santa Barbara County. Landmark Overlook Sonoma County Chardonnay 2011 is a testament to the art of the winemaker. Sourced from multiple vineyards in the Sonoma Coast appellation, Overlook exhibits fragrances of fresh honey and orange blossom. In the mouth rich citrus and tropical fruit flavors combine with soft spice, unexpected florality, and crisp minerality for a wine that is pleasing in both taste and texture. Landmark Kanzler Vineyard Sonoma Coast Pinot Noir 2010 is deep garnet in the glass, with aromas of black cherry, mocha, and a touch of forest floor. Rich cherry flavor is layered with mocha and earth through the smooth yet startlingly bright finish.

LEDSON WINERY & VINEYARDS

7335 Highway 12,
Kenwood, CA 95409,
(707) 537-3810
www.ledson.com

Known as The Castle, Ledson's 16,000-square-foot French Normandy-style winery was originally planned as a home for Steve Ledson and his family, but as the project took on new proportions, Steve decided it was better suited to be a winery. The offspring of dairy farmers and cattle ranchers with a strong family streak of entrepreneurship, Steve was a successful contractor and property developer before going into the wine business. In 1989 he began construction on what was supposed to be someone else's home in the middle of a 17-acre vineyard, and when the buyer pulled out, Steve took over the property for himself. All of Ledson's mind-boggling number of labels are sold directly to consumers at the tasting room, online, or through the 15,000-member wine club. The Ledson family also runs the Ledson Hotel and Centre du Vin on the main plaza in Sonoma. Besides the original 17-acre estate Merlot vineyard, Ledson has 21 acres of Zinfandel in Sonoma and another 5,500 acres in Mendocino County. Ledson Russian River Valley Sauvignon Blanc 2010 is light straw in the glass, with aromas of white peach, jasmine, and a trace of minerality. On the tongue, flavors of lemon, lime, and ripe pear are enhanced by light florality and bracing acidity. Ledson Bertetta Vineyard Russian River Valley "Old Vine" Zinfandel 2009 is almost purple in the glass, with a heady bouquet of blackberry, vanilla bean, and freshly ground pepper. In the mouth full-on berry flavors are backed by a supporting cast of pepper, vanilla custard, and a touch of cigar box, right through the structured, tannic curtain call.

LIMERICK LANE CELLARS

1023 Limerick Lane, Healdsburg CA 95448,
(707) 433-9211
www.limericklanewines.com

Limerick Lane, a 30-acre estate just south of Healdsburg, was first planted to grapes by the Del Fava family in 1910 and was sold to Mike and Tom Collins in the 1970s. The Collins brothers quickly gained a reputation among preeminent wineries as a source of prime Zinfandel and Rhône varieties, and they produced their first estate wines under the Limerick Lane label in 1986. Current owner Jake Bilbro grew up at his family winery, Marietta Cellars. He bought the run-down farm across the road from Limerick Lane in 2007, and he and his wife spent the next two years "bringing it back." In 2009 Mike Collins offered them the opportunity to buy Limerick Lane Cellars and the Collins Vineyard. Jake and his family now live in the original Del Fava family homestead, and in addition to the Pinot Noir, Zinfandel, and Syrah they pick for their own estate production, they sell a small amount of fruit to neighbors such as Carlisle, Bedrock, Robert Biale, and Siduri. Jake Bilbro says you can "taste a bit of the limerick" in his wines, and they inspired us to write a couple as well:

Limerick Lane Block 1910 Russian River Valley Zinfandel 2009:

A fresh nose of chocolate and cherry,
With flavors of mocha and berry,
Elegant and restrained,
True perfection attained.
Do I like it much? Yes, I say, very!

Limerick Lane Block 1970 Russian River Valley Zinfandel 2009:

A tad lighter than Block 1910,
You can sip it again and again,
Savor fruits of the wood
Amidst tannins so good
It could well replace Proust's madeleine.

LITTORAI

788 Gold Ridge Road, Sebastopol, CA 95472,
(707) 823-9586
www.littorai.com

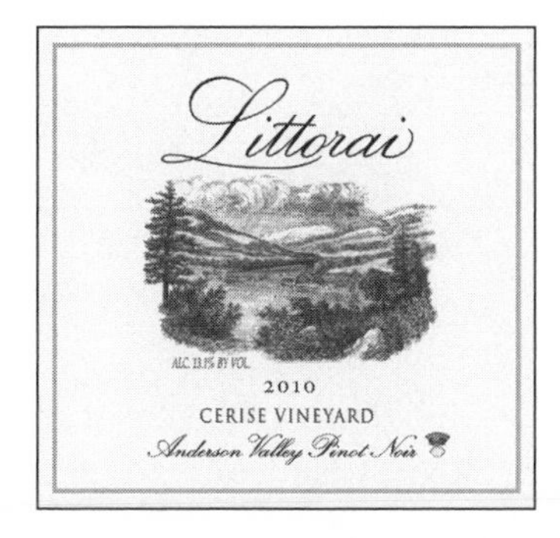

Wine production at Littorai is guided by the philosophy that wine should represent the place it comes from rather than the hand of a winemaker imbued with all that modern technology has to offer. The emphasis is on wine growing as opposed to winemaking, with an additional focus on site selection and vineyard management to create wines with great equilibrium and complexity. Ted and Heidi Lemon established Littorai in 1993 and built their winery in 2008. Ted previously had made wine at some of the finest estates in Burgundy, and he has been a consulting winemaker at outstanding wineries in California, Oregon, and New Zealand. Ted and Heidi employ sustainable practices in their owned and leased vineyards in the Anderson Valley and Sonoma Coast, and they produce exceptional Chardonnay and Pinot Noir. Littorai Cerise Vineyard Anderson Valley Pinot Noir 2010 is garnet in the glass, with a nose of blackberry, clove, and Moroccan spices. On the palate luxurious dark fruit flavors intertwine with spice and herb notes, continuing into the smooth, mineral-driven finish.

LONGBOARD VINEYARDS

5 Fitch Street, Healdsburg, CA 95448,
(707) 433-3473
www.longboardvineyards.com

Longboard's owner and winemaker, Oded Shakked, was born in Israel, was raised around the world, and moved to California to follow his two passions: surfing and wine! Although it may seem at first that winemaking and surfing have little in common, both require balance, perseverance, and respect for nature. Sauvignon Blanc, Pinot Noir, Merlot, Syrah, and Cabernet Sauvignon are sourced from some of Sonoma's finest vineyards, and Longboard has received accolades almost since day one. Their fun tasting room is more surf hangout than stuffy wine bar, so even spongers will feel at home. Longboard Russian River Valley Sauvignon Blanc 2011 is pale straw to the eye and all lemon-lime on the nose. Flavors of lemon-lime sorbet, pear, and passion fruit are enhanced by an undercurrent of lightly toasted vanilla bean. Longboard Russian River Valley Syrah 2007 is almost purple in the glass and offers aromas of mixed-berry pie with a touch of just-dug-up fennel bulb. Rich tannins and spot-on acidity showcase flavors of brambleberries, aniseed, and mocha.

LYNMAR ESTATE

3909 Frei Road,
Sebastopol, CA 95472,
(707) 829-3374
www.lynmarestate.com

Lynn Fritz bought Quail Hill Ranch in 1980 with the idea of using it as his country retreat, a place to relax after traveling the globe in his role as CEO of Fritz Companies. He and his wife, Anisya, moved here permanently

in 2008, and they dwell among 70 acres of Pinot Noir, Chardonnay, and a small block of Syrah, all surrounded by abundant gardens. Planted in 1971, their Quail Hill Vineyard harbors some of the oldest vines in the Russian River Valley. The vineyard team is headed by Jason Saling, and Shane Finley is in charge of winemaking. Lynmar Estate Quail Hill Vineyard Russian River Valley Chardonnay 2010 is medium straw to the eye with a bright meniscus. Fragrances of clementine, jasmine, and ripe Gala apple continue in the mouth, where they are joined by mineral, toast, and butterscotch flavors. Lynmar Estate Quail Hill Vineyard Russian River Valley Pinot Noir 2010 is rich garnet in the glass, and aromas of mixed dark berries and plums waft toward the nose. Strong fruit flavors intertwine with notes of espresso, Turkish delight, and birch root.

MACMURRAY RANCH

3387 Dry Creek Road,
Healdsburg, CA 95448,
(707) 431-5507
www.macmurrayranch.com

MacMurray Ranch's modern era began when actor Fred MacMurray bought the circa-1850 homestead in 1941 and started raising cattle. MacMurray Ranch is now owned by the Gallo family, with Kate MacMurray carrying on her father's legacy. MacMurray Ranch produces Pinot Noir, Pinot Gris, and Chardonnay sourced from its 450-acre Russian River Valley Ranch and prime vineyard sites in California's Sonoma Coast and Central Coast and Oregon's Willamette Valley. Winemaking is under the direction of Chris Munsell, a UC Davis graduate who worked at some of California's finest properties before joining MacMurray. MacMurray Ranch Sonoma Coast Pinot Gris 2011 is an aromatic gem, offering notes of peach, pear tart, and baking spice. On the palate flavors of melon and white peach meld with recurring notes of spice and citrus blossom. MacMurray Ranch Winemakers Block Selection Russian River Valley Pinot Noir 2010 is deep red in the glass, with acute aromas of black cherry and five-spice powder. A finely spun web of tannins and brightness makes a pleasing backdrop for flavors of black cherry, fruits of the wood, and a dash of spice.

MACPHAIL FAMILY WINES

851 Magnolia Drive, Healdsburg, CA 95448,
(707) 433-4780
www.macphailwine.com

At first glance, the MacPhail Family Winery appears to be a vintage barn sharing quarters with winemaker James MacPhail's family home. In actuality, the energy-efficient facility that was completed in 2008 uses a combination of cutting-edge technology and ecologically friendly innovation such as solar power and a purpose-built wetland that reclaims winery wastewater. MacPhail crafts small-batch *terroir*-driven Pinot Noir using fruit from selected vineyards in the Sonoma Coast and Anderson Valley appellations, utilizing traditional techniques such as cold maceration and hand punch-downs while avoiding flourishes such as fining and filtration. Maximum production is capped at 5,000 cases by both the winery's permit and James's focus on quality over quantity. MacPhail Pratt Vineyard Sonoma Coast Pinot Noir 2010 is deep garnet in color. A lush nose of black plum and Christmas spices hints at the flavors of dark berries, aniseed, clove, and cedar that linger on the tongue through the gratifying finish. MacPhail Ferrington Vineyard Anderson Valley Pinot Noir 2010 is dark red to the eye, with aromas of black cherry, cinnamon, star anise, and Dr Pepper. Black cherry and spice continue on the palate, accompanied by raspberry and a touch of Sichuan pepper, interwoven with smooth tannins and vivid acidity.

MACROSTIE WINERY AND VINEYARDS

21481 8th Street East #25, Sonoma, CA 95476,
(707) 996-4480
www.macrostiewinery.com

Steve MacRostie officially founded his winery in 1987 and released his inaugural Carneros Chardonnay the same year. Five years later he released his first Pinot Noir, but it wasn't until 1997, when he entered into a partnership with Nancy and Tony Lilly, that he began planting vines on his own land. Together the group developed Wildcat Mountain Vineyard and made great improvements on this former pastureland by planting 58 acres of Chardonnay, Pinot Noir, and Syrah. In 2004 Steve shifted his focus to the vineyard and to working more closely with his contract growers. Kevin Holt, formerly of Testarossa and Quivira, took over winemaking duties and continues Steve's legacy of fine wine production. MacRostie Winery and Vineyards Sonoma Coast Chardonnay 2011 has notes of lemon curd, citrus blossoms, and green apple in the bouquet. It is full-bodied in the mouth with bright flavors of Anjou pears and stone fruits. It has a persistent finish with a nice minerality. MacRostie Winery and Vineyards Carneros Pinot Noir Rosé 2011 tastes like summer in a glass. Light pink in color, it has aromas of strawberries and cream and candied lemon peel. In the mouth flavors of pink ripe fruits come out with a creamy texture and later morph into a bright, clean finish.

MARCASSIN

3358 River Road, Windsor, CA 95492,
(707) 942-5633

Helen Turley has been called "the Greatest Winemaker in America" by no less than Wine Spectator, and Ms. Turley has been consulting winemaker at a Who's Who of notable California wineries, including Bryant Family, Landmark, Peter Michael, and Martinelli. There is a rumored 14-year wait to join the mailing list at Marcassin, the private winery project that she founded with her viticulturist husband, John Wetlaufer, in 1993. The wines of Marcassin, French for "young wild boar," were produced at the Martinelli Winery before completion of the new Marcassin Winery in 2010. From the 2010 vintage forward, Marcassin has been producing only two wines, Chardonnay and Pinot Noir, from its 20-acre Sonoma Coast vineyard. Grapes previously were sourced from the Martinelli family's Blue Slide Ridge and Three Sisters vineyards in addition to estate vineyards. Wines are aged for five years before release, and prices on the secondary market are often multiples of the original release price. Assistant winemaker Matt Courtney, who had worked under Helen Turley's direction for eight years, left in late 2012 to take on winemaking at Arista. Marcassin Marcassin Vineyard Sonoma County Chardonnay 2008 is golden in the glass, with a heady nose of clementine, jasmine, and rising bread. Rich flavors of tangerine, white peach, honeysuckle, and river stones fill the mouth, culminating in a satisfying finish. If you manage to score a bottle of the 2008, your first impulse will be to drink it immediately, but those who can wait for as long as 10 more years will be rewarded for their efforts.

MARIMAR ESTATE

11400 Graton Road,
Sebastopol, CA 95472,
(707) 823-4365
www.marimarestate.com

Marimar Torres has been immersed in the world of wine her entire life. Before starting her eponymous California estate, Ms. Torres worked closely with her family's well-known Spanish wine brand, Torres. She settled in California in 1975, and in 1986 she began planting her Russian River Valley Don Miguel vineyard, named in honor of her late father, which today is composed of 30 acres each of Chardonnay and Pinot Noir. Marimar's Doña Margarita vineyard, an homage to her late mother, is home to 20 acres of Pinot Noir in the Sonoma Coast AVA. Both vineyards are organically farmed, and all wines are estate-grown. Completed in 1992, Marimar Estate's winery was built in the style of a Catalan farmhouse. An expert in Spanish cuisine and the author of two cookbooks, Marimar Torres has a love of all things Spanish that shines through in the many paella and wine pairing events held at the estate throughout the year. Marimar Estate Don Miguel Vineyard Russian River Valley Acero Chardonnay 2010 offers pleasing fragrances of crisp autumn pear and just-picked green apple. *Acero* is Spanish for "steel," and this unoaked Chardonnay is crisp and clean, with flavors of Granny Smith apple, pear, and light mineral notes. Marimar Estate Don Miguel Vineyard Russian River Valley La Masia Pinot Noir 2009 is garnet in color, with aromas of black cherry, birch root, and orange zest. These notes continue on the palate, mingling with baking spice and freshly picked mushroom, sheathed in gentle tannins.

MARTINELLI WINERY

3360 River Road, Windsor, CA 95492,
(707) 525-0570
www.martinelliwinery.com

Like many of their equally high-profile neighbors, the Martinellis are descendants of Italian immigrants who came to California in the late nineteenth century and began farming grapes and making wine. Giuseppe Martinelli and his bride, Luisa Vellutini Martinelli, set out from their small Tuscan village in 1887, settling in the Russian River Valley. They planted Zinfandel and Muscat of Alexandria vines on the 60-degree slope of what is now known as the Jackass Hill Vineyard (a long story within a long story), and the Martinelli Vineyard was born. Giuseppe and Luisa's son Leno farmed the vineyard from the age of 12 in 1918, finally handing over the keys of his tractor to his son, Lee Sr., in the mid-1990s. In the meantime Lee and his wife, Carolyn, had taken over family orchards in the Russian River Valley and replaced fruit trees with grapevines. After providing grapes for other wineries in the area, they started the Martinelli Winery in the mid-1970s, converting an old triple-roofed hop barn into a winemaking facility and tasting room. In 1992, Lee and Carolyn met Helen Turley, who served as their head winemaker and then consulting winemaker from 1992 through 2010. Bryan Kvamme, who had worked with Turley since 1997, took over full winemaking duties in 2008. Today the third and fourth generations of family members work side by side growing and producing handcrafted Chardonnay, Pinot Noir, Zinfandel, Syrah, and small amounts of Sauvignon Blanc and Muscat of Alexandria. Martinelli Winery Martinelli Road Russian River Valley Chardonnay 2009 is medium straw in the glass, with an alluring nose of citrus, freesia, and caramel. Flavors of lemon curd, Bosc pear, and toffee are underscored by striking minerality and a sumptuous texture. This is a gorgeous Chardonnay that will drink well for several more years. Martinelli Winery Jackass Vineyard Russian River Valley Zinfandel 2009 is inky purple to the eye, yielding aromas of mixed cherry pie and freshly ground black pepper. On the tongue, raspberry and blueberry intertwine with flavors of baking spices, pepper, and a burst of florality, culminating in a surprisingly bright finish.

MATANZAS CREEK WINERY

6097 Bennett Valley Road, Santa Rosa, CA 95404,
(707) 528-6464
www.matanzascreek.com

Although it usually is thought of as a cold grape-growing region, Bennett Valley's Mediterranean climate comes into sharp focus upon visiting Matanzas Creek's luxuriant lavender gardens. Founder Sandra McIver purchased a dairy farm in 1971, added neighboring properties as time went on, planted Merlot—and lavender—and started Matanzas Creek Winery in 1997. The estate is now under the Jackson Family Wines umbrella and specializes in Chardonnay, Sauvignon Blanc, Syrah, and Merlot. Matanzas Creek Winery Bennett Valley Sauvignon Blanc 2011 is light straw to the eye. Fragrant notes of mango, lemon, and apricot jump out of the glass and continue on the palate, mingling with flavors of chopped Thai basil and lemongrass. Matanzas Creek Winery Bennett Valley Merlot 2007 is deep red in the glass, giving off aromas of cassis, herbes de Provence, and anisette. On the palate, luscious cassis, herbal, and spice notes carry through, backed by fluid tannins.

MAZZOCCO SONOMA

1400 Lytton Springs Road, Healdsburg, CA 95448,
(800) 501-8466
www.mazzocco.com

When Mazzocco's Lytton Spring's hilltop vineyards straddling Dry Creek and Alexander Valley became available, it was an opportunity Ken and Diane Wilson just couldn't pass up. Besides giving them more room to make their wines, the vineyards provided the quality of fruit they needed to make their single-vineyard-designated Zinfandels. Their winemaker, Antoine Favero, was born in Champagne and raised in Peru before attending UC Davis. Mazzocco Sonoma Seaton Dry Creek Valley Zinfandel 2011 is inky purple with a violet rim. It has aromas of blackberry, freshly brewed coffee, and lifted notes of rose petals. It has flavors of black fruit, espresso, mocha, bittersweet chocolate, and a smooth, long, sweet tannic finish. Mazzocco Sonoma Serracino Reserve Dry Creek Valley Zinfandel 2011 is inky purple with aromas of black cherry and black raspberry. It tastes of wild brambleberry on the palate, with a smooth mouthfeel and a rich long finish. The tannins are sweet and balanced, and there is a lingering sensation of cocoa powder in the post palate.

MEDLOCK AMES

13414 Chalk Hill Road, Healdsburg, CA 95448,
(707) 431-8845
www.medlockames.com

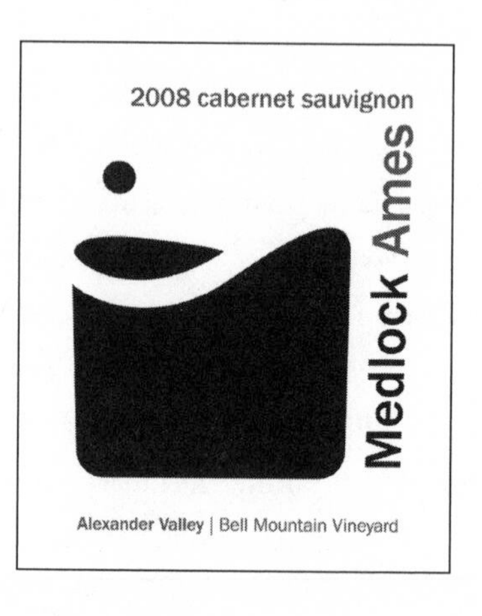

If you're looking for a cocktail in a sea of fine wine, look no farther than Medlock Ames's tasting room just outside Healdsburg. Since opening this winery offshoot, owners Chris James and Ames Morison have created a vibe rarely found along wine roads. After 5 p.m., when the tasting rooms shut down, it's time for a garden-to-glass cocktail in the speakeasy-style Alexander Valley Bar. James and Morison's commitment to gardening is also apparent in their 56 acres of organic vineyards set among over 300 acres of meadow and woodlands just up the road. The spotlight is on estate-grown, handcrafted Chardonnay, Sauvignon Blanc, Merlot, Pinot Noir, and Cabernet Sauvignon. Medlock Ames Bell Mountain

Vineyard Alexander Valley Sauvignon Blanc 2011 is vibrant from the first whiff of citrus, melon, and fresh green herbs. These bright notes endure straight through the piquant finish. Medlock Ames Bell Mountain Vineyard Alexander Valley Cabernet Sauvignon 2008 is deep black cherry in the glass, presenting with a nose of mixed fruits of the wood, red currants, and aniseed. The palate is awash in berries and spice sprinkled with hints of mocha and cigar box, with a refreshing combination of tannins and acidity.

MERRIAM VINEYARDS

11654 Los Amigos Road, Healdsburg, CA 95448,
(707) 433-4032
www.merriamvineyards.com

After specializing in Bordeaux-style red blends from their own Russian River Valley Windacre Vineyard and other local growers, Peter and Diana Merriam expanded their holdings in 2009, planting Pinot Noir and Sauvignon Blanc in their Los Amigos Vineyard. Peter is an avid outdoorsman and Diana loves all things culinary, and their combined passions show through in the vineyard and the glass. Winemakers David Herzberg and Margaret Davenport work alongside Peter to create blends and single-varietal bottlings that reflect both the *terroir* and the vintner's craft. Merriam Vineyards Russian River Valley Miktos 2008 is a blend of 42 percent Cabernet Sauvignon, 23 percent Petite Verdot, 20 percent Cabernet Franc, and 15 percent Merlot. To the eye, it is deep garnet. Black cherry and violet are most evident on the nose, backed by aromas of dark chocolate and graphite. The palate is gently bathed in flavors of fresh and preserved cherry, blackberry, and pleasing notes of forest floor.

MERRY EDWARDS WINERY

2959 Gravenstein Highway North,
Sebastopol, CA 95472,
(707) 823-7466
www.merryedwards.com

Visitors to the Russian River Valley can learn about Merry Edwards's artisanal Sauvignon

Blanc, Chardonnay, and Pinot Noir at the winery she and husband, Ken Coopersmith, completed in 2008 after having used other people's facilities since the founding of her eponymous brand in 1997. The winery sits among the vines of the Coopersmith Vineyard, one of five estate-owned vineyards, named for Merry's husband and business partner. Merry Edwards was one of California's first female winemakers; her career started at Mount Eden Vineyards in 1974. She was the first winemaker at Matanzas Creek Vineyards, where she worked for seven years, before becoming a consulting winemaker on multiple projects throughout California and Oregon. Sustainable practices are utilized in the vineyards and winery, including a solar power system that was installed in 2010. Merry Edwards Olivet Lane Russian River Valley Pinot Noir 2011 is garnet to the eye, yielding aromas of black cherry, cranberry, and black currants. Fruit flavors are joined on the palate by luscious notes of fennel, baking spices, and Turkish delight. Pleasing tannins endure through the smooth finish, balanced by a final note of orange zest. Merry Edwards Russian River Valley Sauvignon Blanc 2012 gives off a nose filled with honeysuckle, grapefruit, and soft spice. A full mouthfeel and zesty acidity abound amid flavors of tropical fruits, Bartlett pear, and kiwi.

MICHEL-SCHLUMBERGER WINE ESTATES

4155 Wine Creek Road,
Healdsburg, CA 95448,
(707) 433-7427
www.michelschlumberger.com

The white stucco and terra-cotta visitor center at Michel-Schlumberger is a testament to the Spanish history and influence in California, while the elegant nature of estate-grown Chardonnay, Cabernet Sauvignon, Cabernet Franc, and Merlot bears witness to the European roots of founding partners Jean-Jacques Michel, a native of Switzerland, and Jacques Pierre Schlumberger, whose family has been making wine in Alsace, France, for four hundred years. Michel first planted his Dry Creek Valley vineyard in 1979, originally calling the estate Domaine Michel, and Schlumberger joined forces with him and was the winemaker from 1991 until his retirement in 2011. Winemaking is now under the direction of Bryan Davison with input from consulting winemaker Kerry Damskey. Total output is about 7,000 cases per year of single varieties and blends. Michel-Schlumberger Benchland Wine Estate La Nue Dry Creek Valley Chardonnay 2011 is pale straw in the glass. Fragrances of peach, honeysuckle, and river stones carry over onto the palate and are joined by flavors of green apple, highlighted by zippy acidity and a fresh finish. Michel-Schlumberger Benchland Wine Estate Dry Creek Valley Maison Rouge 2010 is a blend of 32 percent Merlot, 14 percent Cabernet Franc, 14 percent Carménère, 14 percent Syrah, 10 percent Cabernet Sauvignon, 10 percent Petit Verdot, and 6 percent Malbec. It is deep garnet to the eye, offering a bouquet of black cherry, raspberry, baking spices, and lavender. On the tongue black cherry, cassis, white pepper, and anise cavort with vanilla and violet in a satisfying web of tannins and acidity.

MONTEMAGGIORE

2355 West Dry Creek Road, Healdsburg, CA 95448,
(707) 433-9499
www.montemaggiore.com

For members of a sprawling Italian family with ties to the village of Montemaggiore in southern Italy, Vince and Lise Ciolino keep things simple at their Sonoma winery, focusing on biodynamically farmed Syrah and olive oil. Vince tends their 10 acres of vines in Dry Creek Valley, and Lise makes Syrah, a Cabernet-Syrah blend, and a small amount of 3 Divas, their white Rhône-style blend. Montemaggiore Paolo's Vineyard Syrah 2008 is red violet in color, exhibiting a bouquet of wild cherry, dark chocolate, and white pepper. Cherry coats the tongue in pleasing waves, supported by mocha, spice, and gauzy tannins.

MUELLER WINERY

118 North Street,
Healdsburg, CA 95492
(707) 473-8086
www.muellerwine.com

Bob and Lori Mueller's Cellar Tasting Room, set among their Russian River Valley vineyards, offers guests exactly the sort of laid-back, friendly atmosphere—and exquisite Pinot Noir—that people expect when visiting Sonoma. From the first vintages of Chardonnay in 1991 and Pinot Noir in 1994, Mueller wines have delighted wine lovers and critics alike. Bob Mueller worked at Foppiano, Charles Krug, and Souverain before striking out on his own in 1991, and he and Lori built their 5,000-case-per-year-capacity Windsor winery a decade later. In addition to four different Pinot Noirs and a single Chardonnay, Bob works with Syrah, Zinfandel, and Sauvignon Blanc. Mueller Tempi Russian River Valley Pinot Noir 2010 is deep garnet, with a nose of red raspberry, fennel bulb, and vanilla bean. On the palate, sensuous layers of freshly picked berries saturated with spice and vanilla notes are at play in a bed of soft tannins. Those who can wait until the end of the decade to pop the cork will truly be rewarded for their patience.

MURPHY-GOODE WINERY

20 Matheson Street,
Healdsburg, CA 95448,
(800) 499-7644
www.murphygoodewinery.com

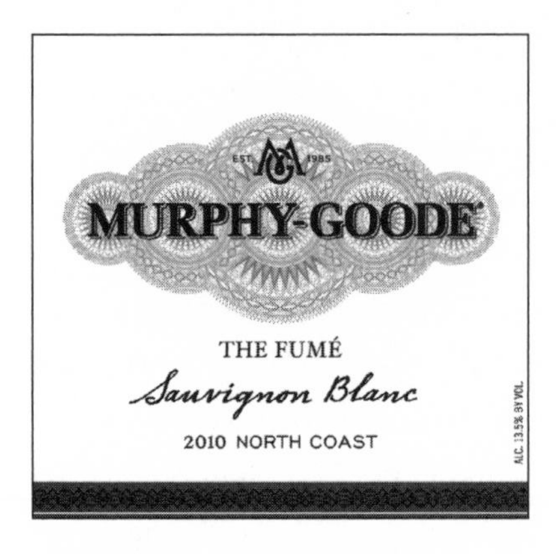

Anyone who opens a winery will tell you it's a gamble, and it is obvious that Tim Murphy, Dale Goode, and Dave Ready's bet paid off. In 1985 while playing liar's dice, the three of them decided to start making their own wines from Murphy-Goode Vineyard and Murphy Ranch Sonoma County Fruit, starting out with Chardonnay and Fumé Blanc. Their love of a good time is celebrated on labels such as Liar's Dice Zinfandel, All In Claret, and Dealer's Choice Cabernet Sauvignon. David Ready Jr. has been working here since 1997 and took over as winemaker in 2001. Murphy-Goode is part of the Jackson Family portfolio. Murphy-Goode The Fumé North Coast Sauvignon Blanc 2010, composed of 95 percent Sauvignon Blanc and 5 percent Sémillon, is pale straw in color, with a bright nose of passion fruit and pineapple. Tropical fruit flavors mingle with peach and cantaloupe, enhanced by floral notes and a hint of smoke. Murphy-Goode Dealer's Choice Alexander Valley Cabernet Sauvignon 2009 is dark red in the glass, presenting aromas of cherry vanilla parfait with Mediterranean herbal notes. Cherry and smooth vanilla lead on the tongue, yielding to flavors of wild raspberry and sage bedecked in a velvety tannic cloak.

MUTT LYNCH

602 Limerick Lane,
Healdsburg, CA 95448,
(707) 942-6180
www.muttlynchwinery.com

If you and your canine companion are inseparable, then book your appointment for a "pawsome" wine tasting experience at Mutt Lynch. Owners Chris and Brenda Lynch—and their rescue greyhound, Patch—hound out the best Sonoma vineyard sites for their Sauvignon Blanc, Chardonnay, Syrah, Zinfandel, Merlot, Cabernet Sauvignon, Petite Sirah, and Primitivo. Serious wines are found behind their fun-loving, dog-centric labels with zany names such as Fou Fou le Blanc, Merlot Over and Play Dead, and Unleashed Chardonnay. Chris and Brenda are also serious about our four-legged friends, donating much time and money each year to animal charities. Their top-of-the-line bottlings bear the MBF designation, shorthand for "Man's Best Friend." Mutt Lynch MBF Zinfandel 2008 is dark garnet in the glass, with aromas of black cherry, blueberry, and fresh black pepper. Vigorous cherry and blueberry appear on the palate as well, mingling with pepper and licorice in a nice tannic framework. Mutt Lunch MBF Primitivo 2010 is deep cherry to the eye, with a bouquet of black cherry, butterscotch, and cigar box. A rich mouthfeel encases flavors of raspberry, black cherry, fresh ground pepper, and a dusting of spice.

NOVY FAMILY WINES

981 Airway Court,
Santa Rosa, CA 95403,
(707) 578-3882
www.novyfamilywines.com

The extended Novy family traces their roots to the former Czechoslovakia, where *Novy* means "new." In that spirit, Adam and Dianna Lee (owners of Siduri Wines) and Dianna's family created this new label together. Adam and Dianna had already found success with their Siduri Pinot Noir, which came to the attention of the wine world when they dropped off a sample of their first vintage with Robert Parker and received a 90-point rating. Joining forces with Dianna's family, they started a new brand in 1998 and quickly gained accolades for this project as well. Both members of the couple share winemaking duties, and they have expanded their focus from single-vineyard Syrah to small batches of Zinfandel, Viognier, Chardonnay, and Grenache. Novy Keefer Ranch Vineyard Chardonnay 2010 offers a clean nose of pear and orange blossom, developing into flavors of pear and clementine with clean mineral undertones. Novy Sonoma County Syrah 2010 yields aromas of black cherry and cassis with a healthy dose of anise. In the mouth fruit yields to bacon and fennel bulb with a touch of chewing tobacco.

PAPAPIETRO PERRY WINERY

4791 Dry Creek Road,
Healdsburg, CA 95448,
(707) 433-0422
www.papapietro-perry.com

Owned by two couples with a passion for wine, food, and fun, Papapietro Perry receives accolades and awards that at first seem extravagant for a small family-owned winery until you taste their wine. Ben Papapietro, a former newspaperman turned winemaker, asked his friend Bruce Perry to join him during harvest at another friend's Sonoma County winery in the early 1980s. Shortly thereafter Ben and Bruce were making wine in Ben's garage each fall, and that hobby gradually turned into a life-changing career move for Papapietro and Perry and their wives, Yolanda and Renae. Ben Papapietro is in charge of winemaking, crafting Zinfandel and single-vineyard-designate and clonal-designate Pinot Noir from the Russian River and Dry Creek valleys. Renae handles sales and marketing, and Yolanda joined the business in 2009, overseeing distributor relations. Papapietro Perry wines have received high scores from a number of wine critics, and their tasting room has been singled out as a place to enjoy wonderful wine in a fun setting. Papapietro Perry 777 Clones Russian River Valley Pinot Noir, made from just a single Pinot Noir clone from different Russian River vineyards, is deep red in the glass, with a nose of fresh cherry and light baking spice. On the tongue bright cherry is enhanced by flavors of vanilla and spice. The rich texture and balanced acidity hold through the lasting finish. Papapietro Perry Leras Family Vineyards Russian River Valley Pinot Noir 2009 is dark garnet in color, giving aromas of cherry, Dr Pepper, and baking bread. Sweet cherry flavor is augmented by a touch of tart cherry with notes of river rock and toasted bread. Smooth tannins endure on the palate through the still-fruity finish.

PAUL HOBBS

3355 Gravenstein Highway North,
Sebastopol, CA 95472,
(707) 824-9879
www.paulhobbswinery.com

It has been a long, winding, and very rewarding wine road that Paul Hobbs has traveled since his first sip of 1962 Château d'Yquem as a teenager. Before starting his own brand, Hobbs made wine and consulted at some of the best-known wineries in California and South America, including Robert Mondavi, Opus One, and Catena Zapata. In addition to his eponymous Sonoma winery, where the CrossBarn label is also produced, Hobbs is at the helm of Viña Cobos in Argentina and

Paul Hobbs Imports. His consulting winemaker duties take him to over twenty wineries around the globe, including California, France, Argentina, Chile, Uruguay, and Armenia. Paul Hobbs Winery was founded in 1991, and in 1998 the land in Sebastopol that later became Katherine Lindsey Estate was purchased. The first vintage at the Sebastopol winery was 2003. Hobbs's wines have received some of the highest accolades possible in the US and international wine press. Grapes are selected from some of the best vineyards in Sonoma County, especially the Russian River Valley, as well as those in Napa Valley. Paul Hobbs Ulises Valdez Vineyard Russian River Valley Pinot Noir 2011 is deep ruby to the eye, offering fragrances of raspberry and violet. A startling combination of power and elegance is at play on the palate, with rich flavors of black cherry, raspberry conserves, Chinese five-spice powder, and white chocolate lingering through a finish notable for velvety tannins and fruit-filled acidity. Paul Hobbs Beckstoffer To Kalon Vineyard Oakville Napa Valley Cabernet Sauvignon 2009 is deep black cherry in the glass, giving off a luxurious bouquet of blueberry, cassis, and cocoa bean. Opulent tannins lay a framework for complex flavors of dark berries, river rocks, and mocha that linger through the sensuous finish.

PEAY VINEYARDS

227 Treadway Drive,
Cloverdale, CA 95425,
(707) 894-8720
www.peayvineyards.com

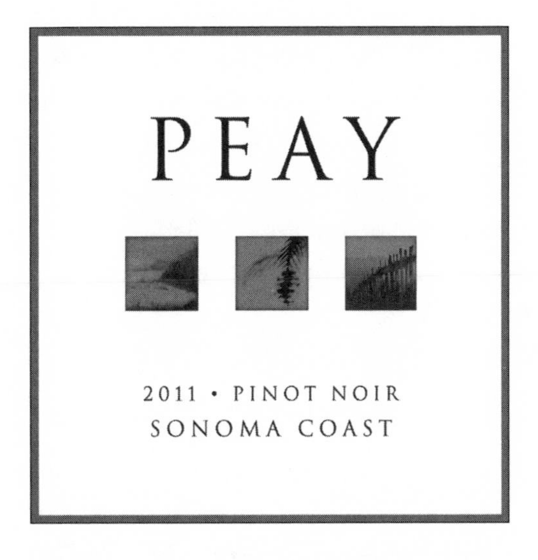

Not wanting to take his parents' advice and become a lawyer, Nick Peay worked his first harvest in 1988 at Schramsberg, loved it, and took a full-time position at La Jota Vineyards the same year. He coaxed his brother Andy into starting their own winery, and along with Nick's wife, Vanessa, the team at Peay makes some delicious cool-weather varieties. Peay Vineyards Estate Chardonnay 2010 is straw colored, with aromas of citrus blossoms, crystallized ginger, and Granny Smith apple. It is crisp yet full-bodied in the mouth, with pleasant levels of minerality and salinity to make it perfectly refreshing. Only 400 cases are made, and that's a shame. Peay Vineyards Sonoma Coast Pinot Noir 2011 is cherry colored, and we're happy that they made a bit more of this one—1,100 cases. It has aromas of Indian spice, orange blossom, and black cherry in the complex bouquet. On the palate it is generous with flavors of sweet fruit and a good level of acidity to make it a perfect wine to pair with grilled lamb or pan-fried duck breast.

PEDRONCELLI

1220 Canyon Road, Geyserville, CA 95441
(800) 836-3894
www.pedroncelli.com

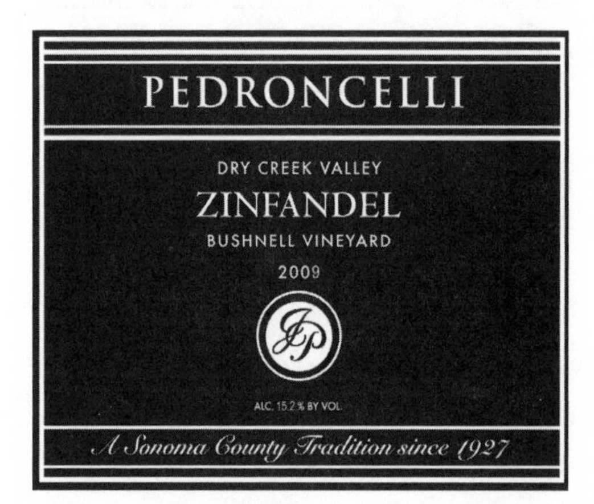

When you stop into the Pedroncelli tasting room, said to be the oldest in Dry Creek Valley, odds are high that your wine will be poured by a member of the family. The fourth generation of Pedroncellis is now old enough to begin working in the vineyards and winery first bought by John Pedroncelli Sr. in 1917. His son John Jr. became the winemaker in 1945 and continues as head winemaker today, working alongside assistant winemaker Montse Reece, cellarmaster Polo Cano, and Lance Blakely, who runs the vineyard and winery operations. The majority of their output is from estate-grown vineyards, and their Cabernet Sauvignon, Zinfandel, Chardonnay, Sangiovese, Petite Sirah, Merlot, and Sauvignon Blanc have won more than their fair share of awards and medals and been featured in major wine magazines. Pedroncelli Vintage Selection Dry Creek Valley Sonoma County Chardonnay 2011 is pale yellow, offering a bouquet of Granny Smith apple, jasmine, and lemon zest. These flavors extend to the palate as well, and the full mouthfeel and zesty acidity make for a satisfying sipper. Pedroncelli Bushnell Vineyard Dry Creek Valley Sonoma County Zinfandel 2009, composed of 96 percent Zinfandel and 4 percent Petite Sirah, is deep violet in the glass. Aromas of mixed-berry compote only hint at the rich blackberry, black cherry, and plum flavors that are encased in a gorgeous structure with whiffs of vanilla and spice.

PETER MICHAEL WINERY

12400 Ida Clayton Road,
Calistoga, CA 94515,
(707) 942-3200
www.petermichaelwinery.com

The Michael family's "100-by-100" plan, envisioning 100 percent family ownership of the Peter Michael Winery and vineyards for at least 100 years, is a very refreshing ideal considering how many seemingly committed vintners sell out to corporate interests as soon as the first offer comes across the table. Sir Peter and Lady Michael, known to friends as Pete and Maggie, purchased over 600 acres of land in Knights Valley in 1982. Within a year, they had planted red Bordeaux varieties, and when their first wineworthy crop came to fruition in 1987, they brought in Helen Turley, the first in a list of prominent winemakers, to craft their first vintage. Current winemaker Nicolas Morlet has been at the helm since 2005, succeeding his brother Luc Morlet. Sir Peter has passed the torch to his son Paul Michael, who, along with his wife, Emily, upholds his parents' ideals of "classical winemaking and limited production." Roughly 95 percent of their wine is produced from estate-grown fruit from the Knights Valley, Sonoma Coast, and Oakville (Napa) appellations. In addition to red and white Bordeaux blends, Peter Michael bottles Chardonnay and Pinot Noir. Peter Michael Winery Les Pavots Single Vineyard Estate Cabernet Blend 2009 is a blend of 66 percent Cabernet Sauvignon, 22 percent Cabernet Franc, 10 percent Merlot, and 2 percent Petit Verdot. It is dark garnet to the eye, with a rich bouquet of cassis, red raspberry, forest floor, and white chocolate. Mouth-filling tannins accompany multihued fruit, spice, and savory flavors of cassis, black cherry, cigar box, black pepper, freshly turned earth, and anise. This wine is perfectly enjoyable now but can withstand aging until your newborn is old enough to drink legally. Peter Michael Winery La Carrière Single Vineyard Estate Chardonnay 2011 has an exquisite nose of clementine, white flowers, buttered brioche, and toasted almonds. A rich mouthfeel shot through with a tantalizing vein of minerality supports pleasing flavors of fresh peach and lemon sorbet.

PORTALUPI

107 North Street,
Healdsburg, CA 95448,
(707) 395-0960
www.portalupiwine.com

Husband-and-wife team Jane Portalupi and Tim Borges first met as children, worked in different areas of the wine business for many years, and started Portalupi in 2002. In the true Italian style of hospitality, they can be found behind the counter of their welcoming Healdsburg tasting room pouring wine by the glass, selling bottles, and sharing their love of wine. Folks who crave Old World style will appreciate a half-gallon jug of Vaso di Marina, a blend of Zinfandel, Cabernet Franc, and Petite Sirah named in honor of Jane's grandmother. Portalupi Bianco 2011, a blend of 47 percent Sauvignon Blanc, 46 percent Chardonnay, and 7 percent Muscat Canelli, is pale straw in color, with a nose of citrus fruit and white flowers. It is crisp and clean on the palate, with flavors of grapefruit, guava, and freesia. Portalupi Dry Creek Valley Zinfandel 2009 is deep cherry red in the glass, offering aromas of raspberry, licorice, and black pepper with a whiff of minerality. Raspberry, pepper, and spice continue onto the palate, where a subtle florality and tangy acidity make their presence known amid opulent tannins.

QUIVIRA VINEYARDS

4900 West Dry Creek Road,
Healdsburg, CA 95448,
(707) 431-8333
www.quivirawine.com

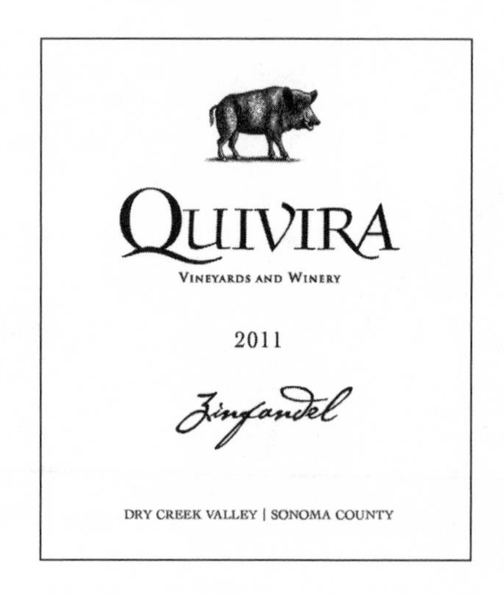

The name Quivira appeared on European maps in the sixteenth to eighteenth centuries, referring to the area that is now Sonoma County. Quivira was a mythical kingdom whose streets were paved with gold, and if that turned out to be an exaggeration, there is no doubt that Quivira's 93 acres of Zinfandel, Sauvignon Blanc, Syrah, Grenache, and Mourvèdre turn to gold in the glass under the hands of winemaker Hugh Chappelle. Owners Pete and Terri Knight took Quivira over from founders Holly and Henry Wendt in 2006; the Wendts had started Quivira 25 years earlier. Their Dry Creek Valley vineyards are farmed using biodynamic and organic techniques, and Pete and Terri have carried on Holly and Henry's vision of protecting the environment and creating better wine through natural vineyard management. Quivira Vineyards and Winery Fig Tree Vineyard Dry Creek Valley Sonoma County Sauvignon Blanc 2011 is pale straw with a slight green meniscus. A nose of tropical fruit and just-cut lawn defers to flavors of Granny Smith apple, passion fruit, lemon, and chopped herbs. Quivira Vineyards and Winery Dry Creek Valley Sonoma County Zinfandel 2011 is deep purple in the glass, offering aromas of mixed wild berries with dried herb and spice flourishes. On the tongue raspberry, blueberry, and Damson plum are backed by Christmas spices and vanilla.

RAMEY WINE CELLARS

25 Healdsburg Avenue, Healdsburg, CA 95448,
(707) 433-0870
www.rameywine.com

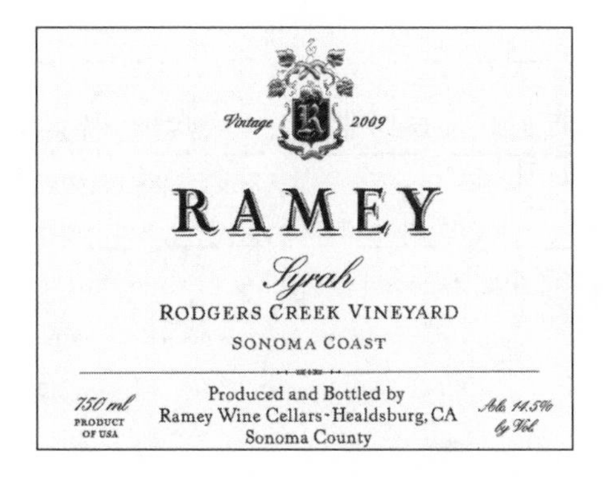

David Ramey is recognized as belonging to a short list of pioneers who helped increase the quality and profile of California wine. After earning a graduate degree in enology from UC Davis, working at the revered Château Pétrus, and being involved in the start-up of wineries such as Chalk Hill, Matanzas Creek, and Dominus, Ramey founded his eponymous winery along with his wife, Anne, in 1996. Using traditional techniques and fruit from throughout Napa and Sonoma, Ramey crafts highly sought after Cabernet blends, Chardonnay, and Syrah. Ramey Platt Vineyard Sonoma Coast Chardonnay 2010, medium straw in color, yields fragrances of tropical fruit, Bosc pear, white peach, and a whisper of ginger liqueur. Flavors of peach, caramelized pineapple, pear compote, Asian spice, and vanilla are at play in a wine that is at once delicate yet expressively complex. Ramey Rodgers Creek Vineyard Sonoma Coast Syrah 2009, a cofermented field blend including 8 percent Viognier, is deep purple violet in the glass, from which it exudes aromas of blueberry, black currants, and freshly ground white pepper. Dense albeit pleasing berry flavors dominate the flavor profile, melding with chocolate-covered espresso bean, smoked pork, and Christmas spice. All in all, it's a delight to drink now, but those who can wait up to 12 years will be richly rewarded for their patience.

RAVENSWOOD

18701 Gehricke Road,
Sonoma, CA 95476,
(707) 938-1960
www.ravenswoodwinery.com

When you get Ravenswood founder Joel Peterson talking about wine, make sure that your glass is full and a bottle of his delicious Zinfandel is within reach. More than just a winemaker, Peterson is a veritable historian of the California wine industry and all the major players of the last 40 years. Since his first vintage of Ravenswood in 1976, the microbiologist turned winemaker became one of those major players himself, and it is almost impossible to talk to anyone about California Zin without Peterson's name popping up. Besides the well-known Single Vineyard Designate and County Zinfandels, Ravenswood produces Cabernet Sauvignon and Merlot, all carefully sourced from many of the same grape growers Joel has worked with from the beginning. Although Ravenswood is now corporate-owned, Joel Peterson is still involved with every step of winemaking from the vineyard to marketing. Many people are familiar with the wines of Ravenswood through the affordable Vintners Blend range, but our idea of a great date with Zinfandel is dinner with Joel tasting through current and past vintages of his single-vineyard Zins. Ravenswood Single Vineyard Designate Barricia Sonoma Valley Zinfandel 2010, composed of 77 percent Zinfandel and 23 percent Petite Sirah, is inky purple in the glass, with aromas of blackberry, cherry preserves, anisette, and black pepper. Velvety tannins abound, and berry flavors cavort on the tongue with notes of tobacco, forest floor, and potent spice. Ravenswood Single Vineyard Designate Belloni Russian River Valley Zinfandel 2010 is deep purple to the eye. Fragrances of plums, blackberry, cassis, anise, and dark chocolate carry over to the palate and endure through the smooth, fruity finish.

RAYMOND BURR VINEYARDS

8339 West Dry Creek Road,
Healdsburg, CA 95448,
(707) 433-4365
www.raymondburrvineyards.com

Older readers—or those who stay up late watching classic TV reruns—know Raymond Burr as the magnetic star of *Perry Mason* (1957–1966) and *Ironside* (1967–1975). Burr met his partner, Robert Benevides, an actor and producer, on the set of *Perry Mason*, and the two shared a life that included an orchid business, a cattle and coconut ranch on an island they owned, and a vineyard and winery. Benevides bought the Dry Creek Valley farm in 1976, and their first grapevines, bearing Cabernet Sauvignon, Chardonnay, and Portuguese varieties, were planted in 1986. The first vintage was produced in 1990 and released in 1995. Burr passed away in 1993 at age 76, and Benevides continues as the face of the vineyard and winery they began together. Winemaker Phyllis Zouzounis creates award-winning Chardonnay, Cabernet Sauvignon, Cabernet Franc, Quartet, a Bordeaux-style blend, and "California port" from estate-grown fruit. Raymond Burr Vineyards Sonoma County Chardonnay 2010 has a bouquet of citrus fruits and vanilla. This is a creamy, mouth-pleasing Chardonnay with flavors of clementine, lemon curd, and vanilla bean. Raymond Burr Vineyards Quartet 2010 is a blend of 53 percent Cabernet Sauvignon, 32 percent Malbec, 9 percent Cabernet Franc, and 6 percent Petit Verdot. It is inky red violet in the glass, with an invigorating nose of wild brambleberries, black pepper, and violet. On the tongue, flavors of mixed berries, spice, and vanilla linger through the persistent finish.

J. ROCHIOLI VINEYARDS & WINERY

6192 Westside Road,
Healdsburg, CA 95448,
(707) 433-2305
www.rochioliwinery.com

The name Rochioli is practically synonymous with handcrafted Russian River Pinot Noir. Their vineyards bordering Westside Road—often referred to as the Rodeo Drive of Sonoma—are each planted to a single clone of Pinot Noir and Chardonnay, and Rochioli's mailing list for its single-vineyard releases has a five-year waiting list. The rest of us can enjoy their more readily available estate-grown Sauvignon Blanc, Pinot Noir, and Chardonnay. Joe Rochioli Sr. first bought this land, which he had previously farmed, in 1938, and today his family, including Joe Jr., carries on the tradition of producing their highly praised site-specific wines. Rochioli Estate Grown Russian River Valley Sauvignon Blanc 2012 is pale straw in the glass, with a fresh nose of tropical fruit. The zippy flavors of grapefruit and lemon, with touches of cut green herbs, are nicely framed by an unexpectedly rich mouthfeel, bright acidity, and a lasting finish. Rochioli Estate Grown Russian River Valley Pinot Noir 2011 is garnet in color. Aromas of cherry conserves, custard, and purple flowers yield to rich flavors of cherry vanilla with a lift of spice, leading to a smooth finish.

RODNEY STRONG VINEYARDS

11455 Old Redwood Highway,
Healdsburg, CA 95448,
(707) 431-1533
www.rodneystrong.com

After retiring from their careers as professional dancers in 1959, Rodney Strong and his new bride, Charlotte Ann Winson, moved to northern California, bought a 100-year-old boardinghouse, and began making wine. Their first vintages were made with purchased juice, but within three years Rod had planted the first Chardonnay in what is now the Chalk Hill AVA, and in 1968 he planted Pinot Noir in the Russian River Valley. In 1970 he built the Russian River Valley winery, which has since become a tasting room and cellar. In 1979 Rick Sayre joined as winemaker, and 10 years later Tom Klein, whose family has been farming in California since the early twentieth century, purchased Rodney Strong Vineyards. Over the years sustainable vineyard practices have been put into use, and in 2003 a large solar power grid was installed. In 2009, the year that marked Rick Sayre's thirtieth anniversary making wine at Rodney Strong and the Klein family's twentieth year as owners, Rodney Strong became the first carbon-neutral winery in Sonoma County. Rick continues as head winemaker, with David Ramey acting as consulting winemaker, and Greg Morthole works on the Reserve and Single Vineyard wines. Multiple varieties are vinified and sold at a broad range of price points under the Sonoma County, Estate, Reserve, and Single Vineyard designations. The Reserve bottlings include Chardonnay, Pinot Noir, Cabernet Sauvignon, and a Meritage blend, while the Single Vineyard line includes small-lot Cabernet Sauvignon. Rodney Strong Reserve Russian River Valley Pinot Noir 2010 is deep garnet to the eye. Aromas of black cherry, blackberry, and crème brûlée continue on the palate, aided by notes of Chinese five-spice and vanilla bean. Rodney Strong Rockaway Single Vineyard Alexander Valley Cabernet Sauvignon 2010 is composed of 88 percent Cabernet Sauvignon, 7 percent Malbec, and 5 percent Petit Verdot. Inky red violet to the eye, it gives off a rich fragrance of blackberry, raspberry, and vanilla. Luscious fruit and vanilla flavors fill the mouth, accented by a touch of spice and black pepper. Chewy tannins and deft acidity dance on the tongue through the show-stopping finish.

RUSSIAN HILL ESTATE

4525 Slusser Road, Windsor, CA 95492,
(707) 575-9428
www.russianhillestate.com

Husband-and-wife team Edward Gomez and Ellen Mack, both of whom are physicians, founded Russian Hill Estate in 1997. They had been searching for a site that could be home to vineyards and a purpose-built winery so that they could control all aspects of winemaking from vineyard to bottle. Their main focus is Pinot Noir and Syrah, and they also produce Chardonnay and Viognier. Ed's nephew Patrick Melley is in charge of winemaking, working with fruit from their own Tara Vineyard and from selected sites owned by noted winemakers and grape growers. Russian Hill Estate Vineyards Russian River Valley Syrah 2009 is deep violet to the eye. Leading with aromas of black currant liqueur, lavender, and cranberry, the palate reveals flavors of black currant, raspberry, blackberry, forest floor, and a hint of restrained florality, sheathed in a network of soft tannins. Russian Hill Tara Vineyard Russian River Valley Pinot Noir 2009 is ruby in the glass, with a bouquet of blackberry, plum, Turkish delight, and hillside herbs. Flavors of ripe black plum, birch root, and cinnamon stick converge on the taste buds, caressing the whole mouth in equal portions of velvety tannins and clean-cut acidity.

ST. FRANCIS WINERY

100 Pythian Road, Santa Rosa, CA 95409,
(707) 538-9463
www.stfranciswine.com

Joe and Emma Martin purchased the 100-acre Behler Ranch in 1971, selling their output to other producers until 1979, when the St. Francis Winery was built. The name is a nod to both the patron saint of animals and nature and the Franciscan priests who were among the first to plant grapes in California. St. Francis's distinctive Mission-style bell tower pays homage to this history as well. Original winemaker Tom Mackey was succeeded in 2012 by Katie Madigan, who started as an intern in 2002. The majority of grapes are sourced from their 600 acres of estate-owned vineyards in the Sonoma and Russian River valleys. St. Francis is known mainly for its outstanding value-driven reds, such as Zinfandel, Cabernet Sauvignon, Syrah,

Petite Sirah, and Merlot, and they also produce Chardonnay, Sauvignon Blanc, and Viognier. In addition to the airy tasting room, the vineyard-view restaurant offers pairing meals ranging from a few small plates to elaborate seven-course tasting menus under the direction of chef David Bush. The Artisan wine series is available only at the tasting room and to club members. St. Francis Sonoma County Merlot 2008 is deep red violet in the glass, with a nose of black cherry, mocha, and white pepper. On the palate, cherry and mocha are joined by flavors of blueberry and mixed spice encased in gentle tannins. St. Francis Sonoma County Old Vines Zinfandel 2010 is dark purple. Aromas of cherry confiture and Christmas spices signal the arrival of flavors of cherry pie, black raspberry, butterscotch, and cracked black pepper.

SAXON BROWN WINES

255 West Napa Street, Sonoma, CA 95476,
(707) 939-9530
www.saxonbrown.com

Owner and winemaker Jeff Gaffner founded Saxon Brown in 1997. He named his winery after the female protagonist in Jack London's *Valley of the Moon*, which was set in the Sonoma Valley. Saxon Brown is well known for its old-vine Zinfandels and field-blended Sémillon. Jeff also produces fine Pinot Noir, Cabernet Sauvignon, Syrah, and Chardonnay, and his annual total production is purposely less than 2,500 cases. Saxon Brown Sonoma Coast Parmelee-Hill, Owl Box Block, Syrah 2007 is opaque garnet purple, with heady aromas of black plum, violets, and black raspberry. It has full-on fruit flavors that coat the entire palate upon entry, with a well-balanced tannic structure and a touch of spiced cedar in the finish. Saxon Brown Sonoma Coast Durell Vineyard, Hayfield Block Pinot Noir 2009 is cherry red, with delightful aromas of dried black cherry, ripe red cherry, and brown baking spice. It is generous in the mouth with lasting flavors of fruit and spice in the complex finish. After tasting this professionally, we enjoyed this wine later that evening with a pan-seared duck breast. It was a match made in heaven.

SBRAGIA FAMILY VINEYARDS

9990 Dry Creek Road,
Geyserville, CA 95441,
(707) 473-2992
www.sbragia.com

Winemaker Ed Sbragia was born and raised in Dry Creek Valley, and he created wines for Beringer for 32 years before he and his wife, Jane, acquired the old Lake Sonoma Winery in 2006. Ed and his son Adam make the wine, and Adam's wife, Cathy, is in charge of hospitality. Ed and Jane's youngest son, Kevin, works in the cellar during harvest, and Jane and daughter Gina help out in the tasting room. Their family history in Dry Creek Valley dates back to 1904, when Ed's grandfather arrived from Tuscany and worked at the Italian Swiss Colony Winery. Sbragia Family Vineyards Dry Creek Valley Home Ranch Chardonnay 2009 is medium straw in the glass, with a nose of fresh citrus and vanilla. Flavors of lemon, citrus blossom, vanilla, and light spice coalesce on the palate, lingering through the bright finish. Sbragia Family Vineyards Dry Creek Valley Gino's Vineyard Zinfandel 2010 is inky violet to the eye, with a bouquet of mixed wild brambleberries, aniseed, and black pepper. Wild blackberry and raspberry dominate the palate, with nice touches of pepper and spice, supported by soft tannins into the lusty finish.

SCHUG CARNEROS ESTATE WINERY

602 Bonneau Road, Sonoma, CA 95476,
(707) 939-9363
www.schugwinery.com

Walter and Gertrud Schug both grew up in the winemaking business in Germany, and shortly after their marriage in 1961 they crossed the Atlantic and headed to California, where they both began working in the fledgling wine industry. Walter worked at E & J Gallo before moving to Joseph Phelps. While at Phelps, he made one of the first varietal Syrahs in the United States and one of the first modern-era California Bordeaux-style blends, Insignia. In 1989 Walter and Gertrud purchased 50 acres in the Sonoma-Carneros appellation and started Schug. All three of their children have been involved in the business, and today their son Axel is the CEO, with his wife, Kristine, acting as the winery chef. Although Walter

still holds the title of winemaker emeritus, winemaking is now headed by Michael Cox. Schug Sonoma Coast Chardonnay 2011 is medium straw in color. A fresh nose of clementine and lemongrass yields to clean flavors of ripe stone fruits with a sprinkle of ginger and nutmeg. Schug Heritage Reserve Sonoma Valley Cabernet Sauvignon 2008, composed of 77 percent Cabernet Sauvignon, 14 percent Merlot, 7 percent Malbec, and 2 percent Cabernet Franc, is inky garnet in the glass, with fragrances of blueberry, purple blossoms, and espresso. Succulent berry, chocolate, and spice flavors caress the tongue, lingering through the harmonious finish.

SEBASTIANI

389 Fourth Street East, Sonoma, CA 95476,
(707) 933-3230
www.sebastiani.com

Now part of the Foley Family Wines portfolio, Sebastiani was established in 1904 by Tuscan stonemason Samuele Sebastiani. The winery remained open during Prohibition by making sacramental and medicinal wine, but Samuele also began canning peaches, pears, and nectarines to keep his workers employed. Samuele's son August carried on his father's legacy from 1944 until 1980, and August's daughter Mary Ann oversaw a major winery and hospitality center renovation in 2001. As president and CEO of Sebastiani, Mary Ann led Sebastiani in the direction of small-lot artisanal winemaking and added many cultural programs to the lineup of visitor experiences. She remained on board until the sale and transition to the Foleys in 2008. Winemaking continues under the direction of Mark Lyon, who has been with the winery since 1978. The Sebastiani Winery is open daily for tours and tastings and a variety of seminars and pairing programs. Sebastiani Cherryblock Sonoma Valley Cabernet Sauvignon 2008, composed of 85 percent Cabernet Sauvignon, 9 percent Merlot, 3.5 percent Malbec, 1.5 percent Petit Verdot, and 1 percent Syrah, is deep red violet to the eye, offering aromas of black cherry, blackberry, forest floor, and anise. Flavors of fresh berries and berry confit nimbly mingle with notes of espresso, anisette, and cranberry through the balanced finish. Sebastiani Patrick's Vineyard Carneros Chardonnay 2011 has a rich nose of ripe summer stone fruits and vanilla bean. Flavors of white peach, nectarine, and almond paste meld on the taste buds, accented by a fleshy mouthfeel and tongue-pleasing acidity.

SEGHESIO FAMILY VINEYARDS

700 Grove Street, Healdsburg, CA 95448
(707) 433-3579
www.seghesio.com

After leaving Italy to head to California and work with the Rossi family, Edoardo Seghesio planted his first Alexander Valley Zinfandel vineyard in 1895. Almost 120 years later, his family farms 300 acres of Zinfandel and Italian varietals throughout the Dry Creek, Alexander, and Russian River valleys. Edoardo's great-grandson Ted Seghesio is the head winemaker, and Ted's brother David is in charge of operations. Their uncle Pete is chief grape grower, and their brother-in-law Jim Neumiller manages the vineyards; Jim's son Ned handles grower relations. Today they are a part of the Crimson Wine Group. Seghesio Home Ranch Alexander Valley Zinfandel 2010 is deep violet to the eye. Wild fruits of the wood and light vanilla begin on the nose and cross over to the palate, enhanced by soft cinnamon and toast flavors. Equitable components of tannic structure and acidity work their magic through the velvety finish.

SIDURI WINES

981 Airport Court, Suites E & F,
Santa Rosa, CA 95403,
(707) 578-3882
www.siduri.com

Self-described wine geeks Adam and Dianna Lee have fulfilled their dream of moving to California and making great Pinot Noir from prize vineyards in Sonoma and the Central Coast. The two met while working together at Neiman Marcus in Texas—Dianna in the fine foods department and Adam in wine—and decided to head to California to immerse themselves in the wine industry, starting Siduri in 1994. One night while drinking wine, they heard that Robert Parker was staying in Napa and decided to leave a bottle at his hotel. Parker gave them 90 points in *Wine Advocate*, and Siduri Wines became an "overnight" sensation. Named for the Babylonian goddess who holds the wine of eternal life, Siduri's bottlings consistently rank among the highest-rated Pinot Noirs California has to offer. Adam makes wine alongside cellarmaster and assistant winemaker Ryan Zepaltas. Siduri Russian River Valley Pinot Noir 2011 is garnet in color, with a nose of blackberry, black cherry, and a touch of strawberry. Fruit is most prevalent on the palate, with nice touches of soft chocolate, vanilla, and citrus zest. It is simultaneously powerful and elegant. Siduri Rosella's Vineyard Pinot Noir 2011 is ruby in the glass. A bright nose of cherry and fennel yields to flavors of black cherry, aniseed, and violets in a sophisticated play of tannins and acidity.

SIMI WINERY

16275 Healdsburg Avenue,
Healdsburg, CA 95448,
(800) 746-4880
www.simiwinery.com

Brothers Giuseppe and Pietro Simi produced their first wines in 1876, and 14 years later the first vintage was made at the winery on Healdsburg Avenue that still bears their family name. Both brothers passed away before their time in 1904, and Giuseppe's daughter Isabelle, then 18, took over the operation, which was highly unusual at the time in light of her gender and age. Simi weathered

Prohibition by selling off vineyards and providing wine via pharmacies to people with medical prescriptions, and in 1934, one year after Prohibition's repeal, Isabelle Simi built a tasting room out of a 25,000-gallon wine barrel, positioning it in front of the stone cellars so that it could be seen from the road. Tasting rooms in the United States were a new phenomenon, and Isabelle would flag down passing cars to let travelers from San Francisco know that wine was available for tasting and purchase. She continued to run the business—and the tasting room—until her retirement in 1970, when she sold Simi to grape grower Russell Green. In 1973 Maryann Graf, the first woman to graduate from an American university with a degree in enology, became head winemaker. Graf was succeeded in 1979 by winemaker Zelma Long, who became the president and CEO. LVMH purchased the winery in 1982, and over the next 10 years Simi significantly added to its vineyard holdings in the Alexander and

Russian River valleys. A new hospitality center was added in 1990, replacing Isabelle's wooden tasting room, and in 1999 Simi became part of Constellation Brands' wine empire. Winemaking continues today under the direction of Susan Lueker, who joined Simi in 2000 after sharpening her skills at Kendall-Jackson and Dry Creek Vineyard. Simi makes a wide variety of wines at varying price points, and many of Lueker's favorite bottlings are available at the tasting room only or on the shaded terrace, where oven-fired pizza is served on summer weekends. Simi Russian River Valley Pinot Gris 2011 has a soft nose of citrus fruit, peach, and white flowers. These continue on the palate as well, and the surprisingly full-bodied wine ends with a touch of spice on the clean finish. Simi Alexander Valley Chardonnay 2010 offers fragrances of crème brûlée, ripe peach, and butterscotch. Bright fruit flavors share the stage with toasted brioche and vanilla, encased in a nice viscosity and a luxurious mouthfeel. Simi Alexander Valley Landslide Vineyard Cabernet Sauvignon 2008 is deep garnet to the eye, with aromas of blackberry and lavender. On the palate blackberry and blueberry fruit flavors show restraint amid grippy tannins, giving way to violet and slate notes that persist through the long finish.

SONOMA-CUTRER WINERY

4401 Slusser Road, Windsor, CA 95492,
(707) 528-1181
www.sonomacutrer.com

Sonoma-Cutrer Chardonnay is one of the most recognized brands among American wine consumers, in no small part because of founder Brice Cutrer Jones's commitment to quality from vineyard to bottle. From its founding in 1973 as a grape-growing company to the establishment of a winery focusing on estate-grown Chardonnay through several growth spurts and ownership changes (the current parent company is Brown-Forman) that emphasis has remained the same. Winemaker Mick Schroeter works with estate-grown fruit from six large vineyards in the Russian River Valley, Sonoma Coast, and Chalk Hill appellations to produce Chardonnay and Pinot Noir. The Russian River Ranches Chardonnay can be found in restaurants and wine shops across the country, but some of the smaller-production labels are available only to wine club members. Sonoma-Cutrer Vineyards

Russian River Ranches Sonoma Coast Estate Bottled Chardonnay 2011, medium straw to the eye, has aromas of Granny Smith apple, tropical fruits, and buttered toast. On the tongue apple flavors meld with citrus fruits, vanilla bean, and a nice play of acidity and shale-tinged minerality.

STEPHEN & WALKER TRUST WINERY

243 Healdsburg Avenue, Healdsburg, CA 95448
(707) 431-8749
www.trustwine.com

Owner-winemakers Nancy Walker and Tony Stephen are both UC Davis grads who have held—and continue to hold—various other positions in winemaking, sales, and consulting in the California wine industry. Most of their outside projects are much larger in scale, but their experience and knowledge show through in the handcrafted wines they make from Napa, Sonoma, Monterey, and Mendocino fruit. The number of awards their wines have won seems far outsized to the small amounts produced, but the quality over quantity ethos is clearly at work here. Stephen & Walker Green Valley of Russian River Valley Sauvignon Blanc 2011 is a tropical fruit delight from the first whiff through the bright finish, with lush aromas and flavors of lime, guava, mango, and orange blossom. Stephen & Walker Dry Creek Valley Petite Sirah 2011 is deep and dark in the glass, with tantalizing aromas of mixed-berry pie and vanilla ice cream. Flavors of blackberry, cherry cola, and crème brûlée are backed by nice notes of spice and sumptuous tannins.

STONESTREET

7111 Highway 128, Healdsburg, CA 95448,
(707) 433-9463
www.stonestreetwines.com

Jess Stonestreet Jackson purchased the former Zellerbach Winery in 1989 and renamed it in honor of his family. Stonestreet's Alexander Mountain estate is in the Mayacamas Mountains, high above the Alexander Valley floor. Over 5,000 acres of rugged landscape nurture 800 acres of grapevines, tended by a team headed by Tony Viramontes and Gabriel Valencia. South Africa native Graham Weerts is in charge of winemaking, working mainly with Chardonnay, Sauvignon Blanc, Cabernet Sauvignon, and Merlot for the Mountain Estate and Single Vineyard series. Stonestreet Gravel Bench Alexander Valley Chardonnay 2010 is medium straw in color, exhibiting aromas of apple pie and baking spice. Green apple fills the palate, balanced by soft flavors of toasted nuts and vanilla, all enhanced by pleasant mineral notes. Stonestreet Alexander Mountain Estate Bear Point Cabernet Sauvignon 2009, deep garnet to the eye, exhibits fragrances of black cherry, violet, and orange zest. Flavors of blueberry and cassis play across the tongue, flecked by notes of tobacco and citrus blossom, leading to a smooth and pleasing finish.

STUHLMULLER VINEYARDS

4951 West Soda Rock Lane, Healdsburg, CA 95448,
(707) 431-7745
www.stuhlmullervineyards.com

Roger and Carmen Stuhlmuller acquired their 150-acre Alexander Valley property in 1982 and, along with their son Fritz, built a small artisanal winery in 1996. When they needed more room a few years later, they renovated a historic barn on the property and designed it to accommodate the fermentation of grapes in small batches. Leo Hansen has been the winemaker since 2004, and currently Stuhlmuller Vineyards produces 6,000 cases of wine a year. Stuhmuller Vineyards Alexander Valley Estate Chardonnay 2011 has aromas of tropical fruits and Anjou pears. In the mouth there are flavors of lemon curd, brown baking spices, and toasted hazelnut. The finish is crisp and clean, with a persistence of minerality. Stuhmuller Vineyards Alexander Valley Estate Zinfandel 2010 has heady aromas of black plum, anise, and crystallized violets. In the mouth flavors of black raspberry sorbet, brown spices, and black plum flow seamlessly into the spicy, persistent finish.

SUACCI CARCIERE WINES

PO Box 2317, Sebastopol, CA 95473,
(707) 829-3283
www.suaccicarciere.com

The Suacci and Carciere families have been friends for over 25 years. Both have Italian backgrounds and grandfathers who made homemade wine, so in 2001 they decided to plant a vineyard and sell the grapes. However, fate prevailed in their fifth year, when they decided to keep the grapes and make their own highly acclaimed wine. Suacci Carciere wines are artisanally made by Ryan Zepaltas, a well-respected and sought-after young winemaker. Suacci Carciere Suacci Vineyard Pinot Noir 2009 has aromas of hickory smoke, dried Mediterranean herbs, and red fruit preserves. It is generous in the mouth with delightful fruit flavors and a touch of creaminess. The acidity and tannins are well balanced, and the finish is long and luscious. Suacci Carciere Heintz Vineyard Chardonnay 2009 is medium yellow with aromas of lemon blossom, lemon curd, and a touch of minerality. It is full and rich in the mouth with a crisp finish.

SUNCÉ WINERY

1839 Olivet Road, Santa Rosa, CA 95401,
(707) 526-9463
www.suncewinery.com

Frane and Janae Franicevic purchased a four-acre horse ranch in 1998 and called it Suncé, the name of their newborn daughter. Translated as "sunshine" from Serbo-Croatian, Suncé Winery began planting its vineyard with Pinot Noir and established itself as a "small, ultra-premium winery" producing wine from small lots of rare varieties of grapes. Suncé Malvasia Bianca 2011 has aromas of honeysuckle, freshly cut pear, and green apples. It is surprisingly round in the mouth, with flavors of lemon curd and custard with a crisp, fruity finish. Suncé RRV Cattich Vineyard Zinfandel 2011 has aromas of mixed red berry and blackberry compote and freshly cracked black pepper. It is fruit-forward in the mouth but not overpowering. It finishes with a balanced tannic structure and restrained elegance.

TEN ACRE

9711 West Dry Creek Road,
Healdsburg, CA 95448,
(707) 473-4418
www.tenacrewinery.com

Scott and Lynn Adams laid down roots in the Russian River Valley with the acquisition of their first vineyard in 1995. Within four years they opened Bella Vineyards and Wine Caves in Dry Creek, and in 2008 they established another microwinery specializing in Chardonnay and Pinot Noir from the Russian River Valley and the Sonoma Coast. They named it Ten Acre after the bucolic spread they share with their grapevines and two children. Charlie Chenowith, whose family has been farming in Sonoma for over 150 years, is in charge of the vineyards, and Michael Zardo, whose résumé includes winemaking at Pisoni, is in charge of winemaking. Ten Acre Green Acre Hills Sangiacomo Sonoma Coast Chardonnay 2011, medium straw in the glass, offers aromas of toasted brioche, lemon curd, and citrus blossom. Flavors of guava, apple cobbler, candied lemon rind, and butterscotch carry through the round finish, which is capped by a final burst of acidity. Ten Acre Cummings Vineyard Russian River Valley Pinot Noir 2010 is ruby in color. A bouquet of dark plums and star anise greets the senses, and the palate is treated to a rich wash of black cherry, raspberry, crème brûlée, and gingerbread spice, nicely wrapped in velvety tannins with a splash of acidity.

VALDEZ FAMILY WINERY

113 Mill Street, Healdsburg, CA 95448,
(707) 433-3710
www.valdezfamilywinery.com

The true American dream success story of Ulises Valdez begins with his crossing of the California–Mexico border in 1985 and his work as an undocumented vineyard worker in Sonoma's Dry Creek Valley. After years of experience and earning respect as a qualified vineyard manager in a partnership with Jack Florence Jr., he applied for amnesty with the Immigration Reform and Control Act of 1986 and eventually gained American citizenship in 1996. In 2003 he bought Jack's share in the company and changed the name to Valdez & Sons Vineyard Management Inc. The two continue to work together as Jack now manages the Valdez Family Winery. Valdez Family Winery Ulises Valdez Rockpile Botticelli Vineyard Zinfandel 2009 is opaque garnet in color, with aromas of black plum, black pepper, and black raspberry. It is fruit-forward in the mouth with amazing complexity and mouthfeel. The finish is long and luscious. Valdez Family Winery Ulises Valdez Vineyard Russian River Valley Pinot Noir 2010 is cherry red, with aromas of dried black cherry, red cherry conserves, and Christmas baking spices. It is restrained and elegant in the palate, with great complexity and a persistent finish.

VÉRITÉ

4611 Thomas Road, Healdsburg, CA 95448,
(707) 433-9000
www.veritewines.com

Pierre Seillan first came to Sonoma in 1998 at the invitation of Jess Jackson, who wanted to make California Merlot to rival that of Bordeaux. Seillan has worked with Merlot and Cabernet Franc for over 40 years, first at his family's estate in Armagnac and eventually as the technical director at seven Bordeaux châteaux. Vérité was started in 1998 as a joint effort between Seillan and Jackson Family Wines. The fruit for Vérité wines comes from small vineyard blocks, which Seillan refers to as "micro-crus," in Alexander Valley, Bennett Valley, Chalk Hill, and

Knights Valley. Under Seillan's direction, Vérité produces only three wines: La Muse, which is mostly Merlot; La Joie, which is predominantly Cabernet Sauvignon; and Le Désir, which is Cabernet Franc–based. The list of accolades and perfect scores these wines have received would be mind-boggling to one who has not experienced the sheer pleasure of a vertical tasting of all three dating back to 2002, plus Seillan's first vintage, from 1998, simply called Vérité, which is 90 percent Merlot and 10 percent Cabernet Franc. As we had expected, this highly lauded wine is still fresh and young in the glass, deep garnet to the eye, with just the faintest hint of iron on the rim. Filled with gorgeous fruit flavors and soft tannins, the 1998 tastes of plum, cassis, black cherry, mint, and black pepper. The freshness of this wine is no surprise considering that recent vintages will easily age well for 20 years or more. Vérité La Joie 2009, a blend of 78 percent Cabernet Sauvignon, 9 percent Merlot, 9 percent Cabernet Franc, and 2 percent each Petit Verdot and Malbec, is a truly beautiful wine. Inky cherry in the glass, with a nose of raspberry and dark chocolate, it unfolds on the palate with lush flavors of blackberry, black currants, espresso bean, and shale. Equipped with a strong tannic backbone and startling acidity, it is truly a joy to drink. Vérité La Muse 2009 is composed of 85 percent Merlot, 9 percent Cabernet Franc, 5 percent Malbec, and 1 percent Cabernet Sauvignon. It is deep dark cherry to the eye, offering fragrances of black cherry, anise, and coffee. Luscious flavors of black cherry, blackberry, mocha, and fennel play on the tongue through the rich, persistent finish, backed by a striking note of minerality.

WILLIAMS SELYEM

7227 Westside Road, Healdsburg, CA 95448,
(707) 433-6425
www.williamsselyem.com

Burt Williams and Ed Selyem produced the first of many award-winning vintages of Pinot Noir in 1981, and in 1998 wine club customer number 2,080—John and Kathe Dyson, who also owned Millbrook Winery in New York State and vineyards on California's Central Coast—bought the winery from its founders. Fortunately, Kathe and John had met Burt and

Ed at a wine dinner several years before, and Kathe convinced them to put her directly on the mailing list rather than the lengthy waiting list. Winemaker and general manager Bob Cabral was also a wine club member—customer number 576, to be exact. A fourth-generation California grape grower, he made wine at DeLoach, Kunde, Alderbrook, and Hartford Court before Burt Williams introduced him to John and Kathe in 1998 and recommended that Bob replace him as winemaker. In 2011 *Wine Enthusiast* honored Bob with the Winemaker of the Year Wine Star Award. In 1998 John and Kathe bought the Drake orchard on the Russian River in Guerneville, planting it to various Pinot Noir clones. Williams Selyem Russian River Valley Pinot Noir 2011 is ruby in color. Fragrances of black cherry, vanilla custard, and Turkish delight set the scene for flavors of black and tart cherries, aniseed, birch root, and forest floor. Fruit flavors with light herbal touches endure through the smooth finish.

WOODENHEAD VINTNERS

5700 River Road, Santa Rosa, CA 95401,
(707) 887-2703
www.woodenheadwine.com

Building contractor turned vintner Nikolai Stez started making homemade garage wines

in 1986. He partnered with Zina Bower, who handles the bookkeeping and management side of the business, and together they are responsible for the small-batch delicious wines from Woodenhead Vintners. Their wines have garnered medals and acclaim at the San Francisco Chronicle Wine Competition as well as recommendations from Food & Wine magazine. Woodenhead Russian River Bertoli Zinfandel 2010 has aromas of sweet red and black fruits. There's a touch of salinity and baking spices in the bouquet as well. In the mouth there are flavors of black cherry, black raspberry, and aromatic brown spices, with a whiff of lifted clove just before the long, luscious finish.

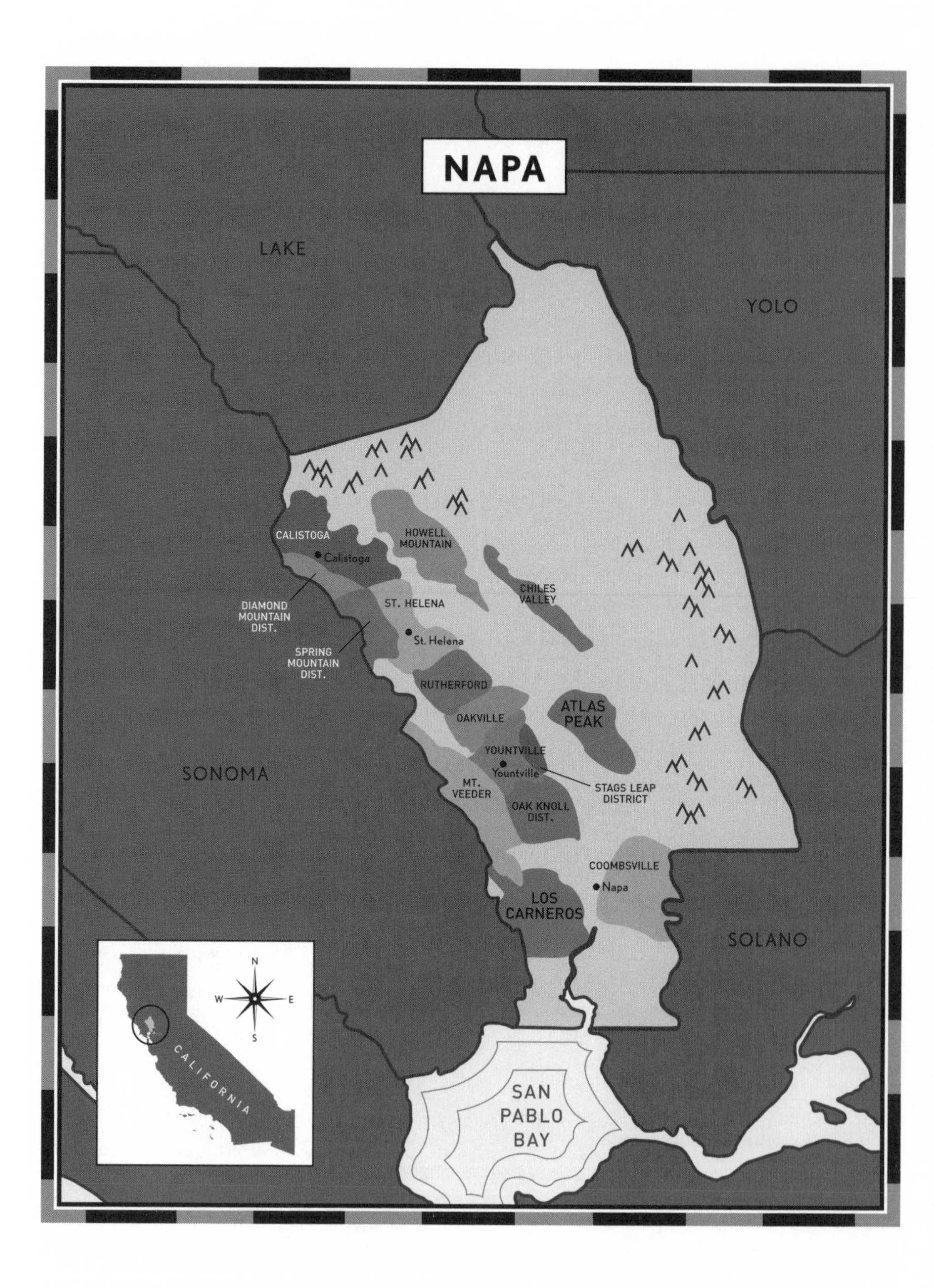
NAPA
LAKE
YOLO
CALISTOGA
Calistoga
HOWELL MOUNTAIN
CHILES VALLEY
DIAMOND MOUNTAIN DIST.
ST. HELENA
St. Helena
SPRING MOUNTAIN DIST.
RUTHERFORD
OAKVILLE
ATLAS PEAK
YOUNTVILLE
Yountville
STAGS LEAP DISTRICT
SONOMA
MT. VEEDER
OAK KNOLL DIST.
COOMBSVILLE
Napa
LOS CARNEROS
SOLANO
SAN PABLO BAY
N
W
E
S
CALIFORNIA

CHAPTER 3

NAPA VALLEY

NAPA VALLEY IS A LITTLE AVA WITH A BIG reputation. Just 30 miles long and 5 miles wide, covering almost the whole of Napa County, it is responsible for only 4 percent of California wine, yet this region has gained world renown in the modern era, squarely placing itself—and the whole state—on the global wine map. The first recognized AVA in California, established in February 1981, Napa Valley has an official status that even predates the surrounding North Coast appellation, which was granted AVA acknowledgment over two years later in October 1983.

Although grape growing here dates back to 1839, when George Calvert Yount, the founder of Yountville, planted the first vineyard in the valley, Napa's preeminence among wine regions emerged in 1976 with the famous Judgment of Paris wine competition. As you may recall, this blind tasting pitted California Chardonnay and Cabernet Sauvignon against their counterparts from Burgundy and Bordeaux and was arranged by British wine merchant Steven Spurrier, who went on to become a well-known wine journalist, author, and educator. When the final denouement was announced, much to the shock of the nine French sommeliers, restaurateurs, winemakers, and winery owners who had tasted and rated the wines, wine from California took top honors in both the white and red categories: Chateau Montelena Chardonnay 1973 and Stag's Leap Wine Cellars Cabernet Sauvignon from the same vintage.

What may be even more shocking to the French is that this AVA covering a mere 225,280 acres, about the same size as Burgundy's Côte d'Or and approximately one-eighth the size of Bordeaux, is home to 45,000 acres of vines whose top five varieties by volume are from not one but both of these esteemed regions: Cabernet Sauvignon, Chardonnay, Merlot, Pinot Noir, and Sauvignon Blanc. Further subdivided into 16 distinct AVAs, Napa Valley is far more diverse than a quick scan of the most prolific grapes would lead you to believe. Over 60 varieties are grown here in some amount and made into wine by 450 wineries, the majority of them family-owned and relatively small.

Napa Valley Cabernet Sauvignon is grown on 19,516 acres, accounting for about one-quarter of all the Cabernet Sauvignon in the state. Next in line is Chardonnay, which blankets 7,165 acres, with significant additional acreage in the Los Carneros AVA, which straddles Napa and Sonoma counties. Merlot, the third most cultivated variety, is grown in 5,975 acres of Napa Valley soil. Pinot Noir, the red transplant from Burgundy, grows on 2,979 acres here, and Sauvignon Blanc covers 2,736 acres in Napa Valley. California's specialty, Zinfandel, is present in the valley, grown on 1,492 acres, as is another variety that seems almost native to the state, Petite Sirah, which graces 845 acres.

Where there is Cabernet Sauvignon and Merlot, the other Bordeaux grapes follow. Cabernet Franc is grown on 1,219 acres, Petit Verdot on 753 acres, and Malbec on 392 acres. Although large proportions of these last three are used in Bordeaux-style or Meritage blends, they often are bottled as single varieties, usually found in tasting rooms and restaurants rather than on wine shop shelves.

Grape growing took off in Napa County in the years following the Gold Rush, especially the 1860s and 1870s, as immigrants from Europe who had come to the United States to seek their fortune turned to the land and planted the same crops they had in the old country. A settler named John Patchett planted vineyards for winemaking in Napa starting in 1860 and hired Prussian immigrant Charles Krug to make wine using a cider press. In 1861 Krug opened his own eponymous winery, which is still in operation, owned today by Peter Mondavi Sr. and his family. Jacob Schram planted what has been called the first hillside vineyard in Napa in 1862, establishing Schramsberg Winery that same year. Another German immigrant, Jacob Beringer, who had worked with Krug, bought land in Napa Valley in 1875 along with his brother Frederick and founded the Beringer Winery. Still in business and owned today by Treasury Wine Estates, Beringer is said to be the oldest continually operating winery in Napa Valley.

By the end of the nineteenth century Napa Valley had a young but thriving winemaking industry. Captain Gustave Niebaum's Inglenook Wine, which is claimed to have been the first Bordeaux-style wine in the United States, took a gold medal at the Paris World's Fair in 1889. In that year there were 140 wineries in Napa, with almost 16,000 acres of planted grapes. Within a few short years phylloxera attacked European rootstock that had been transplanted to Napa Valley, and by 1900 there were only 2,000 acres of grapevines remaining there. The early part of the twentieth century was unkind to the wine industry: before vineyards could be fully restored, the combined effects of World War I, Prohibition, and the Great Depression took their toll on the economy in general and wine in particular, leaving Napa Valley in a state of disrepair.

André Tchelistcheff is one of the people credited with bringing back the vineyards and reputation of Napa Valley after the repeal of Prohibition. George de Latour, the founder of Napa's Beaulieu Vineyards, met Tchelistcheff at the French National Agronomy Institute in 1938 and invited him to come to Napa to become his head winemaker. Tchelistcheff focused his attention on high-quality California Cabernet Sauvignon and is said to have introduced the practice of aging wine in small French oak barrels to California. He also made important advances in the implementation of now-common techniques such as cold fermentation, vineyard frost protection, and malolactic fermentation. In addition, he was instrumental in the development of vineyard sites in Carneros and other California regions. He stayed on at Beaulieu until his retirement in 1973, after which he consulted for a number of high-profile wineries in Napa and Sonoma and throughout the Pacific Northwest. Many prominent winemakers who have been in the business since the 1960s and 1970s list Tchelistcheff among their most important mentors or influences in the wine business.

Robert Mondavi left his family's Charles Krug winery in 1965. In that same year, he and his son Michael established the first large, purpose-built winery in Napa Valley since the start of Prohibition. Mondavi was among the first in California to begin labeling wines with varietal names, such as Cabernet Sauvignon and Chardonnay, as opposed to names of famed European wine regions, such as Burgundy for red wines and Chablis for white, regardless of the grape varieties used in production. During this time American wine drinkers had begun to develop more sophisticated palates, and the fashion in wine changed from sweet to dry and food-friendly. This was the beginning of a new gold rush in Napa, with a growth spurt in the number of new wineries and a meteoric rise in the quality of the wine produced there. By the time Steven Spurrier's France vs. California wine faceoff took place, there were more than fifty wineries in Napa Valley and the scene had been set for its emergence as the premier wine region in the United States.

Bordered to the west by the Mayacamas Mountains, which divide Napa and Sonoma counties, and to the east by the Vaca Mountain Range, which divides Napa and Solano counties, Napa starts out flat in the south and rises in elevation as you head north. The southern end of the valley is cooled by the marine influence of nearby San Pablo Bay, whose estuaries are at sea level. On either side of the valley, in the mountains to the east and west, elevations rise as high as 2,500 feet, and as anyone who has ever bicycled the Silverado Trail can tell you, the valley floor rises almost steadily uphill toward the 4,000-foot Mount St. Helena at its north end. The Napa River runs north to south

through the center of the valley, and Lake Berryessa, a 15-mile-long man-made reservoir, is at the county's eastern edge.

Summers are usually hot and dry, with a minimum of rainfall through the summer growing season. During the day, as hot air in the valley rises, it creates conditions that draw in cool air from the Pacific Ocean, inducing fog that protects the grapes from the rays of the daytime sun. With the cooling influence of San Pablo Bay, the temperature variation from south to north can be as great as 10 to 15 degrees Fahrenheit in summer, and day-to-night temperature variation can be as great as 40 degrees. Napa Valley's sixteen sub-AVAs each provide a variety of soil types, slope, elevation, and orientation that in combination offer subtle influences on the characteristics of finished wine.

Tradition and innovation operate side by side to ensure that the best-quality wines are produced here. While vineyards are tended to and harvested by hand and wine is crafted in diminutive quantities, often measured by the single barrel, viticulturists in Napa Valley were among the first to employ NASA satellite technology to survey vineyard sites to achieve the best possible layout. The University of California, Davis, in neighboring Yolo County maintains a 40-acre experimental vineyard and research facility in Napa Valley's Oakville AVA so that students of enology and viticulture can observe and analyze the effects of wine industry innovation in a natural setting.

The smaller appellations within Napa Valley vary in size from the 2,700-acre Stags Leap District to the 15,000-acre Mount Veeder AVA. Some are named for geographical features, such as Atlas Peak and Howell Mountain, and others are named for the towns they surround, such as Yountville, Oakville, Rutherford, St. Helena, and Calistoga. Downtown Napa, toward the southern end of the valley, features twenty wine tasting rooms, forty hotels and inns, and seventy restaurants, all within walking distance of the revitalized waterfront. The Oxbow Market offers artisanal products, freshly prepared food, local produce, and even an outpost of Gott's Roadside, Napa Valley's hometown burger joint. You can head up the valley on the fast-paced Route 29, but sometimes it's nicer to drive a little more slowly and enjoy the vineyard views on the parallel Silverado Trail. Each of the valley's towns offers its own local style and charm, from Yountville's handful of Michelin-starred restaurants to the spas and mud baths of Calistoga.

ATLAS PEAK AVA

First planted with grapevines in 1870, Atlas Peak was granted AVA status in October 1992. Only 1,500 acres—less than a third of 1 percent of all the cultivated acres in Napa County—are planted with grapes, out of a total area of 11,400 acres. East of Yountville and Oakville and northeast of Napa, Atlas Peak takes its name from the highest peak in the region, which rises to 2,663 feet in altitude, projecting from the Vaca Range. Vineyards in this mountainous AVA vary from 760 to over 2,600 feet and are accessible via only two roads leading from foothills near the valley floor. The shallow, well-drained soils of the region tend to be rocky and volcanic in origin, often with strong tones of red basalt. There are ten wineries and about as many growers in the AVA, and over eighty wineries throughout Napa Valley proudly bottle wine under the Atlas Peak AVA. Although the superstar variety is Cabernet Sauvignon, other reds that do well here are Cabernet Franc, Malbec, Petit Verdot, Sangiovese, Syrah, and Zinfandel. Chardonnay, Sauvignon Blanc, and white Rhône varieties are also cultivated in Atlas Peak.

CALISTOGA AVA

One of Napa Valley's newest AVAs, Calistoga received official status in January 2010. Covering about 4,500 acres in the northwest of Napa Valley, it sits between the Mayacamas Mountains and the Vaca Range. The northernmost AVA in the valley, it is bordered to the south by the St. Helena AVA and to the southwest by the Diamond Mountain AVA. The Howell Mountain AVA is to the east. Unlike most AVAs farther south in Napa Valley, Calistoga has a very small proportion of vineyards planted on the valley floor. Instead, vines are cultivated on hillsides and slopes, with elevations from 300 to 1,200 feet above sea level. Due to its position at the top of the valley, Calistoga enjoys cool Pacific air that moves across Sonoma and enters Napa Valley through gaps in the northwestern hills. Diurnal temperature variation in summer can be close to 60 degrees Fahrenheit, reaching 100 degrees during the day and plummeting into the 40s after the sun sets and cool night air infiltrates the region. As would be expected in an area dominated by hot springs—including the famed geyser Old Faithful—soils are volcanic in nature.

Samuel Brannan, one of Calistoga's founding fathers, purchased 2,000 acres of land here after becoming enamored of the area's hot springs, opening the Indian Springs Resort in 1862. Having been influenced by similar geological formations offering health benefits in Saratoga Springs, New York, Brannan set out to make this town the "Saratoga of California," combining the names to create Calistoga. It is said that wine grapes were first planted here 10 years before the opening of Indian Springs, in 1852. Chateau Montelena was founded here by Alfred L. Tubbs in 1882; current winemaker Bo Barrett and his father, Jim, who passed away in 2013, were the fiercest proponents of the establishment of the Calistoga AVA. Red grapes dominate here, primarily Cabernet Sauvignon, Petite Sirah, and Zinfandel. As everywhere else in Napa Valley, growth is occurring at a prodigious rate: there are close to thirty wineries within the Calistoga AVA at this time, up from just thirteen 25 years ago.

The town of Calistoga retains its small-town feel thanks to the absence of fast-food restaurants and the fact that Highway 29 narrows down to a two-lane road several towns south of here, near Yountville.

CHILES VALLEY AVA

Named for Joseph Ballinger Chiles, who received a Mexican land grant in 1841, Chiles Valley is in the northeast of Napa Valley, east of the Howell Mountain and St. Helena AVAs and the town of St. Helena. Lake Berryessa is due east. This long, narrow AVA in the Vaca Mountain Range is home to vineyards planted at altitudes of 600 to 1,200 feet above sea level. Grapes have been grown here since the arrival of Swiss immigrants in the 1880s, with some vineyards among the AVA's 1,000 planted acres dating back to that era. Granted AVA status in April 1999, Chiles Valley covers a total area of 6,000 acres. Red varieties predominate, primarily Zinfandel, Cabernet Sauvignon, and Cabernet Franc, and there are plantings of Chardonnay and Sauvignon Blanc here as well. As a result of its inland location, Chiles Valley does not receive the cooling effects of the Pacific Ocean, so day-to-night temperature variations are due to elevation rather than maritime influences. There are just seven wineries within its borders.

COOMBSVILLE AVA

The newest AVA in Napa Valley, Coombsville was welcomed to the fold in December 2011. It is in a small valley to the east of downtown Napa and the Napa River and just west of the Wild Horse Valley AVA and the Solano County line. Just south of Atlas Peak, in the foothills of the Vaca Mountains, Coombsville has a footprint of 11,000 acres, on which 1,400 acres of grapes are cultivated. With about forty vineyards and growers in the region, the AVA is known for Cabernet Sauvignon and other Bordeaux reds, which grow in warm hillside vineyards, whereas Chardonnay, Pinot Noir, and Syrah do well in cooler locations. Summer temperatures are moderated by the marine effects of San Pablo Bay. Most vineyards are at elevations between 100 and 500 feet, but some sites rise as high as 1,000 feet above sea level. The volcanic soils here are filled with the detritus of the long-ago eruptions of Mount George.

DIAMOND MOUNTAIN DISTRICT AVA

In the northwestern corner of Napa Valley, the Diamond Mountain District AVA is on the eastern side of the Mayacamas Mountains, southwest of Calistoga and north of the Spring Mountain District AVA. It was established in July 2001, and 500 acres of vines are planted within its 5,000-acre outline, mostly at high elevation. Granular soils with a powdery consistency are the remains of ancient volcanic activity. Vineyards are planted at altitudes of 400 to 2,200 feet. Grapes have been grown here since the early 1860s, when Jacob Schram, founder of Schramsberg, planted his first vines. High vineyard elevations aid in cooling ripening grapes after the sun goes down; this is fortunate because high vineyard elevations are beyond the reach of daytime fog. There are ten wineries within the Diamond Mountain District AVA, and although it is best known for Cabernet Sauvignon and Cabernet Franc, we are seeing more cold-weather whites planted here as well.

HOWELL MOUNTAIN AVA

The first sub-AVA within Napa Valley, Howell Mountain received its formal designation in January 1984. With an overall size of 14,080 acres, Howell Mountain is home to 600 acres of vines and almost fifty wineries. The Howell Mountain AVA is in the northeast of Napa Valley in the Vaca Mountains, east of Calistoga and St. Helena but west of Chiles Valley. Vineyard elevations range from 600 to 2,600 feet, with the majority planted between 1,400 and 2,200 feet, sometimes offering commanding views of St. Helena. Vineyards planted in well-drained volcanic soils sit mainly above the fog line, benefiting from full-day sun that aids in ripening and sugar development. Fortunately, hot days are countered by cool, elevation-derived nights, preserving acid balance in the Cabernet Sauvignon (Howell Mountain's standout variety), Sauvignon Blanc, Merlot, Zinfandel, and Viognier planted here.

Named for Isaac Howell, an early settler who arrived in 1847, Howell Mountain has a history as a grape-growing region that reaches back to the 1880s, when Jean Brun and Jean V. Chaix planted vineyards and opened a winery here. They won a Bronze Medal at the Paris Exhibition of 1889, and their original winery is today the fully renovated home of Ladera Vineyards. In addition to the wineries here, a veritable A-list of wineries elsewhere in Napa Valley purchase fruit from the AVA, bottled with the Howell Mountain designation.

LOS CARNEROS AVA

Also referred to simply as Carneros, *Los Carneros* is Spanish for "the rams," a reference to this wine region's former role as pastureland for grazing sheep. Crossing county borders, it is shared by both Napa and Sonoma counties. Wineries in the eastern portion may be identified as coming from the Napa Valley AVA as well as Carneros, and on the other side of the county line bottles from Carneros may also be labeled with the Sonoma County and Sonoma Valley appellations. Its total surface area is 32,000 acres, of which 8,000 are cultivated with grapes. Twenty-two wineries make their home here, and from the early 1980s onward (the AVA was established in 1983) it has been the American vineyard and winery base of a prominent catalog of European sparkling wine producers, including Moët & Chandon (Chandon), Champagne Taittinger (Domaine Carneros), Freixenet (Gloria Ferrer), Champagne G.H. Mumm (Mumm Napa), and Codorniu (Artesa, previously Codorniu Napa).

Because of its proximity to San Pablo Bay and its east-west orientation (both Napa and Sonoma valleys run north to south) Los Carneros is generally a cold-weather region, although its former title of "coldest" has been rightfully claimed by AVAs farther north and west, in Sonoma County. Both Pinot Noir and Chardonnay have been grown here for many years, although a late-1980s phylloxera outbreak necessitated a major replanting effort. Both of these varieties are made into still and sparkling wines, and they have recently been joined by sizable plantings of Merlot and Syrah.

MOUNT VEEDER AVA

At 15,000 acres in size, Mount Veeder is the largest sub-AVA in Napa Valley, although with almost twenty-five wineries, twenty growers, and 1,000 acres of grapevines the appellation is responsible for only 1.3 percent of Napa Valley's total yearly wine output. On the western edge of the valley, nestled in the Mayacamas Mountains, Mount Veeder was named for Peter Veeder, a German Presbyterian minister who lived here in the 1860s. It is said that Veeder enjoyed hiking among the mountain's soaring evergreens, which cover a good part of the area to this day. It is said that the first wine made from Mount Veeder grapes was in 1864, produced by Captain Stelman Wing. His legacy lives on today in the Wing Canyon Vineyard. The area was home to German immigrants throughout the last two decades of the nineteenth century, and by the beginning of the twentieth century there were twenty vineyards and six wineries on the slopes of Mount Veeder.

After Prohibition the first new wineries in the area were built in the 1950s and 1960s. It is said that the first Petit Verdot in Napa Valley was planted here in 1975, and the first Napa Valley vineyard featuring all five Bordeaux varieties is said to have been planted on Mount Veeder as well. The AVA was established in March 1990.

Planted elevations range from 500 to 2,400 feet above sea level. The highest vineyard in

Napa Valley is here, the Mayacamas Vineyard, at 2,400 feet, as is the winery at the highest altitude, the 2,100-foot-high Sky Vineyard. Most soils are shallow clay seabed soils that offer excellent drainage. Cooled by the breezes of San Pablo Bay and blessed by high elevations, the slopes of Mount Veeder do not suffer from excessive daytime heat, providing for a long, slow ripening season. Cabernet Sauvignon is the preeminent variety, grown in well over half of all planted vineyards and responsible for 64 percent of the AVA's wine production, but almost twenty varieties are grown on the slopes of Mount Veeder. There are considerable plantings of Malbec, Merlot, Cabernet Franc, and Petit Verdot as well as significant acreage of Chardonnay, Syrah, and Viognier.

OAK KNOLL DISTRICT OF NAPA VALLEY AVA

Established in April 2004, the Oak Knoll District of Napa Valley AVA, commonly called Oak Knoll, is home to 3,500 acres of vineyards spread out among 8,300 acres of land on both sides of Route 29. One of the more southern appellations in Napa Valley, Oak Knoll is north of Los Carneros and south of the Yountville AVA, just east of Mount Veeder. Its eastern boundary is the Napa River. Valley floor vineyards are at sea level, with the highest elevations rising to 800 feet. Soils at lower elevations are alluvial in nature, primarily gravel and loam, whereas coarse volcanic soils are present at higher elevations in the western portion of the AVA.

Nearby San Pablo Bay provides Oak Knoll with cool marine air and early morning fog that provide a counterpoint to the heat of summer days. Cabernet Sauvignon is the champion variety of the region both in acreage planted and in reputation, although Merlot, Chardonnay, Pinot Noir, Sauvignon Blanc, and Riesling also do well here. A dozen wineries call the Oak Knoll District home, but a good deal of fruit from here adds the finishing touch to many a bottle of Napa Valley AVA wine.

OAKVILLE AVA

The most densely planted of any Napa Valley appellation, Oakville's 5,760 acres of land play host to 5,000 acres of grapevines. Although real estate prices are stratospheric in the 94562 ZIP Code, any development is purely in the form of winery expansion and vineyard upgrades. As of the most recent census, Oakville's population is 71 people—a number that soars daily as wine-loving tourists make their way up Route 29 and the Silverado Trail to visit some of the country's most esteemed wineries and hallowed vineyards.

North of the town of Yountville and south of Rutherford, Oakville spans the breadth of the valley floor from the Mayacamas Mountains in the west to the Vaca Range in the east. Vineyards in the center of the valley rest at sea level, while those in the hilly edges of the AVA can rise to altitudes of 500 feet. The first vineyard in Oakville was planted by H.W. Crabb in 1868. Crabb dubbed his vineyard *To Kalon*, which is Greek for "most beautiful," and within 10 years he had 130 acres of vines on 240 acres of land. This vineyard is now owned in part by Robert Mondavi Winery—founded by another Oakville pioneer almost 100 years after Crabb's first cuttings took root—and Andy Beckstoffer, who bought the remaining portion of the vineyard from his former employer, Heublein, in 1973. UC Davis's Oakville Experimental Vineyard, a 40-acre training ground for winemakers and viticulturists of the future, is also positioned in this famed vineyard.

Established in August 1993, Oakville has two main soil types. The flatter portion in the center of the AVA has a mix of sandy loam and clay, offering good drainage, while vineyards to the east and west, at a higher elevation, are planted in sedimentary sand and gravel, which offers even better drainage. Daytime hours are hot through the growing season, but breezes and fog that are strong enough to get farther north than Yountville temper the heat of the sun in the early and late parts of the day. There are forty wineries here and a total of sixty growers, and Cabernet Sauvignon, the backbone of Napa Valley, reigns here at its physical core. Some of the most revered wineries in the world are situated here or use Oakville fruit for big-ticket Cabernet Sauvignon or Bordeaux-style blends whose extravagant prices can be justified by the high ratings they have received from wine critics and by the small quantities produced. In addition to Cabernet Sauvignon, Oakville is known for Sauvignon Blanc and Chardonnay and for other Bordeaux reds, especially Merlot and Cabernet Franc.

RUTHERFORD AVA

Situated between St. Helena to the north and Oakville to the south, Rutherford has a total area of 6,840 acres, 3,518 of which are planted to grapevines. Of those, 71 percent are planted with Cabernet Sauvignon. Red grapes lead the pack here; trailing behind Cabernet Sauvignon's 2,484 acres are 295 acres of Merlot and 70 acres of Cabernet Franc, but white varieties hold their own in Rutherford. Three hundred five acres are planted with Sauvignon Blanc, while Chardonnay holds court on 105 acres of Rutherford soil. Vineyards are at elevations of 172 feet in the center of the valley floor up to 500 feet in the east and west, nearer the Vaca Range and Mayacamas Mountains. Rutherford boasts forty-eight wineries and seventy-seven vineyard owners. The oldest winery in the region, Inglenook, now owned by filmmaker Francis Ford Coppola, was founded in

1879, and the oldest continuously bonded winery in Rutherford, Beaulieu Vineyard, opened its doors in 1900.

George Yount, the founder of Yountville, is credited with planting the first vineyard in Napa County. In 1864 his granddaughter Elizabeth married Thomas Rutherford, and Yount gave the couple 1,040 acres of land at the northern end of his ranch. Carrying on a Napa Valley tradition started by his wife's grandfather, Rutherford planted vines and built a reputation as a producer and grower of top-notch wines, expanding his vineyard holdings through 1880. In the same period Captain Gustave Niebaum purchased several plots of land around Rutherford Station, and in 1887 he began construction on his Inglenook winery. Frenchman George de Latour founded Beaulieu Winery in Rutherford in 1900, and he persevered through Prohibition by producing sacramental wine for the Catholic Church. Although many other wineries shut their doors and vineyards lay fallow during the long period of forced temperance in the United States, de Latour is credited with bringing back Rutherford and all of Napa Valley when he hired André Tchelistcheff in 1938. The Russian émigré set his sights on Cabernet Sauvignon and homed in on the best spots for planting this variety and others, changing the direction of winemaking here for the foreseeable future. Tchelistcheff's contemporary, John Daniel Jr., the great-nephew and heir to Niebaum's Inglenook estate, is also considered one of the fathers of Rutherford Cabernet Sauvignon. The AVA received recognition by the TTB in August 1993.

As a result of Rutherford's position at the widest point of Napa Valley, its grapes spend a great portion of their days in the sun, without shade thrown by mountain peaks. Diurnal temperature variations are swift to set in; temperatures may drop 12 degrees Fahrenheit within moments of the sun setting beyond the Mayacamas Mountains and continue to drop as the night wears on. Deep soils with good drainage are alluvial in formation, with gravel, sand, and loam components. Try as one might, the taste of Rutherford dust may not be immediately apparent in even the finest wines of the appellation. When André Tchelistcheff said, "It takes Rutherford dust to grow great Cabernet," he was talking about that rare essence of *terroir* and climate that produces exceptional wine as opposed to an attribute of wine that can be discerned by the human palate.

ST. HELENA AVA

Shaped like a pear, St. Helena is bounded to the south by Rutherford and to the north by Calistoga, with the Spring Mountain AVA and the Mayacamas Mountains running along its western border. St. Helena achieved AVA status in October 1995, but its winemaking past extends back to 1861 and the founding of Charles Krug's winery. By 1880 there were more than a hundred people producing wine in St. Helena. Other wineries surviving from that era are Spottswoode Estate, founded in 1882 and originally called Kraft Winery; Freemark Abbey, which was established under another name in 1886; and Beringer Vineyards, which was established the same year. Today there are fifty wineries and thirty growers in the St. Helena AVA, and just shy of 1,000 acres of grapes are cultivated within its 9,060-acre silhouette. St. Helena became an AVA in October 1995.

Named for Mount St. Helena, one of whose peaks is the highest point in Napa County (the tallest peak, at 4,342 feet, is on the Sonoma side of the mountain), St. Helena's vineyards are at elevations of 100 to 700 feet. Summer days are mostly warm, and temperatures can approach 100 degrees Fahrenheit on many days. Any effects from the Pacific Ocean are minimized by the Mayacamas Mountains to the west, as are obvious benefits from San Pablo Bay at the southern end of the valley. Soils on the western side of the AVA and across the center of the valley are sedimentary, with compositions of gravel and clay, whereas those on the east side, toward the Vaca Range, are volcanic in nature. Cabernet Sauvignon is the number one variety grown here, followed by Sauvignon Blanc, Merlot, and Cabernet Franc.

The small city of St. Helena, with a population of 6,000, most of whom work in the overlapping worlds of wine and food, is home to some of the finest restaurants and cafés in the valley. The imposing West Coast campus of the Culinary Institute of America is based here, as is the famed Meadowood Resort, whose restaurant earned three Michelin stars.

SPRING MOUNTAIN DISTRICT AVA

Spring Mountain is named for the many small springs and streams that run through its terrain—which also receives more rainfall than any other area in Napa Valley—rather than a particular mountain peak. Situated south of the Diamond Mountain AVA and northwest of St. Helena, the Spring Mountain AVA is on the west side of the Napa Valley, in the Mayacamas Mountains, bordering Sonoma County. Vineyard altitudes begin at 600 feet and climb to 2,600 feet, and maritime breezes from the Pacific Ocean cross a low-lying ridge in the Mayacamas and keep Spring Mountain cooler than would otherwise be expected during the hours of daylight. However, because most vineyards are higher than the fog line, mornings on the east-facing slopes can be quite warm in relation to the cold nights. Soils are alluvial at lower elevations and closest to the valley floor, transitioning to sedimentary heading westward and moving upward, with volcanic soils in the higher, more westerly vineyards.

The first recorded grape growing occurred here in 1874, when Charles Lemme planted his 25-acre La Perla Vineyard. Frederick and Jacob Beringer, founders of their namesake winery in nearby St. Helena, planted vines on Spring Mountain in the mid-1880s, and a few years after that a Frenchman with the romantic name Fortune Chevalier built a winery and began growing vines on 25 acres of land. Around the same time San Francisco businessman Tiburcio Parrott started a vineyard that he called Miravalle. Parrott's wines took first place at the San Francisco Midwinter Fair in 1894 and a gold medal at the World's Fair of 1896 in Berlin. Today three of these original vineyards—Miravalle, La Perla, and Chevalier—are part of Spring Mountain Vineyard.

Among its 8,600 acres of mountainous territory, Spring Mountain has 1,000 acres planted to vineyards. There are thirty wineries here, and the most frequently planted variety is Cabernet Sauvignon, followed by Chardonnay, Merlot, and Riesling. Spring Mountain District entered the pantheon of Napa Valley AVAs in June 1993.

STAGS LEAP DISTRICT AVA

Stags Leap—the AVA—has no apostrophe in its name, as opposed to the two wineries within its boundaries with very similar monikers except for the side of the "s" on which the apostrophe is placed. Home to twenty wineries and 850 acres of grapevines, the Stags Leap District AVA is 2,700 acres in size and is due east of Yountville and west of Atlas Peak. Bordered to the east by the Stags Leap Palisades, named for an agile stag that cavorted across mountain peaks, frustrating the huntsmen who would have made him their prey, Stags Leap is much kinder to grape farmers than to native hunter-gatherers. Its western border is the Napa River, where vineyards are at or near sea level, rising to 500 feet as they head eastward.

Grapes have been grown here since the middle of the nineteenth century, and the area's first winery, Occidental Winery (now Regusci Winery), was built in 1878. The first winery with the Stags' Leap name was founded in 1893 by Horace Chase, and it is owned today by Treasury Wine Estates. By the end of the nineteenth century, Stags' Leap Winery alone was bottling 40,000 gallons of wine a year, before phylloxera and Prohibition took their toll on the region and the whole of the Napa Valley. Fast-forward to the modern era, whose inauguration in Stags Leap occurred when Nathan Fay planted 70 acres of Cabernet Sauvignon near the Silverado Trail. Fast-forward 15 more years to 1976, when a Stag's Leap Wine Cellars Cabernet Sauvignon from 1973 came in first place at the Judgment of Paris wine tasting, catapulting the region's reputation into the stratosphere with a single bottle. AVA status came 13 years later, in February 1989.

Stags Leap is planted with mostly red Bordeaux varieties, with the district's largest plantings being Cabernet Sauvignon and Merlot, followed by Sauvignon Blanc. Chardonnay and Sangiovese are grown as well.

WILD HORSE VALLEY AVA

The small Wild Horse Valley AVA consists of 3,300 acres—with only 40 acres of grapes—wedged between Coombsville to the west and Solano County Green Valley to the east. Elevations range from 400 to 1,500 feet, and soils are volcanic with red pigmentation, which is typical of basalt. Wild Horse Valley AVA is home to one winery; its best varieties to date are Cabernet Sauvignon and Sangiovese, which benefit from hot days tempered by the cooling effects from nearby Suisun Bay and San Pablo Bay. It was granted AVA status in December 1988.

YOUNTVILLE AVA

Originally called Yount Mill, Yountville is named for George Calvert Yount, who planted the first commercial vineyard in Napa Valley in 1836. Today "downtown" Yountville boasts a population of about 3,000 and four Michelin-starred restaurants; it is said to have the highest ratio of Michelin stars per square mile of any town or city in the world. Yountville achieved AVA recognition in May 1999, and its 8,260 acres are blessed with 4,000 acres of grapevines and fifteen wineries. The Yountville AVA is north of the Oak Knoll District and south of Oakville, with Stags Leap to the east and Mount Veeder to the west.

The lowest-lying of any appellation in Napa County, Yountville has vineyards that start at 20 feet above sea level and rise to a whopping 200 feet in elevation. Soils are volcanic in nature near the AVA's eastern border with ancient marine deposits; heading west, soils are both alluvial and sedimentary, with areas of sandy loam, gravel-based loam, and clay. San Pablo Bay is the source of cool currents of air that move northward throughout the day, stalling at the heavily forested 450-foot hill called the Yountville Mounts and then lingering over sun-drenched vineyards. Cabernet Sauvignon, Merlot, and Cabernet Franc are the three leading varieties grown in the Yountville AVA in terms of both acreage and renown. Malbec and Petit Verdot are cultivated here as well, as are Zinfandel, Syrah, Petite Sirah, Chardonnay, and Sauvignon Blanc.

THE WINERIES

ACACIA VINEYARDS

2750 Las Amigas Road,
Napa, CA 94559,
(707) 226-9991
www.acaciavineyard.com

Started in 1979 by Mike Richmond and Larry Brooks, Acacia was one of the first California wineries to designate its Pinot Noir by vineyard. Currently, the estate consists of 150 acres planted with Chardonnay and Pinot Noir vines. Senior winemaker Matthew Glynn's experience in California as well as New Zealand and France certainly influences the characteristic style of Acacia's wines. Acacia Vineyard Chardonnay Carneros 2009 is straw colored in the glass, with aromas of freesia and Granny Smith apple. In the mouth it is supple with nuanced flavors of caramelized apples and toasted cashews and has a crisp, clean finish. Acacia Vineyard Estate Pinot Noir Carneros Lone Tree Vineyard 2009 is cherry colored, with notes of cherry pie and lifted purple flowers in the bouquet. Full and round in the mouth, with flavors of ripe sour cherry and cherry jam, this wine has a luxurious finish.

ANCIEN

PO Box 10667, Napa, CA 94581,
(707) 255-3908
www.ancienwines.com

Ken Bernards caught the wine bug in 1986 when he worked his first harvest in Oregon and then went on to work at Truchard Vineyards from 1993 to 1997. In 1998 he began making Pinot Noir, Chardonnay, and Pinot Gris under his own Ancien label. Ken's experimental style has taken him around the world and even prompted him to import whole grapes from France and vinify them back home in California. Ancien has long-term contracts with ten family-owned vineyards in eight appellations, including Morey St. Denis in Burgundy. Ancien Carneros Sangiacomo Vineyard Pinot Gris 2011 is pale straw colored, with aromas of tropical fruits, river rock, and sweet almond blossoms. In the mouth it is bright and rich, with pronounced citrus flavors and a clean lingering finish. Ancien Sta. Rita Hills Fiddlestix Vineyard Pinot Noir 2010 has notes of orange zest, lemon blossom, and ripe black cherry in the bouquet. On the palate the black cherry comes forward with spicy elements, including cherry coke and chewing tobacco. The finish is bright, refreshing, and elegant.

ANDERSON'S CONN FAMILY VINEYARDS

680 Rossi Road, St. Helena, CA 94574,
(707) 963-8600
www.connvalleyvineyards.com

The Anderson family has owned and operated Anderson Conn Family Vineyards since 1983. Their Conn Valley estate consists of 40 acres just south of Howell Mountain. They are well known for their Bordeaux-style blends as well as crisp, clean Chardonnay that does not undergo malolactic fermentation. Conn Valley Vineyards Napa Valley Chardonnay 2008 is straw yellow, with aromas of white stone fruits and fresh pineapple. It has a pleasant level of acidity, great minerality, and a touch of salinity in the finish. Conn Creek Napa Valley St. Helena Holystone Vineyard Cabernet Sauvignon 2008 has aromas of cassis and red plums. In the mouth the fruit flavors are supported by a nice oak frame with flavors of dried herbs and dark cocoa powder in the finish. Conn Creek Napa Valley Anthology 2009 is a blend of 51 percent Cabernet Sauvignon, 16 percent Malbec, 15 percent Merlot, 10 percent Cabernet Franc, and 8 percent Petit Verdot. It is dark garnet colored with notes of blueberry pie, black raspberry, and anise in the complex bouquet. It has flavors of dark berries and a touch of creamy vanilla in the balanced tannic finish.

ANTICA NAPA VALLEY

3700 Soda Canyon Road,
Napa, CA 94558,
(707) 265-8866
www.anticanapavalley.com

Italy's Piero Antinori first visited Napa Valley in 1966 and returned 20 years later as a part owner in a joint venture with France's Bollinger and England's Whitbread companies. In 1993 Piero bought out his partners' shares and took full ownership of the estate. In 2006 he named the estate Antica, which is a combination of "Anti" from Antinori and "ca" for California. The Antinori family also likes to point out that *antica* is the Italian word for "ancient," and the name also symbolizes their long-term commitment to making fine wines in the Napa Valley. Antica Napa Valley Chardonnay 2011 is straw colored, with notes of tropical and stone fruits in the bouquet. In the mouth it is rich and balanced with tastes of pear and citrus blossoms. It has a long, elegant finish. Antica Napa Valley Pinot Noir 2010 is ruby red, with aromas of strawberry preserves and fruits of the wood. On the palate there is a touch of freshly ground black pepper and baking spices underlying the rich fruit flavors. There's a bright splash of citrus on the post palate with a long-lasting finish.

ARAUJO ESTATE

2155 Pickett Road,
Calistoga, CA 94515,
(707) 942-6061
www.araujoestatewines.com

Situated in the northeastern corner of Napa Valley, Araujo Estate is composed of 38 acres of the famed Eislele Vineyard that was established well over 120 years ago. In 1964 the vineyard was replanted with Cabernet Sauvignon, and since that time it has been renowned for producing excellent fruit. Bart and Daphne Araujo took over stewardship in 1990, establishing a tradition of producing excellent wines; they sold the estate to the Pinault family of Bordeaux's Château Latour in 2013. International wine consultant Michel Rolland has been part of the team since 2000. Araujo produces wonderful estate-grown wines: Eisele Vineyard Cabernet Sauvignon, Eisele Vineyard Syrah, Eisele Vineyard Sauvignon Blanc, and Eisele Vineyard Viognier. Araujo Altagracia is produced from estate-grown grapes as well as grapes sourced from neighboring vineyards. Araujo Estate Eisele Vineyard Napa Valley Cabernet Sauvignon 2009 has a rich garnet color, with aromas of purple flowers, Mediterranean spices, dark cherry, and black raspberry. It is luscious on the palate with flavors of sweet stone fruits and a long, luxurious finish. Araujo Estate Eisele Vineyard Napa Valley Syrah 2009 is inky purple, with notes of smoked meats, pencil lead, and strawberry confit. In the mouth the complex flavors evolve to include Asian spice, dried ginger, and bitter chocolate. The tannins are fine and elegant, and the finish is long and lush.

ARIETTA

3468 Silverado Trail,
St. Helena, CA 94574,
(707) 963-5918
www.ariettawine.com

Noted wine auctioneer Fritz Hatton added the title of vintner to his vast repertoire in 1998. He is well known for organizing some of the country's largest wine auctions, including those for Christie's, Zachys, and the Napa Valley Vintners. He and his wife, Caren, initially partnered with John and Maggy Kongsgaard and subsequently assumed sole ownership in 2005. Current winemaker Andy Erickson has been with them since that time. All the wines are named to reflect Fritz and Caren's passion for music. The Arietta portfolio includes four red wines—Quartet, Cabernet Sauvignon, Variation One, and H Block Hudson—as well as one white wine, On The White Keys. Arietta On The White Keys 2011 is a blend of 79 percent Sauvignon Blanc and 21 percent Sémillon. It is pale straw in color, with aromas of citrus blossoms, Ruby Red grapefruit zest, and lemon flan. It is generous in the mouth with flavors of caramelized pineapple, tropical fruits, and a lovely level of pleasant acidity. The finish is clean and balanced and keeps inviting you in for another sip. Arietta Quartet 2010 is composed of 50 percent Cabernet Sauvignon, 29 percent Merlot, 19 percent Cabernet Franc, and 2 percent Petit Verdot. It is garnet, with aromas of black currant, black plum, and Mediterranean herbs. It is juicy on the palate with ripe fruit notes, dried sage, restrained minerality, and supple tannins. The finish is long, luxurious, and elegant.

ARTESA VINEYARDS & WINERY

1345 Henry Road, Napa, CA 94559,
(707) 224-1668
www.artesawinery.com

Artesa began its life in Napa Valley as Codorniu Napa in 1991 with the purpose of making quality sparkling California wine utilizing the Champenoise method. The owners, the Ravento family from Spain, officially changed the name to Artesa Vineyards & Winery in 1997. Mark Beringer, a fifth-generation Napa winemaker and great-great-grandson of Jacob Beringer, is the head winemaker. He is making some wonderful wines from French varieties such as Cabernet Sauvignon, Merlot, Chardonnay, Pinot Noir, Pinot Blanc, and Cabernet Franc as well as limited-release wines from Spanish varieties that include Albariño and Tempranillo. Artesa Vineyards & Winery Artisan Series Cabernet Sauvignon 2009 is composed of 93 percent Cabernet Sauvignon, 4 percent Merlot, and 3 percent Petit Verdot and is garnet in color. It has aromas of black plums, black currants, cigar box, and a touch of crème brûlée. The fruit flavors open up on the palate, and the firm tannic structure leads the way to a persistent finish. Artesa Vineyards & Winery Carneros Pinot Noir 2009 is cherry colored in the glass, with notes of fresh red cherry, rose hips, and dried black cherry in the bouquet. The fruit expression is lovely on the palate, with a pleasant acidic finish.

AUGUST BRIGGS WINERY

1307 Lincoln Avenue, Calistoga, CA 94515,
(707) 942-4912
www.augustbriggswines.com

This winery was founded in 1995 by August "Joe" Briggs, who used his experience as a consulting winemaker to source some of the best grapes in Napa Valley to make his small-batch artisanal wines. His wife, Sally, and he gave control of the winery to their nephew and co-winemaker Jesse Inman as well as other longtime employees in 2011, making it an employee-owned winery. The team also makes delicious boutique wines for the race car driver Jeff Gordon. August Briggs Carneros Leveroni Vineyard Chardonnay 2010 is bright straw yellow, with aromas of caramelized pineapple, citrus blossom, and white stone fruits. It is full bodied in the mouth, with flavors of apple, melon, and creamy lemon curd. There is a touch of minerality, making this a nice wine to pair with delicate cuisine. August Briggs Napa Valley Old Vines Zinfandel 2009 is garnet purple, with notes of black cherry, black plum, and cigar box in the bouquet. In the mouth the fruit flavors are accentuated by flavors of espresso bean and chocolate with a well-balanced tannic finish.

B CELLARS

400 Silverado Trail, Calistoga, CA 94515,
(707) 709-8787
www.bcellars.com

Founded in 2003 by Jim Borsack and Duffy Keys, B Cellars wines get consistent accolades and praise from prominent wine journalists. The "B" in the name refers to the wine term "Brix," which is a nod to the wine geek in all of us. Winemaking is under the direction of Kirk Venge, who was named "One of the Top 20 New Winemakers in the World" in 2005 by *Food & Wine* magazine. B Cellars Caldwell's Kreuzer Canyon Syrah 2008 is deep purple, with aromas of black plums and blueberry in the nose. On the palate flavors of black raspberry and black currant are delightful before the long fruit-filled finish. B Cellars Blend 23 2011 is a full-bodied white composed of 51 percent Chardonnay, 37 percent Sauvignon Blanc, and 12 percent Viognier. It is medium yellow in the glass, and the nose exhibits wet river rock, pineapple, white citrus flowers, and a touch of beeswax. In the mouth it is full and balanced with a crisp finish and flavors of lemon curd and floral blossoms.

BACIO DIVINO CELLARS

PO Box 131, Rutherford, CA 94573,
(707) 942-8101
www.baciodivino.com

Canadian Claus Janzen began his love affair with wine while working during ski season in Switzerland's Berner Oberland. After moving his family to Napa from Winnipeg, he made his first vintage of Bacio Divino Sangiovese in 1993. Claus, along with his wife, Diane; his son Kyle; winemaker Kirk Venge; and vineyard manager David Bartolucci, make delicious wines together under five labels: Bacio Divino, Pazzo, Vagabond, Janzen, and Lucie. Janzen Beckstoffer Missouri Hopper Vineyard Napa Valley Cabernet Sauvignon 2008 is dark garnet, with aromas of ripe black cherries, black currants, and cherry vanilla. It is smooth in the mouth with an elegant structure and fine tannins.

BARNETT VINEYARDS

4070 Spring Mountain Road,
St. Helena, CA 94574,
(707) 963-7075
www.barnettvineyards.com

Hal and Fiona Barnett produced 100 cases of wine in 1989 after purchasing this property in 1983. Today their total production is around 6,000 cases, with about half of that dedicated to quality Cabernet Sauvignon. They also produce small amounts of single-vineyard Chardonnay, Pinot Noir, and Merlot with fruit sourced from other appellations. The estate vineyards grow Cabernet Sauvignon, Cabernet Franc, and Merlot and are completely farmed by hand because of the steep grades at the top of Spring Mountain. Barnett Vineyards Spring Mountain Cabernet Sauvignon 2010 is a blend of 89 percent Cabernet Sauvignon, 8 percent Cabernet Franc, and 3 percent Petit Verdot. It is deep purple in the glass, with prevalent aromas of black currants and black plums and underlying notes of spicy anise and perfumed talc powder. It's big in the mouth with balanced minerality and a persistent finish. Barnett Vineyards Rattlesnake Hill Cabernet

Sauvignon 2010 is made from 100 percent estate-sourced Cabernet Sauvignon. It has rich notes of black fruits, forest floor, and baking spices in the bouquet. In the mouth the fruit flavors open up nicely before a silky finish. Drink it now or hold it for 10 to 15 years, if you have the patience.

BENESSERE VINEYARDS

1010 Big Tree Road, St. Helena, CA 94574,
(707) 963-5853
www.benesserevineyards.com

The Benish family purchased this property in 1994 with an eye to making Italian-style wines in the Napa Valley. The estate plantings include Zinfandel, Syrah, Merlot, Cabernet Sauvignon, Sangiovese, Moscato di Canelli, and Sagrantino. Grapes sourced from neighbors are used in Benessere's Aglianico and Pinot Grigio. Winemaking is directed by Leo Martinez, along with Italian wine consultant Alberto Antonini. Benessere Napa Valley Carneros Pinot Grigio 2011 is pale straw colored, with aromas of citrus blossom and wet river stones. Light and crisp in the mouth, it's perfect on its own or with fresh seafood. Benessere Napa Valley Sagrantino 2009 is ruby to garnet red in the glass, with notes of black plums, cassis, and black raspberries. There's a touch of purple flowers on the palate, followed by an explosion of dark fruits and balanced tannins.

BERINGER

2000 Main Street, St. Helena, CA 94574,
(707) 967-4412
www.beringer.com

Jacob Beringer's brother Frederick emigrated to New York from Mainz, Germany, and wrote letters to his younger brother detailing the exciting opportunities in the New World. Finally succumbing to his older brother's wishes, Jacob crossed the Atlantic in 1868. Not impressed with New York City, Jacob continued west and ended up in the Napa Valley in 1870, and Frederick followed suit. Both brothers bought land in 1875 and founded Beringer Winery in 1876. Frederick built a replica of his family home, and today the seventeen-room Rhine House mansion is home to Beringer's reserve and library tastings. Jacob's house, the Hudson House, is home to the Beringer Vineyards Culinary Arts Center. The estate was listed on the National Register of Historic Places and is the oldest continuously operating winery in the Napa Valley. Laurie Hook is the current winemaker, and Ed Sbragia enjoys his status as winemaker emeritus. Beringer Napa Valley Private Reserve Chardonnay 2011 is straw colored, with aromas of caramelized pineapple, toasted almonds, and citrus blossoms. It is full-bodied and creamy in the mouth, with a pleasant splash of acidity on the finish. Beringer Napa Valley Private Reserve Cabernet Sauvignon 2009 has top notes of mocha, cigar box, and pencil lead over heady aromas of rich, ripe dark fruits. It is elegant yet restrained in the mouth with well-structured tannins and a luscious finish.

BLACKBIRD VINEYARDS

1330 Oak Knoll Avenue, Napa, CA 94558,
(707) 252-4444
www.blackbirdvineyards.com

Before Michael Polenske purchased Blackbird Vineyards and began making wine under his own label, many of the Merlot grapes grown here were used in making award-winning wines for other wineries. His first bottling in 2003 was extremely well received, and today Blackbird continues to garner praise from a variety of wine experts. Blackbird Vineyards Arise 2010 is a blend of 61 percent Merlot, 20 percent Cabernet Sauvignon, and 19 percent Cabernet Franc from the Oak Knoll District. It is aged in French oak for 21 months and is a deep garnet in color. Aromas of forest floor, ripe black cherry, and black plum give way to a luscious fruit-filled expression in the mouth and a lingering finish. Blackbird Vineyards Arriviste Rosé 2011 is pearlescent pink in the glass, with aromas of citrus blossom and wild strawberries. In the mouth it is clean and refreshing with pronounced flavors of freshly picked summer fruits.

BLACK STALLION WINERY

4089 Silverado Trail, Napa, CA 94558,
(707) 253-1400
www.blackstallionwinery.com

Named because it sits on the property of the historic Silverado Horseman's Center, Black Stallion winery came under the stewardship of the Indelicato Family in 2010. Visitors to the winery can see the thirty-six original horse stalls and witness wine production in the former indoor horse track. The estate vineyards that surround the winery are planted to three different Cabernet Sauvignon clones, and visitors can taste Black Stallion wines at the large round tasting bar or sit on the landscaped outdoor terrace and admire the view. Black Stallion Winery Bucephalus Red Blend 2009 is garnet red, with aromas of black currant, black plum, and black raspberry. It is full-bodied in the mouth, with flavors of deep, dark ripe fruits and a touch of vanilla in the long, elegant finish. Black Stallion Winery Napa Valley Merlot 2010 has aromas of purple flowers, candied violets, and a touch of Christmas baking spices. On the palate flavors of black plum, ripe red cherries, and dark chocolate lead into a silky smooth finish.

BOND ESTATES

PO Box 426, Oakville, CA 94562,
(707) 944-9445
www.bondestates.com

The team at Bond Estates crafts wines from five Napa Valley vineyards they consider "Grand Crus": Melbury, Quella, St. Eden, Vecina, and Pluribus. The company feels that its experience working with more than sixty vineyards over the years has enabled it to choose these five plots ranging in size from 7 to 11 acres that share a covenant, commitment, and bond to produce the best expression of *terroir* in winemaking. Bond Estate wines are highly coveted by wine enthusiasts, collectors, and critics alike. The team consists of proprietor H. William Harlan of Harlan Estates, winemaker Cory Empting, vineyard manager Mary Maher, and Robert Levy, director of winegrowing. Bond Melbury Napa

Valley 2008 is purple garnet, with aromas of freshly picked black cherries, red plums, red cherries, cigar box, and forest floor. It is rich and elegant in the mouth, with fruit flavors accented by a touch of violet. The finish is long and luscious. Bond Vecina Napa Valley 2008 is inky purple with aromas of lifted peppermint, graphite, and red fruits. It is big in the mouth with nice balanced levels of fruit and minerality. Although both of these wines are drinking nicely right now, lay them down a few years for added pleasure.

BOUCHAINE VINEYARD

1075 Buchli Station Road, Napa, CA 94559,
(707) 252-9065
www.bouchaine.com

Gerret and Tatiana Copeland purchased what is today called Bouchaine Vineyards from the Beringer Brothers, but the history of this property goes back to the 1800s, when early settler Boon Fly first planted vines. Italian immigrant Johnny Garetto purchased the property in 1927 and opened what is considered to be the area's first tasting room before selling to Beringer in 1951. When the Copelands took over the reins in 1981, they performed extensive renovations on the original structures and hired current general manager and winemaker Michael Richmond. Bouchaine Estate Napa Valley-Carneros Chardonnay 2009 is straw colored, with aromas of citrus blossoms and grapefruit peel. In the mouth it is generous and full, with a light touch of vanilla on the post palate. Bouchaine Copeland Estate Napa Valley Carneros Pinot Noir 2009 is ruby colored, with notes of fresh red cherries and dried black cherries in the bouquet. It has a velvety feel in the mouth and an elegant pronounced finish. It is a delicious Pinot Noir.

BRYANT FAMILY VINEYARD

1567 Sage Canyon Road, St. Helena, CA 94574,
(707) 963-0483
www.bryantwines.com

Art collector and CEO of the Bryant Group, Donald L. Bryant Jr. purchased this property in 1985 and immediately decided to plant vines because of the site's excellent potential for grape growing. Little did he know back then that his wines would become cult icons

and garner amazingly high scores from Robert Parker's *Wine Advocate* and other influential publications. Helen Turley was the first winemaker, and the first vintage release was in 1992. Other luminary winemakers have included Philippe Melka, Mark Aubert, and Helen Keplinger. Todd Alexander was promoted from assistant winemaker to head winemaker in 2012 and continues the esteemed tradition of crafting complex and expressive wines of the highest quality. International wine consultant Michel Rolland has been with the project since 2002 and visits the property regularly to work closely with the winemaker and manager. Donald Bryant has been quoted by *Decanter* as saying, "Michel Rolland is the greatest blender there is." Bryant Family Vineyard Cabernet Sauvignon 2009 is rich garnet purple, with enticing aromas of black cherry, black plum, cassis, and just a whiff of graphite. It is luscious and supple in the mouth with big and bold yet restrained dark fruit flavors, balanced minerality, and an intensely long, smooth tannic finish. This is a perfect example of a well-made and exquisitely balanced Napa Valley Cabernet Sauvignon. Bryant Family Vineyard Bettina 2009 is named for Donald's wife, Bettina, a former dancer in the American Ballet Theater in New York City. It is a delicious proprietary blend of Cabernet Sauvignon, Cabernet Franc, Petit Verdot, and Merlot made with grapes from David Abreu vineyards in St. Helena and on Howell Mountain. It has delightful aromas of ripe dark fruits, black plums, and purple flowers. It is fruit-forward and elegant, with nuances of dried herbs on the palate. This wine truly dances on your tongue before the balanced tannins give way to a long and velvety finish.

BUCCELLA

PO Box 11, Yountville, CA 94599,
(707) 944-1000
www.buccella.com

Founders Bill and Alicia Deem still have the cork from the bottle of Gaja they shared on their first date. It reminds them every day that "dreams really do come true." The name Buccella is taken from the Latin word meaning "mouthful" to evoke the spirit of their big and bold wines. Buccella wines have been very well received by international publications, including *Wine Advocate* and Steven Tanzer's *International Wine Cellar*. Buccella Napa Valley Cabernet Sauvignon 2009 is garnet purple, with aromas of cherry liqueur, purple flowers, and blueberry pie. It is bold and fruit-forward on the palate with mouth-filling tannins and an elegant and restrained finish. It is drinking nicely now and will continue to do so through the next 10 to 12 years.

BURGESS CELLARS

1108 Deer Park Road, St. Helena, CA 94574,
(707) 963-4766
www.burgesscellars.com

After traveling around Europe in the 1960s Tom Burgess decided to purchase a small winery and call Napa Valley home in 1972. His wines are produced from grapes sourced from two vineyards on Howell Mountain and Triere Vineyard in the Oak Knoll District. Winemaking has been under the direction of Bill Sorenson since the winery's inception. Burgess Cellars Estate Vineyards Reserve Napa Valley is a Bordeaux-style red blend that is garnet colored in the glass. Aromas of black currants, black raspberry, and toasted brioche lead to a full mouthful of fruit flavors with a touch of black pepper. The finish is long and luscious. Too bad only 200 cases were produced. Burgess Cellars Estate Napa Valley Cabernet Sauvignon 2008 is a blend of 79 percent Cabernet Sauvignon, 9 percent Cabernet Franc, 4 percent Merlot, 4 percent Petit Verdot, and 4 percent Malbec. It displays a ruby red color, with aromas of toasted vanilla, black cherry, and black fruits of the wood. It is fruit-forward and generous on the palate with a persistent finish.

CADE ESTATE WINERY

360 Howell Mountain Road South,
Angwin, CA 94508,
(707) 945-1220
www.cadewinery.com

Founded in 2005 by John Conover, Gordon Getty, and Gavin Newsom, Cade Estate Winery is a sister winery to PlumpJack. The name Cade comes from a Shakespearean term used to describe wine barrels that were employed to transport Bordeaux wine from France to England. The vineyard estate is above the Howell Mountain fog line at 1,800 feet and consists of 21 acres under plantation with Cabernet Sauvignon and Merlot vines. Cade Estate Winery enjoys the distinction of being the first gold-certified Leadership in Energy and Environmental Design (LEED) winery in the Napa Valley. Cade Winery Napa Valley Sauvignon Blanc 2011 is light straw colored and is composed of 95 percent Sauvignon Blanc, 2 percent Sauvignon Blanc Musque, 2 percent Sémillon, and 1 percent Viognier. It has aromas of citrus blossom, grapefruit rind, Granny Smith apples, and wet shale in the bouquet. In the mouth there are flavors of lemon confit and green apple with a nice amount of minerality and a crisp finish. Cade Winery Cuvée Cabernet Sauvignon Napa Valley is composed of 76 percent Cabernet Sauvignon, 10 percent Petit Verdot, 7 percent Malbec, 5 percent Cabernet Franc, and 2 percent Merlot. It is garnet in color, with notes of black plums, black raspberry, and cocoa powder, followed by flavors of black raspberry, mocha, and cherry vanilla ice cream. The tannic structure is balanced, and the finish is persistent.

CAIN VINEYARD AND WINERY

3800 Langtry Road,
St. Helena, CA 94574,
(707) 963-1616
www.cainfive.com

Joyce and Jerry Cain purchased more than 500 acres of the historic McCormick Ranch in 1980 and planted Cabernet Franc, Merlot, Malbec, Petit Verdot, and of course Cabernet Sauvignon. Their first vintage was 1985, and the next year they entered into a partnership with Nancy and Jim Meadlock, who have run the day-to-day business since the 1991 retirement of the Cains. Christopher Howell makes the wines. Cain Vineyard and Winery Cain Five 2008 is a blend of 61 percent Cabernet Sauvignon, 15 percent Merlot, 13 percent Cabernet Franc, 6 percent Malbec, and 5 percent Petit Verdot and is garnet red in color. It has aromas of purple flowers, especially violet, with a touch of herbs and aromas of black raspberry and cassis. It is juicy and fruity in the mouth with a firm tannic structure. Cain Vineyard and Winery Cain Concept–The Benchland 2008 is a combination of 48 percent Cabernet Sauvignon, 25 percent Merlot, 18 percent Cabernet Franc, and 9 percent Petit Verdot and is ruby red in the glass. Beautiful aromas of black cherry, baking spices, and espresso bean lead you in for another sip of this big, bold Bordeaux-style blend.

CAKEBREAD CELLARS

8300 St. Helena Highway,
Rutherford, CA 94573,
(707) 963-5221
www.cakebread.com

Jack Cakebread, auto mechanic and photographer, was commissioned to take photos of vineyards for Nathan Chroman's 1972 book *The Treasury of American Wines*. Jack had studied with Ansel Adams, and while in Napa he fell in love with the valley and casually mentioned that he would be interested in purchasing some land. His wife of 22 years, Dolores, agreed, and the family began splitting their time between Cakebread's Garage in Oakland and Cakebread Cellars. Their sons Dennis and Bruce were on board with the decision, and in 1979 Bruce became Cakebread Cellars' official winemaker. The winery was designed in 1985 and expanded in 1995 and again in 2007. The Cakebread family is very much involved in Napa activities, including the American Harvest Workshop, and Bruce currently serves on the board of the Napa Valley Vintners. Cakebread Cellars Dancing Bear Ranch Howell Mountain Napa Valley 2009 Cabernet Sauvignon is composed of 94 percent Cabernet Sauvignon and 6 percent Cabernet Franc. It is deep garnet, with aromas of black raspberry, dark cherry, and dark chocolate. In the mouth there are wonderful flavors of dark fruit and chewy tannins. It is delightful to drink now but will continue to improve over the next 7 to 10 years. Cakebread Cellars Napa Valley Cabernet Sauvignon 2009 is composed of 76 percent Cabernet Sauvignon, 13 percent Merlot, 8 percent Cabernet Franc, and 3 percent Petit Verdot. It has notes of black fruits, black currant, and black figs, with flavors that continue onto the palate. It has luscious fruit characteristics and a complex finish with a touch of surprising minerality.

CARDINALE

7600 St. Helena Highway, Oakville, CA 94562,
(707) 948-2643
www.cardinale.com

Winemaker Christopher Carpenter makes only one Cabernet Sauvignon each year, using fruit sourced from the higher slopes of Mount Veeder, Howell Mountain, Diamond Mountain, and Spring Mountain. Cardinale 2009 is composed of 91 percent Cabernet Sauvignon and 9 percent Merlot. It receives 22 months of aging in new French oak barrels. It is dark garnet, with aromas of red plums, baking spice, and a touch of lifted eucalyptus. In the mouth generous fruit and dark chocolate give way to a firm tannic structure. Drink it now or hold it for 15 years; you won't be disappointed either way.

CASTELLO DI AMOROSA

4045 North St. Helena Highway,
Calistoga, CA 94515,
(707) 942-8200
www.castellodiamorosa.com

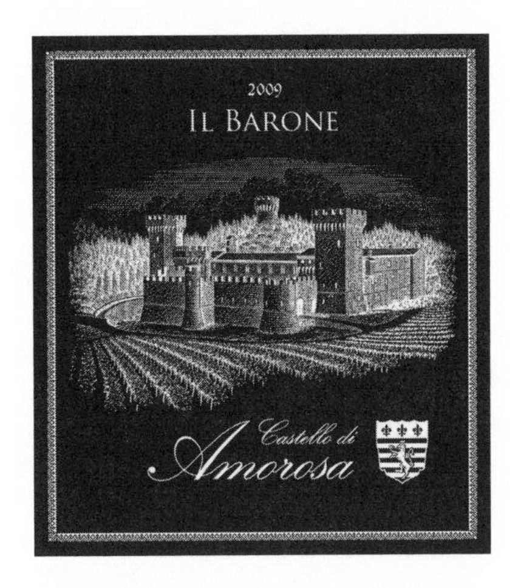

You'll definitely rub your eyes in disbelief and swear you've been transported to Italy as you first gaze upon Castello di Amorosa. Built in the style of a medieval Tuscan castle, the property is certainly a sight to see when one is visiting Napa. Owner Dario Sattui began building his dream property in 1995 after spending countless days researching ancient building techniques in Italy. Enduring years and years of building challenges, Castello di Amorosa opened its doors to the public in 2007. The delicious wines are made using fruit from vines planted in the period 1994–1996 and are held in high esteem by consumers and experts, including those at *Wine Advocate.* Castello di Amorosa La Castellana 2008 is a blend of 70 percent Cabernet Sauvignon, 16 percent Merlot, and 14 percent Sangiovese. It has aromas of red cherry, dried black cherry, black cassis, and dried Mediterranean herbs in the complex bouquet. In the mouth it is velvety smooth, with pronounced red fruit flavors and a luxurious finish. Castello di Amorosa Il Barone Reserve Cabernet Sauvignon, Napa Valley 2009 has luscious aromas of black plum, cassis, and fennel bulb. It is fruit-driven yet elegant and restrained, with silky tannins and a delightful finish. Drink it now or hold it if you have the patience to wait.

CAYMUS

8700 Conn Creek Road, Rutherford, CA 94573,
(707) 963-4204
www.caymus.com

Charlie and Lorna Belle Glos Wagner were just about to sell the ranch and move to Australia in 1971 if their son Chuck declined their offer to set up a family winery. We're happy that Chuck said yes because Caymus has been producing delicious Cabernet Sauvignon since 1972. Their first vintage produced only 240 cases, but today the family-owned company produces 65,000 cases of wine. Caymus Napa Valley Cabernet Sauvignon 2010 has aromas of forest floor, baking spice, and black fruits. In the mouth there are flavors of black plum, ripe black cherries, and cola. The finish is long with just a dusting of dark cocoa powder in the post palate.

CEJA VINEYARDS

1248 1st Street, Napa, CA 94559,
(707) 255-3954
www.cejavineyards.com

Ceja began as an American dream of Mexican immigrants Pablo and Juanita Ceja and their children when they pooled their hard-earned resources and purchased 15 acres of land in 1983. Soon afterward they planted Pinot Noir and celebrated their first harvest in 1988. Today the family has three generations in California and owns 113 acres of vines, with numerous plans for expansion. Ceja currently produces quality Pinot Noir, Chardonnay, Syrah, Sauvignon Blanc, Merlot, and Cabernet Sauvignon. Ceja Carneros Pinot Noir 2008 is cherry red in the glass, with notes of black cherry, cherry cola, and black stone fruits in the bouquet. In the mouth flavors of dried cherries and black raspberries intertwine with black pepper and dried orange zest. There is a delightful splash of acidity in the post palate before the long tasty finish. Ceja Carneros Merlot 2008 is inky red, with aromas of red plums and dark chocolate. On the palate it is velvety with pronounced cassis flavors and juicy tannins.

CHAPPELLET WINERY

1581 Sage Canyon Road, St. Helena, CA 94574,
(707) 286-4219
www.chappellet.com

It is generally agreed that Donn and Molly Chappellet were the first to follow André Tchelistcheff's advice and plant vines on Pritchard Hill in 1967. Their wines consistently received high scores and accolades from major wine publications and continue to do so. Winemaking has been under the direction of Phillip Corallo-Titus since 1990, and he is passionate about separately fermenting and aging different vineyard blocks to achieve the full potential of the *terroir*. Chappellet's portfolio includes its famous Cabernet Sauvignon but also Cabernet Franc, Chenin Blanc, Merlot, and Chardonnay.

Chappellet Pritchard Hill Estate Cabernet Sauvignon 2009 is a blend of 75 percent Cabernet Sauvignon, 15 percent Petit Verdot, and 10 percent Malbec. It is dark garnet in the glass, with notes of black currants, blackberry preserves, red plum, and licorice in the complex bouquet. Fruit flavors come to life in the mouth, with subtle flavors of coffee bean and cacao nib in the long elegant finish. Chappellet Napa Valley Chardonnay 2011 is lively straw colored, with aromas of citrus blossom, lemon zest, and Anjou pears in the bouquet. On the palate flavors of caramelized apples and butter remind one of a well-made tarte Tatin. The finish is decidedly French with a splash of minerality and wet river rock.

CHARLES KRUG

2800 Main Street, St. Helena, CA 94574,
(800) 237-0033
www.charleskrug.com

Prussian immigrant Charles Krug founded his eponymous winery in 1861. He is widely credited as being the first to adapt the cider press for use in winemaking, and his winery was and still is widely credited as the very first commercial winery in Napa Valley. He was well known as a teacher and proponent of the intellectual movement of the nineteenth century and was the editor of the first German newspaper on the

West Coast. After his death the winery was sold to James Moffitt, who sold it to Cesare Mondavi in 1943 for the sum of $75,000. Today the winery continues under the stewardship of the indefatigable Peter Mondavi Sr., who also serves as the company's ambassador, and his sons Peter Jr. and Marc. Peter Mondavi Sr. is well known for his numerous innovations in the world of wine, including cold fermentation and sterile filtration. Innovation must run in the family's genes as Marc and Peter Jr. are known for quite a few of their own contributions to California winemaking. We have had the pleasure of sitting down with this hospitable family to enjoy their delicious and highly regarded wines. Charles Krug Vintage Selection Estate Bottled Napa Valley Cabernet Sauvignon 2009 is 100 percent Cabernet Sauvignon. It is dark garnet, with aromas of black currants, cherries, and mocha. In the mouth the fruit flavors intensify with velvety tannins and a smooth and smoky finish. Charles Krug Carneros Chardonnay 2011 is medium golden yellow, with soft aromas of citrus blossom and lemon curd. In the mouth the lemon scent evolves to flavors of lemon custard and butterscotch with a bracing finish.

CHATEAU MONTELENA

1429 Tubbs Lane, Calistoga, CA 94515,
(707) 942-5105
www.montelena.com

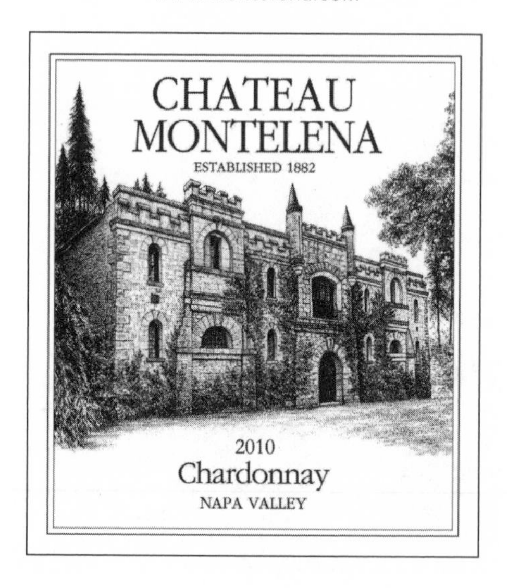

Alfred L. Tubbs purchased 254 acres of land just north of Calistoga in 1882, planted vines, and built his beloved Chateau Montelena, so named because of its proximity to Mount St. Helena. The Tubbs family sold the winery in 1958, and it soon was sold again. Under the guidance of the late Jim Barrett, the château was modernized and the vineyards were replanted. It is widely known that Chateau Montelena Chardonnay 1973 won first prize for white wine in the famous 1976 Judgment of Paris. Chateau Montelena continues to garner high praise and awards from many influential wine publications. Chateau Montelena Napa

Valley Chardonnay 2010 is pale straw yellow with green reflections. It has aromas of citrus blossoms, lemon-lime zest, and Ruby Red grapefruit juice. It is crisp yet creamy in the mouth, with a lingering finish and a touch of almond paste in the post palate. Chateau Montelena Estate Cabernet Sauvignon 2009 is ruby garnet, with notes of black plum, black cherry, and caramelized fennel bulb in the bouquet. It is big yet soft in the mouth, with juicy fruit flavors and a touch of spice in the finish.

CHIARELLO FAMILY VINEYARDS

6525 Washington Street,
Yountville, CA 94599,
(707) 256-0750
www.chiarellovineyards.com

Noted chef and television personality Michael Chiarello is making wine from very old Zinfandel and Petite Sirah vines, some of which were planted in the 1890s. The vineyards were restored to good health more recently with the help of Larry Turley and are organically farmed. Vineyard management is under the direction of Amigo Bob Cantisano, and Thomas Rivers Brown has been the winemaker since 2000. Chiarello Family concentrates on producing 2,000 cases of wine from estate-grown and single-vineyard fruit. Chiarello Family Vineyards Eileen Cabernet Sauvignon 2009 has rich aromas of black raspberries, tobacco leaves, and brown baking spices. It is big and bold in the mouth with restrained elegance in the finish. Chiarello Family Vineyards Bambino Cabernet Sauvignon 2010 has strong delightful aromas of ripe black plums, black cherries, and black raspberries. It has good acidic and tannic balance and should be enjoyed over the next 5 to 10 years.

CHIMNEY ROCK WINERY

5350 Silverado Trail, Napa, CA 94558,
(707) 257-2641
www.chimneyrock.com

Founded in 1980, Chimney Rock Winery brought Hack and Stella Wilson's love of South African architecture to Napa Valley. It was purchased as a 180-acre plot of land complete with a golf course, but the Wilsons quickly began planting vines. Their first vintage was in 1989. Chimney Rock has been lovingly owned by the Terlato family since 2004, and today the estate consists of 119 acres of vines divided into 28 different blocks. Winemaking is carried out by the Terlato Wine Group VP of Winemaking, Doug Fletcher, and Chimney Rock winemaker Elizabeth Vianna. Chimney Rock Cabernet Sauvignon Stags Leap District 2009 is garnet, with notes of cassis, black cherry, purple flowers, and baking spices in the bouquet. In the mouth it is soft and silky with a smooth yet persistent finish. Chimney Rock Sauvignon Gris Stags Leap District 2010 is pale straw in the glass, with aromas of guava and mango. On the palate it is surprisingly rich and full-bodied. This is the type of wine that keeps inviting you in for another pleasant sip.

CIMAROSSA

1185 Friesen Road,
Angwin, CA 94508,
(707) 307-3130
www.cimarossa.com

Dino Dina and his wife, Corry Dekker, met while working at Chiron, a company noted as a leader in biotechnology. Although the two maintain their current day jobs—Dino at Dynavax and Corry at Stanford University and as an adviser to the Centers for Disease Control and Prevention (CDC) in the area of human disease and vaccination—they produce some of Napa's most sought-after and highly rated wines. The name Cimarossa comes from the Italian word for "red hilltop," and it certainly is one of Howell Mountain's most beautiful estates with its terraced vineyards and olive trees. Make sure to try the estate's olive oil—it's as delicious as the products of many Tuscan oil producers. Mia Klein makes the wines. Cimarossa Howell Mountain Riva di Ponente Cabernet Sauvignon 2009 is garnet colored, with aromas of blueberry, black plum, and black cherry. It's broad in the mouth, with flavors of juicy fruits and fine tannins in the smooth finish. Cimarossa Howell Mountain Rian Cabernet Sauvignon 2009 has aromas of dark fruits, cigar box, anise, and a touch of eucalyptus in the bouquet. It is big in the mouth, with grippy tannins that make this a wine that will continue to improve with age.

CK MONDAVI AND SONS

2800 Main Street, St. Helena, CA 94574,
(707) 967-2200
www.ckmondavi.com

Cesare and Rosa Mondavi purchased the Charles Krug winery in 1943 and subsequently started CK Mondavi with their sons Peter and Robert. At almost 100 years, old, Peter Mondavi Sr. continues to act as the company's ambassador, although the day-to-day business of the company is run by the third-generation sons, Marc and Peter Jr. John Moynier has been the winemaker for more than 25 years. CK Mondavi wines are well known in the marketplace for offering quality and value to consumers. CK Mondavi California Chardonnay 2011 is straw yellow, with aromas of citrus blossoms and white stone fruit. It is crisp and clean in the mouth with a pleasant acidic finish. CK Mondavi California Cabernet Sauvignon 2010 is garnet in color, with aromas of black raspberry and black plum that carry through to the fruit-filled palate.

CLIFF LEDE VINEYARDS

1473 Yountville Cross Road,
Yountville, CA 94599,
(707) 944-8642
www.cliffledevineyards.com

Canadian Cliff Lede started making wine in his mother's basement when he was in his twenties and later was introduced to fine wines from Bordeaux. He is still quite passionate about Bordeaux but equally passionate about wines from his Stags Leap estate. His 60-acre property is planted to Cabernet Sauvignon, Merlot, Malbec, Petit Verdot, and Cabernet Franc, and his wines are much sought after by wine lovers and collectors alike. Cliff Lede wines are highly rated by many of the international wine publications. His staff includes the very capable Chris Tynan and Remi Cohen as winemaker and viticulturist, respectively. Cliff Lede Napa Valley Sauvignon Blanc 2011 is pale straw colored, with aromas of citrus zest, white flowers, and Anjou pears. In the mouth it shows tropical fruits and crisp minerality before the long finish. Cliff Lede Poetry Napa Valley Stags Leap District Cabernet Sauvignon 2009 has notes of rose, black plum, and blueberry pie in the complex bouquet. On the palate fruit flavors come forward while secondary characteristics of Indian spice and dark chocolate delight the senses. The finish is tight and elegant. Drink now or hold for 10 to 15 years.

CLOS DU VAL

5330 Silverado Trail, Napa, CA 94558,
(707) 261-5251
www.closduval.com

In 1970 John Goelet hired Bordeaux-raised Bernard Portet to search the world for land on which to build a wine estate. In 1970 the men found themselves in Napa Valley, and in 1973 John Goelet acquired a 178-acre winery property in the Stags Leap District and purchased another 180 acres in Carneros. Their 1972 vintage Cabernet Sauvignon had the distinction of being chosen as one of the six California Cabernet Sauvignons to be entered into the famous Paris Tasting. Clos Du Val Winery Napa Valley Reserve Cabernet Sauvignon 2008 is deep plum colored in the glass. Aromas of dark chocolate, tobacco, cedar, and black raspberries entice you into taking a deep sip. After it opens with luscious fruit intensity, flavors of espresso and black plum linger on your tongue before the well-structured tannic finish. Clos Du Val Winery Carneros Reserve Chardonnay is light straw with green reflections in the glass, with notes of mango, guava, and pineapple to tease the nose. This full-bodied wine coats the inside of the mouth with lemon zest and butter before ending in a clean, crisp finish.

CLOS PEGASE

1060 Dunaweal Lane, Calistoga, CA 94515,
(707) 942-4981
www.clospegase.com

Jan Shrem and his late wife, Mitsuko, purchased their initial 50-acre estate in Calistoga in 1983. Before that Jan made his living in Japan by translating English-language technical books into Japanese and fell in love with the country and the woman who would become his wife. He studied at the University of Bordeaux, moved to the United States, and enlisted the help of André Tchelistcheff; the rest, as they say, is history. The family later acquired an additional 400 acres in various locations in the northern and southern AVAs of Napa Valley and built a winery designed by famed architect Michael Graves. Besides making amazing and highly rated wine, Clos Pegase is well known for numerous art installations that draw praise from wine lovers and art admirers alike. In 2013 Shrem sold the winery to Vintage Wine Estates, backed by Leslie Rudd, the owner of Dean & DeLuca and a fellow Napa Valley vintner. Clos Pegase Cabernet Sauvignon 2008 is dark garnet, with aromas of black plum, currant, and black cherry as well as secondary notes of cigar box and cocoa powder in the complex bouquet. It is voluptuous in the mouth, with great fruit flavors and a luxuriously long finish. Clos Pegase Mitsuko's Vineyard Pinot Noir 2008 is cherry red with notes of red cherry, dried black cherry, and Christmas baking spices. It has a balanced mouthfeel and a pleasant finish with a delightful splash of acidity on the post palate.

COLGIN CELLARS

PO Box 254,
St. Helena, CA 94574,
(707) 963-0999
www.colgincellars.com

A true artist who began her career with a master of arts degree from New York University, Ann Barry Colgin started using her artistic talents to make art in the bottle in 1992. She is well known around the country for her tireless promotion of handcrafted small-production wines. Today Colgin Cellars is situated in the Pritchard Hill district and produces only four distinct wines: IX Estate Syrah, IX Estate Napa Valley Red Wine, Tychson Hill Vineyard Cabernet Sauvignon, and Cariad Napa Valley Red Wine. Ann still keeps her hand in the art world and serves as a consultant to Sotheby's wine department as well as a charity auctioneer. Her donations of library wine to auctions have raised more than $6 million for health-care and art-minded charities. Colgin Cellars IX Estate Syrah 2009 is inky purple, with aromas of black fruits, citrus blossoms, and cured charcuterie. In the mouth flavors of cacao and blackberry confiture come through before the long, well-balanced tannic finish. Colgin Cellars Tychson Hill Cabernet Sauvignon is blended with less than 5 percent of Cabernet Franc and Petit Verdot to make a delicious wine. It is dark garnet in the glass, with lifted notes of anise and white flowers to entice your nose as you dive in for a full mouth burst of fruit flavors followed by a smooth, silky tannic finish.

CONTINUUM

1677 Sage Canyon Road,
St. Helena, CA 94574,
(707) 944-8100
www.continuumestate.com

Tim Mondavi and his sister Marcia, along with their children and other extended family members, make only one quality wine per year at Continuum. Their wine is ranked consistently among the top-quality wines each year and is sought after by critics and collectors alike. This 172-acre Mondavi property enjoys a privileged location on top of Pritchard Hill. Only four varieties are grown on the property: Cabernet Sauvignon, Cabernet Franc, Petit Verdot, and Merlot. Continuum 2009 is a blend of 77 percent Cabernet Sauvignon, 12 percent Cabernet Franc, 7 percent Petit Verdot, and 4 percent Merlot. It is dark inky garnet, with aromas of blackberry, cassis, coffee bean, and anise. In the mouth it is a big, bold, delicious wine with a pleasant tannic grip and a lingering finish.

COQUEREL FAMILY WINE ESTATES

3180 Highway 128, Calistoga, CA 94515,
(707) 942-4534
www.coquerelwines.com

Clay and Brenda Cockerell visited Napa Valley on their wedding anniversary and fell in love with the region. They purchased grapes in 2004 and 2005 and made small quantities of white wine for their family and friends. In 2008 they purchased a second parcel of land so that they could make red wine as well. Today Coquerel makes decidedly French-style wines from Petite Sirah, Merlot, Tempranillo, Verdelho, Chardonnay, and Sauvignon Blanc grapes. Coquerel La Petite Sirah 2010 is inky purple, with aromas of black raspberry, black plum, and Christmas baking spices. It is big and fruity in the mouth with a soft, round tannic finish. Coquerel Verdelho 2011 is pale straw colored, with aromas of tropical fruit and Ruby Red grapefruit rind. It is crisp and clean in the mouth with a refreshing acidic finish.

CORISON WINERY

987 St. Helena Highway, St. Helena, CA 94574,
(707) 963-0826
www.corison.com

A true small-family operation, Corison Winery is making wonderful wines to be reckoned with. Winemaker Cathy Corison and her husband, William Martin, run the day-to-day operations of the winery as well as maintaining their organically farmed Kronos Vineyard. Cathy's history as a winemaker includes stints at Long Meadow Ranch, York Creek Vineyards, and Chappellet Vineyards. Her first vintage of her very own Cabernet was made in 1987, and she's been doing it ever since. Corison Cabernet Sauvignon 2009 exhibits a beautiful garnet color and has aromas of dried black cherries, cigar box, cinnamon, and violets. On the palate it's like a mouthful of blueberry pie sprinkled with powdered cocoa. The finish is long and luscious. Corison Kronos Vineyard Cabernet Sauvignon 2008 is garnet ruby colored in the glass. Notes of black raspberries, black currants, and black plum are present in the bouquet. In the mouth flavors of fruit burst through the underlying notes of licorice, baking spices, and dark chocolate. The tannins are round and smooth, and the finish is lovely.

COSENTINO WINERY

7415 St. Helena Highway, Yountville, CA 94599,
(707) 921-2809
www.cosentinowinery.com

Established in 1980, Cosentino Winery first made wines under the labels Cosentino Wine Company and Crystal Valley Cellars and is recognized by some historians to be one of the first California wines to use the designation "Meritage." Its 1986 vintage of The Poet was officially licensed as a Meritage wine in 1989. Cosentino Winery moved to Yountville in 1990 to be closer to some of the growers with whom it maintained long-term relationships. Cosentino is known for its Cabernet Sauvignon, Cabernet Franc, Chardonnay, Merlot, and Meritage wines. Cosentino Winery Cabernet Sauvignon Napa County 2008 is garnet colored in the glass, with notes of cassis and black raspberry in the bouquet. It has a rich mouthfeel and heft on the palate before a long, balanced finish. Cosentino Winery Chardonnay Napa Valley 2010 is straw colored, with aromas of flan, caramelized sugar, and Granny Smith apples. In the mouth it opens up and releases a refreshing acidity on the finish.

CUVAISON ESTATE

1221 Duhig Road, Napa, CA 94559,
(707) 942-2455
www.cuvaison.com

Cuvaison Estate was established in 1969 with 27 acres of vines in Calistoga and quickly grew to more than 400 acres with its acquisition by the Swiss Schmidheiny family in 1979. In 1998 the family purchased the historic Brandlin Ranch on Mount Veeder and acquired an additional 170 acres. Today Cuvaison is known for its state-of-the-art winery that produces quality Napa Valley wine by using sustainable solar energy. Cuvaison Carneros Chardonnay 2010 shows a beautiful golden tint in the glass, with aromas of tropical fruits, orange and lime zest, and a light florality in the bouquet. On the palate it is like liquid velvet with a pleasant zing and minerality to the finish. Cuvaison Mount Veeder Cabernet Sauvignon 2010 is garnet colored, with notes of black plums, dark cherry, espresso, and cassis that entice the nose before a mouthful of fruit in the first sip. The tannic structure has a firm grip, so drink now or hold in your cellar for a few years.

DALLA VALLE VINEYARDS

PO Box 329, Oakville, CA 94562,
(707) 944-2676
www.dallavallevineyards.com

Gustav and Naoko Dalla Valle acquired the estate that was to become Dalla Valle Vineyards in 1982. They began planting vines at an altitude of 400 feet overlooking Oakville and the Silverado Trail and moved on to making wine, and relatively soon their wines began receiving international attention. Day-to-day winemaking is under the direction of Andy Erickson with the assistance of consulting enologist Michel Rolland. Dalla Valle wines are highly rated by all the prestigious wine publications. Dalla Valle Vineyards Maya 2010 has aromas of dark fruits, bittersweet chocolate, and a touch of purple flowers in the bouquet. It is rich in the mid palate, with flavors of dark fruits and bittersweet chocolate. The finish has delightful flavors of espresso and black currant and a balanced tannic structure. Drink it now or over the next 20 years. Dalla Valle Vineyards Cabernet Sauvignon 2010 has heady aromas of black currant, black plum, and Christmas baking spices. It is big and bold in the mouth, with a fair amount of heft on the palate and a delightful balanced tannic finish. Although it is drinking beautifully now, don't be afraid to hold this one for a decade or two.

DARIOUSH

4240 Silverado Trail, Napa, CA 94558,
(707) 257-2345
www.darioush.com

When you drive up to Darioush's front steps, sixteen very tall travertine columns quickly signal that you have entered another world. Designed by architects Ardeshir and Roshan

Nozari, using stone imported from Persepolis, Darioush Winery welcomes you in the style of true Persian hospitality. Founded by Iranian civil engineer turned grocery store mogul Darioush Khaledi in 2004, the winery is known for its Bordeaux-style estate wines. Winemaker Steve Devitt sources grapes from 95 acres of estate-owned vineyards in the Mount Veeder, Oak Knoll, and Napa Valley AVAs. Darioush grows Shiraz, Merlot, Cabernet Sauvignon, Malbec, and Petit Verdot for its single-varietal and red blends as well as Chardonnay and Viognier for its handcrafted whites. Darioush Duel 2009 is composed of 65 percent Shiraz and 35 percent Cabernet Sauvignon. It is inky purple in the glass, with aromas of juicy black plums, ripe black cherries, and Christmas baking spices. In the mouth stone fruit flavors entice the taste buds before delivering a fruit-filled finish to the entire palate. Darioush Signature Napa Valley Viognier 2010 has tropical fruit and white flower notes in the bouquet. On the palate flavors of Granny Smith apples, carambola, and citrus zest dance on the tongue. The finish is clean and crisp and invites you in for another sip.

DEL DOTTO VINEYARDS

1055 Atlas Peak Road, Napa, CA 94558,
(707) 963-2134
www.deldottovineyards.com

While on vacation in 1988, David and Yolanda Del Dotto fell in love with a historic Frank Lloyd Wright–designed house situated amid 17 acres of land. Two short years later they began planting Merlot, Cabernet Sauvignon, Cabernet Franc, and Sangiovese in homage to Dave's Italian heritage. Their wines became instant cult favorites and quickly garnered high ratings from *Wine Spectator* and Robert Parker. Today visitors to the winery always enjoy the underground caves and barrel-tasting experience. Del Dotto is one of the few Napa Valley wineries that make wine in ancient clay amphorae buried in the ground. Del Dotto Chardonnay

2011 has aromas of lemon blossoms, peach, and lemon curd. In the mouth it has flavors of tropical fruits, almond paste, and a refreshing minerality in the crisp finish. Del Dotto Sonoma Coast Cinghiale Vineyard Pinot Noir 2010 has aromas of red raspberry, mushrooms, fresh cherries, and anise. It has lovely fruit on the palate, with top notes of Indian spice and Earl Grey tea. It has nice weight, a great mouthfeel, and a long finish.

DERENONCOURT CALIFORNIA

335 West Lane, Angwin, CA 94508,
(707) 363-7990
www.derenoncourtca.com

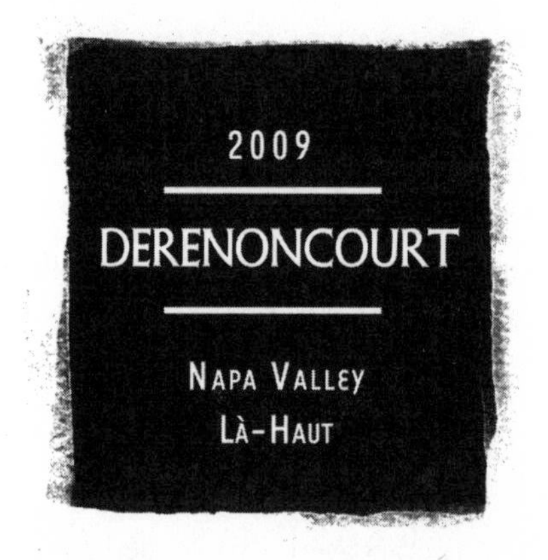

Stéphane Derenoncourt, international wine consultant, began producing quality California wine under his own name in 2006. We first met Stéphane when we interviewed him for *Wine Enthusiast* magazine in 2010 and have been fans of his wines ever since. He currently owns two wineries, Derenoncourt California and Domaine de l'A in Bordeaux, both known for their critically acclaimed wines. Stéphane first began making wine at Château Pavie-Macquin in Saint-Émilion in the early 1990s and made his mark soon afterward when his 1996 vintage of La Mondotte shocked and delighted critics and collectors alike. He currently consults for over 60 wineries around the world, and it's always a pleasure to catch up with him for a glass or two when he is in New York, California, or Bordeaux. Derenoncourt Stagecoach Vineyard Napa Valley Merlot 2009 is made from grapes sourced from an altitude over 2,000 feet on Atlas Peak. In the bouquet aromas of Mediterranean herbs, luscious red plums, and red raspberries entice you in for a big sip. On the palate flavors of ripe red cherries and boysenberries delight the taste buds before the lingering silky finish. Too bad he produced only 140 cases of this delicious wine. Derenoncourt Meritage Là-Haut Napa Valley 2009 is a blend of 75 percent Cabernet Franc and 25 percent Cabernet Sauvignon sourced from Howell Mountain. Notes of dried saucisson, cigar box, and dried cherries are found in the bouquet, while flavors of dark cassis berries and juicy black plums are delightful on the palate. Chewy tannins and a bit of grip carry you nicely into the persistent finish. This great wine will drink finely over the next 15 years, so buy plenty for your cellar.

DIAMOND CREEK VINEYARDS

1500 Diamond Mountain Road,
Calistoga, CA 94515,
(707) 942-6926
www.diamondcreekvineyards.com

Boots Brounstein and her late husband, Al, founded Diamond Creek Vineyards in 1968. It was their goal to create California's first exclusively Cabernet Sauvignon estate vineyard, and to this day Boots, her son Phil Ross, and winemaker Phil Steinschreiber produce excellent and highly rated Cabs. The 20-acre estate has three distinctly different soil types: Red Rock Terrace has iron-rich soil, the soil in Gravelly Meadow is composed of small pebbles, and Volcanic Hill's soil is lighter and has more ash in its composition. Diamond Creek Red Rock Terrace Napa Valley Cabernet Sauvignon 2009 is ruby garnet, with aromas of black cherry, cassis, and a touch of lifted peppermint in the bouquet. It has rich flavors of dark fruits and a silky smooth tannic finish. Diamond Creek Gravelly Meadow Napa Valley Cabernet Sauvignon 2009 has aromas of forest floor, cigar box, and mixed black fruit conserves. It is luscious in the mouth with a touch of spice in the finish.

DOMAINE CARNEROS

1240 Duhig Road, Napa, CA 94559,
(707) 257-0101
www.domainecarneros.com

As you drive up the entranceway to Domaine Carneros, you'll swear that you and your car have been transported to France and that the large château in front of you was built in Reims. Owned by the revered Champagne house of Taittinger, Domaine Carneros is a delight for all the senses. With beautiful entrance foyers, a stunning tasting room, and café tables overlooking the vines, it's no wonder Domaine Carneros is so popular with visitors. We always enjoy sitting in the manicured gardens and enjoying a glass or two of winemaker Eileen Crane's decidedly French-style California sparkling wines. Domaine Carneros Brut Cuvée Sparkling 2009 is straw colored and robust *moussant* with persistent *perlage*. It has delightful aromas of Granny Smith apples and freshly baked brioche. It is crisp and clean in the mouth, with flavors that keep inviting you in for another sip. Domaine Carneros Cuvée de la Pompadour Brut Rose NV is pale pink in color, with aromas of white peach, rose petal, and freshly sliced strawberries. It has wonderful acidity and nice minerality, making it a wine to enjoy with food or on its own as an aperitif.

DOMAINE CHANDON

1 California Drive,
Yountville, CA 94599,
(888) 242-6366
www.chandon.com

The well-known French Champagne house Moët & Chandon began searching for new areas to produce great sparkling wine, and in 1968 they found sites in Mount Veeder, Carneros, and Yountville. They quickly got to work planting vineyards and released their first sparkling wines in 1976. Tom Tiburzi has been the winemaker at Domaine Chandon for more than 20 years and has more recently been assisted by Champagne-born Pauline Lhote. Besides Chandon's delicious and highly rated sparkling wines, the house makes still wine from Pinot Noir, Chardonnay, Petit Meunier, and Cabernet Sauvignon grape varieties. Visitors to the estate are always impressed (as are we) by the delectable cuisine at Chandon's signature restaurant *étoile.* Chandon Limited Edition Brut Classic 2013 has millions of tiny bubbles and a creamy mousse. It has flavors of Anjou pear and Granny Smith apple in the mouth and a touch of freshly baked bread in the nose. This is the perfect bubbly to sip while sitting on a yacht in Monterey Bay. Domaine Chandon Carneros Chardonnay 2010 is straw colored, with aromas of white flowers, white stone fruits, and freshly cut apples. It is crisp yet fruity in the mouth with a bright acidic finish.

DOMINUS ESTATE

2570 Napa Nook Road,
Yountville, CA 94599,
(707) 944-8954
www.dominusestate.com

One of the most famous sons of Bordeaux, Christian Moueix discovered the 124-acre estate he now solely owns in 1981, and in 1995

he changed the name to Dominus, a Latin word symbolizing his commitment to the land. Christian is well known for producing wine at Trotanoy, Hosanna, and Magdelaine, among others, in Bordeaux, but he is probably best known for his consultancy at Château Pétrus. His love of California and the Napa Valley started when he studied at University of California, Davis, in the 1960s. His love of California *terroir* and commitment to the land are easily discernible in the quality of his delicious and well-balanced wines. Dominus 2009 is composed of 86 percent Cabernet Sauvignon, 10 percent Cabernet Franc, and 4 percent Petit Verdot. It is dark garnet in the glass, with aromas of dark plums, blackberries, and cedar. It's like liquid velvet on the palate, with rich fruit flavors and round tannins. The finish is lingering, silky, and sexy. Simply put, this is an excellent wine.

DUCKHORN VINEYARDS

1000 Lodi Lane,
St. Helena, CA 94574,
(707) 963-7108
www.duckhorn.com

Dan and Margaret Duckhorn founded Duckhorn Vineyards in 1976, and because of their extensive travel to Pomerol and Saint-Émilion, they started with a primary focus on

the cultivation of Merlot. Today Duckhorn Vineyards sources fruit from eight estate-owned Napa Valley vineyards—Candlestick Ridge, Stout, Monitor Ledge, Three Palms, Rector Creek, Marlee's, Cork Tree, and Patzimaro—as well as grapes from independent growers. Executive winemaker Bill Nancarrow originally hails from Hawkes Bay, New Zealand, and brings a decidedly global style to California winemaking. Duckhorn Vineyards Estate Grown Stout Vineyard Merlot 2008 is made from 100 percent Merlot. Aromas of dark cherry, juicy red plum, and cherry cola are present in the nose. In the mouth subtle flavors of toffee, dark stone fruits, and black raspberry are noted before the big tannic finish. Drink it now or hold it for a few years. Duckhorn Vineyards Howell Mountain Cabernet Sauvignon 2008 is a blend of 77 percent Cabernet Sauvignon,

20 percent Merlot, 2.5 percent Cabernet Franc, and 0.5 percent Petit Verdot. It spends 26 months in French oak barrels and is inky garnet in the glass. It has notes of black raspberry, cassis, mocha, and cedar in the bouquet. In the mouth the fruit flavors become more pronounced before the savory finish is punctuated by subtle nuances of brown baking spices. Duckhorn also makes quality wine under a variety of labels, including, Decoy, Paraduxx, Goldeneye, and Migration.

EHLERS ESTATE

3222 Ehlers Lane, St. Helena, CA 94574,
(707) 963-5972
www.ehlersestate.com

Ehlers Estate was founded in 1985 by French entrepreneur Jean Leducq and to this day continues the tradition of his philanthropy by donating 100 percent of its profits to the Leducq Foundation, which focuses on cardiovascular research. The original historic stone winery was built in 1886 by Bernard Ehlers and is the namesake of their award-winning 1886 Cabernet Sauvignon. Under the direction of winemaker Kevin Morrisey, Ehlers Estate began producing organic and biodynamic wines in 2005, and in 2008 it was awarded organic certification from California Certified Organic Farmers. Biodynamic certification was received in 2011 from Demeter USA, and today Ehlers continues to produce world-class wines that are Napa Valley–*terroir* driven. Ehlers Estate 1886 Cabernet Sauvignon 2009 has aromas of purple flowers, dark chocolate, black cherry, and mocha in the bouquet. In the mouth it has flavors of luscious black fruits and cocoa. The finish is elegant and persistent. Ehlers Estate One Twenty Over Eighty Cabernet Sauvignon 2009 is composed of 85 percent Cabernet Sauvignon, 9 percent Cabernet France, 3 percent Merlot, and 3 percent Petit Verdot. It is garnet colored, with notes of black raspberry preserves, mocha, and forest floor in the nose. In the mouth it has a large presence with flavors of black fruits and Christmas baking spices and a fine tannic finish.

ENVY

1170 Tubbs Lane,
Calistoga, CA 94515,
(707) 942-4677
www.envywines.com

Pack a picnic lunch, buy a bottle of award-winning wine from the tasting room, and have a picnic on Envy's front lawn. Every 40 minutes or so you'll be treated to the spectacle of the Old Faithful geyser right across the street. Founded by Richard Carter and Nils Venge, Envy wines and its winemakers are consistently ranked highly by a number of wine publications, including *Wine Spectator* and *Wine Advocate.* Planted with Cabernet Sauvignon, Sauvignon Blanc, Merlot, and Petite Syrah, all the estate's wines are produced in a decidedly Bordelaise style. Envy Sauvignon Blanc 2011 is straw colored, with aromas of honeysuckle, white flowers, and sweet nectarine in the bouquet. In the mouth it is crisp and refreshing and invites you in for another sip. Envy Bee Bee's Blend 2009 is composed of estate-grown Cabernet Sauvignon, Merlot, and Petite Syrah. Notes of chocolate and dried cherries excite your nose before flavors of black raspberry, toasted almond, and baking spice delight the palate.

ETUDE WINES

1250 Cuttings Wharf Road,
Napa, CA 94559,
(877) 586-9361
www.etudewines.com

Founded by Tony Soter more than 25 years ago, Etude Wines takes its name from the classical term for a musical composition that allows the musician to practice a specific technique over and over. Both Tony and current winemaker Jon Priest believe that deliberate concentration on specific technique helps them make better wine. They also believe the wines they craft should by themselves be a source of enjoyment. We've had the opportunity to sit down with Jon and experience Etude's wines and the pleasure they can bring to lovers of expertly crafted, luscious, and delicious wine. Etude makes highly acclaimed wines from Pinot Noir, Cabernet Sauvignon, Pinot Gris, Pinot Blanc, and Merlot varieties. Etude Carneros Pinot Gris 2011 has subtle aromas of white peach, freshly cut green apple, and citrus blossom. It is crisp and clean, with a rounded mouthfeel and a mineral-driven finish. Etude Napa Valley Cabernet Sauvignon 2009 is 100 percent Cabernet Sauvignon and has a ruby garnet color. It has aromas of black plum and black raspberry with a top note of caramelized anise. It is rich in the mouth with bold fruit flavors, velvety tannins, and a persistent finish.

FAMA WINES

No visitor facilities.
(415) 250-7505
www.famawines.com

As a little girl, Heather Munden wanted to be a lion tamer, but a chance meeting with Robert Mondavi introduced her to the world of wine, where she made quite a name for herself. After 17 years of making wine for other people and large companies, she struck out on her own with her new label, Fama. She is truly a small-batch artisanal winemaker in every sense of the word. Her third vintage in 2012 produced only 123 cases of Chardonnay and 25 cases of her proprietary red blend aptly named The Partners. We had the pleasure of visiting Heather's home to taste her wines on a brisk November evening. We arrived for what we thought would be a quick tasting, but four hours later we were stuffed on her homemade sausage and charcuterie made from pigs she had raised and butchered herself. We also enjoyed vegetables from her garden roasted in the brick oven she had built in the backyard. Freshly killed roast chicken and hand-gathered eggs rounded out the feast. Heather is truly a hands-on woman and a wonderful winemaker whom we have our eye on for continued greatness. Fama Hudson Vineyards Carneros Napa Valley Chardonnay 2009 is luminescent straw yellow, with enticing aromas of lemon curd, lime blossom, Granny Smith apples, and Anjou pears. On the palate there are pronounced fruit flavors, a fully rounded mouthfeel, and a delightful crisp, clean, saline-driven finish that invites you in for another, and another, and another sip.

FAR NIENTE

1350 Acacia Drive, Oakville, CA 94562,
(707) 944-2861
www.farniente.com

Founded in 1885 by Gold Rush–era entrepreneur John Benson, Far Niente enjoyed a privileged run in the world of wine until the start of Prohibition. Far Niente's winery was designed by the same architect who did Christian Brothers yet lay in a state of disrepair from 1919 until 1979, when it was acquired by the late Gil Nickel. Today Far Niente is owned by partners Erik Nickel, Jeremy Nickel, Beth Nickel, Dirk Hampson, and Larry Maguire. Far Niente provides a wonderful visitor's experience, and lovers of vintage and exotic cars are always impressed by Gil Nickel's extensive collection. Far Niente Estate Bottled Napa Valley Chardonnay 2011 is deep straw colored, with aromas of buttered brioche, butterscotch, wet river rocks, lemon blossom, and lemon pulp in the bouquet. In the mouth it is robust, voluminous, and well rounded with flavors of tropical fruits and buttered toast. It has a luscious and bright finish. Far Niente Estate Bottled Napa Valley Oakville Cabernet Sauvignon 2009 is deep garnet, almost purple, with a violet rim. It has aromas of boysenberry, black licorice, blueberry pie, and a cherry jam whiff at the end. In the mouth it has flavors of blackberry conserves, clove, and tart cherry preserves. It is rich with a linear tannic structure and has a surprising but pleasant bright acidic lift in the mid palate.

FORMAN VINEYARDS

1501 Big Rock Road,
St. Helena, CA 94574,
(707) 963-3900
www.formanvineyard.com

Owner Ric Forman purchased his winery in 1978 and began producing classically made Cabernet Sauvignon and Chardonnay in 1983 using traditional French methods. He crafts handmade wines using grapes sourced from 8.5 acres at the winery site, 20 acres above the winery, and 60 acres in the Rutherford Bench. Ric's red wines are fermented in stainless steel and then moved to oak barrels to undergo malolactic fermentation; his white wines are fermented in oak and do not see malolactic fermentation. Forman Vineyards Napa Valley Chardonnay 2010 is light straw with green tinges and has aromas of Seckel pears, honeycomb, and citrus blossoms. It is big in volume, creamy, and round in the mouth, and flavors of stone fruits with a bracing minerality add to the intrigue of this wine. Foreman Vineyards Napa Valley Cabernet Sauvignon is composed of 75 percent Cabernet Sauvignon, 11 percent Cabernet Franc, 8 percent Petit Verdot, and 7 percent Merlot. It is deep ruby colored, with aromas of black fruit conserves and fruits of the wood in the bouquet. In the mouth this is a big wine with lots of juicy fruit flavors noted before the well-structured tannic finish.

FRANCISCAN

1178 Galleron Road, St. Helena, CA 94574,
(707) 963-7111
www.franciscan.com

In 1972 Justin Meyer and Raymond Duncan planted the original Oakville Estate vines, and Meyer officially purchased Franciscan in 1975. In the same year the winery celebrated its first vintage from estate-grown grapes. Winemaker Agustin Huneeus introduced Franciscan's iconic Magnificat in 1985, and two years later winemaker Greg Upton was the first to ferment Napa Valley Chardonnay using wild yeast. Today winemaking is under the direction of Janet Myers, and she is credited for creating Franciscan's signature reserve Cabernet Sauvignon, Stylus. Franciscan Estate Napa Valley Chardonnay 2011 is pale straw colored, with notes of Granny Smith apple, citrus blossom, and vanilla in the bouquet. It has flavors of tarte Tatin, fresh pear, and lemon curd. The mouthfeel is creamy, and the finish is acidic and persistent. Franciscan Estate Napa Valley Cabernet Sauvignon is composed of 85 percent Cabernet Sauvignon, 11 percent Merlot, 3 percent Syrah, and 1 percent Malbec and is dark garnet in the glass. It has aromas of black cherry, purple flowers, and cigar box, and on the palate flavors of cassis and licorice come out before the elegant finish.

FRANK FAMILY VINEYARDS

1091 Larkmead Lane, Calistoga, CA 94515,
(707) 942-0859
www.frankfamilyvineyards.com

Frank Family Vineyards' previous incarnation was the Larkmead Winery, which had its humble beginnings in 1884. Refurbished in 1906 and still standing, it is on the list of California State Points of Historical Interest as well as the

National Register of Historic Places. Current owners Richard Frank and Connie Frank produce well-regarded Cabernet Sauvignon, Chardonnay, Zinfandel, and Sangiovese wines. Before becoming a Napa Valley vintner, Rich was the president of the Academy of Television Arts and Sciences for six years, chairman of Walt Disney Television, and president of Walt Disney Studios. Frank Family wines are award-winning and consistently garner high points from numerous wine publications. Frank Family Vineyards Napa Valley Chardonnay 2011 is light straw colored, with notes of tropical fruits, Fuji apple, and toasted almonds. In the mouth it has flavors of homemade applesauce, stone fruits, and cinnamon. It has a rich mouthfeel and a crisp acidic finish. Frank Family Vineyards Napa Valley Cabernet Sauvignon 2009 has notes of saddle leather, purple flowers, and cigar box lifted above aromas of black cherry preserves. On the palate it is fruit-filled and luscious with a balanced tannic structure and a persistent finish.

FREEMARK ABBEY

3022 St. Helena Highway, St. Helena, CA 94574,
(707) 963-9694
www.freemarkabbey.com

Freemark Abbey's original winery was established in 1889 by Josephine Tychson, who was one of Napa Valley's first female winegrowers. The current name was created in 1939 by combining the three owners' names: Charles Freeman, Markquand Foster, and Abbey Ahern. The winery was then purchased by seven partners in 1967, and in 1976 history was made at the Judgment of Paris, with Freemark Abbey as the only American winery to have two wines entered, a Chardonnay and a Cabernet Sauvignon. Ted Edwards has been the winemaker since 1985, and Freemark's wines receive consistent accolades from consumers and the press. Freemark Abbey Napa Valley Chardonnay 2011 is straw yellow, with aromas of lemon curd, Granny Smith apple, and lime blossoms. In the mouth there is a pleasant amount of oak characteristics as well as vibrant stone fruit flavors. Freemark Abbey Napa Valley Merlot 2011 is ruby garnet, with notes of black raspberry, baking spice, and vanilla. It is full-bodied in the mouth, with pleasant tastes of dried black cherry, mocha, and just a hint of black pepper in the finish.

FROG'S LEAP

8815 Conn Creek Road,
Rutherford, CA 94573,
(707) 963-4704
www.frogsleap.com

Frog's Leap is housed in the historic Adamson Winery, which was built in 1884. It sits among 130 acres of vineyards in Rutherford and was renovated in 1994 to become Frog's Leap's self-proclaimed "permanent home." Winemakers John Williams and Paula Moschetti use Napa Valley Rutherford-grown grapes to make their award-winning Cabernet Sauvignon, Sauvignon Blanc, Merlot, Zinfandel, and Chardonnay wines. Frog's Leap Napa Valley Rutherford Sauvignon Blanc 2011 has aromas of citrus blossoms and wet river rocks in the nose. It is light and crisp with a fair amount of acidity, perfect with shellfish and seafood. Frog's Leap Napa Valley Rutherford Cabernet Sauvignon 2010 is garnet colored in the glass, with aromas of black cherry and black plums leading to restrained dark fruit flavors in the mouth. The finish is elegant and persistent. Drink now or hold for 10 to 15 years. You won't be disappointed either way.

GIRARD WINERY

6795 Washington Street, Yountville, CA 94599,
(707) 968-9297
www.girardwinery.com

Current owner Pat Roney began his career as a sommelier at Chicago's Pump Room while attending Northwestern University. Upon his return to California, he began working for Seagram's and furthered his career as the president of both Chateau St. Jean and Kunde wineries. In 2000 he purchased Girard Winery, and to this day the wines consistently receive high points and accolades from a variety of wine publications. Winemaking is under the direction of Texas native Glenn Hugo. Girard Diamond Mountain Napa Valley Cabernet Sauvignon 2010 has notes of black raspberries, black plums, and spice in the nose. In the mouth it has lots of fruit enhanced by subtle flavors of espresso and chocolate. The tannins are soft, and the finish is silky smooth. Girard Petite Sirah Napa Valley 2010 has aromas of mocha, Mediterranean herbs, and black raspberry preserves. In the mouth the fruit flavors step forward to the front of the palate, and the sultry tannins invite you in for another and another and another sip.

GRACE FAMILY VINEYARDS

1210 Rockland Drive, St. Helena, CA 94574, (707) 963-0808
www.gracefamilyvineyards.com

Ann and Dick Grace left the San Francisco suburbs in the mid-1970s in search of a better life for themselves and their three children. They fell in love with a fixer-upper Victorian homestead in Napa Valley, planted vine cuttings obtained from a neighbor, and harvested their first vintage in 1978. Today their simple winery is a very serene and peaceful place, built to resemble Buddhist temples in Nepal. Grace Family wines are extremely well received by consumers and critics alike and have been known to fetch high prices at charity auctions. A 12-liter bottle of Grace Family 2003 Cabernet raised $90,000 at the Naples Wine Auction in 2006. The family also maintains the Grace Family Vineyards Foundation, which donates money to a variety of charitable organizations. Grace Family Vineyards Napa Valley Cabernet Sauvignon 2009 has a delightful bouquet of black cherry, mocha, Christmas baking spices, and Mediterranean herbs. In the mouth the fruit is big but restrained and elegant, and the finish is long-lasting and luscious.

GRGICH HILLS

1829 St. Helena Highway, Rutherford, CA 94573, (800) 532-3057
www.grgich.com

In 1954 Mike (Miljenko) Grgich emigrated from Croatia (at that time part of Yugoslavia), bound for America with only ten winemaking books and $32 in the soles of his shoes. A few years later he found himself in Napa Valley, worked at various wineries, and in 1976 learned by telegram that a wine he'd crafted, Chateau, Montelena Chardonnay 1973 was the winning white wine in the famous 1976 Judgment of Paris. On July 4, 1977, along with partners from the Hill Bros. Coffee Company, he broke ground on the winery now known as Grgich Hills. For his numerous contributions to the California wine industry Mike was inducted into the Vintner Hall of Fame in 2008. Grgich Hills Estate Grown Napa Valley Chardonnay 2010 is straw colored, with aromas of citrus blossom and white peach in the bouquet. In the mouth it is crisp and clean, with flavors of pineapple and guava alongside a nice touch of minerality. Grgich Hills Estate Grown Miljenko's Old Vines Zinfandel 2009 is garnet colored, with notes of freshly ground black pepper, dried cherries, and black plums. On the palate it opens up nicely and has a touch of spice in the long, balanced finish.

GROTH VINEYARDS AND WINERY

750 Oakville Cross Road,
Oakville, CA 94562,
(707) 944-0290
www.grothwines.com

Dennis and Judith Groth had their heart set on buying a vineyard in Sonoma and producing Chardonnay wine until Ren Harris, a Napa grape farmer, persuaded them to drive over the mountain and take a look at vineyards on the other side. They immediately fell in love with the sea of Cabernet Sauvignon vines in Napa and purchased 121 acres on the Oakville Cross Road in 1981. The next year they purchased 44 acres in Yountville planted to Chardonnay and Merlot. Their winery was completed in 1990 and renovated again in 2007 to reach its current size of 48,000 square feet. Michael Weis has been the winemaker at Groth since 1994, and his philosophy is simple: "Be true to varietal integrity." Groth Vineyard and Winery Oakville Napa Valley Cabernet Sauvignon 2010 is all a Cabernet should be. It has loads of ripe black and red fruit in the bouquet that transfer effortlessly onto the palate. This is a big Napa Cab with soft tannins and a lingering flavor of cherry vanilla in the post palate. Groth Vineyards and Winery Napa Valley Chardonnay 2011 is straw colored, with notes of pineapple and citrus blossom in the nose and flavors of tropical fruits and soft minerality in the mouth.

HALL NAPA VALLEY

401 St. Helena Highway S., St. Helena, CA 94574,
(707) 967-2626
www.hallwines.com

Craig Hall, founder of the Dallas-based Hall Financial Group, and his wife, Kathryn Hall, former ambassador to Austria, founded Hall Napa Valley with their acquisition of the historic Bergfeld Winery in 2003. Together they are very much involved in charitable contributions and funded a Fulbright Scholarship to teach entrepreneurism in Eastern Europe. In 2005 they unveiled a new renovation of their winery and are the first California winery to achieve LEED-Gold Certification (Leadership in Energy and Environmental Design) from the U.S. Green Building Council's LEED Green Building Rating System. LEED certification takes into account environmental impact, water efficiency, and decreased energy use, among other parameters. Hall Napa Valley Estate is composed of over 500 acres of Sauvignon Blanc, Cabernet Sauvignon, and Merlot vines. Hall Napa Valley Kathryn Hall Cabernet Sauvignon 2009 is deep garnet colored, with aromas of freshly baked cherry pie, anise, purple flowers, and Christmas baking spices. In the mouth the fruit moves to the front of the palate with a layer of mocha undertones. The finish is long and luscious with a touch of anise at the very end.

Hall Napa Valley Napa River Ranch Merlot 2009 is garnet colored, with notes of black plums and anise in the nose. In the mouth flavors of fruit compote and cigar box are revealed in this delicious fruit-driven wine. Enjoy it now while the ripe fruit flavors are big and powerful; you won't be disappointed.

HARTWELL ESTATE VINEYARDS

5795 Silverado Trail, Napa, CA 94558,
(707) 255-4269
www.hartwellvineyards.com

Bob and Blanca Hartwell purchased their estate from Harry See of the See's Candy Company in 1986. They started with a single acre of Cabernet Sauvignon and produced their first wine in 1990, using their neighbor Dick Grace's facility. In 1999 they built the current Hartwell Estate winery and purchased another vineyard in Carneros to plant Sauvignon Blanc. The Hartwells are blending modern technology with Old World traditions and use a variety of fermenters, including wood tanks and concrete eggs. Hartwell Estate Merlot 2009 is garnet colored, with notes of black plum, dried cherry, and leather in the bouquet. In the mouth plum and cherry are accented by nuanced flavors of licorice and dark spices. Hartwell Estate Sauvignon Blanc 2011 is pale straw, with aromas of tropical fruits and citrus zest. On the palate citrus flavors come to life with crisp acidity and a refreshing mineral-driven finish.

HEITZ WINE CELLARS

500 Taplin Road, St. Helena, CA 94574,
(707) 963-3542
www.heitzcellar.com

Founded by Joe and Alice Heitz in 1961, Heitz Wine Cellars is one of a few Napa midcentury wineries to remain independent and family-owned. Joe Heitz received a bachelor of science degree in 1948 and worked for seven years with André Tchelistcheff at Beaulieu Vineyards before purchasing a 160-acre ranch in 1964. Heitz Wine Cellars was one of the first wineries to designate a specific vineyard with its 1966 Martha's Vineyard Cabernet Sauvignon. Today the winery is run by second-generation Kathleen Heitz Myers as president and David Heitz, her brother, as the winemaker. Heitz wines are consistently highly scored by a variety of international wine publications, including *Wine Advocate*, *Wine Enthusiast*, *Decanter*, and *Wine Spectator*. Heitz Wine Cellars Martha's Vineyard Cabernet Sauvignon 2007 is inky garnet, with aromas of black plum, Grandma's blueberry pie, and crushed spearmint leaves. It is full-bodied in the mouth with great balance and an elegant finish, a truly stunning Napa Cab! Heitz Wine Cellars Napa Valley Chardonnay 2011 is straw colored, with aromas of citrus blossom, Anjou pears, and honeydew melon. It is voluptuous in the mouth, with a crisp, clean finish that invites you in for another sip.

HENDRY RANCH WINES

3104 Redwood Road, Napa, CA 94558,
(707) 226-8320
www.hendrywines.com

Margaret and George Hendry moved to Napa Valley in 1939 and purchased what was to become the Hendry Ranch. It originally was planted by Frederick and John Sigrist in 1859, and most historians believe that this land was home to some of the first planted vineyards in the Napa Valley. After extensive replanting in the 1970s the Hendry family continued to sell their grapes to neighboring wineries, and in 1992 the first vintage under the Hendry label was produced. The vineyard was expanded in 1994 with the purchase of additional land, and today the Hendry Ranch is composed of 117 acres divided into 47 vineyard blocks. Ten different varieties are grown, including Cabernet Sauvignon and Pinot Gris. Hendry Ranch Napa Valley HRW Cabernet Sauvignon 2008 is garnet red, with aromas of dried cherry, black plum, tobacco, and spice in the nose. In the mouth it is medium-bodied with full-on fruit flavors and a pleasant finish. Hendry Ranch Napa Valley Pinot Gris 2010 is light straw, with notes of white flowers and citrus blossom. It is crisp and clean with a bracing acidity that makes it ideal as an aperitif or paired with raw shellfish.

HESS COLLECTION

4411 Redwood Road, Napa, CA 94558,
(707) 255-1144
www.hesscollection.com

Donald Hess acquired his first Mount Veeder vineyard in 1978, and today the Hess Collection owns 704 acres in Napa Valley and 330 in other California AVAs. An avid lover of the arts, Donald is consistently rated as one of the top 200 art collectors in the world. Visitors to the winery are able to enjoy a well-curated sampling of some of his favorite sculptures, paintings, mixed-media pieces, and, of course, wines. Hess Collection 19 Block Cuvée Mount Veeder Napa Valley 2009 is a blend of 63 percent Cabernet Sauvignon, 20 percent Malbec, 9 percent Syrah, 7 percent Merlot, and 1 percent Petit Verdot. It has notes of rich black plum, blackberry, cigar box, and wild anise. It is full-bodied in the mouth, with ripe fruit flavors and a touch of vanilla and lanolin. The tannins are smooth and sexy; drink it now or over the next five years. Hess Collection Mount Veeder Napa Valley Chardonnay 2009 has aromas of stone fruit, Anjou pear, and white flowers. On the palate there is a rich, round mouthfeel with tastes of lemon curd, crisp fruit flavors, and clean acidity. The Hess Collection also includes wines made under the Artezin label, which uses predominantly sourced fruit to make well-crafted wines. Artezin Mendocino County Zinfandel 2011 has aromas of red raspberry, black raspberry, and cracked black pepper, with a big and bold mouthfeel that calls out for a grilled steak. Artezin Mendocino County Petite Sirah 2010 is opaque purple, with aromas of black raspberry and cassis that flow seamlessly onto the palate and finish with balanced tannins and a touch of spice.

HEWITT VINEYARD

1695 St. Helena Highway,
Rutherford CA, 94573,
(707) 968-3638
www.hewittvineyard.com

William A. Hewitt, head of the John Deere Company, purchased the estate in 1962. He enlisted the assistance of André Tchelistcheff and replanted the land with Cabernet Sauvignon vines. For many years Hewitt sold its grapes to other wineries, but in 2001 the estate launched Hewitt Vineyard Single Vineyard Cabernet Sauvignon, and the release was met with glowing accolades. Winemaking is under the direction of Tom Rinaldi, and when he is not tending to the vines, he can be found riding around Napa on his racing bicycle or flying through the air above the vines in his glider. Hewitt Vineyard Estate Cabernet Sauvignon Rutherford 2008 is deep garnet with a violet rim. It has notes of black raspberry, black plum, and dried red cherry along with espresso and cigar box characteristics in the complex bouquet. It is bold in the mouth, with flavors of cassis and dark fruits with a balanced and persistent finish.

HONIG VINEYARD AND WINERY

850 Rutherford Road,
Rutherford, CA 94573,
(707) 963-5618
www.honigwine.com

Twenty-two-year-old Michael Honig took over the management of his grandfather's ranch in 1984 and focused on getting his wines into high-end restaurants. Over the years additional family members joined the business, and in 1998 they enlisted the help of winemaker Kristen Belair. Michael is currently active with the Napa Valley Vintners Association, the California Farm Service Agency State Committee, and the California Sustainable Winegrowing Alliance. Honig Vineyard and Winery Napa Valley Sauvignon Blanc 2011 is pale straw, with notes of white flowers, lemon zest, and tropical fruits in the bouquet. In the mouth it is medium-bodied and has a clean, mineral-driven finish. Honig Vineyard and Winery Napa Valley Cabernet Sauvignon 2010 is composed of 91.6 percent Cabernet Sauvignon, 5.2 percent Cabernet Franc, and 3.2 percent Petit Verdot. It is garnet colored, with aromas of dark fruits and Christmas baking spices. On the palate it is big with lingering flavors of licorice and spice. The tannins are round and well integrated.

HOURGLASS BLUELINE ESTATE WINES

1104 Adams Street,
St. Helena, CA 94574,
(707) 968-9332
www.hourglasswines.com

Ned and Marge Smith purchased a six-acre parcel in 1976, planted some fruit trees, and sadly, watched them wither and die. After Ted's death, his widow planned to sell the land until her son Jeff brought in soil experts from UC

Davis who convinced the family that the soil was perfect for the cultivation of vines. In 1992 Jeff planted Cabernet Sauvignon and later released his 1997 vintage with great acclaim and immediately sold his entire stock. He, his wife, and two other couples subsequently purchased another 41-acre property in 2006 and named it Blueline Vineyard. Hourglass Blueline Estate Wines Cabernet Franc 2010 is composed of 94 percent Cabernet Franc, 3 percent Cabernet Sauvignon, and 3 percent Petit Verdot. It is garnet colored, with aromas of violets, Mediterranean herbs, Indian spice, and intense dark berries, including cassis and black cherry. In the mouth the dark, rich fruit flavors are complemented by a touch of cherry tobacco in the elegant, persistent finish.

HYDE DE VILLAINE HDV WINES

588 Trancas Street,
Napa CA, 94558,
(707) 251-9121
www.hdvwines.com

Any lover of Burgundy knows the history of Aubert de Villaine, his wines, and his family. What few people know is that his wife, Pamela Fairbanks de Villaine, is a cousin to the Hyde family of California. HdV is a joint venture between the de Villaine family of Burgundy and the Hyde family of Napa Valley. The wines are bottled using the coat of arms and the name "de la Guerra," which is the historic family line from which both Pamela and the Hydes descend. HdV de la Guerra Chardonnay 2010 is straw colored, with aromas of white flowers and citrus blossom. In the mouth flavors of white peach and nectarine are noted before the pleasant mineral-laden finish. HdV Californio Syrah 2008 is deep garnet, with aromas of black plum, black raspberry, and brown baking spices. On the palate it has flavors of rich dark fruits and cinnamon. The tannins are well structured with a bit of grip. Drink it now or hold it for a few years.

INGLENOOK

1991 St. Helena Highway, Rutherford, CA 94573,
(707) 968-1100
www.inglenook.com

Founded in 1879 by Gustav Niebaum, a Finnish sea captain, Inglenook has had a gloried *and* storied past, and as of April 11, 2011, it looks like it is on its way to glory again. After Niebaum's death in 1908 and then the onset of Prohibition, Inglenook thrived under Gustav's great-nephew John Daniel Jr. from 1939 until the 1960s. But tough financial times forced Daniel to sell the estate, and over the years it was divided and managed by a number of owners, including Heublein, Nabisco, and Constellation. In 1975 film director Francis Ford Coppola purchased 1,500 acres and named it Niebaum-Coppola and then Rubicon, but the historic winery, trademarked name, and additional 94 acres remained out of his hands—that is, until April 11, 2011. On that historic day decades of dedication to the Inglenook memory and name became fruitful, and because of Francis Ford and Eleanor Coppola's undying persistence, Inglenook is once again whole. Today winemaking is carried out by Philippe Bascaules of Château Margaux provenance and Stéphane Derenoncourt, the famed French consultant. Inglenook Blancaneaux 2011 is a blend of Roussanne, Marsanne, and Viognier. It is pale straw colored, with aromas of citrus blossom, Bartlett pear, and ruby pink grapefruit. It is crisp yet silky on the palate with a delightful mouthfeel and a clean finish. Rubicon 2008 is composed of 87 percent Cabernet Sauvignon, 6 percent Cabernet Franc, 4 percent Petit Verdot, and 3 percent Merlot. It is garnet purple, with aromas of fresh blueberry, black currant, and dried black cherries. In the mouth it has great heft and fruit flavors accented by anise and mocha. The tannins are silky and smooth, and the finish is long and luxurious.

JARVIS ESTATE

2970 Monticello Road, Napa, CA 94558,
(707) 255-5280
www.jarviswines.com

In addition to being known for their fine wine, William and Leticia Jarvis are well known

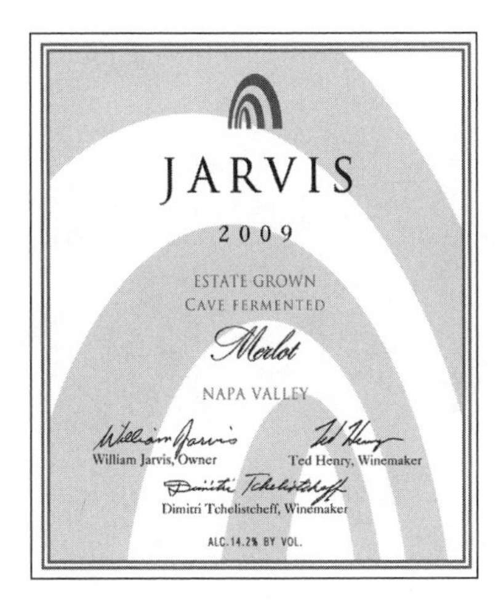

in Napa for their patronage of the Jarvis Conservatory, which brings master classes in classical opera, dance, and film to the valley. Having spent a great deal of time in France and Spain, the couple found it natural to combine their interest in the arts and the art of winemaking when they moved to the Napa Valley. The Jarvis Estate Winery encompasses 1,320 acres with a 45,000-square-foot cave built purposely underground so as not to spoil the natural beauty of the land. Thirty-seven acres are devoted to plantings of Cabernet Franc, Petit Verdot, Merlot, Chardonnay, and Tempranillo used in the production of estate-grown wines. Jarvis Estate Winery Merlot 2009 is cherry garnet in color, with aromas of ripe black cherries and baking spice in the bouquet. In the mouth it has a round velvetlike tannic structure and flavors of black plum and black currants. Jarvis Estate Winery Finch Hollow Chardonnay 2010 is straw yellow, with aromas of green apple and top notes of vanilla and English butter toffee. It is rich and round in the mouth with an elegant finish; it's everything a California Chardonnay should be.

JOEL GOTT WINES

PO Box 539, St. Helena, CA 94574,
(707) 963-3365
www.gottwines.com

Joel Gott's family has been making wine in California for five generations. His first job outside the family winery was at Kenwood Winery in Sonoma County. He and his brother took over the Calistoga Palisades

Market in 1993 and began making wine in 1996. In 1999 he took over management of the iconic Taylor's Refresher in St. Helena that was famous for great burgers and milk shakes. Although it is now named Gott's Roadside and there are additional locations in Napa's Oxbow Public Market and San Francisco's Ferry Building Marketplace, no visit to Napa Valley would be complete without at least one pilgrimage. Don't forget to order a bottle of Joel Gott's wine to pair with your burger. Joel Gott California Alakai 2011 is a blend of Grenache, Syrah, Mourvèdre, and Carignane and has aromas of freshly ground black pepper, red raspberry, and red cherry in the bouquet. In the mouth there are pronounced fruit flavors and silky smooth tannins. Joel Gott California Cabernet Sauvignon 2010 is garnet red, with a fragrance that includes black plum, cherry cola, and Mediterranean herbs. It is both fruity and acidic in the mouth with a soft tannic finish.

JOSEPH PHELPS VINEYARDS

200 Taplin Road, St. Helena, CA 94574,
(800) 707-5789
www.josephphelps.com

Looking for a career change, builder Joseph Phelps bought a 600-acre cattle ranch in

Spring Valley and began planting vines, building a winery in 1973. The estate's current holdings include the original Spring Valley Home Ranch, Las Rocas and Barboza vineyards in Stags Leap, Backus Vineyard in Oakville, Banca Dorada in Rutherford, Suscol Vineyard in South Napa, Yountville Vineyard in Oak Knoll, and Larry Hyde & Sons Vineyard in Carneros. Insignia, a Bordeaux-style blend, is Joseph Phelps's flagship wine, and the company is proud to say that twenty-nine of the last thirty-four vintages of Insignia have been rated 90 points or higher by numerous wine publications. Winemaking is performed by a talented team that includes Damian Parker, the director of winemaking; Ashley Hepworth, the Napa winemaker; and Philippe Pessereau, the director of vineyard operations. Kelly Fields and Justin Ennis assist the team. The sister winery, Freestone Vineyards in Sonoma, focuses on wines made from Chardonnay and Pinot Noir. Joseph Phelps Insignia Napa Valley Estate 2009 is dark purple garnet, with notes of blueberry pie, freshly picked black raspberries, and tobacco leaf in the bouquet. In the mouth it has restrained and elegant fruit characteristics and well-integrated tannins. The finish is long and luxurious. Joseph Phelps Sauvignon Blanc 2011 is straw colored, with aromas of citrus blossom and grapefruit zest. It is voluptuous in the mouth with dancing flavors of tropical fruits and a crisp, clean finish.

KAPCSÁNDY FAMILY WINERY

1001 State Lane, Yountville, CA 94599,
(707) 948-3100
www.kapcsandywines.com

Lou Kapcsándy Sr. fled his homeland during the 1956 Hungarian Revolution and eventually found himself on the West Coast of the United States, but it wasn't until 1998 on a trip to Bordeaux that he and his wife decided to start a winery for their retirement years. In 2000 they acquired the former Beringer Estate State Lane Vineyard and began replanting Cabernet Sauvignon and Merlot vines. Their current winery was completed in 2005, and their wines are consistently rated highly in *Wine Spectator*, *Wine Enthusiast*, and *Wine Advocate*. Kapcsándy Family Winery Cabernet Sauvignon Grand Vin 2009 is a blend of 96 percent Cabernet Sauvignon, 3 percent Merlot, and 1 percent Cabernet Franc. It is garnet colored, with aromas of purple flowers, anise, and juicy red plums. In the mouth the fruit flavors come forward with a touch of brown baking spices before the long elegant finish. Kapcsándy Family Winery Roberta's Reserve 2009 is composed of 96 percent Merlot and 4 percent Cabernet Franc. It has aromas of ripe black plums and red raspberries in the bouquet. On the palate it is big and rich, with flavors of anise and well-worn saddle leather under the fruit components, and has a very pleasant persistent finish.

KONGSGAARD

4375 Atlas Peak Road, Napa, CA 94558,
(707) 226-2190
www.kongsgaardwine.com

John Kongsgaard's family has lived in the Napa Valley for five generations. He and his wife, Maggy, began planting vines together in 1970, but their eponymous wines were not introduced until 1996. Kongsgaard wines are fiercely handmade with very limited production by John, Maggy, and their son, Alex. Kongsgaard is consistently rated highly by wine lovers and critics alike. Kongsgaard The Judge Napa Valley Chardonnay 2010 is medium straw yellow, with aromas of citrus blossom and rich lemon curd. It is velvety smooth in the mouth, with delicious fruit flavors and just the right amount of minerality. It's hard to believe that this isn't a Grand Cru Burgundian wine. Too bad the family produced only 340 cases of this delicious wine. Kongsgaard Napa Valley Cabernet Sauvignon 2010 has aromas of rich red fruits that carry through to the palate. It is big and round with a luxurious finish. Again, too bad only 280 cases were produced.

KRUPP BROTHERS

3267 Soda Canyon Road, Napa, CA 94558,
(707) 226-2215
www.kruppbrothers.com

Physician Jan Krupp turned vintner when he purchased 41 acres in 1991. He got his brother Bart involved a few years later, and together they purchased an additional 750 acres and created Krupp Vineyard, Krupp Brothers Vineyard, and Stagecoach Vineyard. Krupp Brothers Black Bart Stagecoach Vineyard Syrah 2008 is garnet with inky tones and has aromas of purple flowers, charcuterie, cigar box, and black fruits. The fruit flavors become seamlessly pronounced on the palate with pleasant notes of vanilla and oak in the finish. Krupp Brothers Stagecoach M5 Cabernet Sauvignon 2009 is composed of 90 percent Cabernet Sauvignon, 8 percent Merlot, and 2 percent Cabernet Franc. It has notes of cassis, dark chocolate, and black raspberries in the complex bouquet. It is big and viscous on the palate with a gorgeous mouthfeel. The finish is elegant and smooth with well-structured tannins.

KULETO ESTATE

2470 Sage Canyon Road, St. Helena, CA 94574,
(707) 302-2209
www.kuletoestate.com

Restaurateur Pat Kuleto acquired 761 acres of eastern Napa Valley's mountainous terrain in 1992 and began planting Cabernet Sauvignon, Pinot Noir, Chardonnay, and Sangiovese. He then set upon the task of building a 17,000-square-foot gravity-flow winery in 2001. Winemaking has been under the direction of Dave Lattin since 2002, and Alberto Ochoa handles vineyard management. Bill Foley, owner of Foley Family Wines, purchased Kuleto in 2009 and remains at the helm today. Kuleto

Estate Chardonnay 2010 is straw colored, with aromas of Granny Smith apples and citrus blossom. It is big, bold, and refreshing in the mouth with a pleasant finish. Kuleto Estate Syrah 2010 is composed of 82 percent Syrah, 8 percent Cabernet Sauvignon, 5 percent Cabernet Franc, and 5 percent Petit Verdot. It is inky, with notes of black plum and violet in the bouquet. It is soft and round in the mouth with a persistent finish. Kuleto also makes wines under the Native Son, Frog Prince, and India Ink labels.

LADERA VINEYARDS

150 White Cottage Road South,
Angwin, CA 94508,
(707) 965-2445
www.laderavineyards.com

Pat and Anne Stotesbery met while attending Stanford and the University of San Francisco and eventually moved to Montana to become cattle farmers. A serendipitous trip to Napa Valley changed their lives, and today the couple are custodians of a circa-1886 historical stone winery. Winemaking at Ladera is carried out by New Zealander Jade Barrett with consulting winemaker Karen Culler, and vineyard management is handled by Gabriel Reyes. Ladera Vineyards Howell Mountain Cabernet Sauvignon 2008 is 100 percent Cabernet Sauvignon and is deep

garnet, with aromas of black raspberry, blueberry, and cocoa nibs. It is rich and juicy in the mouth with balanced tannins and a long fruit-filled finish. Ladera Vineyards Napa Valley Cabernet Sauvignon 2008 is composed of 95 percent Cabernet Sauvignon, 3 percent Petit Verdot, and 2 percent Malbec. It is deep garnet, with notes of black raspberry, cherry cola, and anise in the bouquet. In the mouth the fruit flavors are pronounced, with well-structured tannins that carry you through the long finish.

LAMBORN FAMILY VINEYARDS

1984 Summit Lake Drive, Angwin, CA 94563,
(925) 254-0511
www.lamborn.com

After his divorce Bob Lamborn needed a change from his career as a private investigator in the

San Francisco Bay Area, so in 1971 he convinced his son Mike to buy a plot of Howell Mountain land adjacent to his. The two got to work clearing land and planting vines, and in 1982 they produced their first 100 cases of wine. In 1996 the Lamborn Family Wine Company brought in winemaker Heidi Barrett, and today the production is over 1,000 cases per year. Lamborn Family Vineyards Vintage VII Cabernet Sauvignon 2009 is garnet colored, with notes of dark fruits, black plum, black cherry, and toffee in the complex bouquet. It is bold yet luscious in the mouth with balanced tannins and a silky finish. Lamborn Family Vineyards Howell Mountain Proprietor Grown Zinfandel The Abundant Vintage 2009 is dark garnet, with aromas of black plums, black raspberry preserves, and freshly ground black pepper. It is fruit-forward on the palate, with notes of black currant and French toast in the finish.

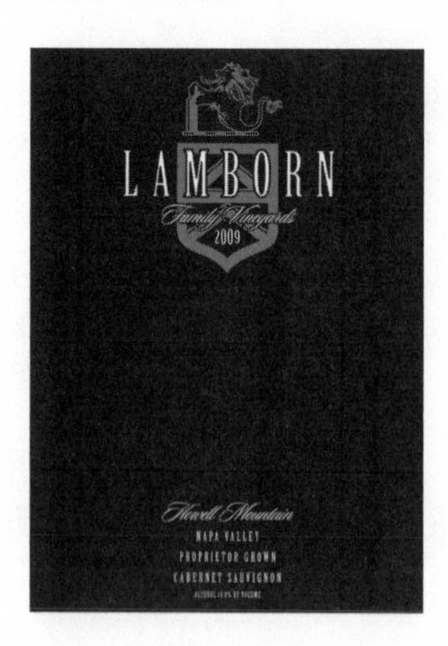

LA SIRENA

3520 Evey Road, Calistoga, CA 94515,
(707) 942-1105
www.lasirenawine.com

Heidi Barrett is well known in the world of wine. She's been called "the Wine Diva of Napa Valley" by *Time* magazine, and Robert Parker has labeled her "the First Lady of Wine." Anybody who has ever heard of Screaming Eagle knows that the 1992 and 1997 vintages she made received perfect 100 point scores from Parker and a 6-liter bottle of the 1992 set a record at the 2000 Napa Auction when it sold for $500,000. Heidi's 1992 and 1993 Dalla Valle Vineyards also received 100 points. So what's a girl to do after all this success? Heidi's answer to the question was to make wine under her own label, La Sirena. Named after the Spanish and Italian word for "mermaid," La Sirena represents Heidi's love of winemaking and scuba diving. We've been lucky enough to sit across the table from this amazing woman and enjoy her well-made and delicious wines. La Sirena Cabernet Sauvignon 2009 is a blend of 83 percent Cabernet Sauvignon, 11 percent Merlot, 4 percent Petit Verdot, and 2 percent Cabernet Franc. It is deep ruby to garnet red, with aromas of cherry vanilla ice cream, cassis, and dark plums. It is big and bold in the mouth with silky smooth tannins. Heidi thinks that 2009 is one of the best vintages of the decade, and we couldn't agree more. La Sirena Le Barrettage 2009 is a blend of Syrah from a few different vineyards. It is ruby red in the glass, with notes of black fruits, brown spice, and smoked meats in the bouquet. It opens up in the mouth with pronounced fruit and spice flavors and a smooth tannic finish.

LIPARITA

No visitor facilities. (415) 606-4640
www.liparita.com

Spencer Hoopes has resurrected the spirit of Liparita, one of Napa Valley's original ghost wineries—one of those with a storied past that eventually was forgotten after it fell into a state of disrepair. W.F. Keyes built the original stone cellar in 1880 on top of Howell Mountain, and the wines received international acclaim at the Paris Exposition in 1900 and a gold medal at the St. Louis Expo in 1904. Spencer and winemaker Jason Fisher are dedicated to bringing back Liparita's glorious past. Liparita Oakville Cabernet Sauvignon 2009 is garnet colored, with aromas of ripe cherries, red raspberries, and a whiff of anise. In the mouth the fruit flavors are front and center, with a touch of freshly ground black pepper in the finish. Liparita V Block Yountville Cabernet Sauvignon 2009 is garnet colored, with luscious ripe black fruit aromas in the nose and big berry flavors in the mouth. The tannins are quite linear and firm. This is a delicious California Cab.

LOKOYA

7600 St. Helena Highway, Oakville, CA 94558,
(707) 948-1968
www.lokoya.com

Named for the indigenous American tribe that lived on Mount Veeder, Lokoya is a boutique winery that concentrates on making ultra-premium wines. A member of the Jackson Family Wine portfolio, Lokoya consistently garners high scores from *Wine Spectator, Wine Advocate*, and *Wine Enthusiast.* Christopher Carpenter is responsible for winemaking. Lokoya Howell Mountain Cabernet Sauvignon 2010 has big aromas of blueberry, black raspberry, licorice, and forest floor. It is full-bodied in the mouth with rich fruit flavors and lifted notes of mint and menthol in the luscious finish.

LONG MEADOW RANCH WINERY

728 Main Street, St. Helena, CA 94574,
(707) 963-4555
www.longmeadowranch.com

The original deed for the land now known as Long Meadow Ranch was signed in 1872 by President Ulysses S. Grant. It had plantings of olives, apples, and grapes that were used for wine until the ranch was abandoned because of Prohibition. In 1989 it was acquired by Ted Hall and his family, who began the arduous process of restoring the ranch to its former status. Today Ted is the president of Long Meadow Ranch and Affiliates, which is a group of family-owned companies that raise grass-fed beef, organic fruits and vegetables, olive oil, and of course grapes for their delicious wines. Whenever we're in St. Helena, we make sure to visit the farmer's market at Long Meadow Ranch held every Friday morning for some of the best local and seasonal produce. Long Meadow Ranch Winery Napa Valley Sauvignon Blanc 2011 is straw colored, with aromas of tropical fruits and honeydew melon and a top note of white flowers such as freesia. In the mouth it is smooth and silky with a crisp finish and pleasant minerality. Long Meadow Ranch Winery Cabernet Sauvignon 2009 is garnet colored, with aromas of black raspberries, cigar box, and licorice in the enticing bouquet. It is big but restrained on the palate with a pleasant persistent finish. Drink it now or any time in the next 7 to 10 years.

LONG VINEYARDS

PO Box 50, St. Helena, CA 94574,
(707) 963-2496
www.longvineyards.com

Once-married couple Bob and Zelma Long started Long Vineyards in 1977 and produced one of Napa Valley's first barrel-fermented Chardonnays from vines planted in 1967. The family-owned estate winery and vineyards are on Pritchard Hill at an elevation of 800 to 1,100 feet. Long Vineyards currently produces 1,200 cases of Chardonnay from estate-grown fruit, 500 cases of Cabernet Sauvignon, and 80 cases of Sangiovese from fruit sourced from Seghesio Vineyards in Geyserville. The winemaking team consists of Zelma Long, Bob Long, and Sandi Belcher, and the vineyards are under the management of Dr. Phil Freese

(Zelma Long's husband) and John Arns. Long Vineyards Estate Napa Valley Chardonnay 2008 is straw yellow, with delightful aromas of citrus blossom, toasted hazelnut, and citrus zest. It is generous on the palate with a creamy mouthfeel and nice heft. It has tantalizing flavors of Granny Smith apple and lemon curd, with a long and lush finish.

LOUIS M. MARTINI WINERY

254 St. Helena Highway, St. Helena, CA 94574,
(707) 963-2736
www.louismartini.com

Louis M. Martini emigrated from Genoa in 1899 but returned to Italy a few years later to learn winemaking. In 1922, during Prohibition, he opened LM Martini Grape Products Company, which made wine for the Catholic Church and supplied grape concentrate to home winemakers. He built his eponymous winery in 1933 and passed the baton to his son Louis P. Martini in 1954. Today Louis M. Martini's grandson Mike Martini runs the family business under the auspices of the Gallo family. Louis M. Martini Napa Valley Cabernet Sauvignon 2010 is garnet colored, with aromas of anise, cigar box, and black fruits. It is nicely structured and has a good amount of weight on the palate. There are flavors of ripe fruit, Christmas baking spices, and vanilla in the persistent finish.

MARKHAM VINEYARDS

2812 St. Helena Highway North,
St. Helena, CA 94574,
(707) 963-5292
www.markhamvineyards.com

Bruce Markham purchased his eponymous winery in 1978. Built in 1879, it was originally called Laurent and is the fourth oldest winery in Napa Valley that has been continuously operated since its inception. Markham Vineyards currently owns 350 acres of grapevines in Napa Valley. Winemaking is under the direction of Kimberlee Nicholls, who enjoys "weaving together the rich fruit flavors" to make her elegant wines. Markham Vineyards Cellar 1879 Red Blend Napa Valley 2010 is composed of 65 percent Merlot, 29 percent Cabernet Sauvignon, 3 percent Petit Verdot, and 3 percent Petite Sirah. It is ruby garnet colored, with aromas of black cherry and charcuterie.

In the mouth it is rich and fruity—think cherry cola—with silky tannins and a persistent finish. Markham Vineyards Merlot 2010 is ruby colored, with aromas of rich black fruits and vanilla ice cream. It is soft and elegant in the mouth with a rich cherry finish.

MARSTON FAMILY VINEYARD

3600 White Sulphur Springs Road,
St. Helena, CA 94574,
(707) 963-8490
www.marstonfamilyvineyard.com

Vines were planted on what is now known as the Marston Family Vineyard in the mid-1890s. In 1969 Michael and Alexandra Marston took over stewardship of this beautiful property, and today approximately 50 acres of their 500-acre estate are dedicated solely to Cabernet Sauvignon. In addition, the Marstons have donated over 200 acres to natural conservation efforts in the Napa Valley. Marston Family Vineyard Spring Mountain District Cabernet Sauvignon 2009 has delightful top notes of purple flowers, red rose, and licorice wafting above rich, bold fruit aromas of red raspberries and black plums. In the mouth the fruit flavors move forward to the mid palate, with subtle tastes of cigar box and cocoa powder in the post palate. Well-balanced tannins provide for an extremely pleasant and persistent finish.

MAYACAMAS VINEYARDS

1155 Lokoya Road,
Napa, CA 94558,
(707) 224-4030
www.mayacamas.com

The original winery was built in 1889 by John Fisher, a German immigrant who first worked as a sword engraver and then as a pickle merchant and later founded Fisher and Sons, a Napa-based company that made wine from the vines they had planted on their land. Robert and Elinor Travers purchased Mayacamas Vineyards in 1968. The Traverses were extremely proud when their 1971 vintage Cabernet was chosen for the famous 1976 Judgment of Paris. Although it received seventh place in the original tasting, it placed second in 1986 and third in the final tasting of 2006. Mayacamas Vineyards wines are well known today for their ability to age; in fact, we tasted a collection of their library wines dating back to their 1989 Cabernet Sauvignon and were extremely pleased. Mayacamas Vineyards was sold in May 2013 to a group that included Charles Banks and his wife, Ali, who were the former owners of Screaming Eagle and Jonata. Mayacamas Vineyards Cabernet Sauvignon 2007 is garnet colored, with aromas of black plum, red raspberry, and purple flowers in the bouquet. In the mouth it is full-bodied, with flavors of fresh dark fruits and a touch of eucalyptus before the lingering well-balanced tannic finish. Mayacamas Vineyards Chardonnay 2009 is straw colored, with aromas of lemon blossom, green apple, and tropical fruits. In the mouth flavors of Anjou pear and stone fruits come out. The finish is crisp and clean with just a touch of oak.

MELKA WINES

PO Box 82,
Oakville, CA 94562,
(707) 963-6008
www.melkawines.com

Philippe Melka began his study of wine under the tutelage of some of the world's finest Bordeaux winemakers: Christian Moueix from Pétrus, Michel Rolland from Château Le Bon Pasteur, and Jean Delmas from Haut-Brion. After traveling around the world, Philippe chose Napa Valley to hone his craft and currently works as a consultant to many well-known wineries. He and his wife, Cherie, decided to settle down in the valley, raise a family, and make wines under the Melka name. Their wines are very well rated, and recently Robert Parker named Philippe one of the top nine wine consultants in the world. Melka Wines CJ Napa Valley Cabernet Sauvignon 2009 is composed of 83 percent Cabernet Sauvignon, 7 percent Cabernet Franc, 6 percent Petit Verdot, and 4 percent Merlot and has delightful aromas of black currant, black cherry, and a touch of cigar box in the complex bouquet. It is big and lush in the mouth, with distinct fruit flavors and lifted Indian spices. There are powerful yet soft tannins and a long, supple finish. Melka Wines Métisse Napa Valley Jumping Goat Vineyard 2009 is a blend of 80 percent Cabernet Sauvignon, 13 percent Merlot, and 7 percent Petit Verdot. It is ruby garnet colored, with aromas of dark fruit and black currant with top notes of cedar and tobacco leaf. It fills your mouth with luscious fruit and supple tannins before the persistent and elegant finish.

MERUS WINES

424 Crystal Springs Road,
St. Helena, CA 94574,
(707) 251-5551
www.meruswines.com

Erika Gottl and Mark Herold began making wine in the two-car garage behind their home. Their first vintage was 1998, and they soon achieved international acclaim. Merus was purchased by Bill Foley in 2007, and today the winery is making award-winning wines that are available only to winery members and those lucky enough to find them on select restaurant wine lists. Merus Cabernet Sauvignon 2009 is garnet colored, with aromas of black plums and black raspberries with a touch of anise and cigar box top notes. It is full-bodied and elegant in the mouth with pronounced fruit flavors and a lingering finish.

MICHAEL MONDAVI FAMILY ESTATE

1285 Dealy Lane,
Napa, CA 94559,
(707) 256-2757
www.michaelmondavifamilyestate.com

We had the privilege of walking the vines with Michael Mondavi at his Animo Vineyard atop Atlas Peak and listening to his memories of his late grandfather, who taught him that "all great winemakers must have respect for their soil and make good wine from the ground up." In addition to learning from his grandfather, Michael's winemaking experience includes responsibility for the wines made from 1966 through 1975 at Robert Mondavi Winery. Over the years his assistants there included winemaking luminaries such as Mike Ggrich, Zelma Long, and Warren Wirniarski. Grapes for Michael's iconic M Cabernet Sauvignon are sourced solely from Animo, which is the Italian word for "soul." Winemaking remains a family affair at Michael Mondavi Family Estate; his lovely wife, Isabel, son, Rob, and daughter, Dina, are all involved. The family is joined by Tony Coltrin, who assists with all the winemaking and produces wine under his own label, Oberon. Rob Mondavi Jr.'s label is named Spellbound, and he also is responsible for making wine for his mother's label, Isabel. Michael, Rob, and Dina are all involved in making wine under the Emblem label. In addition, the family makes wines under the labels Medusa and Hangtime. After all that walking in the vineyard we worked up quite a thirst and were extremely happy when we sat down on the sunny early autumn afternoon with Michael, Rob, and Tony for a tasting of their portfolio.

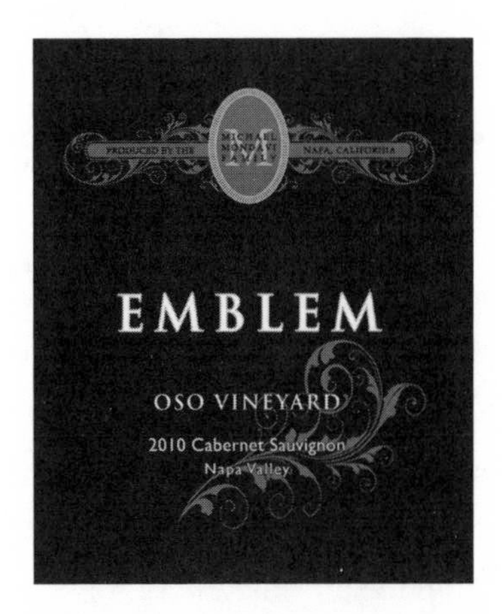

M by Michael Mondavi Cabernet Sauvignon 2009 is deep garnet in the glass, with enticing aromas of fruits of the wood, black plum, and a hint of tobacco leaf. On the palate it has a luxurious mouthfeel and big yet restrained flavors of dark fruit and spice. The exquisitely balanced tannins glide effortlessly into the long, elegant finish. The only word we could muster after our initial sip was "WOW!" Stylistically, we both feel that Michael's M is reminiscent of the great Mondavi Cabs made in the early 1970s. Spellbound Petite Sirah 2012 is dark garnet, with notes of mint, mocha, black raspberry, and plum in the bouquet. In the mouth it is full-bodied and has rich tannins and refreshing acidity. Emblem Oso Vineyard Cabernet Sauvignon 2010 is dark ruby, with aromas of black cherry, blackberry, and toffee. In the mouth fruit flavors are complemented by touches of espresso, vanilla bean, and dark chocolate. Isabel Mondavi Carneros Chardonnay 2012 is brilliantly golden-colored in the glass. There are notes of Seckel pear, Granny Smith apple, and orange blossom in the bouquet. Crisp and clean on the palate with medium body and refreshing minerality, this is a wine that one could sip all afternoon.

As the day progressed and the sun hung lower in the sky, the conversation turned to food and cooking, as it often does, and amid the early evening fog we're pretty sure that we promised to cook an Italian dinner for the Mondavi family the next time we visit Napa. We look forward to making good on that promise.

MINER FAMILY WINERY

7850 Silverado Trail,
Napa, CA 94558,
(707) 944-9500
www.minerwines.com

Dave Miner left the world of corporate software in 1993 and joined Oakville Ranch Vineyards, which at that time was owned by his late uncle Robert Miner. He and his wife, Emily, met while working at Oakville Ranch, and in 1999 they married and started the Miner Family Winery. Their first wine was released the same year, and their hopes are that the Miner Family Winery legacy will continue with their daughters Sophie and Calla. Miner Family Wines are consistently well received by *Wine Spectator* and *Wine Enthusiast* magazines. Their flagship, Miner Family Winery The Oracle Napa Valley 2007, is a delicious Bordeaux-style blend. It is ruby garnet colored, with primary aromas of black cherry, black raspberry, and coffee and top notes of black olive and cigar box. The tannic structure is firm yet sweet. Drink it now or through 2020.

MI SUEÑO WINERY

910 Enterprise Way,
Napa, CA 94558,
(707) 258-6358
www.misuenowinery.com

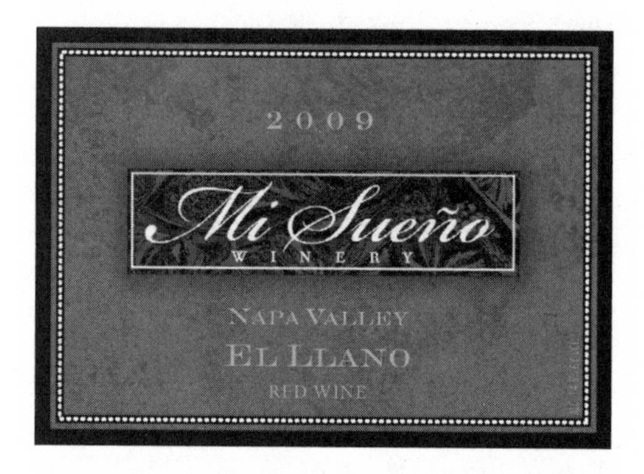

We first met Rolando Herrera in 2008 at a Napa Valley Vintners tasting in New York City and were impressed with his family history as well as his wines. Rolando's family emigrated from Mexico when he was young, and he began his wine country career very humbly as a dishwasher at Auberge du Soleil. Over the next 20 years he worked his way up at Stag's Leap Wine Cellars, Chateau Potelle, and Paul Hobbs Wine Consulting and eventually opened his "dream" winery—Mi Sueño. Although his current winery is in an industrial park just south of Napa, Rolando's dream of attaining a large estate winery with rolling vineyards could very well happen in the near future because of his vision, drive, and commitment to quality wine production. Mi Sueño El Llano Red 2009 is a proprietary blend of Syrah and Cabernet Sauvignon. It has aromas of espresso beans, dried cherries, and red plum in the bouquet. In the mouth the fruit flavors are big and pronounced with silky textured tannins before the long finish. Mi Sueño Los Carneros Chardonnay 2009 is straw colored, with aromas of lemon blossom, orange pith, and white flowers. It has bright flavors of green apple and lemon curd and a crisp, clean finish.

MOUNT VEEDER WINERY

1178 Galleron Road,
Napa, CA 94574,
(877) 545-4932
www.mtveeder.com

Michael and Arlene Bernstein purchased what was to become the Mount Veeder Winery in the early 1960s. It was originally a plum orchard, and Michael and Arlene planted vines and produced their first Cabernet Sauvignon in 1973. Today, Matt Ashby is the vineyard manager and Janet Myers is the winemaker responsible for crafting Mount Veeder Winery's delicious wines. Mount Veeder Winery Cabernet Sauvignon 2009 is composed of 82 percent Cabernet Sauvignon, 12 percent Merlot, 4 percent Petit Verdot, 1 percent Malbec, and 1 percent Syrah. It is ruby garnet in the glass, with aromas of cassis and black plums. Also present are top notes of licorice and Christmas baking spices. In the mouth it is well balanced with flavors of ripe dark fruits and just a hint of chocolate-covered coffee beans. Mount Veeder Winery Cabernet Franc 2008 is garnet colored, with aromas of chocolate-covered cherries and black olive tapenade. It is composed of 76 percent Cabernet Franc, 14 percent Cabernet Sauvignon, and 10 percent Merlot. It is big in the mouth, with lots of fruit and a persistent lush finish.

MUMM NAPA

8445 Silverado Trail,
Rutherford, CA 94573,
(707) 967-7770
www.mummnapa.com

The notable French Champagne house GH Mumm sent its attaché Guy Devaux to the United States in 1979 on a quest to find suitable *terroir* in which to grow traditional Champagne grapes. His search ended in Napa Valley, and in 1986 Mumm Cuvée Napa was established. Monsieur Devaux passed away in 1995, but the spirit of his winemaking is carried on by Champagne-born winemaker Ludovic Dervin. Before joining Mumm, Dervin worked at Charles Heidsieck, California's Piper Sonoma, and harvests in South Africa and Greece. Mumm Napa Blanc de Blancs 2008 is straw colored, with delightful *perlage* of very fine bubbles. It has aromas of toasted brioche, green apple, hazelnut, and a touch of lifted cinnamon as a top note. It is crisp and clean in the mouth with a mineral-driven finish. Mumm Napa Devaux Ranch 2008 is 100 percent Chardonnay and has bubbles that gently tickle the nose. It has notes of freshly cooked vanilla French toast and lemon curd. It is crisp yet generous on the palate with a lovely finish that keeps inviting you in for another sip.

NAPA CELLARS

PO Box 248, St. Helena, CA 94574,
(707) 963-3104
www.napacellars.com

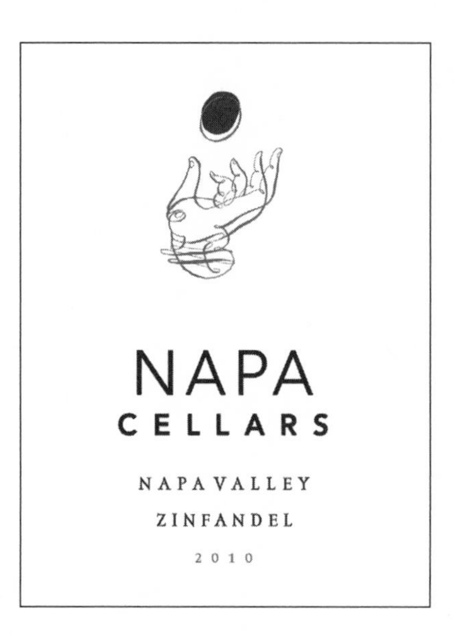

Napa Cellars prides itself on its award-winning wines, each one blended to represent the best possible expression of the variety. Winemaking and blending are under the direction of Joe Shirley, a native Californian who left a premed trajectory to get a master of science in enology at the University of California, Davis. Joe worked at Trinchero Winery in 1999 and in 2007 accepted the position as head winemaker at Napa Cellars. Napa Cellars also makes wines from Sonoma County grapes under a second label, Folie à Deux. Napa Cellars Napa Valley Zinfandel 2010 is inky reddish purple, with aromas of red raspberry, black currants, and Christmas baking spices. In the mouth there are flavors of cherry pie and fresh black fruits, with firm acidity and well-structured tannins. Napa Cellars Napa Valley Cabernet Sauvignon 2010 is garnet colored, with notes of cigar box, black plum, and brown spice in the bouquet. On the palate the fruit flavors move forward in the mouth, and the balanced acidity leads to a persistent finish.

NEWTON VINEYARD

2555 Madrona Avenue,
Yountville, CA 94599,
(707) 963-9000
www.newtonvineyard.com

Su Hua and Peter Newton purchased a square mile of land on Spring Mountain in 1997 and soon thereafter planted Cabernet Sauvignon, Merlot, Petit Verdot, and Cabernet Franc vines in 112 separate blocks around existing trees to avoid upsetting the natural balance of the landscape. Visitors to the winery are always delighted by the Chinese pagoda representing Su Hua's heritage, the British telephone booth representing Peter's British roots, and Solo Pino, a single pine tree that stands over 100 feet tall and graces Newton's wine label. Guests also love the formal English parterre garden that sits atop the winery's Chardonnay barrel room. We have enjoyed tasting Newton's delicious wines in New York City and Napa with winemaker Chris Millard. Newton Vineyard Unfiltered Chardonnay 2010 is medium straw colored, with notes of honeydew melon, white stone fruits, and honeycomb in the bouquet. Upon entry into the mouth, the first impression is that of pineapple upside-down cake followed by luscious tropical fruit flavors. The finish is creamy and delightful. Newton Vineyard Red Label Cabernet Sauvignon 2010 is garnet colored, with aromas of black raspberry, red plum, and Mediterranean herbs. It is fruity on the palate with a persistent and pleasant herbal finish.

NICKEL & NICKEL

8164 St. Helena Highway, Rutherford, CA 94573,
(707) 967-9600
www.nickelandnickel.com

In 1997 the partners at Far Niente decided to produce 100 percent single-varietal, single-vineyard wines, and the winery known as Nickel & Nickel was born. The team acquired the 42-acre John C. Sullenger Vineyard and began construction of a modern winery within the 1880s farmhouse that graces the property. Nickel & Nickel Napa Valley Yountville State Ranch Vineyard Cabernet Sauvignon 2009 is garnet colored, with aromas of rich berries, Christmas baking spices, and tobacco. In the mouth there is a pleasant heft on the palate, with flavors of black fruits and silky tannins. Nickel & Nickel Napa Valley Oakville Branding Iron Vineyard Cabernet Sauvignon 2009 is ruby to garnet colored, with notes of forest floor, spice, and black cherry in the complex bouquet. On the palate the fruit flavors move forward as flavors of toasted oak and soft Tahitian vanilla prepare the mouth for the luscious fruit-filled finish. Although it is drinking nicely now, age this one for a few years and you will be even more impressed.

OAKVILLE RANCH VINEYARDS

7781 Silverado Trail, Napa, CA 94558,
(707) 944-9665
www.oakvilleranchwinery.com

English-born Mary MacInnes met Bob Miner while she was working in Paris. Soon thereafter the couple married, moved to Napa Valley, and acquired the Oakville Ranch in 1989. Oakville Ranch wines are well received by *Wine Enthusiast* and *Decanter*. It takes a team to make their well-made wines. Winemaking is under the direction of Anne Vawter, who received her degree at University of California, Davis, and vineyard management is headed by Phil Coturri, who maintains both organic and biodynamic principles. Oakville Ranch Napa Valley Chardonnay 2011 is straw colored and has aromas of apple pie, pear compote, and white flowers. It is medium-bodied in the mouth, with a slight vanilla nuance and a bright finish. Oakville Ranch Napa Valley Robert's Cabernet Franc 2009 is garnet colored, with a violet rim. Aromas of fresh blackberries and blueberry pie follow through to the palate. The tannic structure is slightly grippy but pleasant, making this a nice wine to go with heavy foods.

OAKVILLE WINERY

7830 St. Helena Highway, Oakville, CA 94562,
(866) 422-4818
www.oakvillewinery.com

First established as Brun & Chaix in 1877 and reestablished in 1993, Oakville Winery strives to produce "Napa Valley's best quality at reasonable prices" with its Bonded Winery #9 Portfolio. Oakville Winery Napa Valley Cabernet Sauvignon 2009 is an intense garnet color, with aromas of black currant, black raspberry, and candied violets. It is round on the palate, with rich fruit flavors and a touch of cigar box and mint in the post palate. Drink it now or over the next 10 years.

OBERON

1285 Dealy Lane,Napa, CA 94559,
(707) 256-2757
www.oberonwines.com

Oberon wines are expertly crafted by Napa-born winemaker Tony Coltrin at the Michael

Mondavi Family Winery. We had the pleasure of tasting Oberon with both Tony and Michael at the property on a picture-perfect autumn day. Because Tony and Michael source quality fruit from some of the best vineyards in Napa Valley, they are able to make big, bold, and delicious wines for Oberon's Sauvignon Blanc, Merlot, and Cabernet Sauvignon varieties. As Tony poured Oberon Napa Valley Cabernet 2010, he explained that the grapes were sourced from Rutherford, Oak Knoll, Oso Vineyard, and Wooden Valley and that after fermentation the wine spent 18 months in French oak. The wine in our glasses was a luminescent ruby-garnet color, with aromas of black plum, black currant, and black raspberry that continued seamlessly onto the palate. The wine had great mouthfeel, a supple tannic structure, and an elegant finish. Oberon Napa Valley Sauvignon Blanc 2011 was bright straw colored, with notes of Granny Smith apple and citrus blossom in the bouquet. The grapes were sourced from the Oso and Milliken vineyards. In the mouth it was bright and had flavors of tropical fruit, Anjou pear, and honeydew melon. Each sip was crisp and clean and called out for another, and another, and another.

OPUS ONE

7900 St. Helena Highway,
Oakville, CA 94562,
(707) 944-9442
www.opusonewinery.com

In 1970 Baron Philippe de Rothschild and Robert Mondavi met for the first time in Hawaii and subsequently formed a partnership that would release wine under the Opus One label. A single case was sold in 1981 at the first Napa Valley Wine Auction, and the first commercial release was in 1984. Within a year Opus One was known as the first American ultra-premium wine, and by 1987 production grew to 11,000 cases. Construction on the winery was completed in 1991, and production grew again to 25,000 cases, making it one of the world's most sought-after wines. Although Baron Philippe has passed away, his daughter, Baroness Philippine, remains calm and steady at the helm. CEO David Pearson has been responsible for Opus One since 2004, and winemaking is currently under the direction of Michael Silacci. Opus One wines have consistently been praised by all the major wine magazines in the world. Opus One 2009 is composed of 81 percent Cabernet Sauvignon, 9 percent Cabernet Franc, 6 percent Petit Verdot, 3 percent Merlot, and 1 percent Malbec. It is dark garnet purple, with heady aromas of freshly picked black currant, blueberry pie, fennel bulb, and olive tapenade. In the mouth it is rich and full-bodied, with luscious dark fruit flavors and top notes of mocha and cherry cola. It has a nice amount of heft on the palate, with silky yet pleasantly grippy tannins in the finish. Drink it now or hold for a decade or so; you won't be disappointed either way.

O'SHAUGHNESSY ESTATE WINERY

1150 Friesen Drive, Angwin, CA 94508,
(707) 965-2898
www.oshaughnessywinery.com

Originally from the state of Minnesota, Betty O'Shaughnessy owned a cooking school in Minneapolis before moving to Oakville in 1990. She met her husband, Paul Woolls, at a wine tasting soon thereafter, and today they run O'Shaughnessy Estate Winery as both partners in life and partners in winemaking. Sean Capiaux is their president and founding winemaker, and he is aided by the winemaking team of Aaron Elam and Orlando Preciado. O'Shaughnessy Estate Winery Howell Mountain Cabernet Sauvignon 2009 is composed of 76 percent Cabernet Sauvignon, 7 percent Malbec, 5 percent Merlot, 5 percent St. Macaire, 5 percent Petit Verdot, and 2 percent Cabernet Franc. It is inky purple, with aromas of cassis, pencil lead, and black raspberry. It is bold on the palate, with flavors of blueberry pie and fresh blackberries. It has a balanced tannic structure and a lasting finish. O'Shaughnessy Estate Winery Mount Veeder Cabernet Sauvignon 2009 is 100 percent Cabernet Sauvignon with aromas of anise, charcuterie, black plums, and black raspberry that continue onto the palate. The powerful tannins are delightful and call out for a juicy steak but will decrease over time, so either drink now or cellar this one for a few years.

PAHLMEYER WINERY

811 St. Helena Highway South, Suite 202,
St. Helena, CA 94574,
(707) 255-2321
www.pahlmeyer.com

Jayson Pahlmeyer admits that he likes a bit of international intrigue. There's a local legend surrounding the winery and French vines that were "imported" by one of Jayson's partners through Canada. The intriguing part of the story is whether those vines crossed the US border labeled correctly as French vines or incorrectly labeled as vines purchased at UC Davis. It's hard to say what really happened, but that was long ago, and what most people care about today is that Jayson's wines have a decidedly French flavor profile. His goal has always been to create a "California Mouton," and it's our opinion that he has come pretty darn close. Helen Turley held the title of winemaker in 1993; Kale Anderson continues the legacy today. Pahlmeyer Proprietary Red Napa Valley 2009 is a Bordeaux-style blend of 82 percent Cabernet Sauvignon, 7 percent Merlot, 7 percent Cabernet Franc, 3 percent Petit Verdot, and 1 percent Malbec. It is inky purple, with notes of purple flowers, black currants, cigar box, and charcuterie present in the bouquet. In the mouth the tannic structure is smooth and velvety, with flavors of dark fruits and a nuance of Indian spice at the finish. Pahlmeyer Napa Valley Chardonnay 2010 is straw yellow, with aromas of mango, guava, and pineapple. In the mouth it is full-bodied, with citrus flavors and a touch of buttered brioche.

PARADIGM WINERY

1277 Dwyer Road, Oakville, CA 94562,
(707) 944-1683
www.paradigmwinery.com

Ren and Marilyn Harris acquired Paradigm Vineyards in 1976. Since their first vintage in 1991, Heidi Peterson Barrett has been the winemaker, and her father, Dick Peterson, is credited for the winery's layout and design. The annual production is around 5,000 cases, which account for only about 30 percent of the grapes grown on the estate. The balance of the fruit is sold to neighbors who focus on premium wine. Paradigm is well known for its acclaimed Cabernet Sauvignon and Merlot, and its wines continue to receive high scores from all the major wine publications. Paradigm Winery Napa Valley Oakville Cabernet Sauvignon 2009 is ruby garnet, with aromas of black cherry and cigar box. It is big and bold yet round on the palate, with a well-structured tannic finish. Paradigm Winery Napa Valley Oakville Cabernet Sauvignon 2008 is garnet colored, with notes of red plum and black raspberry in the bouquet. There is a touch of spice on the palate, with a burst of red cherry in the finish.

PARADUXX

7257 Silverado Trail, Napa, CA 94558,
(707) 945-0890
www.paraduxx.com

Paraduxx was founded by Dan Duckhorn of Duckhorn Wine Company to allow his winemakers the stylistic freedom to work with varieties other than Duckhorn's signature Bordeaux varieties. It was founded in 1994 with the idea of making wines that would appeal to current tastes and cuisines. The modern winery was opened in 2005 and features a ten-sided fermentation building designed to look like a traditional round barn. The fruit for Paraduxx is sourced from four different estate vineyards: Candlestick Vineyard, Monitor Ledge Vineyard, Stout Vineyard, and Rector Creek Vineyard. Paraduxx Z Blend Napa Valley Red Wine 2009 is inky purple, with aromas of blueberry pie, black plum, and fresh blackberries. Entry into the mouth is smooth with velvetlike tannins and a persistent finish. This is a deliciously modern Zinfandel-based blend that is extremely food-friendly.

PARALLEL NAPA VALLEY

169 Kreuzer Lane,
St. Helena, CA 94559,
(707) 255-1294
www.parallelwines.com

Three couples met while skiing in Park City, Utah, in the 1970s. In 1999 they found themselves winemaking partners when they purchased their first vineyard on Maple Lane in Calistoga. In 2001 they hired Philippe

Melka, and in 2005 they released their first vintage of Parallel Napa Valley Cabernet Sauvignon 2003 at Deer Park ski resort in their old stomping grounds. Since its inception Parallel has won numerous awards and raised impressive sums of money for charitable organizations. Parallel Napa Valley Cabernet Sauvignon 2009 is dark garnet colored, with aromas of anise and ripe red plums and flavors of sweet red cherry and black raspberry. The tannins are soft and well balanced, and the finish is long and elegant. The name Parallel Napa Valley Black Diamonds Cabernet Sauvignon 2009 is a playful interpretation of the designation for ski trail difficulty. It is deep garnet, with notes of black plum, dark cherry, and licorice in the bouquet. It is round and opulent on the palate, with wonderful fruit expression and a well-integrated tannic structure.

PATZ & HALL

851 Napa Valley Corporate Way,
Napa, CA 94558,
(707) 265-7700
www.patzhall.com

Started in 1988 by four friends and partners—Donald Patz, James Hall, Heather Patz, and Anne Moses—Patz & Hall strives to create widely acclaimed single-vineyard Pinot Noir and Chardonnay wines. They source their grapes from vineyards in Napa Valley, the Sonoma Coast, the Russian River Valley, Mendocino County, and the Santa Lucia Highlands. An interesting aspect of this boutique winery is that its Salon Society focuses on private seated tastings for guests at the Patz & Hall Tasting Salon. Their wines have been extremely well received by *Wine Spectator* and *Wine Advocate*. Patz & Hall Hyde Vineyard Carneros Chardonnay 2010 is straw colored, with aromas of almond paste, fresh grapefruit, caramelized pineapple, and candied lemon peel. It is full and round in the mouth, with delicious citrus fruit flavors coming forward before the long, luscious finish. Patz & Hall Sonoma Coast Pinot Noir 2010 is cherry colored, with aromas of purple flowers, rose petals, and red cherries. In the mouth the bright acidity upon entry gives way to warm flavors of dried black cherry and red raspberry. The finish is velvety and persistent.

PEJU FAMILY ESTATE WINERY

8466 St. Helena Highway,
Rutherford, CA 94573,
(707) 963-3600
www.peju.com

In 1982 Anthony Peju purchased 30 acres of Rutherford vineyards that included Cabernet Sauvignon and French Colombard vines that were over 60 years old. He and his wife, HB, began selling their wine commercially just three years later, with HB running the tasting room. Tony and HB currently own more than 450 acres in the Napa Valley and produce 35,000 cases of estate-grown wines. Visitors to the tasting room can spot HB working in the flower garden and meet the next generation of the Peju family, Lisa and Ariana. Peju Fifty/Fifty Rutherford Estate Vineyard 2010 is composed of 50 percent Cabernet Sauvignon and 50 percent Merlot. It is garnet colored, with aromas of dark cherry, cigar box, cedar, and red raspberry. It is full on the palate, with dark fruit flavors and a hint of cocoa powder and caramelized orange peel on the post palate. The finish is long and elegant. Peju Rutherford Estate Vineyard Reserve Cabernet Sauvignon 2008 is vibrant garnet, with notes of dark black cherry, cassis, and fresh cracked black pepper in the bouquet. It has nice heft on the palate, with dark fruit flavors and top notes of Indian spice and tobacco leaf before the supple finish.

PHILIP TOGNI VINEYARD

3780 Spring Mountain Road,
St. Helena, CA 94574,
(707) 963-373
www.philiptognivineyard.com

Philip Togni received his winemaking degree from the University of Bordeaux and worked at Château Lascombes. His wife, Birgitta, usually can be found toiling in the vineyard. Together with their daughter Lisa, the Togni family has made internationally acclaimed wines for years. Their first wines, a Sauvignon Blanc and a Cabernet Sauvignon, were bottled in 1983, and today the family concentrates on Bordeaux-style blends made from grapes grown on their 25 acres of Cabernet Sauvignon, Cabernet Franc, Merlot, and Petit Verdot. Annual production is limited to 2,000 cases, and most wines are sold through high-end wine stores in the United States, Europe, and Asia. Philip Togni Estate Cabernet Sauvignon 2010 is garnet colored, with aromas of black plums, dark fruits, pencil lead, and air-dried charcuterie. In the mouth flavors of fresh fruits and purple flowers are accented by a rising whiff of eucalyptus in the post palate. The finish is long and muscular. If you can control yourself for a few years, it can only get better in your cellar.

PINE RIDGE VINEYARDS

5901 Silverado Trail, Napa, CA 94558,
(707) 253-7500
www.pineridgevineyards.com

Pine Ridge was founded in 1978 by the late Gary Andrus, an early supporter of Napa Valley who believed its wines could rival those of Bordeaux. To that end he planted Cabernet Franc, Cabernet Sauvignon, Malbec, and Petit Verdot and named the vineyard for the impressive ridge of pine trees above. Over time the vineyard grew, and today the estate's 200 acres span five different Napa Valley AVAs: Howell Mountain, Carneros, Oakville, Rutherford, and Stags Leap District. We had the pleasure of dining with winemaker Michael Beaulac and tasting wines sourced from all these renowned vineyards. Over dinner Michael explained that his tenure at Markham Vineyards, Merry Edwards, and Murphy-Goode and his work with international consultant Michel Rolland helped shape his winemaking philosophy. We really enjoyed his crisp and clean Pine Ridge Chenin Blanc + Viognier 2012. It was light straw colored and had aromas of tropical fruits and white flowers. In the mouth flavors of white stone fruit, Cavaillon melon, grapefruit rind, and honeycomb all combined to make a delicious off-dry wine that paired perfectly with Asian-inspired cuisine. Pine Ridge Vineyards Napa Valley Cabernet Sauvignon 2010, dark ruby to the eye, offers fragrances of cherry conserves, black plum, star anise, and a hint of pine needle. On the tongue flavors of fresh and gently cooked cherry and blackberry mingle with notes of mocha, crème brûlée, and a dash of violet that leads into the persistent finish.

PLUMPJACK WINERY

620 Oakville Cross Road,
Oakville, CA 94558,
(707) 945-1220
www.plumpjack.com

Gavin Newsom and Gordon Getty founded their curiously named winery in 1995, named after Shakespeare's character Sir John "PlumpJack" Falstaff, whose famous line about wine consumption—"God help the wicked"—echoed Newsom and Getty's sentiments. Known for delicious Cabernet Sauvignons, PlumpJack is in Oakville in the center of the Napa Valley. The winery and the surrounding 42-acre estate vineyard date back to the 1800s. Today winemaker Aaron Miller bottles approximately half of PlumpJack's reserve wines under screw caps, and many agree that PlumpJack Winery is one of the first, if not *the* first, Napa Valley winery to use screw caps on super-premium wines. PlumpJack Oakville Estate Cabernet Sauvignon 2010 is dark garnet, with aromas of black raspberry, freshly ground black peppercorns, and dried black cherry with a pleasant top note of peppermint. Dark fruit flavors explode in the mouth and lead into a restrained yet elegant tannic finish.

PRIDE MOUNTAIN VINEYARDS

4026 Spring Mountain Road, St. Helena, CA 94574, (707) 963-4949
www.pridewines.com

Carolyn and Jim Pride fell in love with the former Summit Ranch in 1989 and bottled their first vintage in 1991. Before the Pride family's ownership, the ranch was home to a dilapidated winery that once served the entire mountain community, but because it currently sits on the county line, Pride Mountain Vineyards now must legally maintain two separate facilities, one in Sonoma County and one in Napa County. There's a dividing line down the middle of the crush pad, and some wines are labeled Napa and others are labeled Sonoma. In 1999 the family dug a 23,000-square-foot cave to house approximately 2,400 of its barrels. Pride Mountain Vineyard Vintner Select Chardonnay 2011 is straw colored, with aromas of Granny Smith apple, white flowers, and honeydew melon. In the mouth the fruit notes are more pronounced with just a touch of creaminess. The finish is crisp and clean. Pride Mountain Vineyard Syrah 2010 is inky purple, with notes of purple flowers and black plum in the bouquet. On the palate it is softly textured with flavors of cassis and smoked sausage. There is a pleasant touch of Indian curry spices in the persistent finish.

QUINTESSA

1601 Silverado Trail South, St. Helena, CA 94574, (707) 967-1601
www.quintessa.com

Chilean-born Agustin Huneeus began his career in the world of wine in 1960 as the CEO of Concha y Toro. He later worked with Seagram's and Noble Vineyard and was a partner at Franciscan Estates. He was awarded the Distinguished Service Award by *Wine Spectator* in 1996, and not one to sit on his laurels, he can be found today focusing his creative energy and extraordinary talent on Quintessa. His estate consists of 280 acres, with 170 of them under vines. There are 129 acres of Cabernet Sauvignon, 26 acres of Merlot, 7 acres of Cabernet Franc, 4 acres of Petit Verdot, and 4 acres of Carménère. The name Quintessa was coined by Agustin and his wife, Valeria, and refers to the property's five distinct hills and five different microclimates. His son, Agustin Jr., is now deeply involved in the family business and helps run the company in California and Chile. Quintessa 2009 is composed of Cabernet Sauvignon, Merlot, and Petit Verdot. It spends 20 months in 100 percent French oak and has delightful aromas of purple flowers, black plums, black raspberries, and cassis in the bouquet. On the palate the fruit flavors move toward the back of the tongue, revealing touches of toasted brioche, vanilla, and Christmas baking spices. The finish is lush and elegant with well-structured tannins. Although it is drinking wonderfully now, try to control yourself and put it in your cellar for a few years. You won't be disappointed. Ten years after the release of his first bottle of Quintessa, Agustin Huneeus is proud to release Faust Napa Valley Cabernet Sauvignon 2010. It is composed of 83 percent Cabernet Sauvignon, 13 percent Merlot, 3 percent Malbec, and 1 percent Cabernet Franc. It has a dark ruby garnet color, with notes of black raspberry, ripe cherry, and black currant in the bouquet. On the palate the rich fruit notes hit the middle of the tongue while flavors of dark chocolate and mocha tickle the sides of the mouth. It has a great fruit-filled finish. Drink it now or hold it for four to six years.

RAYMOND VINEYARDS

849 Zinfandel Lane, St. Helena, CA 94574,
(707) 963-3141
www.raymondvineyards.com

Roy Raymond moved to the Napa Valley in 1933, married Martha Jane Beringer a few years later, and worked at her family's winery for more than 35 years before deciding to put his name on a wine label. His first crush was in 1974, and the family continued to make quality wine under its own name for the next 35 years. In 2009

French wine scion Jean-Charles Boisset and his family purchased the property, and under Jean-Charles's stewardship as president Raymond Vineyards continues to produce excellent-quality wine. The new ownership has been extremely well received, and the wines have been highly rated by every major wine publication. *Wine Enthusiast* honored Jean-Charles as Innovator of the Year in 2008, in 2012 Raymond Vineyards was named New World Winery of the Year, and *Decanter* has named Jean-Charles as one of the Top 50 Power Brokers in the global wine industry. Stephanie Putnam is the director of winemaking at Raymond Vineyards, Kathy George is the assistant winemaker, and Eric Pooler is the vineyard manager who oversees 300 acres of estate-owned vineyards. Raymond Vineyards Generations Napa Valley Cabernet Sauvignon 2009 is inky purple, with aromas of black cherry, Christmas baking spices, and black raspberry. It is full-bodied and generous on the palate, with balanced tannins and a lingering finish. Drink it now or cellar it for up to 12 years for flavor development and added complexity. It will only get better in the bottle. Raymond Vineyards District Collection Napa Valley Calistoga Cabernet Sauvignon 2009 is purple garnet, with notes of blueberry pie, anise, and black currants in the complex bouquet. It has great heft on the palate, with flavors of black cherry and mocha before the balanced tannins take you into a long and luxurious finish. Grab this wine while you can, as only 224 cases were produced.

REYNOLDS FAMILY WINERY

3266 Silverado Trail, Napa, CA 94558,
(707) 258-2558
www.reynoldsfamilywinery.com

With the blessing of his wife, Suzie, former dentist Steve Reynolds traded in his chair and drills for construction tools and farm implements in 1994. The couple purchased a 100-year-old chicken ranch and immediately set themselves the task of cleaning it up, renovating the existing structures, and building new ones. They planted 10 acres of Cabernet Sauvignon in 1996, built a Tuscan-style winery, and produced their first vintage in 1999. Reynolds Family Winery Persistence 2008 is a blend of 57 percent Cabernet Sauvignon, 14 percent Merlot, and small percentages of Syrah, Cabernet Franc, and Petit Verdot. In the nose notes of black plum, cassis, and truffle add to the bouquet, and in the mouth the fruit flavors and velvety tannic structure come to life and contribute to the long, persistent finish. Reynolds Family Winery Cabernet Sauvignon 2008 is made from 100 percent estate-grown grapes. It is garnet colored, with aromas of black fruits, Christmas baking spices, and saddle leather. On the palate flavors of black raspberry and black plum combine with a touch of freshly ground black pepper. The tannins are well structured, and the finish is long and elegant.

ROBERT BIALE VINEYARDS

4038 Big Ranch Road, Napa, CA 94558,
(707) 257-7555
www.robertbialevineyards.com

Pietro Biale immigrated to the Napa Valley from Genoa, Italy, and began raising chickens and planting Zinfandel vines in 1937. His son Aldo discreetly sold Zinfandel wine to help the family through the Depression; the code words his buyers would use to order a jug of his homemade wine were "black chicken." In 1991, Aldo and his son Robert began commercially selling Zinfandel made from the old family vineyard named Aldo's Vineyard. The current winemaker, Tres Goetting, is well known in the industry for his prowess with Zin. Robert Biale Vineyards Napa Valley Black Chicken Zinfandel 2011 is purple, with aromas of black raspberry, black cherry, and Christmas baking spices. It is big in the mouth, with lush fruit flavors and soft tannins in the finish. Robert Biale Founding Farmers Napa Valley Zinfandel 2011 has aromas of blackberry preserves, red plum, and cinnamon. In the mouth it is fruit-forward with balanced tannins and a soft finish.

ROBERT CRAIG WINERY

625 Imperial Way,
Napa, CA 94559,
(707) 252-2250
www.robertcraigwine.com

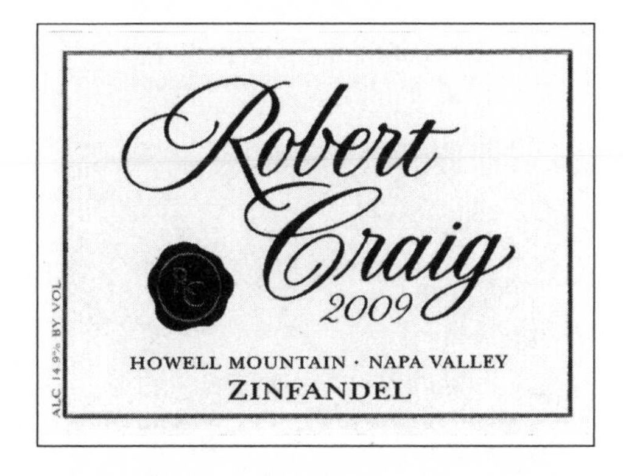

Robert Craig started his winery as a joint venture with three partners in 1992 and released his first wine in 1995, but it wasn't until 2002 that the Craig family finished their long-awaited winery on the top of Howell Mountain. Robert Craig wines have received numerous accolades from a variety of publications. Robert Craig Affinity Napa Valley Cabernet Sauvignon 2009 is garnet purple, with aromas of pencil lead, Mediterranean spices, and rich dark berries. On the palate it is fruit-forward but restrained and complex in its finish. Robert Craig Howell Mountain

Zinfandel 2009 is dark purple, almost black, with aromas of dark flowers, dark fruits, and cigar box. In the mouth it is powerful and complex with a firm tannic finish. Drink it now or hold it for up to eight years.

ROBERT FOLEY VINEYARDS

PO Box 847, Angwin, CA 94508,
(707) 0965-2669
www.robertfoleyvineyards.com

Bob Foley's wines have received a high level of praise by *Wine Advocate* and *Wine Spectator*, and we couldn't agree more. Bob began making wine in Napa in 1977, and in 1998 he bottled his flagship claret. Today he's known for producing fine wine on Napa Valley's Howell Mountain, and when he's not at the winery, you might find him performing with his rock band, the Robert Foley Band. Robert Foley Vineyards Napa Valley Merlot 2010 is dark ruby red, with aromas of black raspberries and Grandma's blueberry pie. In the mouth flavors of chocolate, coffee bean, and vanilla come out and carry you into a long luscious finish. Robert Foley Vineyards Napa Valley Cabernet Sauvignon 2009 is rich with ripe fruit. It has aromas of cherry vanilla ice cream topped with dried black cherries and fresh black raspberries. It is generous on the palate with balanced tannins and a long, long, long finish.

ROBERT MONDAVI WINERY

7801 St. Helena Highway, Oakville, CA 94574,
(707) 226-1395
www.robertmondaviwinery.com

When Robert Mondavi walked through To Kalon, he knew that it was a very special, almost mystical place and established his eponymous winery in 1966 in Oakville. He has been widely credited as a California winemaking legend, and his winery remains highly regarded for its delicious, well-rated wines. He was a traditionalist who believed that wines should reflect their origins as well as an innovator who embraced the latest techniques. Robert is credited for developing his winery's signature wine, Fumé Blanc.

Today, visitors to the winery founded by Robert and his son Michael walk through the now-famous arch and into a beautiful art-filled courtyard. Robert's widow, Margrit Mondavi, is known for curating stunning sculptures and mixed-media art installations. A vast variety of food and wine tours are available, making Robert Mondavi Winery a very popular destination on Napa Valley visitors' itineraries. There's even a seasonal schedule of musical performances on the central courtyard. Robert Mondavi Winery Napa Valley Reserve Cabernet Sauvignon 2009 is composed of 88 percent Cabernet Sauvignon, 8 percent Cabernet Franc, and 4 percent Petit Verdot. It is ruby garnet, with aromas of black currant, licorice, candied violets, and smoked meats. The rich fruit flavors are pronounced on the palate, and there's a touch of olive tapenade and dark cocoa powder in the persistent finish. Robert Mondavi Winery Napa Valley Reserve Fumé Blanc 2011 is composed of 98 percent Sauvignon Blanc and 2 percent Sémillon. It is light straw colored, with aromas of citrus blossom, lychee fruit, and dried fragrant herbs. It is fruity, crisp, and creamy in the mouth, with touches of almond paste and toasted oak in the finish.

ROBERT SINSKEY VINEYARDS

6320 Silverado Trail, Napa, CA 94558,
(707) 944-9090
www.robertsinskey.com

California-born and New York–educated, Robert Sinskey is not your typical winemaker and has never let the fact that he didn't attend winemaking school hold him back. Over the last 20 years he has increased his holdings to over 200 acres of biodynamic and organic-certified vineyards in Stags Leap, Carneros, and Sonoma Valley. His wines are highly rated and well received by consumers and critics alike. Robert Sinskey Pinot Gris 2011 is pale straw colored, with aromas of white flowers, lemon-lime, and wet river rock. In the mouth it has crisp and refreshing flavors of white stone fruits, pear, and citrus blossom. This wine is ideal as an aperitif or paired with light cuisine. Robert Sinskey POV 2009 is a proprietary blend of Merlot, Cabernet Franc, and Cabernet Sauvignon. It is dark garnet, with aromas of black plums and black cherries. In the mouth the fruit flavors come alive and then recede as secondary characteristics of black olive tapenade and Mediterranean herbal notes are revealed. The finish is long and elegant.

ROCCA FAMILY VINEYARDS

129 Devlin Road,
Napa, CA 94558,
(707) 257-8467
www.roccawines.com

Dentist Mary Rocca and physician Eric Grigsby dreamed of reestablishing their childhood connection with farming, and so they purchased 21 acres in the Napa Valley and founded Rocca Family Vineyards in 1999. The duo brought in Celia Welch as their winemaker and produced their initial bottling in 2000. Mary subsequently purchased the 11-acre Collinetta Vineyard in the Coombsville appellation. Today the winemaker is Paul Colantuoni, and he carries on the tradition of making highly regarded wines. Rocca Family Vineyards Estate Collinetta Vineyard Cabernet Sauvignon 2009 is opaque garnet, with aromas of black raspberries, cassis, and dried blueberries. In the mouth there are flavors of black cherry, purple flowers, and a touch of dark chocolate before the long-lasting finish. Rocca Family Vineyards Vespera 2009 is a blend of 75 percent Cabernet Sauvignon, 12 percent Petite Sirah, 12 percent Petit Verdot, and 1 percent Syrah. It has aromas of cassis, black cherry, and Christmas baking spices. It is big and fruit-forward in the mouth with silky tannins and a persistent finish.

ROMBAUER WINERY

3522 Silverado Trail North,
St. Helena, CA 94574,
(800) 622-2206
www.rombauer.com

The Rombauer ancestors come from the Rheingau wine region of Germany, but it wasn't until 1980 that the American branch of the family started their Napa wine legacy. The Rombauers have food and wine pairing down to a science, and many of the wines are expertly paired with recipes written by Koerner Rombauer's great-aunt Irma Rombauer, the author of the famous cookbook *Joy of Cooking*. The Rombauer estate has stunning views of the valley and a beautiful garden in which to take a relaxing stroll. Rombauer wines are highly rated by critics and coveted by collectors. Rombauer Winery Carneros Merlot 2009 is ruby to garnet, with aromas of black cherry, red plum, cigar box, and peppermint. It is juicy in the mouth, with velvety tannins and a soft finish. Rombauer Winery Carneros Chardonnay 2011 is bright straw colored, with notes of caramelized peach, melon, and white flowers in the bouquet. It is fat and creamy in the mouth, with a pleasant finish that keeps inviting you in for another sip.

ROOTS RUN DEEP WINERY

83 Zinfandel Lane, Building C,
St. Helena, CA 94574,
(707) 945-1045
www.rootsrundeep.com

Mark Albrecht worked for 20 years in the wine business before launching his Roots Run Deep brand. His marketing strategy has always been to offer great wines at affordable prices, and he's dedicated to producing lower-cost wines that can compete with wines that command more than $50 per bottle. Winemaking is under the direction of Barry Gnekow, who has been called "one of the best consulting winemakers in the industry" by the *San Francisco Chronicle.* Roots Run Deep Winery Hypothesis Napa Valley Cabernet Sauvignon 2010 is composed of 87 percent Cabernet Sauvignon, 9 percent Cabernet Franc, and 4 percent Petit Verdot. It is garnet purple, with notes of rich, ripe black fruits that transfer seamlessly onto the palate. It has a great mouthfeel with a complex, lingering finish. Roots Run Deep Winery Educated Guess Napa Valley Cabernet Sauvignon 2010 is composed of 85 percent Cabernet Sauvignon, 8 percent Merlot, 4 percent Cabernet Franc, and 3 percent Petit Verdot. It is aged 12 months in French and American oak and has aromas of black raspberry, dried black cherry, dark chocolate, and a touch of lifted eucalyptus in the bouquet. In the mouth it is a serious Cab with a silky, smooth mouthfeel and a persistent finish.

ROY ESTATE

Visits only by prior appointment.
(707) 255-4409
www.royestate.com

We had the pleasure of meeting Shirley Roy and her late husband, Charles, at a Napa Valley Vintners tasting in New York City in 2009 and have been fans of their wines ever since. Both from the East Coast, Shirley and Charles fell in love with the Napa Valley and in 1999 purchased Johnny Miller's estate. In 2005 they brought in winemaker Philippe Melka, who put Roy Estate on the map of fine winemaking. Roy Estate Cabernet Sauvignon 2008 is composed of 95 percent Cabernet Sauvignon and 5 percent Petit Verdot. It is garnet colored, with aromas of black raspberry, brown spices, and purple flowers in the complex bouquet. It is generous in the mouth, with flavors of black fruits and just a touch of anise. The finish is long and elegant. Drink it now or cellar it for up to 15 years. Roy Estate Proprietary Red Wine 2008 is a blend of 71 percent Cabernet Sauvignon, 22 percent Merlot, and 7 percent Petit Verdot. It is dark garnet, with notes of black cherry, rose petal, and forest floor. The palate comes alive with fresh fruit flavors and secondary characteristics of dark chocolate and mocha.

RUDD WINERY

500 Oakville Cross Road, Oakville, CA 94562,
(707) 944-8577
www.ruddwines.com

Leslie Rudd acquired Rudd Winery in 1996 and has been passionately growing Bordeaux grape varieties since that time. He immediately set to work to expand the cellar facilities, and today there are over 20,000 square feet of caves below the property. Whenever we visit we always enjoy a walk through the color-coordinated two-acre garden created by his wife, Susan. Along with landscape architect Thomas Hobbs, she chose only plants that fit her desired color scheme of green, burgundy, and silver. Organic vegetables are grown here for the family's Press Restaurant in St. Helena. Winemaking is under the direction of Patrick Sullivan, and Rudd wines have received high scores from a variety of prestigious publications. Rudd Winery Mount Veeder Sauvignon Blanc 2011 is pale straw colored, with aromas of lime zest and white stone fruits. In the mouth flavors of peach are pronounced, and the finish has a very pleasant touch of brown baking spices. Rudd Oakville Estate Red 2008 is a blend of 59 percent Cabernet Sauvignon, 23 percent Cabernet Franc, 9 percent Petit Verdot, and 9 percent Malbec. It is deep garnet colored, with aromas of cassis, espresso, and dark chocolate. It is generous in the mouth with grippy tannins and a persistent finish. Drink it now or hold it for a decade or so; this delicious wine will continue to evolve with age.

RUTHERFORD GROVE WINERY AND VINEYARDS

1673 Highway 29,
Rutherford, CA 94573,
(707) 963-0544
www.rutherfordgrove.com

Italian immigrant Albino Pestoni planted the vineyards that became Bonded Winery 935 in 1892, and in 1963 his descendants created a composting facility for discarded grape seeds, skins, and stems—the first of its kind in the valley. In the mid-1990s the family acquired another small winery and created Rutherford Grove. They currently make about 4,000 cases of wine entirely from estate vineyards grown on 60 acres in four different AVAs: Rutherford, St. Helena, Howell Mountain, and Lake County. Rutherford Grove Winery and Vineyards Rutherford Estate Cabernet Sauvignon 2008 is dark garnet, with aromas of dried cherries, cassis, and vanilla. On the palate there are flavors of black fruits and cherry vanilla, with a persistent finish. Rutherford Grove Winery and Vineyards Pestoni Family Estate Reserve Merlot 2008 has aromas of brown spices, saddle leather, cigar box, and dark fruits. In the mouth flavors of black cherries, black raspberries, and anise combine to make a delicious Merlot with a luxurious fruity finish.

RUTHERFORD HILL

200 Rutherford Hill Road,
Rutherford, CA 94573,
(707) 963-1871
www.rutherfordhill.com

Rutherford Hill was purchased by Anthony Terlato and his sons, Bill and John, in 1996 and continues the tradition of making elegant Rutherford Bench Merlot-based wines from its select vineyards. As Anthony states, "Quality is a way of life . . . for Rutherford Hill it begins in the vineyard." Rutherford Hill Barrel Select Red Blend 2008 is composed of 77 percent Merlot, 14 percent Cabernet Sauvignon, and 9 percent Cabernet Franc. It is ruby garnet red, with notes of fennel bulb, blueberry pie, and cassis in the bouquet. On the palate it has big flavors of black plum and black cherry, and silky tannins lead to a bright splash of acidity on the finish. Rutherford Hill Merlot 2007 is composed of 76 percent Merlot, 16 percent Cabernet Sauvignon, 7 percent Cabernet Franc, and 1 percent Syrah. It is garnet colored, with aromas of black cherry and black plum. It is fruity on the palate with silky tannins and a long finish.

SAINTSBURY

1500 Los Carneros Avenue, Napa, CA 94559,
(707) 252-0592
www.saintsbury.com

Richard Ward and David Graves met in 1977 in a beer brewing class at the University of California, Davis. Both men enjoyed a hearty home brew but also shared a passion for wines from Burgundy. The next year they were roommates during harvests at Chappellet and Stag's Leap Wine Cellar, and in 1981 they cofounded Saintsbury. Over the years a few winemakers passed through their doors, making them the quality producers they are known to be today. The tradition and quality continue with French-born winemaker Jérome Chéry, who took over the helm in 2004. We had the unexpected opportunity to sit down with Jérome on a picture-perfect fall afternoon and taste his wines in Saintsbury's gardens. Saintsbury Carneros Pinot Noir 2010 is garnet cherry colored, with notes of black cherry, fruits of the wood, and ripe red cherry. It is voluptuous in the mouth with a persistent finish. There is a pleasant splash of bright acidity in the post palate. Saintsbury Carneros Chardonnay 2010 has aromas of Anjou pear, Granny Smith apple, and citrus blossom. It is rich on the palate with a pleasant astringent finish. This is the type of Chardonnay that keeps inviting you in for sip after sip, which is exactly what we did on that beautiful fall afternoon.

ST. SUPÉRY ESTATE VINEYARDS AND WINERY

8440 St. Helena Highway,
Rutherford, CA 94573,
(707) 963-4507
www.stsupery.com

Founded by French businessman Robert Skalli and his family in 1982, St. Supéry began with the purchase of the 1,531-acre Dollarhide Ranch, which dates back to the late 1800s. There are over 500 acres under vine at elevations that range from 600 to 1,100 feet. Sauvignon Blanc vines account for 202 acres and Cabernet Sauvignon for 186, and the rest are planted to Merlot, Chardonnay, Muscat Canelli, Sémillon, Malbec, Petit Verdot, and Cabernet Franc. The Skalli family lays claim to being the "largest family-owned, sustainably-farmed, and estate-produced winery in Napa Valley." They continue, "All of our estate wines are created by St. Supéry Estate from grape to bottle, with no purchased fruit, offsite production, or storage." Winemaking is carried out by Michael Scholz, who received his bachelor of science degree in enology at Roseworthy College in Australia. St. Supéry Napa Valley Estate Sauvignon Blanc 2012 is pale straw yellow with green reflections. It has aromas of bright lime zest and pink grapefruit, and in the mouth it is clean and crisp with persistent flavors of tropical fruits. St. Supéry Napa Valley Estate Cabernet Sauvignon is purple garnet, with aromas of black plums, cassis, and mocha in the bouquet. It is full-bodied in the mouth, with persistent flavors of fruit and dark cocoa powder. The finish is elegant and long.

SCHRADER CELLARS

PO Box 1004, Calistoga, CA 94515,
(707) 942-1540
www.schradercellars.com

Fred Schrader caught the winemaking bug when he first attended Auction Napa Valley in 1988. He soon cofounded Colgin-Schrader Cellars, and in 1998 he started his eponymous Schrader Cellars. Winemaking is under the direction of Thomas Brown, and Schrader wines are consistently well received and highly scored by *Wine Advocate* and *Wine Spectator*. When Fred is not at the winery, you might find him driving on Napa's back-country roads in one of his vintage sports cars. Schrader Cellars CCS Beckstoffer To Kalon Vineyard Cabernet Sauvignon 2009 is bold, with aromas of anise, eucalyptus, cigar box, ripe dark fruits, and purple flowers. It is big in the mouth with a strong yet balanced tannic finish. Drink it now or hold it for a decade or so. Schrader Cellars Beckstoffer To Kalon Vineyard Cabernet Sauvignon 2009 has aromas of black currant, Christmas baking spice, dark chocolate, and espresso bean that progress nicely onto the palate. The tannic structure is linear but will round out over time. It's delicious now, but if you can restrain yourself, hold it for a few years.

SCHRAMSBERG

1400 Schramsberg Road,
Calistoga, CA 94515,
(707) 942-4558
www.schramsberg.com

Jacob Schram emigrated from Germany in 1826 and eventually found himself in Napa Valley. As the son of a winemaker, he cleared trees and planted vines on the large piece of land he purchased in 1862, and thus Schramsberg began. His production reached

12,000 gallons of wine per year by 1876, and he began shipping wine across the country to New York. His wines were very highly scored in local and international competitions. Schramsberg had numerous owners after Jacob's death, but its modern-day incarnation began with its acquisition by Jack and Jamie Davies in 1965. The Davieses were committed to making "America's most prestigious, select, and admired sparkling wine." Schramsberg Blanc de Blancs was served at President Nixon's historical 1972 "Toast to Peace" with Chinese Premier Zhou Enlai and has been served at official state events by every administration since that time. Schramsberg Blanc de Blancs 2010 is made from 100 percent Chardonnay and has aromas of tropical fruit, citrus rind, freshly baked bread, and Granny Smith apple. The fruit flavors come alive on the palate with a crisp acidic finish. Schramsberg makes other delicious sparkling wines, including Blanc de Noir, Brut Rosé, and Mirabelle Brut, as well as one red, J. Davies Diamond Mountain District Cabernet Sauvignon 2009. It has aromas of blueberry pie, blackberry, and licorice and flavors of ripe sweet black cherry, black raspberry preserves, and tobacco leaves. The tannins are well integrated, and the finish is long and elegant.

SCHWEIGER VINEYARDS

4015 Spring Mountain Road,
St. Helena, CA 94574,
(707) 963-4882
www.schweigervineyards.com

The Schweiger family purchased land on Spring Mountain in the early 1960s but did not start to plant vines until the early 1980s. At first grapes were sold to area wineries, including Stags' Leap Winery and Newton, and in 1994 the family began labeling its bottles with the Schweiger name. The family is very environmentally conscious; the new winery was constructed using eco-friendly technology, and all the winery's electricity is generated by its own solar panels. Schweiger Vineyards Sauvignon Blanc 2011 is composed of 89 percent Sauvignon Blanc and 11 percent Sauvignon Musqué. It is light straw colored, with aromas of Granny Smith apples and lemongrass. It is crisp and refreshing on the palate with a fair bit of pleasant acidity. Schweiger Vineyards Dedication 2007 is a blend of 49 percent Cabernet Sauvignon, 39 percent Merlot, 8 percent Cabernet Franc, and 4 percent Malbec. It is garnet colored, with notes of dark ripe berries and pencil lead in the bouquet. It is rich but restrained in the mouth, with a lingering finish.

SCIANDRI FAMILY VINEYARDS

50 Kreuse Canyon Drive, Napa, CA 94559,
(707) 277-4999
www.sciandrivineyards.com

It is very much a family affair at Sciandri Family Vineyards. Descended from Italians who emigrated from the province of Tuscany, Ron and Roberta, Ron Jr., Ryan, and Rebecca and Andy make delicious wine with grapes grown on their Cabernet Sauvignon, Petit Verdot, Cabernet Franc, Malbec, and Merlot vines. The family dog, Fudge, a Chocolate Labrador, is part of the welcome committee. Winemaking is under the direction of Don Baker, and vineyard management is handled by Javier Rentoria. Sciandri Family Vineyards Napa Valley Coombsville Cabernet Sauvignon 2009 is inky garnet, with enticing aromas of black raspberry, black plum, and purple flowers. It is fruit-forward in the mouth with a nice heft and mouthfeel. It is elegant and restrained with a delightfully balanced tannic finish.

SCREAMING EAGLE

PO Box 12, Oakville, CA 94562,
(707) 944-0749
www.screamingeagle.com

Almost everyone who knows a thing or two about California wine has heard of Screaming Eagle, but the wine is made in such small quantities that it is extremely difficult to source. Thankfully, we have generous friends with deep cellars (and pockets) who opened a bottle over dinner one evening. Founder Jean Phillips hired Heidi Peterson Barrett as Screaming Eagle's first winemaker. Their 1992 vintage was awarded 99 points by Robert Parker upon its release, securing Screaming Eagle's place of honor in the world of California cult wine. Screaming Eagle garnered a perfect score—100 points—from Robert Parker for the 1997 and 2007 vintages. Phillips sold the estate in 2006, and today Screaming Eagle is owned by Stan Kroenke. Screaming Eagle 2008 is inky garnet, with abundant delightful aromas of black raspberry, black currant, and just a touch of graphite in the enticing bouquet. It starts out full and bold upon entry into the mouth, with amazing fruit flavors and great tannic structure. As it fills the mouth, it is both elegant and restrained. The finish is superlong and satisfying. This is a truly special wine; too bad it's so hard to get.

SEAVEY VINEYARD

1310 Conn Valley Road,
St. Helena, CA 94574,
(707) 963-8339
www.seaveyvineyard.com

Mary and William Seavey purchased the historical Franco-Swiss Farming Company estate in 1979 from a family friend. It had most recently been used as a cattle ranch, but it was originally planted as a vineyard in the late 1800s. While William worked during the week in San Francisco, he and the family replanted vines on weekends and during school vacations. Although Mary passed away in 2008, William and the family continue to run the winery and make exceptional wines that have been highly rated by numerous publications, including *Wine Enthusiast*. Seavey Cabernet Sauvignon 2009 is garnet purple, with aromas of Indian spice, cigar box, and rich ripe black fruits. It is generous in the mouth, with a fruit-filled finish complemented by a gripping tannic structure. Seavey Chardonnay 2010 is straw colored, with notes of white stone fruits and citrus blossoms in the bouquet. It is crisp and clean in the mouth with a delightful minerality.

SEQUOIA GROVE

8338 St. Helena Highway,
Rutherford, CA 94558,
(707) 944-2945
www.sequoiagrove.com

Whenever we drive up to the entrance, whether by bicycle or by car, to Sequoia Grove's 150-year-old barn cum tasting room, we're amazed at the height of the majestic sequoia trees surrounding the building. The winery sits on 22 acres of mineral-rich alluvial soils on the Rutherford Bench valley floor and truly fits into its natural surroundings. Director of winemaking Michael Trujillo has been with Sequoia Grove since its inception in 1982 and is assisted on a day-to-day basis by winemaker Molly Hill. Together they make wonderful wines from 100 percent Napa Valley grapes. Sequoia Grove Winery has launched a partnership with the Sequoia Parks Foundation, an organization dedicated to preserving the natural environs of the giant sequoia tree. A percentage of sales from the winery is donated to the SPF project. Sequoia Grove Napa Valley Cabernet Sauvignon 2010 is garnet black, with notes of black raspberry, black cherry, and mocha in the complex bouquet. It is full-bodied on the palate, with flavors of dark fruit, clove, and dark chocolate. The tannins are ripe and well balanced, and the finish is persistent. Sequoia Grove Cambium 2008 is highly rated by *Wine*

Enthusiast and *Wine Spectator*. It is garnet colored, with aromas of ripe cherry, mocha, and cigar box. In the mouth it is luscious and full-bodied, with flavors of rich ripe fruit, French toast, and dark chocolate. This is a truly delicious wine made to enjoy now, but if you can restrain yourself, lay it down for a few years. You won't be disappointed.

SHAFER VINEYARDS

6154 Silverado Trail,
Napa, CA 94558,
(707) 944-2877
www.shafervineyards.com

Publisher turned winery owner John Shafer purchased a 210-acre estate in Stags Leap District and moved his family to Napa Valley in 1972. There was plenty of work to do, as many of the original vines that dated back to the 1920s needed to be replanted. The current vineyard is composed of 50 acres under plantation. Former winemaker and now president of the winery Doug Shafer graduated from the University of California, Davis, in 1983 and got together with winemaker Elias Fernandez to form Shafer's winemaking team. Shafer Vineyards Red Shoulder Ranch Chardonnay 2011 is straw colored, with notes of tropical fruits and caramelized pineapple in the bouquet. It is big on the palate, with extended fruit flavors and a lovely persistent finish. Shafer Vineyards Napa Valley Relentless 2009 is a blend of Syrah and Petite Sirah. It is densely purple in color, with aromas of black raspberry, charcuterie, and Indian spice. There is a lot of ripe fruit on the palate, with a complex finish.

SILVERADO VINEYARDS

6121 Silverado Trail,
Napa, CA 94558,
(707) 259-6617
www.silveradovineyards.com

Diane Disney Miller and her mother first visited the Napa Valley in 1975 to tour two wineries that were for sale. As time progressed, more vineyard parcels became available. In a bold investment, Diane and her husband, Ron, bought one parcel of land and Diane's mother purchased another. The Millers chose architect Richard Keith to design their winery and hired Jack Stuart as their first winemaker. Over the years the Millers have purchased additional vineyards in Carneros, Mount George, and Soda Canyon. Jack Stuart retired in 2004, and winemaking currently is carried out by Jon Emmerich, Elena Franceschi, Fred Hansen, and Rick Thomas. Silverado Vineyards Estate Cabernet Sauvignon 2009 is deeply colored and has aromas of black plum, Christmas baking spices, and anise.

It is fruit-forward in the mouth with just the right amount of acid to be well balanced. Silverado Vineyards Carneros Chardonnay 2010 is medium straw colored, with aromas of lime zest, lemon curd, and tropical fruits. It is creamy in the mouth, with a hint of buttered brioche and lots of crisp minerality in the finish.

SILVER OAK CELLARS

915 Oakville Cross Road,
Oakville, CA 94562,
(707) 942-7022
www.silveroak.com

Raymond T. Duncan first visited Napa in the late 1960s and began buying land in both Napa and Alexander valleys. In 1972 he purchased an old dairy farm in Oakville and began planting vines with the help of Justin Meyer. The duo produced their first wine the same year using Alexander Valley fruit, but it wasn't until 1979 that they produced their first Napa Valley Cabernet Sauvignon. Since 1979 Silver Oak has produced two wines each vintage: a Cabernet Sauvignon from Napa Valley and a Cabernet Sauvignon from Alexander Valley. In 2001 Justin Meyer sold his share of the company to the Duncan family, and a new winery was built on the Oakville property in 2008. Silver Oak Cellars Napa Valley Cabernet Sauvignon 2008 is dark ruby, with aromas of black raspberry, black plum, and a touch of spice. It is big and bold in the mouth, with silky tannins in the finish. Silver Oak Cellars Alexander Valley Cabernet Sauvignon 2008 is dark garnet, with aromas of black fruits, Indian spice, and smoked meats. It is velvety in the mouth, with flavors of black plum and dark chocolate. The tannins are a bit chewy, making this a wine to drink now or lay down for 15 years or so. When you find yourself on the other side of the hill in the Alexander Valley, make sure to visit Silver Oak Cellars at its other location on Chianti Road in Geyserville.

SMITH-MADRONE VINEYARDS AND WINERY

4022 Spring Mountain Road,
St. Helena, CA 94574,
(707) 963-2283
www.smithmadrone.com

December 5 is a lucky day in the history of Smith-Madrone Vineyards and Winery. President Chester A. Arthur signed the real estate deed for what is today known as Smith-Madrone Vineyards on December 5, 1884, and on December 5, 1933, Prohibition was repealed. December 5, 2012, marks another milestone with the release of the winery's very first reserve wine, Cooks Flat Reserve, named in honor of George Cook, who first owned the property in 1884. Each bottle is numbered; only 2,052 bottles were made, and each bears a copy of the 1884 US Land Office deed. If you can't get your hands on one of those bottles, try Smith-Madrone Napa Valley Spring Mountain District Cabernet Sauvignon 2007. It is garnet colored, with aromas of cassis, blueberry pie, and tobacco leaf. It is round in the mouth with a balanced tannic structure. Smith-Madrone Napa Valley Spring Mountain District Chardonnay 2010 is straw colored, with aromas of pear, citrus blossom, and Golden Delicious apple. It is round and smooth in the mouth with a pleasant acidic finish.

SNOWDEN VINEYARDS

1478 Railroad Avenue, St. Helena, CA 94574,
(707) 963-4292
www.snowdenvineyards.com

Wayne and Virginia Snowden purchased seven acres of vines and six acres of fruit orchards in 1955, and for years they sold their grapes to local cooperatives. In 1962 they began planting Cabernet Sauvignon vines, and after Wayne's death in 1977 their sons Scott and Randy replanted the fruit orchards with Cabernet Sauvignon. The family continued to sell most of their grapes over the next 15 years, but in 1993 they decided to produce wine under their own label. We're glad they did. Snowden Vineyards Napa Valley Reserve Cabernet Sauvignon 2009 is composed of 75.5 percent Cabernet Sauvignon, 19.1 percent Merlot, 3.8 percent Cabernet Franc, and 1.6 percent Petit Verdot. It is garnet colored, with aromas of red plums, violets, and cigar box. On the palate there are flavors of ripe fruit with secondary characteristics of anise and eucalyptus. The finish is powerful and balanced. It is very delicious, indeed. Snowden Vineyards Lost Vineyard Napa Valley Merlot 2010 has soft aromas of red fruits, purple flowers, and a touch of sweet baking spices. It is generous in the mouth, with sweet tannins and a touch of bright red fruit in the finish.

SPRING MOUNTAIN VINEYARD

2805 Spring Mountain Road, St. Helena, CA 94574, (707) 967-4188
www.springmountainvineyard.com

Once three separate properties, each with its own winery, Spring Mountain Vineyard includes some of the first vineyards planted by Frederick and Jacob, the Beringer brothers, in 1882. The old Chateau Chevalier property was acquired in 1993, and La Perla and Miravalle were acquired in 1996. The old buildings and vineyards are really a sight to see and should not be missed when visiting Napa Valley. Spring Mountain Vineyard wines have been highly rated by *Decanter*, *Wine Spectator*, and *Wine Enthusiast* and are sought after by consumers and collectors alike. Spring Mountain Vineyard Elivette 2009 is a blend of 55 percent Cabernet Sauvignon, 22 percent Cabernet Franc, 12 percent Petit Verdot, 10 percent Merlot, and 1 percent Malbec. It is inky garnet in color, with aromas of black currant, Chinese five-spice powder, and cherry cola in the complex bouquet. It is full-bodied in the mouth, with fruit flavors as well as mocha and espresso beans in the persistent finish. Spring Mountain Vineyard Estate Sauvignon Blanc 2010 is light straw colored, with notes of white flowers, kumquat, and tropical fruits. It is clean and refreshing with flavors of white stone fruits and citrus blossom.

STAG'S LEAP WINE CELLARS

5766 Silverado Trail, Napa, CA 94558, (707) 944-2020
www.cask23.com

Stag's Leap Wine Cellars was founded in 1970, and its S.L.V. Cabernet Sauvignon 1973 was rated number one at the 1976 Judgment of Paris, using grapes from vines that were only three years old! Since that time Stag's Leap Wine Cellars wines have been acclaimed by numerous wine critics, served on Her Majesty Queen Elizabeth II's royal yacht, and installed into the permanent collection at the Smithsonian National Museum of American History. Winemaking is under the direction of podiatrist turned winemaker Nicki Pruss, and vineyard management is handled by Kirk Grace. Stag's Leap Wine Cellars Artemis Cabernet Sauvignon 2010 is named for Artemis, the Greek goddess of the hunt. It is composed of 88 percent Cabernet Sauvignon and 12 percent Merlot and is dark garnet in the glass. It has aromas of dark plums and black raspberries, with a touch of graphite in the bouquet. In the mouth it is big, fruit-forward, yet elegant, a wonderful example of an excellent Napa wine. Stag's Leap Wine Cellars Karia Chardonnay 2010 is straw yellow, with aromas of Anjou pear, Granny Smith apple, and citrus blossom. It has a nice mouthfeel with citrus flavors braced by subtle minerality. The name "Karia" comes from the Greek word meaning "graceful," and we feel that this wine embodies that spirit.

STAGS' LEAP WINERY

6150 Silverado Trail,
Napa, CA 94558,
(800) 395-2441
www.stagsleap.com

It's a bit of a wine journalism conundrum that with the two Stags Leap wineries, one has to remember whether the apostrophe is to the right of the *s* or to the left when discussing the two. They are both situated in the Stags Leap AVA, but after years of contentious lawsuits between the two—it's still difficult for most people to sort out who actually won—this Stags' Leap Winery has its apostrophe to the right. Like the other winery and the AVA, Stags' Leap Winery takes its name from the tale of the stag that eluded hunters by leaping to safety. Stags' Leap Winery was established in 1893, but modern-day wine production began in 1971 when Carl Doumani purchased the property. Today Stags' Leap Winery is owned by Treasury Wine Estates and is known for producing fine wine. We happen to be big fans of its Petite Sirah. Stags' Leap Winery Petite Sirah 2008 has delightful aromas of blackberries, red plums, and Christmas baking spices. It is soft upon entry to the mouth yet powerful with concentrated fruit flavors, English toffee nuances, and just a pinch of finely ground white pepper at the finish.

STONY HILL VINEYARD

3331 St. Helena Highway,
St. Helena, CA 94574,
(707) 963-2636
www.stonyhillvineyard.com

Eleanor and Fred McCrea purchased a 160-acre goat farm on Spring Mountain in 1943. Because of their love of white wine from Burgundy, they began planting Chardonnay vines in 1947. They built a small winery and produced their first Chardonnay in 1952. Peter, their son, and his wife, Willinda, along with their children, Frederick and Sarah, are the second and third generations working at the family business. Mike Chelini is in charge of both winery and vineyard operations. Stony Hill Vineyard Cabernet Sauvignon 2009 has aromas of dried black cherry, olive tapenade, and black plum. In the mouth there are flavors of ripe red fruits and a touch of bittersweet chocolate. The finish is long and powerful with a persistence of smoked meats and cocoa powder. Stony Hill Vineyard Chardonnay 2010 is pale yellow, with aromas of lemon blossoms, Granny Smith apples, and powdered chalk. It is luscious on the palate, with great fruit flavors and a rich mouthfeel. The finish has a nice touch of crisp acidity.

STORYBOOK MOUNTAIN VINEYARDS

3835 Highway 128,
Calistoga, CA 94515,
(707) 942-5282
www.storybookwines.com

In 1976 Jerry and Sigrid Seps purchased 90 acres and an abandoned ghost winery that was built by Adam Grimm in 1883. They began replanting Zinfandel vines, and in 1983 they released their first wine. Jerry was one of the founding members of ZAP (Zinfandel Advocates and Producers) and served as its president for the first five years. Storybook Zinfandel has been served to Nobel laureates in Sweden. It also has been served to White House guests on three occasions, most recently by President Obama in 2011. In 2012 Storybook Mountain Vineyards had the distinct honor of being named one of the "Top 100 Wineries" for the ninth time by *Wine & Spirits*. Storybook Mountain Vineyards Estate Reserve Zinfandel 2009 has aromas of black raspberry, crystallized violet petals, and sweet red fruits. It is sophisticated and elegant in the mouth, with pronounced fruit flavors and a sweet tannic finish.

TERLATO FAMILY VINEYARDS

200 Rutherford Hill Road,
Rutherford, CA 94573,
(888) 241-0259
www.terlatovineyards.com

Anthony Terlato is well known and revered in the world of wine. He was one of the first importers to bring Italian Pinot Grigio into the American market, and Santa Margarita, a brand he has been importing for years, is one of the industry leaders in the United States. More recently he and his sons, Bill and John, decided to become winemakers in the Napa Valley, and so they began their search for the right climate conditions and soil in which to make their quality wines. Besides their eponymous Terlato Family Wines, the family makes wine under the Chimney Rock, Sanford, Rutherford Hill, and Alderbrook labels. Terlato Family Vineyards Russian River Valley Pinot Grigio 2010 is light straw colored, with aromas of white flowers, white peach, and citrus blossom. It is delightful on the palate, with flavors of green apples and peach. It has a crisp finish. Terlato Family Vineyards Devils' Peak Napa Valley 2008 is a Bordeaux-style blend of 50 percent Cabernet Franc, 39 percent Merlot, 6 percent Malbec, and 5 percent Cabernet Sauvignon. It is ruby garnet and has aromas of fresh baked blueberry pie and violets. It is full-bodied with flavors of ripe berries and a long finish.

TOR KENWARD WINES

1241 Adams Street, #1045,
St. Helena, CA 94574,
(707) 963-3100
www.torwines.com

Tor Kenward started his eponymous label in 2001 after working at Beringer Vineyards for 27 years. He notes that he has had some great mentors along the way, including Ed Sbragia and Bob Steinhauer, as well as lots of help and support from his wife, Susan. TOR Napa Valley Oakville Tierra Roja Vineyard Cabernet Sauvignon 2010 has great aromas of rich dark cherries, black raspberry, black plum, and a whiff of lifted spearmint. In the mouth the fruit flavors come to life with a touch of spice in the post palate. The finish is long and luxurious. Tor Napa Valley Beckstoffer To Kalon Anniversary Cuvée Cabernet Sauvignon 2010 is simply amazing—too bad only 150 cases were made. It has concentrated aromas of red raspberries, black plums, forest floor, and smoked meats. It is big and bold but maintains restraint and elegance. We wish we had more in our cellar, as we expect it to only get better with age.

TREFETHEN FAMILY VINEYARDS

1160 Oak Knoll Avenue,
Napa, CA 94558,
(866) 895-7696
www.trefethen.com

Gene Trefethen was involved in the planning and building of the San Francisco Bay Bridge and the Hoover and Shasta dams. After he retired in 1968 he and his wife, Catherine, moved to the Napa Valley and purchased six contiguous farms as well as the dilapidated Eschol Winery to create their 600-acre estate. Their plan was to sell all their grapes, but their son John changed their minds when Trefethen's third-vintage 1976 Chardonnay was awarded "Best Chardonnay in the World" at the 1979 Gault Millau World Wine Olympics in Paris. Trefethen Family Vineyards Chardonnay 2011 has beautiful nuances of freesia, jasmine, and honeysuckle along with white stone fruit aromas. It has nice body on the palate, with bright acidity and a touch of minerality in the finish. Trefethen Family Vineyards Dragon's Tooth Red Wine 2010 is a combination of 58 percent Malbec, 22 percent Cabernet Sauvignon, and 20 percent Petit Verdot. It has rich aromas of black currant, brambleberry, cinnamon, and nutmeg. It has flavors of dark fruits and dark chocolate with a sweet, rounded tannic finish.

TRINCHERO NAPA VALLEY FAMILY VINEYARDS

3070 St. Helena Highway, St. Helena, CA 94574,
(707) 963-1160
www.trincheronapavalley.com

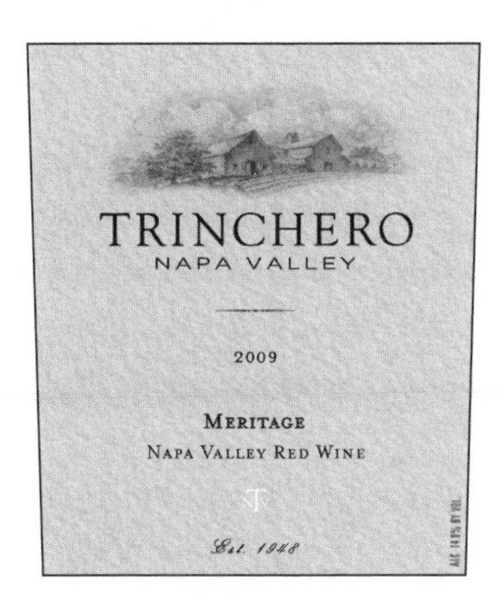

Mary and Mario Trinchero and their three children left bustling New York City for the laid-back Napa Valley in 1948 and purchased the abandoned Sutter Home Winery. Their son Bob is known industrywide for crafting the first "White Zinfandel" in 1972 and thereby creating an entirely new category of wine for the marketplace. By 2007 the family had acquired more than 200 acres of Napa vineyards, and in 2009 it released its first estate-grown wines bearing the Trinchero name. In total, fewer than 12,000 cases of Trinchero Napa Valley Family wines are produced. Trinchero St. Helena Napa Valley Mario's Vineyard Cabernet Sauvignon 2009 is dark garnet, with aromas of black cherry, cigar box, and lavender. In the mouth it has flavors of rich red raspberry and ripe cherry and velvety tannins. Trinchero Napa Valley Meritage 2009 is composed of 72 percent Cabernet Sauvignon, 15 percent Merlot, 8 percent Petit Verdot, and 5 percent Cabernet Franc. It is reddish-purple in the glass with notes of rich black fruits in the complex bouquet. In the mouth the fresh berries come alive along with flavors of mixed-berry preserves. The mouthfeel is velvety, and the finish is persistent.

TUCK BECKSTOFFER WINES

807 St. Helena Highway South,
St. Helena, CA 94574,
(707) 200-4410
www.tbwines.com

The Beckstoffer family moved to the Napa Valley in 1975, and from a young age Tuck developed a love of farming. In his teen years he worked in the vineyards of Mendocino and Napa counties, and after college he returned to Napa to work for Beckstoffer Vineyards. He began producing wine under the Tuck Beckstoffer label in 1997. Although St. Helena is his center of operations, Tuck sources fruit from premium vineyards throughout the state to make his fine wines. Tuck Beckstoffer Semper Silver Eagle Vineyard Pinot Noir 2009 is made from Sonoma Coast fruit and is cherry red to garnet colored in the glass. It has aromas of freshly picked red cherries and red plums and a top note of Christmas baking spices. It is fruit-forward in the mouth, with flavors of crushed black pepper and toffee combining to give it a spicy but well-rounded mouthfeel and finish. Tuck Beckstoffer Seventy Five Wine Company The Sum 2011 is a blend of 75 percent Cabernet Sauvignon, 15 percent Petite Syrah, and 10 percent Syrah. It has aromas of anise, pencil lead, smoked meats, and dark fruits. It is juicy and full-bodied on the palate, with a long-lasting fruit-focused finish.

TWOMEY

1183 Dunaweal Lane, Calistoga, CA 94515,
(707) 942-7026
www.twomey.com

The Duncan family decided to name its winery Twomey to honor Ray Duncan's mother and her maiden name. The family makes what they consider their most labor-intensive wine from Merlot grapes at this Calistoga winery. Visitors to the winery enjoy sitting and drinking Twomey's fine wines in their sunny courtyard. Twomey Single Vineyard Merlot 2008 is garnet, almost purplish, in color, with aromas of freshly picked black cherries, candied violet, and Christmas baking spices. In the mouth there are vibrant fruit flavors, good heft, and a balanced tannic finish with just the right touch of cocoa powder in the post palate. When visiting Sonoma, make sure to check out Twomey's sister winery on Westside Road in Healdsburg.

VIADER ESTATE

1120 Deer Park Road, Deer Park, CA 94576,
(707) 963-3816
www.viader.com

Argentine-born Delia Viader established her eponymous winery in 1986. Her wines have been well respected and highly rated for years. Delia hired family friend Michel Rolland as her consultant in 2006, and her children have returned to the family business after attending school. Her son Alan is the director of operations and winemaking; his wife, Mariela, is the director of the culinary program; and daughter Janet is director of marketing and sales. Viader Estate Limited Edition Black Label 2010 is composed of 40 percent Cabernet Sauvignon, 29 percent Syrah, 26 percent Cabernet Franc, and 5 percent Malbec. It is garnet to purple, with aromas of black raspberry, red plum, pencil lead, and a touch of forest floor. It is full-bodied, with flavors of black cherry, Chinese tea, and red fruits. The tannins are well balanced, and the finish is persistent. Viader Estate Liquid Cashmere 2009 is 70 percent Cabernet Sauvignon and 30 percent Cabernet Franc and, as the name implies, is smooth and silky in the palate with an elegant mouthfeel. Aromas of cigar box, black fruits, and dark cocoa powder transfer seamlessly onto the palate with great expression of both the fruit and the secondary flavors. Drink it now for immediate pleasure, but if you can control yourself, put it in your cellar for a few years; you won't be disappointed.

VILLA MOUNT EDEN

No visitor facilities., St. Helena, CA 94574,
(866) 931-1624
www.villamteden.com

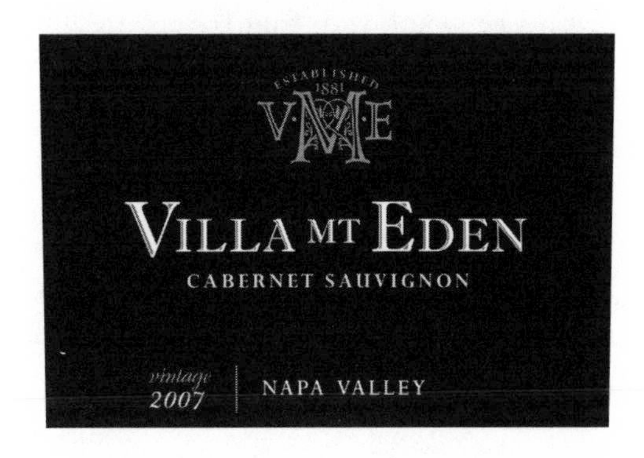

Villa Mount Eden was the eleventh bonded winery in Napa in 1881 under George W. Meyers's ownership. Meyers planted Riesling and Zinfandel, and eventually the winery was sold to Nick Fagiani in 1913. The winery changed hands a few times after Prohibition, and in 1969 it was purchased by James and Anne McWilliams. Nils Venge was brought in as general manager and winemaker in 1974 and handed over the baton to Mike McGrath in 1983. Villa Mount Eden has been named a best-value wine by a variety of publications and has the honor of being placed in *Wine Spectator*'s "Top 100" five times. Villa Mount Eden Napa Valley Cabernet Sauvignon 2007 is composed of 84 percent Cabernet Sauvignon, 9 percent Syrah, 4 percent

Cabernet Franc, 2 percent Petit Verdot, and 1 percent Merlot. It has aromas of freshly picked black raspberries and dried black cherries, with a touch of crystallized violet petals. It is rich in the mouth with fruit flavors, freshly ground black pepper, and chewy, balanced tannins that lead you into the long finish.

VINEYARD 7 & 8

4028 Spring Mountain Road, St. Helena, CA 94574, (707) 963-9425
www.vineyard7and8.com

The New Jersey/New York–based investment adviser Launny Steffens and his wife, Weezie, purchased land on Spring Mountain in 1999 and began Vineyard 7 & 8. Only their youngest son, Wesley, lives locally in Yountville, and he serves as the winery manager and assistant winemaker. The winemaker, Luc Morlet, trained in Bordeaux and Champagne before calling Napa Valley his home. Vineyard 7 & 8 Spring Mountain District Cabernet Sauvignon 2009 is dark garnet, with aromas of black cherry, blueberry pie, and anise. It is big and bold in the mouth with a burst of fruit and smooth lingering tannins in the finish.

WHITEHALL LANE WINERY AND VINEYARDS

1563 St. Helena Highway, St. Helena, CA 94574, (707) 963-9454
www.whitehalllane.com

San Francisco businessman Tom Leonardini purchased Whitehall Lane Winery in 1993. He immediately got to work purchasing new winemaking equipment, replanting vineyards, and implementing new barrel-aging protocols. He also scaled down the production to focus on four varieties: Merlot, Cabernet Sauvignon, Sauvignon Blanc, and Chardonnay. Unlike Tom's other business ventures, Whitehall Lane is a family affair. He, his wife, and their five children are directly involved in running the winery, and Tom hopes that his grandchildren and their children will continue the business for generations. Whitehall Lane Reserve Cabernet Sauvignon 2009 has delightful aromas of black plum, black raspberry, and a touch of purple flowers. It is fruit-forward on the palate with nice fruit flavors and a persistent finish. Drink now or keep for a few years; you won't be disappointed either way.

WISE ACRE VINEYARD

768 Sunnyside Road, St. Helena, CA 94574,
(707) 968-9094
www.wiseacrevineyard.com

Wise Acre Vineyard is probably one of Napa Valley's smallest commercial vineyard-wineries, measuring just half an acre. Founded in 2003 by Kirk and Lynn Grace, with Gary Brookman as their winemaker, the winery made its first release with its 2008 Cabernet Sauvignon. The vines were planted in 2005 and were grafted to the Bosche Cabernet Sauvignon clones from Kirk's parents' vineyard: the Grace Family Vineyard. We tasted their 2010 Cab and were impressed with the balance and complexity. Although this is a very young winery, we feel it's an up-and-comer and one to watch. Wise Acre Vineyard Cabernet 2010 is dark purplish garnet, with aromas of dark plums, cassis, wild herbs, and pencil lead. In the mouth the fruit flavors are full and rich, complemented by rounded tannins.

YAO FAMILY WINES

PO Box 111, Napa, CA 94515,
(707) 968-7470
www.yaofamilywines.com

Founded by former NBA All-Star and Olympian Yao Ming, Yao Family Wines entered the US wine market in 2012 with the introduction of its Napa Valley Cabernet Sauvignon 2009 and Family Reserve Cabernet Sauvignon 2009. Both wines were and continue to be extremely well received by the American and international press. Yao Family Wines sources grapes from established Napa Valley vineyards, and winemaking is under the direction of Tom Hinde, who was the CEO for Flowers Vineyard and Winery and general manager for Kendall-Jackson Wine Estates. Larry Bradley is the consulting viticulturist; he has worked at Clos du Val, Flowers, and wineries in France and Australia. Yao Family Wines Yao Ming Napa Valley Cabernet Sauvignon 2009 is deep garnet with a bright rim. It has aromas of lush black fruits and a touch of confectioner's sugar. It has bright fruit in the mouth—blackberry and strawberry—and notes of dried herbs and talc. The finish is round with a pleasant acidic rinse across the mid palate. Yao Family Wines Yao Ming Family Reserve Napa Valley Cabernet Sauvignon 2009 is inky garnet, with aromas of blackberry and red raspberry. It is smooth and velvety in the mouth, with flavors of fruits of the wood, lavender, white pepper, and candied watermelon rind. There is a nice touch of savory herbs on the finish.

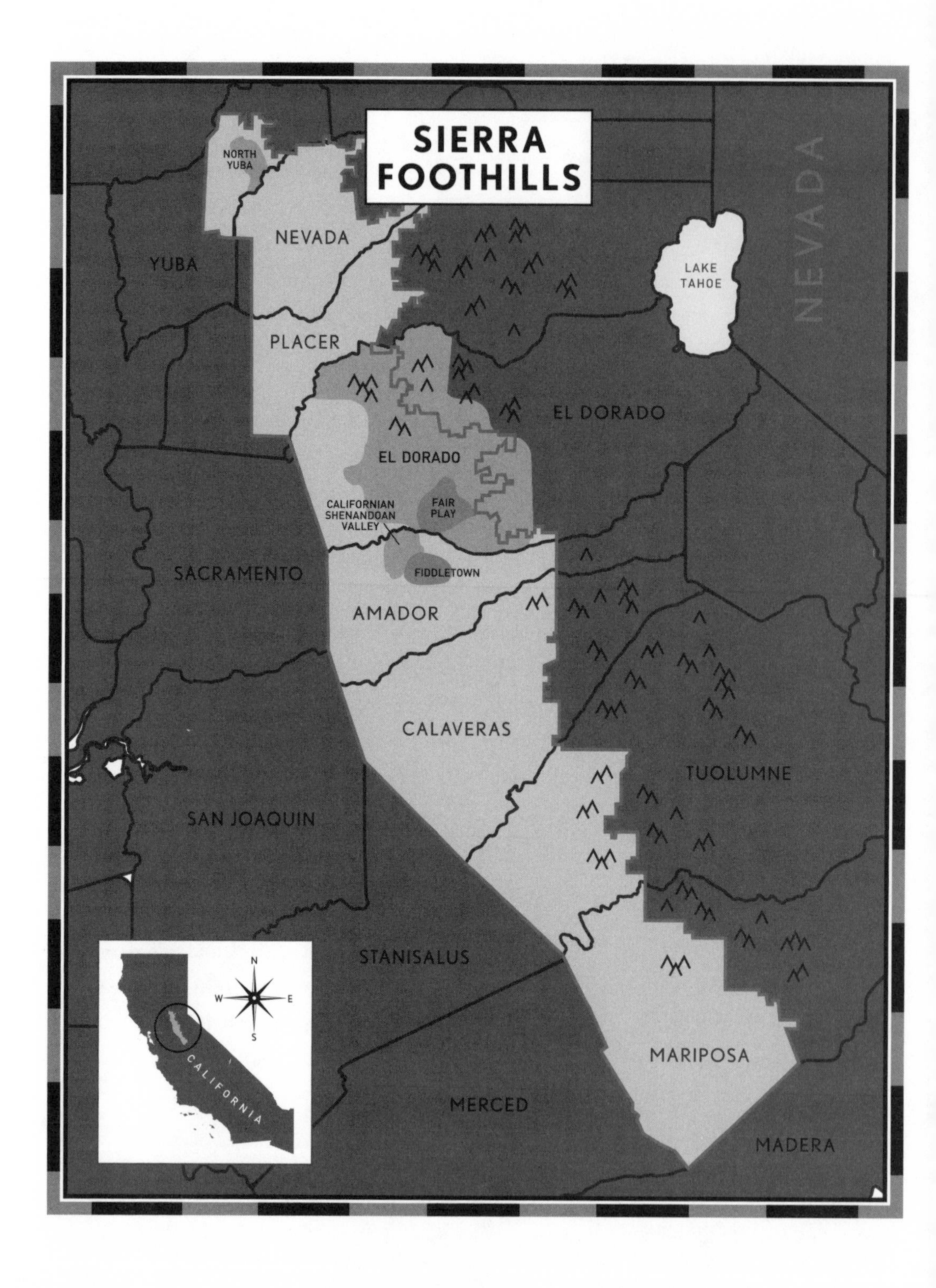

SIERRA FOOTHILLS
NORTH YUBA
NEVADA
YUBA
PLACER
LAKE TAHOE
NEVADA
EL DORADO
EL DORADO
CALIFORNIAN SHENANDOAN VALLEY
FAIR PLAY
FIDDLETOWN
SACRAMENTO
AMADOR
CALAVERAS
TUOLUMNE
SAN JOAQUIN
STANISALUS
N
W
E
S
CALIFORNIA
MARIPOSA
MERCED
MADERA

CHAPTER 4

SIERRA FOOTHILLS

WHEN JAMES MARSHALL HAPPENED UPON gold at Sutter's Mill in Coloma, California, on January 24, 1848, neither he nor his employer, Captain John Sutter, could have imagined the vast changes that the discovery of gold would bring. California was not even a US territory at the time, much less a state, and as word spread, fortune seekers from around the globe rapidly made their way to this mythical place in the American West. The Gold Rush of 1849—which lasted through 1855—brought a wave of immigration that would immutably alter the course of California's history. Over 300,000 people headed to this newfound Promised Land, and while some brought pans, sieves, and pickaxes, others arrived with carefully transported grape cuttings, which they planted in the mineral-rich soils of the Sierra Foothills. By the end of the nineteenth century there were over 100 wineries in the area, which shrank back to next to nothing during the years of Prohibition. A new wave of pioneer winemakers arrived in the 1970s and 1980s, and the number of wineries is finally back up to pre-twentieth-century levels.

Marshall's first gold sighting took place in modern-day El Dorado County in the Sierra Foothills AVA. El Dorado translates from Spanish as "The Golden," and although the gold is mostly long gone, grapes still thrive here and in adjacent counties in the Sierra Foothills AVA. Present-day Coloma is part museum and part ghost town, but among the remnants of the Gold Rush era are some of the oldest Zinfandel vines in the country. Although the term "old vine" may be applied willy-nilly in various parts of the world, here the meaning is exactly as intended: Sierra Foothills grapevines can date back to the 1860s or possibly even earlier. The Sierra Foothills AVA, one of four very large viticultural areas in the state, covers an area of 2,600,000 acres across eight counties and contains five sub-AVAs: California Shenandoah Valley, El Dorado, Fair Play, Fiddletown, and North Yuba.

The Sierra Foothills AVA stretches for 160 miles between California's Central Valley and the Sierra Nevada, and the main wine-growing regions are due east of the northern portions of Napa and Sonoma. Established in 1987, the region is composed of portions of eight counties: from north to south, Yuba, Nevada, Placer, El Dorado, Amador, Calaveras, Tuolumne, and Mariposa. Wine grapes are planted on just 5,700 acres of the 2,600,000 acres in the Sierra Foothills, which is less than a quarter of 1 percent of the total available land. Desertlike conditions, infertile soil, extreme elevation, and inaccessible locations make much of the area within the AVA inhospitable if not downright impossible for the cultivation of grapes. Vineyard elevations generally range from 1,500 to 3,000 feet, and rocky soils offer vines the high stress they need to produce richly flavored grapes.

At last count, Zinfandel, the undisputed king of the region, was grown on over 2,400 acres, a good portion of it in dry-farmed vineyards dating back to the 1860s. The second most prolific grape is Cabernet Sauvignon on 625 acres, followed by Syrah on 559 acres. Among the diverse plantings are 297 acres of Chardonnay, 283 acres of Merlot, and 244 acres of Barbera. There is a smattering of Sangiovese, which was one of the first varieties planted by nineteenth-century Italian immigrants. White Rhône varieties—Roussanne, Marsanne, Viognier, and Grenache Blanc—seem to be gaining the most traction in the region. In all, over sixty varieties are grown here, and there are over a hundred wineries, mostly small family-run affairs, throughout the AVA.

The largest of the subregions is El Dorado, bordered to the north by the Rubicon River and partly bordered to the south by the Cosumnes River. On a map, the borders of the El Dorado AVA, which sits completely in the county of the same name, look like the edges of a very complicated puzzle piece. The smaller California Shenandoah Valley and Fiddletown AVAs, in neighboring Amador County, jut out toward the southwest corner, separated from the main portion of the AVA by the Cosumnes River. El Dorado's sub-AVA Fair Play is just to the northwest of this jigsaw tab, on the north side of the river. The one noncontiguous AVA within the larger Sierra Foothills footprint is North Yuba, situated in Yuba County, at the northern edge of the Sierra Foothills AVA. North Yuba is 30 square miles in size and features loam and clay soils with high mineral content.

The El Dorado AVA is at high elevations: 1,200 feet at its eastern edge, ranging up to 3,500 feet to the west. Whereas elevation is responsible for maintaining lower temperatures than might be expected, cooling air from the coast moves inland in a direct line from the Carquinez Strait, between Suisun

Bay and San Francisco Bay. The chilling effect moderates the heat of the summer sun, offering necessary protection to fragile grapes surviving on minimal groundwater, especially in the southern portions of El Dorado and in the Fair Play AVA. Fair Play's vineyards are at elevations of 2,000 to 3,000 feet, and this area is said to have the highest average elevation of any AVA in the state. Totaling 36 square miles, it is planted with 350 acres of vines, mainly within ridges between river canyons. Soils in El Dorado are composed of sandy loams and coarse sandy loams, and Fair Play's soils are said to be the deepest and most fertile in the entire region. The El Dorado AVA was established in 1983 and finalized in 1987, and the Fair Play AVA was carved out in 2001.

The California Shenandoah Valley AVA, first established in 1982 and amended in 1987, is so named to avoid confusion with the Shenandoah Valley AVA on the East Coast of the United States, near the Blue Ridge Mountains in Virginia and West Virginia. Vines here start at elevations of 500 feet, running up to heights of 2,000 feet. Fiddletown, its neighbor to the southeast, features vines at slightly higher elevations. Both are in Amador County, and soils there are made up of sandy clay loam over fragmented granite and volcanic stone. Fiddletown, first established in 1983, was finalized as an AVA in 1987.

THE WINERIES

BOEGER WINERY

1709 Carson Road, Placerville, CA 95667,
(530) 622-8094
www.boegerwinery.com

Greg Boeger followed in his Swiss-Italian grandfather's footsteps when he purchased a former vineyard site in El Dorado County, planted vines, and opened his eponymous winery in 1972. His son Justin recently joined the family tradition, assuming the role of winemaker and thereby leaving Greg more time to work in the vineyards. Boeger Winery Sauvignon Blanc 2011 is composed of 87 percent Sauvignon Blanc, 7 percent Flora, 4 percent Sémillon, and 2 percent White Riesling. It is 100 percent estate-grown and has aromas of citrus blossoms and white stone fruits. In the mouth it has flavors of white peach and honeycomb, with a refreshing persistent finish. Boeger Winery Barbera 2010 consists of 95 percent Barbera, 2 percent Cabernet Sauvignon, 2 percent Cabernet Franc, and 1 percent Petit Verdot. It is garnet colored, and it has aromas of dark cherry, black pepper, and a touch of Christmas baking spices. On the palate it is big and round with a long and fruity finish.

GROS VENTRE

8054 Fairplay Road, Somerset, CA 95684,
(707) 955-5788
www.grosventrecellars.com

Winemaker Chris Pittenger makes Pinot Noir in El Dorado with fruit he sources from the Sonoma Coast, Russian River Valley, and Anderson Valley. The *San Francisco Chronicle* selected him as a winemaker to watch in 2013, and we couldn't agree more. Gros Ventre is his personal project, but he makes his wine at Skinner Vineyards and

Winery, where he is employed as a winemaker. The name Gros Ventre is French for "big belly" and was named for his wife, Sarah, during her pregnancy. Gros Ventre Cerise Vineyard Pinot Noir 2011 is made from grapes sourced from the Anderson Valley; only 176 cases were produced. It is cherry red in the glass, with aromas of black cherry, tobacco leaf, cranberry juice, and rose hips. It is bright in the mouth with lovely fruit flavors and an herb-infused savory finish.

HOLLY'S HILL VINEYARDS

3680 Leisure Lane, Placerville, CA 95667,
(530) 344-0227
www.hollyshill.com

Tom and Holly Cooper shared their first bottle of Châteauneuf-du-Pape on their honeymoon, and their love of Rhône varieties was born. Holly's Hill Vineyards concentrates on making fine wine from Grenache, Mourvèdre, Syrah, Counoise, Roussanne, and Viognier grapes. Winemaking is under the direction of husband-and-wife team Josh and Carrie Bendick. Visitors to the winery are always impressed by the panoramic views over the valley because the tasting room is perched at 2,700 feet of altitude. Holly's Hill Vineyards Viognier 2012 is straw colored, with aromas of clementine, Anjou Pear, and white stone fruits. It is crisp and balanced in the mouth, with a touch of florality in the finish. Holly's Hill Vineyards Grenache Blanc 2012 is pale straw, with notes of lemon-lime zest and white flowers in the nose. It is fruit-forward and clean on the palate, with just the right zing of acidity in the finish.

LAVA CAP WINERY

2221 Fruitridge Road, Placerville, CA 95667,
(530) 621-0175
www.lavacap.com

David and Jeanne Jones and family founded Lava Cap Winery when they planted their first vines in 1981. This family of geologists chose the name because a cap of lava and volcanic soil exists on the property. The winery opened in 1986, and today Tom Jones continues the tradition of winemaking while his brother Charlie manages the vineyards.

Lava Cap Estate Bottled El Dorado Petite Sirah 2009 is deep violet red with aromas of black cherry, blackberry, and spice in the bouquet. It has good acidity with soft tannins and a touch of anise on the finish. Lava Cap Estate Bottled El Dorado Barbera 2009 is dark garnet in color, with aromas of black raspberry, dark cherry, and vanilla. In the mouth it is full-bodied yet soft, with a lingering nuance of chocolate-covered cherries in the finish.

MADROÑA VINEYARDS

2560 High Hill Road, Camino, CA 95709,
(530) 644-5948
www.madronavineyards.com

Dick and Leslie Bush were captivated by the charm of the high foothills of the Sierra Nevada in the 1970s and decided to plant vineyards. At that time their vines were among the highest in the state. Perched at 3,000 feet in the El Dorado AVA, Madroña is composed of three family-owned vineyards growing twenty-six varieties of grapes: Madroña Vineyard in Apple Hill and Sumu-Kaw Vineyard and Enye Vineyard in Pleasant Valley. Dick and Leslie's sons Paul and David and their wives have joined the family business. Madroña Vineyards Hillside Collection Zinfandel 2010 is garnet purple, with aromas of red raspberry, black raspberry, and cranberry sauce. It is fruit-forward in the mouth, with flavors of sweet cherry washing the palate before the balanced tannic finish. Madroña Hillside Collection Gewürztraminer 2011 is pale straw, with aromas of Cavaillon melon, Ruby Red grapefruit, and white stone fruits. Entry into the mouth is smooth and silky with great fruit flavors and a crisp acidic finish.

MIRAFLORES WINERY

2120 Four Springs Trail,
Placerville, CA 95667, (530) 647-8505
www.mirafloreswinery.com

MIRAFLORES

The architecture of the Miraflores tasting room will make you think you have been transported to a Mediterranean winery. Colombian-born owner Victor Alvarez is not only a vintner, he is also a practicing pathologist whose love of wine moved him to establish Miraflores in 2003. The winery sits on a 254-acre estate, 40 of which are under vine. Miraflores Pinot Grigio 2012 is pale straw colored, with aromas of citrus blossoms and white stone fruit. It is crisp and clean on the palate with a delightfully acidic finish. Miraflores Estate Zinfandel 2009 has aromas of black cherry preserves, cherry vanilla ice cream, and purple flowers. It is fruit-forward in the mouth with ripe tannins that carry on to the persistent finish.

MOUNT AUKUM WINERY

6781 Tower Road, Somerset, CA 95684, (530) 620-1675
www.mountaukum.com

Winemaker Michel Prod'hon learned winemaking at a young age in his childhood village of Chaumount in the Champagne region of France. Most of the grapes he uses to craft his artisanal small-batch wines are grown on his estate in the Fair Play AVA. The winery sits at a privileged elevation of 2,615 feet on the peak of Mount Aukum, and Michel invites visitors to bring a picnic lunch to enjoy the majestic view. Mount Aukum Winery Estate Fair Play El Dorado Sangiovese 2009 has a medium dark cherry color, with tart cherry and Mediterranean herbal notes in the bouquet. It is big and round in the mouth, with a sweet tannic finish and a fair bit of acidity. Mount Aukum Winery El Dorado Zinfandel 2009 is deep reddish-purple, with aromas of dark fruits, anise, blueberry, and clove. On the palate there is an herbal note that comes out with flavors of ripe juicy fruits and licorice. The finish is laden with smooth, soft tannins.

SKINNER VINEYARDS AND WINERY

8054 Fairplay Road, Somerset, CA 95684, (530) 620-2220
www.skinnervineyards.com

Scottish immigrant James Skinner crossed the United States to mine for gold and eventually saved enough money to buy some land, build a house, and plant some vines. By 1861 his wines and distilled brandy had developed a local following. Over time his land changed hands, and in 2006 Carey and Mike Skinner found a great piece of property on a ridge overlooking the Sierra Nevada and decided to reestablish the Skinner name in the wine business. Today Mike and Carey are joined by their family and winemaker Chris Pittenger and are making wines that are capturing some nice buzz and media attention. Skinner Vineyards Seven Generations 2010 is a blend of 46 percent Roussanne, 26 percent Marsanne, 13 percent Viognier, 13 percent Picpoul Blanc, and 2 percent Grenache Blanc. It has aromas of citrus blossom, tropical fruits, and orange vanilla sherbet. It is clean and crisp in the mouth, with a touch of vanilla and baking spice in the finish. Skinner Vineyards Grenache 2011 is dark cherry red, with aromas of red raspberry, freshly picked strawberry, and a touch of forest floor. It is fruit-forward in the mouth with a balanced tannic finish.

TERRA D'ORO WINERY

20680 Shenandoah School Road,
Plymouth, CA 95669,
(209) 245-6942
www.terradorowinery.com

Named for the gold diggers lured to this "land of gold" in the Sierra Foothills, Terra d'Oro Winery was first known as Montevina when it was founded by Cary Gott and Walter Field in 1970. It has the distinction of being the first winery to make wine in Amador County after the repeal of Prohibition and today boasts 400 acres of

estate vines, including plantings of Sangiovese, Zinfandel, Barbera, Pinot Grigio, and Moscato. Terra d'Oro Winery Amador County Sangiovese 2010 is composed of 91 percent Sangiovese and 9 percent Barbera. It is garnet colored, with notes of black raspberry, rose petals, and cardamom in the bouquet. In the mouth Indian spices and a smooth tannic finish accent flavors of black cherry and cassis. Terra d'Oro Winery Amador County Zinfandel 2010 is garnet red, with aromas of black cherry, Christmas baking spices, and a touch of cherry vanilla ice cream in the bouquet. On the palate ripe fruit flavors combine with notes of black pepper and nutmeg that blend into the soft, round tannic finish.

TERRE ROUGE EASTON WINES

PO Box 41, Fiddletown, CA 95629,
(209) 245-5415
www.terrerougewines.com

Named for the red earth of the region, Terre Rouge makes wines from Rhône varieties, including Marsanne, Roussanne, Viognier, Mourvèdre, Grenache, and Syrah. Winemaker Bill Easton also makes non-Rhône varieties under his eponymous Easton label. He is currently working with Sauvignon Blanc, Cabernet Sauvignon, Barbera, and Zinfandel. Production at Terre Rouge and Easton Wines is small. Although twenty different wines are made between the two labels, they are made in small lots of only 300 to 500 cases each. Terre Rouge Sierra Foothills Vin Gris d'Amador 2011 is a blend of 61 percent Mourvèdre, 35 percent Grenache, and 4 percent Syrah. It is pale pink in the glass, with aromas of freshly picked strawberries, red cherry juice, and Christmas baking spices. It is creamy in the mouth with a nice acidic finish. Terre Rouge Fiddletown Early Release Viognier 2012 is pale straw colored, with aromas of white flowers, white stone fruits, and dried apricots. The peach and apricot flavors come out on the palate, with a nice touch of florality in the finish.

YORBA WINES

51 Hanford Street,
Sutter Creek, CA 95685,
(209) 267-5055
www.yorbawines.com

The Kraemer Family continues to use the name Yorba to honor their great-grandmother Angelina Yorba, descended from Jose Antonio Yorba, who came to California in 1769. The family planted 34 acres of vines at Shake Ridge Vineyards in 2003, and an additional 12 acres were planted in 2009. Family member Ann Kraemer manages the vineyards, and Ken Bernards handles the charge of winemaking. Yorba Zinfandel 2007 has delightful aromas of dried herbs, red cherries, and black raspberries. It is voluptuous in the mouth with balanced tannins and a nice bright note in the finish. Yorba Syrah 2008 is inky purple in the glass with aromas of purple flowers, black raspberry, licorice, and dried Mediterranean herbs. The fruit flavors pass seamlessly onto the palate, with silky tannins and a long, luxurious finish.

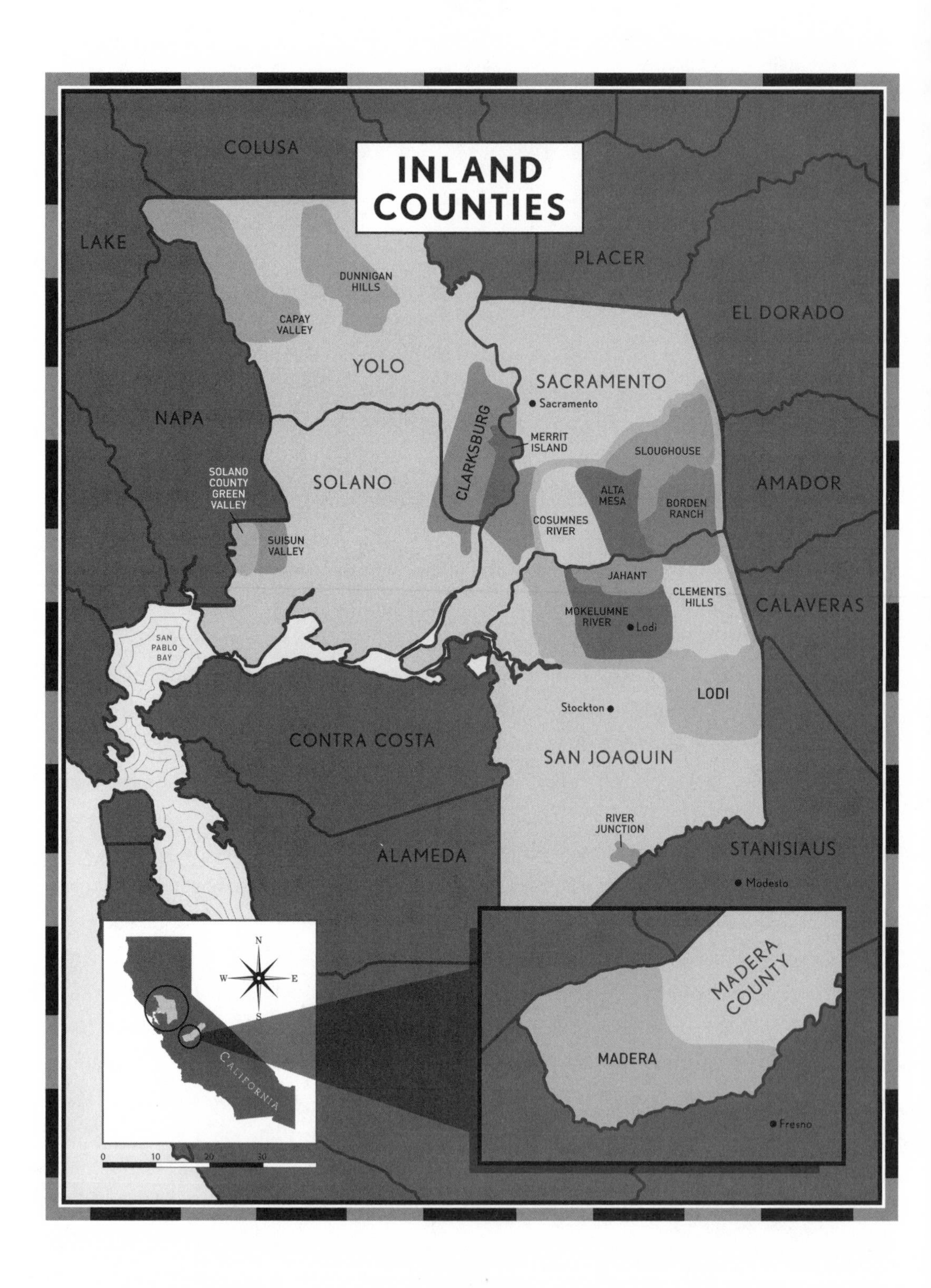

INLAND COUNTIES
COLUSA
LAKE
PLACER
EL DORADO
DUNNIGAN HILLS
CAPAY VALLEY
YOLO
SACRAMENTO
Sacramento
NAPA
CLARKSBURG
MERRIT ISLAND
SLOUGHHOUSE
SOLANO
AMADOR
SOLANO COUNTY GREEN VALLEY
ALTA MESA
BORDEN RANCH
COSUMNES RIVER
SUISUN VALLEY
JAHANT
CLEMENTS HILLS
CALAVERAS
MOKELUMNE RIVER
Lodi
SAN PABLO BAY
LODI
Stockton
CONTRA COSTA
SAN JOAQUIN
RIVER JUNCTION
ALAMEDA
STANISIAUS
Modesto
N
W
E
S
CALIFORNIA
MADERA COUNTY
MADERA
Fresno
0
10
20
30

CHAPTER 5

CENTRAL VALLEY AND THE INLAND COUNTIES

CENTRAL CALIFORNIA, BETWEEN THE Coastal Mountain Range to the west and the Sierra Nevada to the east, is the nation's produce stand. It is where a vast majority of the country's vegetables come from, just about any fruit or vegetable you can think of, from asparagus to zucchini. Known as the Central Valley, it is composed of two valleys, the San Joaquin in the south and Sacramento in the north, and at 450 miles long by 60 miles at its widest point it is larger than any of the nine smallest states in the United States: Maryland, Hawaii, Massachusetts, Vermont, New Hampshire, New Jersey, Connecticut, Delaware, and Rhode Island.

The Central Valley runs through a string of inland counties, including Yolo, Solano, Sacramento, San Joaquin, Stanislaus, Merced, Madera, and Fresno. Blessed with fertile soils (designated Class 1, the best, by the US Department of Agriculture), 300 days of sunshine per year, and abundant water, it is home to over 230 crops, including wine grapes. The wine regions of California's inland counties do not fall within the boundaries of the state's four large AVAs; they are east of the North Coast and Central Coast AVAs and west of a portion of the Sierra Foothills AVA. Snowmelt from the Sierra Nevada is used to irrigate vegetable fields, fruit orchards, and vineyards alike. The Sacramento River flows through the northern reaches of Sacramento Valley, and the San Joaquin River traverses the length of the San Joaquin Valley. Lodi and its subappellations grew up in the propitious soils surrounding the Cosumnes and Mokelumne rivers, which give their names to two of the AVAs within Lodi.

Grapes first were planted throughout central California in the late nineteenth century, after the boom and bust of the Gold Rush. Immigrants who had come seeking their fortune turned their hands to the productive soils of Lodi and Madera, many growing melons and other crops alongside their vineyards. Lodi was a hotbed of grape farming during Prohibition. It was during that dark era in American history that Italian immigrant Cesare Mondavi relocated his family from Minnesota to Lodi and began growing grapes to ship by rail to winemakers back east. Immediately after Prohibition ended, Ernest and Julio Gallo founded their eponymous winery in Modesto, to the south of Lodi. From this period through the 1960s Americans preferred sweet wines, and many wines labeled "port" but produced in Central California had nothing to do with the grapes or *terroir* of Portugal, but rather were made with Lodi grapes. In the 1960s and 1970s, as wine drinking caught on in the United States, large-volume wineries such as Gallo and Franzia used Lodi and nonappellation Central Valley grapes for their inexpensive bottles and boxes. Robert Mondavi, who grew up in Lodi, struck out on his own in 1966 and founded his winery in Napa Valley, continuing to use Lodi as a source of grapes for his entry-level wines.

LODI AND ITS SUB-AVAS

Even before Italian and German settlers planted *Vitis vinifera* vines there in the 1850s, Lodi was home to indigenous *Vitis labrusca* grapes. Abundant wild grapevines were first noted by trappers, who called one local stream Wine Creek. By the 1880s immigrants had planted Alicante, Tokay, and Zinfandel. Today Lodi's grape growers have christened the region the Zinfandel Capital of the World, in part because of the 2,000 acres of old-vine Zinfandel rooted here. Lodi is also responsible for 32 percent of all the Zinfandel grown in the state of California. In addition to this distinctly Californian variety with a mysterious Mediterranean provenance, Lodi is home to proportionally high amounts of Chardonnay, Cabernet Sauvignon, Merlot, Pinot Grigio, Petite Sirah, Syrah, and Sauvignon Blanc. It is also home to five very large wineries—Robert Mondavi Woodbridge, Turner Road Vintners, Sutter Home Winery, Bear Creek Winery, and Oak Ridge Winery—and close to eighty small family-owned wineries. Many well-known California wineries buy grapes from Lodi, including Ravenswood, Fetzer, Beringer, and Delicato.

Although many of the well-known varieties of grapes that are grown in large amounts are used by the big wineries in the area or sold elsewhere, boutique Lodi wineries are working with an intriguing catalog of varieties, most notably from Southern Europe, including Albariño, Alicante Bouschet, Carignane, Petit Verdot, Sangiovese, Tempranillo, Touriga Nacional, Vermentino, and Viognier. About 750 growers farm 100,000 acres of grapes in Lodi and its sub-AVAs. The Lodi AVA was established in March 1986 and amended in 2002, and the eight smaller appellations were created in August 2006 to better reflect the diversity of climates and soils within Lodi. They are Alta Mesa, Borden Ranch, Clement Hills, Cosumnes River, Jahant, Mokelumne River, River Junction, and Sloughhouse. Lodi's total size is 551,000 acres, and it straddles three counties: San Joaquin, Sacramento, and Solano. The seven sub-AVAs fill in the outline of the original 458,000 acres that were simply designated Lodi from 1986 to 2006, and the area that is now just called Lodi without a subappellation, in the southern and western portion of the AVA, consists of the 93,000 acres that were added when the Lodi AVA was amended in 2002.

The two rivers that run through Lodi, the Mokelumne and Cosumnes, are responsible for the granitic alluvial soils closest to their shores. Lodi is due east of a huge gap in the Coastal Range, at the entrance to San Francisco Bay, which offers cool maritime air that is denied to other inland grape-growing regions.

The Alta Mesa AVA, bordered to the west by the Cosumnes River AVA and to the east by Sloughhouse and Borden Ranch, is composed of flat terrain with red clay and gravel soils. Its name is Spanish for "high table" because it is at a slightly higher elevation than the surrounding areas. Of its 55,400 acres, roughly 10 percent are covered with vines. It is known primarily known for red grapes, notably Zinfandel, Syrah, and Cabernet Sauvignon. The Borden Ranch AVA, to the east, has the widest-ranging altitudes within Lodi, running from 73 feet in the west to 520 in the east. Its stone-filled soils offer good drainage for red varieties. It covers an area of 70,000 acres, of which 12,000 are planted to grapes.

The Clements Hills AVA, whose delineating feature is the hills and cliffs at the bottom of the Sierra Foothills, is also home to mainly red varieties. The Mokelumne River runs through its northern portion, and the Calaveras River forms its southern border with the greater Lodi AVA. Warmer and wetter than its neighboring regions, it is also the obvious habitat for red varieties. Soils include a mixture of loam and clay overlying granite and volcanic rock. Approximately 25 percent of its 85,400 acres are cultivated with grapevines. The Cosumnes River AVA, in Lodi's northwest, sits between Alta Mesa and the neighboring Clarksburg AVA. Elevations are low here—from 5 to 48 feet above sea level—and the cool, wet climate is particularly suited to white varieties. Among a total 54,700 acres, grapes are grown on 3,500.

Named for its pink Rocklin-Jahant loam soils, Lodi's smallest AVA, Jahant, covers 28,000 acres, with 9,000 of them planted to wine grapes. Central to the region and surrounded by five of the other sub-AVAs, Jahant has borders that were determined by the natural boundaries of this soil type. Its closeness to the Mokelumne River and the Sacramento–San Joaquin Delta offers cooling effects to the AVA. Whereas Jahant may be the physical center of the Lodi AVA, its neighbor to the south, the Mokelumne River AVA, is the region's historical center. The city of Lodi is in its midst, as is the twisting course of its namesake body of water. The AVA's total area is

87,500 acres, and about half of that is home to grapevines, a much higher percentage than in any other appellation within Lodi. Its soils are mainly alluvial, with varying degrees of sand and loam. The majority of old-vine Zinfandel within the Lodi appellation is grown here.

The northeastern piece of the puzzle that Lodi resembles is the Sloughhouse AVA, which is also in the foothills of the Sierra Nevada. The Cosumnes River passes through Sloughhouse, which is noted to be the warmest of Lodi's sub-regions. Elevations range as high as 590 feet above sea level. Of 78,000 total acres, fewer than 10 percent are planted to grapes.

CLARKSBURG

To the west of Lodi and just 20 minutes by car from downtown Sacramento, the Clarksburg AVA straddles three counties: Yolo, Sacramento, and Solano. Established in February 1984, Clarksburg covers 64,640 acres, with over 20,000 acres cultivated with grapevines. The Sacramento River passes north to south through Clarksburg and its sub-AVA, Merritt Island (5,000 acres, established February 1987), which is indeed an island. Named for its founder, Robert C. Clark, who settled here in 1859, Clarksburg is still home to many of its earliest farming families, including the Bogle family, who started farming here in the 1850s.

The Clarksburg Wine Growers and Vintners Association boasts twenty-eight growers and twelve wineries, and over thirty-five different varieties of grapes are planted here. Although the area was noted in the past for red grapes such as Zinfandel, Merlot, and Petite Sirah, the proximity of the Sacramento River and the maritime effects from San Francisco Bay make this an ideal climate for white varieties, in particular Chardonnay, Pinot Grigio, Sauvignon Blanc, and Chenin Blanc. Pinot Noir has overtaken the other red varieties and now accounts for more than half of the red grapes grown in Clarksburg.

SOLANO COUNTY GREEN VALLEY AND SUISUN VALLEY

Two relatively small AVAs that abut Napa County—just over Howell Mountain to the east—are Solano County Green Valley and Suisun Valley. They were established one month apart, Suisun Valley in December 1982 and Solano County Green Valley in January 1983. They are both on the other side of the county line but just south of Napa's Stags Leap District. The smaller of the two, Green Valley, is wedged between Suisun Valley to the east and Napa's Coombsville AVA to the west. Solano County Green Valley has a total area of 2,560 acres, and enjoys cool afternoon winds and moisture from San Pablo Bay.

Suisun Valley's 15,360 acres are home to 3,000 acres of grapevines and ten wineries. Red varieties such as Cabernet Sauvignon, Zinfandel,

Syrah, Petite Sirah, and Pinot Noir are grown here, as are Chardonnay, Riesling, Sauvignon Blanc, and white Rhône varieties. Elevations vary from 100 feet on the valley floor to over 2,100 feet toward the western border. This valley was named for the indigenous Suisun Indians, and its first winery was built in the 1860s; there were several others before Prohibition. Suisun Valley is the second oldest AVA in the United States, established 22 months after Napa Valley.

CAPAY VALLEY AND DUNNIGAN HILLS

Capay Valley, just over the Coastal Range from Napa Valley, borders both Napa and Lake counties and is situated in the northwest corner of Yolo County. Established as an AVA in 2002, it covers an area of 102,400 acres, of which fewer than 100 acres are planted to grapes. The first winery in Yolo County was founded here in 1860, and the petitioner for AVA status was the owner of Capay Valley Winery, the biggest winery in the AVA. Its neighbor to the east, the Dunnigan Hills AVA, is 89,000 acres in size but has substantially more plantings, including 1,300 acres of estate vineyards belonging to R.H. Phillips Winery, the producers of Toasted Head Wine. A growers and producers group known as Roots to Wine has ten member wineries in western Yolo and northern Solano counties. The wineries belonging to this coalition range in size from boutique to behemoth, but their common goals include a higher consumer profile for the wines of the region and an increase in tourism to the area.

MADERA

Established in 1984 and amended in 1985 and 1987, the Madera AVA covers an expanse of 230,000 acres; about 17 percent of that is planted to grapes. In addition to grapes, Madera County plays an important role in the Central Valley's fruit and vegetable production. Situated between the San Joaquin River and the Sierra Nevada, Madera (Spanish for "wood") County is known as the Gateway to Yosemite. Grape growing began as a tradition here toward the end of the nineteenth century, founded by transplants from far-flung countries such as Italy, France, and Armenia. Many of the grapes grown here are shipped elsewhere and make their way into inexpensive California appellation bottlings, but a handful of small wineries are now gaining lots of attention for their small-batch, handcrafted wines. Some are trading on the heritage of the Madera County sweet wine that was popularized in the early twentieth century and continued to be produced in the early years following the repeal of Prohibition. A visit to the Madera Wine Trail will no doubt include wine being poured by many of the same people who tend the vines and make the wine.

THE WINERIES

BOGLE VINEYARDS

37783 County Road 144, Clarksburg, CA 95612,
(916) 744-1139
www.boglewinery.com

Warren Bogle planted his first 20 acres of vines in Clarksburg in 1968, but his family had been farmers in the region since the mid-1800s. Bogle Vineyards is a large winery but remains a family-run company. His son, Warren W. Bogle, studied agriculture at California State University, Chico, and returned in 1997 to the 1,500-acre family ranch, where he currently serves as company president. His older sister Jody is in charge of customer relations and international sales, and his younger brother Ryan serves as vice president. Bogle wines are consistently rated as "best buys" and "biggest bargains" in many wine publications. Bogle Vineyards Petite Sirah 2010 is deep purple in the glass, with aromas of black plum, cranberry, raspberry preserves, and violets. In the mouth there are flavors of black cherry, blackberry, purple flowers, and spice. This is certainly a wine that overperforms for the price. Bogle Vineyards Old Vine Zinfandel is red violet in color, with aromas of black pepper, lilac talcum powder, and fruits of the wood in the bouquet. In the mouth it is medium-bodied, with flavors of black cherry, blackberry, thyme, and a touch of milk chocolate on the finish.

CAPAY VALLEY VINEYARDS

13757 Highway 16, Brooks, CA 95606,
(530) 796-4110
www.capayvalleyvineyards.com

Tom Frederick and Pam Welch founded Capay Valley Vineyards in 1998. Tom is well known for his earlier career in the race car industry. In the 1960s he was crew chief for a variety of drivers, including Jim Hall and Al Unser Jr., but he transitioned out of the competition circuit in the 1980s to a career in restoring vintage racing cars for drivers and collectors. Today he can be found at

Capay Valley Vineyards working alongside winemaker Terri Strain. Tom, Pam, and Terri are proud that a Capay Valley winery was hailed as "the finest vineyard in the state" in 1861. Today the team strives to bring history full circle and make the best possible wines from this venerated region. Capay Valley Vineyards Capay Valley Viognier 2012 is straw colored, with aromas of tropical fruits and melons. It is crisp and clean in the mouth with balanced acidity and a persistent finish. Too bad only 200 cases were made. Capay Valley Vineyards Capay Valley Tempranillo 2009 is garnet colored, with aromas of black cherry and smoked meats. It is fruit-forward in the palate, with balanced tannins and a persistent finish.

CASEY FLAT RANCH

PO Box 1274, Tiburon, CA 94920,
(415) 435-2225
www.caseyflatranch.com

Named for one of Capay Valley's pioneer homesteaders, John Casey, Casey Flat Ranch was originally part of the Rancho Canada de Capay in the historic 1846 Mexican Land Grant. Currently owned by the Robert and Maura Morey family, the ranch is home to Casey Flat Vineyards, Open Range wines, CFR, and a purebred longhorn cattle operation. There are 24 acres of vineyards, including Sauvignon Blanc, Bordeaux, and Rhône varieties, planted amid the ranch's 6,000 total acres. Casey Flat Ranch Capay Valley Sauvignon Blanc 2011 has aromas of Cavaillon melon, dried apricot, and white stone fruits. In the mouth flavors of peach and apricot integrate with subtle herbaceous notes to create a delightfully complex palate. The finish is clean with an appropriate amount of crisp acidity that would make this ideal as an aperitif or paired with shellfish. Casey Flat Ranch Capay Valley Estate Red Wine 2009 is a blend of 50 percent Syrah, 30 percent Cabernet Sauvignon, and 20 percent Cabernet Franc. It is garnet colored, with notes of black raspberry and black plum in the bouquet. Flavors of fruit are joined by nuances of Mediterranean herbs in the mouth before the firm tannic finish.

CREW WINE COMPANY

12300 County Road 92B, Zamora, CA 95698,
(530) 662-1032
www.crewwines.com

Situated in Zamora, Crew Wine Company was founded by John, Lane, and Karl Giguiere. No strangers to the wine and grape-growing industry, John, along with his wife and brother, started RH Phillips Winery in 1983, sold the company to Vincor in 2000, and in August 2005 began Crew Wine Company. Their wines are made under a variety of labels, including Mossback, Matchbook, Sawbuck, and Chasing Venus. Matchbook Dunnigan Hills Tinto Rey 2008 is a blend of 54 percent Tempranillo, 34 percent Syrah, 7 percent Cabernet Sauvignon, and 5 percent Graciano. It is big, bold, and fruit-driven and has aromas of violets, espresso, dark chocolate, and dark fruits. The tannins are pleasantly grippy, and the finish is long with a burst of fruit on the posterior palate. Mossback Russian River Valley Chalk Hill Cabernet Sauvignon 2009 is composed of 77 percent Cabernet Sauvignon and 23 percent Merlot. It is dark garnet, with aromas of dried cherry, cigar box, and freshly grated white pepper. It is soft in the mouth with a big and balanced finish.

DELICATO FAMILY VINEYARDS

12001 South Highway 99, Manteca, CA 95336,
(877) 824-3600
www.dfvwines.com

Italian immigrant Gaspare Indelicato first planted vines in 1924 and sold grapes to home winemakers during Prohibition, and today the company he started has become DFV, one of the leading family winegrowers in the United States. Under the dutiful watch of Gaspare's sons and grandchildren, DFV grows grapes across California from their Clay Station Vineyard in Lodi to the San Bernabe Vineyard in Monterey. Delicato Family Vineyards has won numerous awards, including "Best American Winery" at the London International Wine and Spirit Competition. They produce wine under a variety of labels, including Noble, Gnarly Head, Twisted, Bota Box, Fog Head, HandCraft, and Irony. Noble Vines 337 Cabernet Sauvignon 2010 is dark garnet to purple in color, with aromas of cassis, mocha, and black cherry. In the mouth there are full-on fruit flavors with notes of Mediterranean herbs and cracked blacked pepper in the long luxurious finish. Gnarly Head Authentic Red 2011 is a blend of Zinfandel, Merlot, Cabernet Sauvignon, Syrah, and Petite Sirah. It has aromas of black cherry, black plum, and mocha with rounded fruit flavors in the mouth and a finish that begs for a burger or baby back ribs. HandCraft Artisan Collection Inspiration Red Wine 2011, a blend of Syrah, Zinfandel, Merlot, Malbec, and Sangiovese, is cherry red in the glass, with a nose of bright cherry and baking spices. A truly easy-drinking red, it offers full-on fruit flavors of cherry and red raspberry with just a tiny dollop of sweetness.

FIELDS FAMILY WINES

3803 East Woodbridge Road, Acampo, CA 95220, (209) 896-6012
www.fieldsfamilywines.com

Russ Fields and his family bought their property in Lodi in 2005 and started in right away building the winery and two homes. Business partner Ryan Sherman, the realtor who helped find the vineyard, is the winemaker at Fields Family, working with estate-grown Syrah, Lodi Zinfandel and Tempranillo, and Cabernet Sauvignon and Merlot from Napa Valley. In addition to tours and tastings at the winery, tastings are available at its wine bar in downtown Lodi, which also features art exhibits and live music. Fields Family Wines Sherman Family Vineyards Lodi Old Vine Zinfandel 2010 is deep reddish-purple in the glass, with a nose of black plums, blueberry, cassis, and clove. These flavors continue on the palate, with a very nice balance between fruit and spice flavors with a touch of herbs. A nice note of black licorice continues through the smooth finish.

GALLO

600 Yosemite Boulevard, Modesto, CA 95354,
(877) 687-9463
www.gallo.com

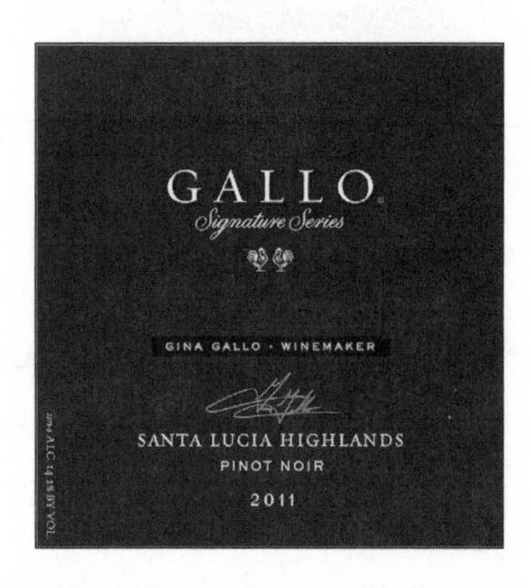

Brothers Ernest and Julio Gallo started Gallo Winery in 1933, and today the company is the world's largest family-owned winery. Multiple generations of the Gallo family, including children, grandchildren, and great-grandchildren, work side by side to continue the legacy of Ernest and Julio. The Gallo family continues to be the largest exporter of California wine to the world. The Gallo headquarters are in Modesto, Stanislaus County, but the company makes wine from AVAs all over the state. They produce over sixty brands, including Gallo Signature Series, Apothic Red, Bella Sera, Ecco Domani, Frei Brothers, Indigo Hills, Mirassou, Turning Leaf, Barefoot, Night Train, Thunderbird, Boone's Farm, and Bartles & James Wine Coolers. Gallo is a global business serving more than ninety countries and has multiple production facilities, including those in Modesto, St. Helena, and Dry Creek Valley. We were honored to have winemaker Gina Gallo pour Gallo Signature Series Napa Valley Cabernet Sauvignon 2008 into our glasses. It was deep garnet purple, with aromas of black currants, black raspberries, dark cherries, and a touch of powdered cocoa. In the mouth it is fruit-forward yet restrained and elegant with velvety tannins and a long finish. It is truly a delicious Napa Cab. Gallo Signature Series Santa Lucia Highlands Pinot Noir 2011 is certainly inspired by Gina's love of Burgundy. It is cherry colored, with aromas of black cherries, Christmas baking spices, and purple flowers in the complex bouquet. It is juicy on the palate with flavors of black currant, cherry vanilla, and pomegranate. There's nice weight and velvety tannins in the mouth before the persistent finish that keeps inviting you in for another sip.

HARNEY LANE WINERY

9010 East Harney Lane,
Lodi, CA95240,
(209) 365-1900
www.harneylane.com

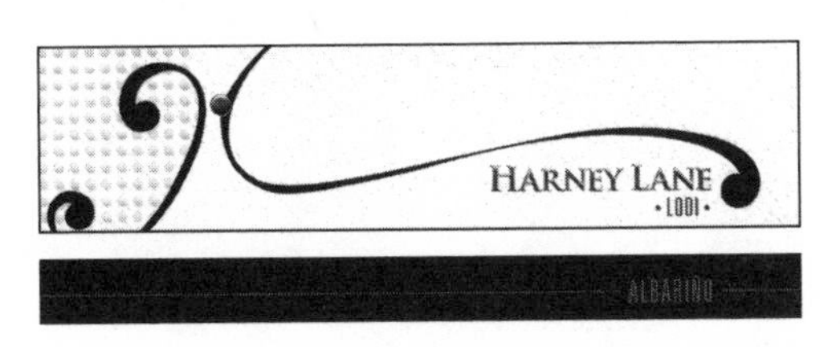

The Harney Lane story harkens back to 1907, when George Mettler's great-grandfather, Fred Schnaidt, bought land on Harney Lane and planted a vineyard. George's family has farmed this land for over a hundred years. Joined in this endeavor by wife, Kathleen; daughter Jorja; and her husband, Kyle Lerner, George and family now bottle award-winning wines, including Tempranillo, Petite Sirah, Chardonnay, Zinfandel, and Albariño. Their Lizzy James Vineyard is named in honor of Jorja and Kyle's two children, the sixth generation to live and work on this family farm. Harney Lane Winery Lodi Albariño 2011, pale straw in color, presents aromas of lemon-lime, citrus blossom, and wet stones. After an initial burst of lime sorbet, this easy-drinking quaffer offers refreshing citrus flavors.

IRONSTONE VINEYARDS

1894 Six Mile Road,
Murphys, CA 95247,
(209)728-1251
www.ironstonevineyards.com

The Sierra Foothills' Gold Rush town of Murphys is home to Ironstone Vineyard and its seven-story winery and entertainment complex. The replica of an 1859 mill includes a tasting room, delicatessen, aging cavern, conference center, and Heritage Museum and Jewelry Shoppe. The Ironstone Amphitheater summer concert series features an eclectic lineup of current and classic pop and country stars, and winery visits can include a lesson in panning for gold. Winemaker Steve Millier came aboard in 1989, joining the Kautz family, fourth-generation grape growers who own more than 5,000 acres of vineyards in the Sierra Foothills and Lodi. Ironstone produces a wide variety of whites and reds, including Verdelho, Muscat Canelli, Viognier, Cabernet Franc, Cabernet Sauvignon, Malbec, Zinfandel, Syrah, and Meritage blends. Ironstone Reserve Lodi Malbec 2009, composed of 95 percent Malbec and 5 percent Zinfandel, is deep garnet with a violet rim. A bouquet of boysenberry, geranium, tomato leaf, and rose petal sets the scene for bright fruits-of-the-wood flavors with a nice herbal wash across the mid palate and a fair bit of acidity on the finish.

KIDDER FAMILY WINERY

17266 Hillside Drive,
Lodi, CA 95240,
(209) 727-0728
www.kidderwines.com

Aaron Kidder and his wife, Linda, were both destined for stardom at an early age. Linda Hauck Kidder, a Lodi native, was the Lodi Kiddie Parade Queen while still a young girl, and Aaron, his two brothers, and his father, Don, a tightly knit barbershop quartet, sang on the *Ed Sullivan Show.* Aaron and Linda met in Lodi and married in 1994, and after they planted a vineyard and Aaron studied at UC Davis, they started making wine in

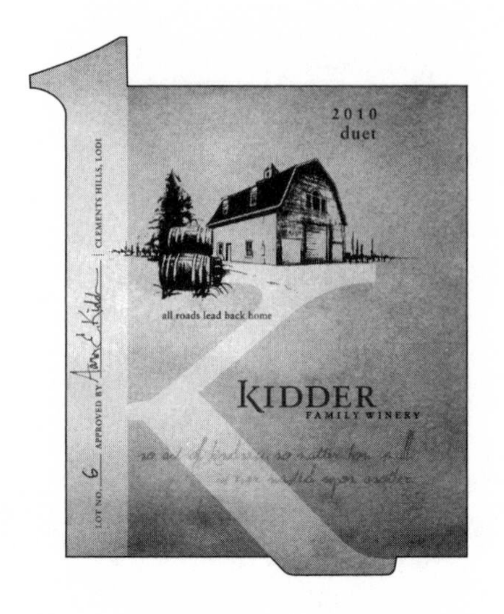

2001. Seven and a half acres of vineyards are home to mainly Syrah and small amounts of Petite Sirah, Graciano, and Tempranillo. The Dutch-style barn depicted on Kidder's labels is an image of the winery and tasting room in Lodi's Clements Hills appellation. Kidder Family Winery Duet 2010, a blend of 57 percent Graciano and 43 percent Tempranillo, is deep purple in the glass, with a nose of strawberry preserves, Turkish delight, and cocoa powder. In the mouth it exhibits flavors of blackberry, strawberry, and rose petal, with a hint of milk chocolate on the rich tannic finish.

KLINKER BRICK WINERY

15887 Alpine Road, Lodi, CA 95240,
(209) 224-5156
www.klinkerbrickwinery.com

Fifth-generation grape growers Steve and Lori Felten should be very happy, as are we, that over 100 years ago their ancestors gave up growing watermelons in Lodi, converting their fields over to grapevines, including Zinfandel, Tokay, Carignane, and Alicante. Winemaker Barry Gnekow, a UC Davis graduate with more than 25 years of winemaking under his belt, is also a family member, and so is Klinker Brick president Lynne White Barnard, who is in charge of sales and marketing efforts. Their fifteen blocks of old-vine Zinfandel range in age from 35 to over 100 years old, and after growing grapes for and selling bulk wine to other wineries, Klinker Brick, named for a distinctive style of heavy brick used in the area, was founded in 2000. Curious about the name? Bang two klinker bricks together and tell us what sound they make. Klinker Brick Lodi Syrah 2010 is inky purple in color. Aromas of black cherry, cherry cola, and violet talcum powder prime the taste buds for flavors of chocolate-covered cherries, cassis, star anise, and Szechuan pepper. Chewy tannins pave the way for a refreshing finish.

LANGE TWINS WINERY AND VINEYARDS

1525 East Jahant Road, Acampo, CA 95220,
(209) 334-9780
www.langetwins.com

Yes, there is actually a set of Lange twins, Brad and Randall, whose great-grandparents Johann and Maria Lange came to Lodi in the 1870s. In 1916 they planted their first grapes, having first grown watermelons. Randall and Brad continued to farm their family land, striking out on their own in 1974 and building a winery in 2006. Lange Twins is truly a family affair. Randall's wife, Charlene, and Brad's wife, Susan, are actively involved in winery and vineyard operations, as are the two couples' five grown children, Marissa, Aaron, Philip, Kendra, and Joe. Based in Acampo, just outside the town of Lodi, Lange Twins' grape-growing efforts spread across San Joaquin, Sacramento, Solano, and Yolo counties, growing a true A-to-Z range of varieties, including Albariño, Barbera, Cabernet Sauvignon, Chardonnay, Malbec, Petit Verdot, Pinot Noir, Sauvignon Blanc, Syrah, Viognier, and Zinfandel, primarily from the Lodi, Clements Hills, and Clarksburg appellations. Lange Twins Winery Estate Grown Musqué Clone Lodi Sauvignon Blanc 2011, pale straw in the glass, proffers aromas of passion fruit mingling with freshly cut grass. It is pleasant on the tongue, with flavors of grapefruit, fresh pineapple, and gardenia.

MACCHIA WINES

7099 East Peltier Road,
Acampo, CA 95220,
(209) 333-2600
www.macchiawines.com

Tim and Lani Holdener, the husband-and-wife team who started Macchia in 2001, source grapes for their well-priced Zinfandel from prime vineyards in Lodi and Amador County. They make a range of Zinfandels, including some single-vineyard bottlings and others that are combined from multiple vineyards to bring out the best of the variety. They also produce Amador County Barbera and Sangiovese. Italian for "the spot," Macchia has a tasting room that is filled with visitors and wine club members every weekend.

Macchia Wines "Mischievous" Lodi Old Vine Zinfandel 2010, deep red-violet to the eye, has a classic nose of black cherry, vanilla, and cocoa powder. Prominent flavors of mixed-berry pie, vanilla, and baking spice play on the palate, with persistent acidity and sweetness of fruit through the pleasant finish.

METTLER FAMILY VINEYARDS

7889 East Harney Lane, Lodi CA 95240,
(888) 509-5969
www.mettlerwine.com

The history of winemaking in the Mettler family stretches back to the late eighteenth century, and they have been growing grapes in Lodi since the end of the nineteenth century. When sixth-generation grape farmer Carl Mettler married Gladys Handel in the 1940s, two families—and their vineyard holdings—were joined. Both Carl and his son Larry have been inducted into the Agricultural Hall of Fame. Larry, his wife, Charlene, and their three grown children started making their own wine in 2001 and have received great praise and recognition since the first vintage. In addition to Cabernet Sauvignon, their first bottling, they produce Zinfandel and Petite Sirah from their certified-organic vineyards. Mettler Family Vineyards Estate Grown Cabernet

Sauvignon 2010, inky purple with a bright rim, has a nose of blackberry, bacon, and dried oregano. Smooth flavors of blackberry, strawberry confiture, air-cured Spanish ham, and chocolate-covered espresso coalesce on the tongue, aided by keen balance and pleasurable acidity.

MICHAEL DAVID WINERY

4580 Highway 12,
Lodi, CA 95242,
(209) 368-7384
www.michaeldavidwinery.com

Brothers Michael and David Phillips represent the fifth generation of their family to grow grapes in Lodi, now joined by the sixth, Kevin Phillips and Melissa Phillips Stroud. Under the direction of winemaker Adam Mettler, himself a member of a multigenerational Lodi grape-growing family, Michael David produces a wide variety of labels, including the well-known 7 Deadly Zins and 7 Heavenly Chards. In addition to estate-grown fruit from their Bare Ranch and Windmill Estate, grapes for specific bottlings are sourced from throughout Lodi and from Sonoma and Monterey. Michael David Winery Inkblot Lodi Cabernet Franc 2010 is inky purple red to the eye. Fragrances of black plum, grilled red pepper, purple flowers, and cocoa set the scene for flavors of strawberry preserves, black raspberry, and chocolate-covered cherries. A light floral lift immediately precedes the pleasant mineral finish.

QUADY

13181 Road 24,
Madera, CA 93637,
(559) 673-8068
www.quadywinery.com

Quady is well known for highly respected and acclaimed sweet wines. Quady's motto is "Keeping it sweet since 1975"; the company was started by Andrew and Laurel Quady in that year. In 1977 the couple built their own small winery behind their home in Madera and began making port-style wines, but the brand really took off in 1980 when they made a fortified dessert wine from Orange Muscat grapes. They named the wine Essensia, and the rest is history. Quady Essensia 2010 is straw yellow in color and viscous. It has aromas of sweet orange, candied orange peel, white flowers, and caramelized sugar. It is big on the palate with great presence and heft and delightfully sweet flavors of orange, tangerine, and lime sherbet. Quady Elysium Black Muscat 2011 is stained reddish-purple, with aromas of red currants and red fruit preserves. It has nice weight on the palate with rich fruit flavors and a balanced acidic sweet finish.

SORELLE WINERY

9599 North Highway 88, Stockton, CA 95212,
(209) 931-4350
www.sorellewinery.com

Named for the sisters who oversee the day-to-day operation of the family business, Kim and Melissa Scott, Sorelle, Italian for "sister," produces fine wines from Italian grape varieties. Visitors to the winery always enjoy visiting the Dodge House, named for Jonathan Holt Dodge, a gold miner who purchased the property in 1857. He was the first to plant 50 acres of grapevines on this land, and the Scott sisters have honored his heritage by replanting vines and building a winery in 2007. Sorelle Winery Grazia Clarksburg Pinot Grigio 2012 is pale straw colored, with aromas of Cavaillon melon, Mission fig, and cantaloupe. It has nice heft on the palate with a crisp, clean finish. Sorelle Winery Troppo Bella Lodi Sangiovese 2010 has aromas of black currant, blueberry pie, smoked meats, and a touch of dried Mediterranean herbs. It has pronounced fruit flavors in the mouth with a nice mouthfeel and a persistent finish.

UVAGGIO

PO Box 10708, Napa, CA 94581,
(707) 224-2254
www.uvaggio.com

After a successful career that included crafting award-winning wines for Robert Mondavi, Jim Moore wanted to move away from California's fascination with Cabernet Sauvignon and Chardonnay and focus instead on his beloved Italian varieties, which makes perfect sense given California's Mediterranean climate. Uvaggio's current lineup consists of Barbera, Moscato, Primitivo, Sangiovese, and Vermentino. Although Moore is serious about winemaking, he seems to take a light-hearted approach to just about everything else. Uvaggio Lodi Vermentino 2011 is light straw in color. A bright nose of fresh citrus gives way to refreshing flavors of citrus fruits, honeysuckle, and shale.

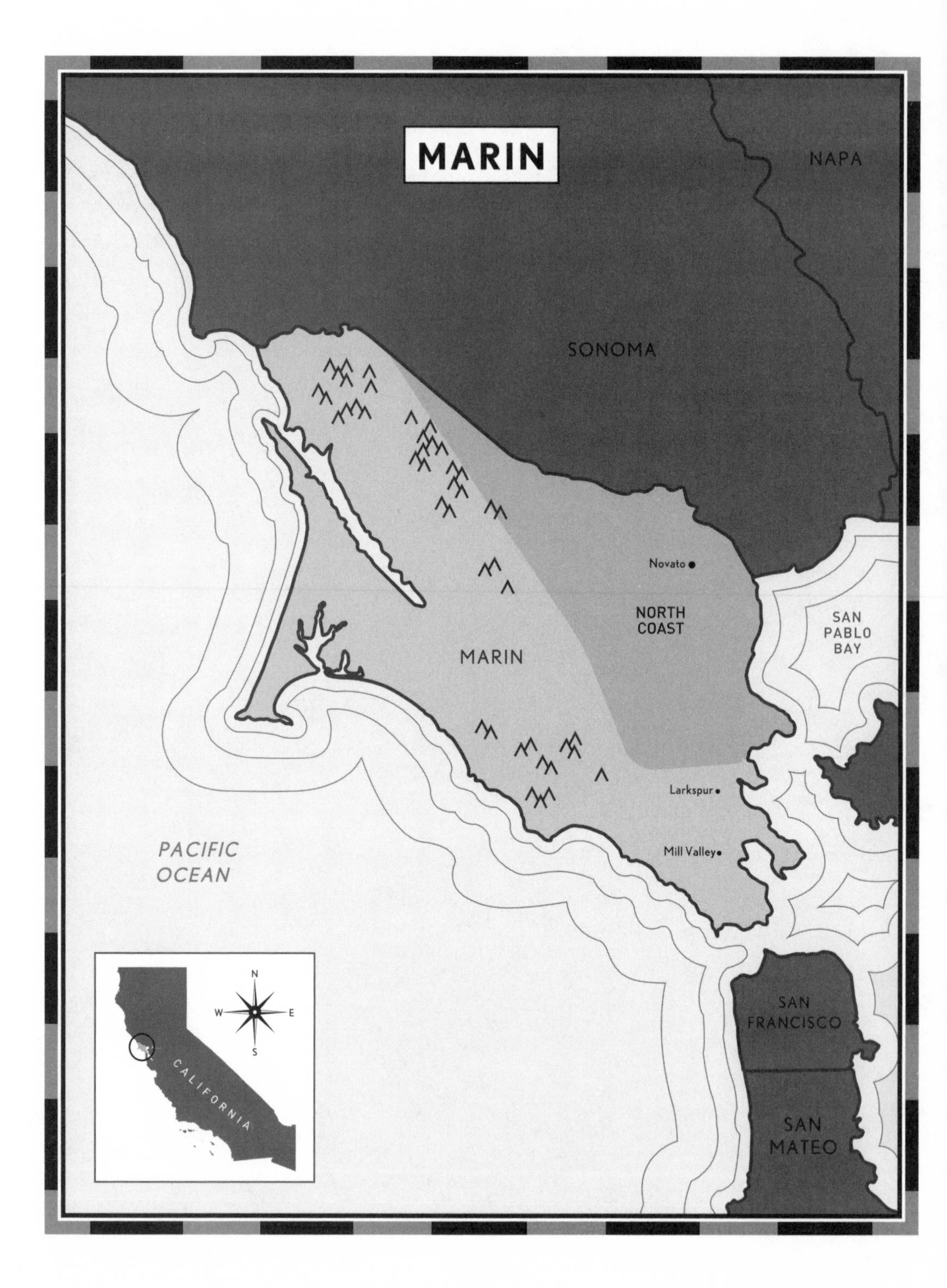
MARIN
NAPA
SONOMA
Novato
NORTH COAST
SAN PABLO BAY
MARIN
Larkspur
Mill Valley
PACIFIC OCEAN
N
W
E
S
CALIFORNIA
SAN FRANCISCO
SAN MATEO

CHAPTER 6

MARIN COUNTY

LOCATED ON THE "OTHER SIDE" OF THE Golden Gate Bridge north of San Francisco, Marin County is the city's gateway to the well-known wine regions just beyond its uppermost border: Sonoma and Napa. Known for its high household income and natural beauty, Marin is home to the Point Reyes Natural Seashore, the Muir Woods National Monument redwood forest, the Marin Headlands, part of the Golden Gate National Recreation Area, and Mount Tamalpais, said to be the spot where mountain biking was invented.

The northeastern portion of the county, divided along a diagonal roughly parallel to Highway 1, is in the larger North Coast AVA. Marin is a peninsula bordered to the northeast by Sonoma County, to the west by the Pacific Ocean, and to the east by San Pablo Bay. The southeast borders the uppermost portion of San Francisco Bay, and San Francisco sits across the bay from the city of Sausalito, which is itself due north of the exclusive enclave of Mill Valley. Although the areas closest to San Francisco are somewhat heavily populated, the western portion of Marin is dominated by farmland. It has long been a dairy farming area, and some of the best-known local cheese producers, a key component of the thriving farm-to-table movement, are here, including Point Reyes Farmstead Cheese, Cowgirl Creamery, and Marin French Cheese.

As in most of California, grapes came to Marin County with Spanish missionary priests and were planted around the same time Mission San Rafael was constructed in 1817. It is said that some of those vines were transplanted to General Mariano Vallejo's Sonoma County ranch about 20 years later. Hermann Zopf, an immigrant from Germany who ran a San Rafael grocery store and saloon popular with vacationers from San Francisco, also planted grapes and made wine. French expatriate Jean Escalle planted almost 25 acres of vines on his land in Larkspur. His original winery, built in the last decade of the nineteenth century, is now the host location for the Marin County Pinot Noir Celebration held each June the last few years.

Its position between the Pacific Ocean and two bays gives Marin rainy winters, cool springs, and cooling effects from the nearby bodies of water that protect grapes from the harsh heat of the summer sun. The rolling hills of the county, home to far more acres of pasture than grapevines, have a multitude of soil types, including gravelly loam that offers good drainage and silt-filled clay that holds moisture even in the driest season. Both volcanic and alluvial influences shaped the topography here and left their mark on the soil. While the habitat really offers everything that grapes need to mature, Prohibition all but destroyed the hundreds of acres of vineyards that existed in the early part of the twentieth century. A thriving real estate market makes available land in the county much more attractive to developers than to grape farmers. Today only about 200 acres of grapes are cultivated in Marin, mostly on the less-developed western side of the county.

The handful of producers in Marin County work with a combination of locally sourced fruit, much coming from estate vineyards, and small amounts of grapes sourced from other regions. The primary varieties grown here are Pinot Noir and Chardonnay, with a smattering of grapes such as Cabernet Sauvignon, Syrah, and Zinfandel. All the wineries in Marin are small, focusing on handcrafted artisanal wines.

THE WINERIES

KALIN CELLARS

61 Galli Drive, Novato, CA 94949,
(415) 883-3543
www.kalincellars.com

Kalin Cellars prides itself on the use of traditional European techniques to create small-batch wines in Marin County. Annual production is less than 7,000 cases, and both red and white wines are fermented in oak with no fining or filtering. Kalin produces exclusively 100 percent single-vineyard wines. It is among the few wineries that cellar their wine for a long period—sometimes for more than 10 years—before releasing them to the public. Kalin Cellars Cuvée LV Chardonnay

1995 was not released until September 2012. It is remarkably youthful, with aromas of fresh citrus blossom, candied orange peel, and white flowers. It is powerful yet restrained with an elegant finish. It's definitely worth the wait.

KENDRIC VINEYARDS

48 Tamalpais Avenue,
San Anselmo, CA 94960,
(415) 806-4944
www.kendricvineyards.com

Named in memory of the father of Stewart Johnson, Kendric Vineyards produces Pinot Noir and Viognier from estate vineyards in Marin County. Stewart likes to tell people that he handles all phases of the winemaking process: planting the vines, tending to them, picking the grapes, crushing them, and making the wine. He admits that his wife, Eileen Burke, helps with the marketing as well as managing the kids and running a busy San Francisco law practice. Kendric Vineyards Marin County Pinot Noir 2009 is cherry red, with aromas of red cherries, toasted hazelnut, and Indian spices. It exhibits nice fruit flavors in the mouth with a balanced level of acidity, soft tannins, and a clean finish.

PACHECO RANCH WINERY

235 Alameda Del Prado,
Novato, CA 94949,
(415) 883-5583
www.pachecoranchwinery.com

Situated on the same land granted to Ignacio Pacheco in 1840, Pacheco Ranch Winery was replanted in 1970 by his descendants and their winery partners and has been making handcrafted wines for over 30 years. Winemaking is under the direction of Jamie Meves, who cellars many of the wines for at least five years before release. Pacheco Ranch Winery Cabernet Sauvignon 2005 has aromas of dried black cherry, cassis, and pencil lead. There is a top note of Indian spice that carries on to the palate, and the finish is long, lean, and luxurious.

PEY-MARIN VINEYARDS

PO Box 912,
San Anselmo, CA 94960,
(415) 455-9463
www.scenicrootwinegrowers.com

Jonathan and Susan Pey made wine for other vintners around the world and started Pey-Marin Vineyards in 1999. They believed that although Marin County was virtually unknown as a wine region, it had a lot of untapped potential. Jonathan and Susan have

made quite a name for themselves in the county and currently specialize in small-lot, artisanally made Pinot Noir and dry Riesling with grapes grown on the western side of the county. Pey-Marin Vineyards The Shell Mound, Marin County Riesling 2012 is pale straw colored, with aromas of Anjou pears, citrus blossom, and candied lemon peel. It is crisp and clean in the mouth with balanced acidity and a touch of spiciness in the finish.

Pey-Marin Vineyards Trois Filles, Marin County Pinot Noir 2010 is garnet colored, with aromas of cherry cola, red raspberry, and Christmas baking spices. It has nice weight on the palate, juicy red fruit flavors, and a pleasant amount of spice in the finish.

POINT REYES VINEYARDS

12700 Highway 1, Point Reyes Station, CA 94956,
(415) 663-1011
www.ptreyesvineyardinn.com

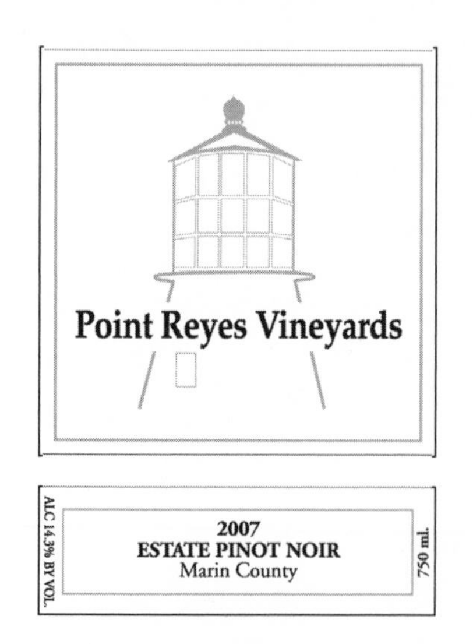

The Doughty family is widely credited with opening the first tasting room in Marin County since 1930. The family has been farming the land for three generations, and in 1990 they decided to plant grapevines of their own. There's a small inn and villa on the property that's very popular with brides and grooms from San Francisco. Owners Steve and Sharon Doughty are the consummate hosts—splurge for the Champagne suite with views overlooking the vineyard. The family sources grapes from nearby growers and also grows Pinot Noir on their own estate. Point Reyes Vineyards Estate Pinot

Noir 2007 is cherry red with aromas of black cherry, dried red cherries, and a touch of menthol in the bouquet. It has nice heft on the palate with fruit flavors and a well-balanced tannic finish that has just a hint of black pepper in the post palate.

SEAN THACKREY

240 Overlook Drive, Bolinas, CA 94924
www.wine-maker.net

Sean Thackrey looks at winemaking from a different angle. The art gallery owner turned winemaker likes to let his grapes rest under the stars before crushing, a process we have yet to encounter elsewhere in our travels. He has been cited claiming that the early Greeks used this technique and that Hesiod described the procedure in his early poems. Thackrey moved to Bolinas in 1964 and became a bonded winemaker in 1981. Thackrey's ideas may be unconventional, but he does make some delicious wines. Sean Thackrey Cassiopeia Wentzel Vineyard Anderson Valley Pinot Noir 2010 is named after the celestial constellation Cassiopeia. It is cherry red, with aromas of purple flowers, dried Provencal herbs, ripe red raspberries, and red plums. It is medium-bodied in the mouth, with a good expression of fruit and a touch of spice in the well-balanced finish.

STARRY NIGHT WINERY

359 Bel Marin Keys Boulevard, Suite 5,
Novato, CA 94949,
(415) 382-6200
www.starrynightwinery.com

Winemakers and friends Wayne Hansen, Bruce Walker, Skip Granger, and Mike Miller began making wine in Wayne's basement. Their first crush produced 50 cases of Zinfandel, Cabernet Sauvignon, and Chardonnay. Turning their hobby into a vocation, they became bonded as a legitimate winery a few weeks before the 1999 harvest. They still strive for minimal intervention in their winemaking and use small open-top fermentation tanks as well as employing manual rather than mechanical punchdowns of the grapes during fermentation. The guys definitely like making Zinfandel, and Bruce is currently on ZAP's (Zinfandel Advocates and Producers) board of directors. Starry Night Winery Moonhead Red Petite Sirah Zinfandel Blend 2010 is purple red in the glass, with aromas of black plums, black raspberries, and black cherries. It is rich and fruit-forward in the mouth, with a light dusting of licorice and finely ground black pepper in the finish. Starry Night Winery Lake County Terre Vermeille Vineyard Cabernet Franc 2010 has rich aromas of black currant, blueberry pie, freshly cut green pepper, and black raspberry in the bouquet. It has medium weight on the palate and a well-balanced tannic finish.

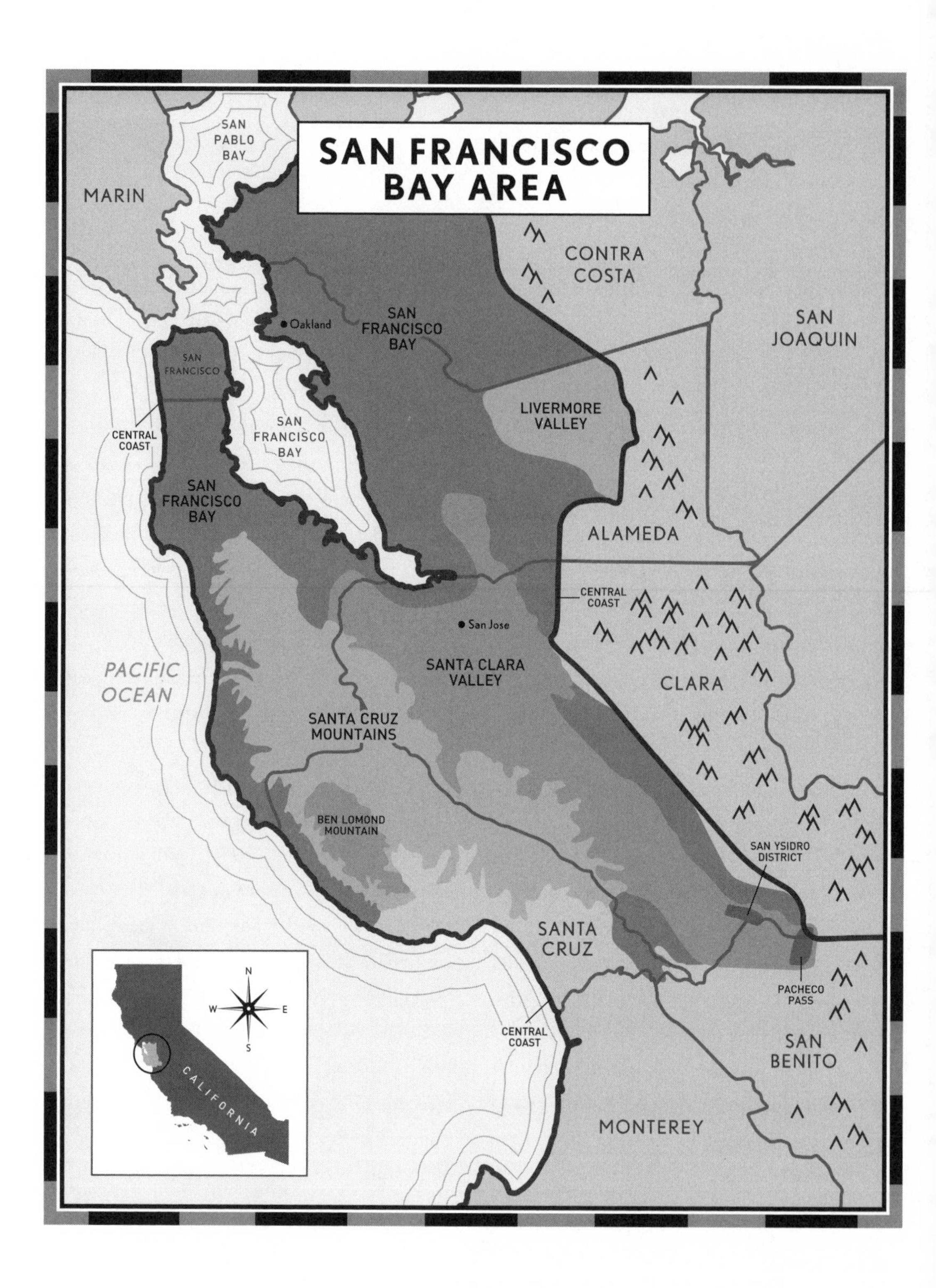
SAN FRANCISCO BAY AREA
SAN PABLO BAY
MARIN
CONTRA COSTA
Oakland
SAN FRANCISCO BAY
SAN JOAQUIN
SAN FRANCISCO
CENTRAL COAST
SAN FRANCISCO BAY
LIVERMORE VALLEY
SAN FRANCISCO BAY
ALAMEDA
CENTRAL COAST
San Jose
PACIFIC OCEAN
SANTA CLARA VALLEY
CLARA
SANTA CRUZ MOUNTAINS
BEN LOMOND MOUNTAIN
SAN YSIDRO DISTRICT
SANTA CRUZ
PACHECO PASS
N
W
E
S
CENTRAL COAST
SAN BENITO
CALIFORNIA
MONTEREY

CHAPTER 7

SAN FRANCISCO BAY AND THE SURROUNDING AREA

THE BAY AREA, AS IT IS KNOWN, IS HOME TO the rebirth of the farm-to-table movement that has taken hold across the entire country, so it was only a matter of time before winemakers would be joining chefs, organic farmers, cheese makers, and artisanal food producers as the local heroes of the region. Berkeley, San Francisco, and Oakland have thriving food scenes—and have had them for several decades—and those truly committed to eating and drinking local no longer have to look to the other side of the Golden Gate Bridge for a good bottle of wine.

The San Francisco Bay AVA is a large viticultural area that is the farthest north within the even more enormous Central Coast AVA. It includes portions of six counties: Contra Costa, San Francisco, San Mateo, Alameda, Santa Cruz, and Santa Clara. There are about 6,500 acres of vines planted in the San Francisco Bay AVA and over 100 wineries, made up of an interesting combination of funky newcomers and the current generation descended from notable forerunners of the California wine industry. The Livermore Valley AVA is within its borders and is an important grape-growing region, as are areas in Contra Costa County. The large Santa Cruz Mountain AVA runs north to south through portions of San Mateo, Santa Clara, and Santa Cruz counties. When one looks at a map of California AVAs, the Santa Cruz Mountain AVA and Ben Lomond Mountain AVA fall within the outlines of the San Francisco Bay AVA and Central Coast AVA, but for official purposes neither is considered part of the Central Coast AVA.

First established in 1999 and then amended in 2006, the San Francisco Bay AVA is also home to the sub-AVAs Pacheco Pass, San Ysidro District, and Santa Clara Valley. Although vineyards tend to be in the more rural portions of the region and many winemakers source their fruit from a combination of local and distant growers, there are a handful of small-scale urban winery operations and tasting rooms in San Francisco, Oakland, and Berkeley. The most prevalent grape in the AVA as a whole is Chardonnay, followed by Cabernet Sauvignon and Merlot. Grapes planted in well-drained gravel soils benefit from hot days, cool nights, and coastal fog through the late morning.

The first grapes in what is now the Livermore Valley AVA, in Alameda County, were planted by Spanish missionaries in the 1760s. About 80 years later commercial vineyards were planted by immigrant pioneers, and in the 1880s the Wente, Concannon, and Wetmore families founded the first commercial wineries in the region. In 1889 a wine from Livermore Valley brought acclaim to the California wine industry by winning a gold medal at the Paris Exhibition. Approved as an AVA in 1982, Livermore Valley is now home to about fifty wineries—the same number that existed before Prohibition—and has over 4,000 acres of grapevines, mainly Petite Sirah, Sauvignon Blanc, Sémillon, and some newer plantings of Merlot.

Wine has been produced in Contra Costa County, mainly near Oakley, in the northeastern corner of the county, for over 100 years. One of the first vineyards in the county was planted farther to the west, in Pinole, in the early part of the nineteenth century by Don Ignacio Martinez. There were over 3,000 acres of vines in Contra Costa in 1891, and by 1897 that number had grown to 6,000 acres. Forty percent of the farmland in the county was planted with grapes by 1919, but the onset of Prohibition caused farmers to either abandon their vineyards or convert to more salable crops. Today there are almost 2,000 acres of Oakley-area old-vine vineyards bearing Zinfandel, Carignane, and Mourvèdre, many originally farmed by Valeriano Jacuzzi (of hot tub and spa fame). Jacuzzi's grandson Fred Cline still sources grapes from those family-owned vineyards for wine produced and bottled in his eponymous Sonoma winery.

To the south, the Santa Cruz Mountain AVA is home to some of the finest vineyards in the region, including the famed Ridge Monte Bello Vineyard, which produces extraordinary Cabernet Sauvignon. Other notable varieties emanating from the Santa Cruz Mountains are Chardonnay and Pinot Noir. Achieving AVA status in December 1981, the Santa Cruz Mountains AVA covers a total area of about 322,000 acres from Half Moon Bay in the north to Watsonville in the south. There are more than 200 mainly small vineyards, with total grapevine acreage covering about 1,500 acres. Vineyard elevations in the AVA roughly follow the fog line down the coast, ranging primarily between 400 feet and 800 feet, with some ridges reaching as high as 2,500 feet or more. Two wines from the Santa Cruz Mountains participated in the 1976 Judgment of Paris tasting: David Bruce Winery Chardonnay 1973 and Ridge Vineyards Monte Bello Cabernet Sauvignon 1971.

BONNY DOON VINEYARD

328 Ingalls Street, Santa Cruz, CA 95060,
(831) 425-3625
www.bonnydoonvineyard.com

In 1979 Randall Grahm set out to produce what he called "the great American Pinot Noir," but after Pierce's disease decimated his Bonny Doon Estate Vineyard, he replanted to Syrah, Roussanne, Marsanne, and Viognier. Besides being a great winemaker, Randall is an accomplished author and blogger. His unique style of writing has garnered awards from James Beard, Born Digital, and the Georges Duboeuf Wine Book of the Year in 2010. Bonny Doon Vin Gris de Cigare 2012 is a blend of 62 percent Grenache, 17 percent Mourvèdre, 9 percent Roussanne, 6 percent Grenache Blanc, and 6 percent Cinsault. It is salmon pink in color, with aromas of peach, ripe strawberry, and citrus zest. It has nice minerality in the palate with waves of fresh fruit in the finish. Bonny Doon Le Pousseur Syrah 2010 is inky purple, with aromas of black plum, black raspberry, and air-cured meats. This is a big and juicy wine on your palate with a viscous mouthfeel and great texture. It is fruit-driven, but then the balanced tannins take you into the long and luxurious finish.

BROPHY CLARK CELLARS

PO Box 955, Nipomo, CA 93444,
(805) 296-3017
www.brophyclarkcellars.com

A collaboration between the husband-and-wife team of winemaker John Clark and viticulturist Kelley Brophy, Brophy Clark Cellars was founded in 1996. Their mission is simple: to produce the best possible wines from the Central Coast. In doing so, the couple focus on Zinfandel, Pinot Noir, Syrah, Chardonnay, and Sauvignon Blanc because they believe those varieties are best expressed here. John and Kelley limit their small-lot production to 2,500 cases per year. Brophy Clark Santa Maria Valley Chardonnay 2010 is medium straw colored, with aromas of pear, peach, papaya, guava, and buttered brioche. In the mouth the flavors of the fruit come forward before the rich, lingering creamy finish. There is a pleasant splash of citrus in the post palate. Brophy Clark Santa Maria Valley Pinot Noir 2010 is medium cherry colored, with aromas of strawberries and cream, red cherry, and cherry cola. The fruit flavors are lively in the mouth, with a pleasant acidic splash to the finish.

CLOS LACHANCE

1 Hummingbird Lane, San Martin, CA 95046,
(800) 487-9463
www.clos.com

Bill Murphy and Brenda LaChance Murphy began looking to purchase vineyards and came across a parcel of land large enough for their

needs in San Martin. Then luck intervened, and they partnered with CordeValle Resort to plant 40,000 vines and build a new winery that could handle production of 60,000 cases of wine per year. The winery was finished in August 2001 in time for the harvest, and the visitor center was opened in May 2002. Today winemaker Stephen Tebb oversees winemaking from the estate's 150 acres. His provenance includes Codorniu Napa, Mirassou, and Chateau St Jean. He was joined by Jason Robideaux as associate winemaker in 2007. Clos LaChance Estate Central Coast Sauvignon Blanc 2011 is composed of 87 percent Sauvignon Blanc and 13 percent Sémillon. It is straw colored and has aromas of lemon zest, white flowers, and freshly cut grass. It is crisp and clean on the palate with a delightful zing in the finish. Clos LaChance Estate Zinfandel 2008 has aromas of red and black fruits. It is generous in the mouth with balanced tannins and a bright note of fruit in the finish.

CONCANNON VINEYARD

4590 Tesla Road, Livermore, CA 94550,
(800) 258-9866
www.concannonvineyard.com

James Concannon planted vineyards and built his eponymous winery in 1883. Today the fourth-generation family is very proud that Concannon Vineyard was one of the first successful wineries founded by an Irish immigrant, and they were one of the first to have a female winemaker, Katherine Vajda, who joined the team in 1961. The Concannon family is widely credited as being the first to bottle and label Petite Sirah as a variety. Concannon Captain Joe's Reserve Petite Sirah 2010 is inky purple, with aromas of Christmas baking spices, cassis, and black raspberry. It is fruit-forward in the mouth, with just a touch of smoked meats in the finish. Concannon Selected Vineyards Cabernet Sauvignon 2010 has aromas of black raspberry, black plum, and black olive tapenade. In the mouth the berry flavors transfer seamlessly onto the palate. The tannins are well balanced, and the finish is long-lasting.

CUDA RIDGE WINES

2400 Arroyo Road, Livermore, CA 94550,
(510) 304-0914
www.cudaridgewines.com

Founders Larry and Margie Dino like to say that Cuda Ridge Wines is truly a family and friends endeavor. They make small-lot, artisanally produced wines, and visitors to the winery can always meet a family member and a few friends in the tasting room. Cuda Ridge's new winery, opened in August 2013, brought production capacity up to about 1,600 cases of Bordeaux-style wines from Sémillon, Cabernet Sauvignon, Merlot, Cabernet Franc, Sauvignon Blanc, Malbec, and Petit Verdot. Cuda Ridge Livermore Valley Sauvignon Blanc 2011 is pale straw colored, with aromas of Cavaillon melon, grapefruit zest, and citrus blossom. It has a high but balanced level of acidity, making it a perfect wine to pair with fish and shellfish. Cuda Ridge Livermore Valley Merlot 2010 is composed of 80 percent Merlot, 10 percent Cabernet Sauvignon, 5 percent Petit Verdot, and 5 percent Malbec.

It is garnet purple, with aromas of freshly picked cherries, blueberry pie, and cranberry sauce. It is juicy in the mouth with a touch of Christmas baking spices in the well-balanced tannic finish.

DARCIE KENT VINEYARDS

7000 Tesla Road, Livermore, CA 94550,
(925) 243-9040
www.darciekentvineyards.com

Darcie Kent Vineyards was founded in 1996 by Darcie Kent as a family-owned winery. In addition to estate-grown grapes, they source fruit from a variety of family-owned vineyards, including DeMayo Vineyards, Madden Ranch, Picazo Vineyard, Rava's Black Jack Vineyard, and West Pinnacle Vineyard. Darcie Kent Vineyards Rava Blackjack Vineyard Pinot Noir 2010 is garnet colored, with aromas of red raspberries, dried strawberries, violet, and cotton candy. In the mouth you find flavors of strawberry, blackberry, and black cherries before the bright and balanced finish. Darcie Kent Vineyards DeMayo Vineyard Chardonnay 2010 is light straw colored, with notes of pineapple, vanilla, and fennel fronds in the bouquet. On the palate there are flavors of caramelized pineapple, lemon-lime soda, anise, and mint before the bright finish.

DASHE CELLARS

55 4th Street, Oakland, CA 94607,
(510) 452-1800
www.dashecellars.com

Michael and Anne Dashe founded Dashe Cellars in 1996. Their winery is in downtown Oakland, near Jack London Square. They are recognized as urban artisanal winemakers, and together they produce about 10,000 cases per year. The couple has 40 years of combined experience working at Ridge Vineyards, Far Niente, Chappellet, and Château Lafite Rothschild, among others, and they source fruit from a variety of AVAs in California. Dashe Cellars Potter Valley McFadden Farms Dry Riesling 2012 is pale straw colored, with aromas of Anjou pear, white flowers, and a touch of salinity. In the mouth it is generous with fruit flavors and has a touch of crisp minerality in the finish. Dashe Cellars Alexander Valley Todd Brothers

Ranch Petite Sirah 2010 has aromas of cassis, black raspberry, and black plum. There's a nice mouthfeel, with rich fruit flavors giving way to a balanced tannic finish.

DONKEY & GOAT WINERY

1340 5th Street, Berkeley, CA 94710,
(510) 868-9174
www.donkeyandgoat.com

Tracey and Jared Brandt learned natural wine-making in France and brought those techniques back to Berkeley. The couple has been called "Winemakers to Watch for in 2011" by the *San Francisco Chronicle,* and together they make delicious wine from Chardonnay, Pinot Noir, and Rhône varieties. Donkey & Goat is a fun place to visit in downtown Berkeley; it draws a hip crowd and has a cool vibe, and there's always something going on. Donkey & Goat El Dorado Grenache Blanc 2011 is pale straw-colored, with aromas of Cavaillon melon, white peach, and honeysuckle. It has great citrus notes in the mouth with refreshing minerality in the finish. Donkey & Goat Improbable El Dorado Chardonnay 2011 is straw yellow, with enticing aromas of white stone fruits and lemon blossoms. It is crisp and clean in the mouth with nice minerality and acidity in the finish.

HEART O' THE MOUNTAIN

No visitor facilities. Scotts Valley, CA 95066,
(831) 406-1881
www.heartothemountain.com

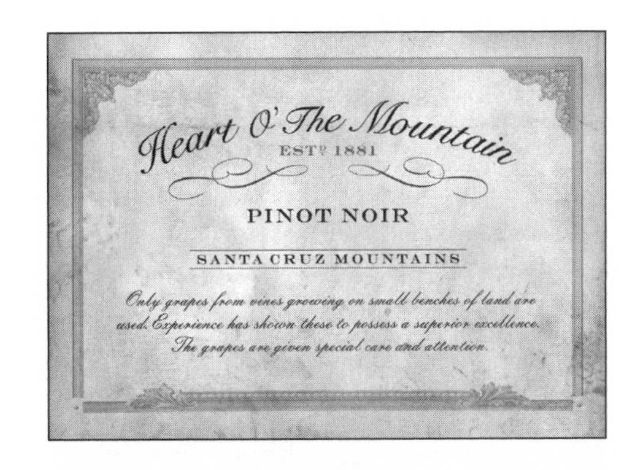

In 1940 Hollywood director Alfred Hitchcock purchased the property originally planted by Pierre and Sada Cornwall in 1880. The Cornwalls named the property Heart O' The Mountain, planted vines, and made wine until Prohibition. In 1978 Bob and Judy Brassfield acquired the property, replanted vines, and began preservation of the historic estate. The Brassfields are true Burgundian wine lovers and have planted five different Dijon and Pommard clones of Pinot Noir. Heart O' The Mountain Estate Pinot Noir 2009 is a blend of Dijon clones 777, 667, 828, and 115. It is cherry red in color, with aromas of spice, cracked black pepper, fresh red cherries, and dried black cherry. It is fruit-forward in the mouth with refreshing acidity and a persistent finish that has just a dusting of cocoa powder in the post palate.

JC CELLARS

55 4th Street, Oakland, CA 94607,
(510) 465-5900
www.jccellars.com

Urban winemaker Jeff Cohn makes twenty-one different labels at his Oakland warehouse winery. His provenance includes Rosenblum Cellars, and his long-standing relationships with quality grapegrowers around the state enable him to source stellar fruit for his wines. JC Cellars Iron Hill Vineyard Zinfandel 2010 is garnet purple, with notes of black plum, blackberry, and cherry preserves. It has jammy flavors of dark fruits, anise, and just a touch of finely ground white pepper in the long, luxurious finish. JC Cellars Stagecoach Vineyard Marsanne 2008 has delightful aromas of white flowers, freesia, and white peaches. It is crisp and clean in the mouth with a nice level of minerality in the finish.

LA ROCHELLE WINERY

5433 Tesla Road, Livermore, CA 94550,
(925) 243-6442
www.lrwine.com

Steven Kent Mirassou's great-great-great-grandfather crossed the Atlantic from France from the port of La Rochelle, hence the name of his winery. His family is credited with being one of the first, if not *the* first, to plant Pinot Noir in California in the 1850s. Steven also makes wine under the Steven Kent label and the Lineage label. At La Rochelle Steven's commitment to Pinot Noir remains true, and he and winemaker Tom Stutz make some delicious varietally correct Pinots. La Rochelle Santa Lucia Highlands Soberanes Vineyard Pinot Noir 2010 has rich aromas of orange blossom, blackberry, dried black cherries, and just a touch of lifted cocoa powder. It has an excellent mouthfeel and good weight on the palate. The finish is long and linear and keeps inviting you in for another sip.

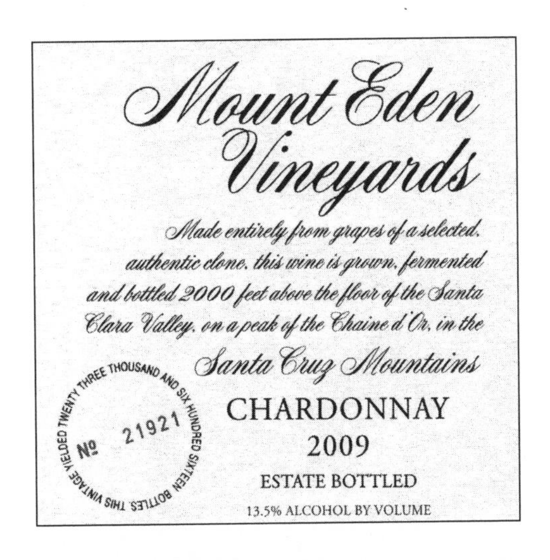

MOUNT EDEN VINEYARDS

22020 Mount Eden Road, Saratoga, CA 95070,
(888) 865-9463
www.mounteden.com

The legacy of Mount Eden Vineyards begins with Burgundian winemaker Paul Masson and Martin Ray, who purchased the Frenchman's Champagne Company after the repeal of Prohibition. Ray sold the property in 1943 and moved up to a higher peak called Mount Eden. He planted Pinot Noir and Chardonnay and brought in investors in the 1960s. Ray produced his last vintage in 1970, and today winemakers Jeffrey and Ellie Patterson run the winery and are the majority shareholders. They live in the original house built by Martin Ray with their two children, Sophie and Reid. Mount Eden Vineyards Estate Santa Cruz Mountains Chardonnay 2009 is straw yellow, with aromas of lemon rind, fennel bulb, and Provencal herbs. It has a healthy heft on the palate, with a nice level of creaminess in the finish. Drink it now or hold it for a few years. Mount Eden Vineyards Estate Pinot Noir Santa Cruz Mountains Pinot Noir 2010 is cherry red, with aromas of Indian spice, black cherry, and red plum. It has a good level of acidity in the palate, making this a wine to enjoy now or, better yet, lay down for a few years. It will continue to develop.

MURRIETA'S WELL

3005 Mines Road,
Livermore, CA 94550,
(925) 456 2390
www.murrietaswell.com

Named for Joaquin Murrieta, the infamous local bandito who frequented the artesian well that graces the property, Murrieta's Well's original winery was built by Louis Mel in the 1870s. The property was purchased in the 1990s by Philip Wente and Sergio Traverso, and today the winery is owned by the Wente family, with Sergio staying on as the consulting winemaker. Murrieta's Well produces approximately 12,000 cases of wine per year, and its 92 acres are planted with Cabernet Sauvignon, Sauvignon Blanc, Sémillon, Cabernet Franc, Merlot, Zinfandel, Petit Verdot, Tempranillo, Mourvèdre, Souzão, Touriga Nacional, and Touriga Francesa. Murrieta's Well The Spur Livermore Valley 2010 is a blend of 48 percent Cabernet Sauvignon, 24 percent Petit Verdot, 23 percent Malbec, and 5 percent Petite Sirah. It is garnet colored, with aromas of dark cherry, blueberry pie, and mocha. In the mouth the fruit flavors move forward before the secondary tastes of dark chocolate and licorice. The finish is smooth and persistent.

RHYS VINEYARDS

No visitor facilities.
(650) 419-2050
www.rhysvineyards.com

Owner Kevin Harvey, winegrower Javier Meza, and winemaker Jeff Brinkman select grapes from five different sites in the Santa Cruz Mountains to make their delicious wines at Rhys Vineyards. The team concentrates on Chardonnay, Pinot Noir, and Syrah grapes that are grown using organic and biodynamic principles. Rhys Family Farm Vineyard Pinot Noir 2009 has aromas of dried black cherries, ripe red cherries, and a touch of Mediterranean herbs. It has a nice balance of fruit sweetness and acidity on the palate, with a persistent finish. Drink it now or hold it for a few years.

RIDGE VINEYARDS

17100 Monte Bello Road, Cupertino, CA 95014,
(408) 867-3233
www.ridgewine.com

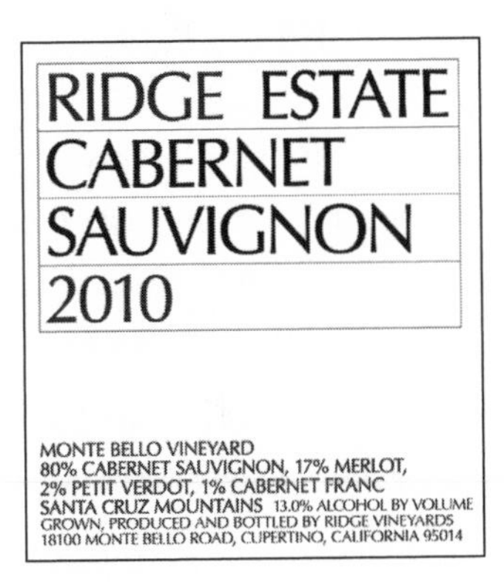

Dr. Osea Perrone was the first to plant terraced vines on 180 acres of land on Monte Bello Ridge in 1885. The vines were abandoned during Prohibition and changed hands a few times before Paul Draper joined the owners in 1969. He had just returned from setting up a winery in Chile and was known as a practical winemaker. In 1991 the group acquired Lytton Springs in Sonoma County. Although the original site is on Monte Bello Road, Ridge makes fine wine in Cupertino as well as wine from a variety of California AVAs, including those grown, produced, and bottled by Ridge Vineyards at the Lytton Springs Road facility in Healdsburg. Ridge Estate Santa Cruz Mountains Monte Bello Vineyard Cabernet Sauvignon 2010 is composed of 80 percent Cabernet Sauvignon, 17 percent Merlot, and 2 percent Petit Verdot. It is garnet purple in the glass, with aromas of black currant, black raspberries, purple flowers, and anise. In the mouth it is rich with fruit flavors that are accented by dark chocolate, brown spice, and a pleasant minerality. The finish is long with smooth and chalky tannins. Ridge Estate Santa Cruz Mountains Monte Bello Estate Vineyard Chardonnay 2011 has aromas of caramelized pineapple, tropical fruits, freesia, and honeycomb in the bouquet. On the palate it has great texture with ripe stone fruits and a crisp, clean, satisfying finish.

ROSENBLUM CELLARS

2900 Main Street, Suite 1100, Alameda, CA 94501
(510) 995-4100
www.rosenblumcellars.com

If you like to drink Zinfandel, Rosenblum Cellars is the place for you. Boasting more than twenty different variations on Zinfandel, including old-vine Zin, big-attitude Zin, and high-altitude Zin, Rosenblum is a founding member of ZAP (Zinfandel Advocates & Producers) and sources its fruit from all over the state of California. Kent Rosenblum started Rosenblum Cellars among the docks and shipyards of Alameda in 1978 and has been called "the King of Zin" by more than one person.

Rosenblum Cellars Sonoma Valley Monte Rosso Vineyard Reserve Zinfandel 2009 is inky garnet purple, with aromas of red fruits, black plums, and brown spice. It is fruit-forward in the mouth with fruit flavors, black pepper, and a touch of bramble. The finish is smooth and silky. Rosenblum Cellars Reserve Cullinane Zinfandel 2009 has delightful aromas of black plum, black raspberry, and black cherry. There's a touch of spearmint or even eucalyptus as an enchanting top note. It's big and bold in the mouth with juicy fruit flavors and secondary flavors of cigar box and English toffee. The finish is long and luscious.

TESTAROSSA WINERY

300 College Avenue, Los Gatos, CA 95030, (408) 354-6150
www.testarossa.com

The historic building that houses Testarossa was originally built as Novitiate Winery in 1888 by the Jesuit Fathers to fund the building of Santa Clara College. The priests enjoyed a 98-year run—even during Prohibition—until they closed the doors in 1986. It was purchased by Rob and Diana Jensen for production of wine under the Testarossa label in 1997 and is currently the fourth oldest continuously operating winery in California. Today production is approximately 20,000 cases of wine per year.

Testarossa Jensen Reserve Diana's Chardonnay 2010 is medium straw colored, with delightful aromas of citrus blossom, lemon curd, and Granny Smith apple. It is medium-bodied in the mouth, with creamy fruit flavors and just a touch of acidity in the post palate leading the way to a long, clean finish. Testarossa Rosella's Vineyard Santa Lucia Highlands Pinot Noir 2011 has enticing aromas of red fruits, dried black cherries, and a touch of brown spice. There are nicely rounded fruit flavors on the palate and a pinch of black pepper in the finish.

THOMAS FOGARTY WINERY

19501 Skyline Boulevard, Woodside, CA 94062, (650) 851-6777
www.fogartywinery.com

Vascular surgeon Thomas Fogarty planted his first grapes in 1978, started making wine in a small cabin, and established his eponymous commercial winery in 1981. The estate sits at 2,000 feet of elevation and has a total of 325 acres, with 25 under plantation of vines. The site has unparalleled views of the San Francisco Bay Area and can accommodate 220 people under its pavilion, making it very popular for large events. Winemaking has been under the direction of Michael Martella since the inception of the winery. He is assisted by Nathan Kandler and cellarmaster Ryan Teeter. Thomas

Fogarty Skyline Riesling 2011 is straw colored, with aromas of Granny Smith apples, freesia, jasmine, and citrus blossom. It has flavors of stone fruits and crisp apple in the mouth with brisk acidity in the finish. Thomas Fogarty Santa Cruz Mountains Pinot Noir 2010 has notes of red cherries, wet leaves, and brown spice in the complex bouquet. It is well structured in the mouth, with fruit flavors leading to a balanced tannic finish.

WENTE VINEYARDS

5565 Tesla Road, Livermore, CA 94550,
(925) 456-2300
www.wentevineyards.com

At over 130 years old, Wente Vineyards lays claim to being the country's oldest continuously operated family-owned winery. German immigrant C.H. Wente learned winemaking from Charles Krug and opened his own winery in 1883. His original vineyard was 48 acres, and today, in the fifth generation of Wente ownership, the family maintains 2,800 acres of vineyards. Wente Vineyards has the distinction of being one of California's leading wine country destinations, offering great food, great wine, and a championship golf course designed by Greg Norman. Visitors to the winery also love the concert series featuring performances by Styx, Chicago, and REO Speedwagon, to name only a few. Wente Estate Grown Riva Ranch Chardonnay 2010 is medium straw yellow, with aromas of pineapple, beeswax, and white flowers—especially freesia. In the mouth flavors of tropical fruits come to life with a light oak frame and nuances of butter and toffee. The finish is long and fruit-filled. Wente Vineyards Nth Degree Cabernet Sauvignon 2010 is inky garnet with aromas of black currant, mocha, and black plums. In the mouth there are flavors of black cherry, Chinese black tea, and espresso. There is a nice heft on the palate with a long balanced tannic finish.

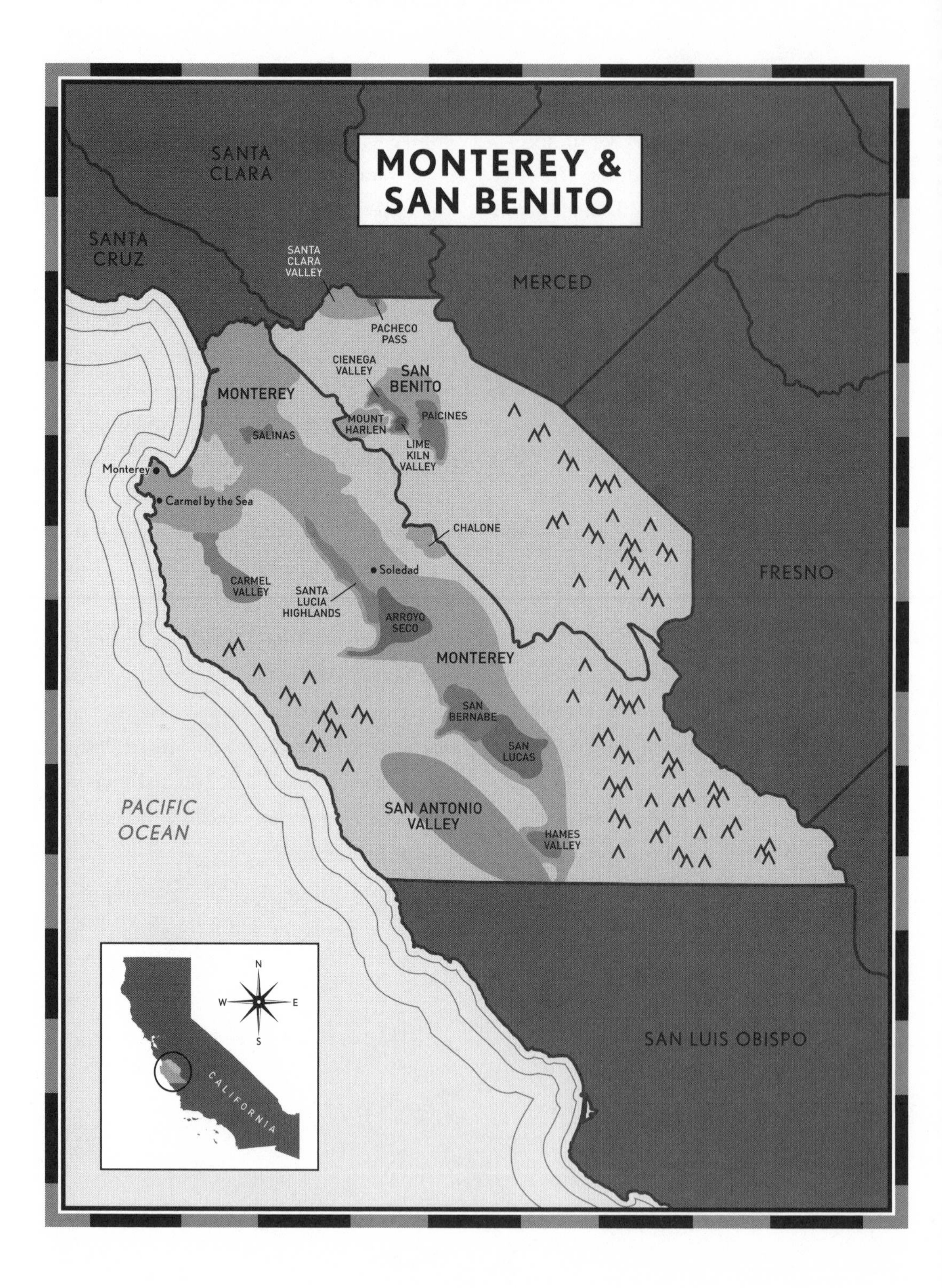

MONTEREY &
SAN BENITO
SANTA CLARA
SANTA CRUZ
MERCED
FRESNO
SAN LUIS OBISPO
PACIFIC OCEAN
SANTA CLARA VALLEY
PACHECO PASS
CIENEGA VALLEY
SAN BENITO
PAICINES
MOUNT HARLEN
LIME KILN VALLEY
MONTEREY
SALINAS
Monterey
Carmel by the Sea
CHALONE
Soledad
CARMEL VALLEY
SANTA LUCIA HIGHLANDS
ARROYO SECO
MONTEREY
SAN BERNABE
SAN LUCAS
SAN ANTONIO VALLEY
HAMES VALLEY
N
W
E
S
CALIFORNIA

CHAPTER 8

MONTEREY AND SAN BENITO COUNTIES

MONTEREY COUNTY MAY JUST HAVE IT ALL: rugged cliffs; sandy beaches; elegant resorts; outstanding cuisine; the allure of Carmel, Big Sur, and Pebble Beach; more than 40,000 acres of wine grapes grown in nine AVAs; and more than 100 wineries and tasting rooms. Tourists flock to the galleries, shops, restaurants, and wine bars of Cannery Row, Fisherman's Wharf, and Carmel-by-the-Sea, but grapes are grown and wine is made farther inland, in the broad valley bordered to the west by the Santa Lucia Mountains and to the east by the Gabilan Mountain Range.

Monterey and its eight sub-AVAs, along with the much smaller San Benito and Harlan Mountain AVAs in neighboring San Benito County, are part of the large Central Coast AVA that stretches from San Francisco, Oakland, and Berkeley in the north to Santa Barbara in the south. The Monterey AVA, established in 1984, runs the length of Monterey County, 80 miles from stem to stern, with widely varying growing conditions resulting from variations in temperature and soil. The other AVAs in Monterey are Santa Lucia Highlands, Arroyo Seco, San Lucas, Carmel Valley, Chalone, Hames Valley, San Antonio Valley, and San Bernabe.

Grapes were first grown here with the founding of California's thirteenth Spanish mission, Nuestra Señora de la Soledad, established on October 9, 1791, which grew to become the city of Soledad. Once famous for lettuce and spinach—and the setting for John Steinbeck's *Of Mice and Men*—Soledad is now at the center of a valley whose agricultural cachet rests more on the laurels of its finest bottles of wine than on its status as the home of the world's largest precut salad plant.

Modern-day grape growers first looked to the soils of Monterey in the late 1960s. In 1960 the pioneering research of UC Davis's A.J. Winkler and Maynard Amerine produced the Winkler scale, a classification system describing the climate of wine regions, which categorized Monterey County as comparable to Burgundy, Bordeaux, Sonoma, and Napa. Before long, well-known wineries in dire need of more vineyard space began spreading their holdings south, planting vineyards and building new facilities. There were not even five acres of wine grapes planted in the county in 1966, and by 1970 there were over 2,000 acres. Since that time new plantings in Monterey have averaged 1,000 acres annually, multiplying to today's total of nearly 45,000 acres covered with every commercially viable grape variety.

Due to its proximity to the Pacific and Monterey Bay, the Monterey AVA is blessed with cool days throughout the long growing season, although the temperature differential from north to south makes the northernmost areas of Monterey ideal for Chardonnay (the number one grape here, totaling just over 40 percent of plantings), Pinot Noir, Pinot Gris, and Riesling. Farther south, where daytime temperatures can be five degrees higher than in the northern reaches of Monterey, Bordeaux varieties such as Cabernet Sauvignon and Merlot grow side by side with Syrah, Sangiovese, and Touriga Nacional. Although the Salinas River runs through the center of the valley, sandy soils and an almost complete lack of rainfall during the growing season make irrigation a must in most of the region.

The Carmel Valley AVA, established in 1983, has just 300 acres planted to grapevines out of a total of 19,000 acres of land. It is south of the city of Monterey and Carmel-by-the-Sea. Vines are planted at altitudes running between 200 feet and 2,762 feet, and soils are mainly sandy loam. Just southeast of Monterey Bay, Carmel Valley is subject to cool coastal influences. Higher-elevation vineyards that sit above the fog line rely on altitude and summer diurnal temperature variations of up to 60 degrees Fahrenheit to retain freshness in the grapes. Bordeaux varieties are the most prevalent, with Cabernet Sauvignon and Merlot accounting for more than 70 percent of the plantings. A few small plantings of Pinot Noir and Chardonnay have also garnered attention.

The Santa Lucia Highlands AVA was first planted with Mission grapes at the tail end of the eighteenth century. A more recent planting boom that started in the early 1970s set the stage for this mountainside AVA to be lauded by wine lovers and critics alike for its high-quality output, especially Pinot Noir. Santa Lucia Highlands gained AVA status in 1991 and has grown to include just over 6,000 acres of vineyards planted at altitudes of 100 to 2,350 feet on the eastern side of the Santa Lucia Mountains, just west of Salinas. Morning sun aids in sugar and flavor development before the afternoon's heavy fog and strong pelagic winds off the Monterey Bay make additional contributions to elevation-derived coolness, delaying ripening for two to three weeks beyond comparable regions elsewhere in the state. Beside Pinot Noir, Chardonnay thrives in the soils of the Santa Lucia Highlands, while Syrah and other Rhône varieties do well in sheltered canyons and slopes beyond the reach of chilling winds. Many famed Santa Lucia Highlands vineyards provide fruit for Pinot Noir–focused producers in other regions; you will find the appellation listed on small-batch bottlings from wineries up and down the California coast.

Arroyo Seco received AVA approval in 1983, about 20 years after the first commercial plantings in the area and almost 200 years after the first Mission grapes were cultivated by Spanish priests. Spanish for "dry riverbed," Arroyo Seco runs from a high-tapered gorge in the Santa Lucia Mountains to the more open floor of the Salinas Valley. Grapes are planted on 7,000 acres of sand and loam out of a potential 14,000 acres in the AVA. Vineyards on the east-facing slopes of the Santa Lucia range as high as 1,670 feet, running down to 266 feet nearer the valley's center.

Canyons offer shelter from late-day winds, whereas more open vineyards on the valley floor benefit from cooling Pacific Ocean breezes. Soil types vary too: inhospitable canyon soils force vines to dig deep for water and nutrients, while in the valley fist-sized stones called Greenfield Potatoes (named for the nearby town of Greenfield) offer drainage to the roots of grapevines and retain warmth from the rays of the sun, radiating it back at night and preventing frost damage to delicate vines. Cooler areas of Arroyo Seco are home to Chardonnay and Riesling, and red Bordeaux and Rhône varieties and Zinfandel are planted in the warmer areas of the AVA. In the past it was common to blend Arroyo Seco fruit into large bottlings of California or Central Coast Chardonnay, but now even large producers are setting aside tanks of prized Arroyo Seco juice for smaller amounts of appellation-based bottlings.

Granted AVA status in 1982, the Chalone AVA has a long history of grape growing in the twentieth century, dating back before Prohibition. Its 300 planted acres include Chardonnay, Pinot Noir, Pinot Blanc, Chenin Blanc, and Syrah. Vineyards range in altitude from 1,200 to 2,323 feet, with an average elevation of 1,800 feet. The vineyards are set in the Gabilan (also spelled Gavilan) Mountain Range to the east of the Monterey AVA, against the impressive background of Pinnacles National Monument. The majority of the vines planted in the region's granite and limestone soils belong to Chalone Vineyard, one of just two wineries in the AVA.

Named after Saint Barnabas by a Spanish missionary in 1776, San Bernabe became an AVA in 2004. It consists of an 11,000-acre single vineyard called San Bernabe Vineyard that is touted by its owners, Delicato Family Vineyards, as the largest contiguous vineyard in the world. Twenty varieties are grown here, including Merlot, Syrah, Pinot Noir, Chardonnay, and Riesling, which make their way into various Delicato brands or are sold to other wineries.

Previously home to grazing cattle, the San Lucas AVA on the southwestern border of the Salinas Valley was granted official recognition in 1987. Home to 8,000 acres of grapes, mainly Cabernet Sauvignon, Merlot, Chardonnay, and Sauvignon Blanc, San Lucas is less affected by maritime breezes and provides grapes with a warmer climate than other AVAs in Monterey County. Grapes have been planted here since the 1970s in shale and sandstone of an alluvial nature.

The San Antonio Valley AVA to the west of San Bernabe, San Lucas, Hames Valley, and the southernmost portion of the Monterey AVA is the most recent addition to Monterey County's roster of viticultural areas. It was established in 2006, although the first grapes were planted here in 1772 at the Mission of San Antonio de Padua, which stands to this day. Warm days are moderated by the maritime influences of the nearby Pacific and lacustrine effects from Lake San Antonio. More than 800 acres of grapes are grown in gravelly loam and clay soils, mainly red Rhône and Bordeaux varieties.

Hames Valley was granted AVA designation in 1994. The southernmost AVA in Monterey County, Hames Valley has the warmest daytime temperatures and is said to have the largest day-to-night temperature variation in the region. Syrah and other red Rhône varieties predominate among its 2,000 acres of vines.

Over the Gabilan Range and across the San Benito County line are the San Benito AVA and its subregions and the Mount Harlan AVA. The latter received AVA status in 1990, and the only commercial winery in the Mount Harlan appellation is Calera, whose founder, Josh Jensen, petitioned for AVA status. The soils here are almost all limestone, and Jensen chose the site because of Pinot Noir's affinity for this soil type. Chardonnay, Aligoté, and Viognier are also grown here at elevations between 1,800 and 2,200 feet.

The San Benito AVA contains three sub-AVAs: Cienega Valley, Lime Kiln Valley, and Paicines. The total area is 45,000 acres and was established in 1987. Before 1984 Almaden acquired a large portion of its grapes from the vineyards of San Benito, specifically Cienega Valley and Paicines, but after Almaden's sale to Constellation in the mid-1980s plantings dwindled to fewer than 1,000 acres. A handful of small-scale wineries and a couple of larger operations have discovered San Benito, and the total planted area is back up to almost 3,000 acres. Cienega Valley's AVA recognition predates San Benito's, having been granted in 1982, as do Lime Kiln Valley's (also 1982, amended in 1987, and itself a sub-AVA of Cienega Valley) and Paicines, established in 1982 as well. A wide array of grape varieties are grown in San Benito, including Chardonnay, Pinot Noir, red Rhône varieties, Tempranillo, and Barbera.

The Lime Kiln Valley AVA is home to one winery, Enz Vineyards, and Paicine's largest vineyard (500 acres), now in the hands of Sonoma-based superstar winery Williams Selyem, was formerly a major supplier for Almaden.

THE WINERIES

BERNARDUS WINERY

5 West Carmel Valley Road,
Carmel Valley, CA 93924,
(831) 659-1900
www.bernardus.com

Netherlands native Bernardus Pons was born into the world of wine—his family owns the oldest wine distribution house in Holland. A lifelong sportsman, he has raced six times at Le Mans and competed in the 1972 Olympics as a skeet shooter. He and his wife, Ingrid, decided to put down roots in the Carmel Valley, where they planted vines on 50 acres of their 220-acre estate. They primarily grow Bordeaux varieties, including Cabernet Franc, Cabernet Sauvignon, Petit Verdot, and Merlot. Winemaking is under the direction of American-born, Burgundian-trained Dean DeKorth, who oversees the day-to-day activities at the winery. Bernardus Winery Ingrid's Vineyard Estate Chardonnay 2010 is straw colored, with aromas of Granny Smith apples, pear compote, and brown spice. In the mouth the fruit flavors recede as subtle flavors of creamy lemon curd come to the forefront. The finish is clean and crisp with good persistence. Bernardus Winery Ingrid's Vineyard Estate Pinot Noir 2010 has aromas of cherry preserves and fresh red raspberry. On the palate it is medium-bodied with good mouthfeel, juicy fruit flavors, and a silky smooth tannic finish.

CALERA WINES

11300 Cienega Road, Hollister, CA 95023,
(831) 637-9170
www.calerawine.com

Josh Jensen returned to California from Burgundy in 1971 and began searching for a site to plant vines. He stumbled on an old lime kiln in the Gabilan Mountains and found the limestone-rich *terroir* he was looking for to plant Pinot Noir. In 1975 he planted 24 acres of Pinot Noir in three separate parcels. The Jensen Vineyard has 14 acres, the Selleck Vineyard has 5 acres, and the Reed Vineyard has 5 acres. Calera Mount Harlan Chardonnay 2011 is straw colored, with aromas of Indian spices, white flowers, and citrus blossoms. In the mouth there are lovely flavors of Anjou pear, Granny Smith apple, and creamy lemon curd. There is a crisp and clean finish. Drink it now or over the next three to four years. Calera Mount Harlan Jensen Vineyard Pinot Noir 2010 has notes of black raspberry, red plum, and Provencal spice in the bouquet. It is fruit-forward on the palate, with flavors of red cherry and candied violet and just a touch of cinnamon on the elegant finish.

CHALONE VINEYARD ESTATE

32020 Stonewall Canyon Road, Soledad CA 93960,
(800) 407-9047
www.chalonevineyard.com

Charles Tamm planted the first grapevines on Chalone Peak in 1919, and in 1960 the first wine to bear the Chalone label was made by Philip Togni. In 1966 Dick Graff produced the first commercial vintage, and the 1970s, 1980s, and 1990s saw extensive expansion. Today there are over 1,000 acres of property, with 250 acres under plantation. Currently, Chalone is one of just two wineries in the Chalone AVA. At the time of this writing there were no visitor facilities, but plans for a visitor center are said to be under way. Chalone Vineyard Estate Chalone Appellation Chardonnay 2010 is brilliant straw colored, with aromas of Anjou pear, white stone fruits, and citrus blossoms. There are lovely fruit flavors in the mouth with pronounced minerality in the finish. Chalone Vineyard Estate Chalone Appellation Pinot Noir 2010 has notes of ripe cherry, red raspberry, and sage in the bouquet with ripe fruit flavors on the palate. The finish is complemented by smooth tannins and balanced acidity.

HAHN FAMILY WINERY

37700 Foothill Road, Soledad, CA 93960,
(866) 925-7994
www.hahnwinery.com

When you visit Hahn Family Winery, make sure to take the ATV tour through its vineyards in the Santa Lucia Highlands and bring a picnic lunch to accompany some of the best views of the Salinas Valley—don't worry, they will supply the wine. Swiss-born Nicolaus "Nicky" Hahn realized the potential of Monterey as a wine-growing region over 30 years ago. Today, Paul Clifton is the director of winemaking and Greg Freeman is the winemaker. Hahn Winery Monterey Chardonnay 2011 is a brilliant straw color, with aromas of candied lemon rind and caramelized pineapple. It is medium-bodied in the mouth with flavors of Bartlett pear and white peach and a crisp, clean finish. Hahn Winery Exclusive Monterey GSM 2010 is composed of

53 percent Grenache, 41 percent Syrah, and 6 percent Mourvèdre. It has a ruby garnet color, with aromas of red raspberry, red plum, and Mediterranean herbs. There are juicy flavors of red fruits and firm tannins on the palate.

MORGAN WINERY

590 Brunken Avenue, Salinas, CA 93901,
(831) 751-7777
www.morganwinery.com

Dan Morgan Lee and Donna George made their first 2,000 cases of Monterey Chardonnay in 1982 and immediately gained national acclaim when they received a platinum medal from *Wine & Spirits*. Thirty-five years and numerous medals and awards later, they opened Taste Morgan, their hip and fun visitor center and tasting room at the Crossroads Shopping Village in Carmel. Gianni Abate, formerly of Woodbridge, Delicato, Robert Mondavi, and Bronco, is the current winemaker. Morgan Winery Rosella's Vineyard Chardonnay 2011 has aromas of lemon curd, dried apricots, and white peach. It is full and creamy in the mouth with a good mouthfeel and a pleasant acidic finish. Morgan Winery Gary's Vineyard Pinot Noir 2011 is cherry red, with aromas of red raspberry, red cherry, and a touch of cedar in the bouquet. On the palate it shows ripe fruit and subtle floral notes—overall, a very nice Pinot Noir from the Santa Lucia Highlands.

PARAISO VINEYARDS

38060 Paraiso Springs Road, Soledad, CA 93960,
(831) 678-0300
www.paraisovineyards.com

Rich and Claudia Smith began planting vines in 1973, and today their 400-acre estate is home to more than 150,000 vines in sixteen different blocks. Very much a family affair, Paraiso—or Paradise—Vineyards is owned, operated, and managed by Mom, Dad, the kids, their spouses, and their dogs. Besides making great wines, the Smith family is very much involved in their community and a variety of charitable organizations, including Ag Against Hunger. Paraiso Vineyards Santa Lucia Highlands Riesling 2010 has heady aromas of dried apricot, Anjou pear, and Christmas baking spices. It is floral and pleasantly acidic on the palate, making it a perfect wine to pair with spicy Asian cuisine. Paraiso Vineyards Faite Pinot Noir 2009 has aromas of red cherry, dried black cherry, and cedar. In the mouth there are flavors of red raspberry and red cherry with balanced tannins and a persistent finish.

PISONI VINEYARDS

PO Box 908,
Gonzales, CA 93926,
(831) 675-7500
www.pisonivineyards.com

Gary Pisoni and his vineyard have been called the "rock star and grand cru site of the Santa Lucia Highlands" by Robert Parker. Gary's parents, Jane and Eddie Pisoni, had been farming since 1952, and their profit from the celery crop of 1979 became the down payment for the current vineyard site in the Santa Lucia Highlands. Gary began planting vines in 1982, growing grapes for an impressive array of amazing wines that are consistently highly praised and highly scored, including, now, many of their own. The vineyards are at an altitude of 1,300 feet, and Gary's vineyard management style calls for very low yields and extremely high-quality fruit. Gary's sons are following in the family business, with Mark as the vineyard manager and Jeff as the winemaker. In addition to visiting the family's vineyards, we had a chance to catch up with Jeff in New York City and taste his recent releases over dinner. Pisoni Santa Lucia Highlands Pinot Noir 2011 is cherry garnet colored, with delightful aromas of ripe black cherry, dried red cherry, and a touch of dried sage. It is full and rich in the mouth with flavors of red fruits, dried Mediterranean herbs, and just a touch of lifted mint. The finish is long, elegant, and generous. Pisoni Santa Lucia Highlands Soberanes Chardonnay 2011 is medium straw colored, with aromas of white stone fruits, tropical blossoms, and caramelized pineapple. In the mouth it is full-bodied with luxurious texture and a persistent finish that keeps inviting you in for another sip.

ROAR WINES

32721 River Road,
Soledad, CA 93960,
(831) 675-1681
www.roarwines.com

Both Gary and Rosella Franscioni, who grew up in the Santa Lucia Highlands, recognized

the potential for grape growing and winemaking early on. In 1996 they planted their first vines in Rosella's Vineyard. Roar is named for the sound of the Monterey Bay winds that whip through their vineyard and keep the grapes cool at night. Roar Wines Santa Lucia Highlands Pinot Noir 2011 is deep cherry red, with aromas of dark cherry, red cherry, and brown baking spice. In the mouth there are fresh fruit flavors—namely, red raspberry and ripe cherry—good acidity, and a nice grip to the tannic finish. Roar Wines Sierra Mar Vineyard Viognier 2011 is pale straw colored, with aromas of citrus zest and white stone fruits. It is richer and rounder than most Viogniers, and that makes this a special wine. It has great flavors of white peach, anise bulb, and a touch of Christmas baking spices, especially star anise and nutmeg in the finish. It's great to drink on its own as an aperitif or with Asian cuisine.

SCHEID VINEYARDS

1972 Hobson Avenue, Greenfield, CA 93927,
(831) 386-0316
www.scheidvineyards.com

Scheid Vineyards was started in 1972 by investment banker Al Scheid. Today Scheid owns ten estate vineyards and farms 4,200 acres. In addition to a large high-capacity winery that produces custom-made wine for other brands, Scheid also has a smaller reserve winery, where the Scheid Vineyards wines are made. One of Scheid's new high-profile brands is GIFFT, a wine created in partnership with dynamic daytime television host Kathy Lee Gifford, who brings wine into homes of millions of viewers every day. GIFFT Estate Grown Monterey Chardonnay 2012 has a nose of apricot, peach and white flowers, with flavors of peach, apple, and a hint of toast. This wine is clean and crisp, with refreshing acidity. GIFFT Estate Grown Monterey Red Blend 2011 is a blend of ten grapes, mainly Merlot with Petite Sirah, Syrah, and Petit Verdot. Aromas of black cherry, blueberry, and violet talc yield to flavors of black plum, cherry, vanilla, and rose petal, wrapped up in a web of soft, easy-drinking tannins. Scheid Vineyards Pinot Noir 2011 offers aromas of fruit of the wood, Turkish delight, and nutmeg. Flavors of black cherry and brambly berries with a touch of clove persist through the bright finish.

TALBOTT VINEYARDS

53 East Carmel Valley Road,
Carmel Valley, CA 93924,
(831) 659-3500
www.talbottvineyards.com

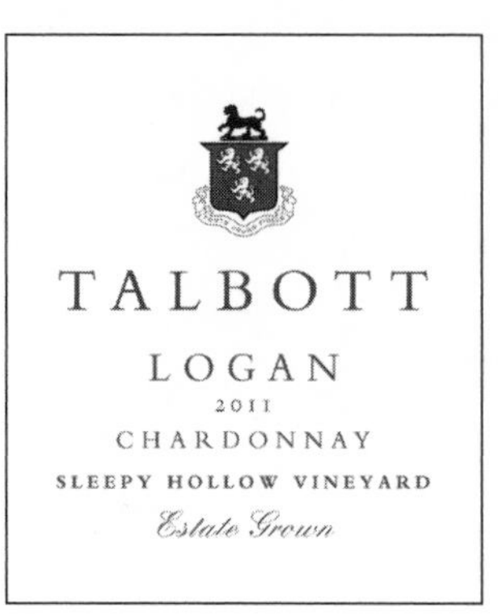

Robb Talbott grew up in Carmel Valley and left for college in Colorado, but in 1972 he returned home and built a log cabin on the property that would become his Diamond T Vineyards. He planted vines in 1982, enlisted the help of his wife and children, and today runs both Talbott Vineyards and his family's Robert Talbott Tie Company. Talbott Vineyards Logan Sleepy Hollow Vineyard Chardonnay 2011 is straw colored, with aromas of white peach and Granny Smith apples. It is powerful on the palate with focused acidity. Talbott Vineyards Diamond T Vineyard Monterey Pinot Noir 2010 is medium cherry red, with aromas of black cherry, red plum, and brown spice. It is rich in the mouth with pleasant acidity and supple tannins.

TONDRE WINES

PO Box 866, Gonzales, CA 93926,
(831) 675-3214
www.tondrewines.com

Father-and-son team Tondre and Joe Alarid planted their first six acres in 1997, and today Tondre Wines has 80 acres of Pinot Noir vines and 21 acres of Chardonnay vines. Tondre Wines remains a passion-driven family project, with both men and their respective families living on the property 24/7. Their wines have won numerous medals and are consistently highly rated by *Wine Enthusiast.* Tondre Santa Lucia Highlands Pinot Noir 2010 has aromas of ripe red cherries and dried black cherry with a touch of cinnamon toast in the nose. The wine shows lots of fruit on the palate and beautifully balanced tannins on the finish. Tondre Debut Vintage Chardonnay 2010 has notes of mango, guava, and pineapple in the bouquet. It is crisp yet creamy in the mouth with good heft and a pleasant acidic finish.

VENTANA VINEYARDS

2999 Salinas Highway,
Monterey, CA 93940,
(831) 372-7415
www.ventanawines.com

Situated within Monterey County in the Arroyo Seco AVA, Ventana Vineyards benefits from a cool climate and brisk evening winds that are perfect for the cultivation of Chardonnay, Riesling, and Pinot Noir. The 300 acres of vineyards are tended by Steve McIntyre, who introduced sustainable farming practices, and management is under the direction of Randy Pura. Ventana Vineyards Riesling 2010 is pale straw colored, with aromas of candied orange peel and dried apricot. It has flavors of white peach, orange zest, and a touch of dried sage in the bouquet. Nice and dry, this wine would pair well with spicy Thai or Vietnamese cuisine. Ventana Vineyards Chardonnay 2011 has aromas of guava, pineapple upside-down cake, and lemon blossom. In the mouth flavors of crisp apple and pear compote dance on the tongue, with just a touch of honeysuckle in the finish.

WRATH WINES

35801 Foothill Road,
Soledad, CA 93960,
(831) 678 2212
www.wrathwines.com

Inspired by the similarities between Salinas Valley and the Italian countryside, archaeologist Michael Thomas and his mother, Barbara Wrath, purchased San Saba Vineyards in 2007 and since then have been producing wines that have been highly acclaimed by

critics and wine enthusiasts alike. When he is not digging in the vineyards or making wine in Monterey, you might find Michael digging on an archaeological site near Pompeii. Wrath San Saba Vineyard Monterey Chardonnay 2010 is medium straw in color with a brilliant rim and aromas of caramelized pineapple and white flowers. It is smooth and medium-bodied in the mouth with nice viscosity. It has flavors of vanilla, lemon curd, and hazelnuts with a nice streak of acidity down the center of the tongue. Wrath Boekenoogen Vineyard Santa Lucia Highlands Pinot Noir 2010 is dark red violet colored, with aromas of cherry cola and dried black cherries. In the mouth there is a burst of bright fruit upon entry and flavors of black cherry, black raspberry, mint, oregano, and sage. It has nice complexity with a soft tannic finish.

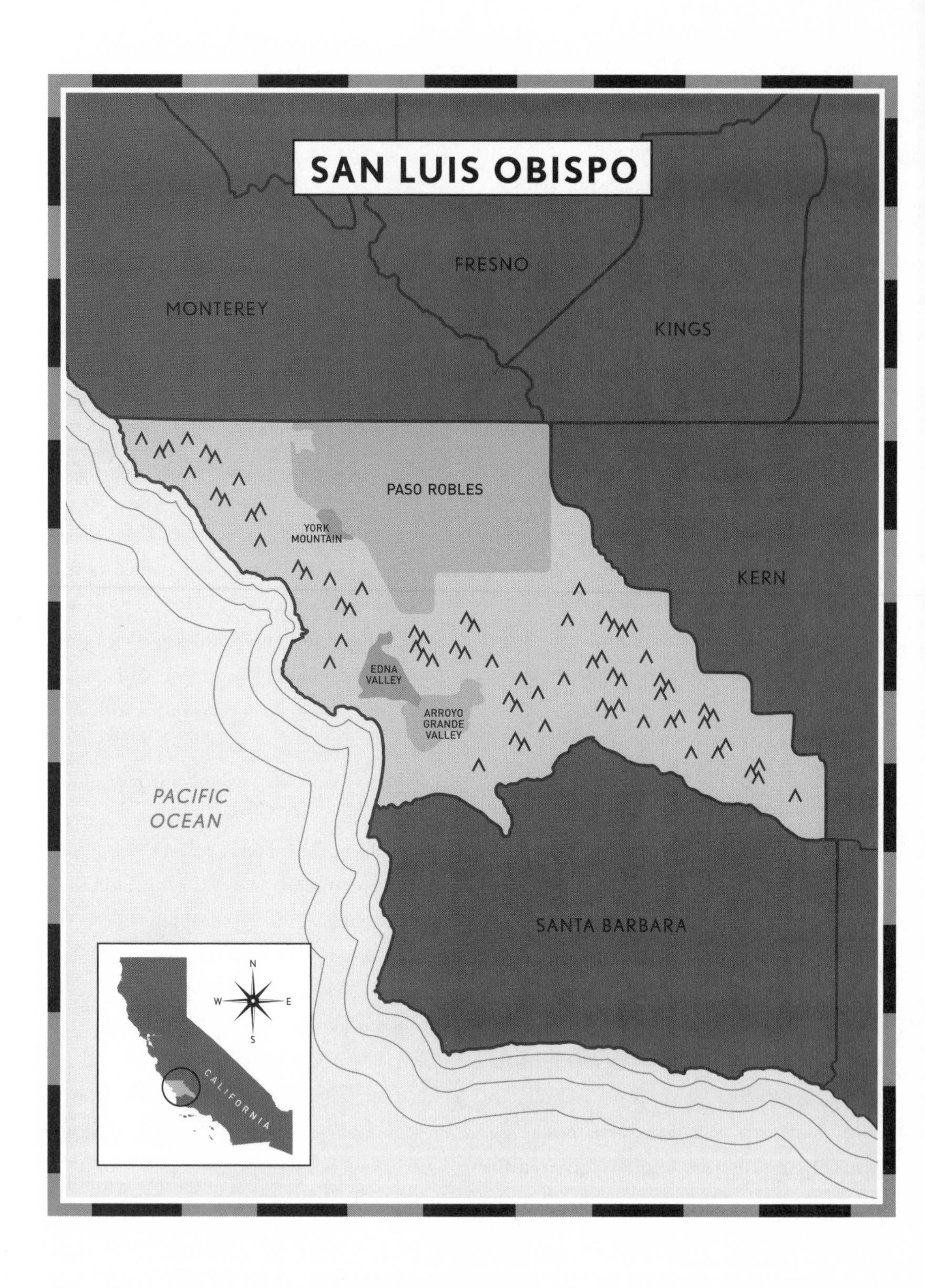
SAN LUIS OBISPO
FRESNO
MONTEREY
KINGS
PASO ROBLES
YORK
MOUNTAIN
KERN
EDNA
VALLEY
ARROYO
GRANDE
VALLEY
PACIFIC
OCEAN
SANTA BARBARA
N
W
E
S
CALIFORNIA

CHAPTER 9

SAN LUIS OBISPO COUNTY AND PASO ROBLES

UNLIKE THE "GENTLEMAN FARMERS" found in some other wine regions, Paso Robles—by far the largest AVA within San Luis Obispo County—is home to multigenerational farming families, and large cattle ranches sit alongside fertile vineyards. Here ranchers and grape growers wear cowboy hats to keep the sun out of their eyes and off the back of their necks, not to make a fashion statement. Famous outlaws of the American Wild West such as Jesse James made Paso Robles their home, and well-worn jeeps and pickup trucks are more common than luxury cars.

San Luis Obispo County is part of the large Central Coast AVA, bordered to the north by Monterey County and to the south by Santa Barbara County, which are also part of the Central Coast AVA. The city of San Luis Obispo, which today has just under 50,000 residents, gradually sprung up around Mission San Luis Obispo de Toloso. The original mission was founded by Father Junípero Serra, called the father of California wine, in 1772. Named after Saint Louis of Anjou, the bishop of Toulouse (*obispo* is the Spanish word for "bishop"), the mission church remains in use as a Catholic parish church in the Diocese of Monterey and is a state historic landmark. Before Spanish settlement the native Chumash people populated the area. Spanish Mission style remains the primary architectural influence in this laid-back city, which is known statewide simply as SLO. Cal Poly SLO's programs in viticulture, enology, and wine business supply the area and the state with a steady supply of well-trained graduates eager to join their neighbors and family members in the thriving wine industry.

Although American Viticultural Areas to the north and south also reside within the Central Coast AVA, when people in California talk about "the Central Coast," they generally mean San Luis Obispo County and the Paso Robles AVA. The county itself is an AVA, and besides Paso Robles there are three smaller ones within it as well: York Mountain, Edna Valley, and Arroyo Grande Valley. (A small portion of the Santa Maria Valley crosses over into San Luis Obispo County, but that AVA is discussed in Chapter 10.) As a whole, the county is agricultural, and its green hills are dotted with small towns, farms, and vineyards. The beautiful and rugged coastline is home to Montaña de Oro State Park, Morro Bay, William R. Hearst Memorial State Beach, and Hearst Castle.

The county is blanketed with 29,000 acres of wine grapes. Cabernet Sauvignon is the most widely planted variety, covering over 10,000 acres, followed by Merlot, Syrah, Zinfandel, Chardonnay, and Petite Sirah. Although Bordeaux-style and Meritage blends are common, it is not unusual to find Cabernet Sauvignon blended with Syrah, Petite Sirah, or Zinfandel. More than 90 percent of the county's 250-plus wineries are in the sprawling Paso Robles AVA, which is also responsible for 90 percent of the grapes grown here. Fifty-eight percent of the grapes grown in the AVA are sold elsewhere in the state, and two-thirds of those grapes are used in entry-level wines with the California or Central Coast AVA designation.

Despite the predominance of Cabernet Sauvignon, the Paso Robles AVA has become known in the wine world as the home of Rhône varietals: mainly Syrah, Grenache, and Mourvèdre for the red grapes and Viognier, Marsanne, and Roussanne for the whites. The area's Rhone Rangers chapter boasts has over forty members. Paso Robles actually produces a surprising number of different types of grapes and wine, including Pinot Noir, Zinfandel, Albariño, Tempranillo, Sangiovese, Aglianico, and Nebbiolo. Many of the wines are rated as "best buys" for their excellent quality-to-price ratio, and you will also find wines that will age well and are meant to be shared on special occasions with family and friends alike.

A long-standing farming community, Paso Robles was home to cattle ranches, horse farms, fruit orchards, and fields of vegetables and wheat long before grapes were planted in any significant manner, and that tradition continues today. There is a very strong farm-to-table ethos among local food producers and restaurants. Downtown Paso Robles is home to a number of restaurants serving locally grown food and locally made wine. Residents argue about which is the best restaurant in town, and don't get them started on their favorite taco shop. Besides the Wild West–era town of Paso Robles, other charming spots in the area are Templeton and Atascadero, both south of Paso Robles, and the coastal communities of Cambria and Cayucos to the west.

The earliest known vineyards here were planted in the late eighteenth century, near the Asistencia chapel on the Santa Margarita Ranch. San Luis Obispo was incorporated as a county when California became a state in 1850; at around that same time immigrants from Europe, primarily Italy and Germany, were beginning to plant grapes and make wine here. Andrew York, a transplanted rancher from Indiana, founded the Ascension Winery in 1882. The name was later changed to York Mountain Winery, and it is said to be the oldest operating winery in the region. York's original vineyards are part of the York Mountain AVA, adjacent to the Paso Robles AVA.

More Italians arrived in the early twentieth century, and many of the oldest vineyards were planted during Prohibition, growing grapes, especially Zinfandel, to be shipped east to home winemakers. At that time Polish piano virtuoso Ignace Paderewski came to Paso Robles to visit the area's hot springs (he had begun to experience pain in his hands that interfered with his playing) and purchased 2,000 acres of land, which he planted to Petite Sirah and Zinfandel. After Prohibition, Padarewski's grapes were vinified at York Mountain Winery.

The first modern large-scale winery, Hoffman Mountain Ranch Winery, was established in 1964 by Stanley Hoffman. Heeding the advice of noted enologist André Tchelistcheff and with further insight from researchers at UC Davis, he planted vineyards next to Padarewski's, in the Adelaida Hills. Tchelistcheff had recommended that Hoffman plant Pinot Noir, Chardonnay, and Cabernet Sauvignon, and within 10 years the wines achieved widespread acclaim. From that point forward development proceeded at a rapid pace, with vineyards spreading from what is now known as the "West Side," west of the Salinas River, to the flatter and warmer "East Side," to the east of the river, which divides the region in two. Gary Eberle, one of the pioneers of the 1970s, is credited with planting the first Syrah vines here.

The Paso Robles AVA and the York Mountain AVA were established in 1983. Paso Robles encompasses an area of 617,000 acres, and York Mountain has 6,400 acres. Because of the wide variety of terrain and climactic conditions within Paso Robles, there is currently a petition before the TTB to create eleven sub-AVAs within the larger AVA. The petition was accepted in March 2007, and it is highly possible that the following will have become official AVAs by the time this book is published: Adelaida District, Creston District, El Pomar District, Paso Robles Estrella District, Paso Robles Geneseo District, Paso Robles Highlands District, San Juan Creek, San Miguel District, Santa Margarita District, Paso Robles Willow Creek District, and Templeton Gap.

In 2005 Robert Parker predicted that within a decade Paso Robles (among other AVAs) would be as well known as Napa. As his forecast comes to pass, there is some concern among winemakers that there may be no additional value to using new, more particular

AVA names at the same moment that there is growing consumer recognition of the quality of wine from Paso Robles. That said, there is little dispute that the creation of subappellations is important in terms of expression of *terroir* and recognition of prime varieties from a specific zone within the AVA.

Vineyard altitudes in Paso Robles range from 720 to 2,400 feet above sea level. The area is crisscrossed with fault lines, most notably the San Andreas Fault, which have created the hot springs that first brought many settlers to the region. The Salinas River runs more or less through the center, and the Santa Lucia Mountains run along the coastline. Soils to the west of the river tend to be sedimentary clay and loam with calcareous and silicone elements. Soils to the east are alluvial in nature, with a predominance of gravel, clay, and sand. Mineral content increases at higher altitudes. Diurnal temperature variations of up to 50 degrees Fahrenheit in the growing season aid proper sugar development and acid retention in the grapes. Areas closest to the Pacific receive the most rainfall and cooling fogs and breezes, whereas those farther east often require irrigation and aggressive canopy management.

A good way to sample everything that Paso Robles has to offer is to visit during special festival weekends throughout the year, such as Zinfandel Weekend in March, CABS of Distinction in April, Paso Robles Wine Festival in May, Wine Country Auction in August, and Harvest Wine Weekend in October. CABS of Distinction is organized by the CAB Collective, which stands for Cabernet and Bordeaux Collective, an organization dedicated to promoting the wines some consider to be the most ageworthy and collectible in the region.

The Edna Valley AVA, established in 1982, is south of San Luis Obispo and just north of the town of Arroyo Grande. Of the 22,400 acres in the AVA, just under 3,000 are planted with grapevines. The AVA is best known for Pinot Noir and Chardonnay, and Syrah is grown there as well. The most well known winery in Edna Valley is Chamisal. The Arroyo Grande AVA was established in 1990. The 16-mile long winding valley includes a total area of just less than 40,000 acres with 1,200 acres of vineyards. Its east-to-northeast orientation allows breezes and fog from the Pacific to temper morning and midday temperatures, protecting grapes from the harsh rays of the sun. Chardonnay and Pinot Noir thrive in the cooler areas in the center of the valley, and Zinfandel, Petite Sirah, and red Rhône varieties grow in the vicinity of Lopez Lake.

THE WINERIES

ALTA COLINA

2725 Adelaida Road, Paso Robles, CA 93446,
(805) 227-4191
www.altacolinawine.com

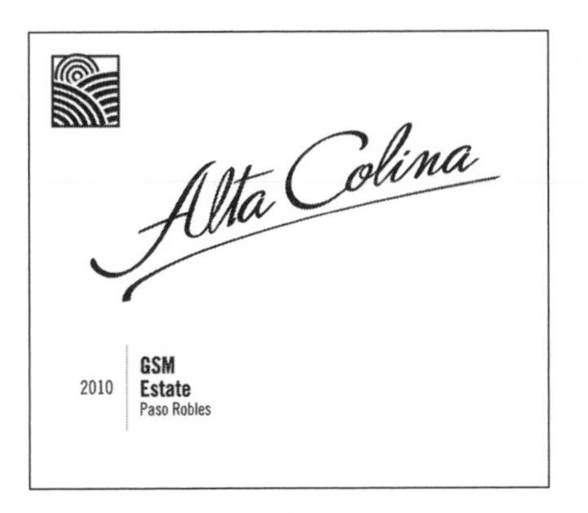

After 35 years in what he describes as the "high-tech business world," Bob Tillman and his wife, Lynn, started Alta Colina in 2003. Consulting winemaker Jeff Cohn joined the team in 2011 and provides coaching and guidance in producing Rhône blends from Alta Colina's vineyards. Alta Colina Estate GSM 2010 is 45 percent Grenache, 30 percent Mourvèdre, and 25 percent Syrah. It is garnet colored, with aromas of black cherry and espresso. It is fruity in the mouth with flavors of black cherry, raspberry, and freshly ground black pepper that continue into the finish. Alta Colina Old 900 Estate Syrah 2010 is composed of 95 percent Syrah, 4 percent Mourvèdre, and 1 percent Viognier. It is deep purple in color, with aromas of blackberry, sandalwood, and mixed white flowers. It has flavors of black cherry and crème brûlée, with a floral lift at the end.

ANCIENT PEAKS WINERY

22720 El Camino Real,
Santa Margarita, CA 93453,
(805) 365-7045
www.ancientpeaks.com

When we arrived at Ancient Peaks Winery to tour the property and taste the wines, we were greeted by Karl Wittstrom, who handed us each a harness and a helmet and then politely explained that the best way to see the vineyards was on his newly constructed zipline. Never one to turn down an adventure, we quickly agreed. In minutes we were soaring high above the vines, and you can too; just remember to save the actual wine tasting part until last. Part of an original Mexican land grant, Ancient Peaks Winery and the town of Santa Margarita sit right in the middle of the Santa Margarita Ranch. Ancient Peaks is owned by Karl, Doug Filipponi, and Rob Rossi, and winemaking is under the direction of Mike Sinor, who has been recognized as one of the Central Coast's highest-scoring winemakers by a variety of well-respected publications. Ancient Peaks Winery Paso Robles Renegade 2010 is a blend of 51 percent Syrah, 25 percent Malbec, and 24 percent Petit Verdot. It is inky purple, with aromas of violet, dark fruits, and black plums. It is full-bodied in the mouth, with rich fruit flavors and a touch of milk chocolate on the finish. Ancient Peaks Winery Paso Robles Oyster Ridge 2010 is garnet to inky purple with a violet rim. It has aromas of black fruits, toasted brioche, white pepper, and red plums. Flavors of black cherry, cassis, and black plums make up the mid palate, and the finish has a touch of spice and espresso bean.

ARONHILL VINEYARDS

3745 West Highway 46, Templeton, CA 93465,
(805) 434-3066
www.aronhillvineyards.com

Judy Hill Aron planted AronHill Vineyards in 1996 and made her first vintage in 2004. We had the pleasure of celebrating Judy's birthday lunch at her beautiful terraced restaurant cantilevered above her vineyards. We were joined by her winemaker, Michael Olsten, and viticulturist, Richard Sauret. AronHill produces 2,000 cases of wine in total, with 1,300 of them produced from estate-grown fruit. AronHill Vineyards Cabernet Sauvignon 2008 is opaque garnet, with aromas of dark cherry, violet, and Mediterranean herbs. In the mouth flavors of cherry vanilla and ripe black cherry entice your palate before the smooth finish with an integrated tannic structure. AronHill

Primitivo 2007 is garnet colored, with aromas of vanilla and red plum. The nuanced fruit flavors change to a smooth yet flinty full-on cherry vanilla before the creamy milk chocolate finish.

BAILEYANA WINERY

5828 Orcutt Road, San Luis Obispo, CA 93401,
(805) 269-8200
www.baileyana.com

One of the Niven Family collection of wine estates, Baileyana is a winery that harks back to founder Catharine Niven's original vision of crafting wines that are Old World–inspired, made with New World standards, and sustainably grown. Raised and schooled in Burgundy, winemaker Christian Rougenant continues the family tradition by making delicious wines that decidedly skew Burgundian in style and flavor. Baileyana Edna Valley Firepeak Vineyard Chardonnay 2010 is medium yellow, with aromas of white stone fruits, citrus blossoms, and lemon curd. It is medium-bodied on the palate with nice fruit flavors and a clean finish. Baileyana Edna Valley Firepeak Vineyard Pinot Noir 2010 has aromas of dried red cherries, ripe black cherries, and red raspberries. It has nice heft in the mouth with lifted notes of dried Provencal herbs in the finish.

BOOKER VINEYARD

2640 Anderson Road,
Paso Robles, CA 93446,
(805) 237-7367
www.bookerwines.com

Lisa and Eric Jensen acquired a parcel of 72 acres of land in 2001 from the original 1,200-acre Booker Estate. Eric made wine with Stephan Asseo of L'Aventure Wines for two years and Justin Smith of Saxum for five years before venturing out on his own. The 2005 vintage was Booker Vineyard's first release. Eric was kind enough to take a few hours out of making wine and coaching his youth basketball team to sit down with us and taste a few of his wines. Booker Vineyard Ripper Grenache 2010 is cherry red, with aromas of Mediterranean herbs, predominantly oregano, and sweet black cherry. In the mouth it has intense fruit flavors with nuances of fine dark chocolate and cocoa powder. Booker Vineyard Oublié 2010 is a blend of 43 percent Syrah, 26 percent Mourvèdre, 16 percent Counoise, and 15 percent Grenache. It has notes of fresh red fruits and dried herbs in the bouquet. The structure is well balanced with excellent acidity and freshness. Drink it now or over the next 15 years.

CALCAREOUS VINEYARD

3430 Peachy Canyon Road,
Paso Robles, CA 93446,
(805) 239-0289
www.calcareous.com

CALCAREOUS
VINEYARD
Moose
2009
PASO ROBLES
88% Syrah, 12% Petit Verdot
15.5% Alc. By Vol.

Lloyd Messer and his daughter Dana Brown established Calcareous Vineyards in 2000. Both wine distributors from Iowa, they decided to name the 342-acre vineyard for the solid calcareous rock and soil on which it sits. Calcareous Vineyard Tres Violet 2009 is a blend of 36 percent Mourvèdre, 34 percent Syrah, and 30 percent Grenache and is the color of black cherry. It has aromas of cassis, candied violets, and red raspberry and has flavors of fruits of the wood, licorice, and a touch of menthol. It has sweet, rounded tannins and a delightful finish. Calcareous Vineyard Moose 2009 is a blend of 88 percent Syrah and 12 percent Petit Verdot. It is inky purple, with aromas of plum, tart cherry, and freshly roasted espresso beans. There are flavors of black cherry, ripe black raspberry, and caramelized fennel bulb. The tannins are smooth, and there is a bounce of brightness in the finish.

CAYUCOS CELLARS

131 North Ocean Avenue, Cayucos, CA 93430,
(805) 995-3036
www.cayucoscellars.com

Situated in an old dairy barn on a working ranch, Cayucos Cellars is the real-deal family-owned coastal winery. Only five people run every aspect of the business: winemaker Stuart Selkirk; his wife, Linda; his two sons, Clay and Ross; and his daughter, Paige. The tasting room is in downtown Cayucos—famous for beaches and surfers—because, as Stuart puts it, "We don't want anyone being flattened by a tractor." So put down your surfboard and visit the Selkirk family; you'll be glad you did. Cayucos Cellars Chardonnay 2007 was kept *sur lie* for two years in French oak before racking. It is a well-aged, round Chardonnay with medium straw coloring. It has aromas of baked brioche, fruit compote, and lemon curd and flavors of baked apples and poached pears. Cayucos Cellars Estate Barrel #2 Pinot Noir 2008 is cherry red with aromas of cherry confiture and vanilla. It is medium-bodied with delightful fresh and cooked fruit flavors and a pleasant finish that showcases a touch of allspice and cloves.

CHAMISAL VINEYARDS

7525 Orcutt Road, San Luis Obispo, CA 93401,
(805) 541-9463
www.chamisalvineyards.com

Named for the Chamise flowering shrub that grows wildly in the vineyard, Chamisal holds the distinction of being the first vineyard planted in the Edna Valley AVA, in 1973. The 80-acre property was part of the original Spanish land grant named Domaine Alfred and is currently planted with Chardonnay, Pinot Noir, Grenache, Pinot Gris, and Syrah vines. Winemaking has been under the direction of New Zealander Fintan du Fresne since 2006, and his wines have received accolades from a variety of publications. Chamisal Vineyards Central Coast Stainless Chardonnay 2011 is medium straw colored, with aromas of preserved Moroccan lemons, lemon blossom, butterscotch, and pineapple. In the mouth there are flavors of lemon curd, pineapples, and citrus blossom with nice heft on the palate and a refreshing acidic finish. Chamisal Estate Pinot Noir 2009 is cherry colored in the glass, with notes of red raspberry and cigar box in the bouquet. On the palate the fruit flavors are bright and balanced with a restrained, elegant finish.

CHATEAU MARGENE

4385 La Panza Road, Creston, CA 93432,
(805) 238-2321
www.chateaumargene.com

Businessman turned winemaker Mike Mooney's family history in Paso Robles goes back seven generations to a soldier in the 1775 expedition led by Juan Batista de Anza. Chateau Margene is named for Mike's wife, and together they produce well-crafted distinctive wines that are highly rated by numerous publications. Chateau Margene Cabernet Franc 2008 is composed of 80 percent Cabernet Franc and 20 percent Cabernet Sauvignon. It is ruby red in the glass, with aromas of black raspberry and bell pepper. Flavors of black cherry and cassis are present on the palate along with a touch of minerality. The balanced structure is delightful now, yet the grippy tannins make this a wine to lay down for a few years. Chateau Margene Beau Mélange 2007 is a blend of 45 percent Cabernet Sauvignon, 33 percent Cabernet Franc, and 22 percent Merlot. It is garnet with a purple rim and has notes of violet, lavender, and black fruit in the elegant bouquet. It has a smooth tannic finish with great black fruit flavors. When visiting the winery, make sure to ask for a sample of the sons' wines to taste the next generation of the family's wines.

CHRONIC CELLARS

2020 Nacimiento Lake Drive,
Paso Robles, CA 93446,
(805) 237-7848
www.chroniccellars.com

Josh and Jake Beckett grew up in Paso Robles wine country. After college they both did a stint at Peachy Canyon Winery and decided to open Chronic Cellars a few years later. When they're not making wine, you can find Josh surfing the waves and Jake tearing up the dirt on his cross-country motorcycle. All their wines have fun names. Chronic Cellars Sofa King Bueno (go ahead, say it fast) 2011 is a blend of 79 percent Syrah, 12 percent Mourvèdre, 5 percent Petite Sirah, and 4 percent Grenache. It is tattoo ink purple in color, with aromas of anise, dried herbs, and black fruits. In the mouth there are tastes of black plum, Christmas baking spices, and purple flowers. It's big and bold with supple tannins and a long finish. Chronic Cellars Dead Nuts 2011 is a blend of 37 percent Zinfandel, 26 percent Tempranillo, 24 percent Petite Sirah, and 13 percent Tannat. It has aromas of fresh dark fruits, cigar box, and freshly chopped toasted nuts. It's fleshy in the mouth with a finish of just-baked cherry pie.

CLAUTIERE VINEYARD

1340 Penman Springs Road, Paso Robles, CA 93446,
(805) 237-3789
www.clautiere.com

Serious winemaking and serious fun go hand in hand at Clautiere Vineyard. It was named one of *Wine Enthusiast*'s most unusual tasting rooms because of a "play-room" filled with wigs and hats, and visitors and guests have very little trouble letting their childish side come out, especially after a few glasses of wine. The brainchild of

Claudine Blackwell and Terry Brady, Clautiere Vineyard was founded in 1999 and is known in the area for its fun parties and great concerts. Clautiere Vineyards Estate BDX 2007 is a blend of 70 percent Cabernet Sauvignon, 20 percent Cabernet Franc, 5 percent Petit Verdot, and 5 percent Counoise. It has aromas of blueberry pie and dried black cherries and a whiff of cigar box. It is round in the mouth with a firm tannic finish. Clautiere Vineyards Syrah 2009 is inky purple, with notes of ripe red cherry and blueberry preserves in the bouquet. There is a nice touch of spice on the palate that comes through in the persistent finish.

CLAYHOUSE WINES

849 13th Street, Paso Robles, CA 93446,
(805) 238-7055
www.clayhousewines.com

Named for the 150-year-old adobe structure that sits in the middle of their vineyards, Clayhouse Wines was founded by fourth-generation agriculturist Rick Middleton and his family. Ben Mello manages the vineyard, and winemaking is overseen by Blake Kuhn. Clayhouse Estate Old Vine Petite Sirah 2010 is inky purple, with aromas of dried cherry, black raspberry confit, and cherry vanilla. It is medium-bodied in the mouth, with dark fruit flavors and chewy tannins. Clayhouse Estate Cuvée Blanc Red Cedar Vineyard 2011 is a blend of 70 percent Grenache and 30 percent Viognier. It has notes of white flowers, almond cookies, and citrus zest. Tropical fruit flavors come alive with a rich mouth presence and a finish that keeps inviting you in for another sip.

CLOS SOLÈNE

2815 Live Oak Road, Paso Robles, CA 93446,
(805) 296-0027
www.clossolene.com

When winemaker Guillaume Fabre met his future wife, Solène, in a tiny French village, it was, as he describes it, a *coup de foudre*—a lightning bolt—or love at first sight. Now, in a new country and years later, Guillaume crafts high-quality, limited-production wines using Bordeaux and Rhône varieties with his lovely muse at his side. We're big fans of their wines, which are highly rated by a number of prestigious wine publications.

Clos Solène L'Insolent 2010 is a blend of 60 percent Cabernet Sauvignon and 40 percent Petit Verdot. It has aromas of dark plums, cassis, and graphite in the complex bouquet. On the palate there are fresh fruit flavors and a touch of brown spice, with well-structured tannins in the luxuriously long finish. Clos Solène Hommage à Nos Pairs Reserve 2010 is Guillaume's homage to his mentors. It is composed of 95 percent Syrah, 3 percent Grenache, and 2 percent Mourvèdre, with a beautiful purple-garnet color. It has delightful aromas of violet, lavender, and ripe dark fruit that integrate seamlessly on the palate. This is a big, bold wine with restrained European elegance and a delicious Old World finish.

CROAD VINEYARDS

3550 Vinedo Robles Lane,
Paso Robles, CA 93446,
(805) 226-9899
www.croadvineyards.com

New Zealander Martin Croad is making solid wines with distinctive Kiwi flavor profiles from California vines planted in the early 1900s. He enjoys working with Zinfandel and Rhône varieties, including Syrah, Grenache, and Mourvèdre, as well as Sauvignon Blanc grapes that he uses to make a refreshing wine that brings us back to Marlborough with every sip. Croad Vineyards Sauvignon Blanc 2011 is pale straw colored with green reflections. It has aromas of Granny Smith apple and freshly zested lemon peel. It is crisp and clean in the mouth, a classic New Zealand–style Sauvignon Blanc. Croad Vineyards Syrah 2009 is purple ink colored, with notes of violet, cassis, and black pepper in the bouquet. In the mouth there are a ton of sweet fruit flavors and a pleasant fruit-filled finish.

CYPHER WINERY

3750 Highway 46 West, Templeton, CA 93465,
(805) 237-0055
www.cypherwinery.com

Co-owners Christian Tietje, aka ZinBitch, and Susan Mahler, the "Queen Executive

Officer," aka ZinPunk, make really great wines with totally funky names; just look at what they call themselves! After working together at the 140,000-cases-per-year Four Vines Winery, Christian and Susan longed to make petit-batch artisanal wines and run a smaller winery. Thus, the concept of Cypher Winery was born. Cypher Winery Freakshow ZinBitch Paso Robles Zinfandel 2010 has notes of violet, black raspberry, and dried cranberry in the bouquet. In the mouth flavors of blueberry pie and black raspberry mingle with good heft. The finish is smooth and velvety. Cypher Winery Freakshow Anarchy 2009 is a blend of Zinfandel, Mourvèdre, and Syrah. It is loaded with red and black fruits with a touch of baking spices and Mediterranean herbs. It is broad and generous on the palate with a lingering finish of dark ripe fruit in the back of your throat.

DERBY WINE ESTATES

5620 Highway 46 East, Paso Robles, CA 93447, (805) 238-6911
www.derbywineestates.com

Thinking of their retirement, Pam and Ray Derby relocated to the Central Coast in the early 1990s, but as luck would have it, they purchased their first vineyard in 1998 and then another a few years later until all thoughts of a sedentary lifestyle were dashed. They use only 10 percent of the grapes that they grow to make Derby wines, with the remaining 90 percent sold to neighboring wineries. Derby Wine Estates Derbyshire Vineyard Pinot Gris 2011 is pale straw colored, with aromas of Anjou pear and honeysuckle and flavors of pear cobbler and lemon curd.

EBERLE WINERY

3810 California 46, Paso Robles, CA 93446, (805) 238-9607
www.eberlewinery.com

Gary Eberle started his wine career in 1973 while working at his family's Estrella River Winery. In 1980 he was one of the men responsible for establishing the Paso Robles AVA, and in 1983 he founded his eponymous winery. He currently produces 25,000 cases of wine that are consistently showered with glowing accolades by the leading wine publications. In 1992 Gary oversaw the excavation of a 17,000-square-foot underground cave in which to age his red wines. We had the pleasure of having dinner with Gary, and he explained that the name Eberle translates to "small wild boar" in German. He went on to tell us about the bronze boar fountain at his winery where guests rub the nose for good luck and toss a few coins. Given this man's generous spirit, it was not a surprise to hear that all the money collected is donated to local children's charities. Eberle Winery produces wine from a large number of varieties, including Chardonnay, Viognier, Syrah, Sangiovese, Barbera, Zinfandel, and Cabernet Sauvignon, among others. Eberle Winery Estate Cabernet Sauvignon 2009 is garnet with a violet rim. In the nose there are notes of blackberry, dried cherry, graphite, and slate. The finish has great fruit, a balanced tannic structure, and a persistent finish. We were amazed when Gary pulled a bottle of his 1980 Estate Cabernet Sauvignon from beneath the table and pulled the cork. If anyone at the table had ever had any doubts about the ageability of Paso Robles Cabernets, those myths were quickly dispelled by this amazingly fresh and young-tasting wine. Our tasting note consisted of only one word—"WOW"—scribbled in our notebook.

EPOCH ESTATE WINES

7505 York Mountain Road, Templeton, CA 93465,
(805) 237-7575
www.epochwines.com

We were lucky enough to sit with the charming, talented, and beautiful winemaker Jordan Fiorentini while we tasted her wines at a shaded picnic table perched high on a hill overlooking Epoch Estate vineyards. Epoch Estate is owned by geologists Liz and Bill Armstrong, who fell in love with the area and the Paderewski Vineyards named for former owner and famed Polish pianist Ignace Jan Paderewski. Justin Smith of Saxum is the consulting winemaker, and Tim and Diana Rovenstine are the ranch managers. Epoch Estate Wines Ingenuity 2010 is a blend of 62 percent Syrah, 14 percent Mourvèdre, 12 percent Grenache, and 12 percent Petite Sirah. It is dark purple, with aromas of big fruit and seductive notes of brown spice and Mediterranean herbs. In the mouth the fruit flavors burst on the tongue with a heightened level of lusciousness before the well-integrated tannins wipe the mouth clean for the next sip. Epoch Estates Block B Syrah 2010 is bright garnet, with aromas of fresh black cherries. Flavors of ripe fruit, black pepper, cherry, and blackberry entice the tongue with secondary notes of lavender and rosemary. The finish is long and elegant.

GIORNATA WINES

3855 High Grove Road, Templeton, CA 93465,
(805) 434-3075
www.giornatawines.com

Giornata Wines is the lifelong dream of Brian Terrizzi and his wife, Stephanie. Brian's previous experience included making wine at Rosenblum Cellars and Isole e Olena in Italy. We had the chance to sit down with Brian and enjoy his wines, many of them made from Italian grape varieties, with delicious Italian cuisine, and we couldn't help feeling like we were sitting in a Tuscan hillside village. One of our favorite wines was made from Nebbiolo. Giornata Luna Matta Vineyard Paso Robles Nebbiolo 2009 has notes of black cherry, cigar box, cranberry, and tar in the bouquet. In the mouth there are flavors of dark cherry, saddle leather, cranberry juice, and Indian spice. The finish is elegant and persistent.

HALTER RANCH VINEYARD

8910 Adelaida Road, Paso Robles, CA 93446,
(805) 226-9455
www.halterranch.com

Founded by Hansjörg Wyss in 2000, Halter Ranch has grown from the original 40 acres to its current 280 acres of vines planted amid this beautiful 1,000-acre ranch. There are over twenty varieties planted in fifty-seven separate vineyard blocks, including most Bordeaux and Rhône varieties. Winemaking has been under the direction of Kevin Sass since 2011. Halter Ranch Vineyard Cabernet Sauvignon 2008 is composed of 81 percent Cabernet Sauvignon, 9 percent Petit Verdot, 5 percent Malbec, 3 percent Merlot, and 2 percent Cabernet Franc. It is dark ruby garnet, with aromas of Mediterranean spices, cassis, and black raspberry. In the mouth it has black fruit flavors—especially black plum—and a rounded, velvety tannic finish. Halter Ranch Vineyard Côtes de Paso 2010 is a blend of 48 percent Grenache, 20 percent Mourvèdre, 17 percent Syrah, 11 percent Tannat, and 4 percent Counoise. This southern Rhône-style blend is ruby colored, with notes of dark fruit, espresso, rose petals, and oregano in the bouquet. On the palate dark fruit flavors are framed nicely by oak, and the finish is persistent and elegant.

HAMMERSKY VINEYARDS AND INN

7725 Vineyard Drive, Paso Robles, CA 93446,
(949) 338-7813
www.hammersky.com

Named for the family's two young sons, Hamilton and Skyler, HammerSky Vineyards were planted in 1997 by dentist Douglas Hauck and his wife, Kim. The family members concentrate on Bordeaux varieties and pride themselves on their Bordeaux-style blends. The on-premise inn is a great place to stay and is very popular for wedding parties. HammerSky Vineyards Estate Grown Party of Four 2009 is garnet purple, with aromas of black raspberry, black plum, anise, and vanilla. It is smooth on entry with ripe fruit flavors and a persistent finish. HammerSky Vineyards Estate Grown Red Handed 2009 is ruby garnet, with aromas of red plums, cloves, and red raspberry. It is fruit-forward on the palate with a pleasant tannic grip in the finish.

HEARST RANCH WINERY

442 SLO San Simeon Road,
San Simeon, CA 93452,
(805) 927-4100
www.hearstranchwinery.com

The first time we arrived at Hearst Ranch Winery to meet Steve Hearst and taste his wines, the very first thing he said to us was, "Hop in the pickup—let's go for a ride." Not ones to say no to the publishing magnate turned winery owner, we jumped into the cab of his truck and enjoyed a personalized tour of his cattle ranch, the Pacific Coast Highway, and San Simeon Point. We've returned many times to visit Steve and his business partner, Jim Saunders, and are big fans of their wines. The winery's tasting room is inside the historic Sebastian's General Store that continues to supply groceries and basic necessities to fisherman, campers, and tourists, and the grapes are sourced from Saunders Vineyard in Paso Robles. Hearst Ranch Wines have garnered numerous medals and "best in show" awards. Hearst Ranch Winery Glacier Ridge Chardonnay 2011 is luminescent gold-colored, with aromas of citrus blossoms, tropical fruits, and a touch of vanilla. It has nice heft on the palate with flavors of caramelized pineapple, lemon curd, and bright lemon zest in the pleasant finish. Hearst Ranch Winery The Point is composed of 60 percent Cabernet Sauvignon, 14 percent Merlot, 9 percent Cabernet Franc, 9 percent Petit Verdot, and 8 percent Petite Sirah. It is inky garnet, with complex aromas of black raspberry, black currant, smoked meats, and brown baking spices. In the mouth the fruit flavors come to life seamlessly with notes of freshly baked cherry pie and cherry cola before the ripe tannic finish.

HOPE FAMILY WINES

PO Box 3260, Paso Robles, CA 93447,
(805) 238-6979
www.hopefamilywines.com

When the Hope family moved to Paso Robles over 30 years ago, they planted grapevines and apple orchards. Although their apple orchards are long gone, the Hope family continues to concentrate on making quality wines from Cabernet Sauvignon, Merlot, Syrah, Mourvèdre, and Grenache grapes. Austin Hope is the president and head winemaker, and Jason Diefenderfer is the winemaker. Hope Family Wines consists of five individual brands: Troublemaker, Austin Hope, Treana, Liberty School, and Candor. Hope Family Wines Treana Red 2009 is 70 percent Cabernet Sauvignon and 30 percent Syrah; it is inky purple, with aromas of red and black fruits and purple flowers. It is fruit-driven on the palate with a touch of spice on the finish. Hope Family Wines Liberty School Cabernet Sauvignon 2010 is garnet colored, with fragrances of dark cherry, black fruit, and purple flowers. There are bright fruit and nice spice notes on the palate.

J. LOHR

6169 Airport Road, Paso Robles, CA 93446,
(805) 239-8900
www.jlohr.com

Raised in a South Dakota farming family, Jerry Lohr began searching for potential vineyard sites in California in the late 1960s and acquired his first vineyard in Monterey County in 1971. In 1986 he began planting in Paso Robles, and today he has more than 2,000 acres of vineyards there, 900 acres in Monterey, and 33 acres in the Napa Valley. In 2001 the J. Lohr Paso Robles Wine Center opened its doors, and visitors are treated to expansive views over estate-owned vineyards. J. Lohr Estates Seven Oaks Paso Robles Cabernet Sauvignon 2010 is a blend of 76 percent Cabernet Sauvignon, 12 percent Merlot, 5 percent Petit Verdot, 4 percent Petite Sirah, and 1 percent Syrah and is inky purple and dark red in the glass. It has notes of ripe black raspberries and blueberries. It is big in the mouth with a generous heft and a lingering finish. J. Lohr Cuvée Paso Robles Cuvée Pau 2009 is composed of 73 percent Cabernet Sauvignon, 15 percent Malbec, 10 percent Petit Verdot, and 2 percent Cabernet Franc. It is garnet colored, with aromas of black plums and black currant. It is fruit-forward on the palate with a bright finish of red cherry.

JACK CREEK CELLARS

5265 Jack Creek Road,
Paso Robles, CA 93446,
(805) 226-8283
www.jackcreekcellars.com

Doug and Sabrina Kruse purchased their initial 75 acres on Jack Creek Road in 1997 and started planting Chardonnay, Pinot Noir, Grenache, and Syrah vines. Their vineyards are on the southern end of the Santa Lucia Mountain Range approximately seven miles

from the coast, giving them a unique microclimate in which to grow their grapes.

We had the pleasure of tasting Doug and Sabrina's wines at their newly renovated home with stunning views over the vineyards. The couple is very talented as winemakers and could not be any nicer to have a glass of wine with. Jack Creek Cellars Concrete Blond 2010 is straw yellow, with aromas of tropical fruits and caramelized pineapple. It is aged on concrete and sees no oak at all. It provides a fair amount of acid in the mouth, which makes this a perfect wine to pair with lighter cuisine and seafood. Jack Creek Cellars Stained Pinot Noir 2010 is the inaugural vintage from the estate's vineyard. There are strong aromas of freshly picked red cherries and dried black cherry. In the mouth it is very balanced and has an elegant mouthfeel. The finish is lingering with a pleasant sensation of milk chocolate and spice.

JUSTIN VINEYARDS & WINERY

11680 Chimney Rock Road, Paso Robles, CA 93446,
(805) 591-3200
www.justinwine.com

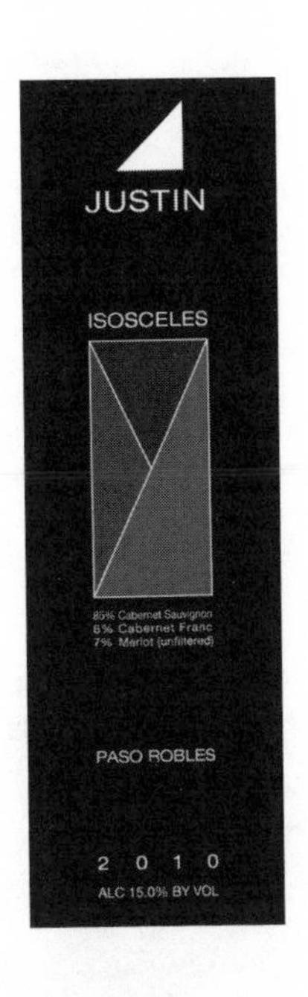

Justin Vineyards & Winery was founded in 1981 by Justin Baldwin, who had the vision and drive to produce quality Central Coast wines from the major Bordeaux varieties. Justin's wines have received numerous accolades from *Wine Spectator*, *Wine Enthusiast*, *Wine Advocate*, and *Decanter* and continue to delight critics and collectors alike. The property has beautiful accommodations—the Just Inn B&B—and offers a world-class dining experience at The Restaurant at Justin. Justin

Vineyards & Winery Isosceles 2010 is bright ruby garnet. It is composed of 85 percent Cabernet Sauvignon, 8 percent Cabernet Franc, and 7 percent Merlot. It has notes of dark black cherry, anise, and cigar box in the complex bouquet. In the mouth there are flavors of dark fruits, black currants, mocha, and a touch of lifted eucalyptus on the persistent finish. Drink it now or over the next 10 years.

KENNETH VOLK VINEYARDS

2485 Highway 46 West, Paso Robles, CA 93446, (805) 237-7896
www.volkwines.com

Ken Volk started making wine in the Central Coast in the 1970s and released his first commercial Pinot Noir for Wild Horse Winery in 1983. He is well known in Paso Robles and the Santa Maria Valley for crafting world-class wines from Chardonnay and Pinot Noir grapes, and just recently he has begun to release wines under his own name. We have had the opportunity to have dinner with this quiet and modest small-batch artisanal producer in Paso Robles and in New York City. Although Ken's winery is in Santa Maria, he has no problem crossing county lines and maintains an inviting tasting room in Paso Robles. Kenneth Volk Vineyards Jaybird Chardonnay 2011 is straw colored, with aromas of green apple, lemon blossom, and red grapefruit zest. In the mouth flavors of tropical fruits, apple, and Anjou pear lead up to a crisp, clean finish with just the right touch of minerality. Kenneth Volk Vineyards Touriga Nacional 2010 is garnet colored with a purple rim. It has aromas of dark fruit, black cherries, violet, and lavender. It has a smooth tannic structure, nice body, and a pleasant acidic finish that makes it a perfect food-friendly wine.

KUKKULA WINERY

9515 Chimney Rock Road, Paso Robles, CA 93446, (805) 227-0111
www.kukkulawine.com

Named for the Finnish word for "hill or high place," Kukkula consists of 80 acres of land with 29 acres under vine, 34 acres with mature walnut trees, and 8 acres with olive trees. The ultra-modern Kukkula Winery

was completed in 2010. Owner Kevin Jussila first fell in love with winemaking when he and two friends purchased a half ton of Russian River Valley Pinot Noir in 1991, but a 1995 vacation in Provence sealed his fate as a winemaker. We enjoyed tasting Kevin's wines over dinner in Paso Robles. Kukkula Sisu 2010 is a blend of Grenache, Syrah, and Mourvèdre and has aromas of purple flowers, anise, baking spices, and black raspberry. It has wonderful complexity in the mouth with flavors of black fruits and bramble with sweet, smooth tannins. Kukkula i.p.o. Paso Robles 2008 is a blend of Cabernet Sauvignon, Syrah, and Zinfandel. It is garnet purplish in color, with aromas of black cherry preserves, cassis, and anise. It is juicy in the mouth with sweet fruit flavors and a touch of spice in the persistent finish.

L'AVENTURE

2815 Live Oak Road, Paso Robles, CA 93446, (805) 227-1588
www.aventurewine.com

Stephan Asseo was educated in Macon, Burgundy, and in 1982 he and his family purchased Château Robin and Château Fleur Cardinale in Bordeaux. After honing his winemaking skills in France for 15 years, he fell in love with Paso Robles in 1996, began a new adventure in his life, and established L'Aventure Winery. L'Aventure Estate Rosé 2011 is composed of 70 percent Syrah, 20 percent Mourvèdre, and 10 percent Grenache. The color is gray pink, like a true Vin Gris, and there are aromas of fresh strawberry and strawberry conserves in the bouquet. In the mouth there is more heft than one would expect from a rosé, but then again, this is a wine that will stand up to food. L'Aventure Optimus 2010 is a blend of 55 percent Syrah, 27 percent Cabernet

Sauvignon, and 18 percent Petit Verdot. It has heady aromas of fresh red raspberries, black cherry, and cocoa powder. It is fruity on the palate with a touch of black pepper in the finish.

LAZARRE WINES

5678 Lone Pine Place, Paso Robles, CA 93446, (831) 402-1153
www.lazarrewines.com

Adam LaZarre has always been a behind-the-scenes kind of guy, and with a mere 20 years of experience in winemaking, he is also one of the most frequently awarded winemakers, having won three "best of show" awards at the prestigious Los Angles International Wine Competition. He has been named "Winemaker of the Year" by the *Sacramento Bee* and "One of the Top Five Winemakers" in the *San Francisco Chronicle*. Adam has made wine for *American Idol* producers Nigel Lythgoe and Ken Warwick as well as Hahn Estates. We have tasted Adam's wines many times over the years and feel that this is one winemaker to keep your eye on. LaZarre Albariño 2011 is pale straw, with aromas of Anjou pear, Granny Smith apple, and white stone fruits. It is big in the mouth with nice heft—it has rich, ripe flavors with just a touch of fruit sweetness before the elegant dry finish. This is one of those wines that keep inviting you in for another and another sip. LaZarre Central Coast Pinot Noir 2010 is cherry red, with aromas of red raspberry, cherry cola, wet leaves, and dried black cherries. It is smooth upon entry into the mouth with big fruit flavors, restrained and elegant acidity, and a luxurious, velvety finish.

LINNE CALODO

3030 Vineyard Drive, Paso Robles, CA 93446, (805) 227-0797
www.linnecalodo.com

Founded by Matt and Maureen Trevisan in 1998, Linne Calodo has a cult following in the Central Coast, and for good reason—they're making some pretty exceptional wines. The family lives among the vines, so there's no use of harmful chemicals, and Matt is the grape grower and winemaker. Linne Calodo wines have been well rated by wine lovers and experts alike. Linne Calodo Cherry Red 2010 is a blend of 70 percent Zinfandel, 20 percent Mourvèdre, and 10 percent Syrah. It is garnet purple, with aromas of rich ripe red and black fruits with just a touch of dried herbs. It is full-bodied in the mouth with a persistent finish. Drink it now or through 2018. Linne Calodo Problem Child is composed of 77 percent Zinfandel, 16 percent Syrah, and 7 percent Mourvèdre. It has notes of violets, dried lavender, black plums, and dark fruits that move from the bouquet to the palate seamlessly. The finish is long and luscious and invites you in for another sip.

MIDNIGHT CELLARS WINERY & VINEYARD

2925 Anderson Road, Paso Robles, CA 93446,
(805) 239-8904
www.midnightcellars.com

After a family vacation in 1995, three generations of the Hartenberger family gave up harsh Chicago winters and purchased a 160-acre ranch in Paso Robles. Twenty-eight acres are under plantation with Cabernet Sauvignon, Petit Verdot, Merlot, Chardonnay, and Zinfandel vines. Midnight Cellars Winery & Vineyard Estate Zinfandel 2009 is inky garnet colored, with aromas of dried tarragon, dried cherries, and dark chocolate. In the mouth are flavors of bright fruit with sweet tannins and a bright acidic lift on the finish. Midnight Cellars Winery & Vineyard Mare Nectaris Reserve Red Wine 2007 is inky purple violet, with aromas of violet talc, black plum, and a touch of forest floor in the bouquet. It is a blend of 50 percent Cabernet Sauvignon, 16 percent Merlot, 16 percent Malbec, 9 percent Cabernet Franc, and 9 percent Petit Verdot, and it has flavors of black fruit, black pepper, and dried thyme on the palate before the luxurious, balanced tannic finish.

NINER WINE ESTATES

2400 Highway 46 West, Paso Robles, CA 93446,
(805) 239-2233
www.ninerwine.com

Princeton and Harvard Business School graduate Dick Niner started Niner Wine Estates in 2001 with his acquisition of the 224-acre Bootjack Ranch and the purchase of the

130-acre Heart Hill Vineyard two years later. Varieties planted include Petite Sirah, Cabernet Sauvignon, Merlot, Syrah, Sangiovese, Barbera, and Sauvignon Blanc. Niner Wine Estate Bootjack Ranch Estate Bottled Sangiovese 2010 is ruby garnet, with aromas of cranberry, cherry, and freshly brewed coffee. In the mouth it has flavors of black fruits, blackberry, brown spice, coffee, and mocha. Niner Wine Estates Bootjack Ranch Cabernet Sauvignon 2009 is dark purple with aromas of black cherry, sage, and cherry cola. It has flavors of red fruits, purple flowers, and smoked meats across the midpalate and fresh Greek herbs in the post palate.

PEACHY CANYON WINERY

2025 Nacimiento Lake Drive,
Paso Robles, CA 93446,
(805) 237-1577
www.peachycanyon.com

Established in 1982 by Doug and Nancy Beckett, Peachy Canyon currently has 100 acres of estate vineyards and long-term contracts with over twenty growers to source enough grapes to make 64,000 cases of wine annually. Peachy Canyon was one of the first wineries in the Paso Robles area and over the years has served as the proving ground for many young up-and-coming winemakers to hone their craft. Peachy Canyon Chardonnay 2011 is light straw colored, with aromas of candied orange peel and citrus blossoms. In the mouth there are flavors of caramelized pineapple and white stone fruits. Peachy Canyon Incredible Red Zinfandel 2011 has notes of fresh strawberry and dried black cherry in the bouquet. On the palate there are soft notes of ripe fruit, a touch of saddle leather, and a persistent taste of anise and licorice in the finish.

PIPESTONE VINEYARDS

2040 Niderer Road,
Paso Robles, CA 93446
(805) 227-6385
www.pipestonevineyards.com

Jeff Pipes left a career in environmental law and environmental engineering to grow grapes in Paso Robles and start Pipestone Vineyards with his wife, Florence, a former fashion designer.

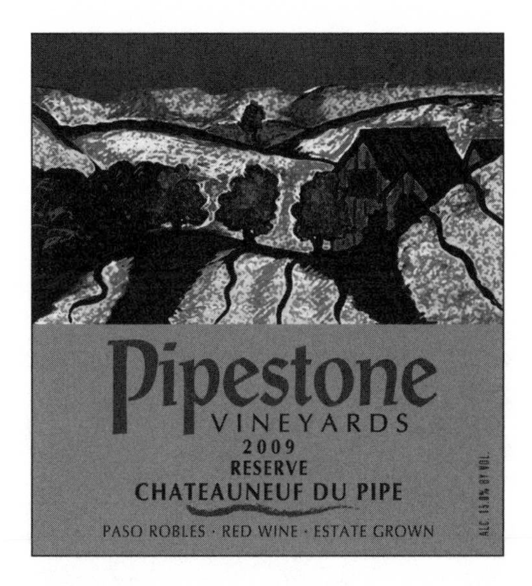

The vineyards are laid out according to the principals of feng shui and are plowed with two draft horses. The vineyard is a certified wildlife habitat, and the winery is solar-powered. Pipestone Vineyards Estate Syrah 2008 is inky purple and has aromas of violet, smoked meats, and black fruits. It is generous in the mouth with a nice balance between depth and brightness. Pipestone Vineyards Reserve Chateauneuf du Pipe is ironically named and is a self-described "super-Rhône." It is deep cherry red, with aromas of fruits of the wood and Mediterranean herbs. It fills the mouth with flavors of blackberry, cassis, and smoked meats.

POMAR JUNCTION VINEYARD AND WINERY

5036 South El Pomar,
Templeton, CA 93465, (805) 238-9940
www.pomarjunction.com

The Merrill family grew grapes for other wineries for more than 30 years before they decided to make and sell their own wines. Today the vineyards remain under the direction of Dana and Marsha; son Matthew acts as the general manager, and Jim Shumate handles the winemaking. Pomar Junction Vineyard and Winery Syrah Rosé 2012 is medium blush-colored and is composed of 95 percent Syrah, 4 percent Viognier, and 1 percent Mourvèdre. It has aromas of freshly picked strawberries and ripe cherry juice. In the mouth there are flavors of cherry vanilla and soft Mediterranean herbs as well as balanced acidity and a touch of salinity. Pomar Junction Vineyard and Winery Train

Wreck 2010 is a blend of 28 percent Cabernet Sauvignon, 28 percent Petite Sirah, 28 percent Zinfandel, 14 percent Syrah, and 2 percent Mourvèdre. It is dark garnet with aromas of blackberry, cassis, mocha, and violet talc. The flavors are a mix of black cherry, tart red cherry, and pomegranate with smooth tannins and an acidic lift on the finish.

RANCHERO CELLARS

No visitor facilities.
(805) 423-3765
www.rancherocellars.com

Amy Jean Butler has made wine for venerated Napa wineries and new ventures in Paso Robles for over 16 years. We have met with Amy a few times over the last few years and are always impressed by her winemaking skills, intense modesty, and wry sense of humor. She's the real deal, and we've got our eye on her for continued greatness in the future. Over a recent dinner we shared a few of her wines and love her new blend, simply called Chrome. Ranchero Cellars La Vista Vineyard Chrome 2011 is a blend of 92 percent Grenache Blanc and 8 percent Viognier. It is pale straw, with aromas of citrus blossom and white flowers. It is delightful in the mouth, with superb roundness and balanced acidity that keeps inviting you in for another sip.

ROBERT HALL WINERY

3443 Mill Road,
Paso Robles, CA 93446,
(805) 239-1616
www.roberthallwinery.com

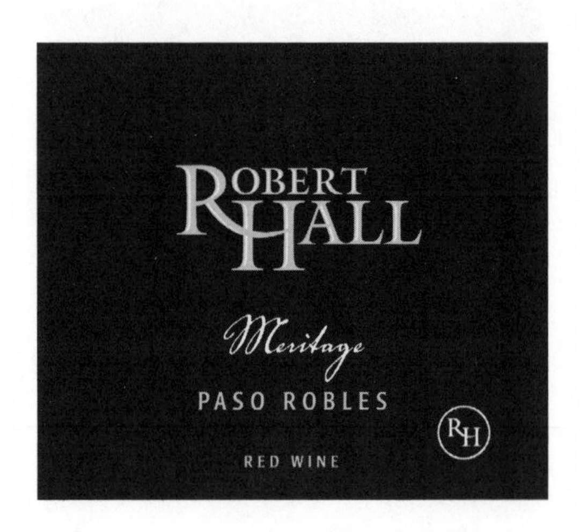

Native Minnesotan Robert L. Hall fell in love with the idea of making wine on a family vacation to France in the 1970s, but it wasn't until 1995 that he found his perfect piece of land in Paso Robles. His acquisition of the Home Ranch was soon joined by the purchase of the Terrace and Bench vineyards. Robert Hall Winery has a worthwhile visitor experience and is architecturally beautiful with an amphitheater and plenty of areas for weddings and corporate celebrations. Robert Hall Winery Merlot 2010 is garnet colored and is composed of 84 percent Merlot, 12 percent Cabernet Franc, and 4 percent Petite

Sirah. It has aromas of black raspberries and black currants. In the mouth the fruit flavors are accentuated by nuances of dried tobacco leaves and forest floor. The finish is silky soft and persistent. Robert Hall Winery Meritage 2010 is a blend of 50 percent Cabernet Sauvignon, 41 percent Merlot, 8 percent Petit Verdot, and 1 percent Cabernet Franc. It is barrel-aged for 18 months and is ruby red in color. It has notes of cassis, black plum, and cigar box in the bouquet. On the palate it has intense dark fruit flavors and smooth yet firm tannins. The finish is long-lasting and elegant.

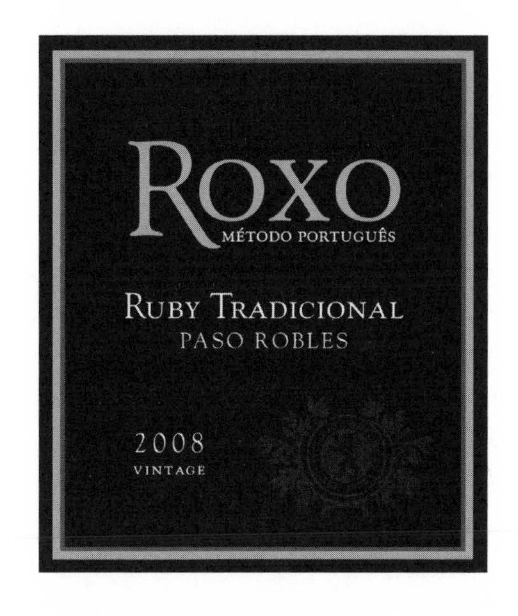

ROXO PORT CELLARS

6996 Peachy Canyon Road,
Paso Robles, CA 93446,
(805) 464 0922
www.roxocellars.com

Founded by Jeff and Kim Steele in 2005, Roxo Port Cellars produces only sweet port-style wines. Fruit is sourced from Paso Robles, San Luis Obispo, and Cienega Valley, and the wines are made in the traditional *Método Português*. When you visit, you just might find Jeff enjoying a fine cigar and port on the front porch of the tasting room that they share with Chateau Margene and Limerock Orchards. Roxo Ruby Tradicional Paso Robles 2008 is composed of 35 percent Touriga Nacional, 35 percent Tinta Roriz, 16 percent Souzão, and 14 percent Bastardo. It is deep ruby red, with aromas of mocha, blueberry pie, and espresso in the bouquet. It is soft and smooth in the mouth with lingering dark berry flavors and a nice touch of warmth at the back of the throat. Roxo Magia Preta Paso Robles 2008 is composed of 50 percent Cabernet Sauvignon and 50 percent Syrah and is extremely dark colored like the "black magic" for which it was named. The nose has subtle cigar box, dark plum, and dark berry notes. In the mouth fruit flavors are framed by a touch of cedar and dark chocolate.

SAXUM VINEYARDS

2810 Willow Creek Road, Paso Robles, CA 93446,
(805) 610-0363
www.saxumvineyards.com

Named for the Latin word for "stone," Saxum was founded by Justin Smith in 2002, and in a few short years Smith's wines have developed a legendary cult following. He keeps his production between 3,000 and 4,000 cases per year and uses grapes from his family's James Berry Vineyard as well as Paderewski Vineyard, Heart Stone Vineyard, Terry Hoage Vineyard, and Booker Vineyards. His Saxum James Berry 2007 won number one wine of the year at the 2010 *Wine Spectator* tasting. Saxum James Berry Vineyard 2010 is a blend of 52 percent Grenache, 26 percent Mourvèdre, and 22 percent Syrah. It is garnet purple, with aromas of red plum, black raspberry, freshly ground black pepper, and brown spice. It has sweet fruit flavors in the mouth with nicely gripping tannins and a long finish.

SCULPTERRA WINERY

5015 Linne Road, Paso Robles, CA 93446,
(888) 302-8881
www.sculpterra.com

New York–educated Warren Frankel practiced medicine for years before moving to Paso Robles in 1979. He and his wife, Kathy, were

searching for a simpler life and began planting pistachio trees and Cabernet Sauvignon vines. In 1997 they expanded their vineyards with the addition of 20 acres of Merlot and Zinfandel. Their winery was completed in 2007, and visitors can enjoy beautifully manicured gardens featuring sculptures by the artist John Jagger. Dr. Frankel and his wife are very involved in charitable organizations, and a portion of their wine profits go to His Healing Hands.

Sculpterra Winery and Sculpture Garden Paso Robles Cabernet Sauvignon 2008 is dark garnet with a violet rim. It has aromas of eucalyptus, cedar, and toasted brioche over notes of red raspberries and pomegranate juice. In the mouth the fruit flavors mingle with chocolate and mocha to produce a smooth and velvety wine. Sculpterra Statuesque 2010 is a blend of 34 percent Cabernet Sauvignon, 33 percent Syrah, and 33 percent Petite Sirah. It is inky purple with aromas of cedar, eucalyptus, black cherry juice, and black plum. There are flavors of black raspberries, espresso, black cherries, and dark chocolate in the mouth before the bright tannic finish.

SINOR-LAVALLEE WINES

PO Box 701, Arroyo Grande, CA 93421,
(805) 801-2502
www.sinorlavallee.com

Mike Sinor and Cheri LaVallee-Sinor met while attending college in San Luis Obispo and began working at local wineries. They freely admit that the "wine bug hit us hard, but the Pinot Noir bug hit us even harder." Their dedication to Pinot Noir skews slightly fanatical, so much so that the couple was married in Burgundy, the indisputable land of their favorite grape. Mike has been known as one of the Central Coast's highest-rated winemakers, and in 2012 he was voted Winemaker of the Year for San Luis Obispo County. Sinor-LaVallee Pinot Gris 2012 is pale straw colored, with lifted floral top notes over heady aromas of white stone fruit and citrus blossom. It is generous in the mouth with refreshing acidity and a crisp, clean finish. Sinor-LaVallee Pinot Noir 2011 has delightful aromas of red cherries, red raspberries, and ultra-fine cocoa powder. It is fruity in the mouth with restrained elegance and a touch of mocha in the persistent finish.

STARR RANCH VINEYARDS

9320 Chimney Rock Road,
Paso Robles, CA 93446,
(805) 227-0144
www.starr-ranch.com

Although she was born and raised on the East Coast, Judy Starr pulled up roots in 2000 and moved her family to the hills of Adelaida to grow grapes. Today her family members continue to grow grapes, but they have also started making their own quality wine. We had a chance to sit down with Judy over dinner in downtown Paso Robles and taste her delicious wine, but she promised that the next time we visit we can spend a weekend in her luxuriously appointed Airstream camper parked in the middle of her vineyards—and you can too. Starr Ranch Vineyards Reserve Syrah 2009 is inky purple, with aromas of blackberry and black plums. It is generous in the mouth, with flavors of black cherry, dried plums, and a touch of chocolate on the finish. Starr Ranch Vineyards Marriage 2010 is a blend of 50 percent Cabernet Sauvignon and 50 percent Merlot and was blended by Judy for her son's wedding. It has rich flavors of ripe red and black fruits with a touch of anise and black pepper in the finish. It has good body in the mouth with pleasant acidity.

STEINBECK VINEYARDS AND WINERY

5940 Union Road,
Paso Robles, CA 93446,
(805) 238-1854
www.steinbeckwines.com

We visited Howie Steinbeck and his daughter, Cindy, to sample wine in their tasting room, but before we knew it, we were riding shotgun in the family's 1958 vintage jeep through the vineyards. If jeep rides are your thing, make sure to join Howie and Cindy on one of their crash courses and learn more about their style of winemaking up close and personal. The Steinbeck Vineyard is the site of a 1956 historic B-26 plane crash that claimed the life of one airman while four others parachuted to safety. Steinbeck Vineyards The Crash 2008 is made in homage to that fateful day. It is a blend of Cabernet Sauvignon, Zinfandel, Merlot, Viognier, and Petite Sirah. It has aromas of freshly baked cherry pie, brown spice, and fresh red fruit in the bouquet. In the mouth the fruit flavors mingle with tastes of mocha and dark chocolate. The finish is long and supple. We found it very interesting that Steinbeck Vineyards uses only 1 percent of the grapes they grow to make their quality wine and sells the other 99 percent to neighboring wineries. Steinbeck Vineyards and Winery Viognier 2010 is medium straw colored, with aromas of lemon zest and green apple. It is creamy in the mouth with a delightful acidic finish.

TABLAS CREEK VINEYARD

9339 Adelaida Road,
Paso Robles, CA 93446,
(805) 237-1231
www.tablascreek.com

Founded in 1985, Tablas Creek Vineyard is a partnership between Robert Haas and the Perrin family of Château de Beaucastel. In 1989 they purchased 120 acres of West Paso Robles land because of its similarities to Châteauneuf-du-Pape. Today, Tablas Creek is known for excellent varietal representation from its Grenache, Syrah, Mourvèdre, Counoise, Marsanne, Viognier, Grenache Blanc, and Roussanne vines. Tablas Creek Vineyard Grenache Blanc 2011 is pale straw colored, with aromas of licorice, green apple, and pear that slide seamlessly onto the palate. There is a crisp mouthfeel with bright acidity and a touch of salinity on the finish. Tablas Creek Vineyard Counoise 2010 has notes of Mission fig, smoked meats, and black fruits in the bouquet. On the palate there are flavors of subdued citrus and cherry cola. The finish is pleasantly tart, making this a perfect companion for grilled meats and barbecue.

TERRY HOAGE VINEYARDS

870 Arbor Road, Paso Robles, CA 93446,
(805) 238-2083
www.terryhoagevineyards.com

Professional football player Terry Hoage moved to Paso Robles to give his family a better life after playing for six teams in the NFL. Now he and his wife, Jennifer, as well as their family team up to produce some delicious Paso wines. Jennifer and Terry share the

duties of viticulturist and winemaker, and Jennifer is proud to say, "If you like the wine, she made it, and if you don't like the wine, Terry made it." We're already fans of Terry's football career and bigger fans of his wines, so we reckon that makes us fans of Jennifer as well. The Hoages have 17 acres under vines, use organic farming principles, and produce about 2,500 cases per year. Terry and Jennifer are very involved in Must! Charities, and $1 from the sale of each bottle goes to the organization. Terry Hoage Skins Grenache 2006 is garnet colored, with aromas of black cherry, toast, and anise. In the mouth there are big fruit flavors and nuances of cherry cola and dried herbs. Terry Hoage The "46" 2009 is a blend of 50 percent Grenache and 50 percent Syrah. It is cherry red to garnet colored, with aromas of red fruit, eucalyptus, cocoa powder, and talc. On the palate there are big flavors of sweet red fruits and sweet-supple tannins before the long finish.

THACHER WINERY

8355 Vineyard Drive, Paso Robles, CA 93446,
(805) 237-0087
www.thacherwinery.com

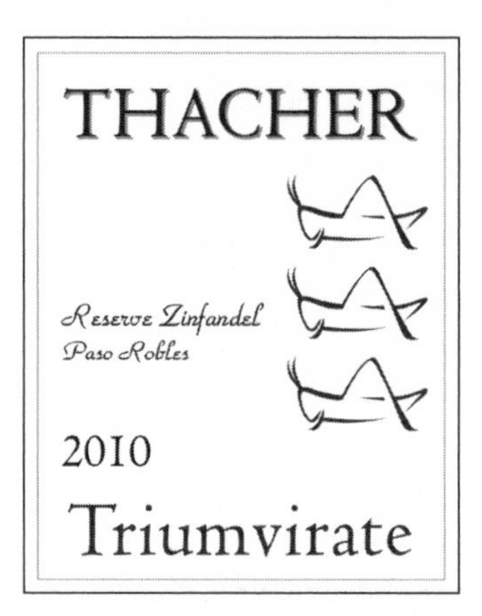

Sherman and Michelle Thacher fell in love with Paso Robles when they attended a 2003 wedding at the Kentucky Ranch, and when the ranch came on the market shortly thereafter, they purchased it and moved from Santa Cruz. Sherman graduated from UC Davis and worked as a beer brewmaster until his first grape harvest and vintage in 2004. Thacher Winery Paso Robles Controlled Chaos 2010 is a blend of 47 percent Mourvèdre, 42 percent Zinfandel, and 11 percent Grenache. It is medium garnet, with aromas of dried Greek herbs and black figs. In the mouth there is a mix of red and black fruits with a sweet, soft tannic finish. Thacher Triumvirate Reserve Zinfandel 2010 is inky garnet, with aromas of red raspberry and fire-roasted red pepper. There are flavors of rich fruit, spice, and milk chocolate before the round tannic finish.

TOBIN JAMES CELLARS

8950 Union Road, Paso Robles, CA 93446,
(805) 239-2204
www.tobinjames.com

When you walk into the tasting room, you can't help feeling that have entered a saloon on the set of an old-fashioned Western movie. And there's good reason: Tobin James Cellars is built on the site of a former stagecoach stop, and the mahogany bar dates back to 1860. Winemaker Toby James worked at Estrella, Eberle, and Peachy Canyon before building his eponymous winery in 1993. In 1996 Toby met Lance and Claire Silver, formed a friendship and then a business partnership, and expanded the winery to what it is today. Tobin James Cellars has an unprecedented 26,000 members in its fun and active wine club, making it one of the, if not *the,* largest wine club in the world. We had a chance to catch Toby, Lance, and Claire and sit down before the trio departed on a cruise around French Polynesia with lucky members of their club. Tobin James 5 Paso Robles 2010 is a blend of Cabernet Sauvignon, Merlot, Petit Verdot, Cabernet Franc, and Malbec. It's dark garnet in the glass, with rich aromas of dark fruits, ripe cherry, and red plum. It's big and bold on the palate, with beautiful fruit flavors and a luxuriously long finish. Tobin James Ballistic Paso Robles Zinfandel 2010 is inky purple, with aromas of blackberry jam, black pepper, and brown spice. Rich black fruits come alive on the tongue before a fruity mouth-filling finish.

VICTOR HUGO WINERY

2850 El Pomar Drive, Templeton, CA 93465,
(805) 434-1128
www.victorhugowinery.com

Although he is not related to the literary icon, Victor Hugo Roberts likes to create intrigue around the names of his wines. His Hunchback is a delightfully popular red blend, and Les Mis is a rosé made from Malbec, Zinfandel, Merlot, and Petit Verdot. Victor Hugo graduated from

UC Davis with an enology degree in 1979 and has been making wine ever since. He enjoys making wine in a 100-year-old converted barn that sits amid 78 acres of vines. Victor Hugo Winery Paso Robles Estate Hunchback 2010 consists of 40 percent Malbec, 34 percent Petit Verdot, 20 percent Petite Sirah, and 6 percent Syrah. It is deep garnet, with aromas of black fruits, rose petals, cassis, and shale. It has flavors of candied violet, black fruits, and tart cherries and a chalky tannic finish. Victor Hugo Winery Paso Robles Estate Opulence 2010 is a blend of 33 percent Cabernet Franc, 26 percent Merlot, 23 percent Cabernet Sauvignon, 13 percent Malbec, and 5 percent Petit Verdot. It is purple garnet and has notes of mocha, black fruits, and cherry cola in the bouquet. In the mouth there are flavors of black fruits, toasted espresso bean, and coffee. There are savory notes in the finish with a predominance of roasted red pepper.

VILLA SAN-JULIETTE

6385 Cross Canyons Road,
San Miguel, CA 93451,
(805) 467-0014
www.villasanjuliette.com

We first met television producers turned winery owners Nigel Lythgoe and Ken Warwick (*American Idol, So You Think You Can Dance?*) at the Paso Robles Wine Festival and Auction and had the pleasure of interviewing Nigel for *Wine Enthusiast* magazine. Their beautiful Villa San-Juliette property consists of 168 acres of vines and a stunning 14,000-square-foot Tuscan-style estate complete with tasting room. The first estate-grown vintage was bottled in 2008 and received nothing but favorable reviews. Villa San-Juliette Reserve Albariño 2011 is pale straw, with aromas of white stone fruits, lemon zest, and Bartlett pears. In the mouth there is pleasant acidity, a touch of minerality, and a crisp, clean finish. Villa San-Juliette Reserve Malbec 2009 is inky purple colored, with aromas of purple flowers, forest floor, black fruits, and cigar box. On the palate fresh fruit flavors are accented by a touch of Mediterranean herbs and smooth, round tannins.

VILLICANA WINERY AND VINEYARD

2725 Adelaida Road, Paso Robles, CA 93446,
(805) 239-9456
www.villicanawinery.com

Culinary student Alex Villicana caught the winemaking bug while he was working at Creston Vineyard and was allowed to hand harvest (and keep) the grapes remaining after the mechanical harvest. In 1996 he and his wife, Monica, purchased 72 acres in Paso Robles and planted Cabernet Sauvignon, Cabernet Franc, Merlot, Zinfandel, Viognier, Grenache, Mourvèdre, and Syrah. In addition to winemaking, the Villicanas began distilling well-crafted vodka and gin under the Re:Find label in 2012. Villicana Estate Grown Paso Robles Cabernet Sauvignon 2009 is garnet colored, with aromas of black currant, black cherry, and oregano in the bouquet. On the palate there is a fruity yet vegetal characteristic with a grippy tannic structure and pronounced, lingering smoked meat finish, making this wine a natural for pairing with grilled meats and ribs.

VINA ROBLES

3700 Mill Road, Paso Robles, CA 93446,
(805) 227-4812
www.vinarobles.com

Swiss-born Hans Nef became enchanted with the Pacific coastline and the cowboy culture that continue to grace Paso Robles back in the mid-1990s. In 1996 he partnered with another Swiss expatriate, Hans R. Michael, and hired Swiss native Matthias Guber as the winemaker in 1999. The team built a beautiful 14,000-square-foot hospitality center in 2007, and in 2013 we donned hard hats for a tour of an outdoor amphitheater that should be completed by the time you are reading this. Their hope is to offer a venue for singers, bands, and orchestras to perform in as they travel the freeway between San Francisco and Los Angeles. Vina Robles Estate Paso Robles Petite Sirah 2009 is garnet colored, with aromas of black plums, black raspberries, and a touch of Christmas baking spices. It is big and round in the mouth with flavors of black plum and a touch of nutmeg. Vina Robles Suendero Meritage Paso Robles 2009 is dark garnet, with notes of black currant, anise, and hazelnuts in the bouquet. On the palate the black fruit flavors emerge with a touch of spice and well-balanced tannins. Too bad only 408 cases were produced.

WILD HORSE WINERY AND VINEYARDS

1437 Wild Horse Winery Court,
Templeton, CA 93465,
(805) 788-6310
www.wildhorsewinery.com

Founded by Ken Volk in 1982, Wild Horse Winery is considered one of the first wineries in the region. The first crush was in 1983, and today Wild Horse continues to make vineyard-designated wines from Cabernet Sauvignon, Syrah, Zinfandel, Chardonnay, and Pinot Noir. Other varieties in limited release include Grenache Blanc, Zinfandel, Syrah, Blaufrankisch, Malvasia Bianca, and Verdelho. Winemaking is under the direction of Chrissy Wittmann, and the vineyards are managed by Emerson Philpot. Wild Horse Winery and Vineyards Cheval Sauvage Santa Maria Valley Pinot Noir 2009 is cherry red, with notes of purple flowers, red fruits, Chinese five-spice powder, and saddle leather in the complex bouquet. It is fruit-forward in the mouth with luxurious persistence. Wild Horse Winery and Vineyards Central Coast Pinot Noir 2011 has aromas of cranberry, black cherry, cherry cola, and a touch of nutmeg. It has flavors of Thanksgiving Day cranberry sauce, cherry cola, and lingering fruit nuances in the lingering finish.

WINDWARD VINEYARD

1380 Live Oak Road, Paso Robles, CA 93446,
(805) 239-2565
www.windwardvineyard.com

Husband and wife Marc Goldberg and Maggie D'Ambrosia planted Windward Vineyard in 1989 with a vision to produce single-vineyard "Monopole" Burgundian-style wines in Paso Robles. Their 15-acre vineyard has four different French clones of Pinot Noir vines, and the couple exclusively produces wines made from the single variety. Windward Vineyard Pinot Noir 2008 has aromas of dried black cherries and cherry vanilla ice cream. It has a decidedly Burgundian characteristic on the palate, with bright fruit flavors and refreshing acidity in the post palate.

ZENAIDA CELLARS

1550 Highway 46 West, Paso Robles, CA 93446,
(805) 227-0382
www.zenaidacellars.com

Biologist turned winemaker Eric Ogorsolka first worked with Ken Volk at Wild Horse Winery and began making wine under his Zenaida Cellars label in 1998. With the help of his wife, Jill, the winery was completed in 2000. The property has 36 acres, 22 of which are under vine. Zenaida Cellars Wanderlust 2010 is a blend of 50 percent Grenache, 35 percent Syrah, and 15 percent Mourvèdre. It is dark ruby garnet, with aromas of wild brambleberries, smoked meats, and a delightful vegetal top note. It has flavors of freshly picked berries, espresso bean, dark chocolate, and a touch of farm stand before the well-balanced finish. Zenaida Cellars Zephyr 2010 is composed of 55 percent Syrah, 40 percent Zinfandel, and 5 percent Viognier. It is deep purple garnet colored, with aromas of freshly picked cherries and violet talc. It is fruit-forward on the palate, with flavors of black plum, blackberry, savory herbs, baking spices, and a touch of mocha on the finish.

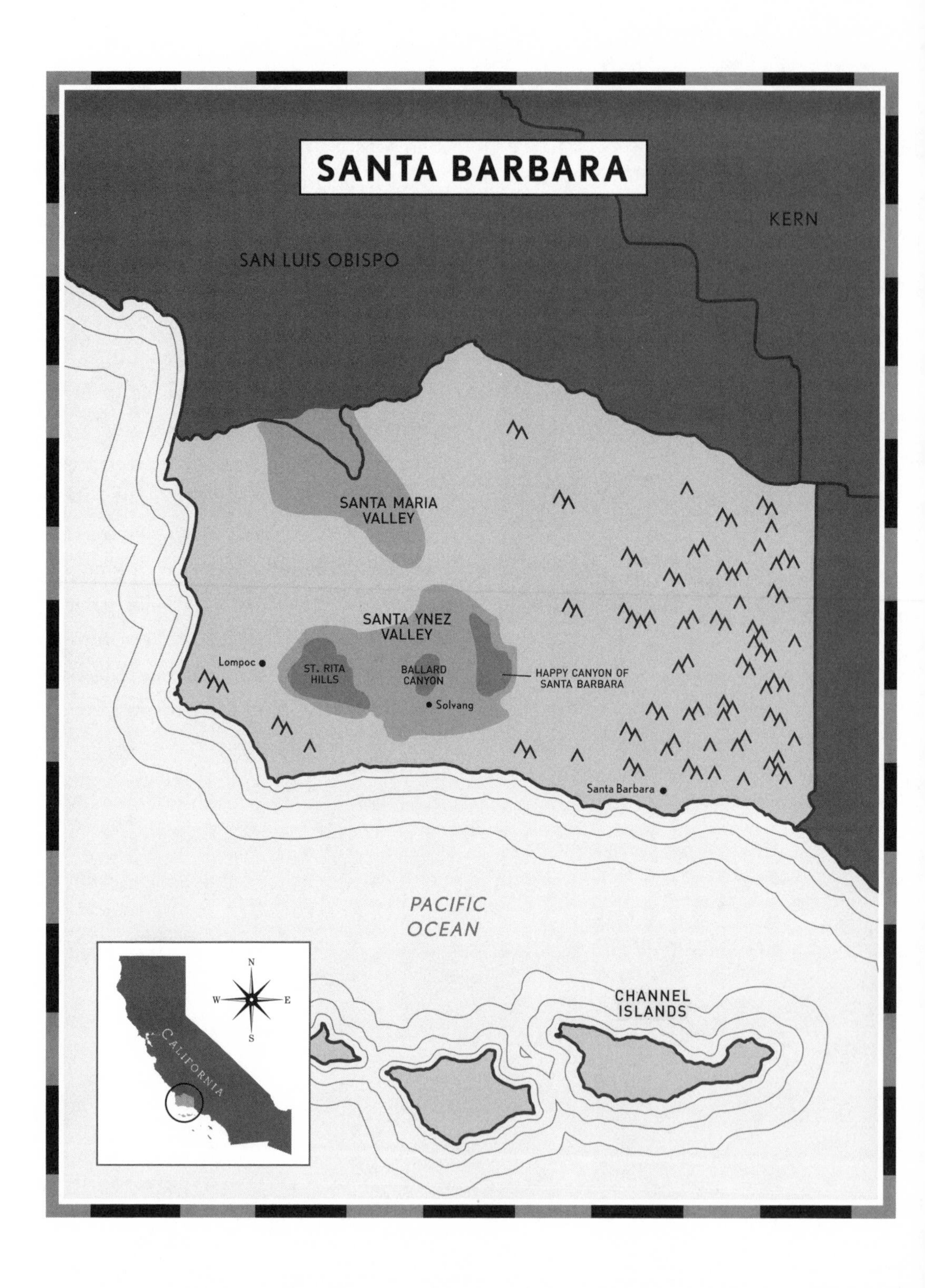
SANTA BARBARA
KERN
SAN LUIS OBISPO
SANTA MARIA VALLEY
SANTA YNEZ VALLEY
Lompoc
ST. RITA HILLS
BALLARD CANYON
Solvang
HAPPY CANYON OF SANTA BARBARA
Santa Barbara
PACIFIC OCEAN
CHANNEL ISLANDS
N
W
E
S
CALIFORNIA

CHAPTER 10

SANTA BARBARA

WINE TOURISTS VISITING THE LOMPOC Wine Ghetto, the industrial park turned winery and tasting room complex, would probably be amused by, and then raise a glass of Pinot Noir to, the fact that Lompoc was originally founded in 1874 as an alcohol-free temperance colony called New Vineland. Lompoc and its sister towns in Santa Barbara County—Solvang, Buellton, Los Alamos, and Los Olivos—may not completely steal the spotlight from the nearby "American Riviera," but with a critical mass of tasting rooms and restaurants featuring local food and wine, Santa Barbara wine country is luring visitors inland to savor all the delights the region has to offer. Although the devious goings-on inside glamorous mansions hidden in the hills above the winding coastline first came to global attention during the tenure of the 1980s-era soap opera *Santa Barbara*, the media focus headed outside to the vineyards of Santa Barbara after the release of the 2004 hit movie *Sideways*. The film chronicled the escapades of down-on-their-luck buddies Miles and Jack, but its real star turned out to be delicately nuanced Pinot Noir produced in the Santa Ynez Valley.

Having been populated by the native Chumash people for over 10,000 years, Santa Barbara received its name in 1602. It was christened by the Spanish explorer Sebastian Vizcaíno, who touched land here after surviving a storm on December 3, the eve of the feast day of Saint Barbara. Spanish colonization took place after the arrival of a larger population, including missionaries under the direction of Father Junípero Serra, in 1769. Padre Serra planted vines bearing Mission grapes here in 1782, and the Mission of Santa Barbara was completed on December 4, 1786. The San Jose Winery, which is now a county landmark, was built in the local adobe style in the early years of the nineteenth century, although the exact date is unknown. By the end of the nineteenth century forty-five different vineyards totaling 260 acres existed in the area, and in 1884 Justinian Caire, a Frenchman who ran a successful ranching operation, planted a large vineyard on nearby Santa Cruz Island. In the early part of the twentieth century, Santa Barbara was home to a relatively small but thriving wine industry.

As it did elsewhere throughout the state, Prohibition took its toll on the burgeoning practice of grape growing, and it was not until the 1960s that wine farming again took hold in Santa Barbara, specifically in the Santa Maria Valley. At that time large commercial growers produced grapes for big operations that dominated the domestic wine industry such as Gallo, Almaden, Paul Masson, and Korbel. Meanwhile the Santa Ynez Valley was starting to be developed by family-owned wineries with an interest in the small-batch, handcrafted wines that remain the hallmark of the region to date.

The Santa Maria Valley AVA is in the northern part of the county, with a portion crossing over into San Luis Obispo County. Established in 1981, it was the third American Viticultural Area in the United States and the first in Santa Barbara. Its original size was 97,483 acres, with another 18,790 added in 2011, bringing the total to 116,273 acres. Because of the east-west orientation of the valley, Pacific fog enters in the morning and often blankets vines until midday, creating cool daytime temperatures ideal for growing Pinot Noir and Chardonnay. The Santa Maria River cuts through Santa Maria Valley, and soils toward the north tend to include thin layers of earth over decomposed shale and limestone. Soils to the south of the river are much deeper, containing a combination of alluvial qualities and sand brought inland over the years via west-to-east wind patterns.

The first large-scale vineyard in the modern era was 100 acres of vines planted by Uriel Nielson in 1964. Originally planted to multiple varieties that were sold to large producers, the Uriel Nielson Vineyard is now home to the two previously mentioned cool-weather varieties. In 1969 the Millers, a fifth-generation California farming family, purchased the two large plots of land, and in 1970 brothers Stephen and Robert planted the Bien Nacido Vineyard. In the early 1970s other vineyards were developed under the direction of the Sanford and Wild Horse wineries.

Much of the history of current-day Santa Barbara is told through the stories of individual winery owners such as Jim Clendenen of Au Bon Climat and Bob Lindquist of Qupé, both of whom founded their wineries in 1982. Each got his start at Zaca Mesa Winery, which launched the careers of their contemporaries Ken Brown and Adam Tolmach. Santa Maria Valley is also home to Fess Parker Winery and Vineyard and the Jackson family's Cambria Winery. There is an unofficial viticultural area known as Los Alamos Valley, wedged between the southern border of Santa Maria Valley and the northwestern corner of Sta. Rita Hills that is beginning to gain traction as a grape-growing region to watch out for.

To the south of Santa Maria Valley is the Santa Ynez Valley AVA, which contains within its borders two sub-AVAs: Sta. Rita Hills to the west and Happy Canyon of Santa Barbara to the east. (Sta. Rita Hills, known as Santa Rita Hills from 2001 through 2006, now uses the Spanish abbreviation for saint, after negotiations with the Chilean wine producer Viña Santa Rita.) There are three petitions before the TTB that concern the Santa Ynez Valley. The first, formally accepted as complete in March 2013, concerns the expansion of the Sta. Rita Hills viticultural area, and the second, accepted as complete by the TTB in April of that year, regards the establishment of the Los Olivos District. The third petition, requesting the establishment of an additional 7,800-acre sub-AVA in the center of the Santa Ynez Valley called the Ballard Canyon AVA, was approved in the fall of 2013. Ballard Canyon features multiple twisting hills and canyons as compared with the more level landscape of the surrounding Santa Ynez Valley.

The Santa Ynez Valley AVA was established in 1983, the same year the Santa Barbara County Vintners Association was formed. Bordered on the north by the Purisima Hills and San Rafael Mountains and to the south by the Santa Ynez Mountains, it is home to the highest concentration of wineries in the county. Santa Ynez Valley is 77,000 acres in size, while Sta. Rita Hills (created in 2001) is 31,000 acres and Happy Canyon (established in 2009) is 24,000 acres. The 92-mile-long Santa Ynez River runs east to west, roughly parallel to Highway 246, ending in the Pacific Ocean just west of Lompoc. The climate is Mediterranean, and soils range from heavy clay in the east to shale, gravel, and sand toward the west. The portion of coastline just below the wine-growing valleys, which runs 50 miles in an east-west direction, is the largest transverse section of coastline on the west coast of the Americas. This orientation provides the valleys of Santa Barbara with cool Pacific breezes and fog during the day, giving grapes protection from the sun's heat during the dry growing season.

The modern history of the Santa Ynez Valley is also told through the narratives of area vineyard pioneers. Richard Sanford planted Pinot Noir in his Sanford & Benedict Vineyard in 1972 despite concerns from many others that the area was too cold for the cultivation of this variety. Leonard Firestone and his son Brooks planted vines here in the early 1970s and founded Firestone Winery, said to be Santa Barbara's first estate winery.

Firestone originally was known for its excellent Chardonnay and Pinot Noir. Pierre Lafond founded Santa Barbara Winery in 1962, the first winery in the county built since the end of Prohibition, planting Pinot Noir at the same time. He built a winery bearing his family name in 1998 and also owns a bistro in Buellton. From the late 1970s into the 1980s, winery and vineyard expansion continued throughout the valley, and the last 25 years have seen exponential growth in both quality and quantity.

Today there are over a hundred wineries in Santa Barbara, with more than sixty grape varieties growing on over 16,000 cultivated acres. Just under 50 percent of the vineyards are in the Santa Maria Valley AVA, with a little more than half divided between Santa Ynez Valley, including subappellations, and the non-AVA designated Los Alamos Valley and other areas throughout the county. The two established subappellations of Santa Ynez Valley, Sta. Rita Hills and Happy Canyon of Santa Barbara, account, respectively, for 12 and 3 percent of the total acreage of grapes grown. Santa Barbara's most recently added AVA, Ballard Canyon, received official designation on November 1, 2013. This 7,800-acre canyon currently has 565 acres of planted vines, most notably Syrah and white Rhône varieties, and is home to eighteen wineries.

In Santa Barbara, the number one variety is Chardonnay, with 37 percent of the total cultivation, followed by Pinot Noir at 27 percent, Syrah at 8 percent, Cabernet Sauvignon and Sauvignon Blanc at 4 percent each, and Grenache with 1 percent of the total. The remaining varieties are divided among a total share of 19 percent of vine-bearing acreage. Vineyards are almost equally divided between red and white grapes. Among the varieties falling into the "other" category are Grenache, Viognier, Marsanne, Roussanne, Albariño, Merlot, Malbec, Petit Verdot, and Sangiovese.

For the last several years January has ushered in the Santa Maria Chardonnay Symposium, a three-day conference featuring fifty producers focused on all things Chardonnay. This is fitting in a region in which this is the most prolific and best-known variety. Many of the plantings date back to the 1970s, and Chardonnay is made here in a variety of styles, from steely-sharp to oak-tinged. As a result of cool coastal influences, the valleys of Santa Barbara are well suited for this variety and for Pinot Noir. Eighty percent of all the vines in Sta. Rita Hills are graced with Pinot Noir grapes, and it too is vinified into a number of different styles, from fresh and fruity to a deeper, more savory fashion.

Although Syrah lags behind Chardonnay and Pinot Noir in production, it is said to be the grape that is produced as a single variety by the highest number of wineries in the county. It is also blended with Grenache and Mourvèdre, alone or in combination, as well as with Cabernet Sauvignon or Zinfandel. And while Sauvignon Blanc makes up only 4 percent of total acreage here, thriving particularly in Happy Canyon, it is a variety whose praises are widely sung by both critics and wine consumers. The bulk of Cabernet Sauvignon is also found in Happy Canyon, where it is vinified as a single variety or in Bordeaux-style blends.

As in other popular wine regions in this agricultural state, there is a very strong farm-to-table movement throughout the wine regions of Santa Barbara. Locals and tourists enjoy local meats and vegetables alongside a bounty of local wine, and it is possible to find yourself seated next to a superstar winemaker or a movie star visiting from nearby Los Angeles. There are goings-on to make a visit special throughout the summer season, from the Los Olivos Jazz and Wine Festival in June through the Harvest Weekend Celebration in mid-October. Many wineries and tasting rooms offer music and other programs throughout the entire year.

ALMA ROSA WINERY & VINEYARDS

7250 Santa Rosa Road, Buellton, CA 93427, (805) 688-9090
www.almarosawinery.com

Truly a pioneer in the Santa Ynez Valley, Richard Sanford is widely credited as one of the first to plant Pinot Noir vines in the Sta. Rita Hills. After returning home from the Vietnam War in 1968, he organized a partnership to purchase a ranch and planted Pinot Noir at Sanford & Benedict vineyard in 1970. He married Thekla Brumder in 1978, and together they started Sanford Winery in 1981. In 2005 they left their shares in Sanford and founded Alma Rosa. Today they produce quality wine from 100 acres of certified-organic vineyards in the Sta. Rita Hills. Richard Sanford has been noted recently as the first person from the Central Coast to be inducted into the Vintners Hall of Fame. Alma Rosa La Encantada Vineyard Sta. Rita Hills Pinot Noir 2011 is ruby colored, with aromas of red raspberry, dried black cherry, and Christmas baking spices. It is full-bodied with supple tannins and a balanced finish. Alma Rosa El Jabali Vineyard Sta. Rita Hills Chardonnay 2011 is straw colored, with aromas of freshly cut Cavaillon melon, white stone fruits, and caramelized pineapple. It is crisp on the palate with balanced acidity and a well-rounded mouthfeel.

ALTA MARIA VINEYARDS

2933 Grand Avenue, Los Olivos, CA 93441, (805) 686-1144
www.altamaria.com

Named for the upper Santa Maria River, Alta Maria Vineyards was founded by winemaker Paul Wilkins and viticulturist James Ontiveros. Together they make small-batch Chardonnay, Sauvignon Blanc, and Pinot Noir. Alta Maria Vineyards Santa Barbara County Sauvignon Blanc 2010 is straw yellow, with aromas of geranium leaf, melon, and mango. In the mouth flavors of tropical fruit and crisp acidity bring you along to its clean finish. Alta Maria Vineyards Santa Maria Valley Pinot Noir 2010 is cherry red, with fruity aromas of dried red cherries and fresh strawberries. It is medium-bodied in the mouth with a touch of Mediterranean herbs in the finish.

ANDREW MURRAY VINEYARDS

2901-A Grand Avenue, Los Olivos, CA 93441,
(805) 693-9644
www.andrewmurrayvineyards.com

Paleontology student turned winemaker Andrew Murray became infatuated with Rhône varieties in France in 1980 and subsequently moved to Australia. He eventually finished his bachelor's degree in enology at the University of California, Davis, and began his own winery. He has been called "one of the shining stars in the Santa Barbara firmament" by Robert Parker and named "Tastemaker of the Year" by *Food & Wine* magazine. His wines are highly scored by *Wine Advocate*, *Wine Spectator*, and *Wine Enthusiast*. Andrew Murray Esperance Red Blend 2011 is composed of Grenache, Syrah, and Mourvèdre. It is ruby purple in the glass, with aromas of purple flowers, freesia, violets, dark fruits, and a touch of minerality. It is big and bold but restrained in the mouth with balanced fruit flavors and a lingering finish. Andrew Murray RGB White Blend 2011 is composed of Roussanne and Grenache Blanc. It is straw colored, with aromas of tropical fruits and banana flowers. It is generous in the mouth with rich fruit flavors and a nice touch of minerality on the finish.

AU BON CLIMAT

813 Anacapa Street, Santa Barbara, CA 93003,
(805) 963-7999
www.aubonclimat.com

Former aspiring lawyer Jim Clendenen visited France for his twenty-first birthday and upon returning to the United States changed course to embark on a new career in wine. He became the assistant winemaker at Zaca Mesa Winery in 1978, and in 1982 he started Au Bon Climat, which roughly translates from the French as "a well-exposed vineyard." His winery was recognized by Robert Parker in 1989 as one of the "Best Wineries in the World," and in 1991 he was one of Oz Clark's picks for "World Creator of Modern Classic Wines." His wines are highly regarded by all leading wine publications, including *Wine Spectator*, *Wine Enthusiast*, and *Food & Wine*, and are coveted by admirers and collectors. Au Bon Climat Santa Barbara County Pinot Noir 2009 is cherry red, with aromas of cherry preserves, freshly picked strawberries, baking spices, and crushed coriander seeds. It is big and full-bodied in the mouth with flavors of sour cherries and red raspberries that produce the balanced acidity that makes this a perfect food wine. Au Bon Climat La Bauge Au-dessus Pinot Noir 2007 is a wild party of red fruit aromas laced with forest floor and Chinese black tea infused with Asian spices. Delightful on the palate, it has a long, lingering finish.

BECKMAN VINEYARDS

2670 Ontiveros Road,Los Olivos, CA 93441,
(805) 688-8664
www.beckmanvineyards.com

Family-run since its inception in 1994, Beckman Vineyards is the fulfillment of the vision of Tom and Steve Beckman. They started with a 40-acre parcel of land and subsequently purchased a 365-acre ranch in Santa Ynez Valley in 1996 that they named Purisima Mountain Vineyard. They vineyard has been farmed biodynamically since 2006. Beckman wines are highly rated by a number of publications, and in 2007 *Wine & Spirits* magazine called them one of the "Top 100 Wineries" in the world. Beckman Vineyards Purisima Mountain Vineyard Whole Cluster Grenache 2010 has notes of ripe cherry, pomegranate, red raspberry, and Provencal lavender in the complex bouquet. In the mouth the fruit flavors move backward on your palate as the balanced tannic finish floods the entire mouth.

BIEN NACIDO VINEYARDS

4705 Santa Maria Mesa Road,
Santa Maria, CA 93454,
(805) 937-2506
www.biennacidovineyards.com

The multigenerational Californian Miller family purchased two parcels of Rancho Tepusquet totaling more than 2,000 acres in 1969 and began planting grapevines soon afterward. The original ranch was part of a Spanish land grant made to Tomas Olivera by the governor of Upper California, Juan Bautista Alvarado, in 1837. "*Bien nacido*" translates from Spanish as "well born," and that concept is carried on today in Bien Nacido's site selection and vineyard management. Bien Nacido Vineyards Santa Maria Valley Chardonnay 2010 has aromas of tropical fruits, lemon blossom, and toasted hazelnuts in the bouquet. In the mouth it is medium-bodied, with pronounced citrus flavors and a clean finish. Bien Nacido Vineyards Santa Maria Valley Pinot Noir 2009 is cherry red, with aromas of dark cherry, dried cranberry, and a touch of mint. It is round on the palate with a pleasant acidic finish.

BLAIR FOX CELLARS

2902 San Marcos Avenue, Los Olivos, CA 93441,
(805) 691-1678
www.blairfoxcellars.com

Once the former winemaker at Fess Parker Winery, Blair Fox was recently named "André Tchelistcheff Winemaker of the Year." In 2004 he planted his own organically farmed vineyards in Los Olivos, and to this day his wines continue to receive high marks from all the major wine magazines. His French style most definitely has been influenced by his travels in the Rhône Valley. Blair Fox Cellars Paradise Road Vineyard Viognier 2010 is zippy and zesty with aromas of ripe white fruits, honeycomb, and Indian spices. In the mouth it runs almost savory with balanced acidity and pronounced minerality. Blair Fox Cellars Thompson Vineyard Syrah 2009 is inky purple, with aromas of black currant, black plum, and black raspberry. There is a fair amount of minerality, namely, iron and calcium, in this rich, fruit-driven well-executed Syrah.

BREWER-CLIFTON

329 North F Street, Lompoc, CA 93436,
(805) 735-9184
www.brewerclifton.com

In their former lives Greg Brewer taught French and Steve Clifton was a surfer who sang

rock 'n' roll. That's not to say that Brewer doesn't still speak French and Clifton doesn't sing anymore. That's all well and good, but what we find interesting is the delicious wine that this duo crafts together mere meters away from the Lompoc Wine Ghetto. Brewer-Clifton Sta. Rita Hills Chardonnay 2010 is a blend of grapes from five different vineyards: Mount Carmel, 3-D, Gnesa, Sea Smoke, and Zotovich. It has heady aromas of citrus flowers, lemon zest, and crystallized ginger. In the mouth it is crisp with a fair bit of linear minerality, making this a perfect wine to pair with any number of cuisines. Brewer-Clifton Ampelos Pinot Noir 2011 has aromas of freshly cracked black pepper, ripe black cherry, and just a touch of cigar box. It has flavors of rich red fruits, pomegranate, and black Chinese tea. It is firm in the mouth with a taut finish.

BYRON WINES

2367 Alamo Pintado Avenue,
Los Olivos, CA 93441,
(805) 938-7365
www.byronwines.com

Ken Brown founded Byron in 1984 with the goal of making quality Chardonnay and Pinot Noir, and by all accounts he succeeded. In 2003 winemaking duties were assigned to Jonathan Nagy, and although production has moved to neighboring Cambria Estate, Byron continues to focus on small-batch, high-quality wines. Byron Santa Maria Valley Chardonnay 2011 is golden straw colored, with aromas of citrus blossoms, Greek fig, and honeysuckle. It is generous on the palate, with flavors of ripe peach and dried apricot with pleasant mineral notes. Byron Santa Maria Valley Pinot Noir 2011 has aromas of dried black cherry, red raspberry, cherry cola, and a touch of brown spice in the bouquet. It is fruit-forward in the mouth with a pleasant lingering finish.

CAMBRIA ESTATE WINERY

5475 Chardonnay Lane, Santa Maria, CA 93454,
(805) 937-8901
www.cambriawines.com

In 1986, Barbara Banke of Jackson Family Wines acquired a large section of an original Mexican land grant, Rancho Tepusquet, to serve as the site for Cambria Winery. The Tepusquet Vineyard originally was planted in 1971, but over the last 20 years it has been replanted and expanded. Cambria Estate Winery Katherine's Vineyard Santa Maria Valley Chardonnay 2011 is golden straw colored, with aromas of Anjou pear, caramelized pineapple, and honeysuckle. It is rich in the mouth with a crisp, acidic finish. Cambria Estate Winery Julia's Vineyard Santa Maria Valley Pinot Noir 2010 is cherry red, with notes of ripe cherry, red plum, and a touch of spice in the bouquet. It is generous on the palate with juicy fruit flavors and a delightful finish.

CARGASACCHI

420 East Highway 246,
Buellton, CA,
(805) 691-1300
www.cargasacchi.com

Winemaker Peter Cargasacchi is the fifth generation of his family in California, but the first born in the New World. His great-great grandfather

2010

came from Italy, but then disappeared. His great grandfather founded a restaurant and hotel in San Francisco, the Saint Gotthard, which was

CARGASACCHI

destroyed in the earthquake and fire of 1906. Subsequent generations, though born in Italy, farmed and made wine in California's Central Coast.

PINOT NOIR

Paintings of Saint Gotthard often show him hanging his cloak on a sunbeam.

Peter Cargasacchi planted his eponymous vineyard in Sta. Rita Hills in 1998 and then planted Jalama Vineyard the next year. Because of and perhaps as a direct result of their shared Italian heritage, he and Julia Manuela Cargasacchi craft fine wines that are indisputably food-friendly. They produce estate-grown Pinot Noir under their own label and Syrah, Pinot Grigio, Chardonnay, and Pinot Noir from estate and purchased grapes under the Point Concepción label, all of which can be sipped at their new tasting room in Buellton. Cargasacchi Cargasacchi-Jalama Vineyard Santa Barbara County Pinot Noir 2010 is ruby garnet, with aromas of red raspberry, red currants, and black raspberry with just a touch of dried herbs. In the mouth it is soft and voluptuous at the same time with great tannic structure and just a touch of balanced minerality.

CASA DUMETZ

388 Bell Street, Los Alamos, CA 93440,
(805) 344-1900
www.casadumetzwines.com

We first met winemaker Sonja Magdevski when we were interviewing her and her fiancé, actor-director-producer Emilio Estevez, for *Wine Enthusiast* magazine. The couple had just dug up their Malibu front yard to plant Pinot Noir grapevines, and Emilio had recently finished filming *The Way*, a thought-provoking film about personal transformation that stars his father, Martin Sheen. We immediately fell in love with the couple's passion for wine and have shared more than a few glasses with them over the last few years. When you're in downtown Los Alamos, make sure to visit Sonja at Babi's Tasting Room, named for her Macedonian grandmother, Babi Ilinka. Casa Dumetz Gewürztraminer 2012 is light straw colored, with delightful aromas of grapefruit peel, clementine, lemon juice, and vanilla. It is fruit-forward and floral on the palate with a crisp, clean finish. Perfect as an aperitif, it invites you in for another and another and another sip. Casa Dumetz Tierra Alta Vineyard Grenache 2012 is garnet colored, with notes of anise, blackberry preserves, and cassis. It is generous on the palate with great fruit flavors and a long luxurious finish.

COLD HEAVEN CELLARS

92 A Second Street, Buellton, CA 93427,
(805) 686-1343
www.coldheavencellars.com

Started in 1996 by winemaker-owner Morgan Clendenen, Cold Heaven Cellars has become well known among wine geeks for expertly crafted cool-climate Viognier. Grapes are sourced from the Clendenen family–owned Le Bon Climat Vineyard in Santa Barbara County and Sanford and Benedict Vineyards in Sta. Rita Hills. But that's not all Morgan produces: since 2003 she has been making delicious Syrah, and in 2008 she added Pinot Noir to her fine portfolio. Cold Heaven Cellars Le Bon Climat Viognier 2010 is pale straw, with aromas of citrus blossom, white flowers, white stone fruits, and honeycomb. The fruit flavors come alive on the tongue, with just the right amount of Indian spice nuances complementing the balanced acidity and pronounced florality of the finish.

DIERBERG VINEYARD

PO Box 217, Santa Ynez, CA 93460,
(805) 697-1467
www.dierbergvineyard.com

Jim and Mary Dierberg have owned Hermannhof Winery in Hermann, Missouri, since 1974, but their love of cool-climate grapes and cool-climate wines brought them to Santa Barbara in 1996. The next year they began planting Pinot Noir and Chardonnay in the Santa Maria Valley. The family brought in winemaker Andy Alba in 2001 for the first crush, and he has been succeeded by Tyler Thomas. Dierberg Santa Maria Valley Dierberg Vineyard Chardonnay 2010 has aromas of lemon zest, orange pith, and toasted almonds. It is delightfully light on the palate, with flavors of green apple and candied orange peel with crisp acidity, balanced minerality, and a clean finish. Dierberg Santa Maria Valley Dierberg Vineyard Pinot Noir 2009 is ruby cherry red, with aromas of black raspberry, black cherry, and wet leaves. It is fruity in the mouth with delicate powdered cocoa and talc on the finish.

EVENING LAND VINEYARDS

1503 East Chestnut Avenue, Lompoc, CA 93436,
(805) 736-9656
www.eveninglandvineyards.com

Mark Tarlov, the legendary Hollywood film producer, founded Evening Land Vineyards in 2005 and together with his talented team crafted some legendary wines. In 2012 he left Sta. Rita Hills to make wine in Oregon and sold his Santa Barbara property to winemaker Sashi Moorman, sommelier Rajat Parr, and their investment partners. Evening Land Bloom's Field Vineyard Sta. Rita Hills Pinot Noir 2010 is cherry red, with aromas of dried black cherry, red raspberry, and a touch of Indian spice. It is medium-bodied, with nice fruit flavors and a pleasant finish. Evening Land Estate Sta. Rita Hills Pinot Noir 2010 has notes of red plum, red cherry, and freshly ground black pepper in the bouquet. Rich fruit flavors hit the palate on the initial entry, and the finish leaves you longing for the next sip.

FESS PARKER WINERY AND VINEYARD

6200 Foxen Canyon Road,
Los Olivos, CA 93441,
(805) 688-1545
www.fessparkerwines.com

Better known as Walt Disney's Daniel Boone or, better yet, Davy Crockett, King of the Wild Frontier, actor Fess Parker purchased a 714-acre ranch in the Santa Ynez Valley in 1987 and began making wines that garnered international

attention. He purchased the Grand Hotel in Los Olivos in 1998 and converted the 21-room Victorian-style inn to the complex now known as Fess Parker's Wine Country Inn and Spa. Although he passed away in 2010, his legacy lives on with his son Eli as director of winemaking and vineyard operations and his daughter Ashley as vice president of marketing and sales. Fess Parker Winery and Vineyard Santa Barbara County Riesling 2011 is pale straw colored, with notes of white stone fruit and honeysuckle blossom that move seamlessly into fresh fruit and jammy flavors in the mouth. It's clean and crisp with a slightly off-dry finish. Fess Parker Winery and Vineyard Bien Nacido Pinot Noir 2010 is cherry red, with aromas of fresh red cherries, dried black cherries, and a touch of peppermint. It has sweet fruit in the mouth with a pleasant acidic finish. It has just the right touch of menthol in the post palate.

FIRESTONE VINEYARDS

5017 Zaca Station Road,
Los Olivos, CA 93441,
(805) 688-3940
www.firestonewine.com

Leonard Firestone and his son Brooks started Firestone Vineyards in 1972 and made quality wine for over 35 years before they sold their holdings to Santa Barbara vintner Bill Foley. The Firestones decided that they wanted to have more time to concentrate on their smaller Curtis Winery and eponymous brewery and knew that Bill Foley would be an excellent steward of their vineyards. Foley and his team oversee all aspects of the production of fine wines from Chardonnay, Merlot, Cabernet Sauvignon, Syrah, and Sauvignon Blanc grapes grown on the estate's 400 acres. Visitors to the winery enjoy the comprehensive tours and picnic areas, and brides and grooms have rated Firestone as one of the best places to plan a wedding. Firestone Vineyards Ambassador Meritage is a blend of 62 percent Cabernet Franc, 12 percent Cabernet Sauvignon, 12 percent Merlot, 10 percent Malbec, and 4 percent Petit Verdot. It is garnet colored, with aromas of black currant, red plum, and black raspberry with top notes of Christmas baking spice. It is fruit-forward in the mouth with soft, balanced tannins and an elegant finish. Firestone Vineyard Clone 174 Syrah 2009 is inky purple, with notes of ripe black raspberry, dried black cherry, and charcuterie. It has flavors of ripe black fruits with nuances of smoked meat and vanilla on the palate. The finish is soft and smooth.

FLYING GOAT CELLARS

1520 East Chestnut Court, Unit A,
Lompoc, CA 93436,
(805) 736-9032
www.flyinggoatcellars.com

Yes, goats do fly. Just visit Flying Goat Cellars and watch the winery's pygmy goat mascots, Never and Epernay, jump, spin, and twist in the air. Winemaker Norm Yost and his wife, Kate Griffith, wanted a fun name for their serious wines and came up with the name to honor their acrobatic pets. The couple source grapes from a variety of quality vineyards, including Bien Nacido, Clos Pepe, Dierberg, Rancho Santa Rosa, Rio Vista, Salisbury, Solomon Hills, and Sierra Madre, and are known for their Pinot Gris, Pinot Noir, and sparkling wines. Flying Goat Cellars Pinot Gris 2012 is straw colored, with aromas of candied orange peel, pineapple upside down cake, and baking spices. It is linear and clean in the mouth with a crisp finish. Goat Bubbles Blanc de Blancs

Sierra Madre Vineyard 2010 is cream straw-colored, with abundant *perlage* and a creamy mousse. It has aromas of citrus blossoms and freshly baked brioche. You can tell these grapes get a lot of maritime influence by the refreshing salinity and minerality.

FOLEY ESTATES VINEYARD & WINERY

6121 East Highway 246, Lompoc, CA 93436,
(805) 737-6222
www.foleywines.com

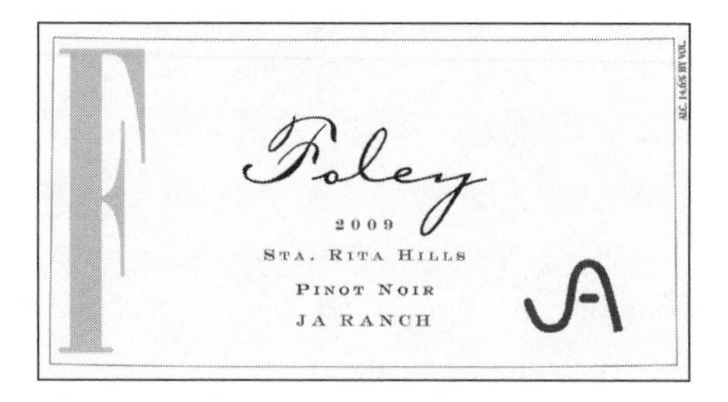

Bill Foley realized his dream to produce world-class, cool-climate wines from Pinot Noir and Chardonnay grapes grown in Santa Barbara County when he established Foley Estates Vineyard & Winery. In 1998 he began planting 230 acres of Pinot Noir, Chardonnay, and Syrah divided into fifty-nine blocks on the 460-acre property known as Rancho Santa Rosa. Leslie Mead Renaud is the winemaker and is aided by Lorna Kreutz Duggan as her assistant. Foley Estates Vineyard & Winery Two Sisters Courtney's Vineyard Sta. Rita Hills Chardonnay 2010 is medium straw colored, with aromas of toasted almonds, citrus blossoms, and a touch of cinnamon. It has linear acidity on the palate, with wonderful balance and delightful minerality in the finish. Foley Estates Vineyard & Winery JA Ranch Pinot Noir is cherry red, with aromas of blueberries, red raspberries, and red cherries and with top notes of Indian spices in the complex bouquet. It is vibrant and bright in the mouth with ripe fruit flavors and nuances of dried Mediterranean herbs and cocoa powder in the finish.

FOXEN WINERY AND VINEYARD

7600 Foxen Canyon Road, Santa Maria, CA 93454,
(805) 937-4251
www.foxenvineyard.com

We get a kick out of Foxen's tag line, "If you you don't know Foxen, you don't know Dick . . . or Bill," and when you visit the winery, you'll get a kick out of Dick Doré and Bill Wathen's wry sense of humor. But for a really fun time join Bill and Dick and their equally fun wives on a food-and-wine cruise around the Mediterranean with their wine club. These guys may joke around once in a while, but when it comes to making serious wine, they know how to deliver. The Foxen boys have been making wine together since 1985, when the duo started Foxen Winery and Vineyard in Santa Barbara County. The winery was named in honor of Dick's great-great-grandfather William Benjamin Foxen, who once owned 9,000 acres in what is now known as Foxen Canyon. The family has managed to retain the 2,000-acre Tinaquaic Ranch on which Foxen Winery operates. Foxen Winery and Vineyard Cuvée Jeanne Marie Williamson Doré Vineyard Santa Ynez Valley 2010 is a blend of 64 percent Grenache, 20 percent Syrah, and 16 percent Mourvèdre. It is garnet purple, with aromas of fresh red raspberry and cherry jam with top notes of menthol and cigar box. It is juicy in the mouth with a pleasantly firm finish.

GAINEY VINEYARD

3950 East Highway 246,
Santa Ynez, CA 93460,
(805) 688-0558
www.gaineyvineyard.com

The 100-acre Gainey Vineyard sits on the 1,800-acre Gainey Home Ranch in Santa Ynez Valley. The remainder of the land is dedicated to Arabian horses, cattle, and the cultivation of organically grown fruits and vegetables. The family also owns two other vineyards, Rancho Esperanza and Evan's Ranch, in the Sta. Rita Hills AVA. Dan J. Gainey and his son, Dan H., first planted 50 acres of vines in 1983 and opened their winery in 1984. It was quickly hailed as "one of the best wineries to visit on California's Central Coast" by *Wine Spectator* magazine. Today Gainey Vineyard produces 18,000 cases of highly regarded wine per year. Gainey Vineyard Limited Selection Riesling 2011 has aromas of white flowers, green apple, and dried apricot. It is full-bodied and generous on the palate, with fruit flavors, nice minerality, and a touch of citrus zest in the balanced acidic finish. Gainey Vineyard Limited Selection Merlot 2010 is garnet colored, with aromas of black plum, cassis, and bittersweet chocolate. It is round in the mouth with pronounced fruit flavors and a savory finish.

GYPSY CANYON

2753 Gypsy Canyon Drive, Lompoc, CA 93436,
(805) 737-0204
www.gypsycanyon.com

While house hunting in 1994, Deborah Hall and her husband, Bill, came across a ramshackle farmhouse on an old lima bean farm in Santa Barbara and decided to make it their early retirement home. While clearing the property, they discovered gnarled grapevines—misidentified at the time as Zinfandel—that had belonged to Doña Marcelina Felix Dominguez, said to be the first female grape grower in California. The vines turned out to be Mission grapes, the variety originally brought to California by Spanish missionaries in the mid-eighteenth century. Bill, who had been in remission from cancer at the time he and Deborah found the property, succumbed to his disease shortly after their purchase. Deborah, a young mother and former surgical assistant, decided to restore the vineyards to their former glory and plunge headfirst into a new career as a winemaker. In addition to using her Mission grapes to make small-batch handcrafted Angelica, a traditional style of fortified dessert wine, which is sold in a hand-blown glass bottle with a wax seal, Deborah produces award-winning Pinot Noir. She also offers a limited number of 300- to 400-year-old collectors bottles each year, available only by special order. Her vineyards have been called the oldest existing vineyards in Santa Barbara County, and she makes Gypsy Canyon Angelica using a late-nineteenth-century formula. Gypsy Canyon Ancient Vine Angelica NV is the color of honey and nearly as viscous. Mouth-pleasing flavors of dried fig, apricots, and toasted almond are backed by a gentle dusting of earthy mountain herbs.

HAPPY CANYON VINEYARD

813 Anacapa Street, Santa Barbara, CA 93101,
(805) 966-9463
www.happycanyonvineyard.com

Thomas Barrack bought Piocho Ranch in 1992 partly for his love of vineyards and partly for his love of polo. All four wines produced at Happy Canyon Vineyard have a relationship to the game: Chukker, Ten Goal, Barrack Brand, and Piocho. There are two regulation-sized polo fields, and late summer brings with it polo teams from around the world and fiery competitions. Piocho means "where the two rivers meet and go to heaven" in the indigenous Chumash language. Winemaking is under the direction of Doug Margerum. Happy Canyon Vineyard Ten Goal 2008 is composed of 90 percent Cabernet Sauvignon, 5 percent Cabernet Franc, and 5 percent Merlot. It is garnet colored, with aromas of black fruits, graphite, and black licorice. It is fruit-forward but restrained on the palate with a luxurious, lingering finish. It's a shame only 179 cases were produced. Happy Canyon Vineyards Piocho Santa Ynez Valley 2010 is a blend of 55 percent Merlot, 23 percent Cabernet Sauvignon, 18 percent Cabernet Franc, 2 percent Petit Verdot, and 2 percent Malbec. It has aromas of black raspberries, black currant, and black cherries. In the mouth the fruit flavors are enhanced by vanilla and a fine-grained oak frame. The finish goes on and on.

HARTLEY OSTINI HITCHING POST WINES

PO Box 2009, 406 East Highway 246,
Buellton, CA 93427, (805) 688-0676
www.hitchingpostwines.com

Every wine lover has seen the movie *Sideways*, whose protagonist, Miles, falls hopelessly in love with a waitress named Maya at The Hitching Post restaurant in Buellton. Although in real life there is no waitress named Maya, there is indeed a restaurant named The Hitching Post that is owned by larger-than-life chef Frank Ostini. Frank and his good friend fisherman Gray Hartley started making homemade wine in 1979 and then moved their operation to local wineries, including Au Bon Climat and Qupé. Hartley Ostini Hitching Post Wines are currently being made at the Terravant Winery, just a short distance from the restaurant. Hartley Ostini Hitching Post Pinks Dry Rosé 2012 is named for the color of pink Alaskan salmon. It is pale pink in color and is made from 48 percent Valdiguié, 47 percent Grenache, and 5 percent Pinot Noir. It has aromas of strawberries and cream, crushed red raspberry, and citrus blossom. It is round yet crisp and refreshing in the mouth with a clean finish. Hartley Ostini Hitching Post Highliner Pinot Noir 2010 is cherry red, with aromas of red raspberries, red cherries, and a touch of Christmas baking spices. The fruit flavors open up on the palate, and the finish is clean and luxurious.

finish. The tannins are large and linear. Drink it now or lay it down for a few years. It's all good.

JAFFURS WINE CELLARS

819 E. Montecito Street, Santa Barbara, CA 93103,
(805) 962-7003
www.jaffurswine.com

Craig Jaffurs is known in Santa Barbara for his production of fine wines from Rhône varieties. He produced his first wine in 1994, and today his production of small-lot wines totals around 3,500 cases. He sources Syrah, Grenache, Petite Sirah, Viognier, and Roussanne grapes from growers in Santa Ynez, Santa Rita, Los Alamos, and Santa Maria. Jaffurs Wine Cellars Stolpman Vineyard Santa Barbara County Roussanne 2011 is pale straw colored. It has intoxicating aromas of lemon zest, lime juice, and white pepper. It has nice heft with linear acidity. It is crisp and clean in the mouth with a refreshing finish. Jaffurs Wine Cellars Santa Barbara County Syrah 2010 is inky purple, with big aromas of cassis, black raspberry conserves, and dried black cherries. It is fruit-forward in the mouth with freshly ground black pepper in the

LARNER VINEYARD

955 Ballard Canyon Road, Solvang, CA 93463,
(805) 350-1435
www.larnervineyard.com

Founded by Stevan and Christine Larner in 1997, Larner Vineyard consists of 134 acres of land with plantation of 34 acres of vines, including Grenache, Mourvèdre, Syrah, and Viognier. At the time of this writing, the Larners are constructing a new winery to be completed in two phases. The existing tasting room at Ballard General Store is undergoing an upgrade and expansion. Larner Vineyard Estate Grown Santa Ynez Valley Syrah 2009 is inky purple, with aromas of cassis, black plum, and black raspberry. It is fruit-forward in the mouth with the presence of fine-grain tannins. The finish is long and luxurious.

LINCOURT

1711 Alamo Pintado Road, Solvang, CA 93464,
(805) 688-8554
www.lincourtwines.com

Named for Bill Foley's daughters Lindsay and Courtney, Lincourt sources grapes from its own estate vineyards situated within Santa Barbara County: Rancho Las Hermanas and Rancho Santa Rosa in the Sta. Rita Hills for Chardonnay, Pinot Noir, and Syrah; Santa Ynez's Alamo Pintado for Sauvignon Blanc; and La Cuesta for Cabernet and Merlot. Lincourt Carol Ann Chardonnay 2010 is medium straw colored, with aromas of Granny Smith apples, citrus blossoms, and just a touch of cinnamon. It is fruit-forward in the glass with restrained elegance and a crisp, clean finish. Lincourt Bouchaine Estate Block 43 Pinot Noir 2010 is cherry red with notes of cherry cola, black currants, and dried black cherries in the complex bouquet. It has nice heft on the palate with refreshing acidity and a long finish.

LONGORIA WINES

2935 Grand Avenue, Los Olivos, CA 93441,
(805) 688-0305
www.longoriawine.com

Many agree that Rick Longoria was one of the first, if not *the* first, of the established wineries in downtown Lompoc. He was the winemaker for J. Carey Cellars and started his own business in 1982 with a loan from his father, producing 500 cases of Chardonnay and Pinot Noir from vineyards in the Santa Maria Valley. He worked as the winemaker for Gainey Vineyards in 1985, and in 1998 he moved his equipment into a 5,400-square-foot building in what has since become the Lompoc Wine Ghetto. Rick had the early insight that Santa Barbara had the potential to produce world-class wines. He continues to produce small-lot handcrafted wines; his annual production is only 3,000 cases. Longoria Sta. Rita Hills Fe Ciega Vineyard Pinot Noir 2010 has aromas of red cherries, dried Mediterranean herbs, and a touch of toasted oak. It is balanced in the palate with prolonged acidity and a persistent finish. Longoria Santa Ynez Valley Clover Creek Vineyard Tempranillo 2009 has aromas of red raspberries, red cherries, and black peppercorns. The flavors of red fruits move seamlessly onto your palate, with soft sweet tannins in the finish.

MARGERUM WINE COMPANY

813 Anacapa Street, Santa Barbara, CA 93003, (805) 845-8435
www.margerumwinecompany.com

Doug Margerum began his career in food and wine in 1981 when his family purchased a locally renowned wine store, the Wine Cask, and expanded it to a bistro and again to a well-respected restaurant. He started his eponymous wine company in 2001 and currently produces 6,000 cases of wine annually under four labels: Sybarite, Über, M5, and Klickitat. Margerum Wine Company M5 Santa Barbara County 2009 is a blend of 51 percent Syrah, 32 percent Grenache, 11 percent Mourvèdre, 3 percent Counoise, and 3 percent Cinsault. It is ruby garnet in color, with aromas of black licorice, black plum, and cigar box. It has nice acidity on the palate with a long, rich finish. Margerum Wine Company Klickitat Pinot Gris 2010 is pale straw, with aromas of citrus blossoms, white flowers, and lemon zest. It is refreshing and pleasant in the mouth with strong acidity and a touch of residual sugar on the finish. It is a perfect match for spicy cuisine.

MELVILLE WINERY

5185 Highway 246, Lompoc, CA 93436, (805) 735-7030
www.melvillewinery.com

Ron Melville's passion for the wines of Burgundy brought him to Lompoc, and in 1996 he planted four different clones of Chardonnay and fourteen different clones of Pinot Noir on 82 acres of land. He subsequently purchased an additional 100 acres in Cat Canyon, north of Los Alamos in Santa Barbara County. His sons Brent and Chad are active in the family business, and winemaking is under the direction of Greg Brewer. Melville Winery Sta. Rita Hills Estate Chardonnay 2011 is medium straw yellow, with aromas of white peach, Cavaillon melon, and citrus blossom. It has bright fruit flavors with a touch of creaminess—think English lemon curd—and a delightful well-rounded finish. Melville Winery Block M Estate Pinot Noir 2011 is ruby red, with aromas of candied orange peel, red fruits, and cherry cola. It has nice heft on the palate with a balanced acidic finish.

OJAI VINEYARD

109 South Montgomery Street, Ojai, CA 93023,
(805) 798-3947
www.ojaivineyard.com

Adam Tolmach studied enology and viticulture at the University of California, Davis, and graduated in 1976. He started his career working at Zaca Mesa Winery and subsequently partnered with fellow employee Jim Clendenen in 1982 to start Au Bon Climat. In 1991 the pair separated; Jim bought Adam's share, and Adam concentrated his efforts on his Ojai vineyards. Today Adam works closely with his wife, Helen, as well as Fabien Castel, and together the team produces approximately 6,500 cases of wine per year. Ojai Vineyards Bien Nacido Vineyard Chardonnay 2009 is straw yellow, with aromas of citrus blossom, white flowers, and white stone fruits. It has nice heft on the palate with balanced acidity and a persistent finish. Ojai Vineyard Kick On Pinot Noir 2009 has aromas of ripe black cherry, cigar box, and fennel bulb. It is big and fruit-forward in the mouth with restrained elegance in the finish.

PALMINA

1520 East Chestnut Court, Lompoc, CA 93436,
(805) 735-2030
www.palminawines.com

Steve Clifton honored his good friend and surrogate grandmother, Palmina, by naming his winery in her memory. His Italian varieties have been acclaimed by numerous publications, and many wine experts agree that his wines rival those produced in Italy. His whites include Arneis, Malvasia Bianca, Pinot Grigio, Tocai Friulano, and Traminer, and his reds include Barbera and Nebbiolo. Palmina Santa Barbara County Barbera 2010 is certainly a food-friendly wine. It has aromas of black raspberries, cassis, and orange zest. It is full-bodied in the mouth with soft tannins and a balanced acidic finish. Palmina Santa Barbara County Malvasia Bianca 2011 is pale straw colored, with aromas of white flowers, citrus blossoms, and green olives. It is light and crisp in the mouth with zesty acidity in the finish. This wine calls out for food; think oysters and shellfish.

QUPÉ WINE CELLARS

2963 Grand Avenue, Los Olivos, CA 93441,
(805) 686-4200
www.qupe.com

Bob Lindquist named his winery Qupé for the indigenous Chumash tribal word for "poppy," which happens to be the California state flower. Bob began his wine career working at Zaca Mesa Winery, and instead of receiving a salary he traded his services for the use of the winery's equipment. His first commercial release was 900 cases of Chardonnay, Syrah, and Pinot Noir Rosé in 1982. In 1989 he partnered with Jim Clendenen, and together they began producing fine wines in conjunction with Bien Nacido Vineyards. In October 2013 investor Charles Banks purchased a majority share in Qupé, with Lindquist remaining on as winemaker and partner. Qupé Wine Cellars Sawyer Lindquist Vineyard Viognier 2012 is light straw colored, with aromas of Anjou pears, white stone fruits, and citrus blossoms. It is full-bodied in the mouth with balanced fruit sweetness and crisp minerality. Qupé Wine Cellars Edna Valley Sawyer Lindquist Vineyard Grenache 2011 is ruby purple, with aromas of freshly picked red cherry and dried Mediterranean herbs. It is fruity on the palate with nice intensity and a persistent finish.

SANFORD WINERY AND VINEYARDS

5010 Santa Rosa Road, Lompoc, CA 93436,
(800) 426-9463
www.sanfordwinery.com

Founded in 1971, Sanford Winery and Vineyards first planted Pinot Noir vines in its Sanford & Benedict Vineyard. Today Sanford is majority-owned by Anthony Terlato and his sons, and with the artistry of winemaker Steve Fennel, it continues to produce quality cool-climate Pinot Noir and Chardonnay. Sanford Winery Sta. Rita Hills Pinot Noir 2009 is bright red in the glass, with aromas of red raspberries, dark cherries, and lavender. In the mouth the fruit flavors pop with a touch of spice, namely, freshly ground black pepper. The finish is pleasantly acidic with round tannins. Sanford Winery Sanford & Benedict Vineyard Pinot Noir 2008 is brilliant ruby red, with notes of red raspberry, Chinese five-spice powder, and dried cherry in the bouquet. There are silky tannins on the palate with a touch of acidity on the finish.

SEA SMOKE CELLARS

No visitor facilities.
(805) 737-1600
www.seasmokecellars.com

Bob Davids acquired the land that was to become Sea Smoke Cellars in 1999. His belief that the vineyard shapes the wine is the reason Sea Smoke makes wine only from estate fruit grown in their vineyard in the Sta. Rita Hills AVA. Sea Smoke is a small operation: only six people work to produce these well-crafted and highly acclaimed wines. Sea Smoke Chardonnay 2010 is golden straw colored, with aromas of pineapple upside-down cake, candied lemon, and green apples. It has flavors of Anjou pear, honeysuckle, and lemon curd and a full-bodied mouthfeel. The finish is clean, inviting you in for another sip. Sea Smoke Southing Pinot Noir 2010 is cherry red, with aromas of cherry cola and red raspberries. It is complex in the mouth with a delightful finish. Hold it for a few years, as the flavors will continue to develop in the bottle.

SINE QUA NON

No visitor facilities. PO Box 1048,
Oak View, CA 93022,
(805) 640-8901
www.sinequanon.com

What started as a hobby in 1994 for Elaine and Manfred Krankl became their life dream when their newly released wine immediately rocketed to cult status. The winery name comes from the Latin "without which [there is] nothing." The couple sources grapes from their four estate vineyards: Eleven Confessions, Cumulus, Third Twin, and Molly Aida. Sine Qua Non wines are produced from Rhône varieties, including Syrah, Grenache, Mourvèdre, Roussanne, and Viognier. Sine Qua Non Five Shooter Grenache 2010 is a blend of all of these. It is garnet to purple in color, with aromas of black and red fruits and a touch of spice in the enticing bouquet. It is fruit-forward yet restrained in the mouth with nice heft on the tongue. The finish is long and luxurious and invites you in for another sip.

STOLPMAN VINEYARDS

2434 Alamo Pintado Avenue, Los Olivos, CA 93441,
(805) 688-0400
www.stolpmanvineyards.com

Marilyn and Tom Stolpman founded their eponymous vineyards in 1990, sold grapes for years, and began making their own wine in 1997.

Vineyard management is handled by Ruben Solorzano, and winemaker Sashi Moorman joined the team in 2001. Stolpman wines are highly rated by a number of prestigious wine magazines. Stolpman Vineyards L'Avion 2010 is composed of 100 percent Roussanne. It has lovely floral aromas—think freesia and honeysuckle—and a strong presence of white stone fruits with a top note of peppermint. It is voluptuous in the mouth with a nice balance of fruit sweetness and acidity. Stolpman Vineyards Syrah 2010 is garnet purple, with aromas of red raspberry, red plum, and purple flowers. It is generous on the palate with ripe fruit flavors and a balanced sweet tannic finish.

TANTARA WINERY

2330 Westgate Road, Santa Maria, CA 93456,
(805) 938-5051
www.tantarawines.com

Named for owner Bill Cate's horse, Tantara has been producing highly rated wines since

1997 from grapes sourced from Solomon Hills, Sanford & Benedict, Bien Nacido, Silacci, Pisoni, Tondre, and Brousseau, among other vineyards. Tantara Winery Bien Nacido Vineyard Chardonnay 2010 is straw colored, with aromas of caramelized pineapple, white stone fruits, and citrus blossom. It is full-bodied on the palate with fruit flavors and balanced minerality. Tantara Winery Bien Nacido Adobe Pinot Noir 2010 is ruby red, with aromas of freshly picked strawberries, red plum, and forest floor. It has balanced acidity and flavors of red fruits accented by a fine dusting of cocoa powder. We wish that more than 213 cases of this delicious wine had been produced.

TENSLEY WINES

2900 Grand Avenue,
Los Olivos, CA 93441,
(805) 688-6761
www.tensleywines.com

Joey Tensley began his winemaking career as a "cellar rat" at Fess Parker Winery in 1993, and in 1998 he launched his eponymous label while maintaining his position as assistant winemaker at Beckmen Vineyards. Today he produces more than 3,000 cases of vineyard-designated Syrah per year while maintaining his artisanal hands-on approach to winemaking. Tensley wines are consistently rated in the mid-90s by

Wine Advocate and *Wine Spectator*, and perhaps Joey's philosophy of "get out of the way and let the vineyard speak for itself" has been responsible for his wide acclaim. We met Joey and his lovely wife, Jennifer, at a tasting in New York City, and when we mentioned that we had just finished a cookbook, they both asked, "When are we invited for dinner at your house?" As luck would have it, the next evening was free for all of us, and while we cooked, the Tensleys opened their wines. Tensley Winery Camp 4 Vineyard Blanc 2011 is a blend of 65 percent Grenache Blanc and 35 percent Roussanne. It is light straw colored, with aromas of Granny Smith apples, Anjou pears, and lemon blossom. In the mouth there is crisp acidity but a smooth rounded mouthfeel and flavors of white stone fruits, honeycomb, and white flowers. Tensley Winery Turner Vineyard Syrah 2011 is garnet colored, with notes of blueberry pie, red raspberry, and freshly ground black pepper in the bouquet. Flavors of blueberry and black plum hit the palate first, followed by nuances of saddle leather and smoked charcuterie. Drink it now or hold it for 10 years; you won't be disappointed either way.

TRANSCENDENCE WINES

313 N. F Street, Lompoc, CA 93436,
(805) 689-5258
www.transcendwines.com

Kenneth "Joey" Gummere has been making wine in Santa Barbara County since 1997. He and his wife, Sarah, make delicious cool-climate small-production wine from Syrah, Pinot Noir, and Chardonnay grapes and are extremely involved in several local and international nonprofit organizations, including Hope Through Opportunity, Fallbrook Healthcare Foundation, and Project Transcend, an organization that educates people living in the shadow of Mount Kilimanjaro. Transcendence Zotovich Vineyard Chardonnay 2011 is straw colored, with aromas of tropical fruits, Anjou pear, and lemon blossoms. It is full in the mouth with a pleasant, bright acidity. Transcendence Lafond Vineyard Pinot Noir 2011 is cherry red, with notes of purple flowers, dried black cherry, and a touch of forest floor in the bouquet. It is supple on the palate with an elegant acidic finish.

ZACA MESA WINERY & VINEYARDS

6905 Foxen Canyon Road,
Los Olivos, CA 93441,
(805) 688-9339
www.zacamesa.com

Started in 1973 by a group of friends, Zaca Mesa Winery & Vineyards is widely credited with planting the first Syrah in Santa Barbara County. The team also planted Grenache, Mourvèdre, Viognier, and Roussanne, allowing the winemakers to create acclaimed Rhône-style blends. Zaca Mesa is proud that its wines have been served by President Bill Clinton to French President Jacques Chirac at the White House and to President Ronald Reagan at his eightieth birthday party at the Beverly Hilton. Zaca Mesa Estate Black Bear Block Santa Ynez Valley Syrah 2009 is dark inky purple, with aromas of black currant, smoked meats, anise, and black plums. In the mouth flavors of dark fruits and balanced sweet tannins are mouth-filling and elegant. Zaca Mesa Z Cuvée 2008 is a blend of 68 percent Grenache, 18 percent Mourvèdre, and 14 percent Syrah. It has delightful aromas of black raspberry and fresh-picked blueberries. It is fruit-forward in the mouth with prominent flavors of dark fruits and has a pleasant long-lasting finish.

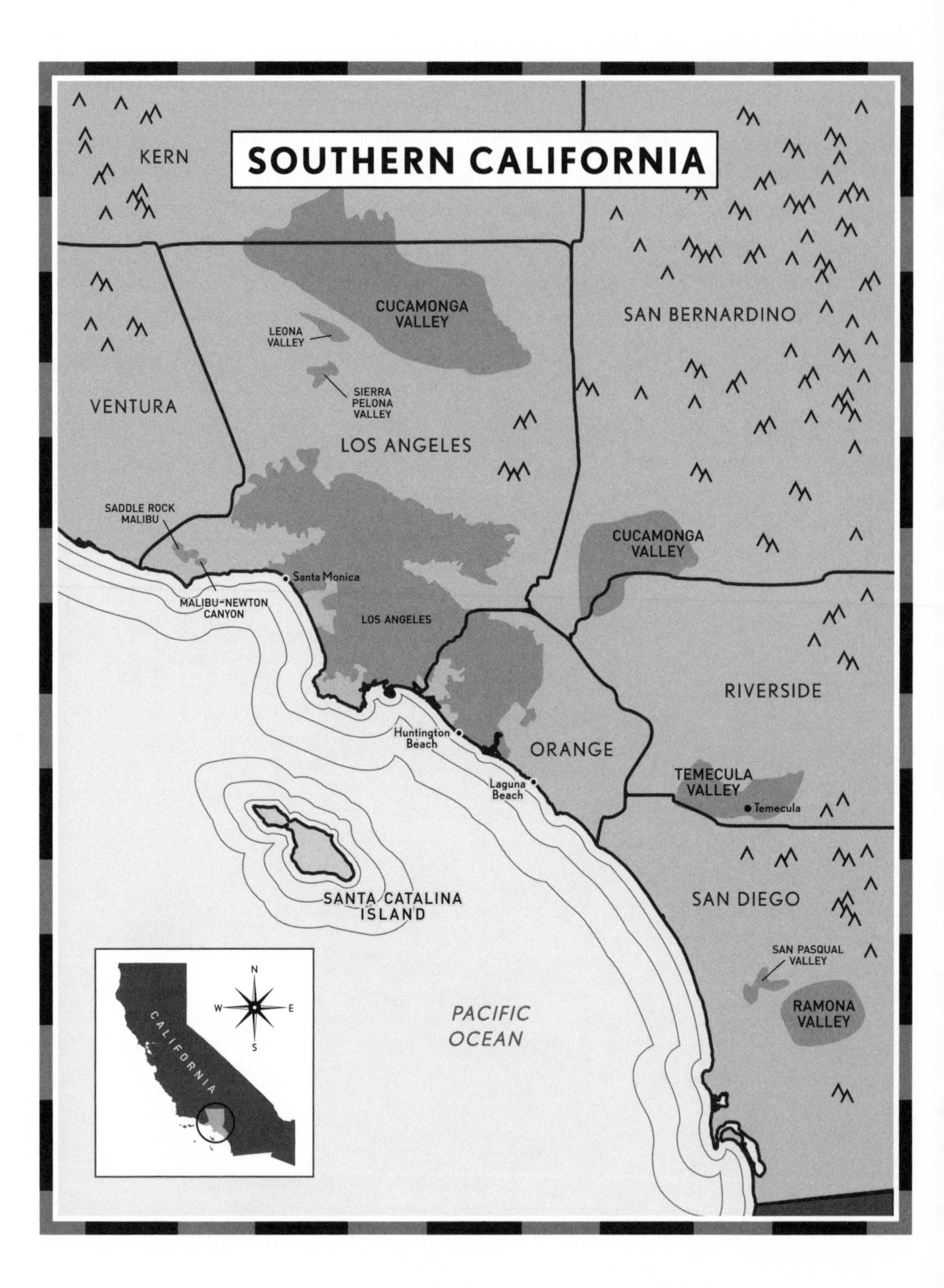

SOUTHERN CALIFORNIA
KERN
VENTURA
LOS ANGELES
SAN BERNARDINO
CUCAMONGA VALLEY
LEONA VALLEY
SIERRA PELONA VALLEY
SADDLE ROCK MALIBU
MALIBU-NEWTON CANYON
Santa Monica
LOS ANGELES
CUCAMONGA VALLEY
RIVERSIDE
ORANGE
Huntington Beach
Laguna Beach
TEMECULA VALLEY
Temecula
SANTA CATALINA ISLAND
SAN DIEGO
SAN PASQUAL VALLEY
RAMONA VALLEY
PACIFIC OCEAN
CALIFORNIA
N
W
E
S

CHAPTER 11

SOUTHERN CALIFORNIA AND THE SOUTH COAST AVA

SOUTHERN CALIFORNIA IS REALLY THE place we all think about when "California Dreamin'" sets in. Our collective imagination can't help but be taken in by images of movie stars, the Academy Awards, Rodeo Drive, convertibles, surfing, and long-legged beauties with sun-streaked hair. Although wine may not be the first thing that comes to mind when picturing the southern part of the state, this is where grape growing and winemaking arrived first. California's first successful vineyard for winemaking was planted near modern-day San Diego in 1779 by Father Junípero Serra. Known today as "the Father of California Wine," Padre Serra planted his vineyard at Mission San Diego de Alcala and built a rudimentary winery on the site a year later. The only grape grown here at the time was Mission, which is known as *Pais* in Chile and *Criolla Chica* in Argentina. In the late 1700s the United States was a brand-new country, and California was years away from becoming a full-fledged state; it was then known as the *Provincia de Las Californias*, part of the Viceroyalty of New Spain.

In 1833, fifteen years before the California Gold Rush and seventeen years before the territory achieved statehood, Frenchman Jean-Louis Vignes had Cabernet Sauvignon and Sauvignon Blanc cuttings brought to him from his native Bordeaux. He had attempted to make drinkable wine using available Mission grapes and was not happy with the outcome. He is said to have been the first person in California to age his wine in wood, using barrels he made himself from lumber forested on his own property in the San Bernardino Mountains. Ten years later he was shipping wine by sea northward to Santa Barbara, Monterey, and San Francisco. By the time California became a state, Vignes was producing more than 150,000 bottles of wine each year.

The AVAs in southern California stretch from just north of the city of Los Angeles to the southern border of the state, where California meets Mexico. North of Los Angeles is the Antelope Valley of the High Desert AVA, which straddles Los Angeles and Kern Counties. The total area is 665 square miles, and the local winegrowers' association has fourteen growers and six wineries. There are two smaller AVAs nearby: Leona Valley and Sierra Pelona Valley.

To the south and directly on the coast are two Malibu AVAs: Malibu-Newton Canyon and Saddle Rock-Malibu. The Malibu-Newton Canyon AVA owes its existence to real estate and hotel mogul George Rosenthal; the majority of the vineyards in the AVA are on Rosenthal's beautiful private estate a couple of miles inland from the Pacific. Because of regulations limiting industry within municipal limits, grapes grown in Malibu generally are vinified elsewhere, such as Santa Barbara, to the north. There is also a petition before the TTB for a designation of the Malibu Coast AVA.

Cucamonga Valley AVA lies due east of Malibu. Located in San Bernardino County, around 15 miles from the city of San Bernardino, Cucamonga Valley has a history of grape growing stretching back to 1838 that came to a rapid end with the onset of Prohibition in 1920. Prior to that time Cucamonga Valley's annual grape production was higher than that of Napa and Sonoma counties put together. Since the repeal of Prohibition in 1933, grapes are still grown in this hot, dry valley with alluvial soils, but urban sprawl from Los Angeles and other nearby areas has encroached on vineyard land. The 109,400-acre AVA was officially established in 1985, and total plantings today are around 1,000 acres, primarily Bordeaux and Rhône varieties. Cucamonga Valley boasts some of the state's finest old-vine Zinfandel vineyards, whose production generally is sold to winemakers elsewhere in the state.

Just to the south is the large South Coast AVA, which encompasses an area of 115,200 acres. This AVA continues south to the Mexican border and contains several other AVAs within its limits: the Temecula Valley (33,000 acres), Ramona Valley (89,000 acres), and San Pasqual Valley (9,000 acres) AVAs. The most densely planted and best known of these is Temecula Valley, which draws many tourists each year from San Diego, Los Angeles, and the surrounding areas.

The Temecula Valley AVA—and the small city of Temecula—is at the center of a triangle, with Los Angeles, San Diego, and Palm Springs at the three corners. The area has been populated for thousands of years, and the Temecula Indians became known as the Luiseño Indians after the founding of the nearby Spanish mission San Luis Rey de Francia. The name Temecula roughly translates from the indigenous language as "the place where the sun breaks through the mist," and it is the sun and the mist hovering over the valley's sedimentary soils, filled with decomposed granite, that make the area perfect for the cultivation of grapes. Although Temecula is in the far southern part of the state, average vineyard elevation is around 1,500 feet, which provides for cooler temperatures than would be expected at a lower elevation. A cooling effect is also achieved by cold Pacific air infiltrating the valley as warm air is drawn upward by the heat of the daytime sun. Cooler daytime air enters the valley through gaps in the Coastal Mountain Range; this helps cool the grapes and keep the finished wine from having a cooked or stewed quality. Large swings between daytime and nighttime temperatures help retain acidity in the grapes, another necessary quality for the production of balanced wines.

The well-drained soil with a minimum of organic matter is inhospitable to phylloxera, but warmer year-round temperatures provide an unfortunately ideal environment for Pierce's disease, which is caused by the bacterium *Xylella fastidiosa*. This bacterium that destroys grapevines is spread by glassy-winged sharpshooters, a type of grasshopper that thrives throughout the American South. Over the last 15 years more than $70 million has been spent in the state to eradicate this pest. Efforts include ripping out and replanting affected vineyards and introducing parasitic wasps whose eggs interfere with the breeding cycle of the glassy-winged sharpshooters.

According to the religious beliefs of the native peoples, life began in the Temecula Valley, and while taking in the natural beauty of the area it is easy to understand why they would think this. The first commercial vineyard was established in this natural paradise in 1968, with a handful of other ventures following in the next several years. The Temecula AVA was officially established in 1984, and the same viticultural area was rechristened the Temecula Valley AVA on June 18, 2004. Today the Temecula Valley Winegrowers Association has thirty-five member wineries, most of which offer tastings and tours. Several feature full-service restaurants and overnight accommodations. Several different styles of wine are produced here, including Zinfandel, Cabernet Sauvignon, and Bordeaux-style blends, both white and red Rhône Valley blends, Italian varieties such as Sangiovese and Nebbiolo, and white wines such as Chardonnay and Sauvignon Blanc.

THE WINERIES

BAILY VINEYARD & WINERY

33440 La Serena Way, Temecula, CA 92591,
(951) 676-9463
www.bailywinery.com

Phil and Carol Baily started growing grapes over 25 years ago, making this one of Temecula's oldest wineries. When you stop in for a wine tasting, make sure to take some time to enjoy a delicious meal at Carol's on-premises restaurant or visit their other locations, Baily's Fine Dining and Front Street Bar and Grill, in the town center.

On a recent visit Phil arranged a vertical tasting from the last four years, and we were quite impressed by his wine's evolution over the years. Baily Vineyard & Winery Estate Bottled Meritage 2009 is a blend of 55 percent Cabernet Sauvignon, 20 percent Cabernet Franc, 20 percent Merlot, and 5 percent Malbec. It is deep cherry colored in the glass, with aromas of black cherry, summer farm stand, and fresh paprika. In the mouth rich flavors of fresh cherry and black raspberry along with notes of freshly ground white pepper, violet, lavender, and brown spices are present before the sweet and elegant tannic finish.

CALLAWAY VINEYARD & WINERY

32720 Rancho California Road, Temecula, CA 92591,
(951) 676-4001
www.callawaywinery.com

Founded over 40 years ago by golf icon Ely Reeves Callaway, Callaway Winery was owned by the Hiram Walker Company and then Allied Domecq until 2005. Callaway has the distinction of being the first dry table wine from Southern California to be served to Queen Elizabeth II at a New York City diplomatic luncheon in 1976. Today the Lin family of San Diego privately owns Callaway Vineyard & Winery, and the wines are available only at the winery. Callaway Vineyard & Winery Winemaker's Reserve Chardonnay 2009 is pale straw, with aromas of butterscotch and Granny Smith apples. It has flavors of honeydew melon, buttered toast, guava, and a nicely oaked finish for lovers of oaky California Chards. Callaway Vineyard & Winery Winemaker's Reserve Calliope Red 2009 is a blend of 42 percent Syrah, 28 percent Mourvèdre, 20 percent Grenache, 5 percent Cinsault, and 5 percent Counoise. It is cherry red in color, with notes of blackberries, red raspberry jam, ripe cassis, cinnamon, and nutmeg in the bouquet. In the mouth there are a lot of red and black fruits with nuances of oregano, black pepper butcher cut, and cremini mushrooms, with a pleasant finish.

DOFFO VINEYARDS

36083 Summitville Street, Temecula, CA 92592,
(951) 676-6989
www.doffowines.com

It is easy to feel the Doffo family's Argentine-Italian hospitality when visiting Doffo Winery in Temecula. Their hearty and heartfelt welcome makes their loyal fans return again and again. Doffo Winery is built on the site of a historic schoolhouse and encompasses 15 acres of planted vines. Motorcycle enthusiasts will love the family's private collection of over 100 vintage and racing motorcycles at its on-premise museum, MotoDoffo. Doffo Vineyards Reserve Syrah 2008 is inky purple with a blueberry-colored rim. It has aromas of blackberry, cassis, strawberry jam, cocoa powder, and a touch of tomato leaf. It has flavors of dark plum, black cherry, tart cherry, and mocha. The soft tannins lead to a refreshing fruit splash at the finish. The unique bottle doubles as its own decanter.

FALKNER WINERY

40620 Calle Contento, Temecula, CA 92591,
(951) 676-8231
www.falknerwinery.com

Ray and Loretta Falkner left jobs in technology and retail, respectively, and opened Falkner Winery on July 1, 2000. The winery

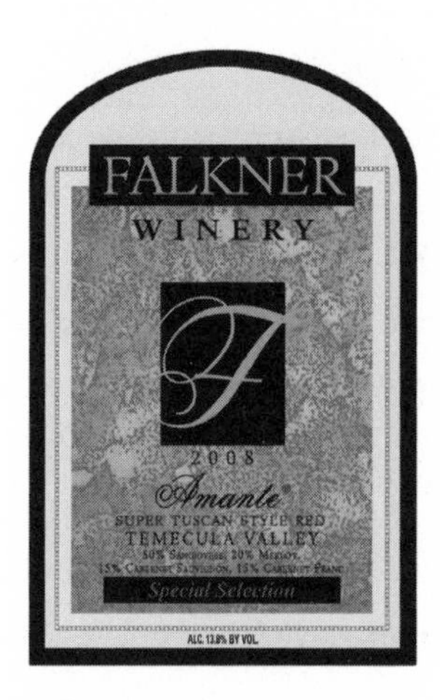

has amazing views from on top of a 1,500-foot hill, and their award-winning Pinnacle restaurant offers Mediterranean cuisine for lunch all year long. At night the Pinnacle becomes a popular space for weddings and private events. Steve Hagata is in charge of the winemaking, and his wines have garnered numerous accolades. Falkner Winery Estate Grown Viognier 2011 is pale straw colored, with a nose of stone fruits, white flowers, and a touch of petrol. In the mouth it is medium-bodied and creamy with flavors of white peach and Cavaillon melon, with a lilting florality in the finish. Falkner Winery Special Selection Amante 2008 is a blend of 50 percent Sangiovese, 20 percent Merlot, 15 percent Cabernet Sauvignon, and 15 percent Cabernet Franc. It is medium ruby in color, with aromas of cherry cola, mocha, espresso, and forest floor. On the palate one finds cherry cola, tobacco, Mediterranean herbs, eucalyptus, and a gripping tannic structure.

HART WINERY

41300 Avenida Biona,
Temecula, CA 92591,
(951) 676-6300
www.hartfamilywinery.com

Joe and Nancy Hart planted their first Cabernet Sauvignon, Cabernet Franc, Merlot, Sauvignon Blanc, Syrah, and Viognier vines in 1974 and in 1980 built their winery and produced their first wines. Today, with their son Jim, they produce about 5,000 cases, and their wines have won numerous gold medals in local competitions. Hart Family Winery Sangiovese 2010 is cherry red in color with a fair amount of brown spice—think cinnamon and nutmeg—in the nose. It has characteristic black cherry and dark plum flavors and a touch of spice in the finish. Hart Family Winery Roussanne 2011 is light straw colored, with notes of citrus blossom and grapefruit pith, with a light florality. In the mouth it is refreshing and crisp.

LEONESS CELLARS

38311 De Portola Road, Temecula, CA 92592,
(951) 302-7601
www.leonesscellars.com

Gary Winder and Mike Rennie founded Leoness Cellars in 2003. Both men had been involved in Temecula Valley agriculture for years, and so the decision to open a winery was natural for them. They chose to name their winery Leoness because as they explain, the word "leoness" translates to "village of dreams." They currently produce highly rated wine from Cabernet Sauvignon, Cinsault, Grenache, Merlot, Cabernet Franc, Syrah, Chardonnay, Muscat Canelli, and Viognier grape varieties. Leoness Cellars Curry Vineyard Syrah 2009 is dark garnet, with a complex bouquet of fruit, leather, spice, and a touch of lifted eucalyptus. In the mouth it has flavors of licorice root and black plum and a splash of bright fruit that lingers on the palate through the finish. The tannins are velvety smooth with a pleasant level of acidity. Leoness Cellars Mélange de Reves 2008 is a proprietary blend of Syrah, Cinsault, and Grenache. It is garnet colored, with notes of black raspberry, dark plum, cigar box, and freshly ground black pepper in the bouquet. There is a touch of eucalyptus upon entry into the mouth, with flavors of sweet black fruits, dried black cherry, fennel, and Mission fig before the sweet tannic finish.

MIRAMONTE WINERY

33410 Rancho California Road,
Temecula, CA 92591,
(951) 506-5500
www.miramontewinery.com

Miramonte has been entertaining its regular customers with live music every Friday and Saturday night since 2001. Cane Vanderhoof founded the winery in 2000, bought a neighboring piece of property in 2008, and currently sources grapes from 44 acres of vineyards in Temecula that he either owns, manages, or maintains long-standing contracts with. Miramonte Winery Tempranillo 2009 is 85 percent Tempranillo and 15 percent Grenache and is bright cherry in color. On the nose there are aromas of blackberry, black pepper, anise, and cherry cola. In the mouth it has flavors of cranberry, boysenberry, smoked meats, and grilled Portobello mushrooms. Miramonte Winery Opulente 2009 is a blend of 50 percent Grenache, 25 percent Syrah, 22 percent Mourvèdre, and 3 percent Cinsault. It is cherry red with a violet tinge and has aromas of cherry, tobacco leaf, and blueberry pie. It is smooth and sensual on the palate with flavors of cherry and waves of mint and eucalyptus.

MONTE DE ORO

35820 Rancho California Road,
Temecula, CA 92591,
(951) 491-6551
www.montedeoro.com

Sixty-eight family owners from the United States, the United Kingdom, and South Africa came together in 2002 and started "OGB," or "One Great Blend." Their simple principle at that time was "Vines, Wine, and People." Monte De Oro's first vineyard, Vista Del Monte, was planted that year with 18 acres of Cabernet Sauvignon and Syrah. Their second vineyards, DePortola and Galway, planted in 2003, are composed of 18 acres and 23 acres, respectively, and are planted with Cabernet Franc, Viognier, Zinfandel, Merlot, Pinot Gris, Sauvignon Blanc, Muscat Canelli, and Chardonnay. Today the group owns 72 acres and produces wine only from its estate-sourced grapes. Monte De Oro Estate Grown Nostimo 2011 is pale straw colored and is a blend of 30 percent Viognier, 30 percent Sauvignon Blanc, 20 percent Pinot Gris, and 20 percent Muscat Canelli. Aromas of grapefruit, citrus blossom, and freesia entice you in for a lingering sip. In the mouth it has pure grapefruit and citrus flavors with a crisp, clean, and refreshing finish. It is ideal as an aperitif or paired with seafood. Monte De Oro Vista Del Monte Estate Grown Syrah 2009 is cherry to garnet colored with a purple rim. The nose has aromas of mixed-berry pie, dark fruit compote, and spice notes of clove and cinnamon. In the mouth it is smooth and silky with a burst of fruit flavors followed by nuances of anise and fennel before the balanced tannic finish.

MORAGA VINEYARDS

650 North Sepulveda Boulevard,
Los Angeles, CA 90049,
(310) 471-8560
www.moragavineyards.com

Considered by many to be "the only commercial vineyard in Los Angeles," Moraga Vineyards was once a horse ranch owned by Hollywood director Victor Fleming, whose masterpieces include *Gone with the Wind* and *The Wizard of Oz*. Tom Jones, the former Northrop Grumman CEO, and his wife, Ruth, purchased and developed the property in 1959 and lived on the estate for many years. Their travels around the world influenced their taste in wine, and their style definitely skews toward Bordeaux. The property is currently owned by media mogul Rupert Murdoch, who purchased the estate in May 2013 for an undisclosed sum. The property includes 7.2 acres of vines: 4 acres of Cabernet Sauvignon, 2 acres of Merlot, 1 acre of Sauvignon Blanc, 0.1 acre of Petit Verdot, and 0.1 acre of Cabernet Franc. It was the first commercial winery to become bonded in Los Angeles after the repeal of Prohibition. Winemaker Tony Soter began working at Moraga in 1987 and later brought in Scott Rich. Moraga Estate White 2011 is produced from Sauvignon Blanc and has a light straw color. Notes of Ruby Red grapefruit juice, lemon zest, and white stone fruits are present in the bouquet. It is fresh and lively in the mouth with persistent flavors of tropical fruits. Moraga Estate Red 2009 is a blend of Cabernet Sauvignon, Merlot, Cabernet Franc, and Petit Verdot. It is garnet colored, with aromas of black fruits, cassis, and graphite in the nose, with rich fruit flavors transferring seamlessly onto the palate. The finish is long and luxurious.

PALUMBO FAMILY VINEYARDS & WINERY

40150 Barksdale Circle, Temecula, CA 92592,
(951) 676-7900
www.palumbofamilyvineyards.com

Nick Palumbo's career in food and wine began when he was living in Williamsburg, Brooklyn, and signed up for culinary courses at the New School. He moved back to San Diego in 1997, and in 1998 he purchased seven acres of existing vineyards and began growing grapes. Soon afterward he purchased additional vineyards and today produces limited-production wine from grapes grown on his estate's 13 acres. Palumbo Family Vineyards & Winery Tre Fratelli Meritage 2009 is a blend of 40 percent Cabernet Sauvignon, 40 percent Merlot, and 20 percent Cabernet Franc. It is deep garnet to deep black cherry colored with a luminous violet rim. On the nose there are notes of blackberry, raspberry, and a touch of smoked meats. In the mouth there are flavors of cherry cola, cassis, baking spices, mint, and pipe tobacco. There is a persistent tannic finish that allows you to drink it now or through the next seven years. Palumbo Family Vineyards & Winery Shiraz/Cabernet Sauvignon 2009 is a blend of 60 percent Shiraz and 40 percent Cabernet Sauvignon. It is garnet red with a bright rim and has aromas of red raspberry, black cherry, and oregano. The mouth is fruit-driven but restrained, with flavors of red raspberry, charcuterie, thyme, and sage.

PONTE FAMILY ESTATE WINERY

35053 Rancho California Road,
Temecula, CA 92592,
(877) 314-9463
www.pontewinery.com

The Ponte family has farmed their vineyards since 1984 and opened their winery in 2003. The winery is surrounded by 300 acres of gardens and vineyards and is a popular site for weddings. Visitors to the winery can also dine at the signature restaurant and stay at the Ponte Vineyard Inn, rated one of the Top Ten Vineyard Hotels in the World by *Departures* magazine. Ponte Family Estate Arneis 2012 is light straw colored, with enticing aromas of Bartlett pear, white stone fruits, and grapefruit rind. It is crisp and clean in the mouth with a refreshing finish. Ponte Family Estate Moscato 2012 has aromas of white flowers and white peaches. It has a fair bit of pleasant sweetness in the mouth, making it ideal as an aperitif on a hot sunny day.

ROBERT RENZONI VINEYARDS

37350 De Portola Road, Temecula, CA 92592,
(951) 302-8466
www.robertrenzonivineyards.com

Federico Renzoni immigrated to the United States in 1912 and began a wine and cordial business with his brother-in-law, Romeo Battistoni, but their new venture was forced to close soon thereafter because of Prohibition. In 1954 Federico's sons Dominic and Romero entered into an alliance with Canandaigua Wine Company (now Constellation Brands) to become the first US distributor for Richards Wild Irish Rose. At that time, the company was based in Buffalo, New York. The family business was eventually sold in 1994, but Federico's great-grandson, Robert Renzoni, has continued the family's passion for making wine since 2008, but this time in the Temecula Valley. Robert Renzoni Vineyards Barile Chardonnay 2011 has aromas of buttered brioche and lemon curd as well as flavors of canned apricots, toffee, and peach pie on the palate. Robert Renzoni Vineyards Cabernet Sauvignon 2008 is garnet colored and has aromas of baking spices, eucalyptus, dark cherries, and purple violets. It has flavors of cassis and black cherry preserves with a touch of mint and spice. The finish is powerful with strong but balanced tannins.

ROSENTHAL MALIBU ESTATE

18741 Pacific Coast Highway,
Malibu, CA 90265,
(310) 456-1392
www.rosenthalestatewines.com

Los Angeles businessman George Rosenthal began planting 32 acres of vines on his 250-acre Malibu estate in 1987 and started making quality wine soon afterward. We had the distinct pleasure and honor of sitting down with George at his Malibu Wine Tasting Room marvelously situated across from the Topanga State Beach on the picturesque Pacific Coast Highway. His winemaker is Christian Roguenant, who crafts delicious wines in a decidedly French style. Rosenthal Malibu Estate Viognier 2010 is pale straw colored, with aromas of freesia, honeysuckle, and white stone fruits in the bouquet. On the palate it has pleasant and crisp acidity with nice minerality, thus allowing the flavors of Granny Smith green apple and white peach to shine. Rosenthal Malibu Estate Malibu-Newton Canyon Cabernet Franc 2008 is dark ruby colored, with aromas of cassis, violet, cigar box, and a touch of minty eucalyptus. In the mouth it has flavors of dark plums, black cherries, freshly ground black pepper, and brown spices. The finish is persistent with a touch of oak and Mediterranean spice.

SOUTH COAST WINERY RESORT & SPA

34843 Rancho California Road,
Temecula, CA 92591,
(951) 587-9463
www.wineresort.com

Jim Carter purchased 400 acres of land in the Temecula Valley in 1981 and eventually placed 38 of them under vine. Today his beautiful resort, winery, and spa sit right in the middle of those vineyards. Jim wants his guests to get the "complete wine country experience" and delivers it to them in the form of great food, delicious wines, relaxing spa treatments, and luxury villas among the vines. Carter's South Coast wines continue to earn awards in the United States, the United Kingdom, Spain, and France. South Coast Winery GVR 2011 is a blend of 44 percent Grenache Blanc, 28 percent Viognier, and 28 percent Roussanne. It is pale straw colored, with delightful aromas of apricot, citrus pith, honeysuckle, and honeycomb. In the mouth it has flavors of white stone fruits, white peach, orange blossoms, and freshly baked brioche with a very pleasant lingering finish. South Coast Winery Carter Estate Private Reserve Malbec 2009 is inky red, almost blue-colored, with aromas of cigar box, tobacco leaf, and dark plums. It has a delightful herbaceous quality in the mouth with restrained fruit, bold spice, chewy tannins, and a lingering finish.

WILSON CREEK WINERY

35960 Rancho California Road,
Temecula, CA 92591,
(951) 699-9463
www.wilsoncreekwinery.com

The Wilson family purchased their 20-acre winery in 1996, and as the family likes to say, they had very little winemaking experience except for Gerry and Rosie Wilson's attempts at making rhubarb and dandelion wine in their Minnesota basement. The times have certainly changed, and the family's wines have won a variety of medals since 2002. Wilson Creek Winery is also a very popular spot for weddings and corporate events. Wilson Creek White Cabernet Sauvignon 2012 is pale straw with a hint of pink like a pale *vin gris.* On the nose there are aromas of fresh cut grass and lemon zest with a tropical fruit—think guava—nuance. In the mouth there are flavors of canned peaches in sugar syrup, candied apricots, toasted pineapple, and a light sprinkling of freshly chopped parsley. There is a nice amount of residual sugar that makes this a perfect pairing with Asian cuisine. Wilson Creek Distinction Vineyard Family Reserve Petite Sirah 2010 is cherry red, with aromas of dried red cherries, cassis, fennel seed, and mocha. On the palate there are flavors of dark chocolate, cherry conserves, fresh red cherry, brown spice, and licorice. The chewy tannins quickly give way to a smooth yet lingering finish.

CLOCKWISE, FROM TOP LEFT: Peter Mondavi Sr., Charles Krug; Cheryl Indelicato, Delicato Family Vineyards; Tom Tiburzi, Domaine Chandon; Joel Peterson, Ravenswood Winery; Gina Gallo, Gallo.

PART 2

IN THEIR OWN WORDS

AGUSTIN F. HUNEEUS JR.

The Huneeus family's holdings, labels, and partnerships include Quintessa, Faust, Illumination, Veramonte, Neyen, Flowers Vineyards and Winery, The Prisoner, and Saldo. Agustin F. Huneeus has worked in the family business for more than 20 years and extends the family tradition as head of the wine portfolio in the United States and abroad.

How did you get involved in the world of wine?
I was born into it as a family business, so I grew up in the vineyards, visiting wineries, first in Chile and then in Argentina and finally in the Napa Valley.

What are some of the biggest changes you have seen in winemaking since you began your career?
In the 20 years I have been in the wine business, I have seen wine go from a niche, unknown product to a mainstream culture where everyone is into wine. You see it in movies, on TV, and being enjoyed in restaurants. Wine is more popular and cooler than I ever imagined possible.

What are some of the exciting changes that you see happening in your area of California?
It's been great to see Napa become such an important producer of Cabernet in the world and to see the growth of Sonoma Coast Pinot Noirs. And of course, the popularity of modern and innovative red blends like The Prisoner.

Where else in the world have you studied, trained, or worked a harvest? How did that influence your winemaking?

I have had the opportunity to make wines in Chile, Argentina, and California, which gives me a unique perspective to think outside the box when we are developing a new blend or harvesting practices.

Which varieties are you working with? Are you experimenting with anything new?

At Flowers Winery, we create Pinot Noir, Chardonnay, and an exciting red blend that also includes Pinot Meunier, which is a very unique blend in the market.

Prisoner Wine Company produces wines with provocative packaging and dramatic Rhône-style blends. This year we are introducing two new wines: a red blend and a white blend that will stand up nicely with the original Prisoner.

At Quintessa, we create two Bordeaux-style wines: a single unique red blend of Cabernet Sauvignon, Merlot, Cabernet Franc, Petit Verdot, and Carménère as well as a white blend, Illumination.

Are there any new areas that you have identified for potential vineyard sites?

We are always looking for properties or opportunities that fit well into our luxury wine portfolio.

What challenges have you faced as a winemaker or winery owner?

We produce high-quality wines with no compromises or shortcuts. And we own our vineyards, so this means we are in the business of farming. Being at the mercy of Mother Nature is always tough as the weather can change the outcome of a harvest overnight. One frost can change yields and sugars for an entire vintage. But to make great wine you have to take risks in farming, and that's what we do each year.

What is your winemaking philosophy?

"Wines are a reflection of place," as my father would say. We create wines with a reason for being that represent where the grapes come from. Flowers and Quintessa could not be made at any other location with any other grapes—we are distinctive.

What would you hope people say about your wine?

Delicious! And I want more.

Do you think that the market should influence winemaking or do you think that winemaking should influence the market?

Perhaps it's both. If you make wine, chances are you're a wine geek. The greatest results come from winemaking having the ability to influence consumers. Pioneers who led the way, like Robert Mondavi, created wine styles that were new and enticing that had a huge impact on the market. But then with wines like The Prisoner, which started slow, this is now a phenomenon due to the market influencing our winemaking choices.

Besides your own wine, what are some of your favorite wines?
When you grow up in the wine business you tend to drink wines your friends are producing or introducing to you, but a few would be Frescobaldi, Rothschild's, and Chateau des Jacques.

What is your opinion on screw cap versus cork closures?
Depending on the wine style, we use both, and each has its benefits as well as challenges.

If you could invite anyone from history, living or dead, to your home for dinner, who would it be? What food would you serve? What wine would you serve?
Leonardo da Vinci, and the food or wine would pale in comparison.

If you were to stay home tonight for a relaxing evening, drinking wine while watching a movie, which movie would you watch? Which wine would you drink? Explain.
With four young children at home, it would most likely be Disney's *Ratatouille,* and I would most likely enjoy one of our own wines, maybe Quintessa or Neyen. We always seem to have some on hand at home.

How do you like to spend your time away from the winery?
I spend time with good friends and family enjoying great food and amazing wines.

Do you collect wine? If so, what is in your cellar?
Yes. I usually collect wines that friends are making or maybe wines that sparked an interest during a trip or perhaps wines related to a project we are developing. Right now I am enjoying wines with a Rhône style.

If you weren't involved in wine, what would you be doing?
I would probably stay home with my kids and enjoy their childhood years.

AUSTIN HOPE

Winemaker Austin Hope has made wine in Paso Robles since he was a teenager. He was named Winemaker of the Year in 2009 at the California Mid-State Fair and is currently on the board of the Paso Robles Wine Country Alliance.

How did you get involved in the world of wine?

I grew up in the wine world. My parents moved to Paso Robles when I was eight years old and planted a vineyard. I grew up helping in the vineyards, learning from my father and uncle. Later, during college, I studied crop science and was helping manage the family vineyard. When we decided to not just grow grapes and actually make wine, I ended up taking the lead role. It has been an amazing roller coaster.

What are some of the biggest changes you have seen in winemaking since you began your career?

Technology. The filtration systems for the wine have come so far. In terms of making the wine taste better and allowing us to make more sound wines, they are amazing.

The other change that was interesting to experience was the ramping up of alcohols, or the "Parkerization"of the wine world. We went from 13 to 16 percent alcohol pretty fast, and it was embraced by the public.

What are some of the exciting changes that you see happening in your area of California?
With Paso Robles, it has been fun to see us become a global player in the wine world. When I was growing up, there were a handful of wineries here, and now people around America and even internationally know of Paso Robles as a wine region. What a quick acceleration.

Where else in the world have you studied, trained, or worked a harvest? How did that influence your winemaking?
I traveled to Italy and France to see how they make their wines. I spent time in both the northern and southern Rhône and really loved that style of wine. I enjoyed seeing the Old World style of winemaking. Back in California, I worked for and studied under Chuck Wagner at Caymus. He was such an open-minded teacher, always encouraging me to try new things to see what happens.

Which varieties are you working with? Are you experimenting with anything new?
We work with lots of Cabernet Sauvignon for our Liberty School and Treana Red programs. For Austin Hope and Troublemaker brands, we focus more on Rhônes. I grow Syrah, Grenache, and Mourvèdre on our ranch and love seeing these varieties develop. We work with Marsanne, Viognier, and Chardonnay for our Treana White and Liberty School as well. We've just released our first Liberty School Pinot Noir and Merlot. That has been a fun project.

Are there any new areas that you have identified for potential vineyard sites?
The thing we love about Paso Robles is the diversity of the AVA. Not only in the varieties we can plant but the diverse microclimates in the area. We are continually finding new vineyards sites with different soils and weather that work great together.

What challenges have you faced as a winemaker or winery owner?
The biggest challenge I've faced as an owner has been consolidation among wineries and distributors. We are always fighting for more attention with the larger companies. Another challenge is the fluctuation in the amount of fruit we get year to year. That swing can be difficult for yearly projections and keeping up with demand.

What is your winemaking philosophy?
My philosophy is to create a New World wine with Old World style. Balanced with finesse, but real tannins and real acidity.

What would you hope people say about your wine?

My goal is for people to say that we overdeliver for the price. That we are consistent—and make great-tasting quality wines at the right prices.

Do you think that the market should influence winemaking or do you think that winemaking should influence the market?

This question is a very difficult one to answer; I think all winemakers would like to say we should influence the market. I say this because we (winemakers) all believe we know what we are doing and people should love the wines that we choose to make. In reality, some winemakers like high-acid wines and some like more soft wines. This gives the consumer a natural selection process by having multiple styles of wines in the market from all our different palates. Now the rest of my answer is where it gets slippery; the US consumers who have just been introduced to wines prefer a sweeter, soft style of wine that most winemakers don't like. However, marketers and owners, etc., get involved and tell the winemakers to make these wines because the trends and volume of sales for those wines are rapidly growing.

So now the question of art and money is poised—does the winemaker become a sellout to their own beliefs because that is what sells or hold firm and make wine to their ideals?

My answer is we can't be prejudiced about these things; our job is to make a great wine that all will enjoy. . . . Trends and styles will continue to change as they have in the past, and we must be open-minded. We can always make a barrel of wine for ourselves to keep our palates happy.

Besides your own wine, what are some of your favorite wines? What do you like about them?

I really enjoy the Didier Dagueneau wines. I love Silex and Pur Sang. I love the purity of those wines—they have piercing acidity yet are so balanced and authentic. I also love white wines from Burgundy—they have that great matchstick characteristic that I love. They do what a wine should do—really balance oak and acid, which is a hard thing to do.

What is your opinion on screw cap versus cork closures?

I'm amazed at the short amount of time that it's taken for them to be embraced. For longevity and for aging wines, I really think cork is the way to go, but for wines that will be consumed young, screw caps are a good alternative. Plus it makes them easy to drink when you're on the run!

If you could invite anyone from history, living or dead, to your home for dinner, who would it be? What food would you serve? What wine would you serve?

I would have dinner with Jim James (My Morning Jacket), Dave Grohl, and Bill Clinton. We'd eat cedar-planked arctic char, grilled Brussels sprouts, and corn with cayenne, Cotija, and fresh lime (street corn on the cob). We'd drink Corton-Charlemagne, one of my favorites from Burgundy.

If you were to stay home tonight for a relaxing evening, drinking wine while watching a movie, which movie would you watch? Which wine would you drink? Explain.

I'd watch *The Shawshank Redemption,* and I'd drink our 1996 Treana White (Marsanne and Viognier blend). It's a timeless movie that you can always watch, and like our Treana White, it ages beautifully. They are a perfect pairing.

How do you like to spend your time away from the winery?

I love to listen to live music and hunt ducks . . . not at the same time.

Do you collect wine? If so, what is in your cellar?

No, I drink it too fast. The only way I age wine is if somebody hides it from me and I find it later.

If you weren't involved in wine, what would you be doing?

Drinking wine and driving a race car.

BARBARA BANKE

Barbara Banke is the chairwoman and proprietor of Jackson Family Wines. She is one of the most successful female winery owners in the world. She and her late husband, Jess Jackson, are the cofounders of the children's charity Sonoma Paradiso Foundation.

How did you get involved in the world of wine?
I was a passionate consumer of wine and enjoyed wine tasting in Napa and Sonoma. Then I met my husband, Jess Jackson, who had a vineyard and a fledgling winery.

What are some of the biggest changes you have seen in winemaking since you began your career?
I have seen the rise and subsequent decline of super-ripe California wines. Now there is more focus on balance, ageability, and maximizing the potential of individual vineyards.

What are some of the exciting changes that you see happening in your area of California?
In Sonoma, Santa Barbara, Monterey, and the Anderson Valley of Mendocino County, Pinot Noirs continue to impress. New clones permit both refined and profound wines. In the Mayacamas Mountains of Sonoma County, mountain vineyards are producing some of the world's best wines in general.

Where else in the world have you studied, trained, or worked a harvest? How did that influence your winemaking?

I have worked in Tuscany and Saint-Émilion, and that has led to a fascination with Cabernet Franc, both alone and in blends.

Which varieties are you working with? Are you experimenting with anything new?
Of course we work with Chardonnay, Pinot Noir, Zinfandel, Sauvignon Blanc, Merlot, Cabernet Franc, and Cabernet Sauvignon in California. We make Shiraz and Grenache in McLaren Vale of Australia. Our newest venture is in the Willamette Valley of Oregon with Pinot Noir and Chardonnay. We specialize in cool-climate wines.

Are there any new areas that you have identified for potential vineyard sites?
We have a beautiful site on Pine Mountain in Mendocino and one overlooking Lake Mendocino.

What challenges have you faced as a winemaker or winery owner?
Mother Nature is always a challenge.

What is your winemaking philosophy?
Showcase the best that a vineyard has to offer with balance, complexity, energy, and refinement.

What would you hope people say about your wine?
I hope that a person would appreciate the heart and soul of the people working on the land and in the winery.

Do you think that the market should influence winemaking or do you think that winemaking should influence the market?
Both. If you make something spectacular, you can find a market for it.

Besides your own wine, what are some of your favorite wines? What do you like about them?
Angela Pinot Noir from Oregon. Ramey Chardonnay. First growths of Bordeaux. Graham Beck Blanc de Blancs.

What is your opinion on screw cap versus cork closures?
Both can be good with the right wines.

If you could invite anyone from history, living or dead, to your home for dinner, who would it be? What food would you serve? What wine would you serve?
Winston Churchill and Margaret Thatcher. I would serve rare meat with Vérité and Lokoya.

If you were to stay home tonight for a relaxing evening, drinking wine while watching a movie, which movie would you watch? Which wine would you drink? Explain.

I would watch *The Maltese Falcon* and drink a fine Anderson Valley Pinot Noir or one from Santa Maria, like Cambria.

How do you like to spend your time away from the winery?

Hiking or watching my horses win.

Do you collect wine? If so, what is in your cellar?

First-growth Bordeaux, excellent California bottlings, and Champagne.

If you weren't involved in wine, what would you be doing?

Watching my horses train.

BO BARRETT

Winemaker Bo Barrett's illustrious career in the world of wine began in 1972 when his family purchased the iconic Chateau Montelena and subsequently became well known for its award-winning white wine in the 1976 Judgment of Paris. He is married to winemaker Heidi Peterson Barrett.

How did you get involved in the world of wine?
My dad bought Chateau Montelena the same year I graduated high school. My grandparents were Irish immigrants, so his philosophy was I had to get a full-time job. I needed money because I was moving to Snowbird to begin my chosen full-time job riding the Snowbird Tram and skiing Utah powder. I needed a source of funds since this was naturally a nonpaying employment, so I went to work in the vineyards. I worked summer and fall at the winery for three or four years to fund my 100-day-a-year skiing job. And then the winemaking got in my blood. I went from Snowbird U to Fresno State in 1976 and have been winemaking full-time ever since.

What are some of the biggest changes you have seen in winemaking since you began your career?
Fruit handling and gentle precision processing. Alcohol-level precision targeting. Much better microbiology.

What are some of the exciting changes that you see happening in your area of California?

Better and better grapes. To make great wine you need the right grape in the right place. The first time you plant a piece of ground it's a crapshoot, then the second planting is usually better, then by the third around we can really fine-tune how to farm that land. Vineyards typically last about 20 years, so since 1972–73 you can do the math. It's been 40 years; so many great vineyards are in the third iteration and better than ever. I bet any winemaker worth a damn answers this similarly.

Where else in the world have you studied, trained, or worked a harvest? How did that influence your winemaking?

In 1981 I took a trip through all the great Euro wine-land regions, and most of what I brought back was from the Rhône and southern Italy. That was mostly fruit handling of the different cultivars. A later trip I took to Austria was to focus on better Riesling.

Which varieties are you working with? Are you experimenting with anything new?

Chateau Montelena is a classic house, so we stick to the traditional varietals: Cab, Chard, and Zin. We did a little Tempranillo last year. We had a vineyard in Paso where I worked with Grenache, Mourvèdre, and Syrah, but we ended that project a few years back. Heidi and I grow Syrah and Muscat for La Sirena wines.

Are there any new areas that you have identified for potential vineyard sites?

Not since 2008. Heidi and I picked up a piece of bare land close to a Chateau Montelena planting we had kept our eye on for years. It's extremely rocky, and it's the most exciting land I have planted in years.

What challenges have you faced as a winemaker or winery owner?

No question: bad government. You can't believe how much pointless and stupid regulation we have in California.

What is your winemaking philosophy?

Capture sunlight with the land and put it in a bottle to make people's lives a little better one glass at a time.

What would you hope people say about your wine?

Yum! That wine is simply delicious! I'd like to buy a case of that! What else you got?

Do you think that the market should influence winemaking or do you think that winemaking should influence the market?

That is a chicken-and-egg question. Yin and yang. Winemaking influences the market by making better and better wines, but we need to get paid to stay in business, so we need to make what people will buy, so the market is the final arbiter.

Besides your own wine, what are some of your favorite wines? What do you like about them?
I'd say I am an omnivore. If it's well grown and well executed and styled, I generally like it regardless of origin. My favorite wine is a good one I've never tried before that I would actually buy, but it's my favorite when someone else paid for it!

What is your opinion on screw cap versus cork closures?
Both are good closures for the appropriately produced and priced product. The best news is that the market acceptance of alternative closure has forced the natural cork producers to make such excellent progress in the quality of the corks. There has been a fantastic improvement in reliability in natural cork from what we saw in the 1980s and '90s. Chateau Montelena is very traditional, and we are a sustainable producer, 100 percent solar, Fish Friendly Farming, and all that good stuff. So in general we use natural cork for our wines. Most of our wines are made to age, and so far cork is still winning that race. The reductive nature of screw caps would change the winemaking methods we traditionalists use.

If you could invite anyone from history, living or dead, to your home for dinner, who would it be? What food would you serve? What wine would you serve?
Leonardo da Vinci. I'd take him up for a helicopter ride, I am certain he would dig that! Since he's probably a bit of an old-school Italian "paisan," I'd probably go with our Zin.

Food? That would depend on the season, whatever was good then. If it was salmon season, I'd probably start with that and some Chateau Montelena Chardonnay.

If you were to stay home tonight for a relaxing evening, drinking wine while watching a movie, which movie would you watch? Which wine would you drink? Explain.
Bottle Shock! Hahahhahahahahahahaha! LOL! We do this almost every night. I'd drink whatever we were having with dinner.

How do you like to spend your time away from the winery?
Outdoors. Preferably on water. I am a water man, and so are Heidi and our kids: scuba diving, fishing, skiing, surfing.

Do you collect wine? If so, what is in your cellar?

Not as much as you would think. I'm a producer, and all my buddies are too. We have a cellar full of what we make and what our friends make.

If you weren't involved in wine, what would you be doing?

Flying. I fly both airplanes and helicopters. I got my pilot's license in 1974; I was 20 years old. And more than likely I would be farming or ranching. I have that crazy farmer gene; I like working with the land.

CHERYL INDELICATO

The granddaughter of Delicato Family Vineyards founder Gaspare Indelicato, Cheryl Indelicato became a registered nurse before returning to the family business in 1990. She runs DFV alongside her siblings and cousins, and in 2010 she launched her own brand, the HandCraft Artisan Collection. A member of Les Dames d'Escoffier, Cheryl is also the Monterey representative to the California Wine Institute.

How did you get involved in the world of wine?

I was born into it . . . you might say I have wine in my blood. I'm a third-generation vintner; my grandfather Gaspare Indelicato planted our first vineyards in 1924 and began making wine several years later. I grew up next door to the winery and always enjoyed being in the vineyards and in the cellar. My father and uncles, knowing how much I loved the family business, put me to work in the cellar when I was five years old.

What are some of the biggest changes you have seen in winemaking since you began your career?

The basics of winemaking haven't changed, but what amazes me is the technology we rely on in all facets of the wine business. The equipment we use is very advanced, from the cellar, to the vineyards, to the computer systems in the tasting rooms. . . . It's quite a change from when I was that little five-year-old working in the cellar.

What are some of the exciting changes that you see happening in your area of California?
I live in Monterey, and I'm so pleased to see this region receiving the recognition it should as a world-class viticultural area. New AVAs are emerging with varietals we never thought would grow well here. The area is also becoming a wine destination, with many new tasting rooms opening in Carmel. When I first moved here over 10 years ago, many of the grapes grown here were shipped to other areas as blenders. It's great to see the growth of Monterey-labeled wines on wine lists and store shelves—both across the nation and abroad.

Which varieties are you working with? Are you experimenting with anything new?
I started working with traditional varietals such as Cabernet Sauvignon, Chardonnay, and Pinot Noir; however, I wanted to create distinctive wines that honored my Italian heritage, so I began experimenting with Italian varieties such as Malvasia Bianca and Sangiovese. I love to cook, and I find blending wine is similar, where small differences can change the flavor and aromatics. I really enjoy it. I kept on with the blending and created two signature wines: Inspiration White, which is a blend of Riesling, Moscato, Sauvignon Blanc, Viognier, and Pinot Grigio, and Inspiration Red, a food-friendly blend of Zinfandel, Merlot, Malbec, and Sangiovese.

Are there any new areas that you have identified for potential vineyard sites?
I love the Pinot Grigio grown in Monterey, at my family's San Bernabe Vineyard—it's full of flavor and bright acidity. My hope is to plant additional acreage of Pinot Grigio at San Bernabe and, fingers crossed, produce a HandCraft Pinot Grigio someday.

Another area that means a lot to my family is Lodi. My grandfather settled in Lodi after making his way across the United States from Ellis Island. I would love to find a vineyard of old, gnarled head-trained Zinfandel in the Lodi area.

What challenges have you faced as a winemaker or winery owner?
As a winery owner, I find myself on the road a lot. I enjoy the travel, especially meeting our customers, but I find that I miss my husband and son quite a bit. Finding that work-life balance is key.

What is your winemaking philosophy?
I want to create wines that are approachable yet distinctive. My wines are fruit-forward and easy to pair with food. The distinctive aspect is the addition of Italian varieties not often

seen in California wines, which makes my wines stand apart from a sensory perspective.

What would you hope people say about your wine?
I love this wine; where can I buy another bottle?

Do you think that the market should influence winemaking or do you think that winemaking should influence the market?
I feel that if you provide consumers with the very best, if you overdeliver on quality, consumers will embrace your product and come back for more. I guess that means winemaking, and I emphasize, quality winemaking, should and will influence the market.

Besides your own wine, what are some of your favorite wines? What do you like about them?
I'm a fan of Napa Valley Cabernet Sauvignon. I love the full-bodied, velvety tannins.

What is your opinion on screw cap versus cork closures?
I guess I'm a bit old-fashioned on this issue, but I feel screw caps perform best on aromatic white wines. I still prefer a cork for red wines.

If you could invite anyone from history, living or dead, to your home for dinner, who would it be? What food would you serve? What wine would you serve?
Wow, that's a hard one. I would say there are three: God, Josh Groban, and Steve Young (former 49ers quarterback). I would serve my Inspiration Red blend along with braised short ribs over polenta.

If you were to stay home tonight for a relaxing evening, drinking wine while watching a movie, which movie would you watch? Which wine would you drink? Explain.
I would watch *The Sound of Music*, one of my old-time favorites, with a glass of HandCraft Cabernet in hand. Why? Well, that's what I would like to sip with Christopher Plummer if he stopped by.

How do you like to spend your time away from the winery?
My favorite thing is cooking and entertaining. I like to prepare seasonal menus, so visiting the local farmers markets is key. I also enjoy kickboxing and long hikes with my dog, Lucy.

Do you collect wine? If so, what is in your cellar?

Lots of Napa Valley Cabernet and other full-bodied reds like Châteauneuf-du-Pape, Pio Cesare Barolo, Nicolas Catena Malbec, and Brancaia Il Blu.

If you weren't involved in wine, what would you be doing?

I am a registered nurse and worked in a hospital setting for some years before returning to the winery. I enjoy teaching and helping others, so if I wasn't working in the wine industry, I would be involved with the Visiting Nurse Association.

EILEEN CRANE

Eileen Crane is often called America's Doyenne of Sparkling Wine. She has been recognized as one of the 75 Most Influential Women in Business by the *San Francisco Business Times.*

How did you get involved in the world of wine?

I became involved in the world of wine when I was eight years old. My father had a wine cellar in New Jersey in the 1950s, which was very unusual. Where I grew up, everyone drank gin and tonic or rye and ginger. So a wine cellar was quite extraordinary.

My father had become interested in wine during World War II. He was among the soldiers who landed on the beaches the morning of D-Day and survived. Later, he directed the International Department for Dean Witter.

When I was about eight years old, he would let me taste a little wine at Sunday dinner. I was fascinated by the wine labels and the stories about where the wines came from, but little girls from New Jersey did not grow up to be winemakers. I assumed that to be a winemaker you needed to grow up in an Italian family in upstate New York, and you certainly were not a woman. So I went on to other jobs, such as social work in Venezuela.

This job inspired me to learn more about nutrition. I went to the University of Connecticut and obtained a master's degree in nutrition in 1975. I then taught for the university for a couple of years and became very interested in the culinary arts.

The CIA [Culinary Institute of America] had started in New Haven, Connecticut, and I knew a great deal about it and the women who had started it. So I took a summer off and went to the CIA for 10 weeks. There I was lucky enough to meet a real-life winemaker through the wine club. He had a book about winemaking from UC Davis, and I was intrigued. Could you study winemaking at Davis? I made some phone calls and found out that you could.

The first professor of enology at Davis I spoke with discouraged me. He said because I was a woman I would not be able to do the barrel work. He suggested I go to the nutrition department and enroll in a PhD program there. I said thank you, but I was going to be a winemaker. He said, "I don't think so," but he did introduce me to Ann Noble, who was just arriving at Davis. Ann agreed to talk to me amid all of her unopened boxes. She encouraged me to take wine classes at Davis as a concurrent student for a few months and then convince somebody that I could do it. That's exactly what I did. I took four months of classes, and then, knowing that it was too early to get a technical job, I took a job as a part-time tour guide at Chandon. I almost starved that summer, but by the end of July there was a job in the laboratory and I was offered it.

Why was I at Chandon, and how did I choose sparkling wine? It's what I wanted in my glass. Six years later I was hired to build and develop Gloria Ferrer. Then, three years later I accepted the position at Domaine Carneros to once again build and oversee the development of a sparkling wine house. Taittinger and I were a match made in heaven. I absolutely love my job. It has morphed over the years, and while the challenges have sometimes seemed overwhelming, I seem to have been able to navigate my way through.

Looking back, even as a child I knew what I wanted to do but could not have conceived that I could make it happen.

What are some of the biggest changes you have seen in winemaking since you began your career?

My career in sparkling and now still winemaking has spanned 35 years. One of the biggest changes that I have seen is the evolution of California sparkling wine from nice, clean little wines to wines that hold their own very successfully on the world stage. California sparkling wines have evolved through realization of the importance of cold-climate appellations, the evolution of individual styles, and the overall appreciation by winemakers and owners that we're no longer playing in the minor leagues.

Other things that have changed, of course, include the corporatization of the industry. Winemaking has become much more sophisticated, and our appellation system has moved into maturity.

What are some of the exciting changes that you see happening in your area in California?
The exciting change that I saw in Carneros was the commitment to better clones and refined grape growing. When I got to Carneros, there were vast stretches of Pinot Noir clones that were undistinguished. As phylloxera wiped out many of the existing vineyards, replantings were done with smaller-producing, more specialized clones and vineyard selections. Wine growing became much more focused on making the very best wines possible, and we started to see the beginning of highly committed winemakers, wineries, and owners striving to grow the absolutely best Pinot Noir possible. This wasn't true for everybody in Carneros, but it certainly was true for very significant numbers of winemakers and wine growers.

Where else in the world have you studied, trained, or worked a harvest? How did that influence your winemaking?
I think the only other place where I could claim to have learned about winemaking would be at the CIA. This was the place that I fine-tuned my early palate.

Which varieties are you working with? Are you experimenting with anything new?
Domaine Carneros works with Chardonnay and Pinot Noir. On occasion we have made Merlot largely because a number of years ago I purchased a small vineyard site that had some extraordinary and healthy Merlot. We couldn't resist seeing what it would do under our tutelage. And just this past year, we brought in a little bit of Pinot Gris for a Blanc de Blancs trial. We are always looking for new, good ideas in clones, varieties, and winemaking. About four years ago we started working on a Pinot Noir made as a white still wine. We call it our Pinot Clair.

Are there any new areas that you have identified for potential vineyard sites?
Domaine Carneros is committed to the Carneros appellation: Carneros and nothing but Carneros. Within that appellation we are always looking for new great vineyard sites. This year we acquired a vineyard that historically was called Tula Vista.

Domaine Carneros is virtually all estate, and in the next few years we will be

100 percent estate. All of our estate vineyards are certified CCOF organic. This has made a huge difference in the quality of our wines.

What challenges have you faced as a winemaker or winery owner?
Some of the big challenges I have faced in my career were building wineries first for Gloria Ferrer and then Domaine Carneros. I had no construction background when I took on the Gloria Ferrer job. I had not even done a major home improvement project. What I did do well was to find a good contractor and ask a lot of questions. Both wineries went up on time and within budget.

Another major challenge for me has been to develop our marketing for the winery. I do not have any kind of marketing background in terms of education; it has been a learn-as-you-go project, a very exciting project.

Another challenge is that after 35 years of making sparkling wine I am still looking for the new, the best, and the next experiment.

What is your winemaking philosophy?
My winemaking philosophy is that the first obligation of any wine is to be delicious. I love wines of finesse with the great nose, good body, and a long finish. I view Domaine Carneros wines as Audrey Hepburn in the little black dress. Everything in place, nothing over the top, elegant, and Kiki.

What would you hope people say about your wine?
Of our wines, I would hope that people would say this is the most memorable wine I have ever had.

Do you think that the market should influence winemaking or do you think that winemaking should influence the market?
I believe that small to midsize wineries that are well respected and have good ways to sell their wines have the luxury of creating wines that are distinctive and in keeping with the winemaker or the winemaking team's palate. Domaine Carneros as the second smallest sparkling house of any size in California has the luxury of being its own thing. Great winemakers, like great artists, need to have the freedom to create from their gut. It has to be inspired and their authentic inspiration.

Besides your own wine, what are some of your favorite wines?
My favorite wine is always the wine that I have in my glass, or at least almost always. I absolutely love bubbles, and I'm happy to drink them five to seven days a week, but occasionally I find myself enjoying a great Sauvignon Blanc, Chardonnay, Gewürztraminer, of course Pinot

Noir, and occasionally Cabernets, Merlots, etc. I like wine, and I like to try a huge variety of them.

What is your opinion on screw cap versus cork closures?
The great advantage with a screw cap is there are no corky bottles and you don't need an opener or to know how to use it. I have no objection to screw caps. I think they're very appropriate for wines that are going to be drunk young. This year we're making a small amount of still rosé, and it will go into a bottle with a screw cap.

If you could invite anyone from history, living or dead, to your home for dinner, who would it be? What food would you serve? What wine would you serve?
I would invite Buddha, Jesus, George Washington, Gandhi, and Desmond Tutu. Well, I would ask Jesus to bring the wine that he made from water for the main course. I would ask George to bring his favorite Madeira for the cheese and dessert, and I would have an eclectic mix of Indian, Middle Eastern, South African, and American food.

If you were to stay home tonight for a relaxing evening, drinking wine while watching a movie, which movie would you watch? Which wine would you drink? Explain.
If I were to stay at home tonight and have a relaxing evening with a little glass of bubbles, I would probably choose something from one of the countries that I am going to visit in the next five weeks. Or I might look at one of the funniest movies that is also an inspiration called *Kinky Boots*.

How do you like to spend your time away from the winery?
Time away from the winery is spent on getting together with friends, wine on the back deck, long walks, some exotic travel, and always a good book.

Do you collect wines? If so, what is in your cellar?
I do not consider myself a wine collector, although I do buy wines that I would like to drink and often I am willing to buy those wines and lay them down. I never buy wine just for its name or hype.

If you weren't involved in wine, what would you be doing?
Do I only get one choice on what I would be doing if I didn't make wine? Well, I'm going to take two. I would either be a perfumer or an anthropologist.

EMILIO ESTEVEZ AND SONJA MAGDEVSKI

Actor, filmmaker, and director Emilio Estevez and his fiancée, winemaker Sonja Magdevski, began their careers in the world of wine when they planted vines in their front yard and began making wine in their garage. Today the couple makes delicious world-class wines at a proper winery and can often be found at their Babi's Tasting Room in Los Alamos.

How did you get involved in the world of wine?
Our involvement with wine transformed once we planted a vineyard on our property in Malibu in 2004. We understood the process from a completely new perspective as we became immersed in it. It is difficult to not become 100 percent committed once you plant vines in your front and backyard! They are now our seasons—life revolves around them.

After planting vines we began making wine in the garage, literally with a small hand-cranked crusher/destemmer and a basket press. We'd call our friends to help harvest and press. It was great fun. Once we decided to increase production, the two barrels in the garage scenario no longer worked. Once we began commercially making wine, the entire dynamic of our production changed. The fun and excitement are still there, though the concentration and intention are different. Wine is now with us on a cellular level instead of just a surface, cerebral level.

When we started, we didn't have a plan; we simply wanted to grow something and share it with our community. Now our goal is to create community while growing something to share—incredible fruit for delicious wine for the wonderful people we meet.

What are some of the biggest changes you have seen in winemaking since you began your career?

Some of the biggest changes in winemaking since we began are not as stark as changes in previous decades, such as increased cleanliness, or planting the first Rhône varietals on the Central Coast, or discovering Pinot Noir grows great in the Sta. Rita Hills. But give us some time and I am sure this short career thus far in the long run will see many changes! In all seriousness, one major change is the greater acceptance of the screw cap or twist-off closures versus cork.

Also, the current conversations about balance or acidity or lower alcohol or minerality are distractions from the actual focus and challenges of making wine. I don't know one winemaker who seeks to make an unbalanced wine or an alcohol bomb or flabby wines. I often say if we didn't put any numbers on the labels I believe people would have a difficult time guessing the correct alcohol level. Consumer perception too often rides with trends versus consumers trusting their own palates, which is the primary reason people should be drinking wine—to enjoy what they like, not what the magazine told them to like. Wine should be personal, if it comes from a jug or box or a magnum with a twist-off (wait; it could be next!). It is a record of the moment.

I distinctly remember a snobby sommelier from a highly lauded (and quite delicious) restaurant in Santa Monica saying to me two years ago, "Syrah is dead." *Hmmm*, I thought. Let's not even discuss the Rhône. But I can name you dozens of producers who have no trouble at all selling their Syrah, who consistently get remarkable points for their wines. In our tasting room, Syrah has no problem selling. Point being, trends are trends, and good wine is what remains.

What are some of the exciting changes that you see happening in your area of California?

The prevalence of great fruit from responsibly farmed vineyards with incredible vineyard managers caring tremendously about what they do. It is difficult to get a bad grape in the Santa Ynez Valley and Santa Barbara County. I do believe we are also gaining greater recognition for this thanks to the pioneers who helped pave the way and continue to make incredible wines with fruit from this area and offer guidance to others. There are numerous people who have worked incredibly hard and have been successful in their efforts and are the benchmarks of our region. To name them all would take paragraphs. I am thankful they followed their passions, which have allowed us to follow ours.

Where else in the world have you studied, trained, or worked a harvest? How did that influence your winemaking?

Both our stories are quite unique. We like to say it is the dark matter in our DNA that led us to this place. Emilio grew up visiting his grandfather Francisco's vineyard in Spain. To him as a child it was the most natural environment he had ever known. For me, Sonja, I grew up running around my family's villages in Macedonia each summer when I'd visit with my family every year. There we had cattle, apple orchards, vineyards, beehives, walnut and chestnut trees, chickens, pigs, everything. The idea of working with the land was integral to our upbringing though not encouraged in school or home for success. And yet we kept coming back to it in various ways. Planting the vineyard was the first step to our ongoing education of a lifetime, though we didn't know it yet.

When my grandmother, God rest her, came to visit us for the first time in Malibu and she saw the vineyard and the garden, the first words out of her mouth were, "I left the village 50 years ago and you have come back to it." That is the driving force toward all we do.

In regard to formal education, we consider a number of wonderful people in the Santa Ynez Valley to be mentors, both formally and informally. Joey Tensley of TensleyWines, Mikael Sigouin of Kaena Wines and head winemaker at Beckman Vineyards, Norm Yost of Flying Goat, and Greg Brewer and Steve Clifton of Brewer-Clifton Wines.

Once I decided to take over the winemaking production, I began to take classes at the local Allan Hancock Community College in Santa Maria. I came to winemaking later in life, and I already had two jobs and two degrees—an undergraduate in political science from the University of Michigan and a master's in journalism from Michigan State University. My thesis was on ethnic issues in the Republic of Macedonia—nothing to do with winemaking—but then again everything to do with my ability to seek out the answers and reasons I was looking for. The decision to continue education at Allan Hancock was perfect, as it draws upon all of the local resources, experience, and brainpower in the area. The director of the program, Alfredo Koch, is such a supportive mentor of his students. John Alban of Alban Vineyards came to speak, as did Philippe Armenier, a wonderful biodynamic, Randall

Grahm of Bonny Doon, and so many more. Being in that program gave me the confidence and determination to continue forward. And it gave me the ability to share and debate everything I had learned with everything I was doing in the winery with Emilio, who is an absolute hands-on learner and a damn good one, too.

Today we say that I am the winemaker and he is my assistant winemaker, while he is the farmer and I am his farmhand with our vineyard in Malibu.

Which varieties are you working with? Are you experimenting with anything new?

We make Pinot Noir from our property in Malibu, which has proven to be the most challenging endeavor most years, and yet when it works, the fruit creates the most unique, velvety wine we have tasted. The issue is that there simply isn't that much of it even in good years. Our primary focus is on Rhône varieties—Viognier, Syrah, Grenache, Roussanne, a Syrah Rosé, and a Sparkling Syrah Rosé, which we call Sonja's Suds. And for good measure a Gewürztraminer that is 100 percent dry with a good portion of the fruit fermented cold on the skins for a few weeks. This is for my grandmother. All of these varieties we source from various vineyards in the Santa Ynez Valley, including Tierra Alta Vineyard, Larner Vineyard, Thompson Vineyard, and Rancho de Vina de Santa Ynez for the Gewürztraminer—the oldest Gewürz plantings in the county.

I'd love to experiment more with skin-fermented whites and cofermentations and perhaps add another sparkling wine to the repertoire. Also with the use of various fermentation and aging vessels in the future. The possibilities are endless, and it is important to keep that playful experimentation alive.

I am a big fan of single-varietal wines. I like the purity of a variety expressed on its own. We would love to experiment with new varieties, particularly Picpoul Blanc, though the problem is finding the fruit. Whatever small amount is planted in the region is already spoken for. Though each year we say we are going to try Tempranillo for Emilio's Spanish heritage. I am waiting for him to take control of that project. Perhaps in the future.

Along these same lines we both have goals of international wine projects: me in Macedonia and Emilio in Spain. It is simply a matter of resources and time, really.

Are there any new areas that you have identified for potential vineyard sites?

Not at this point. The focus has been on working with the incredible variety of fruit already planted in Santa Barbara County and getting our Malibu vineyard to produce delicious healthy fruit consistently year after year. That is a very big challenge for a small property.

What challenges have you faced as a winemaker or winery owner?
Getting the word out. I always say making wine is the easy part—selling wine is the hard part. The beauty of making wine is that everyone has their own story and their own energy expressed in their wine. It is amazing how different wines can taste from the same vineyard harvested one day apart, for instance, using similar winemaking protocols.

What is your winemaking philosophy?
Purity and authenticity achieved through attentiveness, which may mean babying to some or careful consideration to others. And also letting the fruit express itself—I call this wine independence—because it has its own energy and we need to work together to create a cohesive, "balanced" wine. I have to trust the process and the history of the process and remain open to every new idea while keeping grounded in the foundations of our style.

What would you hope people say about your wine?
That it is delicious. I don't want people to overthink or overanalyze the wine—then I have taken them out of the moment of enjoying the wine, which is the reason it is created in the first place. One of the greatest compliments we hear time and again in the tasting room is how people enjoy the entire lineup of wines they have just tasted and their experience with us. And on the same note, I do hope people who do want to deconstruct the wine also can say the same thing, "This is delicious," while smiling and reaching for another glass.

Do you think that the market should influence winemaking or do you think that winemaking should influence the market?
Obviously I think that winemaking should influence the market because I want to make wines that I want to make in the way that I want to make them. This is my artistry and my expression at that moment in life. But that said, everyone needs input and we all need an open mind to understand our environment. Communication in all parts of life is vital to our growth. Though again, for small winemakers like us, I do believe the winemaking does influence the market because once you get people inside the tasting room tasting wines, whatever they believed outside changes once they start tasting. And

if we go back to the comment about trends made above, good wine bucks all trends or marketplace fever.

Besides your own wine, what are some of your favorite wines? What do you like about them?
David Arthur Cabernets are a perennial favorite. David personally inspired Emilio to rethink his approach to wine years ago while barrel sampling. As David was climbing all over barrels, he continually used the word "fun" to describe his wines. That opened the entire wine experience to a new level, particularly because his wines are exceptional and, indeed, fun.

Otherwise we like always try new things and explore what other people in other regions around the world are doing.

What is your opinion on screw cap versus cork closures?
Since we moved all of our wines to screw cap with the 2010 vintage, we love screw cap. Ease of use, 100 percent recyclable. Not that we don't love corks and not that we won't go back to corks at some point, though elegance of a bottle is in its complete package—particularly what is on the inside.

Emilio was more hesitant to switch than me, and now he loves it. For him it was about moving away from tradition. A closure is not a reflection of what is in the bottle. Now that I want to go back to cork, Emilio doesn't want to! Screw caps are here to stay, and it is a personal choice and style. I think it is great that we have the choice to play. Glass closures are considered by some to be the best closure for a wine, though when was the last time you opened a bottle with that closure?

If you could invite anyone from history, living or dead, to your home for dinner, who would it be? What food would you serve? What wine would you serve?
Does family history count? I would invite all of my grandparents and great-grandparents as far as the family tree could reach and have a big feast and celebration in the vineyard with folk music and folk dancing and fresh food from our garden—whatever was in season at the time—with plenty of our wine and homemade slivovica from the villages of Macedonia—and express to them that all of their hard work in their difficult lives does means something and their work and legacies live on. Emilio would do the same. Though perhaps on a separate night! A houseful of rowdy Macedonians and rowdy Spaniards would certainly mean a weeklong party!

If you were to stay home tonight for a relaxing evening, drinking wine while

watching a movie, which movie would you watch? Which wine would you drink? Explain.
Pat Garrett and Billy the Kid directed by Sam Peckinpah, starring James Coburn and Kris Kristofferson and music by Bob Dylan. We are huge Western fans, and this one rates at the top, without a doubt, for mood, performance, characters, and simply a damn great film you can watch over and over again and always be amazed at it all. For this film, we'd open one of the few remaining bottles of the 2009 Casa Dumetz Pinot Noir from our property. Always a special occasion when we get to open it.

How do you like to spend your time away from the winery?
What time away from the winery? Particularly as "winery" includes wine tasting room, outside wine sales, social media, event coordination, and sleeping! As a small business owner the difficulty is balancing it all while not losing sight of life and relationships. This has been difficult. What little time I do get to spend away from work is generally in the garden or hiking and simply exploring new places without a plan—Emilio and I like to just get in the car and drive toward a destination for new discoveries.

Do you collect wine? If so, what is in your cellar?
We do not collect wine now. Not even our own! Emilio has to beg me to save a few cases of each wine each year. Emilio did at one point have a significant collection, only to realize that the collection was controlling him, not the other way around. Today we buy wine and generally drink it soon thereafter. Every day we are in the bonus, so if we have inadvertently collected something, it is because we forgot about it and can be pleasantly surprised when we find it later on in the wine room.

If you weren't involved in wine, what would you be doing?
We are still doing it even while making wine—for me that is writing and for Emilio filmmaking. To watch Emilio on set is the most natural experience in the world for both him and those around him. He commands the set with such ease that it seems effortless, though we all know it is not. He is a marvel to watch in action, and everyone feels comfortable with him. He is such an incredibly sensitive, intuitive, and creative person that he inspires me daily to always strive for greatness. He never stops from the moment he wakes up singing every day to the moment he rests his head on the pillow still making jokes—he is a filmmaker first and foremost, and he is my muse.

GARY EBERLE

Winemaker Gary Eberle began his career in 1973 by heading his family's Estrella River Winery. He was a cofounder of the Paso Robles appellation in 1980 and opened his eponymous winery in 1983.

How did you get involved in the world of wine?

In 1970s I was down in New Orleans working on a doctorate in genetics. One of my professors liked wine, so we'd get together and drink great French wines. I was trying to introduce him to the fine stuff I was drinking—you know, Mateus and Lancers. Turns out he was into wine of slightly higher quality, like Lynch-Bages and Ducru-Beaucaillou. I got the wine bug and I got it bad . . . so I made a trip to UC Davis and packed my U-Haul and old Pontiac and moved to California.

What are some of the biggest changes you have seen in winemaking since you began your career?

When I was at Davis there were only seventeen other students in our class. After graduation, we all got jobs as winemakers; we didn't start out as assistants or cellar rats. We started out as winemakers. So now we see everyone doing an apprenticeship before they become head winemaker, and they are all doing real hands-on work and getting experience. The qualifications of winemakers are so much better now starting out. When I came out of school, I had a degree, but I had never actually made wine.

What are some of the exciting changes that you see happening in your area of California?
Paso Robles is experiencing such an explosion of talent. When people started coming out here, they were basically home winemakers who couldn't afford to get in the game anywhere else, so they came here, bought land, and made their own wine. Paso used to be perfect for the home winemaker, not serious winemakers. People were turning out good wine maybe three out of every five years. What we have now is consistency. We have so many good wines coming out of Paso Robles from young winemakers, it really is amazing.

Where else in the world have you studied, trained, or worked a harvest? How did that influence your winemaking?
In 1976 I made wine with Ed Friedrich at San Martin in Gilroy. He was making delicate but delicious wines that came in at 7, 8, or 9 percent alcohol. I learned how to make softer, fruit-forward wines from him. I also spent some time with Dr. Becker at the Geisenheim Grape Institute in Germany.

Which varieties are you working with?
It would be easier to list what we don't work with. I love Pinot Noir, but it's not something I do. Cabernet has always been my flagship. I planted the first Syrah vines since Prohibition. Are we experimenting with anything new? I love to work with Counoise, Viognier, Tempranillo, Sangiovese, and Barbera. I also make port with the five Portuguese varieties every few years. Our winemaker Ben Mayo is part Hobbit and part mad scientist. He's always coming to me and saying we should work with this grape that somebody just discovered under a rock in Slovenia.

Are there any new areas that you have identified for potential vineyard sites?
The next up-and-coming area in California is Paso Robles.

What challenges have you faced as a winemaker or winery owner?
Number one is marketing. I have made wines that were really outstanding, and people would like them, but especially in the 1970s, Paso Robles was unknown. If I was going to survive as a winemaker, I had to learn how to sell wine. When people come to me and say that they are building a winery and ask me for advice, I tell them that before they even break ground on the winery they better have a marketing plan.

What is your winemaking philosophy?
We make wine that I like, that makes me happy.

What would you hope people say about your wine?

Many people drink their wines too young, and I hope that when they open a bottle of mine that's really too young to drink, they like the flavor and they find it soft, easygoing, and drinkable, not too harsh to drink.

Do you think that the market should influence winemaking or do you think that winemaking should influence the market?

I make 25,000 cases of wine, and it's all wine that makes me happy. I will never have enough people drinking my wine to influence the market, but as winemakers we should be making wine that people want to drink.

Besides your own wine, what are some of your favorite wines? What do you like about them?

I like wines from Jim Clendenen, Ken Volk, Bob Lindquist, Randy Dunn. Also Dick Arrowood, Heidi Peterson, and my classmate Merry Edwards.

What is your opinion on screw cap versus cork closures?

Give me a screw cap any day.

If you could invite anyone from history, living or dead, to your home for dinner, who would it be? What food would you serve? What wine would you serve?

I would love to have John Adams, Ben Franklin, and Thomas Jefferson. I would serve Château Lafite, and dinner would be a Central Coast barbecue, you know, grilled tri-tip, beans, and salsa. Dessert would be strawberries, brown sugar, and sour cream, served with an old port or Madeira.

If you were to stay home tonight for a relaxing evening, drinking wine while watching a movie, which movie would you watch? Which wine would you drink? Explain.

I would drink a Zin or a Syrah. They are fun wines, and I would be laughing. I'm currently waiting for Netflix to deliver *Night Shift* with Henry Winkler and Michael Keaton. I actually know Michael Keaton, he is a distant relative, and I sat at a rehearsal dinner with him one evening and he cracked me up. So the movie and the wine would have to be fun.

How do you like to spend your time away from the winery?

I love to travel, but I am always selling wine. I love to do winemaker cruises, and we get to travel all over the world. I have done 46 cruises since 1976. I also have my own plane, a Cessna 340, and I fly all over the country.

Do you collect wine? If so, what is in your cellar?

Yes. I have about 3,500 bottles, and half of my cellar consists of several bottles of all the wine I have made, with vintages going back to 1976.

If you weren't involved in wine, what would you be doing?

I would love to be a concert pianist with a symphony orchestra. I would also love to be the lead tenor with a great opera company. Too bad I don't play an instrument and I am tone-deaf.

GEORGE ROSENTHAL

George Rosenthal began his career as a real estate developer in 1955, and today his company, Raleigh Enterprises, owns fifteen subsidiaries, including the Raleigh Film and Television Studios, the Sunset Marquis hotel in West Hollywood, and The Malibu Estate, where he grows grapes to make his fine wines.

How did you get involved in the world of wine?
I became involved in the world of wine through the enjoyment of drinking fine wines throughout Europe with a very dear friend from Mexico, Emilio Azcarraga M. In our multiple journeys through various countries in the early '70s, we experienced the finest products from the vineyards throughout France, Spain, Italy, and all the outlying areas of vineyard and wine production. To be able to enjoy a fine glass of wine in either a formal or a very casual setting of an exotic restaurant or on the beaches of Saint-Tropez is a wondrous experience, making any day or meal more complete.

What are some of the biggest changes you have seen in winemaking since you began your career?
The biggest change that I have seen in winemaking has been the advancement of technology, which has allowed the monitoring of juice to occur under controlled and ideal conditions. Although a fine wine in the end is still determined by the quality of the grapes, gaining the ability to control the fermenting

aspects with such a high degree of technology has resulted in less violent swings between production years, and therefore the wines being produced are more consistent in their level of quality.

What are some of the exciting changes that you see happening in your area of California?

In 1987, Rosenthal The Malibu Estate was the first vineyard to be created in the Malibu area. After intensive study with a preeminent viticulturist from Napa and studies in conjunction with the University of California, Davis, we determined that the Malibu area could produce fine wines. Although there were many who doubted our ability to create a high-quality wine, our weather studies, soil studies, and temperate climate six miles inland from the Pacific Coast proved to be ideal. The temperature swings from the mid-nineties to the low sixties in a single day provided an excellent climate for Cabernet Sauvignon. What has been exciting in the past 26 years is that since our beginning there are now seventeen or eighteen vineyards in Malibu producing wines of various varieties. The ability to create wines in different varieties within a relatively small area is conclusive proof that the temperature and climate changes dramatically from the time you are at sea level along the Pacific Coast Highway until you reach Mulholland Highway, a short eight miles from the coast but approximately a 2,000-feet-in-elevation differential. We look forward to the continuation and the development of wines in Malibu as more people become familiar with the ability to enjoy the great viticultural area.

Where else in the world have you studied, trained, or worked a harvest? How did that influence your winemaking?

I have studied winemaking in the Napa area, Paso Robles, Santa Barbara County, and the area of Malibu. What I have personally determined is that each area produces its own unique wines and vintages. We are not trying to emulate any given specific area but are always attempting to produce the finest quality wine from what the *terroir* and climactic conditions provide in Malibu. It is unique; the wines are unique and stand-alone. I have also determined that we will maintain our discipline with respect to alcohol levels and continually maintain a high standard of production quality with very specific and direct attention to the vineyard on a daily basis. This while also working extensively with our winemakers to determine which grapes from each vineyard will produce the best wines without consideration to quantity but maintaining only quality.

Which varieties are you working with? Are you experimenting with anything new?

At the present time we are working with Cabernet Sauvignon, Merlot, Cabernet Franc, Petit Verdot, Chardonnay, Viognier, and Muscat. We have determined over a period of 22 years, after experimenting with other varieties, that our vineyard is best served by maintaining our disciplines with the varieties mentioned above, as they seem to provide us with the best quality in the growing conditions existing within our vineyards.

Are there any new areas that you have identified for potential vineyard sites?

We are presently investigating an opportunity to extend the Rosenthal label into the Napa area. We have not yet determined specifically which part of Northern California where we would best be served.

What challenges have you faced as a winemaker or winery owner?

The greatest challenge ahead is to create an acceptance of wines from Malibu. We have had reasonable success throughout various states in the country and to some degree internationally. However, as a boutique winery without an extensive advertising budget, it has been extremely difficult to get acknowledgment in locales outside of Southern California as to the quality of our wines. We do, however, maintain a very significant wine club with extremely loyal wine club members. As a winery producing approximately 4,000 cases of wine per year, we simply do not have the budget to maintain an extensive sales force, and the distribution networks as they presently exist are reticent to carry boutique wineries' product as the volume they are able to create in sales is not significant enough to them.

What is your winemaking philosophy?

My winemaking philosophy is really quite simple: we will maintain our standard, we will maintain alcohol levels at reasonable amounts, we will not be seduced by the current "flavor of the month/year" style of winemaking, and we will maintain small quantities of fruit, farmed from each vineyard. We will not compromise in what we think is the best wine that we can make each year, and we are not hesitant to reduce our production levels in order to maintain standards.

What would you hope people say about your wine?

I would hope that people who consume Rosenthal the Malibu Estate wines would, at the conclusion of their dinner or social gathering, acknowledge that it was a joyous occasion enhanced by the quality of our wines.

Do you think that the market should influence winemaking or do you think that winemaking should influence the market?

I believe that winemaking should influence the market. However, in truth, what the market perceives as being the wines they enjoy at the moment does influence the winemaking. I have seen in the past two decades significant changes in various aspects of winemaking, and it is unfortunately inevitable that winemaking must follow the palate of the market. Over the years we have seen an increase in the level of alcohol content, which to my mind masks the differential in varieties. I also believe that having high levels of tannin to enhance the long-term quality of the wines in the general marketplace is extremely difficult to be accepted. For the most part, people drink wines within 24 hours of purchase, and therefore it is a balance between creating a wine that is drinkable within a year of its release and still maintaining its ability to lay down for multiple years.

Besides your own wine, what are some of your favorite wines? What do you like about them?

I enjoy wines from multiple areas. If I were to select fine wines from California, at the top of the list would be Harlan, Colgin, and a very small vineyard called Promise. I thoroughly enjoy a bottle of semidry rosé. It conjures up images for me of the beaches at St. Barts, Saint-Tropez, and just a wonderful, enjoyable afternoon with light hors d'oeuvres. In the French wines, I of course love the top-end of Château Margaux, Pétrus, Lafite-Rothschild, and my very favorite, Romanée-Conti. Some special-occasion wines need not be at the top of the viticultural "hit list." For me a special occasion is a good pizza margarita and a wonderful bottle of wine.

What is your opinion on screw cap versus cork closures?

There is no question that there is a romance around cork closures in wine bottles. The very act of removing the cork, the sound of it leaving the bottle, and the psychological aspect of a cork and foil equals fine wines. In truth, I have no objection to a screw cap—we have in fact used them on some of our wines, and I believe that screw caps are coming more into acceptance. There is also the aspect that irrespective of the price one pays for their corks, there is always the opportunity to wind up with bottles "corked." The difficulty is that many people do not know the musty "off" flavor that a cork can create in a fine wine and oftentimes they are put off by a brand simply because they thought that the wine represented something different than that which was actually placed in the bottle and spoiled by the cork. After a bottle of wine is placed in an ice bucket, carafe, etc., the fact that it had a cork in it or was a screw cap becomes rather irrelevant.

If you could invite anyone from history, living or dead, to your home for dinner, who would it be? What food would you serve? What wine would you serve?

If I could invite anyone from history, I would invite Thomas Jefferson. We would serve a wonderful medium-rare rack of lamb with all the appropriate vegetables. We would of course serve Lafite-Rothschild.

If you were to stay home tonight for a relaxing evening, drinking wine while watching a movie, which movie would you watch? Which wine would you drink? Explain.

I cannot name a specific movie that I would watch, but I will say that it would be happy, could be a musical, a wonderfully complete love story, a film that did not have a lot of stress: a heartwarming resolution at the end, and in all probability I would drink a Pinot Grigio. There is an aspect of the Italian social life that is warming to me. Where else in the world is there a country that has confronted such a variety of issues and always winds up smiling, great design, beautiful clothes, wonderful yachts, and Ferraris to enjoy driving? The villages of Italy and the lakes at Como are representative of a wonderful lifestyle where no matter what travails may exist, there is always time for a long and joyful lunch, a bottle of wine on the table, and good conversation.

How do you like to spend your time away from the winery?

My time spent away from the winery covers a multitude of things, but most importantly, time spent with family, enjoyment of skiing, the lake country of Canada, and certainly not last, nor least, cruising the Mediterranean on a private yacht. Also, a nice place to consume a bottle of wine.

Do you collect wine? If so, what is in your cellar?

I have never been a great collector of wine. I have found over the years that oftentimes wine is laid down long enough to spoil without getting back to it for a "special occasion." Therefore, I tend to have a very small collection of wine but enjoy drinking them frequently and add to the inventory as needed.

If you weren't involved in wine, what would you be doing?

My involvement in wine is only one small part of my life. I enjoy on a daily basis the multiple aspects of business, social, and family involvement with which I have been blessed over the years. I enjoy meeting new people, engaging in conversation, and generally have a thirst for new discovery and entrepreneurship. I am doing exactly what I would have fantasized if my fantasies were beyond expectation. I love the varied aspects of my life.

GINA GALLO

Gina Gallo is the granddaughter of California wine pioneer Julio Gallo. She is married to Jean-Charles Boisset, president of the St. Helena–based Boisset Family Estates. She is the winemaker for Gallo Signature Series.

How did you get involved in the world of wine?
Winemaking has been part of the fabric of our family for 80 years. I developed a deep connection to the land at a very young age. As I child, I loved picking fruits and vegetables for my mother and grandmother to use in their recipes. I also spent a lot of time walking in the vineyards with my grandfather Julio. But my family history and my own love of the land didn't translate to a passion for winemaking until after college. I joined the sales division of E. & J. Gallo Winery and started taking coursework in winemaking at UC Davis. Right away, I knew I had found my calling. From that moment on, I wanted to be a winemaker.

What are some of the biggest changes you have seen in winemaking since you began your career?
There are certainly more women winemakers now. It's exciting, because we bring a different perspective to the craft.

It's also fascinating to see how far we've come with Pinot Noir in California. I am what they call a die-hard Pinotphile, so I am enamored with the Pinot sites that have been developed in the Russian River Valley and the Santa Lucia Highlands over the years. We have such a greater understanding now of how Pinot Noir adapts to different clones and different microclimates. With the right site selection, we've been able to plant the right clones exactly where they thrive.

What are some of the exciting changes that you see happening in your area of California?
It is wonderful to see the industrywide effort to move toward sustainable agriculture. My family has always approached farming with a deep respect for the land and the environment—long before sustainability was fashionable. In the past decade, our industry has begun to understand that sustainable agriculture is essential for the preservation of our vineyards and the surrounding land. At Gallo, we have moved very quickly to bring all of our estate vineyards and wineries up to the highest standards of sustainability; in fact, we've been among the first to earn certification for sustainable practices.

Where else in the world have you studied, trained, or worked a harvest? How did that influence your winemaking?
I've spent a lot of time in France, and I always find great inspiration there. The people are a lot like the people here in California—passionate about the land and the grapes and the wine. Given my love of Pinot Noir, Burgundy has always been a great draw for me. I also adore Pinot Gris and have spent time with different winemakers in Alsace. I definitely look to the Old World for a historical foundation, but there is so much to be learned from so many different regions across the globe. I've spent significant time in New Zealand and the cool-climate regions of Australia, getting a different perspective on Pinot Noir.

I also had the incredible opportunity of traveling with my father and brother through the oak forests of France and the United States. I gained such a depth of understanding about how the forests are maintained and how different types of oak can impact a wine. I also spent time with a cooper in Kentucky, diving into the process of crafting barrels and toasting the oak. Winemaking isn't just about the vineyards and the grapes. Oak plays such an integral role, so these experiences have been invaluable for me.

Which varieties are you working with? Are you experimenting with anything new?
My focus is on our Gallo Signature Series collection, which includes Pinot Noir, Chardonnay, and Cabernet Sauvignon. This is a passion project for me, so I get to work

with some of the best grapes from our estate vineyards in Napa, Sonoma, and Monterey. I have always been inspired by Burgundy, so Pinot Noir and Chardonnay are a natural fit for me. Pinot Noir is such a fickle, elegant grape; it presents some challenges that keep things interesting for me. I have a passion for cool-climate Chardonnay, and I am very fortunate to be able to work with phenomenal Chardonnay grapes from the Russian River Valley. Cabernet Sauvignon rounds out the collection with a bolder, richer style.

I am typically drawn to the classic varieties, but I love to experiment with different winemaking techniques. Right now, for example, we are working with concrete egg fermenters for our Sonoma Coast Chardonnay. I am able to better control the temperature and oxidation during fermentation, which in turn allows the wine to develop more complex layers of flavor and a rounder mouthfeel.

Are there any new areas that you have identified for potential vineyard sites?

I have the good fortune of working with grapes from some of the best vineyard sites in California. But we are always looking for those special places that offer a unique *terroir*—all of those intangible elements that make up a great vineyard. My sense is that there are still incredible vineyard sites to be discovered in California. Searching for them is part of the fun.

What challenges have you faced as a winemaker or winery owner?

I think it's always a challenge to be able to express myself through my wines and honor the land in a way that feels true to me and to my family's legacy. That is my life's passion. It's a challenge, but I take it on wholeheartedly.

What is your winemaking philosophy?

My approach is to consider the land—the *terroir* of the vineyard, the grapes that are suited to that site—and convey the story of that specific place in a personal and meaningful way. Given my background, I certainly take a historical perspective, but I also aim to create wines that feel authentic to my own style and true to today's wine culture.

What would you hope people say about your wine?

I hope people get a sense of place from my wines, that they are able to discover the nuances of the grape and the vineyard. I hope people find my wines to be a natural accompaniment for time spent with family and friends. Ultimately, I hope they simply enjoy tasting and sharing my wines.

Do you think that the market should influence winemaking or do you think that winemaking should influence the market?

I think you can't have one without the other. The wine world is a lot like the art world. Creating art for the sake of art has an intrinsic value, but the human connection to that art is just as important. As winemakers, we introduce the market to new varieties and new styles of wine, but ultimately we strive to create wines that people will enjoy. I think there is a healthy push and pull that creates significant influence in both directions—and that is a good thing. It keeps us all moving forward.

Besides your own wine, what are some of your favorite wines? What do you like about them?

I love Clos de Beaujeu Blanc. We served it our wedding, actually. I think it does a beautiful job of balancing that line between elegance and power. And, I am partial to JCB No. 3. It is such an interesting wine—something you never really see—blending Burgundy Pinot Noir and Russian River Pinot Noir. You get the best of both worlds.

What is your opinion on screw cap versus cork closures?

I think both have their place in the modern wine world. There are certain wines that simply beg to have the traditional experience of uncorking the bottle—and all that comes with that. But screw caps offer some incredible benefits in terms of preserving flavors and quality.

If you could invite anyone from history, living or dead, to your home for dinner, who would it be? What food would you serve? What wine would you serve?

I would love to sit down for a meal with Mother Teresa. I am fascinated by her life's work. The menu would be some of my favorites: wild Alaskan halibut over fresh fava beans from the garden. For dessert, a homemade wild berry sorbet with an oatmeal cookie. The wine would have to be our Gallo Estate Chardonnay from our Laguna Ranch Vineyard in the Russian River Valley. This vineyard is very special to me, and it's sustainably farmed. I would choose an older vintage, probably 2005, which is just gorgeous right now.

If you were to stay home tonight for a relaxing evening, drinking wine while watching a movie, which movie would you watch? Which wine would you drink? Explain.

I rarely watch TV; in fact, we don't even have a TV in our living room. But for a relaxing evening, I'd choose something from

Peter Sellars. I tend to reach for something with bubbles or a classic red with a lower alcohol level.

How do you like to spend your time away from the winery?

I've always been a family-oriented person, and I really cherish the time I spend with family. These days, I have my own family, so my focus is on our children—watching them grow and just enjoying being with them.

Do you collect wine? If so, what is in your cellar?

I love to collect wine. Before I met my husband, I was on a 10-year streak of collecting Champagne, Bordeaux, and Burgundy wines as well as Spanish wine. Now the Burgundy side of the cellar has blossomed even more. I also love classic Sonoma and Napa Cabernet, Dry Creek Valley Zinfandel, and Pinot Noir from the Sonoma Coast, the Santa Lucia Highlands, or the Santa Cruz Mountains.

If you weren't involved in wine, what would you be doing?

I would be working with children in some way. I truly believe they are precious gifts from God, so I would probably be doing something in the area of child development.

HEIDI BARRETT

Winemaker Heidi Peterson Barrett is well known in the world of wine for creating some of California's most notable and highly scoring cult wines, including Grace Family Vineyards, Screaming Eagle, and Dalla Valle Vineyards, to name only a few. She is married to winemaker Bo Barrett.

How did you get involved in the world of wine?
I grew up in the Napa Valley with a winemaker father and an artist mother.

What are some of the biggest changes you have seen in winemaking since you began your career?
Huge improvements in winery equipment, farming practices, analysis, even better tasting glasses!

What are some of the exciting changes that you see happening in your area of California?
Winemakers always trying to make better wines and getting creative with blends.

Where else in the world have you studied, trained, or worked a harvest? How did that influence your winemaking?
I learned versatility in Australia. I learned balance in Wittenberg, southern Germany, and South Australia, as well as the Barossa Valley.

Which varieties are you working with? Are you experimenting with anything new?

I am always fine-tuning. Chardonnay, Sauvignon Blanc, Muscat Canelli, Cabernet Sauvignon, Cabernet Franc, Merlot, Syrah, Petit Verdot, Grenache, Petite Sirah, and Zinfandel.

Are there any new areas that you have identified for potential vineyard sites?
No.

What challenges have you faced as a winemaker or winery owner?
Running a business. Well, it's farming, so weather can be a challenge. Juggling multiple clients, scheduling, and planning.

What is your winemaking philosophy?
Wine should be simply delicious. Philosophy—to make the best wine possible from any vineyard property.

What would you hope people say about your wine?
My favorite comment is "WOW." People have told me they are delicious and sometimes the best wine they have ever had.

Do you think that the market should influence winemaking or do you think that winemaking should influence the market?
I just make the best wines I can in a balanced, tasty style and hope people like them.

Besides your own wine, what are some of your favorite wines? What do you like about them?
I like wines that are delicious and make you want another sip. Consistency is important too. Any variety can be made well.

What is your opinion on screw cap versus cork closures?
Screw cap for nonaging wines. Cork is still the best for long-time agers if you get the best quality corks.

If you could invite anyone from history, living or dead, to your home for dinner, who would it be? What food would you serve? What wine would you serve?
I would invite Ronald Reagan, astronaut Gene Cernan, Amelia Earhart, Gustav Dalla Valle, and my dad, Dr. Richard Peterson. I would have a casual barbecue with veggies from my garden and an assortment of wines from my cellar.

If you were to stay home tonight for a relaxing evening, drinking wine while watching a movie, which movie would you watch? Which wine would you drink? Explain.
We do that a lot . . . always different.

How do you like to spend your time away from the winery?

Scuba diving trips, ski trips, doing art, painting, gardening, ceramics, and helicopter flying.

Do you collect wine? If so, what is in your cellar?

Yes, everything I've made, everything Bo has made, trades with friends, and gifts from friends.

If you weren't involved in wine, what would you be doing?

Marine biology, discovering new species and exploration, or teaching art. Or helicopter flights for humanitarian purposes.

JEAN-CHARLES BOISSET

Burgundy-born Jean-Charles Boisset became enchanted with California at the age of 11. He is a member of numerous wine industry organizations, including the Northern California Young Presidents Organization and La Confrérie des Chevaliers du Tastevin. He was named one of the "Top 50 Power Brokers" in the world of wine by *Decanter* and "Innovator of the Year" by *Wine Enthusiast*. He and his wife, Gina Gallo, are very active in many charitable organizations, including Feed The Children.

How did you get involved in the world of wine?
I was born and raised into the world of wine and had the pleasure of growing up in the village of Vougeot in Burgundy, France, where my view was the vineyards of the world-renowned Château du Clos Vougeot. As a child, we played amid the vineyards planted by the Cistercian monks as early as 1110, and my bedroom was literally above the barrel cellar and the winery.

In 1981, when I, age 11, and my sister, 14, had the opportunity to accompany my grandparents on a journey to California, we found ourselves discovering the spirit of the Gold Rush state in Monterey, San Francisco, and Sonoma. When on the square in Sonoma, the birthplace of the California Republic, they noticed a historical landmark—a winery founded in 1857 named Buena Vista. I'll remember forever discovering the oldest stones of the California wine world—a grand winery estate—the first gravity-flow winery, the first caves, and the foundation of modern viniculture in California.

My grandparents allowed us tastes of those incredible Chardonnays in the hotel room, and I was transfixed—such pure, elegant, and tropical notes that we did not know in Burgundy! I recall the moment I declared to my sister, "Wouldn't it be fun one day to make wine in California?"

That dream was realized in 2003 with DeLoach in the Russian River Valley, in 2009 with Raymond in the Napa Valley, and in 2011 when we finally brought Buena Vista Winery, California's first and most historic estate, into our family collection of wineries!

We are now the stewards of an incredible winemaking heritage in California, from the pioneering efforts of DeLoach in the Russian River Valley, to the Raymond family legacy in Napa Valley, and of course of the most historical winery in California—Buena Vista: a long-held dream, now come true.

What are some of the biggest changes you have seen in winemaking since you began your career?

We are excited about the rise of organic and biodynamic practices in the vineyards, a hallmark of Boisset properties worldwide. My family began farming according to biodynamic principles in Burgundy in 1994. Today, Domaine de la Vougeraie is the leading organic and biodynamic domaine in the Cote d'Or with more than 95 acres under cultivation.

In California, we began implementing biodynamic farming at DeLoach Vineyards, which was certified organic by CCOF in 2008 and biodynamic by Demeter USA in 2010. Raymond Vineyard's Napa Valley estate vineyards in Rutherford and St. Helena became certified organic by California Certified Organic Farmers (CCOF) and certified biodynamic by Demeter in April 2013.

What are some of the exciting changes that you see happening in your area of California?

We've seen an increase in smaller, more specific *terroirs* that mirror the classical appellation system in France. This in combination with exploring more wine-growing regions has led to our discovery of some unbelievable vineyards and a new generation of world-class wines.

Where else in the world have you studied, trained, or worked a harvest? How did that influence your winemaking?

I've had the honor and the pleasure to make amazing wines from the Old World, such as Burgundy, Beaujolais, the Rhône, and the south of France, and the New in California's Russian River and Napa valleys, Canada's Quebec and

Niagara, and Uruguay and Chile, where we were one of the first to make Pinot Noir.

Which varieties are you working with? Are you experimenting with anything new?

We work with all of them! At DeLoach Vineyards in the Russian River Valley, we are focused on Pinot Noir, Chardonnay, and Zinfandel. At Raymond in the heart of the Napa Valley, we make Cabernet Sauvignon, Merlot, and Sauvignon Blanc.

When it comes to experimenting, the most exciting winery where we are making unique varieties is Buena Vista. We are making delicious wines with many of the varieties that Count Haraszthy, the founder of Buena Vista, brought back from Europe, such as Charbono, Colombard, Alicante Bouschet, and Valdiguié.

Are there any new areas that you have identified for potential vineyard sites?

We're fascinated by the quality of wines coming from Marin County.

What challenges have you faced as a winemaker or winery owner?

Rebuilding and restoring iconic wineries such as DeLoach, Raymond, and Buena Vista to their original grandeur. One must have patience, passion, and long-term vision to effect change, especially in this business, where change can only be effected over years.

What is your winemaking philosophy?

Our family is as attentive to all of the essential aspects of *terroir*, from the soil to the climate, and importantly, the people and their passion, as it is to the vineyards.

As dedicated as we are to our wines, we are equally passionate about the long-term health and vitality of our *terroir*, so we have a particular focus on biodynamic and organic winemaking practices.

What would you hope people say about your wine?

Our vision today is to hope that our spirit of collaboration and commitment to wine will transcend any divisions . . . that the world will vibrate with a passion and appreciation for the elixir of God and wine's expression of our land and our place. That we can realize our vision that while oceans may separate us, wine unites us!

Do you think that the market should influence winemaking, or do you think that winemaking should influence the market?

Coming from Burgundy, we can only imagine that the vineyards and the wines guide us first, of course!

Besides your own wine, what are some of your favorite wines? What do you like about them?
The wines of my beautiful wife, of course! Gina makes a stunning Chardonnay from the Russian River Valley for one.

What is your opinion on screw cap versus cork closures?
We have always embraced innovation when it serves the quality of the wine, and we are very open to the idea that every wine has its own personality, its own place, and its own time—for some, there is nothing better than to be sealed under a screw cap to preserve the freshness and vibrancy of the wines, and for others, cork is the natural choice. We should expand the conversation to include all the positive alternatives for wine packaging that may help reduce the carbon footprint of the wine world—whether it's the Tetra Pak carton or our Barrel to Barrel!

How do you like to spend your time away from the winery?
With my wife, Gina, the twins, and Frenchie. There's nowhere else I'd rather be!

Do you collect wine? If so, what is in your cellar?
We love old Burgundy!

If you weren't involved in wine, what would you be doing?
I was born into wine. I can't imagine doing anything else!

JIM SAUNDERS - STEVE HEARST

Wine grower Jim Saunders (above right) began his career in wine by designing and building wineries. He purchased a 100-acre ranch, planted grapes, and partnered with Steve Hearst (above left) of the Hearst publishing family to create delicious wines under the Hearst Ranch Winery label.

How did you get involved in the world of wine?
I have been a building contractor for many years. Early in my career, I helped design a small winery. I liked designing and building them so much that I created a niche for myself and became quite busy. I purchased a 100-acre ranch and asked one of my customers, if I planted grapes, would they purchase them.... The answer was "Yes," and I was committed. This worked well for many years, until the grape market became saturated and demand was no longer there. Winemakers would come into my vineyard and "cherry pick" rows of grapes they wanted and leave other rows to rot. It was not a good time for growers. One winemaker and I were speaking of this dilemma, and it was suggested that if I bought the tanks and equipment, they would simply buy the juice from me and I wouldn't have to put up with lunatic winemakers anymore. So I did just that. We then sold juice to many different wineries, using their protocol, and charged them to do so. This arrangement worked well for many years. By now we had planted out the entire ranch and had developed nine blocks of grape varieties.

All of this came to an end when we entered into a partnership with Hearst, and now all of our production of grapes goes directly into our program. In addition, we must purchase many more tons of fruit.

What are some of the biggest changes you have seen in winemaking since you began your career?
I believe the consumer has redirected our winemaking in that we now find that it isn't just quantity, it must also be quality. The consumer is much more sophisticated now than in years past.

What are some of the exciting changes that you see happening in your area of California?
Specifically, people are discovering Paso Robles. That is exciting, especially since we are delivering great quality wines from here.

Where else in the world have you studied, trained, or worked a harvest? How did that influence your winemaking?
I have traveled virtually all over the world but studied wines specifically in Italy, Spain, Switzerland, Germany, and France.

Which varieties are you working with? Are you experimenting with anything new?
We grow five varieties: Malbec, Tempranillo, Syrah, Petite Sirah, and Petit Verdot. We dabble with many different varieties in the quest to keep things exciting.

What challenges have you faced as a winemaker or winery owner?
The biggest challenge is the weather. . . . No question. If you get a good crop, you should be able to make great wine. A close second is money . . . there is never enough money, especially when you are growing; capital is king.

What is your winemaking philosophy?
Simple: "Overdeliver at an affordable price for the consumer."

What would you hope people say about your wine?
"I can't get enough of it," of course, but seriously, a comment I get often is how much people enjoy our wines, not just one or two, but all of them. That is the highest compliment anyone in this business can hope for.

Do you think that the market should influence winemaking or do you think that winemaking should influence the market?
It goes hand in hand. Prima donna winemakers cannot drive the market, although they may think otherwise. And the consumer has to realize what is a good product. Have you ever

been to a friend's home for dinner and they serve what they consider a delicious wine, and you cannot wait to cleanse your palate?

Besides your own wine, what are some of your favorite wines? What do you like about them?
I enjoy wines from all over. Domestically, it is hard to beat Caymus, Saxum, Screaming Eagle, to name a few. These wines are olfactory bombs and solid . . . great fruit and gamy at the same time with adequate oak that they spent a lot of money to purchase and use once. I appreciate that.

What is your opinion on screw cap versus cork closures?
You had to ask. . . . I am old-school and love a great cork. Sorry, but it is part of the romance. Screw caps are a great way to ensure wine integrity, but so what? It's like driving a Rolls-Royce with crank windows. Print that and I'm dead.

If you could invite anyone from history, living or dead, to your home for dinner, who would it be? What food would you serve? What wine would you serve?
That is a really tough one. George Hearst Jr. . . . Hearst Ranch grass-fed beef . . . Hearst Ranch Winery Cab Franc. He didn't drink too much, but one of the best storytellers ever. A truly great person.

If you were to stay home tonight for a relaxing evening, drinking wine while watching a movie, which movie would you watch? Which wine would you drink? Explain.
McLintock or *Rooster Cogburn*. Honestly, I would drink either a Malbec or Cabernet Sauv. I enjoy either one, and no kidding, it would be one we made.

How do you like to spend your time away from the winery?
I love San Simeon. . . . Give me a choice of the world or San Simeon, well, sorry, I love it here. I feel a lot of other countries don't appreciate us and want to rip us off or shoot us. Why bother?

Do you collect wine? If so, what is in your cellar?
Yes, I have some older Burgundies and Bordeaux wine and some fun domestics. I won't say what exactly, but some are older than dirt.

If you weren't involved in wine, what would you be doing?
I have adult ADHD, so who knows? I love to build things, especially that can be appreciated by others and that will be around a long time. I have no intention of retiring, just seizing up someday.

JOEL PETERSON

Joel Peterson has been called the "Godfather of World-Class California Zinfandels." He began his career as an immunology researcher and cofounded Ravenswood Winery in 1976. He is a founding member of Zinfandel Advocates and Producers (ZAP) and past president of the Sonoma Valley Vintners and Growers Alliance.

How did you get involved in the world of wine?

It's not so much that I got involved in the world of wine; it is more like the world of wine involved me. I was taught about wine quite early in my life. My parents discovered wine in 1951 and became early foodies. That of course meant that they were also heavily involved in the developing Bay Area wine culture. By the 1970s I was living in Berkeley doing some wine writing, store consulting, and tasting extensively. It was during the era of the food revolution: Chez Panisse, Pig by the Tail, Peet's Coffee, The Cheese Board were all new, exciting, and singular in their focus on food. Wine was very much intertwined with this.

I met Joe Swan at a tasting at the Vintners Club and began working on a part-time basis with him late in 1972, learning the nuts and bolts of winemaking. By 1976 I felt that I could make my own wine and thus made the first 427 cases of Zinfandel for what became Ravenswood.

What are some of the biggest changes you have seen in winemaking since you began your career?

There are a number of changes. One is the dimension and scale of what is possible for fine wine. The understanding of wine chemistry and wine technology was virtually nonexistent when I began drinking wine. We have better barrels, more international understanding of wine style, and an overall quality improvement of wine in general.

What are some of the exciting changes that you see happening in your area of California?
One of the exciting changes is the return to California's roots and reinvestigation of winemaking style and viticulture by a number of young California winemakers. They have focused on understanding viticulture, taking lessons from California's historic vineyards, and in the process have maintained and enhanced some of California's most historic vineyards and also have made some very exciting wines along the way.

Where else in the world have you studied, trained, or worked a harvest? How did that influence your winemaking?
I have never worked in any winemaking region but California. I have, however, studied European wine extensively. That involved understanding climate and terrain, grape variety, and winemaking approaches that ultimately create a particular flavor and character in a wine. In essence, my winemaking is a synopsis of what I have learned. I try to make wines of place, with typicity, that allow the character of the grape to work in harmony with the influence of winemaking. In short, these are the kinds of wines that have had longevity with wine enthusiasts for many years.

Which varieties are you working with? Are you experimenting with anything new?
I have always had a strong focus on red wine. About 90 percent of what I do is red. While I make Cabernet Sauvignon, Merlot, and Cabernet Franc as well as some other Bordeaux varieties, my major focus has been on traditional California grapes: Zinfandel, Petite Sirah, Carignane, and the like. While I have focused primarily because of market imperatives on varietal wines, with a primary focus on Zinfandel, I have been experimenting with California field blends and attempting to understand the interrelationships between different grape varieties; how they are planted in vineyards and how they influence one another when combined in the winemaking process.

Are there any new areas that you have identified for potential vineyard sites?
No.

What challenges have you faced as a winemaker or winery owner?

The challenges of owning and developing a winery are legion. Regulations, the three-tier system, intrastate compliance, all provide one challenge or another. But the largest challenge I faced after going public in 1999 was the challenge of mandatory growth. It sometimes finds itself in direct conflict with the agricultural nature of winemaking.

What is your winemaking philosophy?

1. Make wine that is pleasing to the senses. Especially my senses.
2. Translate the typicity of the location to the resulting wine accurately.
3. Try to make the winemaking process transparent. The winemaking should be subservient to the character of the grape.

What would you hope people say about your wine?

That they like it, find it interesting, love to share it with friends, will put my best bottles in their cellars, age it, and tell me how much they love it 10 years later. And finally, that they want more.

Do you think that the market should influence winemaking or do you think that winemaking should influence the market?

I think they are intricately intertwined. There is no doubt that a winemaker needs to make wines that he feels are reflective of his personality and of the character of the grape and place of which he is working. On the other hand, no winemaker works in a vacuum. By the very nature of being human, a winemaker is influenced by the social fabric around him. Consumers, sommeliers, wine writers, and indeed his own family all have some influence on how he perceives the wine that he makes. Ultimately, though, a winemaker, to be influential in the market, needs to make wines that he believes in.

Besides your own wine, what are some of your favorite wines? What do you like about them?

Champagne—it's celebratory, and it's a high contrast to anything I do. Wines from the Côtes du Rhône, Cornas in particular. It is wine with a strong sense of place made mostly in a pure style that is reflective of place and personality. Italian—Piedmontese Barbera—in a good year. Satisfying wine of great value. Also very typical of location. And about a hundred others too numerous to list.

What is your opinion on screw cap versus cork closures?

Screw caps are fine and probably even mandatory for aromatic whites and wines that are made for short-term drinking. Things like Riesling, Sauvignon Blanc, rosé, some light reds and their ilk, are perfectly fine under screw cap. But fine wines, particularly big red wines and complex whites like white Burgundy, some California Chardonnay, Sauternes, should never be put under screw cap. We have much traditional and long-term information about how wines develop in cork closures, and these wines seem to benefit and indeed improve in a cork closure.

If you could invite anyone from history, living or dead, to your home for dinner, who would it be? What food would you serve? What wine would you serve?

I would invite Agoston Haraszthy to dinner. We would discuss the myth and the man. We would discuss the whys and hows of early viticulture in Northern California. I would serve him a farm-to-table meal that would reflect the local bounty of Sonoma County: lamb, fresh vegetables, strawberries (which would be a revelation to him), and the like. I would hope that he would feel free to bring wine from his cellar and we would match it with wines of the same type made today. Sparkling wine, historic red field blends, and Zinfandel would all be part of the show. And just for fun, we might throw in a Russian River Pinot and a Napa Valley Cabernet, which undoubtedly would serve up some interesting conversation.

If you were to stay home tonight for a relaxing evening, drinking wine while watching a movie, which movie would you watch? Which wine would you drink? Explain.

I would watch either *Manon of the Spring* or *The Return of Martin Guerre*. I would drink a good chilled bottle of Bandol Rosé, preferably Domaine Tempier.

How do you like to spend your time away from the winery?

Hanging around with family, hiking, gardening, swimming, and traveling to exotic destinations.

Do you collect wine? If so, what is in your cellar?

What is not in my cellar is perhaps a better question. My wine collection is wide ranging and, for me, interesting. Virtually all the wines are wines that I like to drink. Wines that are well made and reflective of the character of the winemaker and their point of origin.

If you weren't involved in wine, what would you be doing?

If I weren't involved in wine, I would undoubtedly be involved in biomedical research of one sort or another.

JON PRIEST

Jon Priest is the winemaker at Etude and continues the vision started by founder Tony Soter. He assumed his current role in 2005. He previously worked at Taz Vineyards in Santa Barbara, Adelaida Cellars in Paso Robles, and Wild Horse with Ken Volk. In addition, he is an accomplished equestrian.

How did you get involved in the world of wine?
I like to say that I started as a student of wine and my study continues to this day. I was fascinated that wine could holistically encompass agriculture, science, art, culture, history, and craftsmanship. And that it is more than merely a glass of wine—it is the telling of a story of a person or a family and of a place and how that place came to be. The more I studied about the history of wine—and the more corks I pulled—the more fascinated I became. I thought that by becoming a winemaker, I could in some small way help tell a story.

What are some of the biggest changes you have seen in winemaking since you began your career?
The overall quality increase in Pinot Noir grown and made around the world has been quite inspiring, particularly around the Pacific Rim. In a relatively short period of time, we have seen a vast increase of knowledge and understanding of where and how to grow the grape for the highest levels of quality.

What are some of the exciting changes that you see happening in your area of California?
Increased interest and focus on Pinot Noir and the acceptance of nontraditional varieties.

Where else in the world have you studied, trained, or worked a harvest? How did that influence your winemaking?

Aside from spending the better part of my winemaking career on California's Central Coast, I have more recently had the opportunity to be involved with grapes and wine in Central Otago, New Zealand, and in the Willamette Valley of Oregon. Since Pinot Noir is so much about the place, I hope to gain valuable perspective and understanding from working with the grape in such varying regions and seeing how others approach the variety. Hopefully, in some way this insight challenges and stretches my base of knowledge.

Which varieties are you working with? Are you experimenting with anything new?

My early winemaking career was as much about my quest for Pinot Noir enlightenment as it was about varietal cross-training. I have worked with over sixty varieties in my life, some certainly more obscure than others. Currently, my focus remains on Pinot Noir, Pinot Gris, Pinot Blanc, Chardonnay, and Napa Valley Cab Sauv, and the urge to experiment with something "new" always resides. Just leave it to a Pinot person to interpret experimentation as something other than varieties. We recently planted new Pinot Noir clones and heirloom selections on our estate ranch, with the ambition of broadening the spectrum of our wines.

Are there any new areas that you have identified for potential vineyard sites?

After 30 years literally rooted in Carneros, Etude is embarking on a foray into other important Pinot Noir regions. While the Carneros estate will remain our home, our journey will take us south to Sta. Rita Hills and Santa Maria Valley, west to Annapolis on the Sonoma Coast, and north to the Willamette Valley.

What challenges have you faced as a winemaker or winery owner?

Mother Nature will always humble. While most vintages are favorable, we cannot predict or influence the weather. A winemaker can adapt and prepare for any type of weather, but we ultimately are at the whim of nature.

What is your winemaking philosophy?

With inspired wine growing, the need for intervention in the winery is diminished. Every vineyard and vintage has a story to tell, and a winemaker's interpretation is a part of the telling.

What would you hope people say about your wine?

Yum. More, please.

Do you think that the market should influence winemaking or do you think that winemaking should influence the market?

We have an obvious and meaningful coexistence. The beauty of a wine is its nuance and expression: grown in a place and brought forth by the wine grower and winemaker. In that sense, the winemaker crafts the wine to fulfill their intent or persuasion.

Besides your own wine, what are some of your favorite wines? What do you like about them?

I enjoy any well-made wine that exhibits a true sense of place, a wine that has a soul and a transparency to the land. Most often, it's a Pinot Noir from a producer that respects the vineyard from anywhere in the world or a grower-producer Champagne.

What is your opinion on screw cap versus cork closures?

Love the sound of a popping cork, but no real issue with screw caps. I ask myself if I have a hang-up about the romance of wine (that a cork can give) or should I get over myself and be more accepting of screw caps. Will we be asking ourselves the same question in 20 years?

If you could invite anyone from history, living or dead, to your home for dinner, who would it be? What food would you serve? What wine would you serve?

I would love to invite Julia Child over for dinner. We would first open a bottle of Etude Rosé while we pondered the menu. On her suggestion, we would probably settle on a simple roast chicken with morel mushrooms, with an older bottle of Etude Heirloom Pinot Noir.

If you were to stay home tonight for a relaxing evening, drinking wine while watching a movie, which movie would you watch? Which wine would you drink? Explain.

The Third Man—because Pinot Noir is the perfect wine to pair with film noir. Or maybe *The Pink Panther*—really just an excuse to laugh with my wife and drink Champagne.

How do you like to spend your time away from the winery?

On my horse, in the mountains, fly rod tied to the saddle, headed to a secluded lake.

Do you collect wine? If so, what is in your cellar?

Accumulate may be a better description than collect, and it is a rather eclectic mix of wines, mostly Pinot Noir from around the world.

If you weren't involved in wine, what would you be doing?

Retracing Marco Polo's journeys on my trusty steed.

KEN VOLK

Ken Volk and his family established Wild Horse Vineyard in 1981 and sold it to Jim Beam Brands in 2003. He opened his eponymous Kenneth Volk Vineyards in 2004 and has been active in many associations, including the Paso Robles Grape Growers Association, the Central Coast Wine Growers Association, the Paso Robles Vintners and Growers Association, and the Santa Barbara County Vintners Association.

How did you get involved in the world of wine?
In short, home winemaking. Long version below.

I have always been a gardener and horticulturist and a small-time truck farmer. I came up to Cal Poly San Luis Obispo to study greenhouse production and fruit science. Cal Poly has student enterprise projects where teams of students farm various fruits and vegetables. I had the berry vine project, down the hill from the campus vineyard. I had some good friends on the grape project, and I bought a couple hundred pounds of Pinot Noir fruit, a new trash can, and I used my Louisville Slugger baseball bat to crush the fruit and then pulled the stems out by hand. The fruit fermented out cleanly, and I drained the free run and pressed the skins by ringing them out in cheesecloth, and I had a beer keg and a couple of five-gallon glass water bottles. All things considered the wine turned out fairly decent for a rookie walk-on. This experience really sparked my interest, and I started reading all the wine books I could get my hands on and took extension classes from UC Davis and was fortunate to attend all the classes of the now-defunct Napa School of Cellaring. I started filling my garage with winemaking equipment and barrels to the shock of my housemates. The epiphany I had was to realize compared to so many crops I was familiar with, wine growing got you out of the perishability issues and flooded markets of agricultural commodities. It allows you to create your own unique branded creation.

What are some of the biggest changes you have seen in winemaking since you began your career?

There have been tremendous strides in all forms of game-changing winemaking technologies that have improved or simplified winemaking. I have always believed wine is made in the vineyard and the greatest improvement in grape growing is applied canopy management. The work of Dr. Richard Smart and his concept of canopy management's impact on wine quality in his publication *Sunlight into Wine* has done more to improve global wine quality than anything else in my lifetime

What are some of the exciting changes that you see happening in your area of California?

I have been an advocate of heirloom grape varieties, and the Central Coast has been on the leading edge of plantings of the seldom seen.

Where else in the world have you studied, trained, or worked a harvest? How did that influence your winemaking?

I have not worked in other countries. However, I have attended wine symposiums and visited winemaking regions of France, Italy, Australia, and New Zealand specifically to get insight into wine growing in those areas.Visiting Australia made me appreciate Verdelho, visiting Campania and tasting from clean cellars gave me appreciation on how much fruit Aglianico can display, visiting Hungary got me fired up on Blaufrankisch and Cabernet Franc.

Which varieties are you working with? Are you experimenting with anything new?

I have the largest portfolios of heirloom vines to be found from Albariño to Zinfandel. I'm a leading advocate of Blaufrankisch, Touriga Nacional and Cabernet Pfeffer (Gros Verdot), Malvasia Bianca, and Verdelho in California.

Aglianico, Albariño, Blaufrankisch, Chardonnay, Cabernet Franc, Cabernet Pfeffer, Cabernet Sauvignon, Negrette, Merlot, Mourvèdre, Torrontés, Malvasia Bianca, Orange Muscat, Verdelho, Tempranillo,

Touriga Nacional, Viognier, Roussanne, Syrah, Grenache, Carigan, Petite Sirah, Gros Verdot, Malbec, Tannat. . .

Are there any new areas that you have identified for potential vineyard sites?
The San Simeon Coast of San Luis Obispo County.

What challenges have you faced as a winemaker or winery owner?
The corporacy of the wine industry. The dysfunctional three-tier system.

What is your winemaking philosophy?
Work with fruit from superior sites and contentious growers who share a desire for greatness.

What would you hope people say about your wine?
Yummy delicious.

Do you think that the market should influence winemaking or do you think that winemaking should influence the market?
It is very hard, dare I say impossible, for winemaking to influence the market without an enormous promotional budget.

Besides your own wine, what are some of your favorite wines? What do you like about them?
I like northern Rhônes and Iberian varieties.

What is your opinion on screw cap versus cork closures?
No closure is perfect. Cork taint in its many forms is such a buzz kill. The cork industry has made great strides from being a cottage industry to utilizing much better technology to vastly improve the quality control procedures from the forest to the winery, yet at least 2 percent of the natural corks have problems. Screw caps are so friendly to open and great for aromatic whites, for it keeps wines fresh and clean. Screw caps are not without their own problems. There can be issues with reduction on reds and some whites in a nonpermeable membrane, which can be a bummer. If you're going to use nonpermeable membrane screw caps on ageworthy reds, it requires treating the wine differently than you would if using a cork. It requires getting the wine further down the road in its development and more dissolved oxygen in the wine at bottling.

I believe that most red wines benefit from the small amount of air that permeates through a cork as wine ages. There are a number of screw cap companies that are working on permeable membranes on screw caps to mimic the oxygen ingress of a cork closure which I have in trialing. When permeable membrane screw caps get perfected, I will use more screw caps in my red wines. For most of my reds I have been using technical corks that have been treated to remove all cork taint and have a consistent density for standardized oxygen transmission. They are not pretty, but they're the best closure available for my winemaking regime.

If you could invite anyone from history, living or dead, to your home for dinner, who would it be? What food would you serve? What wine would you serve?

There are a number of personalities from history that I would like to get to get some firsthand insight from. I would like to have dinner with Pliny the Elder as well as a translator familiar with ancient Roman culture. I would serve a rustic quail, arugula, and bitter green salad paired with Fiano and a roasted spring lamb served with Aglianico. I would hope to get Pliny to educate me on what grapes were used to produce Falernian wines.

If you were to stay home tonight for a relaxing evening, drinking wine while watching a movie, which movie would you watch? Which wine would you drink? Explain.

This is something I rarely get to do. A campy Mel Brooks movie and some Zinfandel.

How do you like to spend your time away from the winery?

Time with my family, sleeping, gardening, fishing.

Do you collect wine? If so, what is in your cellar?

I have sort of slowed down collecting. I have a modest cellar of Bordeaux, Burgundy, and Rhône reds.

If you weren't involved in wine, what would you be doing?

A plant geneticist or greenhouse grower.

MARK BERINGER

Mark Beringer is a fifth-generation Napa Valley winemaker. The great-great-grandson of Beringer Winery cofounder Jacob Beringer, Mark is the vice president of production and winemaking at Artesa Vineyards and Winery.

How did you get involved in the world of wine?
My great-great-grandfather cofounded Beringer Vineyards in 1876, and the wine business has been in my family for generations. For me, I began my training early working in my parents' wine store, went on to work in my uncle's winery doing various cellar jobs, and then after studying enology at California State University, Fresno, joined Glen Ellen Winery, then Duckhorn Vineyards, before coming to work at Artesa in 2009.

What are some of the biggest changes you have seen in winemaking since you began your career?
The biggest change to me has been the shift from family-owned-and-operated wineries to the consolidation of brands that has created mammoth companies that produce huge volumes of wines.

What are some of the exciting changes that you see happening in your area of California?
I am excited to see that there is never a shortage of new brands being developed. Even

as old brands get consolidated away, new fledgling brands emerge on the market.

Where else in the world have you studied, trained, or worked a harvest? How did that influence your winemaking?
I am a fifth-generation winemaker in the Napa Valley and have only worked in the Napa, Sonoma, and Mendocino areas. However, I am lucky to work for an international company with its roots in Spain, so I do get to travel and work with our other winemakers in Europe and Argentina. Working alongside my international counterparts, I have learned the value of a well-balanced wine that pairs well with many types of food. Wine is an integral part of the daily meals in Europe, something that is evolving and gaining momentum in the United States.

Which varieties are you working with? Are you experimenting with anything new?
We have such a unique portfolio, and I am proud to have had a hand in helping to develop it. We make small, ultra-premium lots of the varieties for which Carneros and the Napa Valley are best known—Chardonnay, Pinot Noir, and Cabernet Sauvignon—but we also make wines that honor our Spanish heritage like Tempranillo, Albariño, and our Grand Reserve Sparkling Wine that is still called Codorniu Napa.

Are there any new areas that you have identified for potential vineyard sites?
Currently our focus is to make the absolute best wines we can from our current sites in the Los Carneros and Atlas Peak appellations.

What challenges have you faced as a winemaker or winery owner?
With so many wonderful winery properties in both Napa and Sonoma it is a challenge to establish a point of differentiation from wineries.

Also, we seem to be challenged every vintage by Mother Nature. Climate change has made things much less predictable in the last 10 years or so, and weather events seem to be more extreme than before. It has even been suggested that our area may no longer be able to grow such premium grapes due to the shift in climate.

Another challenge worth mentioning is limitations to direct shipping due to state laws and regulations.

What is your winemaking philosophy?
The philosophy of winemaking at Artesa is to always be true to the place where the grapes were grown. We recognize that grapes are expressions of *terroir* and show distinct regionality and true characteristics of the region. The wine should always overdeliver in

the glass and have the potential to be enjoyed with food or without.

We use a variety of both traditional and modern techniques to create our wines. The modern ones allow us to control temperature, avoid contamination, and lower our risks. The traditional ones allow us to make wines that are true to their place and express their *terroir*. We avoid any technique that is designed to manipulate the wine's flavor and strive to make wines of great character that reflect where they came from. Fermentations are conducted in both stainless-steel and wood vessels, with many types of yeast, and with different temperatures. These techniques create a palate of component wines with a variety of aromas and flavors. We then step into the artistic realm of winemaking as we create blends from the dozens of separate lots we created during the year. Blending is the time when a winemaker is truly able to express his or her artistic side and form the finished wine into the masterpiece they have envisioned from the day the grapes were harvested.

What would you hope people say about your wine?

That was fantastic! Where can I find more of that?

Do you think that the market should influence winemaking or do you think that winemaking should influence the market?

Personally I feel that both should work in synergy. A winemaker can make the best wines, but it hardly matters if nobody wants to buy them. However, I also feel that wines should never be forced into a mold that has been created by a marketing ideal and should always reflect where they came from.

Besides your own wine, what are some of your favorite wines? What do you like about them?

From Napa, I have always loved Shafer. They are still family-owned and have stuck with what works. I also really enjoy drinking wines from all over the world, like the Scala Dei wines from Priorat, Spain. It fascinates me to see that there can be so many differences in what seems to be such a simple ancient beverage.

What is your opinion on screw cap versus cork closures?

I am a bit of a traditionalist when it comes to cork. I feel that screw caps have a place, but they belong on quick-to-drink, aromatic whites for the most part. I am not a fan of them ending up on higher-end wines, especially ones meant for aging.

If you could invite anyone from history, living or dead, to your home for dinner, who would it be? What food would you serve? What wine would you serve?

Abraham Lincoln. He was such a visionary and would lend to some great conversations. I think I would have to serve grilled Pacific salmon with a Carneros Pinot Noir to show him the amazing things that have become of the Golden State.

If you were to stay home tonight for a relaxing evening, drinking wine while watching a movie, which movie would you watch? Which wine would you drink? Explain.

Since the weather has been warm lately, I would go with a nice chilled rosé and a fun comedy like *This Is 40* or *Horrible Bosses.* We always enjoy a good laugh. In the cooler months I would go with a bigger red such as a Napa Cabernet with a good drama or romantic comedy like *The Godfather* or *Forgetting Sarah Marshall.*

How do you like to spend your time away from the winery?

I love to spend time with my wife and three daughters. We do all kinds of activities together like hiking, biking, kayaking, and stand-up paddleboarding. We are also all big fans of roller coasters.

Do you collect wine? If so, what is in your cellar?

I really don't consider myself a collector. I am a wine consumer. I like to keep things around to enjoy rather than collect dust. That said, I do have a few special bottles around such as some older Artesa and Duckhorn wines I made and some old vintages of Beringer from the family.

If you weren't involved in wine, what would you be doing?

I would be a street performer! Not really. I have always been fascinated with engineering and aviation. I guess that's why I love building and improving wineries and working with all the big machinery. My love for aviation might have something to do with me marrying a pilot. . . .

MICHAEL MONDAVI

Michael Mondavi's career in wine began in 1966 when he cofounded the Robert Mondavi Winery in Napa Valley with his father, Robert Mondavi. Over the years he has been actively involved with the Wine Market Council, Napa Valley Vintners Association, Wine Institute, and Winegrowers of California, to name only a few. He is the founder and "coach" of Folio Fine Wine Partners, a company he established in 2004 with his wife, Isabel, and their children, Rob and Dina.

How did you get involved in the world of wine?

I have the luxury of being the third generation growing grapes and making wine in Napa Valley. I grew up at the Charles Krug ranch, surrounded by vineyards; the winery was 100 yards from my home. The cellarmaster was my baby-sitter, and the tanks, barrels, and winemaking equipment were my jungle gym.

What are some of the biggest changes you have seen in winemaking since you began your career?

From a winemaking perspective, in the late '60s and early '70s, intense oak flavor became very important in California wines, specifically trying to understand the proper balance of varietal flavor and character between oak and wine. Through the '90s to today, we are learning that "less is more" and a "kiss" of oak complements the food and enjoyment of the wine more so. We have also learned how to better manage our vineyards to ensure we have a long growing season producing wines with moderate sugar and alcohol levels. Great wines are from great vineyards—today we understand we are wine *growers*, not wine *makers*.

In the '60s and '70s, there were really two types of customers: the European immigrants for whom wine was a standard everyday beverage to be enjoyed with a meal and the international traveler or businessperson brought up enjoying wines in Europe or who used prestige wines for entertaining or enjoying at home. Today, the interest in wine and food is beyond our fondest dreams of 40 years ago, and wine is being embraced by everyone from the young Millennial through the thriving baby boomer generations.

What are some of the exciting changes that you see happening in your area of California?
In 1965 in Napa, there were approximately twelve wineries; only eight of them had labels, and the remaining four produced wine to be sold to other wineries in tank trucks. Today, there are over 450 wineries in Napa Valley, in excess of 1,000 brands, and Napa Valley is considered one of the leading premium wine areas in the world with word-class tourism and dining experiences. The future for our region is just beginning.

Where else in the world have you studied, trained, or worked a harvest? How did that influence your winemaking?
I've had the pleasure of producing wine with my team in Tuscany in Italy, Languedoc-Roussillon in France, Chile, and Australia, in addition to making wines in Napa, Sonoma, and the Central Coast of California. Each area taught me a different heritage and philosophy of winemaking with techniques that varied from the traditional winemaking techniques practiced in Napa in the '60s and '70s to modern scientific techniques. It opened our eyes to innovation and improved techniques, many of which we are applying today.

Which varieties are you working with? Are you experimenting with anything new?
Cabernet Sauvignon is central to our life alongside the classic Bordeaux varieties, plus Sauvignon Blanc, Pinot Noir, and Chardonnay. My son, Rob Jr., has a love affair with Petite Sirah, and he is making some terrific wines under the Spellbound label. We are always looking to experiment with soil-microclimate combinations and how they impart different nuances of aroma and flavor to the wines.

Are there any new areas that you have identified for potential vineyard sites?

The future is the past. Historically, the great wines from Napa in the 1800s were almost exclusively produced from hillside vineyards. From the '60s through the end of the twentieth century, the vast majority of Napa wines were produced in the valley floor. I strongly believe the best wines from Napa Valley will be produced from hillside vineyards. When our family purchased the Animo vineyard in Atlas Peak in the '90s, we knew it had the potential to produce some of the finest Cabernet Sauvignon in the region. We are still only learning the potential of this site, but it is exciting to see what lies ahead.

What challenges have you faced as a winemaker or winery owner?

You face different challenges as a winemaker than you will as a winery owner. The winemaker's objective is to always produce wine with the personality and style that he or she is passionate about; that may not align entirely with the owner's needs. Managing this is a balance of managing a daily business without losing the wine style and the long-term vision of the company. The beauty of working with my son and daughter is we all share common goals and can make decisions as growers, winemakers, owners, and partners for our collective success.

What is your winemaking philosophy?

Mother Nature is truly the winemaker. The soil and microclimate are the genetic parents, and we are the baby-sitter, nanny, and teacher. I learned that I was not a winemaker but a wine grower and therefore able to produce wines that communicated the heritage of my family, the soil, and the microclimate where we grow those grapes.

What would you hope people say about your wine?

1. Could I please have another glass?
2. I would like some of this wine for my cellar.
3. I love it today, and it's going to be even better in the future.

Do you think that the market should influence winemaking or do you think that winemaking should influence the market?

Yes! Both complement one another. Wines have changed over the ages, as food has evolved, and to make wines only for a specific market is shortsighted. Wines should complement and enhance the food of the times. With the array of wonderful fresh ingredients, the dishes are often more delicate, elegant, and complex than in the past. As winemakers, we should strive to make wines that complement and enhance the foods available to us.

Besides your own wine, what are some of your favorite wines? What do you like about them?
I enjoy a broad spectrum of styles of food from different ethnicities and heritages and the same is true of the wines I enjoy, and I prefer to drink young wines—the freshness and vitality of young wines. The wines of Italy are always inviting—Tuscany for its delicate Sangiovese, Piemonte for full-bodied Barolos, and Sicily for beautiful Nero d'Avolas. France for history and traditional styles of wines, and Spain is moving quickly in creating exciting wines for the young consumer.

What is your opinion on screw cap versus cork closures?
Screw caps have been used in winemaking since the '40s and '50s, and the quality of screw cap closures over the last decade has made them almost "zero-defect" and more user-friendly than cork. With the exception of beautiful Cabernet Sauvignons (that would potentially be aged for 25 to 35-plus years), I believe screw cap closures are a superior closure for protecting the wine and being convenient for the consumer.

If you could invite anyone from history, living or dead, to your home for dinner, who would it be? What food would you serve? What wine would you serve?
I had the pleasure about 15 years ago of playing golf and then having lunch with Joe DiMaggio. He was such a humble, inspirational man and such a role model for young children, it was an honor to spend time with him. We shared a few glasses of 1974 Robert Mondavi Reserve Cabernet over a home-cooked meal after an annual golf weekend fund-raiser for the Boys & Girls Club of Napa Valley. And yes, Joe won the golf match!

If you were to stay home tonight for a relaxing evening, drinking wine while watching a movie, which movie would you watch? Which wine would you drink? Explain.
My wife, Isabel, loves old movies, and quite often we will have a relaxing dinner together and watch one of her classic black-and-white movies. She chooses the movie (most likely *Casablanca*), and I choose the wine and cook. I find the process of cooking very relaxing, and if I cook, I don't have to do the dishes!

In the fall and winter months we will pour M by Michael Mondavi Cabernet Sauvignon and Isabel Mondavi Estate Pinot Noir, and during the warmer summer months I enjoy the Isabel Mondavi Chardonnay while cooking and then simply a chilled bottle of my wife's namesake rosé over dinner.

How do you like to spend your time away from the winery?
My family and I enjoy the Big Island of Hawaii and have been traveling there for many years. The change of climate, scenery, and the tremendous array of fresh fish and seafood that's available is quite the change from our home in Napa Valley. My blood pressure drops 20 points as I get off the airplane, and it's straight to the fridge for a glass of Isabel Rocks—my wife's namesake rosé—poured over ice.

Do you collect wine? If so, what is in your cellar?
Over the years I have amassed more than 8,000 bottles—predominantly Napa Valley Cabernets with select producers from Bordeaux, Italy, Spain, and France. I also have small collections of Rieslings from Germany and California. My cellar is a little more extensive than we can manage, and I thoroughly enjoy opening great old bottles to share with guests who come to visit. After all, great wine is to be shared with family and friends.

If you weren't involved in wine, what would you be doing?
I love architecture, I studied it in college, and I would very likely have been an architect, but wine called me back. I thoroughly enjoy creating things, and architects have the creative freedom to create beautiful structures and buildings and are handsomely rewarded for their efforts.

MICHAEL TRUJILLO

Winemaker Michael Trujillo began his career in 1982 when he visited a family friend at Sequoia Grove who then offered him a job. Michael learned his winemaking skills and techniques by working closely with some of California's legends, including André Tchelistcheff and Tony Soter.

How did you get involved in the world of wine?

I got involved in wine by accident. I was raised on a ranch in southern Colorado, and from a young age I loved building things with my own hands. I took a trip to Napa on college spring break in 1981 and never left. Sequoia Grove founder Jim Allen offered me a job. I learned my craft working with Jim and consulting winemakers André Tchelistcheff and Tony Soter and then later at University of California, Davis, and the Napa Valley School of Cellaring.

What are some of the biggest changes you have seen in winemaking since you began your career?

Science has played a big role in changing the way we think about farming and the growing of grapes. When I first started in the '80s, conversations about soil and rootstocks were happening, but now these factors are part of everyday life. Napa Valley used to be a hodgepodge of grape varieties, but science has given us a more in-depth view of the best land for the right grapes. We now work in terms of microclimates, soil types, and *terroir*. For example, we're no longer growing Chardonnay in Calistoga because we know it grows better in cooler-climate Carneros. We know what we want to grow and where and how to grow it.

What are some of the exciting changes that you see happening in your area of California?

Napa Valley is more globally recognized than it was 20 or 30 years ago. We have become a true contender in the world of wine, thanks to a combination of learning where to plant specific grapes and great winemaking. We've discovered dozens of variations of microclimates, sun exposure, and soil compositions from one vineyard to the next. This detailed knowledge of vineyards is similar to that of Burgundy. I really see Napa Valley as an oasis for winemaking in the United States and the crown jewel of the US wine market.

Where else in the world have you studied, trained, or worked a harvest? How did that influence your winemaking?

I haven't worked abroad, but I spend a lot of time visiting wine regions all over the world. What strikes me, particularly in Europe, is the wisdom and patience that comes with working the same land for generations. The older I get, the more I recognize the value of patience found in Old World winemaking.

Which varieties are you working with? Are you experimenting with anything new?

I'm a Bordeaux guy through and through, which is why I've focused mostly on Bordeaux varieties—Cabernet Sauvignon, Cabernet Franc, and Merlot. That said, I am curious and am always experimenting with small projects with everything from Tempranillo to Malbec and Rhône varietals. I constantly experiment with fermentations, extractions, and yeast. I enjoy the scientific side of winemaking and embrace any information new technology can give us, but I also firmly believe in the role of intuition.

Are there any new areas that you have identified for potential vineyard sites?

Most of the plantable land in Napa has been identified and cultivated. My favorite appellation is Rutherford. Cabernet Sauvignon grown on the Rutherford Bench is the best in all of Napa. Our newest vineyard acquisition, Tonella, is a great piece of Rutherford that our vineyard manager, Steve Allen, replanted to select Cabernet Sauvignon clones that take advantage of the "sweet spot" Napa Valley has for Cabernet.

What challenges have you faced as a winemaker or winery owner?

Year in and year out, the biggest challenge for

a winemaker is Mother Nature. The weather is unpredictable and creates a waiting game that can put even the most tenured winemaker on edge. The season can be short or long, hot or cold, dry or rainy, or a combination of all or none of these factors. It's what keeps us on our toes and challenges us. When it comes to the business of running a winery, the biggest challenges are with the markets, such as grape inflation, energy, and operation costs. This is a big part of the reason why we have made controlling our fruit sources such a priority.

What is your winemaking philosophy?

I love to express varietal character and show a wine's true sense of place. You don't need to put too much frosting on the cake, as I like to say about winemaking. I want to make wines that express where they came from, the season they experienced, and the emotion tied to the land. As a winemaker my job is to guide the wine to be an expression of the season and vineyards.

What would you hope people say about your wine?

My goal is to make balanced, sexy wines that stand as true expressions of the land. Wines don't have to be huge to have character. If a wine is balanced from first smell to lingering aftertaste, that is what I call art in a glass.

Do you think that the market should influence winemaking or do you think that winemaking should influence the market?

Winemaking should influence the market. I try to make wines in a balanced, silky style, and there happens to be a specific target audience that has a love and respect for that style. Buyers will follow the winemakers they trust and will be willing to try something new if they have been able to count on that winery or winemaker in the past. Chasing scores and styles doesn't create that trust.

Besides your own wine, what are some of your favorite wines? What do you like about them?

I don't have a favorite wine as much as I have favorite producers and styles. I find myself attracted to producers who make wine in a similar style to mine and are great at telling the story in the bottle. . . . Some of my favorite producers are Peter Michael and Shafer.

What is your opinion on screw cap versus cork closures?

I think there are pros and cons for both. Screw caps do well with a wine that is drunk young, but it's hard to put a screw cap on a wine that needs to sit in the cellar and rest for a few years.

If you could invite anyone from history, living or dead, to your home for dinner, who would

it be? What food would you serve? What wine would you serve?

I would love to have dinner with André Tchelistcheff. I still make wines that I think would please him. I've always loved having my hands in Rutherford, and those are the wines he loved the most. I would prepare a simple steak dinner—a classic Napa Valley Cabernet pairing. We would sit and talk for hours about the complexities of each wine and simply enjoy each other's company.

If you were to stay home tonight for a relaxing evening, drinking wine while watching a movie, which movie would you watch? Which wine would you drink? Explain.

I'm most likely to watch something with a historical reference or background. I most recently really enjoyed the History Channel's *Men Who Built America* miniseries. I find the history of how the world has evolved intriguing. When I relax, I'm not one to grab a lighter white wine or a big and chewy Cabernet Sauvignon. I tend to relax with medium-bodied reds, such as a Pinot Noir or a Bordeaux blend. I love to enjoy an easy-drinking Ancien or Domaine Carneros Pinot Noir with about five years of postrelease bottle age.

How do you like to spend your time away from the winery?

Woodworking is my greatest hobby, and when I'm not in the vineyard, I'm usually in my workshop. I love working with my hands and crafting things out of wood—tearing into a house, renovating a room, or gutting a kitchen—they allow me to work with my hands in a way different from winemaking.

Do you collect wine? If so, what is in your cellar?

I collect a little of everything. I used to collect all of the popular California wines, but I no longer chase the trophies. I'm not as avid of a collector as I once was, but I still try to keep up with wines from new producers and winemakers to keep up with how wines are evolving. Some of my old standbys that I always keep on hand are Stag's Leap, Alpha Omega, and O'Shaughnessy.

If you weren't involved in wine, what would you be doing?

I first started studying architectural engineering and have always wanted to build on a grander scale, such as bridges or skyscrapers. I would have hoped to have been a design architect of some kind.

MIKE BENZIGER

Winemaker Mike Benziger headed west out of New York City in 1973 and began his career working in a wineshop. In 1978 he took an apprenticeship at a winery, and today he and his family make delicious, highly rated wines using biodynamic principles.

How did you get involved in the world of wine?
The day I graduated from college, my girlfriend (my wife of 39 years now) and I drove to California. At that time we had never been west of Philadelphia. When we got to California, we had no money left. By luck, I got a job in a wineshop. It was my first job out of college. I got bit by the wine bug. I fell in love with wine and never looked back.

What are some of the biggest changes you have seen in winemaking since you began your career?
I started in the wine business in 1973. At the wineshop I worked in, which was a good one, the best-selling wine in 750 ml was Charles Krug Chenin Blanc and Wente Grey Riesling. California Chardonnay was not on the radar screen. The wine consumer at that time was a very narrow demographic. Then, there might have been several hundred wines available; today, tens of thousands. The wine business exploded. The biggest changes have been globalization, consolidation, expansion of the demographics who enjoy wine, and how ingrained wine and food are in American culture. Of course, there's more. I expect the rate of change to continue to increase.

What are some of the exciting changes that you see happening in your area of California?
I am very encouraged by the awareness that is now developing with many growers and wineries that many of the things we do to create a healthy environment can have a direct effect on wine quality. We need to think about what kind of land, climate, and environment we will leave our grandchildren. As the Indian Chief Seattle said, "We don't inherit this land from our parents; we borrow it from our children."

It took my family some time to figure it out, but nature is now our best partner in growing grapes and producing distinctive wines. We are constantly debating the differences/similarities between what is modern quality and authenticity/honesty.

Where else in the world have you studied, trained, or worked a harvest? How did that influence your winemaking?
I have been extremely fortunate to learn much of my farming and winemaking from great mentors. They not only presented me with a great example of what to do but, even more importantly, how to be around nature, grapes, and wine.

I can't think of anything more important than traveling the world of wine, food, and general agriculture and maintaining global connections. Without a wider view, you will lose relevance and get messed up quickly.

Which varieties are you working with? Are you experimenting with anything new?
I personally am focused on Pinot Noir and Bordeaux varieties. What Pinot teaches me I adapt to Cabernet Sauvignon. Our experimenting tends to be focused in the field.

Are there any new areas that you have identified for potential vineyard sites?
I am fascinated with farming out close to the ocean. It's kicked our ass. It will take a few lifetimes to figure it out, but that's fun for me.

What challenges have you faced as a winemaker or winery owner?
My family's goal and mine is to remain humble, passionate, and curious about nature. We believe rhythm, pattern, and harmony are key tools for the future. That said, we don't really understand much but have our eyes wide open.

What is your winemaking philosophy?
My growing and winemaking philosophy is to invite nature in to do the heavy lifting. When you harmonize with nature, it reveals more of itself. That's its way of showing gratitude.

What would you hope people say about your wine?
Pure, honest.

Do you think that the market should influence winemaking or do you think that winemaking should influence the market?
I think anyone in this business has to listen deeply to the customer and the market, then stake your ground and hold it.

Besides your own wine, what are some of your favorite wines? What do you like about them?
I really like Jacques Lardiere's whites at Louis Jadot. You can taste Jacques's passion and beautiful personality. Domaine Leflaive, pure electricity. Lucien Le Moine, Rotem & Mounir make razor-sharp wines. Radio-Coteau Pinots. Eric's wines have great balance all the way through, real. Siduri wines, unique, like Adam. Marcel Deiss, total sense of place. James Milton Vineyard, fresh like a sea breeze. Chateau Pichon Lalande, complex textures and contours.

What is your opinion on screw cap versus cork closures?
I like screw caps for early-consumption whites. Other than that, I like what a cork finish does for a wine's evolution.

If you could invite anyone from history, living or dead, to your home for dinner, who would it be? What food would you serve? What wine would you serve?
God, I don't know. On one level, it might be Gurdjieff or Steiner. On the other, it might be John Candy or Jonathan Winters! My mom and dad for sure; they died a long time ago. I would cook a pig (with the help of my son-in-law, who is a chef) and drink a 2001 Tribute and 2007 de Coelo Pinot Noir.

If you were to stay home tonight for a relaxing evening, drinking wine while watching a movie, which movie would you watch? Which wine would you drink? Explain.
One of my favorite things to do! I like Coen brothers movies. I might drink a beer and probably some Pinot. Definitely pass out before the movie ends, probably sleep in my clothes and get yelled at by my wife!

How do you like to spend your time away from the winery?
I like to hang out with my wife, Mary, kids, and grandchildren. If I have time to read, that's cool; I listen to music, too; that's awesome! My wife and I like to travel to food and wine locations around the world.

Do you collect wine? If so, what is in your cellar?

I am a wine collector. I have a pretty good selection of Bordeaux and Burgundy. Some California Pinots, Zins, and Cabs. A good selection of Chardonnays. Also some good Italian wines. I have a few ports. I'm starting to collect some Spanish wines. I drank all my Rhônes.

If you weren't involved in wine, what would you be doing?

Can't imagine that, but I would like to retire to only farming.

MILJENKO "MIKE" GRGICH

Croatian born Miljenko "Mike" Grgich immigrated to the United States in 1958. He is well known in the industry for crafting the 1973 Chateau Montelena Chardonnay that scored higher than the best French Chardonnays at the famous 1976 Judgment of Paris. He celebrated 50 years of winemaking in 2008 and was inducted into the Vintners Hall of Fame the same year.

How did you get involved in the world of wine? My mother, Iva Grgich, switched me from breast milk to wine (half wine and half water, called "Bevanda") at the age of two and a half. At the age of five I was already on wine only. In later years I studied enology and viticulture and graduated from the University of Zagreb in Croatia.

I came to the United States in 1958 to work in wineries. My first job was at Souverain Cellars, then Christian Brothers, then nine years at Beaulieu Vineyards with André Tchelistcheff and four years with Robert Mondavi. I then joined Chateau Montelena as winemaker and limited partner for five years (1972–1977). At Chateau Montelena I crafted the 1973 Chardonnay that bested the best French Chardonnay at the famous 1976 Paris Tasting. That wine was "the champion" of the Paris Tasting with 132 points, the highest score overall, the best white and red French and California wines. The now-historic 1976 Paris Tasting put Napa Valley on the map as the best wine region of the world, energizing the rest of the world to plant more vines and make better wines.

On Independence Day 1977, Austin Hills and I broke ground in Rutherford to build Grgich Hills Cellar. Since starting Grgich Hills, I continued receiving international awards for my wines and have been recognized for being a leader in sustainable vineyard practices. In 2008 I celebrated 50 years of making wine in California, and the same year I was inducted into the Vintners Hall of Fame. Today all 366 acres of Grgich Hills are certified organic, and the winery has converted to solar power and is completely estate-grown.

My contributions to winemaking in the United States and my homeland Croatia drew the attention of Croatian Radio television, and director Milka Barišić created a documentary about my life *Like the Old Vine (Kao Stara Loza)—The Life Story of Miljenko "Mike" Grgich*. The crew filmed in the Napa Valley; the Smithsonian Institute Museum of American History in Washington, D.C.; and my birthplace in Desne, Croatia. The documentary, first shown at the Zagreb Gourmet Weekend in April 2012 and premiered at the Napa Valley Film Festival in November, 2012, describes my achievements and how my "American dream" became a reality. The film later received the Grand Jury's Special Award from the twentieth annual Oenovideo International Grape & Wine Film Festival, and Milka Barišić accepted the Cep d'Or Trophy in the French Senate at the Palais du Luxembourg in Paris, France, on September 27, 2013.

I was one of the winemakers featured when the Smithsonian Institute Museum of American History opened its first major exhibition on food history—"FOOD: Transforming the American Table 1950–2000"—in November 2012. A major section of the exhibition focuses on the revolution in American wine in the second half of the twentieth century and features the 1973 Chardonnay I handcrafted that won the historic 1976 Paris Tasting, which sparked a wine revolution and made Chardonnay the most popular wine in America. The exhibit also includes the small cardboard suitcase I traveled with when I left Croatia in 1954, my winemaking textbooks, and my original beret.

What are some of the biggest changes you have seen in winemaking since you began your career?

When I arrived in Napa Valley in August 1958, most wines had many defects—volatile acid, haze, sediments, off-aromas, and taste. Some wines would referment in the bottle. The best taster was the person who could find more defects in wine. Today, all defects have been eliminated and the best wine taster is the one who can detect more aromas and pleasure in the current wines.

What are some of the exciting changes that you see happening in your area of California?

When I came to California in 1958, there were only four students in the Department of Enology at the University of California, Davis. Today, over 100 students are enrolled every year; hence, more educated winemakers are available. Following my father's rule to "every day do something just a little better" has guided a long list of advances and innovations at Grgich Hills since it was founded in 1977.

Great wine starts in the vineyard, and over the years Grgich Hills has strung together a string of pearls that run through the Napa Valley. Starting with just 18 acres surrounding the winery in Rutherford, we now own and farm five vineyards, with a total of 366 acres. In recognition that all our wines are estate-grown, the winery changed its name to Grgich Hills Estate in 2007.

By having our wine estate-grown, -produced, and -bottled, my winemaking team and I have total control over the entire process. My nephew, Ivo Jeramaz, who is vice president of vineyards and production, started organically farming the vineyards in 2000. Today every acre is farmed naturally, with no artificial fertilizers, pesticides, or fungicides. Just as my father did in Croatia when I was growing up, we treat the earth as a living organism to maintain a harmonious balance between the vines and the earth's soil. As part of my belief in sustainable farming, the winery switched to solar power in 2006. As a result, Grgich Hills Estate wines are crafted "from our vineyard to your glass—naturally."

In the cellar, Gary Ecklin, chief enologist, has brought in OXOline, an ingenious system for stacking and rotating oak barrels, so that the staff can manage the delicate aging process with even greater care. The winemaking team particularly likes the system for the winery's white wines, which allows the cellar crew to regularly rotate each 60-gallon oak barrel, stirring up the lees and giving the wine additional complexity and body.

Innovations extend to every area of the winery. My daughter, Violet Grgich, has taken the reins of sales and marketing, and she has launched a series of advances in sales, marketing, the website, and social media.

Where else in the world have you studied, trained or worked a harvest? How did that influence your winemaking?

I was born in Croatia and educated in enology and viticulture here. I arrived in California at the age of 34.

In 1996 I opened Grgic Vina Winery in Croatia, producing Plavac Mali, a red wine, and Posip, a white wine, with the goal of helping winemakers in my homeland produce world-class wines from local varieties.

I therefore imported French oak barrels for wine aging, set up a modern bottling line, installed air-conditioned storage for aging wines, and brought a rigorous, scientific approach to improve the winemaking.

My goal was for Croatian wines to become recognized internationally. I felt great satisfaction when in 1999 a commission of Croatian winemakers selected Grgic Vina 1977 Posi and Grgic Vina 1977 Plavac Mali to represent the Croatian wine industry along with Croatian food to be served for one month in the Delegates Dining Room of the United Nations in New York. I believe that the wines are great messengers to the world of the high quality of Croatian wines. In my style of wines one can detect some European influence, particularly if the tasting takes place in Europe. My world-class wines are food-friendly and crafted for enjoyment.

Which varieties are you working with? Are you experimenting with anything new?

Grgich Hills Estate owns five vineyards in Napa Valley with a total acreage of 366 acres. We make wines only from our own vineyards—Chardonnay and Sauvignon Blanc—white varieties; Cabernet Sauvignon, Merlot, Zinfandel, and Petite Sirah—red varieties. We constantly experiment as to how we can maximize the enjoyment of wines, always keeping them "balanced." Lately, we are experimenting with a white wine called Posip and a red wine called Plavac Mali in Croatia.

Are there new areas that you have identified for potential vineyard sites?

I was offered to be an original partner to establish Chateau Ste. Michelle in Washington State, the first winery to make premium wines from Yakima Valley grapes (the first AVA established within Washington State).

What challenges have you faced as a winemaker or winery owner?

My biggest challenge as a new winery owner was to get so many permits to start building Grgich Hills Cellar. When we finally got the permits, it was too late to finish the building for our first year's crush in 1977!

What is your winemaking philosophy?

The Grgich Hills Cellar philosophy was and still is to make "château-quality" wines, consistency in quality, balanced wines with longevity. An example of our longevity is that on April 8, 2013, we tasted with the media a 1972 Chardonnay I crafted—after 41 years this white wine was clear, had no sediments, and was still alive!

What would you hope people say about your wine?

I would like people to say about Grgich Hills wines, "from Grgich Hills vineyard to your glass naturally"—naturally farmed and handcrafted wines.

Do you think that the market should influence winemaking or do you think that winemaking should influence the market?

Winemaking should influence the market. At Grgich Hills Estate we do not follow somebody else's style—we set the style, and others follow our style.

Besides your own wine, what are some of your favorite wines? What do you like about them?

I enjoy only Grgich Hills Estate wines; therefore, I cannot say much about wines of other wineries.

What is your opinion on screw cap versus cork closures?

I prefer cork closures because cork helps wines continue to mature naturally.

If you could invite anyone from history, living or dead, to your home for dinner, who would it be? What food would you serve? What wine would you serve?

If I could invite anyone from history it would be the late André Tchelistcheff. I would serve him barbecued lamb to eat paired with Grgich Hills Estate Zinfandel.

If you were to stay home tonight for a relaxing evening, drinking wine while watching a movie, which movie would you watch? Which wine would you drink? Explain.

If I would stay home tonight for a relaxing evening I would watch the documentary *Like the Old Vine/Kao Stara Loza* and drink Grgich Hills Estate 2010 Chardonnay "Paris Tasting." In my winemaking I have had more recognition for Chardonnay. Over 20 percent of Americans drink Chardonnay; only 12 percent drink Cabernet Sauvignon.

How do you like to spend your time away from the winery?

I like to be by the ocean, especially the Bodega Bay.

Do you collect wine? If so, what is in your cellar?

I have Grgich Hills wines and Chateau Montelena wines in my cellar.

If you weren't involved in wine, what would you be doing?

At the age of 90 years old, I'd spend more time in Croatia.

PETER MONDAVI SR.

Simply stated, Peter Mondavi Sr. is a legend in the world of wine. The son of Italian immigrants Cesare and Rosa Mondavi, he attended Stanford University, graduated in 1937, and pursued graduate enology studies at the University of California, Berkeley. He is widely credited for many innovations used in the California winemaking process, including cold fermentation and sterile filtration.

How did you get involved in the world of wine?
I grew up in Lodi, California, where grapes were a major product.

What are some of the biggest changes you have seen in winemaking since you began your career?
Fortified wines with 20 percent alcohol such as Angelica, Muscatel, port, and Sherry, etc., were the first major wines produced. Over the years dinner wines with less than 14 percent alcohol gradually became the major product.

What are some of the exciting changes that you see happening in your area of California?
The major change these past 10 to 15 years was the production of very expensive, higher-than-14-percent-alcohol dinner wines.

Where else in the world have you studied, trained, or worked a harvest? How did that influence your winemaking?
I researched cold fermentation of white grape juice at the University of California at Berkeley. This maintained the fruity character

of the white juice. Upon my graduation from Stanford in 1937, I did laboratory work and assisted the winemaker at Woodbridge Winery for about two years, after which time I was employed as assistant winemaker at Acampo Winery and Distillery until 1942, when I was drafted into the army for World War II.

I was released from the army in 1946 and was soon employed as winemaker at Charles Krug Winery, which my father purchased in 1943.

My brother, Robert, was the general manager, and I was the winemaker. I was the first person in Napa Valley to purchase and use French oak barrels in 1963.

The ambassador to France, who owned a boutique winery in Sonoma County (Hanzell), was the first person in Sonoma County to use French oak barrels; that is where I had the opportunity to taste Chardonnay aged in French oak.

Up until that time I had high hopes about the quality of French oak barrels for all wines but was hesitant at the cost of $35 per barrel. The tasting of Chardonnay in Sonoma County convinced me of the quality regardless of the price.

Which varieties are you working with? Are you experimenting with anything new?

We are presently concentrating on the different soils as well as the different French oak barrels for the production of the best Bordeaux varieties and Chardonnays.

Are there any new areas that you have identified for potential vineyard sites?

In the early years vineyards were developed in the hills. However, Prohibition and the additional cost to operate those mountain vineyards made it a losing business.

Over these past 10 to 15 years the economy improved and wineries, especially the boutique wineries, concentrated on soils best suited for the Bordeaux varieties, which were the most respected varieties.

With the improved economy the wealthy wine enthusiasts could afford to establish boutique wineries for the expensive hillside mountain vineyards, which were found to have excellent soil for the desired Bordeaux grape varieties.

Napa Valley has great soil and climate conditions overall, but the mountain vineyards have proved to be the best for the Bordeaux varieties along with certain valley areas.

I feel the improved economy has been a major factor in the relocating of vineyards in the hills. We ourselves have gradually developed hillside vineyards. It's an expensive operation, but the quality warrants the expense.

Hillside and mountain vineyards are very expensive but have their place, while the valley vineyards offer quality at a more reasonable price. This presents a good balance for us. We hope to add a few more mountain vineyards as our business warrants it.

What challenges have you faced as a winemaker or winery owner?
When Prohibition was repealed, it was a question of learning the production along with the sale of wine. It was a difficult challenge. I keep saying one has to enjoy wine in spite of its many challenges.

Having grown up in the grape-growing area of Lodi and being Italian, it was a natural business for my father and mother and we children.

I've spent 70 years in the wine business along with 3½ years in the US Army during World War II.

Winemaking and sales is a constant challenge, but if you love it, it's well worth it.

What is your winemaking philosophy?
It's a challenge to do the best you can to produce a wine that is a really enjoyable beverage along with a good dinner.

What would you hope people say about your wine?
I would like people to say they really enjoy our wines and recommend our wine to their friends.

Do you think that the market should influence winemaking or do you think that winemaking should influence the market?
I would like to think that winemakers are capable teachers.

Besides your own wine, what are some of your favorite wines? What do you like about them?
Naturally I favor our wines, but there are many other high-quality wines.

What is your opinion on screw cap versus cork closures?
Screw caps are economical and serve a purpose, while good corks are very traditional and relate to outstanding wines.

If you could invite anyone from history, living or dead, to your home for dinner, who would it be? What food would you serve? What wine would you serve?
I would invite my favorite friend who enjoys wines as much as I do. I'd serve my best filet mignon for my main course along with a selection of vegetables, etc., and a bottle of our Generations, which is a Bordeaux blend.

If you were to stay home tonight for a relaxing evening, drinking wine while watching a movie, which movie would you watch? Which wine would you drink? Explain

I'd watch one of the early movies of the top actors in the early days with a glass of Charles Krug Chardonnay because without food it would be lighter and more relaxing than a robust red wine without food.

How do you like to spend your time away from the winery?

I like to watch mainly the news on TV and an occasional professional football game and occasional good movies. I enjoy shopping for deals at Costco. I enjoy fly-fishing on the Snake River, Idaho, with my sons, Marc and Peter Jr. I also look forward to lunch with our old-timers group at various wineries.

Do you collect wine? If so, what is in your cellar?

In the early days I used to purchase the top French wines for comparison, but our Napa Valley wines are of such good quality today that I now have quite a selection of good Napa Valley wines and very few French wines.

If you weren't involved in wines, what would you be doing?

At the age of 98 I still go to my winery office every workday to keep abreast of our winery operations.

PHILIPPE MELKA

Bordeaux-born and -educated, Philippe Melka is a winemaker and winemaking consultant. His client list includes Vineyard 29, Quintessa, and Seavey, for which he makes well-regarded and high-scoring wines. He also makes wine under his eponymous label, Melka Wines, with his wife, Cherie.

How did you get involved in the world of wine?
I was born and raised in Bordeaux, intrigued by the land around me. When it came time for college, I acted on my childhood interests and studied geology at the University of Bordeaux. A class in winemaking propelled me to earn my master's degree from the school in agronomy and enology.

What are some of the biggest changes you have seen in winemaking since you began your career?
Winemakers are beginning to take more into consideration of the importance of how to handle the grapes upon arrival to the winery; for example, many wineries have incorporated gravity-flow techniques. Additionally, winemaking has become more extreme with longer maceration times and longer barrel aging.

What are some of the exciting changes that you see happening in your area of California?
Better knowledge of the land and soil types, which created huge improvement about vineyard plantation with better choices of rootstocks, clones, and density of planting. Also, much better water management with smart irrigation and water monitoring at the winery to minimize usage.

Where else in the world have you studied, trained, or worked a harvest? How did that influence your winemaking?

I've worked in both France and California. My first position was with Château Haut-Brion in 1990. Following my stint with Haut-Brion, I worked with Dominus sister property Château Pétrus from 1991 until 1994. I then set out traveling, dividing time between soil study and winemaking at world-renowned wineries Badia a Coltibuono in Chianti and Chittering Estate in Australia. After returning to Napa full-time in 1995 and for the past 18 years, I've been working as a winemaking consultant for some of Napa's most highly regarded properties, including Vineyard 29, Hundred Acre, Dana Estates, Gemstone Vineyard, and Lail Vineyards. I have combined Bordeaux's classic winemaking techniques with everything Napa and Sonoma have to offer.

Which varieties are you working with? Are you experimenting with anything new?

I've been working with Cabernet Sauvignon, Merlot, and Cabernet Franc. I recently planted Sauvignon Blanc and Chardonnay in Knights Valley.

Are there any new areas that you have identified for potential vineyard sites?

I will potentially be working with vineyards in Paso Robles and Washington State. Although I don't currently have anything in the works at the time, Languedoc and Sicily have intrigued me as possible areas for vineyard sites.

What challenges have you faced as a winemaker or winery owner?

With my family's label, Melka Wines, one challenge is finding vineyard sites that have the ability to express the best combination of New World and Old World. For example, Knights Valley brings a sense of flavors from the New World with the classic *terroir* of Old World grape-growing regions (i.e., clay).

As a consulting winemaker with my consulting company, Atelier Melka, one challenge I've seen with clients is the education aspect of winemaking as some have no background or history of winemaking.

What is your winemaking philosophy?

My winemaking style is to make wines that showcase the purity of fruit and demonstrate finesse while letting the vineyard express itself.

What would you hope people say about your wine?

I would want people to say that the wines are telling the truth and are not superficial—they are storytellers with regard to the vineyard site, the people behind them, the vintage, and the context.

Do you think that the market should influence winemaking or do you think that winemaking should influence the market?
I believe they are interconnected, and I see both points of view—as a winemaker I try to balance the two.

Besides your own wine, what are some of your favorite wines? What do you like about them?
Some of my favorite wines come from the regions of Côtes du Rhône (Chave Hermitage) and Châteauneuf-du-Pape.

What is your opinion on screw cap versus cork closures?
Personally I am all about corks.

If you could invite anyone from history, living or dead, to your home for dinner, who would it be? What food would you serve? What wine would you serve?
Ernest Hemingway. We will serve a gargantuous meal starting with oysters with Sancerre, trout with Riesling or Condrieu, roasted pork with Rioja Alta, rabbit with Pinot Noir from Burgundy (20 years old or more), then a great Rémy Martin cognac with a Cuban cigar.

If you were to stay home tonight for a relaxing evening, drinking wine while watching a movie, which movie would you watch? Which wine would you drink? Explain.
For both wine and movies, sometimes I like something lighthearted and fun and other times I like something in-depth and intense/complex. Ultimately, the wine and movie tends to go hand in hand. With *Sleeper* from Woody Allen, I would keep it light and easy with a rosé from the Languedoc. With Tarantino's *Pulp Fiction*, I will drink exuberant wines from Châteauneuf-du-Pape. For Jim Jarmusch's *Night on Earth* I like to go with Hermitage from the Côtes du Rhône, more classic but still lots of fun, and for Jean-Paul Rappeneau's *Cyrano de Bergerac* and Francois Truffaut's *The Last Metro*, classic French films, I'd go with a 1985 Château La Mission Haut-Brion.

How do you like to spend your time away from the winery?
With my family and friends and surfing in Hawaii and Indonesia.

Do you collect wine? If so, what is in your cellar?
I don't currently collect wine, but I should!

If you weren't involved in wine, what would you be doing?
Architecture.

PIERRE SEILLAN

French-born Pierre Seillan began his career in the world of wine at a very young age while working in his family's vineyards in Gascony. He later moved on to Château de Targé in the Loire Valley and then seven châteaux in Bordeaux before accepting Jess Jackson's invitation to make Vérité wine in California.

How did you get involved in the world of wine?

I started on my family's estate in Gascony, France, at a very young age, working in the vineyards. I learned very early how to be a servant of the soil, to help identify and express the message of the soil.

What are some of the biggest changes you have seen in winemaking since you began your career?

The 2013 harvest will be my forty-seventh vintage. I have seen a lot of changes in 47 years with newer technologies in the vineyards and in the cellar. We now have a grape-sorting table with a Vision computer, we have temperature-controlled tanks, we have mechanical harvesters. When I started out back in France we did not have all of this technology; a lot was done by hand, and we had concrete and wooden tanks.

What are some of the exciting changes that you see happening in your area of California?

I am excited to see that Sonoma is starting to become a star of California; the diversity of the *terroir* and the proximity to the Pacific

Ocean make it one of the best places in the world to make wine.

Where else in the world have you studied, trained, or worked a harvest? How did that influence your winemaking?

I have trained and worked in different regions of the world. I started in Gascony, then I was a trainee developing vineyards in Temecula in 1976. I worked in Saumur-Champigny with Cabernet Franc and managed several châteaux across the different regions of Bordeaux before discovering the diversity of Sonoma. All of this experience helped me develop my micro-cru philosophy and learn about different *terroirs*.

Which varieties are you working with? Are you experimenting with anything new?

For Vérité I am working with the five red Bordeaux varieties, but I also have some small projects that I am developing with some other varieties.

Are there any new areas that you have identified for potential vineyard sites?

Every year I am looking at new micro-crus to add to the complexity of my wines, new vineyards, new planting sites, and existing vines that can be grafted over to a better variety.

What challenges have you faced as a winemaker or winery owner?

I have faced many challenges as a vigneron. I try to always be looking at how to do things better and how we can adapt to new technology to improve and elevate the level of the quality of wine that we can produce. Sometimes it is hard to convince people of new ideas and change. Some people have called me crazy for developing a vineyard a certain way, for using a different technique or protocol, etc., but most of those people are eventually convinced after seeing what we can do; this is what I call improving the tradition!

What is your winemaking philosophy?

My philosophy is that of micro-crus, working with small parcels of vineyards that each have a unique *terroir*, keeping them separate during harvest and through fermentation and barrel aging to let each develop its own message of that particular micro-cru. Using as well as the micro-crus of the best oak forests for my barrels, selecting the best places in twelve to fifteen forests to source trees that will help the complexity of the grapes, and the micro-crus of the cork, to find all of the best places for these to grow, and to find a synergy between all of them. The goal of my winemaking philosophy is to capture the message of the soils to get the signature of the wine!

What would you hope people say about your wine?
I would hope that people enjoy my wine with family and friends, that they will find it to be a unique expression of the diversity of the *terroir* of Sonoma, that it is complex and elegant, a wine that is singing in the glass for happiness around the table.

Do you think that the market should influence winemaking or do you think that winemaking should influence the market?
I think that winemaking should depend on the grapes and the *terroir*, to make a wine that best expresses the message of the *terroir*, the soil, and the grape. I think that winemaking should influence the market. I see some wines influenced by the market to make higher alcohols and higher residual sugars, and I don't think that is good for the wine.

Besides your own wine, what are some of your favorite wines? What do you like about them?
I enjoy the wines from Hartford Estate Winery, from Stonestreet, from Château de Targé, and older red Bordeaux wines and Château d'Yquem.

What is your opinion on screw cap versus cork closures?
I think screw cap is nice for a rosé or for a white wine that is meant to drink young.

If you could invite anyone from history, living or dead, to your home for dinner, who would it be? What food would you serve? What wine would you serve?
I would invite my parents, Madame Pisani-Ferry, Raoul Quancard, and Jess Jackson, because they are all responsible for who I am today. I would serve foie gras with Château d'Yquem, lobster with Hartford Pinot Noir, and Tournedos Rossini with Vérité Le Désir 2005 and cheese.

If you were to stay home tonight for a relaxing evening, which wine would you drink? Explain.
I would drink a Sancerre or Pinot because it helps me to relax.

How do you like to spend your time away from the winery?
I like to spend my time in the garden and taking care of my land. I also enjoy spending time with my family and friends sharing good food and good wine, and I also enjoy watching rugby matches.

Do you collect wine? If so, what is in your cellar?

I do collect wine, but I am lost in my cellar.

If you weren't involved in wine, what would you be doing?

If I wasn't involved in wine, I would still be a farmer, I am very connected with the soil and the land, I still grow grains and sunflowers on my property back in France, but I could've also been an actor in the theater.

ROB MONDAVI JR.

Rob Mondavi Jr. is a fourth-generation California winemaker. In 2004, Rob and his family founded Folio Fine Wine Partners, followed by Michael Mondavi Family Estate in 2006. His role as president of winemaking has enabled him to return to his first passion: today, Rob is the winemaker for Isabel Mondavi Wines and Spellbound.

How did you get involved in the world of wine?

As a member of one of the most prominent winemaking families in the United States, it came naturally to me. Before I was born in 1971, my father and grandfather were laying the foundation and working tirelessly with the dream of creating the best Napa Valley wines. While bearing the Mondavi name carries a great responsibility, it also offers the opportunity to build upon, and push beyond, what has been done in the past.

What are some of the biggest changes you have seen in winemaking since you began your career?

The influence of technology has been enormous. With the development of data technology, we are now able to enter, track, and quantify data electronically, giving us better information for the vineyards and winery and helping us craft better wines. Also, the quality and availability of winery equipment that we have today is extraordinary. From destemmers and presses, to tanks and pumps, it helps us to improve the way we manage our winery.

What are some of the exciting changes that you see happening in your area of California?
In Napa Valley, the driving force of the vintner collective is to advance the style and quality of the region. We have always strived to be great, but today more than ever, there is a new edge, a passion that has people challenging the standard of excellence and raising the bar.

Where else in the world have you studied, trained, or worked a harvest? How did that influence your winemaking?
I was fortunate enough to have worked in our own wineries and vineyards—Robert Mondavi Winery, Vichon, and our joint venture, Opus One, where I worked as one of the opening cellar hands—for many years. While in McLaren Vale, South Australia, I visited twenty different wineries to better understand their fermentation techniques and winemaking philosophy. More recent travels have taken me to Europe, where I have been fortunate enough to meet with some of the best winemakers, including Artadi Viñedos & Vinos in Rioja, Celler Vall Llach in Priorat, and Tuscany's Tenuta dell' Ornellaia. Each of these wineries has a unique perspective that I wanted to understand, and all were willing to offer their time, knowledge, and mentoring.

Which varieties are you working with? Are you experimenting with anything new?
Cabernet Sauvignon is by far my favorite variety, as it yields so much color, aroma, flavor, and texture. I also enjoy being challenged by Petite Sirah, a variety that requires attention both in the vineyard and the winery; its naturally opulent flavors and structured tannins require a deft hand to produce softer tannin profiles while bringing forth the fruit. For both varieties, we have conducted numerous yeast trials, fermentation techniques, and vessels to find winemaking approaches that work for us.

Are there any new areas that you have identified for potential vineyard sites?
From what I have seen over the years, nothing compels me to invest outside of Napa Valley. Here we have nearly 50 percent of the world's soil types; we have the diversity of valley floor through to hillside vineyards; and microclimates that vary from hot to very cool. To me, Napa Valley is a winemaker's nirvana.

What challenges have you faced as a winemaker or winery owner?
The biggest challenge is climate change. Although overall we are blessed with good vintages, the climate is shifting our seasons, and I believe we have seen more variable

climatic conditions over the last decade than we did in the prior 30 to 40 years. These shifts require us to stay nimble in the vineyards and the cellar so we can adapt and shift to make exceptional wines.

What is your winemaking philosophy?
Remember and respect those who went before and learn from them, stay educated and informed on the latest advancements, challenge yourself, challenge your team, and never settle for good wine.

What would you hope people say about your wine?
Rob Mondavi's wines are simply spectacular: they respect a sense a place and are distinctly Napa Valley, yet they showcase the unique attributes of his vineyard sites. The wines are modern, never tied too much to the past, nor before their time. It is this balance of provenance, elegance, structure, and personality that makes these wines so collectable.

Do you think that the market should influence winemaking, or do you think that winemaking should influence the market?
I believe wines need to have a sense of place, but it is also important to understand the market conditions and "styles" to understand what is current to today's wine drinker. This is easier said than done! For example, the leaner Napa Valley Cabernet styles of the early 1970s were appealing to the market at the time but would be out of context in today's Napa Valley Cabernet styles.

Besides your own wine, what are some of your favorite wines? What do you like about them?
From the Napa Valley, my top choices are the wines from Venge Vineyards, Kelham Vineyards, and Macauley Vineyards, as they all are representative of their place and the personalities who make them. When I can taste a sense of place and feel the guiding style of the winemaker, I know I have a special wine.

What is your opinion on screw cap versus cork closures?
I like both. Screw caps are perfect for aromatic whites and reds that will be consumed within one to four years from release. For longer-cellaring reds and whites, I prefer high-quality cork.

If you could invite anyone from history, living or dead, to your home for dinner, who would it be? What food would you serve? What wine would you serve?
Without reservation I would invite my

grandfather Robert Gerald Mondavi. We did not spend as much time together when I was growing up as either of us would have liked. There are so many conversations that I would like to have with him about his inspiration, drive, and choices he made, in order to better understand his life's work and legacy.

We would sit down to a small plate of fresh pasta with shaved truffles, served with a splash of recently pressed olive oil and a wine from Piemonte. Before the main course, a simple dish of flash-fried squash blossoms, followed by an entrée of braised hunter-style hare served with 2001 Masseto and 2010 M by Michael Mondavi Cabernet Sauvignon.

The Masseto holds a special place, as we actually enjoyed this wine together and had a long conversation about its beauty. The 2010 M is a wine I made and am exceptionally proud of, and I would hope he would taste it and share his thoughts on it with me.

If you were to stay home tonight for a relaxing evening, drinking wine while watching a movie, which movie would you watch? Which wine would you drink? Explain.

Lydia's and my favorite movie is *Out of Africa*, a great love story that we can both relate to, since we're steadfast and independent; and with a back drop of Africa we have always found the film to be tremendously relaxing. The movie's length is perfect for cuddling up and finishing off a bottle of Isabel Mondavi Pinot Noir—an elegant and alluring wine that is ideal to sip for a couple of hours.

How do you like to spend your time away from the winery?

My wife, Lydia, and son, Robert Michael III, enjoy the beachside in South Carolina. We are currently building a beach house there where the three of us plan to spend more time together—fishing, digging for clams, throwing a shrimp net, or simply playing on the beach.

Do you collect wine? If so, what is in your cellar?

Yes, and I prefer wines with 10 to 15 years of age. Besides my family's own wines, my Napa Valley selection is predominantly those of my buddies Mac Watson, Kirk Venge, and Ron Nicholsen. The international selection includes many of the producers my family imports. When you represent the best wines of the world, you put them in your cellar! With that, I have an emphasis on Italy, including wines from Tenuta dell Ornellaia and Dal Forno Romano. My love of Spain is enduring, and so is my small selection from Artadi Viñedos & Vinos and Celler Vall Llach.

If you weren't involved in wine, what would you be doing?

Distilling. The art of fermentation and handcrafting is very special to me, and if I could no longer work with grapes, I would distill whiskey, bourbon, gin, and perhaps create an aromatic or bitters. Capturing the essence of the grains or botanicals and then blending to create something extraordinary has allure to me. Distilling encompasses so much of the art of winemaking with an entirely different set of ingredients, methodology, and flavors.

STÉPHANE DERENONCOURT

Stéphane Derenoncourt began his illustrious career as vineyard help and worked at a variety of French châteaux before becoming a winemaking consultant in 1999. Today he and his company consult for more than 90 wineries around the world, including wineries in France, India, Italy, Lebanon, California, and Virginia. He is considered by many to be one of the world's hottest winemakers, and recently he released his own California label, Derenoncourt California.

How did you get involved in the world of wine?

I am a self-taught man; I started as a vineyard worker in Fronsac (in the Gironde). At first I was pulling the vine shoots, then I learned to prune. I love pruning; it's giving the vine its shape and strength back for a new vintage. At 23 I got my first cellar job, and soon enough, at La Fleur Cailleau, the owner, Monsieur Barre, gave me free rein. Then I became cellarmaster and vineyard manager at Pavie-Macquin. From a small success to another one, in 1995 Stephan von Neipperg hired me at Canon-la-Gaffelière, and LaMondotte was being born: a 4.3-hectare parcel that did not get the authorization to be reattached to the château, forcing the count to build a cellar on site where its grapes had to be fermented. The *terroir* wine received quickly a phenomenal success and became what we call a "garage wine." I earned recognition. I started consulting in 1999; today we are 12 in the Derenoncourt team.

What are some of the biggest changes you have seen in winemaking since you began your career?
Nowadays we have a better understanding of the maturities in the vineyard. The cellar equipment has also greatly evolved with sophisticated machines, especially at the reception of the fruits.

What are some of the exciting changes that you see happening in your area of California?
I see a lot more interest in Lake County from writers, consumers, and winemakers for the quality of the wines this place can produce.

Where else in the world have you studied, trained, or worked a harvest? How did that influence your winemaking?
I work in fourteen countries; experiences abroad are always a source of inspiration.

Which varieties are you working with? Are you experimenting with anything new?
Currently in California I work with Merlot, Cabernet Franc, and Cabernet Sauvignon.

Are there any new areas that you have identified for potential vineyard sites?
When I first went to Lake County and more particularly to Red Hills, I saw there was something special the soil could give to the vines. Some sites have great potential to make *terroir* wines.

What challenges have you faced as a winemaker or winery owner?
Unlike Bordeaux, where optimum maturity is often a challenge, in California the climate is very sunny and can be hot. You have to preserve the freshness of the fruit to let the identity of the place express itself through the wine.

What is your winemaking philosophy?
I like to make wines of *terroir* that reveal the identity of a place. There is no technical or rational definition to account for the word, but it starts out as a subsoil, a soil, and an exposure that generate a microclimate. Then the choice of plant material introduced by generations of growers through their experience and history, combined with the type of cultivation that promotes the vine taking firm root to the rock. All of these will draw out the identity of the locality and imprint it on the fruit, thus giving expression to a *terroir*. This could be interpreted as domesticating a place, but we are often reminded to stay humble before the complex work of nature.

What would you hope people say about your wine?
I hope they appreciate the freshness and the elegance.

Do you think that the market should influence winemaking or do you think that winemaking should influence the market?
Both. I think some exceptional wines have influenced the market, but it is generally the market that influences winemakers in their winemaking choices.

Besides your own wine, what are some of your favorite wines? What do you like about them?
The wines born of the Saint-Émilion limestone when they express violets and black truffle notes.

What is your opinion on screw cap versus cork closures?
Screw caps are great for wines of rapid consumption; cork plays a role in the aging of great wines, and it has a huge cultural impact.

If you could invite anyone from history, living or dead, to your home for dinner, who would it be? What food would you serve? What wine would you serve?
I would invite Tom Waits, and we would drink La Mondotte and Pavie-Macquin while listening to some blues.

If you were to stay home tonight for a relaxing evening, drinking wine while watching a movie, which movie would you watch? Which wine would you drink? Explain.
With my wife, we would drink an Yquem and watch a Coppola movie.

How do you like to spend your time away from the winery?
Stay home cooking, play music.

Do you collect wine? If so, what is in your cellar?
I have about 8,000 bottles in my cellar; they come from all over the world.

If you weren't involved in wine, what would you be doing?
I would be a writer.

TOBIN JAMES

Tobin James started his notable career in the world of wine when he made his first award-winning wine from six tons of discarded Zinfandel grapes. He opened his own winery in 1994, and today he enjoys talking to customers at the mahogany bar in his tasting room and chatting with hordes of his active wine club members on the deck of a winery-chartered cruise ship.

How did you get involved in the world of wine?
I grew up on a vineyard my brother started in Indiana 45 years ago. We were real rookies at grape growing, but I learned about farming, and early on I set my sights on the wine business.

What are some of the biggest changes you have seen in winemaking since you began your career?
If you really look at it, we've only made wine in this country in a concerted effort since Prohibition was repealed. Around the world, most countries have been doing it for hundreds of years. In the last 20 years Paso wines have reached world status.

What are some of the exciting changes that you see happening in your area of California?
Paso Robles is now firmly on the wine map. Twenty-five years ago, I would tell a wine buyer I had a winery in Paso Robles, and he would say, "Oh, you have a winery in Texas?" I would say, "No, that's El Paso."

Where else in the world have you studied, trained, or worked a harvest? How did that influence your winemaking?
Southern Indiana and northern Ohio, and it influenced me to move and make wine in California.

Which varieties are you working with? Are you experimenting with anything new?
Zinfandel is our flagship, and every year we love to add a new variety at crush because it's fun and exciting! We make 30 different wines.

Are there any new areas that you have identified for potential vineyard sites?
Not yet. We are very sold on Paso Robles fruit.

What challenges have you faced as a winemaker or winery owner?
None. If there were challenges, I was having too much fun and was so satisfied with people loving our wines that I quickly forgot them!

What is your winemaking philosophy?
No matter how the wine turns out, that's the way we planned it.

What would you hope people say about your wine?
When people are home in their castles drinking our wines, that they enjoy the wines as "gentlemen that fly straight and level." They're sharing them at their table with good food, loved family, and/or great friends.

Do you think that the market should influence winemaking or do you think that winemaking should influence the market?
You have to make what the public enjoys, but if we think we have a cool recipe or new variety we think they should try, we go for it.

Besides your own wine, what are some of your favorite wines? What do you like about them?
I'm faithful to the wines of Paso Robles but also enjoy a cold Château Budweiser!

What is your opinion on screw cap versus cork closures?
I love when wineries use screw caps because it saves more of the good corks for us!

If you could invite anyone from history, living or dead, to your home for dinner, who would it be?
I would invite Tony Bourdain because something tells me that we have a lot in common!

If you were to stay home tonight for a relaxing evening, drinking wine while

watching a movie, which movie would you watch? Which wine would you drink? Explain.
A perfect evening would be a Clint Eastwood Western with some big pasta dish like lasagna. I would drink our James Gang Reserve Zinfandel since I think of that spicy big wine as being like Clint: a confident gunslinger.

How do you like to spend your time away from the winery?
Traveling is my hobby. Countries are like different varieties; they all have their own special flavor.

Do you collect wine? If so, what is in your cellar?
I really don't need to collect wines because we meet so many cool winemakers and people in the business who love to share.

If you weren't involved in wine, what would you be doing?
I'd be in jail!

TOM TIBURZI

Winemaker Tom Tiburzi is in charge of Domaine Chandon's sparkling wine program. He has been at Chandon for 22 years, and his extensive scientific background and exceptional blending skills have led him to develop an exciting range of sparkling cuvées for the house.

How did you get involved in the world of wine?

Both of my parents emigrated from Italy, very much Old World, and we made wine at home. I was raised in my family's wine and spirits shops, so the world of wine was a constant. When I went off to college, I had no idea that my path would lead to winemaking. After receiving a degree in environmental studies in biology at UC Berkeley, I dove into algae and bacteria research, but when the group I was working with moved from the Bay Area, I didn't wish to leave. It was 1989, my wife had been working as pastry chef at the restaurant at Domaine Chandon, and harvest was about to start. I thought it would be interesting to work a harvest, and it turns out they had a research position open. I fit right in working with yeast and bacteria in wine and never left, moving from the lab, to staff microbiologist, to assistant winemaker, to associate winemaker, and in 2005 was appointed to sparkling winemaker to head the program.

What are some of the biggest changes you have seen in winemaking since you began your career?

Some of the biggest changes have been with the technology used in winemaking, things that make for a more efficient process toward producing wine without flaws. For example, cross-flow filtration with media that lasts for many years has replaced diatomaceous earth filtration, a medium that needs to be mined, shipped to the winery, carefully loaded into the filter to avoid health risk, then hauled off to a dump when spent. Another example is using electrodialysis to cold-stabilize the wine, a very "green" method that is quick and easy on the wine and uses very little energy and resources. This replaces conventional cold stabilization, which takes many days of constant mixing, a lot of electricity to run chillers taking the wine to subzero temperature, producing a slurry of tartaric acid that must be filtered out, then many therms of natural gas to warm the wine back up through heat exchangers.

Other changes have been with our knowledge on how to manage tannins so that red wine can be ready to drink sooner, without need for extended bottle aging. Also, we have evolved greater knowledge and new technology toward managing oxygen in the juice before fermentation, making for higher quality.

The supplier industry supporting winemaking has grown to be very competitive; much of the research and development is now done by them, with winemakers reaping the benefits. Only the very biggest wineries now support their own research staff compared to 20 years ago, when many small to medium-size wineries had research enologists or at least staff devoting time to research. The California Enological Research Association (CERA) was very active with wineries doing collaborative research; this still happens, but to a much lesser extent.

What are some of the exciting changes that you see happening in your area of California?

As mentioned above, the most recent exciting change has been in management of oxygen in juice before fermentation. In sparkling winemaking, we take the grapes directly to press, without crushing. We've known for a long time that a certain amount of oxygen contact with the juice is important for quality, minimizing astringency, and in general improving mouthfeel, with the risk being that too much oxygen could damage fruitfulness. We are now able to measure exactly how much oxygen is needed for each tank of new juice and can finely control the delivery of oxygen to the juice in order to maximize reduction in astringency without losing the fruit aromas and flavors.

Where else in the world have you studied, trained, or worked a harvest? How did that influence your winemaking?

Domaine Chandon is the only winery I have worked for; however, being part of LVMH and specifically the Moët Hennessy wine and spirits group, I have had great learning opportunities. Domaine Chandon was founded by Moët and Chandon, which was itself founded in 1743. I've had the privilege to receive the knowledge that has been passed down from winemaker to winemaker from their beginnings. Making sparkling wine is a special craft; to master the art of blending one needs mentors, and it was the blenders of Dom Pérignon that have taught the winemakers at Domaine Chandon. I am the third winemaker in succession at Domaine Chandon, hired by our first winemaker, and have been trained by the same mentors.

Which varieties are you working with? Are you experimenting with anything new?

I predominantly work with the traditional grapes of Champagne: Chardonnay, Pinot Noir, and Pinot Meunier. Muscat Canelli plays a part in our aromatic sparkling wine when there's a need to push the aroma and flavor toward apricots and peaches. I also work with a small amount of Zinfandel, used for blending with Pinot Noir in our sparkling red wine.

Are there any new areas that you have identified for potential vineyard sites?

For sparkling wine, I need cool growing sites to keep acidity high and extend the growing season. If the growing site is too warm, Chardonnay, Pinot Noir, and Pinot Meunier will achieve the 18–20 Brix sugar level too fast for good flavor development. We need to pick at low sugar because we use second fermentation in the bottle to get bubbles into the wine. This adds alcohol, and if we pick grapes above 20 Brix, then the final alcohol is too high, out of balance. Therefore, cooler areas with direct marine influence are potential new growing sites.

What challenges have you faced as a winemaker or winery owner?

One of the biggest challenges is to match supply and demand. When the economy is stable, it is relatively easy to maintain a slow, steady growth rate. But since it takes two to six years, depending on the sparkling wine, to get to market, forecasting how much to make is a challenge during recessions or rapid growth in demand.

What is your winemaking philosophy?

My philosophy in sparkling winemaking is to be true to tradition while leaving room for innovation. When an innovation presents itself, I ask the question, "Would this have been accepted a hundred years ago if available back then?" If yes, then I move forward.

What would you hope people say about your wine?

I like that the sparkling wines from Domaine Chandon are of consistent high quality and a great value.

Do you think that the market should influence winemaking or do you think that winemaking should influence the market?

There are elements of both. Input from the marketing side is essential if you want to sell wine; as winemakers, we want to be artists but not starving artists. Unless you're a boutique brand, the relationship you have with marketing and their relationship with distributors are key to success. At the same time, winemaking creativity can drive interest toward your brand.

Besides your own wine, what are some of your favorite wines? What do you like about them?

I enjoy drinking all types of wines from all regions of the world, especially in the context of food pairings. At least 50 percent of the wines opened in my home are sparkling. Of the rest it is two to one red to white wines. The reds are mostly Cabernet Sauvignon or Bordeaux blends and Pinot Noir, while the whites are mostly Chardonnay and Sauvignon Blanc. Other wines I especially appreciate are Argentine Malbec, Spanish Tempranillo and Albariño, Riesling, and Chenin Blanc. These are great wines with food that have flavors and mouthfeel that I enjoy.

What is your opinion on screw cap versus cork closures?

Screw caps are good closures, and the liners available now can dial in exactly the desired level of oxygen egress into the bottle to match the style of wine being produced. These liners are very similar to the ones in the crown caps that we use on our sparkling wines for second fermentation and aging in the bottle. If these alternative closures were available when stoppers were moving away from wooden plugs and oily pieces of cloth, it is my opinion that cork closures would have never been developed. However, there has been a long history of using cork closures, and cork is a great, renewable resource. The issue is that for the masses of normal corks, you can expect about 1 percent to be tainted, and what other product would you allow that rate of flaw, bottles of juice, jugs of milk? However, there has been great innovation with agglomerated cork processing that removes potential taint; we use this type of cork at Domaine Chandon. I am happy to use these taint-free technical corks since they are a sustainable renewable resource.

If you could invite anyone from history, living or dead, to your home for dinner, who would it be? What food would you serve? What wine would you serve?

My dinner guest would be Julia Child, someone both my wife and I would have loved to have known. We would go out to the garden to see what's ready to be harvested. Then, with that in mind, go to the market and look at the available meats, poultry, and seafood, talk to the purveyors about where things came from, and garner any special insights until inspiration decides what is to be the main course. At this point, dinner planning ensues in the aisles, and any necessary ingredients are acquired before heading home to prepare dinner with bubbly in hand. Whatever the food cooked or wines served, it would be great because of the conversation and the act of living.

If you were to stay home tonight for a relaxing evening, drinking wine while watching a movie, which movie would you watch? Which wine would you drink? Explain.

I would be watching Woody Allen's *Midnight in Paris*, drinking Domaine Chandon's étoile Brut, a modern testament to Chandon's heritage, which is fitting with the movie's theme to relish history but appreciate the time we are living in. Étoile is a statement of finesse and elegant simplicity, and those we aspire to in the movie believe in the simpler things and are moved by inspiration and passion as I am when creating and sharing étoile. The movie overflows with wine, and I especially like how the writers and artists enjoy wine as it should be, seamlessly within their way of living.

How do you like to spend your time away from the winery?

I like to travel, visiting both remote wild areas for their natural beauty and cities for their sights, art museums, and fine restaurants. We like to cook at home and have a kitchen garden all year round. Besides gardening, hobbies include foraging wild mushrooms and stargazing.

Do you collect wine? If so, what is in your cellar?

I do not collect wine. I have a wine cabinet containing an eclectic mix of wines that have been bought, gifted, or traded for, all intending to be consumed.

If you weren't involved in wine, what would you be doing?

I am intrigued by the merging of art and science, where the science facilitates the realization of the art. Winemaking does this; so does photography, which is the field I would otherwise pursue.

ZELMA LONG

Winemaker and winemaking consultant Zelma Long began her career in the world of wine when her in-laws planted grapes in the Napa Valley. She went on to make wine with Mike Grgich and Robert Mondavi and eventually became the chief enologist at Robert Mondavi Winery. She was the winemaker at Simi Winery for years and has consulted for Chandon in Argentina, Ruffino in Chianti, and other many other wineries around the world. Currently she is making wine at Long Vineyards and is a winemaking partner and owner at Vilafonté Wine Estate in South Africa.

How did you get involved in the world of wine?
In the late 1960s, my in-laws bought and planted to grapes a property in the eastern hills of Napa Valley. I had completed my BS at Oregon State and was completing a dietetic internship at UCSF Medical Center. The Longs thought they might start a winery from their vineyard holdings. Making wine sounded intriguing to me. I went back to school at UC Davis to study winemaking and grape growing.

My master's in enology and viticulture was never completed; at harvest 1970 Mike Grgich called me to work with him at Robert Mondavi Winery. It was an amazing opportunity . . . a beautiful new winery, driven by Robert, the visionary, and Mike Grgich, his enologist, who was so talented. I fell in love with winemaking and never returned to school. After Mike left to become winemaker at Chateau Montelena, I took his place as chief enologist at RMW.

What are some of the biggest changes you have seen in winemaking since you began your career?
Changes? It is more accurately transformation. Wine has become part of our American culture. We have learned to grow wine grapes; not just to "produce grapes" . . . resulting in much better wines. The phylloxera problem in the 1990s was expensive but resulted in a major upgrade in the vineyards—better plant material, better planting strategies, better training, all to the benefit of the wines. We are more sensitive to and knowledgeable about our sites and soils, honoring them in the wine growing and winemaking. We are more proficient at selecting the right sites for each grape cultivar we work with.

Wine has always been international, but now winemakers travel the world, so ideas, innovations travel quickly. Our wines are more sophisticated . . . more balanced, more harmonious, more flavorful, more delicious. Mike Grgich won the famous (or infamous, if you are French) Paris Tasting in 1976. The New World of wine opened up and challenged the Old World. Both are better for it.

What are some of the exciting changes that you see happening in your area of California?
The most important technical changes in the vineyard and winery have been the attention to sustainability, to our carbon footprint, to being sensitive to our vineyard environment, better understanding of soil health, essentially the whole panoply of ways that we can grow and make wine to be gentle with our environment.

Where else in the world have you studied, trained, or worked a harvest? How did that influence your winemaking?
Thanks to Bob Mondavi, I was early on able to travel overseas: in 1973 to Germany, in 1978 with his whole team for three weeks to France and Germany.

In 1977 Bob Long and I started Long Vineyards Chardonnay and Riesling. The vineyards were on Pritchard Hill in Napa Valley. This small project continued, produced fine, long-aging Chardonnays. In the early 2000s, his father sold this vineyard and we elected not to continue the wine in the absence of those great old grapes. The heartbreak was that the new owner pulled out the rare and amazing old vines and planted Cabernet . . . of which there is plenty in Napa.

I started work as Simi's winemaker in late 1979; Simi soon came to be owned by LVMH. For them I consulted to Ruffino in Italy, to Chandon in Argentina, and with them I traveled to France and Australia for global meetings of their winemakers from around the world. At Simi I built a new cellar, developed Cabernet and Chardonnay vineyards, and brought that wonderful old winery into a vibrant "new" world of California wine.

My husband, Phil Freese, and I made Riesling, together with Dr. Monica Christmann, in Germany in 1998, 1999, and 2000, which was an extraordinary insight at making wine at 50 degrees N and its impact on grape and wine flavors. Recently I did a vintage in Bordeaux. I have clients in the Rhône and in Israel, in Oregon and Washington, and in Mendocino.

But my deepest and richest overseas work is our South Africa project, Vilafonté, which Phil and I own and run with our South African partner, Mike Ratcliffe. We began in 1997, buying 100 bare acres in the Cape, planting the first tranche of 13 hectares, and making our first wine: two Bordeaux blends, Series C and Series M, for the Vilafonté label in 2003. We are small; we only make wine from our vineyard (which has been expanded) and neither buy nor sell our Cabernet Sauvignon, Merlot, Malbec, and Cabernet Franc grapes.

From the start, I regarded traveling and talking to other winemakers and winegrowers, and wine and vine researchers, and tasting their wines as the best training possible, stimulating, and a source of new ideas and insights.

Which varieties are you working with? Are you experimenting with anything new?

At Vilafonté we grow Cabernet, Cabernet Franc, Merlot—the best I have made anywhere—and Malbec, which together give unique aromatics, soft tannins, high fruit concentration, and considerable longevity to our wines. Malbec, not widely grown in the Cape, is an important part of our blends for its lush palate.

My local project, Rosati Family Winery, is a small vineyard of old Cabernet high on a ridge in Mendocino, planted by Dave Bennion, who planted the Ridge vineyards, including Jimsomere and Monte Rosso. It is classic, fine Cabernet.

Scanning my projects around the globe, my longtime love and focus are Bordeaux *cépages*. However, my Rhône clients are growing Grenache and Syrah at high elevation, and Grenache is definitely a new love. My client Nicole Sierra-Rolet of Chêne Bleu hosted the first International Grenache Symposium several years ago. It's about time that delicious grape with its unique persona gets attention and respect; it makes great wines.

Are there any new areas that you have identified for potential vineyard sites?

Everywhere I go in the New World, vineyards are pushing successfully into new sites. Both my parents were born, raised, and educated in eastern Washington, and in my early life it was wheat or sagebrush. I love eastern Washington sites—the Horse Heaven Hills, Red Mountain, Wahluke Slope,Walla Walla Valley. They are not new but rich both with success and great potential.

South Africa, our "second home," is producing internationally significant wines, and vineyards are pushing out from the Cape in every direction. Until 1994 they faced restraints from exploring new sites, and what is happening there now is exciting and energizing.

What challenges have you faced as a winemaker or winery owner?

What is particular to our winemaking business is the long cycle of growing, fermentation, and aging of wines and the annual nature of that production. We take it for granted, but those coming into wine from other industries can be flummoxed by these realities.

For the winemaker the challenge is to respond at the best level possible to what Mother Nature provides each harvest, and for the winery owner, to respond to the commercial needs of the business, whatever they may be . . . and both are always changing.

Our business is a slow business. The vineyards need time to establish and develop; it takes a year to grow each harvest, then time in the cellar and the bottle. Personally, I love this slow, thoughtful raising of the wine and the fact that we are based in agriculture, our feet in the soil.

What is your winemaking philosophy?

Honor the vintage, honor the site, honor the variety. Learn deeply about each, using observation, experience, and science. Make wines by responding to the grapes rather than directing them. Know that grapes and wines are sensitive to their environment; handle them carefully and protect them. Produce beautiful wines, delicious wines, and, if fortunate, occasionally wines that set a benchmark for others. And finally, never stop learning.

What would you hope people say about your wine?

It is delicious, it is seductive, it makes my mouth water, it is intriguing and complex, it touches and tickles both the mind and the palate. It is wonderful as a young wine and more intriguing as it ages. I want to drink some now and put it away for the future. It is a wine I will not forget!!

Do you think that the market should influence winemaking or do you think that winemaking should influence the market?

I see two broad categories of wines: (1) the

"beverage wines," those of large quantity, good quality, modestly priced for everyday enjoyment with meals, (2) the artistic wines, made to reflect the site and grapes of their origin and the hand of the winemaker. They are more idiosyncratic, have distinct personalities, are made in small quantities, and often are more expensive, like any fine work of art or craft.

The first group must reflect the needs of the market; the second must reflect what and who they are and seek the buyers looking for that.

Besides your own wine, what are some of your favorite wines? What do you like about them?

This is a bit difficult because there are so many wonderful wines, I cannot track them all, but here are some generalities: I love the Sauvignon Blancs of South Africa; they have great fruit expression and refinement. I adore the Grenache of Priorat and the Rhône—Grenache has intense red and black cherry fruit and depth and freshness. I enjoy the more restrained Cabernets of Napa and Alexander Valley for their complexities and balance and the Syrah-based wines and blends of eastern Washington. I love fine Chablis and am pleased with some of the nonwooded Chardonnays now being made for the seductive and fresh flavors of this great grape. I love fine, older German Riesling, amazing for having grown at high latitudes with long cool summers. And Pinot Noir . . . I adore it with the expressiveness of red fruits and a seductive texture on the palate . . . whether a fine Burgundy, a Sonoma Pinot of great finesse, or an intriguing Willamette Valley lovely.

What I look for in a wine is clarity and purity of expression; a true expression of the *cépage* and its area, but the palate is most important—its harmony, length, balance of components, and length and character in its flavors. That, I believe, is hardest to achieve, and it needs to come from both the vineyard and the winemaking; and the legendary winemakers' wines have these qualities.

Although you have said "besides your own wine," I have to mention my Vilafonté wines; they are luscious, delicious, and I believe the finest red wines I have made over a long winemaking life.

What is your opinion on screw cap versus cork closures?

They both have an important role in winemaking. It is necessary to be aware that the wine will age differently in one versus the other, so the proper match of wine and closure must be made; that is a decision of the winemaker given the style of wine she has or wants to make.

If you could invite anyone from history, living or dead, to your home for dinner, who would it be? What food would you serve? What wine would you serve?

I would like to invite the winemaker of Simi Winery's 1935 Cabernet and find out exactly what grapes were in that wine, where they came from, and how it was made. That wine is still very alive, and over my work time at Simi it changed very little, as if it had hit a plateau and was holding its own; an amazing wine.

I would serve food that was delicate in flavor, so not to overwhelm this old lovely, and of course would want to drink it for dinner, drinking history. Yes, there are wines that are older, no doubt greater, but this is one from my home territory, that I lived with and enjoyed on occasion over 20 years, and it is still a mystery.

If you were to stay home tonight for a relaxing evening, drinking wine while watching a movie, which movie would you watch? Which wine would you drink? Explain.

I understand that there is a movie coming out about Martine Saunier, a wise and wonderful woman born French, living as a Californian, who has been importing wines from Burgundy for decades. I would love to see that movie and drink one of the glorious Burgundies she has sold to us . . . let's say a wine from Henri Jayer, the great Burgundian winemaker.

How do you like to spend your time away from the winery?

I am a PhD candidate at UC Davis in performance studies, with a focus on the performance of art. So I spend a great deal of time studying and visiting art exhibits, galleries, and museums. I love and travel to the Southwest and appreciate Native American art—my DE at Davis is in Native American studies.

I enjoy casual photography. Phil and I photograph our vacations; we also do bird-watching and have a life list of southern African birds. I own a Foundation Quarter Horse and ride, not enough. And I am called to travel and explore. I hope one day we can drive around the United States seeing all the country in between the cities I have visited while in the wine business. I spend time with plants; we have a big garden, tending the plants, finding new, interesting, and unusual ones. Gardens, and vineyards, require patience.

Do you collect wine? If so, what is in your cellar?

Yes and no. I don't collect in the sense that serious wine collectors do. Phil and I have wines that we have made in our wine lives;

I also have clients' wines, wines from people I have visited around the world, wines I have tasted elsewhere and liked, wines of winemaker friends, wines that I read or hear about and sound intriguing. We discovered a Spanish Xarel-lo from an organic vineyard, subtle and lovely. We buy and happily consume Grenache-based wines. We have eclectic tastes and can pull just about anything from our cellar: some great wines, many good ones, and no doubt a substantial number that are over the hill.

If you weren't involved in wine, what would you be doing?

Having fun doing something else. However, by accident, I landed in one of the most fun, gratifying, and stimulating businesses on earth; at one end it is agriculture—feet in the soil—and the other end, global, and everything fascinating in between.

CLOCKWISE, FROM TOP LEFT: David Bush, chef, St. Francis Winery; Brigit Binns, chef and author of *The New Wine Country Cookbook*; Spaghettini Cooked in Zinfandel, Chef Michael Chiarello, Chiarello Family Vineyards; Timothy F. Kaulfers, Executive Chef, Arista Winery; Brigit Binns' Strawberry Gallete.

PART 3

THE RECIPES

STARTERS

WILD MUSHROOM BRUSCHETTA WITH TRUFFLES, PECORINO AND BALSAMIC REDUCTION

Courtesy of Matt Bolton, Executive Chef, Highlands Inn

WINE PAIRING: Wrath Chardonnay, Monterey County

MAKES 24 BRUSCHETTA

FOR THE WILD MUSHROOMS

- 4 ounces wild chanterelle mushrooms
- 4 ounces black trumpet mushrooms
- 4 ounces porcini mushrooms
- 4 ounces hedgehog mushrooms
- Salt and freshly ground black pepper to taste
- Canola oil
- 1 bunch fresh thyme leaves
- 1 small shallot, diced
- 1 teaspoon chopped garlic
- 1 tablespoon sherry vinegar
- 1 bunch parsley, cut into chiffonade

PREPARE THE MUSHROOMS

Keeping the mushrooms separate, lightly season them with salt and pepper. Coat a small skillet with canola oil and heat the pan until hot but not smoking. Add the chanterelles and one-quarter of the thyme leaves and pan sear until slightly darker in color. Transfer the mushrooms to a large bowl to cool. Continue to sear the remaining wild mushrooms in the same manner with thyme leaves and transfer each to the same bowl. When all the mushrooms are cool, transfer them to a chopping board and coarsely chop.

Add some canola oil to a large skillet and heat over moderate heat until hot but not smoking. Add the shallot and the garlic and cook until translucent. Stir in the chopped mushrooms and warm them through. Add the sherry vinegar and stir the mixture to deglaze the pan. Remove the pan from the heat and sprinkle with the parsley.

FOR THE BALSAMIC REDUCTION

1 cup aged balsamic vinegar

FOR THE BRUSCHETTA

Extra-virgin olive oil

1 ciabatta bread, sliced into ½-inch slices

Salt and freshly ground black pepper to taste

1 cup arugula leaves

2 ounces sliced truffle

Pecorino cheese

MAKE THE BALSAMIC REDUCTION

Add the balsamic vinegar to a saucepan and reduce over moderate heat until it coats the back of a spoon. Cool slightly and pour into a squeeze bottle.

ASSEMBLE AND PREPARE THE BRUSCHETTA

Preheat a broiler. (Alternatively, if you happen to be grilling, you can use the grill to toast the bread.)

Drizzle some olive oil on the ciabatta slices, season with salt and pepper, and toast the ciabatta slices. Top the toast with the arugula leaves, then a few truffle slices, then the warm mushroom mixture, and finally the pecorino. Place the bruschetta under the broiler briefly to melt the cheese. Drizzle with balsamic reduction and serve immediately.

HITCHING POST GRILLED ARTICHOKES WITH SPICY SMOKED TOMATO MAYONNAISE

Courtesy of Frank Ostini, Chef, Owner, and Winemaker, The Hitching Post Restaurant and Winery, Buellton, California

WINE PAIRING: Hartley Ostini 2012 Pinks

SERVES 6

- 6 artichokes
- Spicy Smoked Tomato Mayonnaise (recipe follows)
- 2 tablespoons butter, melted
- 2 tablespoons olive oil
- 2 tablespoons white wine
- 2 tablespoons lemon juice
- Salt and freshly ground pepper to taste

Break off the small outside leaves of the artichokes. Cut off the tops with a knife and trim the sharp points of the leaves with scissors. Soak the trimmed artichokes in cold water and then wash them again in cold water to remove any sand.

In a large pot fitted with a steamer basket, steam the artichokes until the hearts are tender, about 25 to 35 minutes, depending on size. Let the artichokes cool, then cut in half and remove the choke stickers with a spoon.

Meanwhile, prepare a grill for grilling and make the spicy smoked tomato mayonnaise (see auxiliary recipe below).

After the mayonnaise is prepared, grill the artichoke halves:

Grill the artichokes on the grill, turning them once or twice. Whisk together the butter, oil, white wine, and lemon juice and baste the artichokes occasionally until they are warmed through and the outer leaves are crispy. Season with salt and pepper to taste.

Serve the grilled artichokes with the tomato mayonnaise on the side.

SPICY SMOKED TOMATO MAYONNAISE

YIELDS APPROXIMATELY 1½ QUART

- 4 ounces garlic cloves
- 1 pound large onions, sliced thin
- 4 pasilla peppers, halved
- 4 tomatoes, halved
- 1 teaspoon cayenne pepper
- 1 teaspoon chili powder
- 1 teaspoon paprika
- 1 teaspoon salt
- 1 quart mayonnaise

Prepare a grill for grilling (alternatively, prepare an oak fire for grilling)

Slow roast the garlic cloves and onions on the grill in a grill basket until soft. Dry the pasilla peppers and tomatoes in an oak smoker until semisoft.

Purée the garlic, onions, peppers, and tomatoes, in a blender until smooth. Transfer to a bowl and blend in the spices and mayonnaise.

BLACK COD BRANDADE

Courtesy of Thomas Hill Organic Restaurant, Paso Robles

WINE PAIRING: Clayhouse Estate Cuvee Blanc

SERVES 4

- 1½ pounds fresh black cod
- 5 garlic cloves, peeled
- 3 sprigs thyme
- 2 bay leaves
- 1½ quarts whole milk
- Kosher salt, minced
- 1 pound Yukon gold potatoes
- 1 cup olive oil
- ½ tablespoons cracked black pepper
- 1 teaspoon chili flakes
- Zest and juice of 2 lemons
- 4 anchovies (optional)

TO SERVE

- Toasted crusty bread
- Capers
- Chopped parsley

Place the black cod into a large saucepan with the garlic, thyme, and bay leaves, cover with the milk, and season with 2 teaspoons of the salt. Bring to a very gentle simmer and poach the fish about 5 minutes, or until it flakes easily. Reserving the poaching liquid, transfer the fish with two large spatulas to a platter, and keep warm, loosely covered.

Strain the poaching liquid through a fine sieve into a bowl and return the garlic and milk to the saucepan. Cook the potatoes in the milk with the garlic until just soft. Strain the potatoes and garlic in a colander.

In the bowl of a mixer with the paddle attachment, whip the potatoes and garlic with half the olive oil. With the mixer on the lowest setting gently fold in the fish (be careful not to let the cod disintegrate or turn the potatoes into glue). Continue to gently fold in the rest of the olive oil, black pepper, chili flakes, lemon zest and juice, and anchovies if using. Season with salt to taste.

Serve the brandade on lightly garlic-rubbed toasted crusty bread with a few fried capers and chopped parley.

SALADS AND VEGETABLES

GRILLED WATERMELON SALAD WITH GOAT CHEESE, BABY GREENS, AND BALSAMIC VINAIGRETTE

Courtesy of Jeff Mosher, Chef, Robert Mondavi Winery

WINE PAIRING: Robert Mondavi Winery Napa Valley Fumé Blanc

SERVES 4

- 1 large seedless watermelon, rind removed
- 8 ounces baby arugula
- 8 ounces Lolla Rossa or other small red-leaf lettuce
- 8 ounces Little Gem lettuce or other small green-leaf lettuce
- 1 bunch basil
- 1 medium shallot, minced
- ½ cup balsamic vinegar
- 1¼ cups grape seed oil
- ½ cup extra-virgin olive oil
- Salt and freshly ground black pepper to taste
- 4 ounces fresh goat cheese, such as Laura Chenel

Slice the watermelon flesh into long planks 1 inch thick. Cut the planks into 3-inch by 3-inch squares. Set aside.

Wash the greens and the basil and toss together in a large bowl.

Combine the minced shallot and the vinegar in a bowl and let the shallots macerate for 10 minutes to soften them. Whisk in 1 cup of the grape seed oil and the olive oil, and salt and pepper to taste.

Prepare a grill for grilling.

Brush the remaining ¼ cup grape seed oil onto the watermelon squares and sprinkle them with a dash of salt. Working quickly, grill the watermelon for 30 seconds, turn it, and grill for another 30 seconds. Flip it over and repeat. (You want to get a nice crosshatching of grill marks without letting the watermelon break down.)

Toss the greens with the balsamic vinaigrette and add salt and pepper to taste. Place two watermelon squares on each plate and top with the salad. Crumble the goat cheese over the salad and serve immediately.

SHAVED FENNEL AND AVOCADO SALAD

Recipe courtesy of David Bush, Chef, St. Francis Winery, Sonoma, CA

WINE PAIRING: St. Francis Sonoma County Chardonnay

SERVES 4

- 1 cup sugar
- 2 Ruby Red grapefruits
- 1 orange
- 1 lemon
- ½ shallot, minced
- 1 teaspoon rice wine vinegar
- 1 cup olive oil
- Salt and white pepper to taste
- 2 medium fennel bulbs
- 2 tablespoons fennel fronds, chopped
- 2 ripe Haas avocados
- ½ cup macadamia nuts, roughly chopped
- 2 cups mache, roots removed

Combine 1 cup water and the sugar in a saucepan and bring to a boil, stirring occasionally with a whisk until the sugar has dissolved and the liquid is reduced to syrup. Transfer the simple syrup to a bowl and refrigerate until cold.

Peel the skins off the grapefruit and remove the sections, cutting between the pith and removing any white pith, and transfer the sections to a bowl. Pour the cold simple syrup over the grapefruit and refrigerate, covered.

Zest and juice the orange and the lemon, and transfer to a bowl, whisking to combine. Add the shallot and whisk in the rice wine vinegar, then whisk in the olive oil in a slow stream. Season to taste with a little salt and white pepper, and refrigerate the vinaigrette.

Using a French or Japanese mandoline, shave the fennel paper thin and transfer to a bowl. Add some of the vinaigrette, the chopped fennel fronds, and a little salt and white pepper and toss to coat. Cut the avocados in half and remove the seeds. Using a spoon, remove the avocado halves from the skin and place half on each of four plates. Place the dressed fennel on top of the avocado halves. Drain the grapefruit sections and distribute among the plates. Sprinkle the macadamia nuts on the plates. Divide the mache among the plates and drizzle any remaining vinaigrette on the mache. Serve immediately.

EGGPLANT ROLLATINI

Courtesy of AronHill Vineyards

WINE PAIRING: AronHill Estate Primitivo

SERVES 4

FOR THE SAUCE

- 2 tablespoons olive oil or enough to coat the bottom of the pan
- 2 yellow onions, sliced thin
- 1 (24-ounce) can whole peeled tomatoes
- 3 cups fresh whole basil leaves
- Salt and freshly ground black pepper to taste

FOR THE EGGPLANT

- 2 cups canola oil
- 2 large eggplant, cut into ¼-inch slices
- 3 cups flour
- 6 eggs, beaten
- 3 cups feta cheese
- 5 sun-dried tomatoes, sliced into thin strips
- 2 cups basil leaves
- 3 cups mozzarella, shredded

MAKE THE SAUCE

Heat the olive oil in a large saucepan over moderate heat until hot but not smoking. Add the onions and sauté until translucent. Add the tomatoes, basil, and salt and pepper and cook until the sauce comes to a boil, about 20 minutes. Let cool.

PREPARE THE EGGPLANT AND ASSEMBLE THE DISH

Preheat the oven to 400°F and spread enough of the cooled tomato sauce in the bottom of a large baking dish to cover.

Heat the canola oil in a large skillet over moderate heat until hot but not smoking.

Working with one eggplant slice at a time, use tongs to coat and fry the eggplant: flour both sides, dip the slices in egg to fully coat, then transfer to the hot oil in the skillet. Repeat until the skillet is full but not overcrowded. Cook the eggplant until light brown and transfer with tongs to paper towels to drain and cool. Coat and cook the remaining eggplant in the same manner.

Transfer the eggplant to a work surface. Divide the feta, tomato, and basil at the ends of the slices. Roll up the slices and arrange them, seam side down, on top of the sauce in the baking dish. Top rolls with a little more sauce and add mozzarella.

Bake the rollatini for about 15 minutes, or until bubbly.

PASTAS

CAVATELLI WITH PANCETTA, CHANTERELLES, AND MINT

Courtesy of Chris Kobayashi, Chef, Artisan Restaurant, Paso Robles

WINE PAIRING: Kenneth Volk Vineyards Chardonnay

SERVES 4

- 1 pound freshly made or dried cavatelli
- ¾ pound chanterelle mushrooms, cleaned
- 2 tablespoons extra-virgin olive oil (preferably Olea Farm Arbequina), plus extra for finishing the dish
- ½ pound pancetta, cut into small dice
- 3 cloves garlic, thinly sliced
- Chili flakes to taste
- 2 tablespoons mint, chopped
- 2 tablespoons flat-leaf parsley, chopped
- Parmigiano-Reggiano to taste

Bring a large pot of salted water to a boil and cook the pasta until just soft, about 4 minutes for fresh, or if using dried, follow the package instructions and cook until al dente.

While the pasta is cooking cut the chanterelles into bite-size pieces, or leave them whole if they are small enough. Set aside.

Heat the olive oil in a large skillet over moderate heat until hot but not smoking. Add the pancetta and render out the fat until the pancetta is golden (not too crispy, but not soggy.) Add the mushrooms and sauté for 5 minutes more, or until the mushrooms have exuded all of their moisture. Add the garlic and cook for 1 more minute. Add chili flakes to taste.

When the pasta is cooked, reserve 1 cup pasta cooking water and drain the pasta in a colander. Transfer the pasta to the pancetta and mushroom mixture. If the mixture seems dry, add some of the pasta water to loosen. Season with salt and pepper, add the mint and parsley, and toss to combine.

Transfer the mixture to a serving bowl, drizzle with more olive oil, and shave plenty of Parmigiano-Reggiano on top.

DOUBLE DELIGHT SUMMER SALSA AND PASTA SAUCE

Courtesy of Carol Baily, Baily Winery, Temecula Valley

WINE PAIRING: Baily Sangiovese

Note from Carol: *When my garden produces plenty of fresh peppers and tomatoes, I head to the kitchen to put together this wonderful combination of flavors. Sometimes I simply use it as a salsa; other times I make a pasta sauce. Lots of chopping is involved, but the flavors are wonderful. The Sangiovese pairs perfectly.*

MAKES 8 APPETIZER PORTIONS OR 4 MAIN COURSE PORTIONS

- 8 large ripe tomatoes, chopped
- ½ onion, finely chopped
- 1 green pepper, finely chopped
- 2 Anaheim chiles, finely chopped
- 1 small jalapeño, finely chopped
- 1 clove garlic, minced
- 1 tablespoon red wine vinegar
- 2 tablespoons oil
- 2 tablespoons cilantro, finely chopped
- Salt and freshly ground pepper to taste

Combine all ingredients in a large bowl and let the flavors blend for several hours.

To serve this as a sauce, simmer the mixture in a large skillet over medium heat until the onions and peppers are soft, adding a little white wine to the sauce if you wish. Serve hot over 1 pound spaghetti or linguine cooked according to package directions.

SPAGHETTINI COOKED IN ZINFANDEL WITH SPICY RAPINI AND PECORINO ROMANO

Courtesy of Chef Michael Chiarello, Emmy-Winning Food Network Personality and Founder of Napa Style and Chiarello Family Vineyards

WINE PAIRING: Chiarello Family Vineyards Giana Zinfandel

SERVES 4 AS MAIN COURSE OR 8 AS FIRST COURSE

- 1½ pounds rapini or broccoli rabe
- 1 pound spaghettini
- 1 (750-ml) bottle red wine, preferably Zinfandel
- 1 tablespoon sugar
- ⅓ cup extra-virgin olive oil
- 2 tablespoons sliced garlic (about 4 medium cloves)
- 1 teaspoon Calabrian chili paste
- 1 teaspoon kosher salt or sea salt, preferably gray salt
- ½ teaspoon freshly grated black pepper
- ½ cup Pecorino Romano cheese

Bring an 8-quart pot of salted water to a boil and cook the rapini for about 3 minutes. Transfer the rapini to a sheet pan and spread it out to cool. Using the same pasta cooking water, cook the spaghetti for half the normal time (3 to 5 minutes), stirring occasionally. Reserve 1 cup of the pasta water and then drain the pasta in a colander. Set aside.

Return the empty pasta pot to the stove. Pour the wine and the sugar into the pot, bring to a vigorous boil over high heat, then reduce the mixture by half, about 8 to 10 minutes. Add the spaghetti and shake the pot to prevent the pasta from sticking. Gently stir the pasta with tongs until coated and boil over high heat until most of the liquid is absorbed, about 6 minutes (the pasta will be al dente).

While the pasta cooks in the wine, heat a large, deep skillet until hot and then add the olive oil. When the oil is hot, reduce the heat to medium-low, add the garlic, and cook until pale golden, about 3 minutes. Add the chili paste, the blanched rapini, and the salt and pepper to taste and cook, stirring occasionally for 1 to 2 minutes. Add half of the reserved cooking water.

Add the rapini mixture to the pasta and toss gently to combine. Transfer to plates or one big platter. Top with the cheese.

SIMI PAPPARDELLE WITH DUCK AND MUSHROOM RAGÙ

Courtesy of Kolin Vazzoler, Chef, Simi Winery

WINE PAIRING: Simi Landslide Cabernet Sauvignon

SERVES 8 AS A FIRST COURSE OR 4 AS A MAIN DISH

- 1½ pounds boneless duck leg meat, cut into chunks
- 1 tablespoon sweet paprika
- Salt and freshly ground black pepper
- 2 tablespoons olive oil
- ¼ cup shiitake mushrooms, stemmed and thinly sliced
- ¼ cup button mushrooms, thinly sliced
- ¼ cup oyster mushrooms, stemmed and thinly sliced
- ¼ large onion, diced small
- 1 carrot, diced small
- 1 celery stalk, diced small
- 1 garlic clove, minced
- 1 cup crushed San Marzano tomatoes
- 1 cup Simi Landslide Cabernet Sauvignon
- 8 black peppercorns
- 8 parsley stems
- 2 sprigs rosemary
- 2 sprigs thyme
- 1 bay leaf
- 3 to 4 cups duck stock
- 1 to 1½ pounds fresh or dried pappardelle pasta
- ½ cup grated Grana Padano
- 4 tablespoons unsalted butter

Mix the duck with the paprika, and salt and pepper to taste. Heat the olive oil in a heavy pot until hot but not smoking, then add the duck and sear until golden brown. Transfer the duck to a plate and set aside. Add all the mushrooms, onion, carrot, and celery to the pot and cook, stirring occasionally, until the onion becomes translucent. Add the cooked duck and garlic and cook for 1 more minute. Add the tomatoes, breaking them up with a spoon, and cook for 4 more minutes. Pour in the wine, scraping the pan as you stir, and reduce by half.

Preheat the oven to 325°F.

Wrap the peppercorns, parsley, rosemary, thyme, and bay leaf in cheesecloth and tie to make a pouch. Add the pouch to the ragù mixture and add enough stock to almost cover the meat. Bring the mixture to a simmer and cover the pot with the lid.

Transfer the pot to the oven and cook the ragù for 2 hours, or until duck falls apart and the mixture is thick. Season with salt and pepper to taste.

Bring a large pot of salted water to a boil. Add the pasta and cook until al dente.

Drain the pasta and add to the ragù with half the cheese and all the butter. Mix until the pasta absorbs the sauce and becomes creamy. Season again and serve topped with the rest of the cheese.

BEEF, PORK, AND LAMB

FILET MIGNON WITH BLENDER BÉARNAISE SAUCE

Courtesy of Tyler Florence, Celebrity Chef and Host of Several Food Network Shows

WINE PAIRING: California Crush by Tyler Florence Custom Blended Red

SERVES 4

- 1 large end piece of beef tenderloin (about 3 lbs), tied and trimmed
- Extra-virgin olive oil
- Kosher salt and freshly ground black pepper
- Blender Béarnaise Sauce (recipe follows)

Preheat the oven to 400°F.

Drizzle the beef tenderloin with olive oil and season well all over with plenty of kosher salt and pepper. Bring the meat to room temperature before cooking.

Heat a large cast-iron skillet over medium-high heat until hot but not smoking. Add the meat and sear all over. Transfer the pan to the oven and roast the meat 15 to 17 minutes, or until a thermometer inserted into the thickest part of the meat registers 130°F for medium-rare meat. If you prefer to cook the meat to medium, cook for 3 minutes more. Remove the meat from the oven and from the pan, tent with foil, and let it rest for 10 minutes.

Just before serving, cut the meat. Serve the meat with the béarnaise sauce on the side.

BLENDER BÉARNAISE SAUCE

- 1 bunch fresh tarragon
- 2 shallots, minced
- ¼ cup champagne vinegar
- ¼ cup dry white wine
- 3 egg yolks
- 1 stick butter, melted
- Salt and pepper to taste

MAKE THE BÉARNAISE REDUCTION

Combine half the tarragon, the shallots, the vinegar, and the wine in a small saucepan and simmer over medium-high heat until reduced by half. Remove the pan from the heat and set aside to cool.

FINISH THE SAUCE

In a blender, blend together the yolks and béarnaise reduction. With the blender running, add one-third of the butter in a slow stream. Once it emulsifies, turn the blender speed to high and add the remaining butter. Add the remaining half bunch of fresh tarragon, season with salt and pepper, and blend for a few seconds. Set aside in a warm spot to hold the sauce until serving.

PEBBLE BEACH WOOD-GRILLED PORK CHOP

Courtesty of The Pebble Beach Resort, Pebble Beach, California

WINE PAIRING: Hahn Monterey GSM

Note: *The following recipe calls for a 10-ounce pork chop. This is slightly bigger than precut chops, so ask your butcher to prepare the chop for you. Although this recipe serves one, it can easily be multiplied.*

SERVES 1

- 5 dry juniper berries
- 1 tablespoon fennel seeds
- 1 tablespoon coriander seeds
- 1 teaspoon kosher salt
- 2 cups dry Italian butter beans or other high-quality dry beans
- 12 ounces crushed San Marzano tomatoes
- 1 bunch basil
- Good quality California olive oil as needed
- 1 (10-ounce) pork chop
- 1 bunch broccoli rabe
- 1 preserved lemon (found in the pickles section of most specialty grocery stores), flesh removed and lemon peel diced
- 2 tablespoons whole-grain mustard
- Kosher salt and cracked black pepper as needed

PREPARE THE JUNIPER DRY RUB

Put the juniper berries, fennel seeds, and coriander seeds in a spice grinder (or a coffee grinder) and pulse until finely ground. Transfer to a bowl and combine with salt.

SOAK THE BEANS

At least 1 day before serving the pork chop, soak the dried beans in a large bowl in three times their volume of water and refrigerate overnight.

COOK THE BEANS

Drain the beans in a colander and put them in a heavy pot. Add enough water to cover the beans by 1 inch, cover loosely with the lid, and turn the heat to medium. Bring the beans to a gentle simmer (do not allow the liquid to come up to a boil) and simmer, checking every 15 minutes, until the beans are tender and fluffy on the inside (like mashed potatoes cased in a bean skin). Remove the pot from the heat, add salt to taste, the crushed tomatoes, and two stalks of basil, and let the beans cool in the liquid until you are ready to use them. *The beans can be soaked and cooked up to 2 days before serving.*

COOK THE CHOP

Preheat a charcoal grill (preferably with wood chips added). When the coals have died down, wipe the grate with some olive oil.

Drizzle the chop with olive oil and rub generously with the juniper rub. Place the chop over moderate heat (not on the hottest part of the grill) and grill until desired temperature is reached, (preferably to medium to preserve tenderness.) Allow the chop to rest for about 5 minutes before serving, to preserve the juices.

PREPARE THE BROCCOLI RABE AND BEANS

Trim the broccoli rabe by removing all the oversized stems from the bottom of the bunch and discarding them (ideally, with kitchen scissors). Heat about 2 tablespoons of olive oil in a skillet with tall sides over medium-high heat until hot but not smoking. Add a big handful of the broccoli rabe and a quarter of the diced preserved lemon skin. Once the broccoli rabe begins to wilt, add the beans and some of their liquor (the cooking liquid) and bring to a simmer. Cook only until the broccoli rabe is tender and the beans are hot, adding more of the cooking liquid as needed (you want the broccoli rabe and bean mixture to be brothy). Add the mustard, kosher salt, and pepper to taste and more olive oil.

To serve, slice the pork chop. Put the broccoli rabe and beans on a plate and place the sliced pork on top.

OSSO BUCO

Courtesy of Santos MacDonal, Executive Chef, Il Cortile Restaurant, Paso Robles

WINE PAIRING: Giornata Luna Matta Vineyard Paso Robles Nebbiolo

SERVES 4

4 pork shanks, bone in
Salt and freshly ground black pepper to taste
Flour for dusting the pork shanks
4 cups white wine
3 tablespoons olive oil
1 cup chopped onions
2 tablespoons thyme leaves
Handful of whole basil leaves
4 to 5 whole Roma tomatoes, chopped
5 to 6 bay leaves
4 to 5 cups chicken stock

Preheat oven to 400°F.

Season the pork shanks with salt and pepper to taste, and dust the shanks with flour.

Put the wine in a small saucepan and bring to a simmer to burn off the alcohol.

Heat the olive oil in a large deep-sided skillet until hot but not smoking. Add the shanks and brown on all sides. Transfer to a large braising pot, reserving the oil and any juices from the shanks in the skillet.

Brown the onion in the oil in the skillet over moderate heat. Add the thyme, basil, and tomatoes, and cook, stirring occasionally, for 4 minutes. Add the wine and bay leaves, and cook for 2 more minutes. Add the chicken stock, and simmer for 3 minutes. Pour the mixture over the pork shanks.

Braise the pork shanks, covered tightly, in the oven for 3 to 4 hours, or until the meat is falling off the bone.

Transfer the pork shanks to warm plates and loosely cover. Transfer the juices from the pot to a saucepan and cook the juices for 3 minutes, then pour over the pork shanks. If desired, serve with Parmesan risotto.

SPANISH LAMB STEW WITH SMOKED PAPRIKA, TOMATOES, AND WHITE BEANS

Courtesy of Chef Joanne Weir, Cookbook Author, and Television Personality

WINE PAIRING: Joanne Weir Cabernet Sauvignon

SERVES 6

- 5 tablespoons extra-virgin olive oil
- 2 pounds lamb stew meat from the shoulder or leg, cut into 1-inch pieces
- 1 yellow onion, minced
- Kosher salt and freshly ground black pepper
- 2 tablespoons all-purpose flour
- 3 cloves garlic, minced
- 1½ cups fresh or canned tomatoes, peeled, seeded, and diced
- 1 bay leaf
- 2 pounds fresh white beans, shelled
- ½ pound Spanish chorizo, thinly sliced
- 1 teaspoon sweet paprika
- ½ teaspoon pimentón
- 2 cloves garlic, sliced

Heat 2 tablespoons of the olive oil in a large heavy pot over medium-high heat until hot but not smoking. Add the lamb, onion, and salt and pepper to taste and cook, stirring occasionally, until golden on all sides, 8 to 10 minutes. Sprinkle the flour over the top, stir to combine, and cook for 2 more minutes. Add the minced garlic and sauté for a few minutes, then add the tomatoes, bay leaf, and 4 cups of water and bring to a boil over high heat. Reduce the heat to low and simmer for 1 hour.

Add the beans and chorizo, and simmer 40 minutes. Add additional water as needed.

Heat the remaining 3 tablespoons olive oil in a skillet until hot but not smoking and add the paprika, pimentón, and sliced garlic and stir together (don't let it take on color). Pour this mixture over the beans and stir gently together. Add water if needed. Let simmer for 30 seconds. Season with salt to taste.

OVEN ROASTED LAMB RACK WITH CHORIZO AND FENNEL VINAIGRETTE AND SPRING PEA RISOTTO

Courtesy of Justin Vineyards and Winery, Paso Robles, California

WINE PAIRING: 2011 Justin Cabernet Sauvignon

SERVES 4

FOR THE LAMB

- 1 teaspoon chopped fresh thyme
- 2 cloves garlic, minced
- Salt and freshly ground black pepper to taste
- 2 (1½- to 2-pound) racks of lamb
- 2 tablespoons olive oil

FOR THE CHORIZO AND FENNEL VINAIGRETTE

- 2 links Spanish chorizo, removed from casing and diced into small pieces
- ¼ cup finely diced red onion
- 4 cloves garlic, sliced thin
- 1½ cups sherry vinegar
- ¼ cup finely diced fennel
- Olive oil

PREPARE THE LAMB FOR COOKING

Combine thyme, garlic, salt, and pepper in a small bowl. Rub racks all over with the mixture and put in a sealable plastic bag with the olive oil. Spread oil around so that it coats the lamb completely. Squeeze out as much air as you can from the bag and seal. Place the bag in a bowl or any larger container in case the bag leaks. Let the lamb racks sit in the marinade as it comes to room temperature before cooking.

MAKE THE CHORIZO VINAIGRETTE

Cook the chorizo in a small saucepan over medium-low heat until most of the fat is rendered out of the meat. Transfer the meat with a slotted spoon to paper towels to drain, reserving the fat in the pan. Add the red onion and garlic to the fat and cook, stirring occasionally, until the vegetables are soft. Stir in the vinegar and deglaze pan, stirring occasionally, until reduced by half.

Put the fennel in another saucepan and add just enough olive oil to cover. Bring to a simmer over medium heat and cook until soft. Add to chorizo mixture and toss to combine. Season with salt and pepper to taste. Set aside and reserve in pan.

FOR THE RISOTTO

- 1 cup water
- 4 cups vegetable broth
- ¼ cup olive oil
- ½ onion or shallot, chopped fine
- 1 cup Arborio rice
- ⅓ cup Justin Sauvignon Blanc
- 1½ cups fresh peas (substitute thawed frozen peas if fresh are not available)
- ¼ cup Manchego cheese, shaved or grated
- ½ cup crème fraîche
- Salt and freshly ground black pepper to taste

MAKE THE RISOTTO

Combine 1 cup water and 4 cups broth in a 2-quart saucepan and bring to a simmer over medium heat. Reduce heat to low and keep warm. Heat 2 tablespoons olive oil in a large saucepan over medium heat until hot but not smoking, add the onion, and cook until soft. Add the rice and stir gently until toasted, 3 to 4 minutes. (You want each grain of rice to appear a touch translucent on the edge.) Add the wine and stir until absorbed. Increase the heat to medium-high and stir in 1 cup water-broth mixture. Cook uncovered, stirring frequently, until the liquid is absorbed. Continue stirring and adding the remaining water-broth mixture, 1 cup at a time, allowing each cup to be absorbed before adding the next. Cook for approximately 25 to 30 minutes or until the rice is tender and the mixture has a creamy consistency. Stir in fresh peas, Manchego cheese, and crème fraîche. Add salt and pepper to taste.

COOK THE LAMB

Preheat the oven to 400°F.

Roast the racks in the oven on a baking sheet for 7 minutes, then lower the heat to 300°F. Cook for 7 to 15 minutes longer, or until a meat thermometer inserted into the thickest part of the meat registers 120°F for rare or 130°F for medium rare. Remove the racks from the oven, cover with foil, and let rest for 5 to 10 minutes. (Alternatively, the lamb chops can be grilled.)

SERVE THE DISH

Cut the chops into single or double chop portions and transfer to heated plates. Drizzle the chops with the vinaigrette and serve with the risotto.

FISH AND SHELLFISH

STEAMED MANILA CLAMS WITH GLAZED PORK BELLY, LIME, AND THAI BASIL

Courtesy of Robert Curry, Executive Chef, Auberge du Soleil, from the Relais & Chateaux Cookbook Chefs at Home

WINE PAIRING: Cliff Lede Sauvignon Blanc

SERVES 4

FOR THE PORK BELLY

1¼ pounds fresh pork belly
½ teaspoon whole black peppercorns
1 whole star anise
½ teaspoon whole cloves
½ teaspoon fennel seeds
½ teaspoon ground cinnamon
Salt to taste
1 head of garlic, halved
½ carrot, peeled and sliced
½ onion, peeled and cut into medium dice
½ fennel bulb, cut into medium dice
½ leek, cut into medium dice
½ bunch thyme, tied with butcher's twine
1 bay leaf
1 half bottle (375 ml) dry white wine
1½ quarts chicken stock
1 tablespoon grape seed oil

PREPARE THE PORK BELLY (UP TO 1 DAY IN ADVANCE)

Preheat the oven to 300°F. If the pork has skin attached, remove and discard it. Score the fat on the skin side of the belly with a knife.

Grind together the black peppercorns, star anise, cloves, fennel seeds, and cinnamon. In a small skillet toast the spices over low heat for about 1 minute and transfer to a bowl to cool.

Season the pork belly liberally with salt and rub the pork with the ground spice mix. Heat a medium-heavy pot until hot but not smoking, add the pork, fat side down, and sear well on all sides. Remove the pork from the pot. Add the garlic, carrot, onion, fennel, leek, thyme, and bay leaf to the pot and cook over moderate heat, stirring occasionally, until the vegetables are tender. Add the wine and reduce by half. Return the seared pork belly to the pot along with the chicken stock and bring the liquid to a simmer. Cover the pot with a lid and transfer the pot to the oven. Braise the pork for 2 hours.

FOR THE PORK BELLY GLAZE

4 tablespoons brown sugar
¼ cup soy sauce
¼ cup mirin

FOR THE CLAMS

2 tablespoons grape seed oil
2 tablespoons ginger, peeled and minced
1 tablespoon garlic, peeled and minced
2 tablespoons shallots, peeled and minced
6 pounds Manila clams, shells scrubbed
1 cup dry white wine
2 tablespoons sweet chili sauce
2 tablespoons Thai fish sauce
½ cup lime juice
2 ounces butter
24 Thai basil leaves, cut into chiffonnade
4 green onions, sliced

Remove the pork from the oven and transfer it, with tongs, to a sheet pan. Put another sheet pan on top of the pork and place something heavy on top to weigh it down. Refrigerate the pork for at least 6 hours or overnight.

Cut the pressed pork into at least 12 large diced pieces and reserve. To finish the pork, heat a skillet until hot, then add the grape seed oil and the pork belly and sear it on all sides. Remove any excess fat from the pan and add the ingredients for the glaze. Reduce just until the pork is glazed.

COOK THE CLAMS

Heat the grape seed oil in a large pot until hot but not smoking, then add the ginger, garlic, and shallots and cook for a few minutes to sweat the vegetables. Add the clams, wine, chili sauce, fish sauce, and lime juice, cover the pot with a lid, and increase the heat to high. Steam the clams until they open, about 2 to 4 minutes. Discard any clams that do not open.

SERVE THE DISH

Divide the clams among four warm bowls, reserving the cooking liquid. Whisk the butter into the clam cooking liquid and ladle the liquid over the clams. Place the glazed pork belly on top of the clams. Garnish with the basil and green onions and serve immediately.

JOEL GOTT FISH TACOS

Courtesy of Joel Gott, Winemaker for Joel Gott, Shatter, and The Show Wines and Restaurateur Gott's Roadside Tray Gourmet.

WINE PAIRING: Joel Gott Sauvignon Blanc

SERVES 4 (2 FISH TACOS PER PERSON)

FOR THE ROASTED TOMATILLO SALSA

- 1 pound tomatillos, husks removed, rinsed and quartered
- 1 jalapeño, halved and seeds removed
- 2 tablespoons minced white onion
- ½ cup chopped cilantro
- 1 garlic clove, sliced
- ½ teaspoon kosher salt

FOR THE SLAW

- ½ small green cabbage, thinly sliced and washed (about ½ to ¾ pound)
- ¼ cup canola oil
- ½ teaspoon kosher salt, or to taste
- ½ cup minced white onion
- ½ cup chopped cilantro
- 1 lime, washed and quartered

MAKE THE ROASTED TOMATILLO SALSA

Preheat a broiler and position rack under broiler.

Broil the tomatillos and jalapeños, skin sides up, until soft and lightly browned, about 15 to 20 minutes. Let cool.

Pulse the broiled tomatillos and jalapenos and remaining salsa ingredients in a food processor or blender until it reaches the desired consistency (a fairly chunky puree works well). Set aside.

MAKE THE SLAW

Combine the cabbage, canola oil, salt, white onion, and cilantro in a medium bowl and squeeze the lime over the mixture. Toss until all the ingredients are evenly distributed, and set aside.

FOR THE FISH

- 1 tablespoon canola oil
- 1 pound petrale sole filets, patted dry, seasoned with salt and pepper to taste, and lightly coated in flour (1 tablespoon flour should be sufficient)
- 1 lime, washed and quartered
- 16 corn tortillas (only 8 if using 1 tortilla per taco)

FOR THE TOPPINGS

- 2 avocados, peeled, pitted, and sliced as desired
- ½ bunch radishes, sliced by hand or on a mandoline to 1⁄16-inch thickness or less
- 1 lime, washed and quartered

COOK THE FISH

Heat about ½ tablespoon canola oil in a nonstick 12-inch skillet over moderate heat until the oil shimmers. Add two filets at a time and fry for 2 to 4 minutes per side, or until lightly golden brown and fish is firm to the touch. Transfer to paper towels to drain. Squeeze lime over the filets and cook remaining filets in the same manner.

PREPARE THE TORTILLAS AND BUILD THE TACOS

Heat an ungreased griddle over medium heat. Heat the tortillas on the griddle until warmed through but still pliable. Working with two tortillas at a time, top with one-eighth of the fish, then spoon on the salsa, and top with slaw, avocados, and radishes to taste. Serve each pair of tacos with a quarter of lime.

FOWL

DUCK LEG CONFIT RAVIOLI WITH OYSTER MUSHROOMS, ARUGULA, AND PINOT NOIR POMEGRANATE GASTRIQUE

Courtesy of Timothy F. Kaulfers, Executive Chef, Arista Winery, Russian River Valley, Sonoma

WINE PAIRING: Arista Ferrington Vineyard Pinot Noir

Note from Chef Kaulfers: *This is a recipe with multiple steps, but all you need is some organization and a few commonplace kitchen tools and machines to help you out. Duck and Pinot Noir are a match made in heaven, and at Arista Winery I pair this dish with our Ferrington Vineyard Pinot Noir from the Anderson Valley in Mendocino County. The combination of flavors in both items keeps people hungry for more of both wine and food!*

SERVES 4

FOR THE DUCK CONFIT DRY CURE

- 1 tablespoon black pepper
- 1 tablespoon coriander
- ¼ teaspoon cinnamon
- ¼ teaspoon nutmeg
- 2 tablespoons fresh thyme
- 1 cup kosher salt
- ⅓ cup brown sugar

FOR THE DUCK CONFIT

- 4 duck legs
- ½ recipe of the dry cure
- 1 to 2 quarts duck fat (cooking oil can be substituted)

MAKE THE CURE

Grind the black pepper, coriander, cinnamon, and nutmeg in a spice grinder and transfer to a bowl. Coarsely chop the thyme and add to a bowl along with the salt and brown sugar. Stir until combined well.

PREPARE THE DUCK

The day before cooking the duck, liberally sprinkle the legs with one-half recipe of the cure. Cover and refrigerate overnight.

COOK THE DUCK

Preheat the oven to 325°F.

FOR THE DUCK FILLING

- Meat from 4 duck legs
- 3 tablespoons mascarpone cheese
- ½ tablespoon chopped parsley
- ½ tablespoon dried sour cherries, minced
- Salt and pepper to taste

FOR THE RAVIOLI DOUGH

- 1 cup all-purpose flour
- ½ tablespoon kosher salt
- 3 egg yolks
- 1 whole egg
- ¾ tablespoon olive oil
- ½ tablespoon milk

FOR THE MUSHROOMS AND ARUGULA

- 1 pound oyster mushrooms
- 1 tablespoon olive oil
- Salt and freshly ground black pepper to taste
- 1 tablespoon vegetable stock
- 1 tablespoon butter
- 2 cups packed arugula

FOR THE POMEGRANATE GASTRIQUE

- ½ cup Arista Pinot Noir
- ½ cup POM pomegranate juice
- Splash of sherry vinegar
- ½ tablespoon cornstarch
- A pinch of salt and sugar to taste

RAVIOLI ASSEMBLY

- Pasta roller attachment for mixer
- 1 recipe pasta dough
- ½ cup semolina flour
- Ravioli press or stamp

Wash the cure off the legs with cold running water, pat dry, and place in an oven-safe brazier. Cover the legs with the fat to submerge them completely and cook in the oven for 3½ hours. (Note: It is very important that the legs are completely submerged in fat; using a small vessel helps.)

Remove the legs from the oven and allow to cool. Once cool, pull the meat from the bones, reserving the meat and discarding the skin and bones. (Save the fat for future batches.)

MAKE THE FILLING

In the bowl of a stand mixer fitted with a paddle attachment beat together the duck meat and remaining filling ingredients until fully blended. Taste the mixture and adjust seasoning with salt and pepper to taste. If it is too "dry," you can add a bit more mascarpone. *The filling mixture can be made up to 2 days ahead and refrigerated, covered.*

MAKE THE RAVIOLI DOUGH

Add the flour and salt to the bowl of a food processor (or you can use the well method by hand if you prefer). Add the remaining ingredients to a bowl and whisk together. Turn the processor on and stream the egg mixture through the feed tube in a stream until the mixture looks shaggy.

Flour your hands and the work surface. Transfer the dough with floured hands to the work surface and manually knead the dough for about 10 minutes. Transfer the dough to a clean bowl, cover with plastic, and allow to rest for 1 hour.

PREPARE THE MUSHROOMS AND ARUGULA

Preheat the oven to 425°F.

(continued on following page)

Put the mushrooms in a bowl, drizzle with the olive oil, and sprinkle with salt and pepper to taste. Mix to coat and transfer to a small roasting pan. Roast in the oven until just golden brown, 12 to 14 minutes.

Just before you cook you ravioli, heat a small skillet until hot but not smoking, then add the stock, butter, mushrooms, and arugula and cook just long enough to wilt the arugula. Adjust the seasoning.

MAKE THE GASTRIQUE

Combine the wine, pomegranate juice, and vinegar in a small saucepan and slowly bring the heat up.

Mix the cornstarch with ½ tablespoon cold water and remove all lumps. Whisk cornstarch slurry into the wine mixture and continue whisking until it comes to a boil.

Add a pinch of salt and sugar and adjust the consistency. To thicken add more slurry, or thin it out with a touch of juice. The gastrique will coagulate as it cools; you are looking for a chocolate syrup–like texture.

ROLL OUT THE DOUGH

On the widest roller setting of the pasta roller machine, flatten out one-half recipe of dough and run it through. Fold the dough in half and run it through once more. Now gradually reduce the thickness one setting at a time, passing the dough through twice on each setting until you achieve desired thinness (#6 on a KitchenAid is ideal). Use semolina to help reduce stickiness during this process.

FORM THE RAVIOLI

Using a ravioli press, liberally sprinkle semolina in the crevices of the press. Lay one dough sheet over the press, then lightly press to form the wells. Add the filling, but be sure not to overstuff. Dip your finger in some water and run it where the seams will be to help the top layer adhere. Place remaining dough sheet over the filling, pressing gently to make the doughs adhere. Roll a rolling pin over the press to cut out the ravioli. Gently flip the press over to release the ravioli.

COOK THE RAVIOLI

Bring a pot of salted water to a gentle boil. Add the ravioli and cook until al dente, about 3½ to 4 minutes.

ASSEMBLE THE DISH

Ladle some of the gastrique onto the plates, top it with mushroom and arugula mixture, and top that with the ravioli.

QUAIL A LA PLANCHA WITH ROASTED GRAPES, CRACKED HAZELNUTS, AND SABA

Courtesy of Chef Mark Stark, Owner of Several Healdsburg Restaurants, Including Starks, Bravas, Willi's, and Monti's.

WINE PAIRINGS: Portalupi Russian River 2010 Pinot Noir–Il Migliore (check out their jug wines!) and Hartford Old Vine Zinfandel Jolene's Vineyard 2010

SERVES 4

FOR THE MARINADE

1 clove garlic, minced
2 tablespoons olive oil
2 sprigs fresh lavender, leaves finely minced (you may substitute rosemary)
¼ teaspoon fresh ground black pepper
4 quails, semiboned

FOR THE ROASTED GRAPES

1 bunch red seedless grapes, stems removed
2 tablespoons extra-virgin olive oil
2 tablespoons cognac or brandy
Salt and freshly ground black pepper to taste

FOR THE HAZELNUTS

2 tablespoons butter
½ cup toasted hazelnuts
2 tablespoons of Saba (reduced grape must) or good aged balsamic vinegar
Salt to taste

Combine marinade ingredients and rub quail, inside and out, with it. Let quail marinate, covered, in the refrigerator for at least 4 hours or overnight.

Preheat the oven to 400°F with a sheet pan in the oven. Toss the grapes with the oil, cognac, and salt and pepper to taste. When the sheet pan is hot, put the grapes on the pan and roast the grapes just until they start to pop. Transfer grapes and juices to a bowl.

Heat a cast iron skillet over medium heat until hot. Season the marinated quail with salt, then transfer to the hot pan and cook until brown and crispy, about 2 minutes. Flip the quail over and repeat on the other side. The quail should be well browned but still slightly pink on the inside. Transfer the quail to a serving platter and keep warm. Pour off any fat in the pan and reduce the heat. Add the butter and the cracked hazelnuts and cook for 30 seconds until the nuts are aromatic. Add the roasted grapes and the accumulated juices and cook until the grapes are just warmed through. Season with salt.

Arrange the quail on plates and drizzle with the Saba. Serve with the hazelnuts and roasted grapes.

DESSERTS

ONLY-IN-SEASON STRAWBERRY GALETTE

Courtesy of Brigit Binns, Chef and Author of The New Wine Country Cookbook

WINE PAIRING: Pomar Junction Reserve Late-Harvest Viognier (Paso Robles)

SERVES 5 TO 6

FOR THE DOUGH

- 8 ounces (2 sticks) cold unsalted butter
- 1¾ cups (7½ ounces) all-purpose flour
- ¾ cup coarse cornmeal
- ½ teaspoon minced fresh rosemary
- 1 teaspoon finely grated zest of an organic or well-scrubbed lemon
- 2 tablespoons granulated sugar
- ¼ teaspoon fine sea salt
- 2 large egg yolks, lightly beaten
- 3 to 5 tablespoons ice water

MAKE THE DOUGH

Cut the butter into small pieces, place them on a plate, and chill in the refrigerator for 25 minutes. Combine the flour, cornmeal, rosemary, lemon zest, sugar, and salt in a bowl and chill in the refrigerator for 20 minutes.

Dump the chilled dry ingredients into a food processor and pulse to blend. Scatter the cold butter over the top and give it three or four 5-second pulses, just until the mixture looks like coarse cornmeal. Remove the lid. Add the yolks, drizzle 3 tablespoons of ice water over the top, and pulse for 10 to 15 seconds, until the dough just begins to clump together. If the mixture doesn't clump, add up to 2 more tablespoons water, one at a time, pulsing briefly between pulses (don't overmix).

Turn the dough out onto a lightly floured surface and gather into a thick disk. Wrap in plastic and refrigerate for at least 1 hour or overnight (dough may be frozen for up to 3 months). If chilled for only 1 hour, let the dough stand for 10 minutes before rolling out. If chilled for 8 hours or overnight, let it stand for 30 minutes before rolling.

FOR THE FILLING

- 1 pound strawberries, about 3 cups, hulled (in-season only)
- All-purpose flour for dusting
- ½ cup lavender jelly or ginger or apricot preserves
- 2 tablespoons butter, melted
- 1 tablespoon granulated sugar

ASSEMBLE AND BAKE THE GALETTE

Preheat the oven to 375°F with a rack in the center position.

Slice the strawberries lengthwise ¼-inch thick.

Place a sheet of baking parchment on a work surface and dust generously with flour. Place dough in the center, and roll it out to a 15-inch round, slightly under ¼-inch thick (or four smaller rounds); it's better if the edges are rough and uneven. Slide the parchment onto a large, rimless baking sheet.

Brush the preserves over the dough, leaving a 2-inch border. Arrange the strawberries over the preserves in concentric circles (or just as they come out), overlapping slightly and leaving a 2-inch border. Lift the edges of the dough and fold them in, pleating as you fold. Brush the top of the dough with melted butter and sprinkle the sugar over the whole tart.

Bake the galette in the oven for 45 minutes, or until the crust is bubbling and browned and the strawberries are slightly glazed. Slide the tart from the parchment onto a cooling rack. Transfer to a platter and cut into wedges; serve warm or at room temperature.

FLOATING ISLAND

Courtesy of Patrice Martineau, Executive Chef, El Encanto Hotel, Santa Barbara

WINE PAIRING: Casa Dumetz Sonja's Suds, Sparkling Syrah Rosé

Note from Chef Margineau: *This historic recipe is a popular signature dessert that was offered to guests when the El Encanto property was first operated as a hotel in 1918.*

SERVES 4

FOR THE VANILLA SAUCE

1 cup cream
1 cup milk
½ tablespoon vanilla extract
6 egg yolks
½ cup sugar

FOR THE CARAMEL SAUCE

1 cup granulated sugar
1 cup cream

MAKE THE VANILLA SAUCE

Prepare a large pot with ice water and set aside. Combine cream, milk, and vanilla extract in a saucepan and bring to a boil over medium heat.

Meanwhile, whisk together the yolks and sugar in a large bowl.

When the cream mixture comes to a boil, pour a little into the yolks and sugar mixture and whisk until all has been incorporated. Return the cream mixture to the stove, whisk in the remaining yolks and sugar mixture, and cook over low heat, whisking constantly, until it coats the back of the spoon. Pour the vanilla sauce through a container into a small heatproof bowl and set inside the large pot with ice water to cool quickly. *The sauce can be made up to 5 days ahead and refrigerated, covered.*

MAKE THE CARAMEL SAUCE

Pour the granulated sugar into a large heavy-duty stainless steel pot. Cook, stirring constantly with a wooden spoon, over medium heat until caramel in color. Slowly pour in the cream. (Use caution, as the cream will splatter and steam.) Pour through a strainer into a bowl and let cool completely.

FOR THE CARAMEL CAGE

2 cups granulated sugar
⅛ teaspoon cream of tartar
½ cup water

FOR THE FLOATING ISLANDS

2 egg whites
1 pinch cream of tartar
¼ cup granulated sugar
¼ teaspoon vanilla extract

MAKE THE CARAMEL CAGE

Place all the ingredients in a heavy-duty stainless steel pot. Cook over medium heat, stirring constantly, until all the sugar has dissolved and the sides begin to turn a light amber color. Turn off the heat and allow to cool slightly (the caramel should be cool but still liquid). Drizzle the caramel on a Silpat (silicone baking sheet) in various directions to create a cage look. Allow to cool completely away from moisture.

MAKE THE FLOATING ISLANDS

Whip the egg whites and cream of tartar in the mixing bowl of an electric mixer fitted with the whisk attachment until soft peaks form. Continue to beat and gradually add the sugar. Continue beating until stiff peaks form. Mix in the vanilla.

Pour enough water into a microwave-safe dish to cover the bottom by ¼ inch. Set aside.

Form an egg-shaped meringue with ¼ of the egg whites (use 2 tablespoons to do this). Place it on the water in the dish. Form a second meringue and place it on the water, leaving a space between the two meringues. Microwave on high power for 20 to 30 seconds. Transfer the meringues to a paper towel to drain. Repeat with the remaining egg whites, making a total of four islands. When all the meringues have been cooked and drained, gently transfer them to a plate. Refrigerate until thoroughly chilled, about 20 minutes.

TO SERVE

Divide the vanilla sauce into four dessert bowls. Gently lift the floating islands and place one in each bowl. Drizzle caramel sauce over and around each floating island. Break off a large piece of the caramel cage and place on top of the floating island.

GOAT MILK CHEESECAKE WITH SLOW ROASTED STRAWBERRIES

Courtesy of Nick Flores, Executive Sous Chef and Pastry Chef, The Lark, Santa Barbara

WINE PAIRING: 2011 Tatomer Beerenauslese Riesling, Kick-on Ranch Santa Barbara County

SERVES 12

FOR THE PISTACHIO STREUSEL

8 ounces pistachios, ground fine
4 ounces sugar
3 ounces all-purpose flour
1 teaspoon salt
3½ ounces butter, melted

FOR THE CAKE

8 ounces cream cheese
3½ ounces granulated sugar
1 vanilla bean
12 ounces fresh goat cheese
3½ ounces crème fraîche
2 eggs

MAKE THE PISTACHIO STREUSEL

Combine the ground pistachios, sugar, flour, and salt in the bowl of an electric stand mixer and mix slowly until combined. With mixer running on low, pour in melted butter and mix until just combined. Chill mixture for 1 hour.

Preheat the oven to 300°F.

Press the streusel base into a 10-inch round ceramic soufflé dish. Bake for 10 minutes.

MAKE THE CAKE

Preheat the oven to 275°F. with oven rack in middle of oven.

Combine cream cheese, sugar, and vanilla paste (scraped from inside of the pod) in the bowl of an electric stand mixer bowl fitted with a paddle attachment and slowly blend until smooth. Scrape down the sides of the bowl. Add the goat cheese and crème fraîche and mix again until smooth. While the machine is running add the eggs, one at a time, scraping down the sides between each addition. Pour into the prebaked streusel lined baking dish and cover tightly with foil.

FOR THE ROASTED STRAWBERRIES

- 2 pints strawberries, hulled, halved, and sliced
- 1 ounce granulated sugar, plus additional if necessary
- 2 teaspoons Aleppo pepper
- 1 pinch freshly ground black pepper
- 1 pinch salt
- Lemon juice, if necessary

GARNISHES FOR SERVING

- Fresh tarragon leaves
- Fresh sliced strawberries

Place baking dish into a large baking pan and put in middle of oven on a rack. Slowly add water to the baking pan to reach halfway up the sides of the baking dish. Bake cake until custard is just barely set. Transfer to a rack to cool completely, then chill completely before serving.

ROAST THE STRAWBERRIES

Preheat the oven to 275°F.

Toss sliced strawberries with sugar, Aleppo peppers, black pepper, and salt in a bowl and arrange evenly in a baking dish. Bake in oven for 1 hour, or until berries become "jammy" and water is released from the fruit. Transfer the strawberry jam to a bowl and adjust sweetness with more sugar or lemon juice if necessary

SERVE THE CAKE

Serve slices of cheesecake with a spoonful of roasted strawberries and a garnish of fresh tarragon leaves and fresh sliced strawberries.

ACKNOWLEDGMENTS

We're lucky to have friends and family that live in the great state of California, and we're even luckier to visit them when the weather in New York City turns to winter. This book was made possible thanks to those generous souls who opened their cellars, kitchens, and hearts to us.

It took years to research, compile, and write the book that you are now holding in your hands. Every moment, every winemaker, every meal, every wine, and every new friend we met along the way made the journey an absolute pleasure. As a direct result of writing this book we truly understand the concept of "bicoastal" living and have achieved the dual mentality of "Type A" New Yorkers and "laid-back" Californians. This newly formed duality allows us to enjoy living in the moment *and* worry about meeting our deadlines at the same time. We like to think of it as a perfect balance of Yin and Yang. We're also thankful for the valuable six hours of writing and meditation time that we captured on every transcontinental flight. And let's be honest: the 80,000 miles we each accumulated in frequent flyer points aren't so bad either.

In starting the long list of people that we'd like to thank we must begin with Carlo DeVito for his friendship and support. As our lead editor and the head of the Sterling Epicure team, his guidance and vision helped shape this book. We can't thank his right hand person Diane Abrams enough for her steady grip on the rudder and keeping *Wines of California* on the right course. We'd also like to thank Scott Amerman for his eagle eyes and amazing organizational skills, Brita Vallens for wrangling the artwork, and Christine Heun and Stacey Stambaugh for their stunning art and design skills.

No expression of gratitude would be complete without thanking our manager and friend, Peter Miller, for his undying support, his staunch respect for the written word, and his defense of authors' rights.

We would like to extend heartfelt gratitude to Michael Mondavi and Kevin Zraly for their kind words in our foreword and preface. We have the utmost admiration for these two innovative geniuses in the ever-changing world of wine.

We would also like to thank the various state, regional, and county winemaker and grape grower associations that provided us with assistance in our work. We are pretty sure that we have listed them all here, but if we have omitted a specific association please accept our heartfelt apologies. Let's start with thanking the statewide California Association of Wine Grape Growers for their generous help and continue our deep appreciation in alphabetical order. We'd like to thank Alexander Valley Winegrowers, Amador County Grape Growers Association, Amador Vintners Association, Anderson Valley Winegrowers Association, Calaveras Winegrape Alliance, Carneros Wine Alliance, Central Coast Wine Growers Association, Clarksburg Wine Growers and Vintners Association, El Dorado Wine Grape Growers Association, El Dorado Winery Association, Hospitality de Los Carneros, Humboldt Wine Association, Lake County Winegrape Commission, Lake County Winery Association, Livermore Valley Winegrowers Association, Lodi District Grape Growers Association, Lodi Grower Vintner Alliance, Lodi Winegrape Commission, Madera Vintners Association, Mendocino Winegrowers, Monterey County Vintners and Growers Association, Mount Veeder Appellation Council, Napa Valley Grape Growers, Napa Valley Vintners, Oakville Winegrowers, Paso Robles Wine Country Alliance, Placer County Vintners Association, Placer County Wine and Grape Association, Ramona Vineyard Association, Russian

River Valley Winegrowers, Rutherford Dust Society, San Diego County Vintners Association, San Joaquin Valley Winegrowers Association, San Luis Obispo Vintners Association, Santa Barbara County Vintners Association, Santa Cruz Mountains Winegrowers Association, Santa Maria Valley Wine Country Association, Sierra Grape Growers Association, Sierra Vintners, Silverado Trail Wineries Association, Sonoma County Winegrape Commission, Sonoma County Vintners, Sonoma Valley Vintners and Growers Alliance, Stag's Leap District Winegrowers Association, Sta. Rita Hills Winegrowers Alliance, Suisun Valley Vintners and Grape Growers Association, Temecula Valley Winegrowers Association, Ventura County Winery Association, West Sonoma Coast Vintners, Wine Artisans of Santa Lucia Highlands, Wine Growers of Dry Creek Valley, Wine Growers of Napa County, Wine Road of Northern Sonoma County and Wineries of Santa Clara Valley.

We'd like to thank all of the wonderful people who allowed us to interview them "In Their Own Words," including Agustin F. Huneeus Jr., Austin Hope, Barbara Banke, Bo Barrett, Cheryl Indelicato, Eileen Crane, Emilio Estevez and Sonja Magdevski, Gary Eberle, George Rosenthal, Gina Gallo, Heidi Barrett, Jean Charles Boisset, Jim Saunders, Steve Hearst, Joel Peterson, Jon Priest, Ken Volk, Mark Beringer, Michael Mondavi, Michael Trujillo, Mike Benziger, Mike Grgich, Peter Mondavi Sr., Philippe Melka, Pierre Seillan, Rob Mondavi Jr., Stéphane Derenoncourt, Tobin James, Tom Tiburzi, and Zelma Long.

We'd also like to thank all of the chefs and restaurant owners who graciously provided us with their favorite recipes including Matt Bolton, Frank Ostini, Jeff Mosher, Debbie Thomas, David Bush, Judy Aron, Chris Kobayashi, Carol Baily, Michael Chiarello, Kolin Vazzoler, Tyler Florence, Santos MacDonal, Joanne Weir, Robert Curry, Joel Gott, Timothy Kaulfers, Mark Stark, Brigit Binns, Patrice Martineau, and Nick Flores.

Heartfelt thanks to all of the winemakers, winery owners, and marketing professionals who made sure that we got the samples and information that we needed to compile this comprehensive book.

There are so many people who assisted us on every level, and most of them are named here, but if we've missed a few, it's only because there's not enough paper and ink in the world to list them all. We'd like to thank Virginie Boone, Kathie Lee Gifford, Jennifer Simonetti-Bryan, Peter Mondavi Jr., Mary Beth Bentwood, Isabel Mondavi, Kristin Green, Chris Taranto, Jennifer Porter, Melissa McAvoy, Mark McWilliams, Skye Morgan, Sienna Spencer, Camron King, Kimberly Charles, Jennifer Chin, Bob DeRoose, Katarina Maloney, Suzie Kukaj, Robin Kelley O'Connor, Susan Kostrzewa, Allison Langhoff, Joe Magliocco, David Drucker, Rebecca Hopkins, Michelle Woodruff, Kristina Kelley, Anna Miranda, Katie Calhoun, Sonia Meyer, Kara Hoffman, Holly Evans, Pat Burns, Erika Michelis, Kate Regan, Lisa Klinck-Shea, Amelia Weir, Michelle Flores, Helen Gregory, Mary Anne Sullivan, Kanchan Kinkade, Ken Morris, Randy Martinsen, Elaine Mellis, Natalie Gerke, Keely Garibaldi, Amy Miranov Janish, Helene Mingot, Claire and Lance Silver, Korinne Munson, Colleen Chen, Jannis Swerman, Chris Silva, Phil Baily, Farley Green, Jessica Blanco, Heather Muhleman, Jetty Jane Connor, Andrea Werbel, Carole MacDonal, Tim McDonald, Liam Mayclem, Lea Wilson, Mimi Huggins, Kirsten Hampton, and Terri Stark.

And finally, we'd like to thank all of our friends and colleagues in the wonderful world of wine. Without your support this book would not have been possible.

Whew . . . thank you all so much!

Mike and Jeff

CREDITS

All images courtesy of the wineries with the following additions: x: Library of Congress; 5: Eadweard Muybridge/Courtesy Wikimedia Foundation; 6: Isaiah West Taber/California State Library; 12: Carol M. Highsmith/Library of Congress; 17, 225: © Chris Leschinsky; 24, 26, 50, 150, 264, 274, 292, 298, 312, 324, 362, 392: © Map Resources; 34: © 2013 Brassfield Estate Winery; 36 right: © Alanna Hale; 41: © Jamey Thomas; 69: © Caitlin McCaffrey 2008; 75: © Brent Winebrenner; 81: © Damon Matson; 93 left: © Kaitlin Childers; 96: © Marie Hirsch; 104: © Adrian Gregorutti; 110 left, 530 top left: © Timm Eubanks; 131, 212: © M. J. Wickham; 166: © Kevin Cruff/Courtesy the Antinori Family; 182 left: © Rien van Rijthoven; 189: © Matthew Millman; 203: © Rocco Ceselin; 226 right: © Alex Farnum; 246: Keith Sutter; 258: © Andy Katz Photography; 261 left: © Cathy O'hagain; 323: © Michael Kelley; 329 right: © Matt Wallac; 354 left: © Derek Skalko/7friday.com; 378 right: Kirk Irwin; 383 right: Jeremy Ball of Bottle Branding; 387 right: © Bob McClenahan; 401: LiFT Photos; 406 bottom left, 448: E&J Gallo CS Photography; 415: Intrepid Production; 431: © Andrew Macpherson/Macfly Corp; 456: © Moanalani Jeffrey Photography; 470: Forest Doud; 474: © Briana Marie Photography; 507: © Douglas Thompson; 512: © Steven Rothfeld; 530 center right: © Frankie Frankeny; 530 top right: © Valerie Martin; 530 bottom left: Brigit Binns

INDEX

Note: Page ranges in parentheses, such as (17–28) indicate non-contiguous/intermittent references.
Page numbers in **bold** indicate main discussions of grape varieties. Page numbers in *italics* indicate recipes.

(continued)

(continued)

663.209794 DESIMONE
DeSimone, Mike.
Wines of California
SOF
R4002265949
SOUTH FULTON BRANCH
Atlanta-Fulton Public Library